W9-DBW-379

PROMOTIONAL STRATEGY

Managing the Marketing Communications Process

James F. Engel
Eastern College

Martin R. Warshaw
The University of Michigan

Thomas C. Kinnear
The University of Michigan

Seventh Edition

Homewood, IL 60430
Boston, MA 02116

Sponsoring editor: Elizabeth S. MacDonell
Developmental editor: Andy Winston
Project editor: Jean Lou Hess
Production manager: Diane Palmer
Designer: Maureen McCutcheon
Cover and Part Photographer: Chicago Photographic Company
Artist: Carlisle Communications, Ltd.
Compositor: Carlisle Communications, Ltd.
Typeface: 10/12 Cheltenham Light
Printer: R. R. Donnelley & Sons Company

Library of Congress Cataloging-in-Publication Data

Engel, James F.
    Promotional strategy : managing the marketing communications
process / James F. Engel, Martin R. Warshaw, Thomas C. Kinnear.
        p.   cm.—(The Irwin series in marketing)
        Includes bibliographical references and index.
        ISBN 0–256–08204–9 —0–256–11408–0 (International ed.)
        1. Marketing.   2. Advertising.   3. Marketing—Management.
    I. Warshaw, Martin R.   II. Kinnear, Thomas C., 1943–.
    III. Title.   IV. Series.
    HF5415.E65   1991
    658.8'2 — dc20

                                                    90–44246

Printed in the United States of America

2 3 4 5 6 7 8 9 0 DOC 7 6 5 4 3 2 1

Preface

This book had its beginning in the fall of 1961 when Jim Engel, then an assistant professor of marketing at The University of Michigan, was assigned to teach the promotion course. Available texts proved to be unsatisfactory, thus leading him to contact his graduate school mentor, Hugh Wales, at the University of Illinois. Both agreed to try their hand at an innovative approach which would focus on the entire promotion mix, not just advertising, and build from a solid behavioral foundation.

As they prepared preliminary outlines, they realized that another person was needed to shore up the material on sales management and reseller strategies. The logical candidate was Marty Warshaw, Jim Engel's colleague at Michigan. And so the book was launched. Hugh Wales retired after the third edition, and another Michigan colleague, Tom Kinnear, joined the team.

Our purposes have changed little since the first edition. Our basic conviction is that advertising, sales promotion, personal selling, direct marketing, public relations and publicity, and corporate advertising are all component parts of *one integrated promotional mix*. There is no way that an individual activity, say advertising, can be managed without fully considering these strategic interrelationships.

We are also convinced that marketing strategy must be grounded in realistic research that clearly documents the opportunities and problems to be faced. This requires knowledge of consumer motivation and behavior, the competitive climate, the legal climate, and so on. While this is not a book on research per se, it will help students identify and glean the information needed and teach them how to think strategically once it is in hand.

Since the outset we have provided the reader a thorough grounding in consumer behavior. Initially we felt, with justification, that few students would have course work in that field. Hence, we tried as much as we could to include a summary of Engel, Kollat, and Blackwell, *Consumer Behavior* (now Engel, Blackwell, and Miniard, *Consumer Behavior,* 6th ed). We now are aware that most readers have had a basic exposure to consumer behavior, so in this edition we concentrate on stressing its unique implications for promotional strategy. Our coverage of consumer behavior remains extensive, however, and is foundational to everything else.

We also have always written from the perspective of those who must conceive and execute promotional strategy. Our intent is to mold and shape effective strategic thinking rather than to provide cookbook lists of answers. We avoid simple answers to problems that defy rule-of-thumb solutions. We make no attempt to imply certainty when it does not exist in the real world.

Finally, our goal—and our greatest challenge over the years—has been to make this book both theoretically sound and highly practical. As we have gained experience ourselves both in teaching and in practical marketing strategy, our perspectives understandably have become modified. Certainly a comparison of this edition with the 1967 version would reveal a marked shift toward consistent use of the criterion, *what does this all mean on the firing line?*

Some schools still retain separate courses in advertising and sales management. Although we take an integrated approach, our material is readily adaptable to a more limited course in advertising by skipping the sections that do not directly apply. We strongly recommend the broader integrated approach, however, because of the trend in that direction in business practice.

Long-time users will quickly see that we have retained our traditional focus which has given this text a leading position in the field. But, *this is an altogether new book throughout.* The following are the greatest changes:

1. Professors and students alike consistently tell us to provide even more examples and illustrations. This we have done in every chapter. It makes for much more interesting and relevant reading.

2. We have been urged never to sacrifice our unique grounding in consumer behavior, and certainly we have not done so. But, as noted earlier, the behavioral material is slanted much more specifically toward promotional applications.

3. We have greatly expanded the chapter on The Nature of Communication (Chapter 3) by adding material on semiotics and nonverbal communication for the first time.

4. Chapters 5 and 6 focusing on understanding consumer behavior have been rewritten extensively from the perspective of promotional strategy considerations. Students will especially benefit from the emphasis on diagnosing consumer behavior in the context of expected outcomes.

5. Our treatment of promotional objectives (Chapter 9) is all new and plows fresh ground in tying objectives concretely to information gained from diagnosing consumer behavior.

6. The dynamic issues of channel command and control is highlighted in many chapters. Manufacturers have been forced to some radical new thinking in channel strategy, and students are immersed in the central issues.

7. Direct marketing continues to receive strong emphasis as a type of promotional strategy which has gained all-new importance in the current arena.

8. As usual, we end with a strong section on social and economic considerations. We hope that this is given the coverage it deserves in a world in which ethics all too often seem to be put on the back burner.

ACKNOWLEDGMENTS

Over the 23 years of our existence, we have been the beneficiaries of widespread input from colleagues literally throughout the world. This has proved invaluable. They are far too numerous to acknowledge by name here, but we do want to thank those who have specifically contributed their insights to this edition:

Les Carlson, *University of Arkansas, Fayetteville*

Gilbert Churchill, *University of Wisconsin, Madison*

Mark Fackler, *Wheaton College, Illinois*

John Holmes, *Bowling Green State University, Ohio*

Lawrence Johnson, *University of Kansas, Lawrence*

John Schleede, Jr., *Central Michigan University*

Also a special thank you to Beth Thompson and Ron Kobler for their help in developing materials for this revision.

We have always thanked our families over the years for their forbearance through the tyranny of seven revisions. Jim and Marty are empty nesters, but we still join Tom in expressing appreciation to our wives and kids who always have been partners with us. And, in keeping with our tradition, each of us continues to blame the other guys for errors and omissions in the manuscript.

A Special Tribute to Marion Harper

Over the years we have benefited from the input of leading professionals in the advertising and promotion world. In particular, the Interpublic Group of Companies, Inc. provided the opportunity for the senior author to have unlimited access to company and client resources for an extended period in the 1960s.

This was at the time when Marion Harper was chairperson at Interpublic. He stood out among his contemporaries as a strategic thinker and innovator, and Interpublic under his leadership became a world-recognized trend setter in strategic marketing.

Marion Harper passed away in late 1989. We would like to add our tribute to the many given upon his death. This book never would have achieved the impact it has had over its years of existence without the input and inspiration of Marion Harper and his executive team.

James F. Engel
Martin R. Warshaw
Thomas C. Kinnear

Contents

Part 1

OVERVIEW   **3**

Chapter 1

PROMOTIONAL STRATEGY: AN OVERVIEW   **5**

Promotional Strategy and the Marketing Exchange, 7
  Seven-Up's Promotion: Where's the Marketing Concept? 9

Promotional Strategy and the Marketing Concept, 10
  Manufacturer's Hanover: Consumer Need Defines Product
  Attributes and Promotion Direction, 11

Promotion Defined, 13

Promotional Strategy in Action, 14
  Acura: Quality Product + Promotion Excellence = Success, 14
  MCI: Promotion of New Services Takes a Bit Out of AT&T, 15
  Tupperware Promotion: Advertising and Sales Approach
  Respond to the Changing Consumer, 17

The Marketing Mix Communicates, 20
  The Product Communicates, 21
  Price Communicates, 21
  The Distribution Location Communicates, 25

Structure of this Book, 25

Review and Discussion Questions, 27

Notes, 28

Chapter 2

**PROMOTIONAL STRATEGY: A DECISION-MAKING
FRAMEWORK**   **29**

The Stages in Promotional Planning and Strategy, 30

Utilizing the Framework: Carnival Cruises to the Top, 32

Situation Analysis, 32
  History, 32
  Demand-Target Markets, 35
  Competition, 36
  Internal Organizational Considerations, 36

Establishment of Objectives, 36

Determination of Dollar Appropriation, 36

Specification and Management of Program Elements, 37
    Advertising, 37
    Distribution Channel Support, 37
    Supplemental Communications (Public Relations), 41

Coordination and Integration of Efforts, 41

Measurement of Effectiveness, 42

Evaluation and Follow-Up, 42

The Marketing Manager's Problem, 43

Review and Discussion Questions, 43

Notes, 44

Appendix 2A
PROMOTIONAL STRATEGIES OF CARNIVAL CRUISE LINES'
MAIN DIRECT COMPETITORS   45

Norwegian Caribbean, 45

Princess Cruises, 46

Sitmar, 46

Cunard, 47

American Hawaii, 48

Holland America, 48

Royal Caribbean, 49

Royal Viking, 49

Admiral, 50

Competitive Advertising, 51

Part 2
WHAT PERSUASIVE COMMUNICATION IS ALL ABOUT   57

Chapter 3
THE NATURE OF COMMUNICATION   59

What Communication Is All About, 61
    A Model of the Process, 61
    Bringing about Common Meaning, 62
    The Multiple Ways We Communicate, 68

Communication in Marketing, 74
Personal Selling, 74
Mass Communication, 75
A Summary Comparison, 78

Summary, 79

Review and Discussion Questions, 79

Notes, 80

Chapter 4
CONSUMER RESPONSE TO PERSUASIVE
COMMUNICATION   **83**

Information Processing, 84
The Central Role of Involvement, 87
Exposure, 88
Attention, 90
Comprehension, 96
Acceptance, 99
Retention, 102

Attitude Change and Persuasion, 102
Information Processing and Attitude Change, 103
Manipulation, 105
Deception, 105
Subliminal Influence, 106

Summary, 110

Review and Discussion Questions, 111

Notes, 112

Part 3
UNDERSTANDING THE CONSUMER   **117**

Chapter 5
UNDERSTANDING THE CONSUMER: EXTENDED
PROBLEM SOLVING   **119**

An Overview of Consumer Decision Processes, 122
The Initial Purchase, 123
Repeat Purchases, 126

Diagnosing Consumer Behavior, 126

Extended Problem Solving (EPS), 127
    Need Recognition, 127
    Search for Information, 133
    Alternative Evaluation, 140
    Purchase and Outcomes, 145

Summary, 147

Review and Discussion Questions, 148

Notes, 149

Chapter 6
UNDERSTANDING THE CONSUMER: LIMITED AND
HABITUAL DECISION-PROCESS BEHAVIOR   151

Limited Problem Solving, 152
    Need Recognition, 154
    Search for Information, 155
    Alternative Evaluation, 155
    Purchase, 156
    Outcomes, 156
    Some Clues for Marketing Strategy, 156
    Habitual Decision Making, 165
    Brand Loyalty, 166
    Inertia, 170

Summary, 171

Review and Discussion Questions, 171

Notes, 172

Chapter 7
INFLUENCE OF THE SOCIAL ENVIRONMENT   175

The Cultural Context, 176
    American Values and Their Influence on Promotional
    Strategy, 177

Subcultures, 187

Social Stratification, 187

Reference Groups, 189
    How Reference Groups Function, 190
    Determinants of Impact, 193

Family Influence, 194
    Influence on Buying Decisions, 195
    Family Life-Cycles, 196

Summary, 199

Review and Discussion Questions, 199

Notes, 200

Part 4

BASIC CONSIDERATIONS IN PROMOTIONAL STRATEGY   **203**

Chapter 8
MARKET SEGMENTATION AND
COMPETITIVE POSITIONING   **205**

The Concept of Segmentation, 207
    Criteria of Usable Segments, 208

Bases for Segmentation, 209
    Geographic Variables, 211
    Demographic Characteristics, 212
    Psychographic Characteristics, 219
    Behavioristic Variables, 224
    Benefits Segmentation, 225
    Product Usage Rates, 226
    Undertaking Segmentation Analysis, 227

The Target Market Decision, 228
    Undifferentiated Marketing, 228
    Differentiated Marketing, 228
    Concentrated Marketing, 230
    The Choice of Approach, 230

Competitive Positioning, 230
    Positioning by Attribute, 231
    Positioning by Price and Quality, 231
    Positioning by Use or Application, 231
    Positioning by Product User, 231
    Positioning by Product Class, 234
    Positioning by Competitor, 234
    Developing a Positioning Strategy, 236

Key Strategic Choices: Segment Targeting and Product
Positioning, 238

Summary, 238

Review and Discussion Questions, 239

Notes, 240

Chapter 9
DETERMINATION OF PROMOTIONAL OBJECTIVES   **241**

Background Considerations, 242
    Market Segmentation, 242
    Other Elements of Marketing Strategy, 243
    Sales and Market Share Goals, 243
    Financial Resources, 244

Using Consumer Research to Define the Role for
Promotion, 244

Description of the Market Target, 245

Diagnosing Motivation and Behavior in a Target Segment, 248

The Statement of Objectives, 256
Target Market, 256
Message Platform, 256
Expected Sales Results, 257
Expected Communication Results, 258
Measurement Methods and Criteria, 259

Summary, 259

Review and Discussion Questions, 260

Notes, 261

Chapter 10
THE PROMOTIONAL APPROPRIATION   **263**

Theoretical Foundations of the Outlay Problem, 265

Traditional Appropriation Approaches, 268
Arbitrary Allocation, 268
Percentage of Sales, 270
Return on Investment, 271
Competitive Parity, 272
All You Can Afford, 272
Objective and Task, 274

Conclusions on Determining the Appropriation, 275

Implementing the Objective-and-Task Approach, 275
Isolation of Objectives, 276
Expenditure Estimation through Build-Up Analysis, 276
Comparison Against Industry Percentage-of-Sales
Guidelines, 278
Comparison Against Projected Percentage of Future Sales, 279
Reconciliation of Divergence between Built-Up Costs and
Percentage-of-Sales Figures, 279
Payout Planning, 279
Modification of Estimates in Terms of Company Policies, 280
Specification of When Expenditures Will Be Made, 280
Building in Flexibility, 280
Comments on the Suggested Approach, 281

Geographic Allocation, 281
Corollary Products Index, 282
Industry Sales, 283
General Buying Power Indexes, 283
Custom-Made Indexes, 284

Expenditures for New Products, 286
Payout Planning, 286

Summary, 290

Review and Discussion Questions, 291

Notes, 292

Chapter 11
ORGANIZATION AND USE OF HUMAN RESOURCES   **293**

Organizational Requirements and Structures, 294
    The Requirements of a Modern Marketing Organization, 295
    Organizational Structures, 300

The Advertising Agency, 303
    Organization of the Advertising Agency, 303
    Principles of the Agency-Client Relationship, 305
    Agency Compensation, 308
    Industry Adjustments, 309
    The House Agency, 311

Using Specialized Services, 315
    Direct Marketing Agencies, 315
    Media-Buying Services, 315
    Creative Boutiques, 316
    Research Services, 316
    Market Changes and the Advertising Industry, 316

Summary, 317

Review and Discussion Questions, 318

Notes, 319

Chapter 12
ADAPTATION TO THE LEGAL CLIMATE   **321**

Pertinent Legislation, 323
    Federal Legislation, 323
    The Future of the Federal Trade Commission, 328
    State and Local Regulations, 331
    Self-Regulation, 332

Important Areas of Regulation, 336
    Content of Advertisements, 337
    Type of Product Advertised, 342
    Vertical Cooperative Advertising, 344
    Advertising and Competition, 344
    Remedial Alternatives, 345
    Regulation of Personal Selling, 348

Summary, 350

Review and Discussion Questions, 351

Notes, 352

Part 5

ADVERTISING AND SALES PROMOTION   **355**

Chapter 13
THE ADVERTISING MESSAGE   **357**

Creative Strategy, 359

Creative Execution, 360
  Persuasion through Advertising: Influencing Attitudes
  and Behavior, 361
  Advertising and the Elaboration Likelihood Model
  of Persuasion, 363
  Behavioral Research Findings for Advertising, 364

A Useful Guide to Creative Aspects, 365
  Alternataive Advertising Approaches, 365
  Choosing an Approach for the Product, 370

Designing and Producing Advertising Messages, 390

Analysis of the Message, 390
  Judgemental Analysis: Evaluation of Execution, 391

Summary, 393

Review and Discussion Questions, 393

Notes, 394

Appendix 13
DESIGNING AND PRODUCING THE MASS
COMMUNICATION MESSAGE   **395**

Print Advertising, 395

The Headline, 395
  Classifications of Headlines, 395
  Some Guides for a Persuasive Headline, 397

Copy, 398
  Classification of Copy Approaches, 398
  Some Copy Problems, 399
  Some Guides for Persuasive Copy, 401

Visual Elements, 402
  Classification of Visual Forms, 403
  Some Guides for Persuasive Visualization, 405

Radio and Television, 406

Copy, 406

Notes, 408

Chapter 14
ANALYSIS OF MASS MEDIA RESOURCES   **411**

Expenditure Trends, 413

Newspapers, 413

Characteristics of Newspapers, 415
    Buying Newspaper Space, 420
    The Future of Newspapers, 420

Television, 421
    General Characteristics of Television, 422
    The Network Television Programs, 424
    Buying Network Time, 426
    Spot Announcements, 427
    Buying Spot Time, 428
    The Future of Television, 429

Radio, 435
    Characteristics of Radio, 436
    The Future of Radio, 439

Magazines, 439
    Characteristics of Magazines, 440
    The Future of Magazines, 442

Outdoor Advertising, 444
    Characteristics of Outdoor Advertising, 444
    Purchasing Outdoor Space, 445
    The Future of Outdoor Advertising, 446

New Media: Videotex, 447

Transit Advertising, 447
    Characteristics of Transit Advertising, 447
    Purchasing Transit Space, 449
    The Future of Transit, 450

The Noncommissionable Media, 450
    Direct Mail, 450
    Point-of-Purchase Advertisements, 451

Intermedia Comparison, 451

Summary, 461

Review and Discussion Questions, 461

Notes, 463

Chapter 15
MEDIA STRATEGY   **465**

The Requirements of Creative Strategy, 467

Reaching the Proper Audience, 468
    Media Audience Data, 468

Reach and Frequency, 476
    The Problem of Audience Duplication, 477
    Using Reach, Frequency, and GRP Measures, 478

Competitive Considerations, 482

Cost Considerations, 483

Qualitative Media Characteristics, 486

Distribution Requirements, 487

Scheduling, 487
    Geographical Scheduling, 488
    Seasonal Scheduling, 489
    Flighting, 490
    Putting the Media Plan Together, 493
    Scheduling within Media, 493

Summary, 497

Review and Discussion Questions, 497

Notes, 498

Chapter 16
MEASUREMENT OF ADVERTISING EFFECTIVENESS   **499**

An Ideal Copy-Testing Procedure: PACT, 502

Cell I: Advertising-Related Laboratory Measures for Pretesting, 503
    1. The Consumer Jury, 503
    2. Focus Groups, 506
    3. Portfolio Tests, 506
    4. Readability Tests, 507
    5. Physiological Measures, 508

Cell II: Product-Related Laboratory Measures for Pretesting, 509
    1. Theater Tests, 509
    2. Trailer Tests, 510
    3. Laboratory Stores, 510

Cell III: Advertising-Related Measurement under Real-World
Conditions for Pretesting and Posttesting, 510
    Pretesting Procedures, 511
    Posttesting Procedures, 513

Cell IV: Product-Related Measures under Real-World
Conditions for Pretesting and Posttesting, 522
    Pretesting and Posttesting Procedures, 522

Summary, 536

Review and Discussion Questions, 536

Notes, 537

Chapter 17
MANAGEMENT OF CONSUMER SALES PROMOTION   **539**

Scope and Importance of Sales Promotion, 541

Consumer-Oriented Sales Promotion, 543

Consumer Promotional Alternatives, 545
    Sampling, 545
    Price Incentives, 547
    Couponing, 552
    Premiums, 555
    Contents and Sweepstakes, 558

Packaging, 562
    Promotional Aspects, 563

Summary, 567

Review and Discussion Questions, 568

Notes, 568

Part 6
PERSONAL SELLING   **571**

Chapter 18
PERSONAL SELLING STRATEGY   **573**

Personal Selling in the Promotion Mix, 574

The Influence of the Product-Market Situation, 576
    Proprietary Drug Manufacturer, 576
    Computer Manufacturer, 577
    Electron Beam Welding Service, 578
    Implications of the Cases, 578

What Do Salespeople Do? 579

Salesmanship, 579
    Buyer-Seller Interactions, 580
    Different Selling Situations, 580

Steps of a Sale, 581
    Prospecting, 582
    Preapproach, 582
    The Approach, 582
    The Presentation, 583
    Meeting Objectives, 583
    Closing the Sale, 584
    Follow-Up, 584

Summary, 585

Review and Discussion Questions, 585

Notes, 586

Chapter 19
BUILDING THE SALES FORCE   587

Building the Sales Force, 588
  Job Descriptions and Recruitment, 588
  Selecting Salespeople, 590
  Training Salespeople, 592
  Assignment of Sales Personnel, 594

Sales Force Management—Compensation and Motivation, 596
  Compensating Salespeople, 596
  Motivating Salespeople, 600
  Methods of Communication, 602
  Organizational Variables and Their Impact
  on Sales, 603

Summary, 604

Review and Discussion Questions, 606

Notes, 606

Chapter 20
EVALUATION AND CONTROL OF SALES FORCE
EFFORTS   607

Information Needs, 609

The Evaluation and Control Process, 609
  Developing Performance Standards, 609
  Standards for Measurement of Performance, 611
  Comparing Sellers' Performance to Standards, 612
  Corrective Action, 614

Reallocation of Effort, 615
  Sales Force Sizing and Deployment at Syntex Laboratories, 617
  The Challenges of Model Building, 619
  Conclusions, 621
  Model Implementation and Results, 621

Summary, 625

Review and Discussion Questions, 625

Notes, 626

Part 7

OTHER FORMS OF PROMOTION   629

Chapter 21
WORKING WITH RESELLERS: THE STRUGGLE FOR
CHANNEL CONTROL   631

The Struggle for Market Entry, 632
    Technology and the Power Shift, 632

The Promotional Role of Resellers, 633
    The Impact of Manufacturer Promotional Strategy, 634
    Effects of Product Evolution, 634
    Implications of Reseller's Promotional Role, 637

Improving Reseller Performance, 638
    Training Reseller Salespeople, 638
    Quotas for Resellers, 642
    Advertising and Sales Promotion Assistance, 642

Supplementing Reseller Performance, 653
    Missionary (Specialty) Selling, 653
    Display and Selling Aids, 654
    Consumer Deals, 656

Controlling Reseller Performance, 657
    Adapting to the New Environment, 657
    Selected Resellers, 658
    Nonselected Resellers, 659
    Vertical Integration, 660
    Distribution Programming, 660

Summary, 662

Review and Discussion Questions, 665

Notes, 666

Chapter 22
DIRECT MARKETING   669

A Growth Industry, 670

The Database—The Key to Direct Marketing Success, 672

Direct Marketing Strategies, 674

Managing the Direct-Marketing Process, 684
    Agencies, 684
    Integrated Strategies, 684
    Measurement of Effectiveness, 686
    Managing the Database, 686

Summary, 687

Review and Discussion Questions, 688

Notes, 688

Chapter 23
PUBLIC RELATIONS, CORPORATE ADVERTISING,
AND PUBLICITY   **691**

Internal Communications, 693

External Communications, 695
    Organizational Symbols, 695
    Corporate Advertising, 696
    Customer Relations Programs, 699

Publicity, 703

Case Histories of Successful Public Relations, 704
    Public Relations Strategy for Rescuing Tylenol, 704
    Public Relations Strategy at Carnival Cruise Lines, 706
    The Acquisition of Holland America Lines, 707
    The Commissioning of the *Fantasy,* 710
    Other Public Relations Activities, 710

The Image of Public Relations, 710

Summary, 710

Review and Discussion Questions, 711

Notes, 711

Part 8
EPILOGUE   **715**

Chapter 24
ECONOMIC AND SOCIAL DIMENSIONS   **717**

Effects On Consumer Behavior, 718

Effects On New Products, Prices, and Competition, 723

Validity of the Fundamental Premises, 727
    Is Profit a Valid Measure of Business Responsibility? 731

Strengthening the Free Enterprise System, 732
    Organizational Mission, 732
    Cooperative Efforts, 733

Summary, 737
Review and Discussion Questions, 737
Notes, 738

INDEX   **741**

PROMOTIONAL STRATEGY
Managing the Marketing Communications Process

OVERVIEW

Part 1 of this book introduces concepts that provide a foundation and framework for the chapters that follow.

Chapter 1 stresses the importance of promotional strategy to the success of businesses and nonprofit organizations of all types. This chapter ties promotional activity directly to the marketing concept and to the practice of marketing management. This relationship is presented through a discussion of promotion as the communications activity of marketing and by showing how other parts of the marketing mix—price, distribution, and product—also have communication power.

Chapter 2 describes a framework for analyzing, planning, and implementing decisions that confront the promotion manager. Promotional activities related to the advertising, sales force, and consumer and trade promotion of Carnival Cruise Lines are used to illustrate this framework in depth. The illustration is presented in the context of an overview of the promotional activity of Carnival's competitors. Carnival's promotional activities will be used in other chapters of the book to illustrate the practical application of conceptual material presented in those chapters. In addition, many other practical illustrations will be presented to reinforce the conceptual material.

Promotional Strategy: An Overview

HELENE CURTIS' SALON SELECTIVES STORM THE MARKET WITH SMART PROMOTION

In a slow-growing market (1 percent to 2 percent a year) in which new-product launches are frequent, payback periods have increased to more than 18 months, product life-cycles have decreased from seven to eight years to three to four years, consumers have virtually no brand loyalty, companies must rely on hefty budgets to promote their products. These budgets, which include advertising, consumer promotions, and trade promotions, are used in an attempt to win shelf space and sales from competitors.

Today, because of incredible competition, many companies (e.g., Revlon, Clairol, and Procter & Gamble) assign specific roles to each brand within their hair care product portfolio to strengthen the position of the entire company rather than simply to focus on the market share that each brand controls. For example, one brand's role may be to attract the premium-quality market segment.

Helene Curtis is a prime example of recognizing market needs and responding to them. The company, which offers Suave in the economy segment and Finesse in the premium segment, saw a growing market for salon-style products. Although fancy names at fancy prices abounded, Helene Curtis realized that no one was offering a mass-marketed line that could make a woman feel as though she had just stepped out of a salon. Opportunity knocked. Helene Curtis answered with style in 1987 when it introduced Salon Selectives.

Backed by an advertising budget of $14 million, Salon Selectives captured $40 million in sales during its first year and $90 million during its second year. The third year projection of $125 million was achieved amid some high-spending competition in a brutally competitive, highly fragmented category.

Salon-type shampoos currently account for 10 percent of the total market.

With a 3.6 percent share, Salon Selectives vaulted into second place behind Vidal Sassoon. Its conditioners did equally well, capturing 6 percent of the market in which Sassoon held 6.6 percent and Jhirmack held 5 percent. And all of this was done without cannibalizing the company's upscale Finesse products.

How did Helene Curtis achieve prominence so quickly? It used marketing research to determine what customers wanted and to create certain competitive advantages. For example, Helene Curtis has been a major supplier to salons since the 1940s, and consumers equated its name with salons. Salon Selectives capitalized on the company's heritage by emphasizing the Helene Curtis name on its distinctive package. Another advantage was the unique pink package designed to "leap off the shelf at the consumer," according to Donald Davis, editor of *Drug & Cosmetic Industry* and *Cosmetic Insider's Report*.

Salon Selectives also offered a new system of hair formula differentiation based on consumers' needs and each product's individual benefits. Designers believed that the long-used system of classifying hair products as "dry," "normal," and "oily" was worn out and generic. Salon Selectives' new system used numbers and letters to distinguish different levels of cleansing and conditioning. For example, Level 1 is a superlight cleansing for fine hair, and Level 7 offers a deep cleansing for hair that is frequently sprayed and moussed. Type B conditioners are for consumers who want extra body in their hair. The line's customized, salon-like aura grew.

Part of the credit for its success goes to President and CEO Ron Gidwitz, whose formula for success includes a strong bent for promotional strategy: "Advertising and promotion expenses are real investments in the business." According to Karen Moberly, co-brand manager of Salon Selectives, "Nothing gets you broad-scale awareness faster than TV," so that is exactly where most of the first year's $14 million advertising budget went. Smaller percentages of advertising dollars also went to cable TV and to spot and print ads (see Figure 1–1). Network TV received $8.7 million, $101,500 went to spot TV, $172,000 to cable TV, $1.6 million to syndication, $778,300 to network radio, $98,900 to spot radio, and $2.1 million to magazines. The print media were considered to be more appropriate for knowledge development. Print ads aimed at most of the women's service and beauty books provided an opportunity to educate consumers on the new brand's unique terminology and customized hair care.

Realizing that success would only spur the competition, Helene Curtis supplied samples of its Salon Selectives products to 18 million households through a direct mail campaign. Plans call for an increase of 20 percent in advertising and similar increases in trade and consumer promotions. Increasing or even just holding Salon Selectives' market share will require even stronger support than the effort expended for its initial success.

Source: Based on "Cheap Chic," *Marketing and Media Decisions,* March 1989, pp. 95–98.

PROMOTIONAL STRATEGY AND THE MARKETING EXCHANGE

In the preceding discussion about Helene Curtis, the dynamic nature of the promotional strategy process is illustrated. We see the promotional manager at Helene Curtis being concerned with *advertising, promotions* to consumers and to the retail channel, *package design,* and *brand name*. Although the Helene Curtis sales force is not mentioned in the example, it was actively supporting the sale of the brand to the channel, presenting the special promotions to the trade, and assuring proper logistical support. All of these activities *communicate*. Imagine yourself with the exciting and complex task of effectively developing and implementing these diverse elements of marketing communications.

The need for this communication activity in marketing arises because an informational gap exists between producers of items (goods, services, and ideas) and potential consumers. The consumer needs information to be aware of the existence of alternative products. This information creates information utility so that the consumer can make better choices. Communication activity provides producers access to markets that would otherwise be unavailable because the consumer lacked information about the product.

Thus promotional strategy plays a significant role in marketing—the creation of mutually beneficial exchanges between producers and consumers of goods, services, and ideas. Both sides benefit when promotional strategy operates properly; both can be hurt when it is done improperly.

FIGURE 1–1

 Salon Selectives Advertisement

To be effective, the promotional strategy must be guided by the *marketing concept*. That is, it must focus on consumer needs and integrate all activities of the organization to satisfy these needs. Thus promotional activity must be consistent with the needs of the consumer and integrated with the other elements of the marketing mix, and with other nonmarketing functional areas of the organization. To illustrate, we present an example of a failure to adhere to the marketing concept by Seven-Up and then one of successful use of promotion within the marketing concept by Manufacturers Hanover Trust Company.

Seven-Up's Promotion: Where's the Marketing Concept?

Seven-Up Co.'s two-year-old strategy of introducing new products by leveraging the 7UP trademark[1] has been laid to rest. Failure of its 7UP Gold and declining sales for its Cherry 7UP have forced the company to refocus marketing efforts on its flagship brand 7UP.

Seven-Up launched a $30 million network TV campaign in an attempt to recover some of the market it lost due to 7UP Gold's double whammy. As Paine Webber analyst Manny Goldman put it, "Gold didn't make it, and it had a negative spillover on Cherry 7UP." Volume sales of Cherry 7UP dropped 41.3 percent in 1987, and regular 7UP dropped 8.8 percent.

These losses occurred amidst reemerging cola wars, increased competition from Coca-Cola Co.'s Sprite and Pepsi Co., Inc.'s Slice, and continual decline of the lemon-lime category's share in the total soft-drink industry. The lemon-lime category, which held an 11.3 percent share of the total 1986 soft drink market, fell to a 10.6 percent share in 1987 and a 10.5 percent share in 1988. The numbers showed no significant market demand for new lemon-lime soft-drink products, and the 7UP name was not enough to create one.

Cherry 7UP is the cherry-flavored version of the flagship brand, caffeine-free 7UP. Introduced in 1986, Cherry 7UP was considered a major hit. It was the talk of the industry when it captured over 2 percent of the total beverage market in 1987. This easy-success story was brought back to reality in 1988 when the brand fell to a respectable but unacceptable 1.2 percent market share. Although Cherry 7UP's novelty and the 7UP name may have won the product's initial triumph, they were not enough to ensure long-term success.

7UP Gold is a spicy citrus soft drink containing caffeine. Introduced in April 1988, 7UP Gold was originally positioned as the "Wild Side of 7UP" and aimed at cola drinkers aged 18 to 34. This was yet another new target for the company. It missed its mark. Consumers did not like the taste.

Seven-Up's President and CEO, John Albers, believed that "perhaps in our zeal and in our euphoria over Cherry 7UP we underestimated the trade's growing impatience with new brands . . . and pressure for shelf space."

Despite a $10 million media campaign, 7UP Gold failed to attain its promotional objective of 20 percent of the company's sales volume.

During this period, the two new products were allocated promotional dollars at the expense of the flagship brands, 7UP and Diet 7UP. As a result, the market position of 7UP and Diet 7UP deteriorated. In total, all 7UP versions experienced a market-share decline in the lemon-lime product category of over 9 percent points in five years. The 1990s find the Seven-Up Company struggling to reverse its decline.

What went wrong here? No doubt there were many considerations, but there are signs that management lapsed into a *selling* or a *promotional orientation*. As Kotler puts it:

> The selling concept is a management orientation that assumes that consumers will either not buy or not buy enough of the organization's products unless the organization makes a substantial effort to stimulate their interest in its products.[2]

The selling concept is based on the assumption that a high level of advertising or sales firepower will somehow work to move the product. It almost endows promotion with a kind of magic through which the consumer can be maneuvered in almost any direction management desires.

No one denies the potential impact from skillful use of media, but a selling orientation tends to ignore an absolute fact of business life—*consumer sovereignty*. The consumer tends to see and hear what he or she wants to see and hear, and the firm can do little to overcome this basic human characteristic! We intend to demonstrate in detail just how consumer sovereignty works and what it means for promotional management, but one thing is clear—if the consumer does not want the product or service, the firm is pretty much powerless to do anything except to change what it offers the market.

What this boils down to is that promotion is only one part, albeit an important one, of a total mix of marketing efforts. It cannot, for example, move an unwanted or overpriced product. It simply does not possess that magic.

Seven-Up's lessons were painful ones. Its profitability declined substantially over this period. It had simply gotten out of touch with its current customers, had failed to properly understand the targeted new customers of its new products, and had failed to meet the needs of its distributors and retail outlets.

PROMOTIONAL STRATEGY AND THE MARKETING CONCEPT

Now let's examine a successful use of promotional tools in marketing a financial service package offered by Manufacturers Hanover Trust Company.[3]

Manufacturers Hanover: Consumer Need Defines Product Attributes and Promotion Direction

The deregulation of the banking industry in the 1980s created a mad scramble in the financial services business. Competition became fierce as banks began to introduce a wide variety of innovative products and services. Faced with such a wide range of financial options, many customers began developing multiple relationships with banks and utilizing specific services that were being offered by different sources.

Manufacturers Hanover Trust Co. of New York recognized a marketing opportunity being created by the "pick and choose" attitude of the postderegulation banking customer. While searching for ways to increase profits in its Retail Banking Division, Manufacturers Hanover realized that if customers with multiple banking relationships could be convinced to consolidate their accounts, the bank's deposit base could be increased at a lower cost than otherwise would be possible. At the same time, the bank could attract more lucrative credit business.

The problem lay in developing an "all-in-one" package that would appeal to customers. Experience had shown Manufacturers Hanover that simply introducing new products and services would not be enough to accomplish its goals; it needed a handle to place on top of the programs already in place or being formed. In addition, marketing research indicated that the typical New York customer was somewhat skeptical about the idea that one bank was able to offer adequate reasons for doing more business in one place. The product-by-product buying habits of the customer did not fit into the all-in-one package account concept.

Research did show, however, that if a bank could adequately demonstrate how customers would personally benefit by consolidating more of their accounts, they would do so.

"What we needed was a simple way to better communicate all of our offerings to consumers, and, in particular, to show them the benefits they would receive in return for consolidating more of their business with us," said Robert J. Hutchinson, the vice president, retail banking for Manufacturers Hanover. "Moreover, it had to be flexible enough to allow us to also focus on the specific needs customers may be shopping around to fulfill, so we could bring them in our doors and then quickly show all the other benefits of doing even more business at MHT."

What Manufacturers Hanover decided to develop was a special package account that would serve as an umbrella for its overall advertising campaign. A special study commissioned by the bank indicated that lifestyle was a major influence on a consumer's choice of financial institution. Manufacturers Hanover decided to capitalize on this research by emphasizing the convenience of its program in helping customers to better manage their money.

Introduced in April 1986, the One-For-All Banking program allowed the bank to creatively combine all of its promotional efforts for credit and deposits. The One-For-All package included mutual funds and other financial planning services as well as the more typical checking, savings, and credit services other banks provided. The program offered many benefits: lower fees and service charges, better loan rates, special CD rates for customers maintaining both checking and savings accounts, lower home loan fees, discounts on financial planning seminars and consultations, and access to 10 different mutual funds. A special service offered financial planning information over the phone.

To make the most of the program introduction, the bank created a special promotional package. The product was unveiled with two-page advertising spreads in the major New York papers. A series of print ads and aggressive advertising on local television stations followed. Manufacturers Hanover distributed a comprehensive press kit that gave detailed descriptions of the program's benefits. One-For-All Banking was marketed with special high bonus rates on 7- and 12-month certificates of deposit. In addition, just before the product was launched, employees were given training at special regional sales meetings on how to communicate the One-For-All Banking concept to customers.

The marketing plan was a success: One-For-All Banking contributed to a rise in new checking accounts and higher savings balances that were well above initial projections. The program served as a showcase for all of the bank's products and services and helped build its image as a force in the marketplace. The promotional efforts were particularly successful in identifying differences between the One-For-All program and the linked package accounts offered by competitors. According to Mr. Hutchinson, "These differences matched what marketing research told us were major unmet needs of our target customer base."

The business philosophy of Manufacturers Hanover follows the marketing concept as defined by Kotler:

> The *marketing concept* is a management orientation that holds that the key to achieving organizational goals consists of the organization's determining the needs and wants of target markets and adapting itself to delivering the desired satisfactions more effectively and efficiently than its competitors.[4]

The marketing concept starts with the premise of consumer sovereignty. The product itself, its promotion, its price, and its distribution all are adapted to consumer motivations to attract and hold their loyalty. There is clearly recognition that failure to adopt a marketing orientation can be followed by a marked drop in market standing.

Marketing, then, encompasses a broad mix of efforts (product, price, promotion, and distribution) through which the firm adapts its offerings to a changing environment. No single element of this mix can be managed apart from the others without a potentially disastrous outcome. Also, all elements of the marketing mix have given some information to the consumer, and thus are a concern in promotional strategy.

PROMOTION DEFINED

Promotion has had many meanings over the years. The original connotation in Latin was "to move forward." More recently the meaning has narrowed so that it refers to communication undertaken to persuade others to accept ideas, concepts, or things. As used in this book, promotional strategy is a *controlled integrated program of communication methods and materials designed to present an organization and its products to prospective customers; to communicate need-satisfying attributes of products to facilitate sales and thus contribute to long-run profit performance.* The tools of promotion include:

1. *Advertising*—Paid, nonpersonal communication through various media by business firms, nonprofit organizations, and individuals who are in some way identified in the advertising message and who hope to inform and/or persuade members of a particular audience; includes communication of products, services, institutions, and ideas.
2. *Personal selling*—The process of assisting and persuading a prospect to buy a good or service or to act on an idea through use of person-to-person communication.
3. *Reseller support*—Incentives given to wholesalers and retailers.
4. *Publicity*—Non-paid-for communication of information about the company or product, generally in some media form.
5. *Sales promotion*—Those marketing activities, other than personal selling, advertising, and publicity, that stimulate consumer purchasing and dealer effectiveness, such as displays, shows and exhibitions, demonstrations, and various nonrecurrent selling efforts not in the ordinary routine.[5]

Promotion, then, is the communication function of marketing. It is multifaceted and complex. No single textbook could treat all of these topics in detail. Our concern here is mostly on consumer goods because the whole industrial market raises unique and specialized issues. Therefore, in the book we focus on advertising, personal selling, and stimulation of support in the trade. Activities of a more supplementary nature, such as sales promotion, public relations, and publicity, also are covered but in less depth. Before proceeding, we will illustrate the use of promotional strategy in a number of different contexts.

PROMOTIONAL STRATEGY IN ACTION

In this chapter, we have already seen promotions in action three times. The Helene Curtis Salon Selectives and Manufacturers Hanover examples showed the positive power of effective promotion campaigns. The failure of promotional activity at Seven-Up has helped us recognize the limitations of the power of promotion when no real consumer need or want is being satisfied. This section of the chapter presents three additional examples of promotion in action to demonstrate to the reader the importance, complexity, and capabilities of promotion. These examples also show promotion at work for different types of products and services.

Acura: Quality Product + Promotion Excellence = Success

The introduction of the Acura[6] by the American Honda Motor Company in 1986 was viewed as a risky move. The U.S. luxury car market had long been dominated by European champions such as BMW, Mercedes Benz, Volvo, and Audi. Critics questioned a Japanese auto company's ability to successfully compete in this segment. The figures speak for themselves.

American Honda's Acura division sold 160,000 cars during its first 21 months in operation, including 109,470 in 1987. *Motor Trend* named the Legend Coupe its 1987 Import Car of the Year, and Acura was ranked number one in a customer satisfaction index conducted by J. D. Powers & Associates. Two years after its introduction, this former long shot had become the leader in the import luxury auto market.

Acura's initial strategy was to attract former Honda buyers who were ready to move up to a more expensive model. Since these buyers had traditionally moved into the European luxury car market, Acura directed its advertising against European automakers, using slogans such as "the finest sports coupes no longer have to come from Europe." Early ads sought to distinguish Acura's upscale car line from Honda's other models and its traditional image in the car market; later ads capitalized on Honda's championship racing heritage. TV, radio, and print ads emphasized Acura's high performance and speed, along with its press critiques and awards. Acura increased its 1987 media budget more than 300 percent, from $10 million in 1986 to $32.1 million in 1987. Magazine expenditures increased from $4.5

million to $11 million (see Figure 1–2), network TV increased from $1.1 million to $16.5 million, spot TV decreased from $3.7 million to $2.2 million, network cable increased from $66,800 to $495,900, and newspaper expenditures increased from $638,200 to $2 million.

When the dollar fell against the yen and the mark, Acura found itself in a prime position to attract other segments in the European luxury import market. The price range for Acura's Legend line, $21,000 to $30,000, was still significantly below the price ranges for BMW ($24,000 to $67,000) and Mercedes ($30,000 to $70,000). Potential BMW and Mercedes buyers wandered into Acura dealerships. While BMW's 1987 sales fell 10 percent, Acura's sales increased 52 percent and is expected to continue to rise. Acura used its promotional strategy to seize a lucrative market opportunity and successfully launch the first line of upscale Japanese imports.

MCI: Promotion of New Services Takes a Bite Out of AT&T

Long distance had long been synonymous with AT&T—until 1988.[7] Suddenly, another player made its mark on the phone scene and forced AT&T to rethink its complacent marketing strategy. MCI convinced America that communications companies had more to offer than tradition had previously dictated and that they could offer value-added services with a wide array of products and an excellent support staff. Many consumers decided not to settle for less, and MCI firmly established itself as the country's number two phone company.

MCI did not stumble into this position easily. Its reputation for lousy technology at a great price lasted through late 1987. The technology improved, but the marketing department faced the immense task of changing MCI's image. Promotional strategy that utilized both interpersonal and mass communication was the key.

MCI's ad campaign was based on the theme "Let us show you." It emphasized MCI's commitment to quality service and knowing what today's businesspeople really want. Its "Sales Representative" ad featured an MCI salesperson walking into a customer's suite while an omniscient voice noted that "most people can't write down the name of the sales representative from their long-distance company." The obvious implication was that MCI customers can name their representative and that their ability to do so reflects the fact that MCI salespeople call on clients and prospective clients more often than AT&T salespeople. This theme was expanded as the campaign continued to emphasize MCI's commitment to quality service and knowing what today's business people really want.

Their campaign also targeted MCI's other services. A huge push was made to make MCI's calling card "America's business card." Print ads reinforced television spots. MCI also mailed briefcases containing working MCI

FIGURE 1–2

❖   **Acura Advertisement**

A C U R A   I N T E G R A   1 6 - V A L V E   D O H C

Integra gives comfort a sporting chance. A new dimension in performance, from a new division of American Honda. Exclusively at Acura dealerships.

The Acura Integra.
A more humane approach to performance.

In the pursuit of spirited performance, many drivers have withstood phone booth interiors and nerve numbing suspensions.

This is definitely not our idea of fun.

Thus, the Acura Integra presents a much more humane approach. A three door sports sedan that recognizes the desire for spirited performance and need for creature comforts.

Integra's 16-valve, fuel injected dual overhead cam engine is a descendant of Honda Formula 1 racing technology.

Coupled with sport suspension, four wheel disc brakes, power assist rack and pinion steering and refined front wheel drive.

A long wheelbase and wide track matches agility with smooth, solid stability.

A low hoodline and expansive flush mounted glass increase visibility, while sleek aerodynamics reduce wind noise.

Performance has been well accommodated in an ergonomically precise cockpit. As has room and comfort for five.

Analog instrumentation reads at a glance.

Controls are positioned for easy reaching.

And equally thoughtful standard features increase the pleasures of driving.

Call 1-800-TO-ACURA for the dealer nearest you. And discover the comfort of performance.

ACURA
PRECISION CRAFTED AUTOMOBILES
A division of American Honda Motor Co., Inc.

cards to one group of top executives and sent another mailing of free calling cards to still another target group. Both mailings were supported by follow-up calls from MCI salespeople; 30 percent of the first group and 25 percent of the second group started using the calling card. The MCI 800 service was also featured (see Figure 1–3). MCI's marketing campaign for its fax service, which included fax coupons, was even more elaborate and very effective.

MCI was willing to invest heavily in promotion to support this strategy. During this campaign, network television advertising was increased from $11.4 million to $24.4 million. Spot television tripled to $233,800. Magazine expenditures were $4.9 million with newspaper and cable television also receiving increased allocations.

The results of the campaign were fantastic. Market share jumped 2 percent, revenue increased from $3.94 billion to $5.14 billion, and profits went up fivefold to $346 million. MCI reported a 40 percent increase in calling traffic in one quarter while AT&T's traffic was down 3 percent for the entire year. AT&T flew to the defensive by changing its ads, billing procedures, product line, and business calling rates. It wanted to show that it, too, could offer "impeccable customer service." Figure 1–4 presents an AT&T ad designed to gain back lost ground in these premium services. This drastic response by its competitor was a sure measure of MCI's marketing success.

Tupperware Promotion: Advertising and Sales Approach Respond to the Changing Consumer

Tupperware has long been a household word. Traditional Tupperware products are basically a wide variety of tripolymer food storage containers distinguished by Earl Tupper's air-tight seal. Under the company's original system, products were sold strictly through a houseware party format.[8] Tupperware's salespeople, referred to as *hosts* and *hostesses,* invited guests to their homes for an evening-long Tupperware party. These parties were designed to capitalize on the advantages of personal selling: products were demonstrated and customers could handle the products so they knew exactly what they were ordering.

The company's distribution system created a major bottleneck. Customers placed their orders with and paid the host or hostess. The host or hostess then mailed the orders to the regional distributor, who filled them from inventory and sent them back to the home of the host or hostess where each customer had to pick them up. This process took approximately three weeks.

Changing demographics and awkward distribution systems demand change from young products and old classics alike. Tupperware's marketing system was forced to accommodate today's growing percentage of working

FIGURE 1–3

FIGURE 1–4

❖ AT&T Advertisement

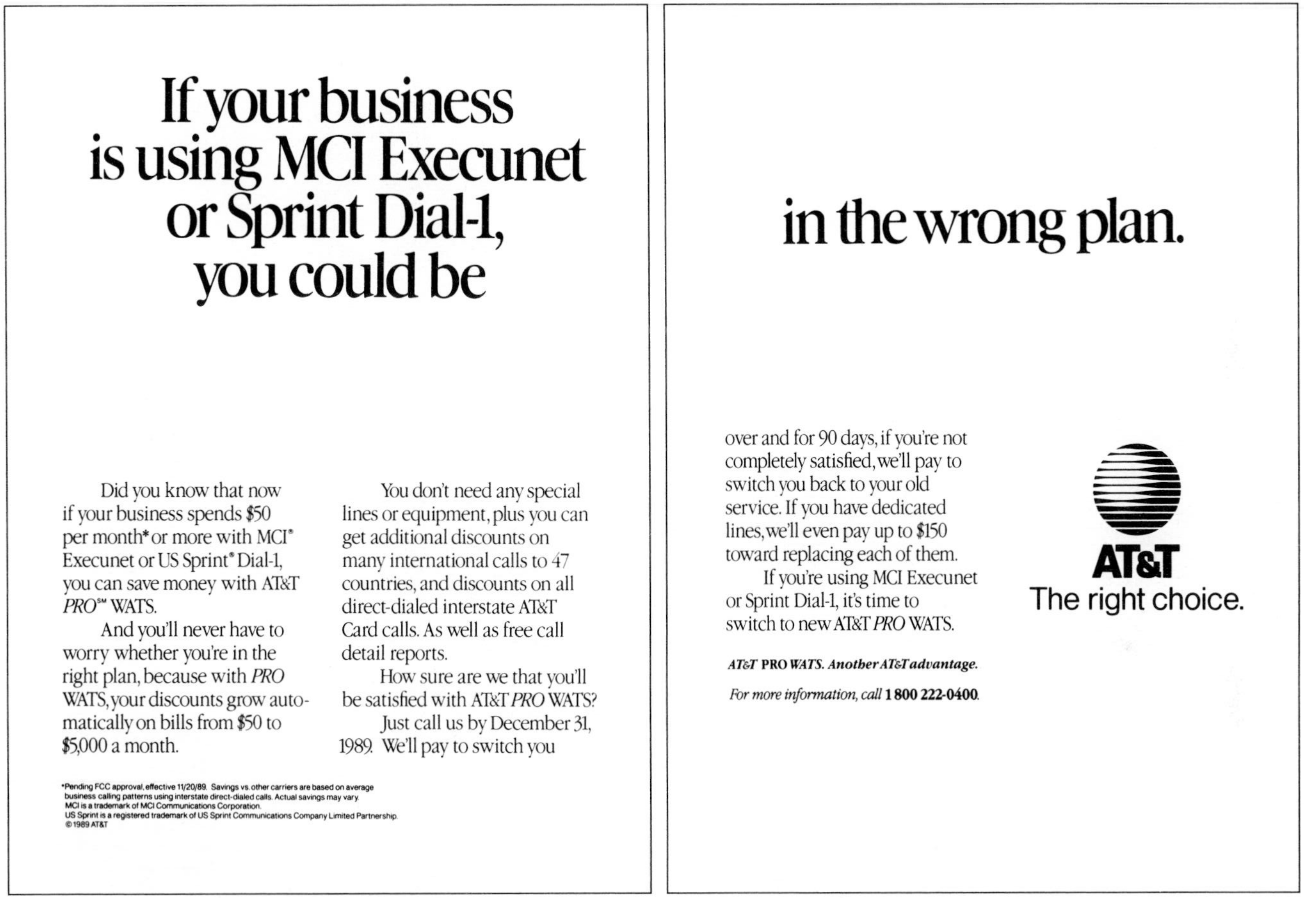

If your business is using MCI Execunet or Sprint Dial-1, you could be

Did you know that now if your business spends $50 per month* or more with MCI* Execunet or US Sprint* Dial-1, you can save money with AT&T *PRO*™ WATS.

And you'll never have to worry whether you're in the right plan, because with *PRO* WATS, your discounts grow automatically on bills from $50 to $5,000 a month.

You don't need any special lines or equipment, plus you can get additional discounts on many international calls to 47 countries, and discounts on all direct-dialed interstate AT&T Card calls. As well as free call detail reports.

How sure are we that you'll be satisfied with AT&T *PRO* WATS? Just call us by December 31, 1989. We'll pay to switch you

*Pending FCC approval, effective 11/20/89. Savings vs. other carriers are based on average business calling patterns using interstate direct-dialed calls. Actual savings may vary.
MCI is a trademark of MCI Communications Corporation.
US Sprint is a registered trademark of US Sprint Communications Company Limited Partnership.
© 1989 AT&T

in the wrong plan.

over and for 90 days, if you're not completely satisfied, we'll pay to switch you back to your old service. If you have dedicated lines, we'll even pay up to $150 toward replacing each of them.

If you're using MCI Execunet or Sprint Dial-1, it's time to switch to new AT&T *PRO* WATS.

AT&T PRO WATS. Another AT&T advantage.

For more information, call **1 800 222-0400.**

AT&T

The right choice.

women. The company's reaction was a multimillion-dollar direct-response campaign.

This campaign was designed to create a more modern image for Tupperware. The company maintained its personal selling approach but modified its party format to accommodate the increasing limitations for working women. The Rush Hour format was designed for after-work visits, and the Stop & Shop format made products and demonstrations available during extended periods for customers who barely had time for a quick visit and order session. Lunchtime office parties were another alternative for both working women and young urbanites who believe that they are above the suburbanism of home parties.

Tupperware also installed a toll-free direct-response number to link customers to a local dealer. This dealer was available to help people interested in hosting the new parties and to send customers the company's color catalog. Although the Tupperware catalogs were originally available only for dealers, hosts, and hostesses, they were made accessible to everyone and reached 30 million people (over one-eighth of the total population) in their first few years of open distribution. The catalogs allowed customers to peruse the products before the demonstration session, thus saving decision and ordering time.

New products were added to Tupperware's traditional product mix. Kitchen innovations included drinkware and Ultra-21, the state-of-the-art Tupperware that is dishwasher-, oven-, and microwave-safe. Nonkitchen additions included traveling desks, drawer organizers, picture frames, and a TupperToy line.

Tupperware was determined to promote consumers' awareness of the company's offerings. The company built on its marketing strengths. It had a strong brand name associated with high quality and held two-thirds of the $1 billion plastic food container market. In a two-year period, the company invested over $30 million in national advertising, spot TV and cable buys in major markets, and print ads in women's service magazines such as *McCall's* and *Ladies Home Journal*.

With this product, distribution, sales, and advertising changes, Tupperware was able to change a declining sales pattern into substantial growth.

THE MARKETING MIX COMMUNICATES

The consumer of goods, services, and ideas is exposed to and actively utilizes communication from all elements of the marketing mix. In this section, we will note (1) the power of attributes of the product itself to communicate, (2) how the price can communicate very loudly to the consumer, and (3) how the type of channel chosen sends a distinct message.

The Product Communicates

The physical product itself communicates a great deal to the consumer, as do the parts of the extended product such as brand name and packaging (including its shape, size, and color). The physical look and quality of the product can have a major impact. These aspects send signals or cues to consumers as to what the product should mean to them. For example, the distinct lines of the Mercury Sable have been demonstrated to mean quality and sportiness to prospective car buyers. This car's overwhelming first-year sales success is in no small part due to the message the product itself gives. The brand name selected, for example, Miller Lite, Head and Shoulders, Elephant Floppy Disks, and Nice and Easy, can communicate to the consumer the intended market position of the product. The package and colors used are no less important. For example, Crest lost substantial market share to Colgate when Colgate introduced the pump-based package to the marketplace. The Crest response is noted in Figure 1–5. This package was rushed to market by Crest. Apparently the pump package symbolized fun and modern product to the consumer. In this section, the Promotion in Action related to the adjustment that European companies must make in their packaging for North America illustrates how package design must meet the needs of consumers.

What all this tells us is that the consumer utilizes cues from all aspects of the marketing offering to make choices. It is imperative that the marketer know (1) how the target consumer will likely respond to the appearance of the product and (2) that all its aspects are consistent with each other in communicating their message.

Price Communicates

Consumers also take cues from the price of a product. A $50,000 price tag on a BMW 633 CSi is a critical element in communicating the product's quality (see Figure 1–6). It is quite likely that it might be less desired by its status-oriented target consumer if it had a lower price tag. General Electric utilizes two different price points in its appliance business. The message communicated is so different that GE utilizes two different brand names, GE and Hotpoint, to go with the higher and lower price points, respectively. Most consumers cannot tell the difference in the taste of beers across a broad spectrum of brands and prices. Yet it is the price of a beer that defines the market segment it will attract and the competitors it will confront. Michelob's position in the superpremium segment is defined by its high price; the regular price of Old Milwaukee puts it squarely in the low end of the market. Consumers use the price cue to define what the product is and to help direct their choice.

FIGURE 1–5

❖ The Package Communicates, the Pump Gives Cues

FIGURE 1-6

AS LONG AS THERE ARE PEOPLE WHO CAN AFFORD PERFECTION, BMW WILL CONTINUE TO PURSUE IT.

style and luxury with definitive performance.

The 635CSi fulfills the first two criteria even before you turn the ignition key.

Its body panels and exterior surfaces are meticulously hand-fitted and hand-examined.

Its amenities include supple hand-stitched leather seats, an electric two-way sunroof and cockpit-like ergonomics. "And everything is put together as if lives depended on the coupe's solidity" (Car and Driver).

But it's when you actually turn the key that you discover just how far this car advances the cause of Grand Touring.

BMW ENHANCES GOING AND STOPPING ALIKE.

The coupe's new 3.5-liter power plant propels it from 0 to 60 in 7.8 seconds. A prowess abetted by a fuel management system that adjusts fuel delivery and ignition timing hundreds of times a second.

You should also appreciate another new 635CSi feature: a computerized ABS anti-lock braking system.

Operating on the same principle that brings jet aircraft to a halt, it prevents brake-locking. And permits steering even during panic stops.

The new 635CSi, in sum, confirms the BMW coupe's position as "the benchmark" without which "you won't know how to judge anything else" (AutoWeek on the 633CSi).

As well as the managerial astuteness of a car company where even the head of finance is an engineer.

A handful are at BMW dealers now, awaiting test drives by automotive enthusiasts who also do not have to report to accountants.

"Life," the accountants often say, "is a series of compromises."

If you can afford to ignore this wisdom, we'd like to present a car that disdains it, too: the new 635CSi coupe.

Priced at about $40,000,* the 635CSi displays what can be achieved when engineers are free from the usual cost constraints of mass production.

And when, of course, they have an ideal worth pursuing in the first place.

THE GRAND COUPE THAT IS UNABASHEDLY GRAND.

In the case of the 635CSi, the ideal is a very aristocratic one: the European Grand Touring tradition, combining uncommon

THE ULTIMATE DRIVING MACHINE.

*Manufacturer's suggested retail price. $41,335. Actual price depends on dealer. Price excludes state and local taxes, dealer prep and handling charges. ©1985 BMW of North America, Inc. The BMW trademark and logo are registered. European Delivery can be arranged through your authorized U.S. BMW dealer.

23

❖
**PROMOTION
IN ACTION
1-1**

Packaging European Products for the Americans: Adjust or Die

According to New York packaging designer Ronald Peterson, European packaging is not always a hit with U.S. consumers. Peterson, managing partner of Peterson & Blyth Associates, Inc., told a U.S. Trademark Association conference in Lisbon, Portugal, that due to differences in packaging and merchandising, European companies should not expect their products to be successful automatically in the U.S. market. Although certain high-end products are highly acclaimed for their original European packages, other more conventional items, such as beer, liquor, and soft drinks, often have to be repackaged for a U.S. product launch.

Peterson recommended that European marketers research package designs to determine whether their product projects what Americans perceive as an "imported look." "To increase a product's chances for success in the U.S. marketplace, its packaging must have a tremendous amount of shelf impact so that consumers will notice it. This includes a demonstrable point of difference that distinguishes it from the competition and package graphics that visually convey its attributes and function."

Several important factors should be considered when evaluating a package's potential in the American market. Peterson believes that since Americans tend to have faith in well-known brands, a prominently displayed brand name is one of the most important packaging elements. Color is often a noticeable point of difference. U.S. packages are generally designed with brighter, cleaner colors that have greater visual impact than traditional European packaging. The relative effectiveness of various package graphics must also be considered. European food packaging relies heavily on illustrations. Although illustrations are often used for U.S. specialty products, American consumers believe that product photography more effectively conveys a food product's quality and ingredients

Peterson advised European companies to check package copy for legibility and to evaluate packaging under lighting conditions similar to those found in U.S. stores. Consumer reaction to graphic imagery should be assessed. Americans need to be visually informed about products with which they are unfamiliar. Ineffective packaging must be discovered early and redesigned if a European product is to succeed in the United States. Employing a U.S. market research firm is a strong option.

Source: "European Products Will Be a Success in the U.S.—If the Packaging Is Right," *Marketing News*, April 25, 1988, p. 1.

The Distribution Location Communicates

Where the marketer places his or her product also communicates to the consumer. Figure 1–7 illustrates this. The availability of Concord watches at Neiman-Marcus provides cues about its quality. This is true even if the consumer has never heard of Concord watches. Consider the different image that a consumer would have of an unknown Concord watch if it were advertised by K mart. A clear fit between the product image and the channel is needed. In the industrial product area, the style, manners, and knowledge of the salesperson or distributor also provide cues to the consumer about the product and company involved.

STRUCTURE OF THIS BOOK

This chapter has presented numerous examples of the use of promotional strategy in the real world of marketing. We see clearly how effective promotion can help make a consumer-driven marketing program a success. We also see that promotional strategy cannot be counted on to make a success of a marketing concept that does not satisfy a real consumer need. Simply put, promotional activity must follow the marketing concept.

This book is concerned with analyzing, planning, and implementing effective promotional programs. In Chapter 2, we will introduce a decision-making framework for promotional decisions. Chapters 3 and 4 (Part 2) begin a solid foundation for promotional decisions by discussing the nature of communication and the way consumers process information. Effective learning about promotional strategy is based on a solid understanding of communication processes and consumer behavior.

Chapters 5 through 7 (Part 3) provide the necessary understanding of consumer behavior that a promotional planner needs. Chapter 5 presents a framework for understanding consumers in complex purchase situations, and Chapter 6 extends this approach to less complex and habitual purchase situations. Chapter 7 discusses the consumer in the context of the social environment.

Part 4 presents the basic considerations of promotional strategy. Chapter 8 discusses the cornerstone concepts of marketing segmentation and product or service competitive positioning. Chapter 9 presents promotional objectives, and Chapter 10 deals with the allocation of funds to promotion. Chapter 11 discusses the application of organizational and human resources to the execution of promotional strategy. Chapter 12 presents a description of the very important legal environment in which promotional strategy takes place.

FIGURE 1-7

❖ **The Distribution Location Communicates**

Part 5 discusses advertising and sales promotion decisions in detail. Chapter 13 discusses the creative aspects of ads, and Chapters 14 and 15 deal with media characteristics and media selection. Chapter 16 describes procedures for assessing advertising effectiveness, and Chapter 17 presents the decisions to be made in sales promotion.

In Part 6 we turn our attention to the sales force. Chapter 18 discusses principles of effective personal selling, and Chapters 19 and 20 present material on the creation and management of the sales force, including selection, training, compensation, and evaluation.

Part 7 deals with the often overlooked areas of promoting to resellers, such as retailers, in Chapter 21. Chapter 22 discusses the growth area of direct marketing. The section concludes with Chapter 23, an overview of public relations, publicity, and institutional advertising.

In Part 8, we address some of the economic and social consequences of promotional strategy in a final chapter.

In summary, this book provides a complete view of promotional strategy from a managerial point of view. It is solidly based on the foundation of understanding consumer behavior and is strongly tied to the real world of promotional decision making. We hope that the extended examples presented in this chapter have given you the flavor of the exciting and challenging world of promotional strategy. Imagine yourself managing the promotional program of Salon Selectives, 7UP, Manufacturers Hanover, Acura, MCI, or Tupperware. Throughout the rest of the book, we will present numerous other examples of real-world applications of promotional strategy. This is a book about the applied world of promotion.

REVIEW AND DISCUSSION QUESTIONS

1. For each of the major examples presented in this chapter (Salon Selectives, 7UP, Manufacturers Hanover, Acura, MCI, and Tupperware):
   a. Identify the elements of promotional strategy used.
   b. Identify the informational gap that exists between marketer and consumer and indicate how promotion helped close this gap. Indicate whether the promotion was successful or not.
   c. Indicate what is being communicated to consumers and how it is being communicated.
   d. Relate the marketing concept to each example.
2. From your personal experience, give an example of a product, its price, and the channel of distribution used to deliver cues to you as a consumer.
3. Bring to class an advertisement and a package that demonstrate effective and ineffective promotion. Be prepared to explain your reason for selecting these ads and packages.

4. In your job search, how do you intend to make effective use of promotion? Be specific and relate your approach to the marketing concept.

NOTES

1. Based on "Seven-Up Concentrates on 7UP," *Advertising Age,* February 20, 1989, p. 62; "Seven-Up Stays Close to Home," *Advertising Age,* August 15, 1988, p. S–10; "Seven-Up Rallies," *Beverage World,* October 1988, p. 51–54; "Seven-Up Puts New Fizzle in Ads," *Advertising Age,* October 17, 1989, p. 34.

2. Philip Kotler, *Principles of Marketing,* 4th ed. (Englewood Cliffs, N.J.: Prentice Hall, 1989), p. 22.

3. Adapted from *Bank Marketing* 19 (December 1987), pp. 18–21.

4. Kotler, *Principles of Marketing,* p. 22.

5. Ralph Alexander, comp., *Marketing Definitions: A Glossary of Marketing Terms* (Chicago: American Marketing Association, 1960). New definitions came from Peter D. Bennett, *Dictionary of Marketing Terms* (Chicago: American Marketing Association, 1988).

6. Based on "The Acura Gambit Pays Off for Honda," *Advertising Age,* February 29, 1988, p. S–2; "Top 200 Brands," *Marketing & Media Decisions,* July 1988, p. 79.

7. Based on "Going the Distance," *Marketing & Media Decisions,* March 1989, pp. 51–56; and "MCI Earnings Rose Fivefold in 4th Quarter," *The Wall Street Journal,* February 2, 1989, p. B2.

8. Based on "Tupperware Locks in New Strategy," *Advertising Age,* February 8, 1988, pp. 30; "Party Animal," *Forbes,* November 16, 1987, p. 262–70; "Finding a Fresher 'World' in Orlando," *Advertising Age,* April 6, 1987, p. 34.

Promotional Strategy: A Decision-Making Framework

GENERAL MILLS AND QUAKER SLUG IT OUT IN THE CEREAL MARKET

A major battle has been waged over the past three years between two giants of the breakfast foods industry. In 1987, General Mills aggressively attacked the king of hot breakfast cereals, the Quaker Oats Company, with a line of new oatmeal products.

General Mills launched an extensive promotional campaign to introduce Total Oatmeal, a collection of vitamin-enriched instant and quick oatmeals. The company hoped that the venerable Total brand name, previously used exclusively on a $110 million cold cereal line, would have a ready-made audience for the hot cereal category. Some officials also believed that Quaker had neglected the oatmeal segment and was vulnerable to competition. "There have been line extensions, but there has not been a single innovation in oatmeal in 10 years, since the introduction of instant," said a General Mills spokesman. "We believe development of the Total brand into oatmeal is both logical and prudent."

General Mills allocated $12 million for the marketing plan, which included the distribution of 175 million coupons. A six-month advertising campaign touted Total Oatmeal as having "more nutrition than any other hot cereal." Special promotional pieces prepared for grocers claimed "we're about to set the hot cereal category on its ear" and showed a box of Total Oatmeal towering over a tipped and leaking box of Quaker Oats.

Although General Mills has done very well recently with new product introductions, this time the company may face overpowering opposition. Quaker Oats is a 110-year-old brand name that totally dominates the hot cereal business, owning a 68 percent market share. The last major competitor that tried to capture some of that territory—the Ralston Purina Co. with its Sun Maid brand oatmeal— saw its brand crushed by Quaker in just two years.

Quaker isn't standing idly by this time, either. The company counterattacked with its own "sensible nutrition" advertising theme. The campaign, "Quaker Oats: It's the Right Thing to Do," featured actor Wilford Brimley as spokesperson. Quaker's objective is to overwhelm Total Oatmeal with its largest oatmeal campaign in five years: a massive promotional plan budgeted at $35 million for the first year and $46 million for the second year. The company gave away 12.5 million packages of its instant oatmeal in boxes of its cold cereal. The promotion also used a special game with 1,500 Amana microwave ovens and 5,000 sets of microwave cookware as prizes.

If Total Oatmeal can capture just a fraction of Quaker's market share, the profits could be tremendous. But faced with the promotional onslaught planned by Quaker, the brand may be doing well just to survive.

Source: Adapted from *Forbes*, July 27, 1987, pp. 86 and 89, and updated based on discussions with industry experts.

The fortunes of the competitors in the hot cereal market are not an accident. Rather they are the result of carefully conceived and executed promotional strategies that are part of broader marketing plans—plans that include all the elements of the marketing mix. In this book, we are concerned primarily with decision making for the promotional aspect of the marketing mix only. What is involved in promotional decision making? After a brief general discussion of the stages involved in the process, we will illustrate the procedure with a detailed example. The stages in promotional planning and strategy described here provide an ordering of the topics in the rest of this book.

THE STAGES IN PROMOTIONAL PLANNING AND STRATEGY

Table 2–1 provides a summary of a systematic approach to promotional planning and strategy. The approach encompasses the following stages: (1) situation analysis, (2) establishment of objectives, (3) determination of dollar appropriation, (4) specification and management of program elements,

TABLE 2–1

Stages in Promotional Planning and Strategy   ❖

STEP
I. Situation analysis
   A. Demand
      1.   Cultural and social influences
      2.   Attitudes
      3.   Individual differences
      4.   Decision processes
   B. Definition and identification of target markets
      1.   Segmentation
      2.   Positioning
   C. Competition
   D. Legal considerations
   E. Internal organizational considerations
      1.   Personnel
      2.   Monetary
      3.   Established policies and procedures
      4.   Operational distinctions
II. Establishment of objectives
   A. Relationship to market targets
   B. Communication of message objectives
   C. Sales objectives
III. Determination of dollar appropriation
IV. Specification and management of program elements
   A. Advertising
      1.   Analysis of media resources
      2.   Selection of advertising media
      3.   Message determination
   B. Personal selling
      1.   Analysis of resources
      2.   Selection, motivation, deployment, compensation, and evaluation
   C. Stimulation of reseller support
      1.   Analysis of reseller resources
      2.   Stimulation of performance
      3.   Improvement and augmentation of performance
   D. Sales promotion
   E. Supplemental communications (public relations)
      1.   Assessment of relevant publics
      2.   Determination of media and message
V. Coordination and integration of efforts
   A. Achievement of proper balance between program elements
   B. Scheduling of execution
   C. Utilization of personnel and outside services
   D. Dollar-appropriation revision
VI. Measurement of effectiveness
VII. Evaluation and follow-up

(5) coordination and integration, (6) measurement of effectiveness, and (7) evaluation and follow-up.

Figure 2–1 presents the same sequence graphically. Note, however, that it is depicted as an "adaptive" process in that it specifically includes systematic procedures for gathering information that then can lead to needed program adaptations. For example, advertising message and media decisions are interrelated. The decisions in one area can lead to modifications in another, as the two-way arrows indicate. Furthermore, a feedback loop represents the fact that the initial budget may have to be modified as planning proceeds. Evaluation and follow-up are shown as providing vital new input to the situation analysis for succeeding planning periods. Thus the continual and ongoing nature of planning is graphically portrayed.

UTILIZING THE FRAMEWORK: CARNIVAL CRUISES TO THE TOP[1]

It is not often that a company is able simultaneously to climb to the top of its industry and lift the entire fortunes of the whole industry. This is exactly what Carnival Cruise Lines was able to do. The success of Carnival, of course, was not an accident. Rather, it was the outcome of some carefully conceived promotional strategy. The story of Carnival's success that follows here is designed to illustrate the use of the framework presented in Figure 2–1.

SITUATION ANALYSIS

The starting point is always an analysis of the environment. In the presentation that follows, we will discuss demand and competition as the key elements of this analysis. Although space limitation prevents us from presenting all aspects of Carnival's situation analysis, we do present a brief history of Carnival Cruise Lines.

History

Ted Arison started Carnival Cruise Lines in 1972 with one used ship (the *Mardi Gras*). The company sought to open the formerly exclusive cruise business to budget-conscious travelers. Through intensive promotion of its moderately priced four- and seven-day cruises, Carnival won the patronage of people who had never dreamed that they could afford a vacation at sea.

In its first three years, Carnival constantly battled to stay afloat, but the company's fortunes turned around in 1975 after Arison assumed full ownership of the company. Carnival's marketing department capitalized on the

FIGURE 2–1

Decision Sequence Analysis of Promotional Planning and Strategy

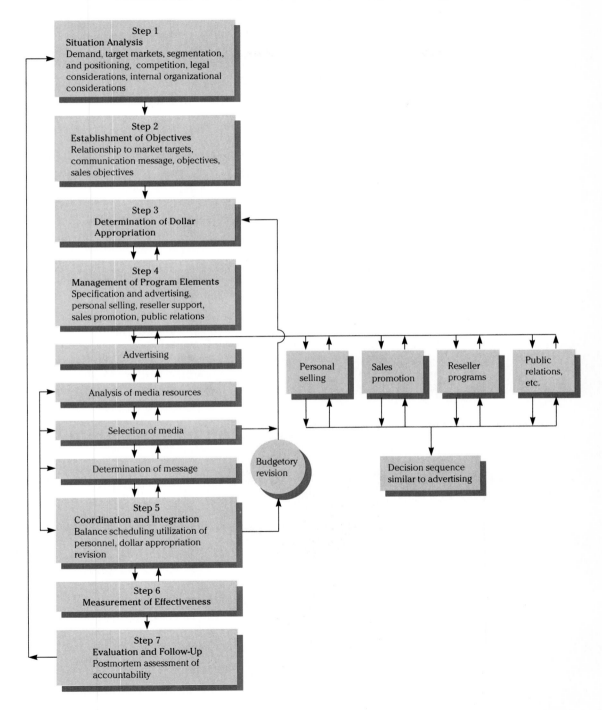

positive reaction to the *Mardi Gras* cruise program, which destroyed traditional class distinctions and pretensions of formality. The cruise line turned the shipboard experience into total recreation rather than a sedate mode of travel, and the Fun Ship concept, which has since become a hallmark of Carnival's success, was born.

Carnival had acquired two other ships by 1978 when Arison made the first of many announcements that shocked and then changed the industry. In the midst of record-high shipbuilding costs, skyrocketing fuel prices, and an industry of medium-sized vessels, Carnival built a new passenger ship, *Tropicale,* with significantly increased capacity. The popularity of this new ship's spaciousness and efficiency sparked more than $1 billion worth of new passenger construction in the 1980s. Encouraged by *Tropicale's* success, Carnival defied the industry again and built three superliners over the next four years. The critics were skeptical, but the passengers loved them!

After building up its capacity, Carnival decided to diversify its product line. After 12 years of offering seven-day cruises, the company capitalized on the American trend toward shorter and more frequent vacations by adding three- and four-day trips to the Bahamas to its schedule in May 1984. Carnival has since become the leader in the short cruise segment of the market. In December 1985, Carnival began offering Thursday and Sunday departures, another new concept in the industry. In November 1986, the company began service from San Juan, giving Carnival a presence in every North American warm water cruise region.

The success of its superliners and the popularity of these line extensions made Carnival the largest cruise line in the world. By 1987, the company held over 25 percent of the total North American market and carried almost twice as many passengers as its nearest competitor. To strengthen this position, Carnival will add three more state-of-the-art passenger ships by 1991: the *Fantasy,* the *Ecstacy,* and the *Sensation.* The *Fantasy* will be the first ship in the industry ever intended for year-round trips in the Bahamas market. The new ships are tentatively scheduled to offer additional three- and four-day trips.

Carnival has continued to expand its vacation/travel market through acquisitions. It acquired Holland America Line (HAL) for $625 million in January 1989. Holland America has four ships that sail to Alaska in the summer and to the eastern Caribbean in the winter. HAL operates in the premium cruise segment. The acquisition furthers Carnival's goal of carving a niche in every segment of the cruise industry. Carnival has chosen to maintain two distinct positioning strategies for its two entities. The Carnival Line is still targeted at the mass market while HAL targets the more upscale traveler. HAL is also priced about 27 percent above Carnival on comparable routes. Chief Executive Officer Micky Arison believes that as Carnival passengers become more affluent and more sophisticated, they will be ready to graduate to Holland America cruises.

Carnival is also constructing three vessels of its own for the luxury market as part of Project Tiffany. The three luxury liners of Project Tiffany will be equipped with suites instead of individual cabins and will carry only 700 passengers to increase spaciousness, comfort, and individual service. According to Karine Armstrong, vice president of marketing for Carnival Cruise Lines, "We have such a humongous repeat factor that there are some people who have traveled on all of our ships. The natural evolution is to move up." Carnival plans to sell this upscale product at a midlevel price.

Carnival is also trying to break into the land-based vacation market with its Crystal Palace Resort & Casino in Nassau. Upon completion, this mega-resort is slated to be the largest gaming complex in the Bahamas and the most elaborate in the Caribbean. Industry analysts are skeptical because Nassau is an expensive and difficult place to do business, and Carnival has yet to prove that it can transfer its on-water success to land.

Demand—Target Markets

Carnival caters to two market segments: the Type A cruise market and the Type B cruise market. Type A is the contemporary cruise market that features cruises lasting from two to seven days, a casual on-board atmosphere, and an average per diem of $200 or less. These cruises, which represent the volume end of the cruise market, appeal to all age groups with annual household incomes of at least $25,000. This market targets the first-time cruiser, and statistics indicate that 240 million North Americans are in this target audience.

The Type B market is the traditional cruise segment, which offers cruises lasting at least 10 days, a more formal on-board atmosphere, and an average brochure per diem of at least $250. These cruises are designed to appeal to the over-50 age market with annual household incomes of at least $40,000. This market targets the repeat cruiser, and statistics indicate that approximately 13 million people in North America are in this target audience.

Carnival has built its strength on the contemporary market. Although approximately 30 percent of its passengers are in the 55 and over segment, another 30 percent are under the age of 35. Carnival targets this younger group by using younger personalities in its advertisements. Working from the company's premise that "the average age [of a cruiser] used to be deceased," Kathie Lee Gifford's "Ain't We Got Fun" commercials are a prime example of Carnival's efforts to lower the average age of its passengers. According to Robert Dickinson, Carnival's senior vice president, sales and marketing, "We're marketing to a younger clientele than the cruise industry." The acquisition of HAL is designed to allow better tapping of the Type B consumer segment.

Competition

Currently 37 cruise lines operate in North America. The largest of these are Norwegian Caribbean, Princess Cruises, Sitmar, Cunard, American Hawaii, Holland America, Royal Caribbean, Royal Viking, and Admiral. These lines compete on the basis of image, target market, destinations, price, and promotions. (See Appendix 2A for a detailed presentation of their respective promotional approaches.) In a poll of 700 travel agents, no agent could name the slogan of even four cruise lines, indicating a low degree of brand identity in the industry. Carnival scored well in this poll in terms of name recognition. A few of the large lines enjoy economies of scale that create cost, product, price, and branding advantages. The smaller lines must carve out market niches to survive. Long-term forecasts predict significant industry consolidation.

Despite this plethora of seagoing competitors, Carnival considers land-based vacation packages, such as an excursion to Hawaii, to be its main competition. Based on this premise, Carnival markets the total cruise ship experience in which the actual trip is more than half of the fun and the ports of call are "mere" bonuses. Carnival capitalizes on its Fun Ships theme and stresses the value of its all-inclusive, up-front prices, which cover transportation, meals, and endless activities.

Internal Organizational Considerations

As indicated in the history section above, Carnival's management is willing to innovate in terms of products, promotion, and taking risks. Management developed skills in promotion and spent aggressively to take market share and to expand the entire market. Carnival's market share dominance generates a cash flow large enough to support the acquisition of new ships and to support even more promotion.

ESTABLISHMENT OF OBJECTIVES

Carnival's objective is to be the market-share leader in the cruise industry. Its promotional goals are to be the number one name in terms of consumer recognition and to be the preferred booking line by travel agents. Its promotional program is designed to reach these goals. A detailed description of these promotional programs is presented below.

DETERMINATION OF DOLLAR APPROPRIATION

Once objectives have been established, a preliminary promotional budget should be determined. This is a difficult task, as later chapters indicate. The initial estimate usually can be only tentative, and modifications generally are required as the planning proceeds. Carnival spends more than $30 million per year to promote itself to consumers and to travel agents through its advertising, sales force, and trade promotions.

SPECIFICATION AND MANAGEMENT OF PROGRAM ELEMENTS

Among the various communication resources available to the firm are advertising, resellers (wholesalers and retailers), direct sales, sales promotion (packaging, price offers, and so forth), and supplemental communication support such as public relations programs. The objective is the best promotional mix, making use of these elements as appropriate. Listed below are some elements of Carnival's activities in these areas.

Advertising

Media   In addition to its large investment in television advertising, Carnival runs newspaper ads in over 200 markets. Most of these ads are in the Sunday travel section of newspapers primarily in the United States and Canada. The company places much less emphasis on magazines but does advertise in a few such as *Cruise Travel, Travel-Holiday,* and the cruise section of *Modern Bride.* Dickinson noted, "We have done some *Sunset* or *Southern Living,* but it takes a real effort to get noticed. They're pretty thick publications."

Carnival leads the industry in media spending with expenditures of about $26 million: $67,600 for magazines, $29,600 for national Sunday magazines, $11.5 million for newspapers, $13.2 million for network television, $1.25 million for spot TV, $289,900 for network cable, and $1,900 for outdoor advertising.

Message   The Fun Ships theme of Carnival's ads was described in the history section above. This approach, as well as Kathie Lee Gifford, the central presenter in Carnival's television ads, has been constant over many years. Figure 2–2 presents examples of Carnival ads and other promotional materials.

Distribution Channel Support

In 1973, 75 percent of Carnival Cruise Line's (CCL's) business came from wholesalers and tour operators. CCL continued to develop its own sales force and by 1975, the company had shifted its focus to direct sales to travel agents. By 1978, 95 percent of CCL's sales were conducted through travel agents; this number reached 99 percent by 1990. CCL employed a direct sales force of 60 representatives in 1989, and that number is expected to

FIGURE 2–2

❖   **Example Carnival Advertisements and Other Promotional Materials**

Example Carnival Advertisements and Other Promotional Materials (continued)

Mardi Gras/3 Day Cruise Itinerary:

DAY	PORT	ARRIVE	DEPART
THURSDAY	FT. LAUDERDALE		5:30 P.M.
FRIDAY	NASSAU	9:00 A.M.	
SATURDAY	DEPART NASSAU FOR FUN DAY AT SEA		6:00 A.M.
SUNDAY	FT. LAUDERDALE	7:00 A.M.	

Mardi Gras/4 Day Cruise Itinerary:

DAY	PORT	ARRIVE	DEPART
SUNDAY	FT. LAUDERDALE		5:30 P.M.
MONDAY	FREEPORT	7:00 A.M.	4:00 P.M.
TUESDAY	NASSAU	7:00 A.M.	
WEDNESDAY	DEPART NASSAU FOR FUN DAY AT SEA		6:00 A.M.
THURSDAY	FT. LAUDERDALE	7:00 A.M.	

Carnivale/3 Day Cruise Itinerary:

DAY	PORT	ARRIVE	DEPART
FRIDAY	MIAMI		4:00 P.M.
SATURDAY	NASSAU	9:00 A.M.	
SUNDAY	DEPART NASSAU FOR FUN DAY AT SEA		8:00 A.M.
MONDAY	MIAMI	7:00 A.M.	

Carnivale/4 Day Cruise Itinerary:

DAY	PORT	ARRIVE	DEPART
MONDAY	MIAMI		4:00 P.M.
TUESDAY	FREEPORT	7:00 A.M.	4:00 P.M.
WEDNESDAY	NASSAU	7:00 A.M.	
THURSDAY	DEPART NASSAU FOR FUN DAY AT SEA		8:00 A.M.
FRIDAY	MIAMI	7:00 A.M.	

33

FIGURE 2-2

3 & 4 Day Cruises
Carnivale & Mardi Gras

Nassau,
Bahamas

Known for its talcom-soft sands and Georgian charm, Nassau is one of the most romantic and interesting islands in the Caribbean. Enjoy a horse drawn carriage tour, see ancient forts or indulge in the cool, clear waters. Don't miss the Las Vegas-style extravaganza and the gambling action at Carnival's Crystal Palace Resort and Casino.

"Fun" Day at Sea

Spend today as you wish with unlimited activities from skeet shooting to limbo lessons. Work out in the gymnasium, then relax under the sun. Fun days melt into enchanted evenings with scrumptious dining and two different nightclub shows.

Freeport,
Grand Bahama

Take a snorkeling tour of this coral rock island and explore the majestic undersea life of tropical fish. Freeport is an incredibly beautiful island filled with colorful flora and fauna. The International Bazaar is the world famous home to some of the Bahamas' best bargains.

Atlantic Ocean

Freeport
Grand Bahama

Ft. Lauderdale

Nassau
The Bahamas

Miami

Caribbean Sea

On Board the Mardi Gras

27,250 tons of fun/entered service in 1962 as Empress of Canada/re-entered service as MARDI GRAS in 1972/refurbished in 1985/Italian officers/international service staff /central air conditioning system throughout the entire ship/private facilities and 110 AC current in each stateroom/2 outdoor swimming pools including children's wading pool/1 indoor pool/Deck sports: trapshooting, table tennis, shuffleboard, golf driving/Flamingo Dining Room/3 meals a day plus midnight buffet, late-night buffet and early morning, mid-morning and afternoon snacks/Showboat Lounge/Showboat Club Casino/Tropicale Bar/Seaview Snack Bar/El Patio Grande/Carousel Lounge/Grand Ballroom/Point After Discotheque/Bourbon Street Arcade/Enclosed Promenades/Cinema/Health Room and Sauna/Exercise Room/Duty-Free Shops/Hairdresser and Barber Shop/Infirmary with doctor and nurse/4 elevators/Registered in Panama.

On Board the Carnivale

27,250 tons of fun/entered service in 1956 as Empress of Britain/completely renovated and re-entered service in 1976 as the CARNIVALE/refurbished in 1984/Italian officers/international service staff/central air conditioning system throughout entire ship/private facilities in each stateroom/piped-in music, telephone and 110 AC current in staterooms/4 outside swimming pools including children's wading pool/1 indoor pool/Deck sports: trapshooting, table tennis, shuffleboard, golf driving/International Dining Room/3 meals a day plus midnight buffet, late-night buffet and early morning, mid-morning and afternoon snacks/Lido Bar/Snack Bar/Fly Aweigh Discotheque/Mardi Gras Nightclub/Riverboat Lounge/Riverboat Club Casino/The Showplace/Enclosed Promenade/Cinema/Sauna/Exercise Room/Duty-Free Shops/Hairdresser and Barber Shop/Infirmary with doctor and nurse/4 elevators/Registered in Panama.

32

increase to 70 by the end of 1990. In addition, Holland America has 34 representatives of its own. The current system allows each CCL representative to effectively serve 500 to 550 travel agents.

Incentives for the sales force are developed based on both past figures and future goals. Sales representatives have no caps on their earnings and they have direct input into their sales quotas. Travel agents receive a base commission of 10 percent, but this figure can increase based on an agent's commitment to CCL and sales volume achieved. Carnival also offers several trade incentives, including free cruises, an agency-of-the-year competition, and mystery vacation contests. In these contests, a Carnival employee posing as a confused traveler visits a travel agent and asks about vacations. Travel agents are awarded $10 if their first suggestion is a cruise, and $1,000 if their suggestion is a Carnival cruise.

Supplemental Communications (Public Relations)

In general, Carnival's public relations (PR) tasks involve communication with three external publics: the trade press, travel editors and free-lance travel writers, and the financial community. Carnival's PR also targets various internal publics, such as the company employees. PR vehicles include in-house newsletters, such as *Carnival Capers* and *Carnivalgrams,* information releases for travel agents' in-house newsletters, daily discussions with the trade press, video news releases, and use of the PR Newswire to communicate any changes in the company's financial status.

For example, Carnival launched a major PR program after it purchased HAL. The program's main purpose was to assure the trade and the public that the union would not lower HAL's quality, that the acquisition would not "turn a Cadillac into a Chevrolet." Public relations also kept the employees of both CCL and HAL informed about the developments and implications of the acquisition. Special video news releases providing both local and national coverage were developed around the announcement.

COORDINATION AND INTEGRATION OF EFFORTS

Coordinated management of various components of the promotion mix obviously is essential. Advertising, for example, should not be overemphasized relative to other types of communication unless the problem calls for dominant use of mass media. Too often one phase is allowed to get out of balance, with the result that profit opportunities are lost.

Coordination also requires skillful use of managerial talent. Decisions must be made regarding the necessity of using outside services such as advertising agencies, research suppliers, and media buying services. Because the advertising agency is in such widespread use, the decision may focus on division of responsibilities between management within the firm and the agency personnel.

Carnival carefully coordinates all aspects of its promotional activities. The advertising is consistent with presentations to travel agents by the sales force, and the advertisements and presentations are timed to support each other.

MEASUREMENT OF EFFECTIVENESS

Occupancy rates are one measure of a cruise line's marketing effectiveness. Since 1980, Carnival has achieved occupancy rates between 108 and 110 percent. (Cabins occupied by two people equal 100 percent occupancy.)

Capacity is another major cruise line statistic. Carnival currently has 8,800 berths. CCL plans to add three new passenger ships in 1990, each of which will have 2,050 berths. These additions will increase Carnival's capacity by 75 percent.

As we have seen, Carnival also excels when measured by market share, controlling 25 percent of the domestic market. Cruise Line International Association (CLIA) compiles market-share data by monitoring the sales of 40 cruise lines worldwide. Any CCL territory with average or lower-than-average market share warrants immediate attention and corrective action. Patterns are identified and examined.

Another indication of success is repeat business. For Carnival, repeats generally account for about 30 percent of its sales. Repeats have increased over the years, which also indicates success. Perhaps, at this point, this trend indicates that the company should concentrate more effort on expanding its markets than on pursuing current customers.

EVALUATION AND FOLLOW-UP

Every effort should be made to assess the strengths and weaknesses of the promotional plan with the objective of cataloging experience for use in future planning. Given that management turnover is a way of life in many organizations, it is not surprising that past mistakes are repeated continually. Part of the problem lies in the fact that records are not kept, perhaps for the reason that managers are avoiding accountability for performance. Whatever the reason, failure to use the results of experience in future planning is inexcusable, and a formal postmortem analysis should be a routine part of the management process.

In the case of Carnival, we see a management that constantly monitors its situation and responds accordingly. This monitoring has been very effective for the company to this point. However, management will have to stay alert to maintain its dominant position because the environment is constantly changing.

THE MARKETING MANAGER'S PROBLEM

It should be stressed that the issues faced in the management of promotion are too complex to allow pat answers. Certain decision routines are developed later, but they are intended only to discipline thinking and to guarantee systematic and rigorous analysis. It is human nature to give way to a "quest for certainty" (a search for concrete and definite answers where none exist). The proper attitude of inquiry, however, calls for an awareness of the state of knowledge and an appreciation of the need for research in areas where knowledge is scanty or missing. A keen appreciation for research and a certain sophistication in its use are central to promotional success. This book is intended to provide the marketing decision maker with a guide to the dynamic, complex, and exciting world of promotional strategy.

REVIEW AND DISCUSSION QUESTIONS

1. In what ways can the external and internal environments of the business firm affect promotional planning and strategy?
2. What reasons can you give for the fact that preselling through advertising has largely precluded the need for personal selling at the retail level? Will this trend continue? In what areas does a role for personal selling remain? Why?
3. Given the decline in the need for retail personal selling, what forms of promotional support can the retailer be expected to offer?
4. Analyze the Carnival case history in terms of the outline given in Table 2–1 and Figure 2–1 and answer the following questions:
   a. Was the situation analysis sufficiently complete to permit realistic planning?
   b. Were the objectives for the campaign reasonable?
   c. Did the emphasis of the television campaign seem appropriate in view of the demand analysis?
   d. Would it be reasonable to use local newspapers, spot radio, Sunday supplements, or other forms of local media rather than spot television?
   e. What role does the sales force play in Carnival's promotion mix?
   f. How does trade promotion impact Carnival's approach to the marketplace?

NOTES

1. Based on "Carnival Tries Sailing Upstream," *Business Week*, September 25, 1989, pp. 82–86; "Liner Notes," *Marketing & Media Decisions*, January 1987, pp. 63–72; "How Carnival Stacks the Decks," *Fortune*, January 16, 1989, pp. 108–16; "Ain't We Got Fun!" *Marketing & Media Decisions*, March 1988, pp. 101–6; internal company documents of Carnival Cruise Lines; and interviews with experts in this industry.

Promotional Strategies of Carnival Cruise Lines' Main Direct Competitors

This appendix presents detailed information on the promotional strategies of the main competitors of Carnival Cruise Lines. It presents the competitive environment in which Carnival's promotion decisions are being made and provides background for the discussion of Carnival presented throughout the book. In addition, it illustrates the dynamic and competitive world of promotion. Imagine being responsible for the promotional activities of Carnival or one of its competitors.

NORWEGIAN CARIBBEAN

Norwegian targets adults between the ages of 35 and 49 with no children at home. Most are married, have had at least some college education, and have annual household incomes of at least $35,000.

Norwegian Caribbean spends about $15 million on media advertising. Network television accounts for 60 percent of this budget, magazines for 30 percent, and newspapers for the remaining 10 percent. The company uses both 15- and 30-second television spots to reach viewers. Norwegian mainly uses mass audience magazines such as *People, Travel & Leisure, Time,* and *Newsweek.* Newspaper promotions have been deemphasized, decreasing from 70 percent of the total media budget to 10 percent currently. Norwegian buys space in the top 20 markets and goes for a newspaper's first section instead of limiting its campaign to the Sunday travel section. Ric Widmer, Norwegian's senior vice president, marketing and sales, notes that "newspapers' own research" has found that 45 to 90 percent of all readers never get to the travel sections.

In the past, Norwegian used consumer promotions, such as a direct mail drop, to several million households offering dollars-off coupons worth $200 to $250 savings on selected cruises. As long as cruise demand holds steady, Norwegian does not discount prices. It also offers trade promotions to its travel agents (who book 100 percent of the company's trips). Depending on available space, agents are offered familiarization cruises, seminars at sea,

Sources: "Liner Notes," *Marketing & Media Decisions,* January 1987, pp. 63–72; "Let's Cruise," *American Demographics,* February 1988, p. 21; and discussions with industry experts.

and "walk-through for the weekend" deals in which agents eat on board a docked ship but stay in a local hotel.

PRINCESS CRUISES

Princess, which sails to worldwide destinations, classifies its product as upscale and targets passengers 35 and over with household incomes of at least $40,000. Michael Hannan, senior vice president, marketing services, notes that since many of the company's offerings are two-week trips, Princess cruises tend to appeal to the 50 and older group who have the time and disposable income for longer excursions.

The "Love Boat" television series increased the popularity of cruises. Princess capitalizes on the "Love Boat" image by using Gavin McLeod, who played the ship's captain on the program, as its spokesperson in all consumer and trade advertisements. Princess spends about $10 million in advertising, the majority of which goes to newspapers. The company advertises mainly in the travel section of Sunday newspapers in the larger market areas. Princess invests over half of its media budget in the western United States since half of its business originates in that region. Princess also advertises in regional lifestyle magazines, such as *Sunset, Southern Living, Los Angeles,* and *The New Yorker*; national magazines, such as *Architectural Digest, National Geographic, Gourmet,* and *Signature*; and several consumer travel magazines including *Travel & Leisure, Travel-Holiday,* and *Cruise Travel.*

Trade promotions are not popular at Princess. Free cruises are not offered to travel agents despite the fact that these agents book 100 percent of the company's trips. According to Hannan, "We prefer to work with travel agents by helping them with sending out brochures, doing presentations, and cooperative advertising on a local basis."

SITMAR

From its humble beginnings as an immigrant transport ship between England and Australia, Sitmar has developed into one of the leading North American cruise lines. Although Australian cruisers still account for 25 percent of its business, most of Sitmar's cruises go to the Caribbean, Alaska, and Mexico. The average age of Sitmar's passengers is 54 and the average household income is $35,000. Sitmar wants to attract "retired older couples, middle-aged working couples, or more mature singles in their 50s." According to William Smith, senior vice president, marketing and sales, "The reason is cruises are longer, so we need to get to that segment with more disposable time or leisure to take a longer cruise."

Sitmar spends about $15 million on media advertising: 25 percent for broadcast ads, 25 percent for trade magazines, and the remaining 50 percent for newspapers. Smith asserted, "We feel it's very important to position ourselves to the consumer and trade. Sitmar is a quality product for the experienced cruiser. Our past advertising was a lot less targeted and specific." TV spots are used mainly for image building. "You can visually depict the setting you're trying to create. Radio or print ads are more effective at driving a price." Based on this premise, Sitmar runs ads with more pricing and details in newspapers, primarily Sunday travel sections and cruise sections of approximately 70 papers in the top 26 markets. The cruise line also advertises in consumer magazines including *Smithsonian, National Geographic,* and *Travel & Leisure* and trade publications including *Travel Weekly, Travel Age West, Travel Age East, Travel Agent, Travel Trade,* and *Tours & Travel News*.

Consumer and trade promotions are prevalent at Sitmar. Supersaver programs, advance-purchase discounts, and group rates are among the consumer offerings. Travel agents, who book almost 100 percent of Sitmar's trips, are eligible for familiarization trips, reduced rates, and incentive programs. A partnership program is available for smaller travel agencies; it allows them to pool their sales in order to compete with the larger agencies for bonus commissions and cooperative dollars. Sitmar also advertises in trade publications.

CUNARD

Cunard, famous for its *Queen Elizabeth* luxury liner, targets the more affluent segment of the population. The income of its passengers falls in the $40,000 to $200,000 range. This cruise line sails around the world in addition to its transatlantic trips.

Cunard spends about $12 million on its media advertising. According to Ron Santangelo, vice president, marketing communications, Cunard is "so targeted that television is not an appropriate medium." Newspapers and magazines get the bulk of Cunard's advertising business. Because the majority of its business comes from New York, California, and Florida, the company places ads only in the travel section of Sunday newspapers in the top 15 markets for those regions. Cunard also runs ads in upscale magazines such as *Gourmet, Vogue, Town & Country, Travel & Leisure, Smithsonian,* and *Architectural Digest*.

Cunard also utilizes consumer and trade promotions. Through direct mail marketing, passengers can get discounts for selected dates or a companion's ticket for half the price of the first ticket. Travel agents book 96 percent of Cunard's cruises, and they can earn a compact disc player for selling a few cabins on Cunard's less luxurious ships. Agents who sell five cabins win a large-screen color television set.

AMERICAN HAWAII

American Hawaii targets adults 35 and over with annual household incomes of at least $30,000. This Pacific cruise line sails to Hawaii and Tahiti. American Hawaii spends about $5.7 million on advertising: $2.5 million for magazines, $651,000 for Sunday magazines, $1.98 million for newspapers, $36,000 for spot television, $434,000 for outdoor ads, and $144,000 for spot radio. American Hawaii runs ads for its Hawaii cruises in 25 newspaper markets nationwide and emphasizes the West Coast markets for the Tahitian cruises.

The cruise line also offers consumer and trade promotions. Passengers can earn discounts by booking six months in advance, or they can earn free hotel accommodations before or after a cruise if they want an extended vacation in the islands. American Hawaii also promotes its services through trade books such as *Travel Age West, Travel Weekly,* and *Travel Agent.* Trade publications such as *Sunset, Travel & Leisure, Signature,* and *Islands* are used as well.

HOLLAND AMERICA

Holland America offers Caribbean and Alaskan leisure cruises. Although its passengers have traditionally been in the 45 and older age group, Rich Skinner, corporate director of public relations and sales promotion, acknowledged that this is changing: "There has been a trend toward skewing into a younger group in the last few years, especially in the Caribbean. Even Alaska seems to have a downward trend." Jan Edmonston, vice president, management supervisor at the company's advertising agency, asserts that Holland America wants "balanced" advertising. "We haven't segmented like other cruises. We don't think we can because demand is so small."

Holland America spends about $4.6 million on media advertising. Most of the budget goes to newspapers, with the remainder going to magazines. Skinner explained that print advertising is used because cruises are a complex product that require study. Because 60 percent of its business comes from the West Coast, most of Holland America's advertising is in the Sunday travel section of daily newspapers in 15 markets on the East and West Coasts. The Alaskan cruises are targeted to a bit older crowd in upscale consumer magazines such as *Smithsonian, Travel & Leisure, National Geographic, Gourmet,* and *Modern Maturity*.

Holland America targets its consumer promotions. A direct mail program sends newsletters and special discounts to the cruise line's "alumni." When a cruise is not filled near its departure date, Holland America uses local newspapers to advertise special discount rates to selected secondary markets. Travel agents book 99 percent of Holland America's trips. Trade promotions include lottery sweepstakes for free cruises and various contests and trivia puzzles. In 1989, Carnival purchased the Holland America Line for $625 million. Currently, Carnival manages Holland America separately in terms of customer targets, branding, and promotional strategy.

ROYAL CARIBBEAN

Concentrated in the Caribbean and based in Miami, Royal Caribbean targets first-time cruisers. Most of its passengers are between the ages of 35 and 54 with annual household incomes over $40,000. Royal Caribbean is well-known for its *Sovereign of the Seas*, "the largest cruise ship in the world."

Royal Caribbean spends about $22.2 million on advertising: $3.8 million for magazines, $6.3 million for network TV, $4.5 million for spot TV, $278,200 for network cable, $1.3 million for national syndications, $15,500 for newspapers, and $15,500 for Sunday magazines. Newspaper advertising is conducted in 25 local markets. According to Mike Petty, director of marketing, this marketing target is intentional. "Ten years ago, 60 to 70 percent of our business came out of the top 20 markets. Now those markets account for 40 percent of [Royal Caribbean] business."

Royal Caribbean does not use special promotions. Petty noted, "Royal Caribbean is unique in the cruise industry in that we do our best not to price promote." He believes that this policy gives the passengers "more for the money [they] are paying."

ROYAL VIKING

Royal Viking offers worldwide destinations, including Leif Ericsson's path to Newfoundland and World War II Pacific battlegrounds. Royal Viking targets 50-year-olds with annual incomes over $50,000 who have sailed before and have taken an international vacation within the past three years. Most of its passengers have incomes around $100,000 and more than 50 percent have sailed with Royal Viking before.

Royal Viking spends about $6 million each year on media advertising and direct marketing. The media budget is split about evenly between magazine and newspaper advertising, with the exception of the 5 percent that goes to cable television's Arts & Entertainment Network. According to John B. Richards, vice president, marketing and planning, "It's done rather well for us. It's the most targeted electronic media available to us. We just can't use broadcast media as effectively."

Print advertising includes a variety of literary, travel, and special interest magazines such as *Travel & Leisure, Harper's, Signature, The New Yorker, The Atlantic, Food & Wine, Gourmet, Bon Appetit, Architectural Digest, Better Homes and Gardens, Sunset,* and *Golfer's Digest*. Theater publications such as *Opera News* are also used. Newspaper ads are run only in the travel section of 35 to 40 Sunday papers in the top 20 markets including the *Christian Science Monitor, New York Times, Los Angeles Times,* and *San Francisco Chronicle*.

Consumer promotions include a direct marketing campaign offering tips on discounts and special interest programs. This program targets past Royal Viking passengers. Travel agents book 98 percent of Royal Viking's cruises. Trade promotions include familiarization trips at attractive rates and special commission rates for large volume producers.

ADMIRAL

Admiral Cruises, Inc., was formed in 1986 by the merger of Eastern Cruise Lines, Western Cruise Lines, and Sundance Cruises. Admiral targets passengers between the ages of 37 and 55 with annual household incomes of $30,000 to $35,000. Although cruises are often associated with couples on romantic getaways, Robert R. Mahmarian, senior vice president, sales and marketing, portrays Admiral's atmosphere as one in which "people alone chaperone each other and have a ball." Mahmarian believes that Admiral is most attractive to women and families because the third or fourth passenger in a group sometimes gets a free cruise as a special promotion. Admiral is also using a shotgun approach with consumers by emphasizing the relative value of cruising as a vacation alternative.

Admiral spends about $11 million on advertising. Approximately 70 percent of the budget goes to newspapers. Ads appear in the Sunday travel section in about 82 markets. The remaining media dollars go to magazine and television advertising. Admiral uses magazines such as *McCall's, Southern Living,* and *Sunset*. Mahmarian notes that the cruise line also advertises in *USA Today* because "about 60 percent of cruises are being decided by men, so a newspaper like *USA Today* is a good opportunity to advertise because it has that kind of mixed reader." He also emphasized that TV commercials are used merely as a veneer for the line's other advertising. "When you're buying a cruise, you need to inspect more. A 30-second commercial can get you interested but can't sell you a cruise."

Travel agents book 100 percent of Admiral's trips. Trade promotions include incentive programs that provide override commissions for large revenue producers. Cooperative advertising programs also allow travel agencies to share ad costs with Admiral.

COMPETITIVE ADVERTISING

Exhibit 2A–1 presents examples of advertisements for some of these competitors. Note the competitive thrust in the statements made in these ads.

BRITTANY HAIFA LAHAINA WATERFORD BALI NICE-SYDNEY TANGIER JUNEAU LENINGRAD FORT-DE-FRANCE SANTAREM CAPRI · LIVORNO PERTH MYKONOS KUALA LUMPUR NEW YORK OSLO PIRAEUS LONDON PAPEETE BORDEAUX BANGKOK QUEBEC BORA BORA BOMBAY SINGAPORE ROME SYRACUSE WHITTIER · AUCKLAND SYDNEY DUBLIN VENICE VILLEFRANCHE HALIFAX SAN FRANCISCO ACAPULCO BARCELONA AMSTERDAM ISTANBUL · COPENHAGEN DUBROVNIK TOKYO GEIRANGER HELSINKI MANAUS HONG KONG BEIJING HONOLULU BERGEN VIGO GDANSK ST CRUZ MOOREA PALMA DE MALLORCA PLAYA DEL CARMEN

A Truly Great Ship Is Something Of A Destination In Itself.

In a world so unfortunately ruled by a point-A-to-point-B mentality, allow us to suggest a unique sanctuary where *how* one arrives still fully eclipses *when*.

It is a place where you'll find 33 chefs, 17,000 bottles of wine, and one staff member for every two guests.

The place is Royal Viking Line—four gleaming white ships, each rated five-stars-plus.

Isn't it time you joined us here? For details see your travel agent or telephone (800) 426-0821. We look forward to seeing you on board.

7:32 p.m. Halfway between Singapore and Sandakan. A finishing touch has been added to your table: freshly-cut yellow roses from the market at Bangkok.

ROYAL VIKING LINE

Bahamian Registry

© Royal Viking Line 1989

THE LOVE BOAT℠

Once Upon A Time A Princess Went To Europe.

This Princess is a storybook ship the likes of which has rarely been seen. She's beautiful, graceful and regal. She's the 5-Star Royal Princess® And she'll pamper you through Europe in royal splendor. Imagine dining on caviar and lobster thermidor as she approaches the fabled French Riviera. Or returning from the fairytale towns of Scandinavia to a magical evening of Broadway-style entertainment. Hans Christian Andersen couldn't have written it better.

Book by Jan. 31, 1990 and save $500 per couple. Fly free. Ask your travel agent about cruises to the Mediterranean, Scandinavia/Russia or to the Black Sea/Greek Isles. Or mail the coupon below.

"It's More Than A Cruise, It's The Love Boat."

Gavin MacLeod

89C-SM12

Yes, send me the full-color Princess brochure.

Name: _____
(Please Print)
Address: _____
City: _____
State: _____ Zip: _____

Princess Cruises, P.O. Box 2089
Warren, MI 48090-9937

British Registry

➤➤ PRINCESS CRUISES®

ALL CRUISE LINES CARRY SPORTING GOODS. WE ALSO CARRY SPORTING GREATS.

Volleyballs, table tennis paddles and ocean-bound golf balls by the bushel basket, Norwegian Cruise Line stocks them all. Of course, so do most other cruise lines.

In NCL's case, however, there's a difference. We also carry a full line of the world's best athletes: Football, basketball and hockey greats. The fact is, we carry athletes of every sport by the score. And if you like keeping score yourself, NCL will keep you busy. With golf, tennis, skeet shooting and more.

Why settle for mere sporting goods when you can have sporting greats? Walk, jog or sprint over to your travel agent soon or call 1-800-262-4NCL to find out more about the pleasure ships of NCL. When it comes to sports cruises, nobody else is in our league. The truth of the matter is, nobody else even makes the playoffs.

NORWEGIAN CRUISE LINE.
The Pleasure Ships.
SHIPS REGISTRY: BAHAMAS ©1990 NORWEGIAN CRUISE LINE.

Suzy Chaffee | Ray Nitschke | Bonnie Blair | Bruce Crampton

Eddie Murray | Peanut Louie Harper | Byron Scott | Steve Lundquist

WHAT PERSUASIVE COMMUNICATION IS ALL ABOUT

The two chapters in this part introduce the subject of communication. Chapter 3 is a review of interpersonal and mass communication from the perspective of the persuasive effectiveness of these two differing approaches. We develop a model of communication processes, drawing on contemporary thinking in the field.

The following is the important question addressed in Chapter 4: How does the consumer process the information he or she receives? Market researchers and consumer psychologists have made great strides in understanding related to this issue. This chapter covers the subject of information processing from a practical marketing point of view.

The Nature of Communication

IS THIS COMMUNICATION?

It's about closing time, and the weary salesperson at the computer counter faces yet another customer. Here is what happened.

	Thoughts	Words
Salesperson	(Oh boy, another one! Won't 9 o'clock ever come?)	(Cheerily). May I help you?
Customer		Yeah, I think I might be interested in a computer.
Salesperson	(Maybe I can get this over with quickly.)	Our Packard Bell Hard Drive System Model PB8810H is on sale. It comes with a Packard Bell 14-inch color RGB monitor for $888.83. This is $200 off list price.
Customer	(What did she say? I'd better not show my ignorance.)	I'm not quite sure what I want.
Salesperson	(I've got to sell one more of these today.)	Well, you'll never find a better system at this price.
Customer	(How do I get out of here?)	I don't know. . . .

	Thoughts	Words
Salesperson	(I had better push harder.)	(interrupting) Look, this is a real deal. It's got a 30 meg hard disk and a floppy drive plus 640K RAM.
Customer	(What in the name of common sense is she saying? Can't she even speak English?)	(hesitating). That's interesting, but . . . .
Salesperson	(OK, I'll clinch this thing right now.)	Tell you what I'll do. I'll also throw in MS DOS 3.3 and GW Basic at no extra price.
Customer	(For crying out loud, I'm out of here.)	I think I'll look a little more. I own the drapery shop around the corner. My partner and I think it's time we got a computer, and this is the first time I've looked.
Salesperson	(Just a neophyte who's looking, huh? Thanks for wasting my time, buddy!)	Sure, here's my card.
Customer	(Fat chance you'll see me again, lady.)	I may be back.

You just read an incident that happens repeatedly in everyday life—*messages are sent without communication taking place!* Look closely at the root meaning of the word *communication: commonness.* We communicate only when meaning is transferred from one person to another and common understanding is achieved.[1]

What went wrong? First, both utterly failed to express in words what they really were thinking. Also, neither bothered to get into the other person's shoes. It is small wonder that there was a communication misfire. Primary blame, however, lies with the salesperson who can succeed only by being a lot more sensitive to the customer's situation and needs.

Promotion is the communication function of marketing. The purpose of this chapter and the following one is to delve into the complexities of promotion—a familiar but sometimes poorly understood process.

We begin by focusing on models of communication. The most crucial issue is *how meaning is established and transferred between two or more parties.* Theories abound ranging from semiology and semantics discussed in this chapter to human information processing covered in Chapter 4.

Then we turn to interpersonal versus mass communication in a marketing context and highlight general principles that shape promotional strategy. You will discover that the key to successful communication lies in understanding your target audience and adapting your message and media strategy accordingly. People see and hear what they want to see and hear. In short, *the audience is sovereign.*

WHAT COMMUNICATION IS ALL ABOUT

A more precise definition of communication is *a transactional process between two or more parties whereby meaning is exchanged through intentional use of symbols.* Notice these important elements:

1. Communication is *intentional*—A deliberate effort is made to bring about an intended response.[2] This is especially true when the purpose is to persuade.
2. Communication is a *transaction*—Messages are exchanged based on the motivations of all participants in expectation of mutual response.
3. Communication is *symbolic*—Symbols (words, pictures, etc.) are deliberately created and used to cause another party to focus on the object or person represented by that symbol.[3]

A Model of the Process

It is helpful to visualize the communication process through the use of a descriptive model that appears in Figure 3–1. This model is a composite of perspectives and theories that have appeared in the vast literature on this subject.[4]

Although writers may differ on details, most agree on the essence of what occurs when communication takes place, but it must be recognized that no simple diagram can reflect all nuances.[5] We have tried to capture the transactional nature of communication by representing both parties as senders and receivers through a continuing process of feedback.

The source and receiver may be either an individual or an organizational entity of some kind. Communication begins when symbols are selected and arranged in a sequence to be transmitted. This is referred to as *encoding.*

The encoded message then is transmitted through some form of medium, ranging from face-to-face interaction to mass media.

The receiver then attempts to *decode* these symbols and uncover their meaning. To complete the process, the receiver becomes a sender by transmitting feedback. As this transaction takes place, meaning is transferred and clarified.

The fidelity or accuracy of communication can be negatively influenced by *noise* that enters into the message itself, the communication channel, or the encoding and decoding process. *Noise* refers to any extraneous factors that can interfere with reception of the message and distort the intended meaning. Examples include the use of contradictory words or inappropriate illustrations, poor printing quality or fuzzy audio reception, a clamor of others for attention while a television show is watched, and so on.

Bringing about Common Meaning

Study carefully the ad in Figure 3–2. What is being advertised here? What meaning do you get from the picture and from the copy? To provide some

FIGURE 3–1

❖   **A Model of the Communication Process**

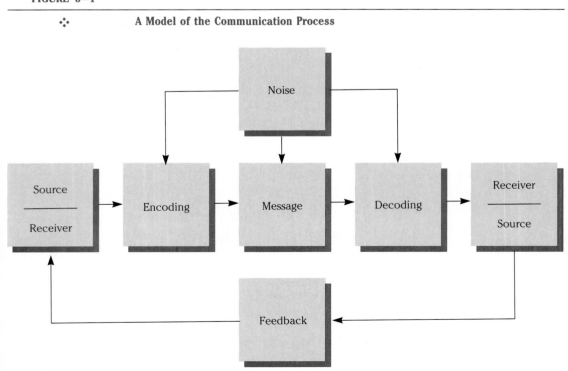

FIGURE 3–2

CANDY IS SWEET, BUT
A DAKIN
IS FOR
KEEPS.

DAKIN. SAN FRANCISCO   GIFTS WITH CHARACTER

insights into this communication, we turn to the field of *semiology* (or *semiotics*), which centers on how meaning is generated in communication messages.[6]

All communication takes place through *signs*. According to eminent semiologist C.S. Peirce, a sign is ". . . anything that stands for something (its object), to somebody (its interpreter), in some respect (its context)."[7]

Broadly speaking, signs fall into three general categories:

1. *Icon*—a sign that visually resembles and signifies the object. In Figure 3–2, the stuffed toy is an icon representing an animal, and the very fact of resemblance signifies that few, if any, would attribute any other meaning to this sign. Also, the picture of the stuffed cat is an iconic sign of the product offered by Dakin gifts.

2. *Index*—a sign that relates to its object by a causal connection. The partially eaten box of candy in Figure 3–2 is an index that the user of this dressing table has eaten the chocolates, although we can only infer this.

3. *Symbol*—an artificial or conventional sign created for the purpose of providing meaning once people have agreed on the sign's form and on what it represents. The Dakin ad in Figure 3–2 is rich in symbolism: the stuffed cat, the partially consumed box of candy, the lace curtain background, and the words used.

Using Symbols Effectively Icon, index, and symbol combine in a complex way in Figure 3–2 to create meaning. It is the symbols, however, that create the greatest difficulty in transferring meaning from one party to another. Fabun puts it this way:

> Most of our present day failures in communication can be traced either to misunderstandings of the role that symbols play in inter-human communication, or to inadequacies in the way we create, transfer and perceive symbols—whether they are spoken or written.[8]

Always remember that symbols, especially words, are something we create and do not have meaning in and of themselves. Words do not have meanings—*only people have meanings.*

Given this fact, how can people ever hope to understand each other using symbols that have no meaning in and of themselves? Part of the answer lies in the way in which languages are learned from birth. Newborn children are initially incapable of symbolic communication. Although they notice people and phenomena of various types, all interaction with others is nonverbal, consisting mostly of a disorganized system of sounds. These sounds, which may serve as signs of their physical state, can be roughly understood only in terms of intensity, pitch, and duration.

Soon infants begin to imitate some of the sounds they hear and repeat them, with the result that they associate words with specific objects. When the word reaches a point that it calls forth the same response as the object itself, it is said to have attained *denotative* meaning. Given the fact that everyone in a society goes through the same process, these meanings are conventionalized and shared in common; thus transfer of meaning is greatly facilitated.

On the other hand, the meaning that is unique to the individual is referred to as *connotative meaning*. For example, a prospective customer who associates the box of chocolates in the Dakin ad with a gift from a loved one may attribute a different meaning to this symbol than someone who does not have this association.

Connotative meanings reflect differences in backgrounds and motivations, thus posing a challenge to the communicator. For this reason, it is necessary to learn *empathy*—the ability to put ourselves in another's shoes. Empathy requires a sensing of needs, background, experiences, and so on. The communicator's goal is to use symbols that are *relevant* and have *shared meaning*. You saw what happened in our chapter opening example when this was not done in the interaction of a customer and a salesperson.

Communication is also facilitated when all parties are as similar as possible in background and outlook. In other words, they should experience an *overlap in psychological fields*. This is especially critical when people have cultural differences. The following are a few examples of what has happened when marketers have attempted to penetrate the Hispanic market without understanding the importance of the overlap in psychological fields[9]:

A cigarette was marketed on the basis of having "less tar," but the translation said "less asphalt."

An ad message attempted to sell the virtues of an upstairs telephone extension by showing a wife saying, "Run downstairs and phone Maria. Tell her we'll be late." This ad completely failed because wives in the Hispanic market usually don't order their spouses around in this way, and Hispanics have a different time language that says "we're expected to be a little late."

A travel contest featured two tickets to Disneyland. But two tickets are not enough for the family-oriented Hispanic.

Band-Aid offered under the Puerto Rican name *banditas* failed to sell in Miami because Cuban Americans did not recognize the name.

Fortunately, social norms (expected uniformities in behavior) come to the communicator's rescue. Norms provide approximate uniformities in ways of thinking and behaving that result from social consensus.

Often two people attempting to communicate are subject to common influences. Perhaps both are from the same Philadelphia suburb, belong to the same church, are graduates of the same college, and are members of the same tennis club. Because of similar environmental influences, they should be able to empathize and transfer meaning with relative ease.

Semiological Analysis   So, then, back to our original question: What is the meaning conveyed to consumers in the Dakin ad (Figure 3–2)? Most would probably say something about the unusual and memorable nature of a Dakin gift, but this would represent only an immediate, spontaneous reaction.

We will learn in Chapter 4 that information processing is more detailed and elaborate than this and that some layers of meaning cannot be verbalized readily. What is signified, for example, by the juxtaposition of the cat and the chocolates? As Sidney J. Levy said in an influential paper more than two decades ago:

❖

**PROMOTION
IN ACTION
3–1**

Symbols, Icons, and Semantics

In just a few years, Lever Brothers Co. built a $300 million fabric softener brand through the charms of a huggable teddy bear named *Snuggle*. Most marketers only dream of creating such a powerful advertising symbol, and Lever didn't want to do anything to jeopardize this little gold mine. It believed it needed to know more about why Snuggle was so successful and how the bear should be used in ads. So Snuggle got psychoanalyzed.

Carol Moog, a psychologist turned advertising consultant, did an analysis of Snuggle that went way beyond cuddliness. "The bear is an ancient symbol of aggression, but when you create a teddy bear, you provide a softer, nurturant side to that aggression," she says. "As a symbol of tamed aggression, the teddy bear is the perfect image for a fabric softener that tames the rough texture of clothing."

Lever had other questions about Snuggle: Should the bear be a boy or girl? Should it interact with humans in the ads? How about blinking its eyes, wiggling its ears, and sniffling the laundry? Blinking, wiggling, and sniffling were all deemed suitable behavior, but Ms. Moog recommended that Snuggle remain genderless and that people not be included in ads. "To keep the magic, it has to be just Snuggle and the viewer communicating," she says. "The teddy bear acts as a bridge between the consumer's rational and more instinctual, emotional side."

Ms. Moog calls her analysis of signs and symbols in advertising "psychological semiotics." Some people refer to it simply as semiotics; others prefer "iconology" or image decoding. Whatever academic jargon they use to describe it, more marketers are turning to social scientists to help them understand the many messages their advertising is transmitting to consumers on both a conscious and subconscious level. Ads have always been rich with psychological imagery, but advertisers now are trying harder to control and manipulate the symbols. Even the penguins in a new Diet Coke com

The things people buy are seen to have personal and social meanings in addition to their functions. Modern goods are recognized as psychological things, as symbolic of personal attributes and goals, as symbolic of social patterns and strivings.[10]

In other words, the meaning of this ad to any given person can be rich and complex, moving far beyond that which is easily verbalized. You will enjoy the report in *Promotion in Action 3–1* on how marketers are beginning to use semiotics.

Symbols, Icons, and Semantics (concluded)

❖
**PROMOTION
IN ACTION
3–1**

mercial aren't there just for humorous effect. SSC&B, an ad agency that practices semiotics, notes that the birds symbolize coolness, refreshment, and friendliness.

"It's mind boggling to try to control all the nonverbal symbols in our creative work," says Elissa Moses, a research executive at the BBDO ad agency. "But if advertisers aren't aware of subtleties, they may inadvertently communicate the wrong message." Consider an ad for Grey Flannel cologne. The marketer was startled to learn from a psychologist that the ad showing only a man's back could be perceived as "rudely giving the consumer the cold shoulder."

Some ad agencies, though, are skeptical of semiotics. They question whether social scientists read too much into commercials, and they chafe at efforts to transform the creative process from an art to a science. "These psychologists tend to be overly intellectual and a little tutti-frutti," says George Lois, chairman of Lois Pitts Gershon Pon/GGK, an ad agency.

Even companies that do semiotic research sometimes take it with a grain of salt. That was the case with executives at American Cyanamid Co., when Ms. Moog, the psychologist, studied a commercial for Pierre Cardin men's fragrance. The ad was designed to show men who are aggressive and in control, but Ms. Moog saw a conflict in an image of the cologne gushing out of a phallic-shaped bottle. She said it symbolized male ejaculation and lack of control. "We recognized that she probably was right," says a marketing official who worked with Ms. Moog, "but we kept the shot of the exploding cologne in the commercial anyway. It's a beautiful product shot, plus it encourages men to use our fragrance liberally."

Source: Adapted from Ronald Alsop, "Agencies Scrutinize Their Ads for Psychological Symbolism," *The Wall Street Journal*, June 11, 1987, p. 25. Used by special permission.

Semiotics offers the marketer tools which augment the direct questions of conventional marketing research and include play, drama, projective techniques, and so on. Also, as Holbrook noted, semiology accepts the researcher's personal, subjective, and introspective inputs as an important part of the analysis.[11]

Some Insights into Strategy   Semiology and its related fields of syntactics and semantics have developed an extensive repertoire of methods that can be used to help ensure that intended meaning is attributed to symbols.[12] We will mention only two: *metaphor* and *contiguity*.

Metaphor   It is possible to transfer through analogy or implied comparison the qualities of one object to another, dissimilar object if imagination is invoked. Notice how the toothbrush topped by the biscuit is a metaphor attempting to connote the teeth-cleaning properties of Milk-Bone Dog Biscuits (see Figure 3–3).

Contiguity   Contiguity, on the other hand, brings other objects, activities, or people into association with an object in order to transfer the qualities of one to the other. This is almost universally used in cigarette advertising, but other products use it as well. The NEC ad in Figure 3–4 certainly associates this product with an upscale and unconstrained baby-boomer lifestyle. Whether this is a socially legitimate tactic has been severely challenged, however.[13]

The Multiple Ways We Communicate

Although we pay greatest conscious attention to the use of visual and spoken symbols, we communicate in many other nonverbal and nonsymbolic ways through the languages of space, artifacts, time, and kinetics, to mention only a few.

The Language of Space   All of us maintain a sense of private space or territoriality. When this space is somehow violated, say in a crowded elevator, people can react with discomfort or even hostility.

On the other hand, space can be used consciously to deliver a clear message. Is there much doubt about the nature of the relationship conveyed in Figure 3–5 or the economic status of the owner of the spacious living room in Figure 3–6?

The Language of Artifacts   Look again at Figure 3–6. You learn even more about the owner by what's in this room (the artifacts) such as contemporary art and sculpture, the oriental rug, and so on. What is your picture of this man or woman? In a very real sense, what we own and display conveys meaning.

The Language of Time   The ways in which we use and express time can be quite revealing, and these expressions vary widely from culture to culture. North Americans can be perplexing for Africans and Latins, who might well disapprove of business people in Figure 3–7 as "too busy for others," even though the image is perfectly suited to the North American target market for which it was created, who will likely associate the same figures with energy, momentum, and success. In short, time is also a language and should be used *consciously* in the development of advertising images.

FIGURE 3–3

A Milk-Bone Metaphor

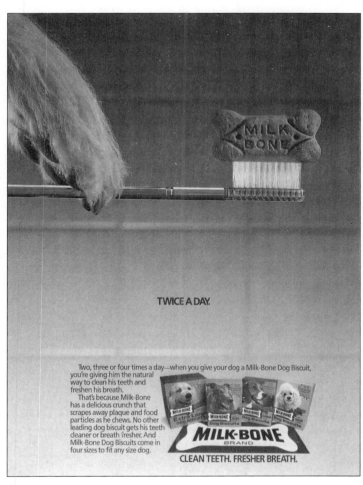

Courtesy Nabisco Brands, Inc.

FIGURE 3-4

❖   **The Product Takes on Meaning by Contiguity**

FIGURE 3–5

The Space between People Says It All

Courtesy Remy Martin Company

FIGURE 3–6

❖ **Space Can Communicate Social Status and Achievement**

ACHIEVEMENT ORIENTED
PANDE CAMERON

For those with top level tastes, a well-appointed room begins at ground level—with Pande Cameron, the who's who in handmade orientals. To get the bigger picture on better living, send $5 (US funds) for our colorful, idea-filled 44-page booklet. Pande Cameron & Co. of New York, Dept. AD108 200 Lexington Ave., New York NY 10016.

Courtesy Pande Cameron & Co.

FIGURE 3–7

Many Messages Are Conveyed by "Nonstop Legs"

Courtesy The Hertz Corporation.

The Language of Kinetics   By *kinetics,* we are referring to gestures and movements. The busy business people in Figure 3–7 send a clear message, supported by artifacts of clothing and briefcases, that they are busy career people on the move. Their facial expressions convey determination, not to be trifled with. They don't want to stop for anything. This is exactly the intent expressed by the ad's joky, briskly worded headline: "Never stop at our counter again."

The Importance of the "Silent Languages"   What other ways in which we communicate can you think of? In addition to those mentioned here, we could add *numerical* (what is the meaning of the number 13 in many societies?), smell (need we say anything about the power of perfume or cologne?), color (don't use the color red if you want to create a calm and nontroubled image), and optics (a darker room is more mysterious and sensual than a brightly lighted scene).

These and other nonverbal signals are frequently referred to as the *silent languages* because they are often used unconsciously. Think of the harm that can be done by inappropriately moving in on someone else's space, violating time expectations, using a wrong gesture (don't wave your hand to call someone in most parts of Asia; you might be surprised what will happen), or an artifact that conveys the wrong impression (wearing an open-collared shirt when making a sales call on a Wall Street lawyer). Such actions can adversely affect credibility. The solution, of course, is to be conscious of the multiple languages and use them purposefully.

COMMUNICATION IN MARKETING

Marketing communication does not differ in essence from communication in any field. The challenge is to make appropriate use of all options ranging from personal selling when needed to wide-scale mass advertising.

Personal Selling

Personal selling is a widely used promotional strategy, especially in industrial goods marketing. Although self-service retailing is becoming increasingly commonplace in the consumer goods field, the demands for effective personal selling still exist in high-service product fields.

Personal selling offers some real strategic advantages:

1. The communication is face to face. Therefore, it is possible for each party to learn all that is necessary about the other party to bring about empathy and meaningful exchange.

2. Feedback is instant. If the first efforts are off target, the skillful use of feedback offers the opportunity to try again and ultimately establish common ground.

3. Exposure is usually voluntary. This means that the customer (receiver) is actively seeking information or help and hence will be receptive to processing what is said.

The marketing challenge lies in answering this question: "Where can I find a good salesperson?" This is a common lament, especially at the retail level. Three chapters in Part 6 will look in detail at the issues related to this problem, but Promotion in Action 3–2 will give you some insights into the steps that progressive companies are taking.

Mass Communication

The economic requirements of reaching a large audience place distinct limits on the use of interpersonal communication in marketing. Therefore, the mass media find widespread use for advertising and public relations.

A diagrammatic model of mass communication appears in Figure 3–8. Actually, the term *mass* is an unfortunate one in one sense. It carries the erroneous connotation to some that the sender has the ability to dominate an unthinking, noninteracting crowd. Nothing could be further from the truth.[14] The audience is *active*, not passive, seeing and hearing what it wants to see and hear, and *interactive* with others who have been exposed.

The source of a mass communication is usually a commercial, governmental, or educational organization. Its purpose is to persuade audience

**PROMOTION
IN ACTION
3–2**

Hart Schaffner & Marx U

Manufacturers not satisfied with the pace of change and worried about how their products are sold are stepping in to help train department store workers. Hartmarx, a manufacturer of expensive men's suits under the Hickey-Freeman, Hart Schaffner & Marx, and other labels, soon will officially open Hart Schaffner & Marx U, as in university. The company will accept students from department and specialty stores who will be taught how to offer the customer a high-quality suit. If a man is going to spend $500 for fancy threads, someone who knows something about the material had better be around, says Hartmarx CEO Harvey Weinberg. "There's too much clerking and not enough selling. We are going to address that."

Source: Bill Saporito, "Retailing's Winners & Losers," *Fortune*, December 18, 1989, p. 74. Used by special permission.

members to accept a particular point of view or to inform and educate them with respect to a particular topic.

The United States Army, for example, had a very effective recruiting campaign in the late 1980s featuring the upbeat slogan, "The Army—Be All You Can Be!" Visualize what must have taken place as this campaign passed through various levels of review, reaching into the highest levels of the Pentagon. Organizational theorists long have recognized what happens—compromises are made and the outcome is institutionally safe and often mediocre. The fact that this was *not* the case with the Army Recruiting campaign underscores the political savvy that must have been exercised to keep the cutting edge intact.

Mass Media and the Promotional Mix   The major reason for the wide use of mass communication is that it can reach a large audience quickly and inexpensively when viewed in terms of cost per individual contacted. Indeed, often no other practical way is available to reach a large and widely dispersed audience.

Although the benefits of mass media are significant, a downside must be recognized. Audiences turn to the mass media for the gratifications offered by entertainment, news, and education. When that is the case, exposure to advertising is usually *involuntary*. As a result, the probability is high that such advertising will be ignored or disregarded through selective information processing discussed in Chapter 4.[15] This dilemma is compounded further by the deluge of competing ads in most media.

FIGURE 3–8

❖   **A Model of the Mass Communication Process**

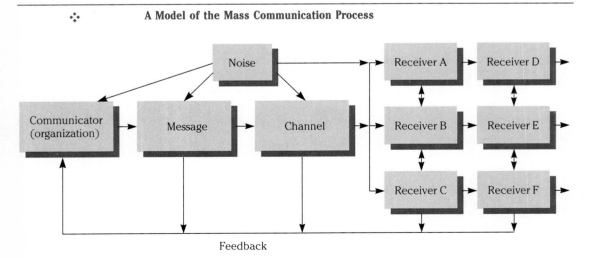

The only exception is when the consumer is engaged in active *extended problem solving* (see Chapter 5) and is interested in scanning ads for information. Now exposure becomes *voluntary,* and the individual actively processes the information that is presented.

An additional difficulty is that effective and timely feedback from mass media communication is difficult and expensive to obtain because the parties are physically separated. At the very least, feedback is delayed because some type of audience survey is usually used.

Use of a survey for feedback cannot adjust content on the spot as a salesperson can do, with the result that the communication opportunity is lost. An audience's reading and viewing can be determined only by asking people what they have read or seen. Standardized techniques for this purpose are discussed in Chapter 16.

Making the Most of the Mass Media   From the perspective of the effective transfer of meaning, the mass media present formidable challenges. But it is possible to use these media with considerable effectiveness if some necessary steps are taken. The following is a brief discussion of these steps.

Isolation of market segments   You will learn in Chapter 9 how to isolate specific groups or segments within the total market that offer the greatest receptivity and to avoid those that are unreceptive. The General Motors Corporation, for example, tried unsuccessfully to broaden the appeal of its Cadillac Eldorado and Seville models to the younger import-oriented buyers. At the same time, GM hoped that the loyal market core in their 50s and 60s would not be alienated by the changed advertising strategy. In reality, the only result was the alienation of the loyal core and the failure to attract import buyers. As a result, sales were less than half of expectations.[16]

This situation could have been prevented if a more careful analysis of buyer motivations and behavior had been undertaken. First, did evidence indicate that younger buyers were wavering in their beliefs regarding the superiority of imported luxury cars? We doubt seriously that this was the situation, in which case the advertising seed was wasted by being sown on nonfertile soil.

Even if the opportunity had existed to make inroads with this approach, a different campaign should have been used for each segment. Some companies that must reach 10 or more segments use different campaigns designed for each. The chances of getting the message across are significantly greater when this segmentation is done skillfully.

Careful media selection   Advertising strategists make every effort to match target audience characteristics with media audience characteristics. The goal is to minimize waste coverage to the maximum extent possible. This is a demanding task, but you will see in Chapters 14 and 15 that dollar productivity is increased when the task is accomplished.

Pretesting appeals There is no chance to try again if an appeal is off target. Therefore, every effort must be made in advance to determine the extent to which an appeal will attract and hold attention and to which the objectives of the message will be achieved. Determining these factors requires pretesting exposure of the message on smaller groups. Pretesting can provide enough information to minimize the probabilities of a communication misfire (see Chapter 16).

Analysis of feedback Feedback, of course, is delayed or absent altogether when mass media are used, whereas the salesperson has the advantage of instantaneous feedback. The advertiser must resort to after-the-fact measures of readership or viewership, comprehension, and response. Although it is too late to change what already has happened, this so-called *postmortem* analysis can prove invaluable in sharpening the impact of future efforts (see Chapter 16).

A Summary Comparison

Table 3–1 enables you to grasp quickly the comparative features of interpersonal and mass media. You can readily understand the benefits of using both in combination whenever possible.

TABLE 3–1

❖

The Comparative Advantages and Limitations of Interpersonal and Mass Communication

Factors	Interpersonal	Mass
Reaching a large audience		
Speed	Slow	Fast
Cost per individual reached	High	Low
Influence on the individual		
Attraction of attention	High	Low
Probability of interest and response	High	Low
Accuracy of comprehension	High	Relatively Low
Feedback		
Direction of message flow	Two-way	One-way
Speed of feedback	High	Low
Accuracy of feedback	High	Low

SUMMARY

This chapter introduced you to the fundamentals of communication, which was defined as a transactional process between two or more parties in which meaning is exchanged through intentional use of symbols. It was stressed that meaning does not lie in words themselves but in individuals.

Communication makes use of symbols—signs designed and used to convey meaning about an object or person. We presented a semiological analysis to understand how symbols are transmitted and are given meaning in the communication process.

Communication goes far beyond the use of verbal and pictorial symbols. As discussed in the chapter, people also use, perhaps unconsciously, such languages as time, kinetics, artifacts, and space. In this realm some of the most serious mistakes are made that undermine the credibility of the communicator.

The differences between interpersonal communication and mass communication in a marketing context were discussed in detail. As noted, interpersonal communication offers the benefits of face-to-face interaction, thus providing a greater opportunity to bring about changes in the other party.

Mass communication, on the other hand, has the advantage of speed and low cost per contact and poses real challenges caused by lack of flexibility and feedback. From this base of understanding, an overview presented the steps required to use communication effectively in marketing strategy.

REVIEW AND DISCUSSION QUESTIONS

1. Refer to the salesperson/customer interaction described at the beginning of the chapter. You are assigned to train this salesperson on how to be more effective. What would you stress in this training?

2. Describe what kinds of connotative meaning most people have for these terms: *affection, love, fondness, tenderness, attachment, endearment, liking, devotion, Republican,* and *Democrat.* How do the connotative meanings differ from denotative meanings?

3. Turn to the Pande Cameron ad in Figure 3–6 (p. 72). Carefully examine this picture and indicate which signs are icons, indexes, and symbols. Compare your analysis with others and see what differences you note. What conclusion can you draw about the uses of semiological analysis?

4. Turn now to the Hertz ad in Figure 3–7 (p. 73). Was any use made of metaphor or contiguity? If so, was the use effective in your opinion?

5. A salesperson is busy selling a wedding gown to a bride-to-be. Given the many languages of communication that we all use, to what specific kinds of feedback should the salesperson be sensitive?

6. A regional soft drink manufacturer has marketed under one brand name since 1904 and still has the original product line consisting of root beer and orange soda. The CEO is being pressed by his board to consider market segmentation. You are asked to comment on this request. How would you define market segmentation? Under what conditions would you recommend it?

NOTES

1. This is the heart of contemporary definitions of communication. See especially Em Griffin, *A First Look at Communication Theory* (New York: McGraw-Hill, in press); Dominic A. Infante, Andrew S. Rancer, and Deanna F. Womack, *Building Communication Theory* (Prospect Heights, Ill.: Waveland Press, 1990), ch. 1; Don Fabun, *Communications: The Transfer of Meaning* (San Francisco, Calif.: International Society for General Semantics, 1987); and Wilbur Schramm, "The Unique Perspective of Communication: A Retrospective View," *Journal of Communication* 33 (Summer 1983), pp. 14–15.

2. Infante et al., *Building Communication Theory*, p. 9.

3. Symbols have long been accepted as being at the very heart of the communication process. See, for example, Kenneth Boulding, *The Image* (Ann Arbor, Mich.: University of Michigan Press, 1956); and Sidney J. Levy, "Symbols for Sale," *Harvard Business Review* 37 (July-August, 1959), pp. 117–24. For a more contemporary statement, see G. Cronkhite, "On the Focus, Scope, and Coherence of the Study of Symbolic Activity," *Quarterly Journal of Speech* 73 (1986), pp. 231–46. Also, David G. Mick, "Consumer Research and Semiotics: Exploring the Morphology of Signs, Symbols, and Significance," *Journal of Consumer Research* 13 (September 1986), pp. 196–213.

4. For an important discussion on changes in the ways in which communication is described and conceptualized, see "Ferment in the Field," *Journal of Communication* 33 (Summer 1983).

5. For a helpful summary of descriptive models, see Infante et al., *Building Communication Theory*, pp. 24–32.

6. This is a difficult and challenging field that involves many theories and conceptualizations. For a good introduction, see Arthur A. Berger, *Signs in Contemporary Culture: An Introduction to Semiotics* (New York: Longman, 1984); John Fisk, *Introduction to Communication Studies* (New York: Methuen, 1982); Arthur A. Berger, *Media Analysis Techniques* (Beverly Hills, Calif.: Sage Publications, 1982), ch. 1; and Mick, "Consumer Research and Semiotics."

7. Quoted in Mick, "Consumer Research and Semiotics," p. 198.

8. Fabun, *Communications: The Transfer of Meaning*, p. 16.

9. Humberto Valencia, "Point of View: Avoid Hispanic Market Blunders," *Journal of Advertising Research* 23 (January 1984), pp. 19–22.

10. Sidney J. Levy, "Symbols by Which We Buy," in *Advancing Marketing Efficiency*, ed. Lynn H. Stockman (Chicago: American Marketing Association, 1959), p. 410.

11. Morris B. Holbrook, "Seven Routes to Facilitating the Semiological Interpretation of Consumption Symbolism and Marketing Imagery in Works of Art: Some Tips for Wildcats," in *Advances in Consumer Research*, ed. Thomas K. Srull, 16 (Provo, Utah: Association for Consumer Research, 1989), p. 420. To discover more about how semiotics has been applied in marketing, see Morris B. Holbrook, "Aims, Concepts, and Methods for the Representation of Individual Differences in Esthetic Responses to Design Features," *Journal of Consumer Research* 13 (December 1986), pp. 337–447.

12. See, for example, Umberto Eco, *A Theory of Semiotics* (Bloomington, Ind.: Indiana University Press, 1976); and Berger, *Media Analysis Techniques*.

13. Grant McCracken and Richard W. Pollay, "Anthropology and the Study of Advertising" (Working Paper #815, Faculty of Commerce and Business Administration, University of British Columbia, 1981).

14. For an excellent introduction to mass communication, see Denis McQuail, *Mass Communication Theory* (Beverly Hills, Calif.: Sage, 1984).

15. See Blaine Goss, *The Psychology of Human Communication* (Prospect Heights, Ill.: Waveland Press, 1989), esp. ch. 4.

16. Russell Mitchell, "GM's New Luxury Cars: Why They're Not Selling," *Business Week*, January 19, 1987, pp. 94ff.

Consumer Response to Persuasive Communication

"MINI-MIZING WOMEN"—ONE OF 10 KEY MARKETING BLUNDERS OF THE 1980S

The fashion industry dictated short skirts in 1987, but women refused to obey. Though many baby boomers had embraced the miniskirt when they were teenagers 20 years earlier, they now had career expectations, family responsibilities, and extra pounds.

Women aged 18 to 24 weigh 132 pounds on average, according to the National Center for Health Statistics. But women aged 35 to 44 weigh 148 pounds. This weight gain is just one sign that middle-aged women have more than fashion on their minds. Almost three-quarters of baby-boom women are mothers. Two in five have attended college; 75 percent are working.

Designers got a chilly reception when the 1987 fall fashions featured miniskirts. Already fed up with the rising costs of clothing and further perturbed by the fashion industry's lack of concern for their real clothing needs, women stopped buying—sending a shock wave through the retail clothing industry. As Mayor Barbara Sigmund of Princeton, New Jersey, explained to the *New York Times,* "Could Lee Iacocca have bailed out Chrysler wearing short pants?" Women in the 1990s can expect more choices and fewer dictates from the fashion industry.

Source: "Missing the Market," *American Demographics* 12 (December 1989), p. 18. Reproduced by special permission.

As our opening example so vividly reveals, the consumer is not a pawn on the marketer's board. Apparently clothing industry executives believed that they could swing clothing preferences by sheer persuasive power. The resulting negative backlash threw the industry into a tailspin that continues as of this writing. This is yet another demonstration of the cornerstone principle of *consumer sovereignty:* consumers have full power to see and hear what they want to see and hear.

This all comes down to the basic proposition discussed in Chapter 3 that, if we are not careful, a marked difference can exist between *meaning intended by the sender* and the *meaning attributed by the receiver.* Why does this happen? To find the answers, we turn to the study of information processing.

Our first purpose is to clarify what happens in the consumer's mind from the exposure to a message to the ultimate response. You will learn quickly that the study of information processing is providing a rich yield of marketing insights. Then we turn more specifically to an exploration of how persuasive communication works to bring about changes in attitudes and behavior.

INFORMATION PROCESSING

Look for a moment at the ad for Kit 'N Kaboodle Brand Cat Food in Figure 4–1. Here's what must happen if this appeal is to have impact on a consumer:

1. *Exposure*—The consumer must have proximity to the message so that one or more senses may be activated.
2. *Attention*—Information processing capacity must be allocated to the stimulus.
3. *Comprehension*—The message must be interpreted and meaning attributed to it.
4. *Acceptance*—The message must be accepted into the structure of existing knowledge, beliefs, and attitudes. Persuasion is said to occur if there also is *yielding*—modification of existing beliefs and attitudes or creation of new ones.
5. *Retention*—The interpreted stimulus is transferred into long-term memory.

This process is shown graphically in Figure 4–2.

According to the information processing model in Figure 4–2, a message must survive five different stages before it is retained in memory. This explodes the folklore that says "you can win them if you just get the message to them." Exposure does *not* guarantee the desired response.

The Kit 'N Kaboodle ad (Figure 4–1) appeared in *Good Housekeeping* magazine. Here are some reasons why it (or any other ad, for that matter) can fall short of intended impact:

FIGURE 4–1

How Will This Ad Be Processed?

Courtesy Ralston-Purina Company

1. Some readers could miss it entirely by scanning or failing to turn to the appropriate page.

2. It does not attract attention. A noncat owner probably would not be interested. In addition, some cat owners do not buy on the basis of brand name and hence will tune out the stimulus.

3. The claim may not be taken seriously and hence will never be fully comprehended. When this is the case, acceptance and retention are unlikely.

Suppose the odds of success at each of the information processing stages are 50 percent (i.e., half of the readers see the ad, half of those pay attention, and so on). This means that the probability of the ad's message

FIGURE 4–2

Information Processing

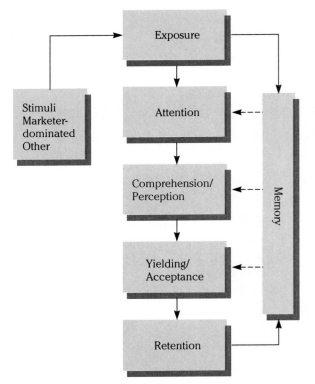

Source: James F. Engel, Roger D. Blackwell, and Paul Miniard, *Consumer Behavior,* 5th ed. (Hinsdale, Ill.: Dryden Press, 1985), p. 52. Reproduced by special permission.

making it into long-term memory and affecting change is only 0.03125 (E.5 × A.5 × C.5 × A.5 × R.5).

Actually, we believe that the Kit 'N Kaboodle ad will be much more successful. Many cat lovers are emotionally involved with their pets and are open and sensitive to relevant information. For that reason alone, this appeal will stand out. Also, the arrangement of the elements is such that the eye is drawn to the pet and from there to the brand name. Skillful use of design principles can greatly enhance the odds of brand awareness and interest.

The Central Role of Involvement

Usually a person has little motivation to process a promotional message unless, first of all, there is high *involvement,* defined as the degree of perceived personal importance and relevance accompanying product and brand choice within a specific situation or context.[1]

Involvement and relevance are personalized issues with some diverse roots:[2]

1. *Perceived risk of negative outcomes.* From time to time, everyone has doubts or fears that purchase expectations will not be met. As an example, the American public has been found to deeply distrust Wall Street to the extent that only 11 percent would turn to a stockbroker for advice on investing a $10,000 windfall.[3] Who could blame the public in view of the sense of powerlessness the average investor had during the sudden stock market declines in October 1987 and October 1989?

2. *Social sanctions.* To the extent that peer group influence defines the "right choice" and becomes an important determinant of choice, involvement correspondingly increases.

3. *Ego relatedness.* Involvement increases to the extent that consumer actions are seen as enhancing or affecting self-image.

When involvement is high, the odds that a message will be processed as intended by the sender are much higher than when this is not the case *if the content is perceived as being relevant.* In other words, the individual is motivated to receive pertinent information and filters are open.

Another outcome of high involvement is *selective perception* in which unwanted or nondesired communication is actively tuned out. In other words, perceptual defenses can be erected and can be difficult to overcome. Certainly, the women's apparel manufacturers referred to at the beginning of this chapter found selective perception to be a common consumer response.

In the discussion that follows, we will frequently explain the information processing consequences at various levels of involvement.

Exposure

Information processing begins when the message reaches at least one of the five senses among target audience members. This requires selection of communication media (interpersonal or mass) that *reach people where they are*. This is the great challenge of media selection discussed in Chapter 15.

Threshold Levels   In the process of exposure, a person's sensory receptors are activated, and the encoded information is transmitted to the brain. This activation is referred to as *sensation* and is affected by four thresholds[4]:

1. *Lower or absolute threshold:* The minimum amount of stimulus energy required for sensation to occur. If this point is not exceeded, effective exposure will not take place.
2. *Recognition threshold:* The point at which a stimulus can be consciously classified.
3. *Terminal threshold:* The point in which increased exposure stimulus intensity no longer affects sensation.
4. *Difference threshold:* The smallest change in intensity that will be noticed.

It often is necessary to detect whether changes in package color or shape and other marketing variables such as price will be noticed. The difference threshold now becomes relevant. Weber's Law may prove to be helpful in assessing the threshold; it takes the form of the following equation,

$$K = \frac{\Delta I}{I}$$

where:

K = A constant that differs across the various senses.
ΔI = The smallest change in stimulus intensity necessary to produce a barely noticeable difference.
I = The stimulus intensity at the point where change occurs.

Weber's Law suggests that a greater amount of change is necessary to produce a barely noticeable difference as initial stimulus intensity increases. Assume that K equals 5 percent in the context of changed package size. A 5 percent increase in the size of a soap bar distributed to hotels would be barely noticeable in the much larger bar usually used in homes.

At other times, the challenge is to make changes without consumers noticing them. This challenge is often the case with price increases. If possible, the change should not reach the level of the barely noticeable difference.

Selective Exposure   Consumers worldwide have become adept at finding ways to avoid exposure to unwanted messages. It has been known for decades that this can happen when involvement is high in order to protect beliefs and practices from attack. When involvement is high, the consumer seeks supportive information but actively avoids contradictory information.

Most products and services, however, do not attain the degree of importance and relevance to incur selective exposure. They do not attain it because low involvement is a fact of life. Does it really matter which brand of toilet paper or motor oil a consumer purchases? Are brand preferences established that must be shielded from attack? We think not in the majority of situations.

Consumers also avoid exposure because they are inundated! Howard Shimmel, vice president for audience research at MTV Networks, estimates that a person watching 30 hours of TV per week is bombarded by 37,822 commercials a year.[5] We cannot help wondering how Mr. Shimmel managed to arrive at such a precise number, but we do not believe that he is far off.

The fact is that consumers have become active *zappers* (actively switching channels during commercials or using the mute button),[6] *zippers* (using the fast forward button on a VCR),[7] and *grazers* (wandering through various channels).[8] In one study, over half of those sampled indicated that they are regular zappers of unwanted commercials, and this is becoming increasingly common.[9] Promotion in Action 4–1 underscores the extent of the problem.

What can be done to thwart the zappers? One suggested strategy is to ignore it. George Garrick, executive vice president of Information Resources, Inc., put it this way:

> If these people are sitting around changing channels all day and night, maybe they're not the kind of people we want to reach anyway. If you bear in mind that the average household is exposed to about 140 commercials per day, it is easy to have a viewer do what he considers to be "a lot" of zapping when, as a percentage of all commercials, he really is doing relatively little.[10]

Accepting Garrick's advice, however, could lead to loss of major market segments, especially baby boomers who lead the "zapping pack." Some methods have proved helpful in holding the viewer and inhibiting zapping. First of all, since most zapping seems to occur during the first and last five minutes of programs, it might be wise to move ads into the interior of the program whenever this is possible.

Research also indicates that people often see a few seconds of a spot before zapping. As a result, major attempts are made to build drama and interest into spots by making them look like a real production before centering on the product (a Middle Ages battle scene selling a computer, for example). Other spots follow quite an opposite strategy and hope to beat the zapping button by hitting the brand name and benefit in less than five seconds.[11]

Finally, it is recognized that programming which holds viewer interest decreases zapping. For example, zapping drops sharply when viewers become embroiled in the legal and sexual maneuvers on "L.A. Law."[12] To the extent that this is true, media choices of ad placement should be made accordingly, but such programs are hard to find.

Attention

Attention is defined as the allocation of processing capacity to the incoming stimulus. Capacity is a limited resource at best, with the result that everyone must be selective in allocation. This means that some stimuli will receive attention and others will be ignored. Attention is influenced by the nature of the stimulus and by such personal considerations as motivations and attittudes.

❖
**PROMOTION
IN ACTION
4–1**

"Zappers Challenge the Giants"

From his bedside in Brooklyn, Bruce Hoenig watches up to three hours of television each night. Remote control glued in hand, he flits continually from channel to channel in a fidgety flight from a stream of TV commercials.

"I'm a zapper," he says. He clicks through a 68-channel cable system and pingpongs among three or four shows at a time. It drives his wife crazy; she retreats to one of three other TV sets in the house. He hasn't found a single show that can keep his zapper in neutral.

But if Mr. Hoenig revels in zapping at bedside, he also worries about it at work. He is media services director at Thomas J. Lipton, Inc., which spends $70 million a year to make and air TV ads for tea bags and other food. If everybody else also zaps, he fears, Lipton isn't getting the audience it's paying for.

He has good reason to worry. A new, experimental ratings system shows that zapping may be far more prevalent—and a bigger problem for advertisers—than most experts believe. Based on a sample of the fickle channel-changing habits in the New York City area, zapping cuts a prime time ad's audience by 10 percent or more. Almost 20 percent of homes are heavy zappers, switching to a new channel so many times that the rate works out to one zap every two minutes on the average.

Source: Dennis Kneale, "Zapping of TV Ads Appears Pervasive," *The Wall Street Journal*, April 25, 1988, p. 21. Reproduced by special permission.

Test for yourself the limitations on your span of attention. How long does it take for you to concentrate on a thought in this book before your mind begins to wander? Not very long? Consider the challenge to marketing communicators in a world of information overload. It is small wonder that there has been a trend toward commercials that air for 15 seconds or less.[13]

Stimulus Determinants   Try paging through a magazine and notice what makes some ads stand out more than others and catch the eye. Advertisers use many devices,[14] one of which is novelty. Notice, for example, how dominance of the letter M on the ad page in Figure 4–3 makes this ad difficult to miss.

Another attention-attracting device is color. It has been found, for example, that four-color, two-page ads scored 53 percent higher in readership than black-and-white ads.[15] In another study involving newspapers, the addition of one color produced 41 percent more sales.[16]

Directionality—the use of visual design to direct a viewer's attention— also can be used effectively. Look first at the Del Monte ad on the left side in Figure 4–4. Where does your eye move? Now do the same thing with the Cool Whip ad on the right side. Do you get the same results? Usually the eye will hit the page in the upper right-hand quadrant. It is important, therefore, to direct the reader's eye toward the brand name or main selling point. We believe that Del Monte accomplished this, but the eye could go either direction off the page without recognizing the Cool Whip name or benefit.

Finally, some stimuli are more noticeable than others because of their location or position. Retailers are well aware of this fact and try to put the fast-moving and high-profit items at the customer's eye level whenever possible.

Position also is important in print media. Greater attention is attracted by ads located in the front part of a magazine, on right-hand pages, and on the inside front, inside back, and outside back covers.[17]

Similarly, broadcast advertisers are well aware that commercials do better when they are separated from the clutter of other commercials at the beginning and end of programs.

Personal Determinants   Our focus now shifts to the individual characteristics and dispositions that affect the allocation of processing capacity.

Needs and motivations   Hundreds of studies dating back to the 1930s document conclusively that needs affect attention by enhancing the likelihood that need-relevant stimuli will be noticed. You no doubt have noticed in your own life how differently you respond to an eye-catching bakery display when you are hungry than when you are not. Marketers long have capitalized on this fact to promote goods at moments or places of high consumer receptivity (i.e., beer and soft drinks at baseball games on a hot summer day).

FIGURE 4–3

❖ The Use of Novelty to Attract Attention

The M-Star logo is a registered trademark of Monroe Systems for Business, Inc.

Beliefs and attitudes   The need to maintain cognitive consistency with the target audience is especially important in promotion efforts. According to cognitive consistency theories (balance theory and cognitive dissonance, for example), all of us strive to maintain a coherent system of beliefs and attitudes. Consequently, there is motivation to be receptive to information that enhances consistency, and to resist information that stimulates inconsistency.[18] For this reason, selective allocation of capacity most often occurs when *involvement is high.* Cognitive consistency is sufficiently important to the individual to activate a filtering process which can prevent some promotional messages from being processed.

One way cognitive consistency is maintained is through *perceptual defense.* A pertinent example of an ad that might activate perceptual defense

FIGURE 4–4

How Does the Eye Move in These Ads?

Courtesy Del Monte   *Courtesy General Foods Corporation*

appears in Figure 4–5. Growing numbers of consumers influenced by the animal rights movement have decided that fur is out, and the industry has been adversely affected.[19] It is likely that many who feel strongly about animal rights would pass right over this ad because their defenses are activated at a subconscious level.

Perceptual vigilance, on the other hand, maintains or enhances consistency by stimulating attention to belief-relevant messages. For example, preferred brand names are often processed more readily than are nonpreferred names.[20] Given this fact, the ad in Figure 4–5 could attract the attention of a consumer segment motivated by the glamour, luxury, and prestige traditionally connoted by fur garments.

Adaptation level Have you ever noticed how you can become so habituated to an always-present stimuli, such as a smell or a noise, that you scarcely notice it at all? What happens is that you develop an *adaptation level* for that stimulus so that it scarcely attracts your attention. Advertising quickly falls victim to this process, especially when the product or service is low in involvement or pertinence.

Burger King introduced a $30 million campaign announcing that the weight of its flagship Whopper hamburger had been increased 20 percent. Such television personalities as Mr. T and Bruce Weitz were the spokespersons for this campaign. During the following month there was a 3.6 percent increase in an awareness of Burger King when consumers were asked to name the first fast-food ads that came to mind. After just one month, however, this awareness dropped 5.6 percent, placing it at one of the lowest levels in that chain's history.[21]

Advertising, in reality, has become part of cultural background noise, and therefore is scarcely noticed, especially when involvement is low. Some of the more intriguing (and controversial) gimmicks for print advertising are described in Promotion in Action 4–2.

The loss of consumer attention is further aggravated by the zapping phenomenon mentioned earlier. Therefore, more and more effort is being focused on stimulus effects that capture and hold attention. Matters have reached the point where some ads virtually become mini-TV series. The New England Telephone & Telegraph Company had an image of being cold and indifferent. To change this image, a series of commercials was built around life situations in which the telephone played a vital role in the solution. One embraced the age-old theme of the prodigal son, for example, and illustrated how a family uses the phone to celebrate and cope with his return.[22]

The trend toward television and print "spectaculars" is likely to continue, but the trend is not without its risks. Attention is commonly attracted to secondary stimulus factors while the main message is completely missed. Marketing communicators must use these elaborate advertising devices to

FIGURE 4–5

The Fur Flies

Courtesy Grosvenor Canada

attract and hold attention in such a way that the brand name and selling proposition are reinforced. Unless this objective is accomplished, the promotional investment can be wasted.

Comprehension

"Warning: This Story Will Be Miscomprehended." So read the headline of a *Marketing News* report on the results of a study designed to measure comprehension/miscomprehension of editorial and ad copy in 18 magazines.[23] This research undertaken by Jacoby and Hoyer found that more than one-third of the people surveyed could not correctly state what they had read.[24] But, surprising to some, *ad content fared slightly better than editorial features.*

What this says, of course, is that exposure and attention do not guarantee that correct meaning is attributed to the message. Understanding has not been created at least one-third of the time, and communication has misfired.

Categorization and Elaboration   Meaning depends, first of all, on how a person categorizes and elaborates a stimulus through the use of existing knowledge and beliefs.[25]

PROMOTION IN ACTION 4–2

Combating the Boredom Barrier with High Tech

Absolut's holiday magazine ad talks. Finlandia's ad is a hologram. Chivas Regal's has pull-up tabs, and Crown Royal uses peel-off stickers.

The race is on to be more exotic, more high-tech, more "big idea" in magazine ads. All kinds of advertisers are coming up with unwieldy magazine "spectaculars," as the overdone ads are called in the trade. Like loud women wearing too much jewelry, these ads stand out in a crowd, touting everything from Porsche to Texas Instruments, which ran an ad with a talking computer chip in a recent issue of *Business Week.*

Jerry Della Femina, whose Della Femina McNamee WCRS agency created the first "spectacular," a pop-up Transamerica ad, contends that a splashy insert ad "puts people in the mood to look at advertising, and I think they pay more attention to it."

Bill Tragos, chairman of TBWA Advertising, agrees. TBWA is credited— and blamed—for starting the escalating high-tech liquor ad war with a 1987 musical Christmas ad for Absolut. No matter that the tinny version of "Jingle Bells" malfunctioned in scores of magazines, causing them to play endlessly; the competition for more elaborate ads was on.

Source: Joanne Lipman, "Ads That Sing Out, Pop Up Getting the Thumbs Down," *The Wall Street Journal,* November 8, 1989, p. B1. Used by special permission.

Categorization   Processing an incoming stimulus involves comparing it with memory content so that it can be classified as to its physical properties and assigned meaning. In other words, the stimulus undergoes something analogous to an unconscious filing process.

We are beginning to understand more about how memory is organized. Although many theories attempt to explain that organization, the current literature suggests that memory is organized at the least complex level in the form of an *associative network*.[26] From this perspective, memory is viewed as consisting of a series of nodes (concepts) and links (associations between nodes). Figure 4–6 displays how such an associative network might look for a consumer's recall of a VCR brand.

A link between two or more nodes forms a *belief* (or proposition) such as "Brand A is a reliable VCR." These beliefs, in turn, combine to create a higher-order knowledge structure now referred to as a *schema*.[27] Schemas might include expectations as to the extent to which brands vary in terms of

FIGURE 4–6

An Associative Knowledge Network for a VCR Brand

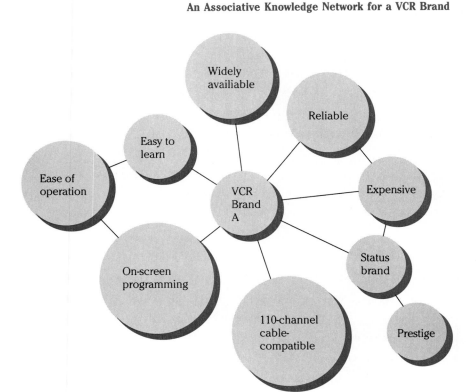

features and important attributes. When a schema contains knowledge about temporal action sequences that occur during an event, it is designated as a *script.*[28]

The weight of evidence suggests that most schemas used in consumer decision making are brand-based in their organization, reflecting important attributes and features.[29] It is possible to generate a pictorial representation through computerized perceptual mapping, a simplified example of which appears in Figure 4–7.

Beliefs, schemas, and scripts become activated as filters during information processing and directly affect the meaning attributed to a stimulus. Those who hold a perceptual map similar to the one in Figure 4–7 most likely would interpret a Blue Cross promotional message within the schema of "community oriented," "solid," and "stable."

Elaboration In addition to categorization, comprehension is also affected by the extent of *elaboration* that takes place (i.e., integration—or personal connections—between new information and existing knowledge). This typically is conceived as a continuum ranging from low to high (or shallow to deep)[30] and is detected by analysis of thoughts during exposure.

Stimulus Determinants Message elements such as words, graphics, and design affect attribution of meaning. In the early 1980s, two engineers formed a company to sell portable computers and tentatively chose Gateway as the company name. There was substantial unrest among potential inves-

FIGURE 4–7

How Health Care Alternatives Stack Up Perceptually

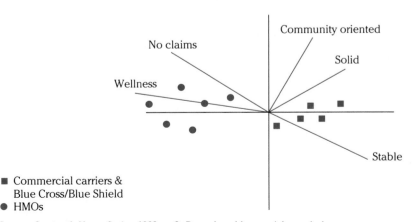

■ Commercial carriers &
  Blue Cross/Blue Shield
● HMOs

Source: *Sawtooth News*, Spring 1989, p. 3. Reproduced by special permission.

tors over this choice of name. "What does it connote?" is the question that was asked.

At this point, the semiology discussed in the previous chapter has direct application. Would Cortex, Cognipack, or Suntek be a better choice? It all depends on the connotations. The company selected the name Compaq, which reflected an important feature of the company's computer—portability. Apparently this was a good choice because the company set an industry record for sales volume in its first year.[31]

Color can also be used to symbolize moods or emotions. Green and blue, for example, connote security. Given these connotations, IBM should be happy with the nickname, Big Blue.

In 1985, Cadillac introduced slimmed-down versions of its popular Seville and Eldorado models. Sales dropped as much as 50 percent because these models appeared nearly identical to other GM cars offered at much lower prices.[32] Once the original length and more extravagant exterior ornamentation were reintroduced, sales began to rebound. Small size in this case was not a virtue.

Personal Determinants   Just as involvement and motivation can influence the attention process, they have a similar effect on comprehension.[33] Deeper and more elaborate information processing is likely when an important need is activated by emotional and complex message symbolism.

Such complex symbolism is used in the Carrington ad in Figure 4–8. Perfumes and fragrances can represent the ultimate of high involvement for many users. The linkage of this motivation with the Carrington name is an especially interesting strategy. Krystle Carrington, a popular television character, is portrayed to connote wealth, power, sophistication, and influence. The goal of this campaign no doubt was to transfer these connotations to the Krystle Carrington line of fragrances.

A person's expectations or perceptual set will affect the attribution of meaning. It is well-known that taste tests conducted with the brand name highly visible are often quite different than when the name is not visible. The management at the Coca-Cola Company learned this lesson when new Coke was blind tested. The taste-testing edge given the formulation of new Coke without identification of brand name did not hold up once the product was introduced to the market.[34] Consumers may have liked the new Coke formula, but they were not ready to change their tried and true Coca-Cola.

Acceptance

Turn once again to the fur coat ad in Figure 4–5. Do you think that this ad will be effective? By *effective,* we mean will it result in sufficient modification or change in existing beliefs and attitudes to lead to appropriate buying action? We noted earlier that negative attitudes by animal rights activists can serve as a potent barrier resulting in this ad never being accepted into memory. *Comprehension does not necessarily lead to acceptance.*

Three responses are possible as information is being categorized. First, the information can be filtered out with no effect on existing beliefs, schemas,

---

FIGURE 4–8

❖   **"The Love That Lives Forever"—A Potent Appeal or Not?**

Courtesy Carrington Parfums Ltd.

and scripts. This result is especially likely when involvement is high and the contradiction with existing cognitions is high.

A more favorable outcome is *assimilation*—integration into existing cognitive structures. The best outcome of all is *accommodation* in which existing schemas are changed or all new schemas are created to handle the new concept.[35]

Cognitive Responses   Growing evidence suggests that *cognitive responses* (mental reactions as information is processed) are indicators of the degree to which acceptance and yielding actually happen, especially when involvement is high[36] and the consumer is actively engaging in brand evaluation.[37] These responses are classified as follows:

1. Counterarguments—Disagreement with message claims.
2. Support arguments—Agreement with and support of message claims.
3. Source derogations—Negative response to the source of the message.

Evidence to date indicates the following:

1. The greater the extent of counterargumentation, the less the probability of change in beliefs, attitudes, and behavior.
2. Support arguments and probability of acceptance are positively related.
3. Source derogation may entirely rule out acceptance and yielding.
4. When involvement is low, acceptance is determined more by cognitive responses to the executional elements of the message than by the content.[38]

Back once again to our fur coat ad (Figure 4–5). If a person is not sympathetic to the animal rights cause and also has an active need for this product, the person would be expected to offer support arguments: "Great looking coat," "An interesting color."

The opponent, on the other hand, could counterargue, "What a bunch of baloney. Anybody who wears this thing is committing a crime." You also would expect to hear source derogations such as, "You'll never catch me anywhere near a fur store."

The marketer can often anticipate counterarguments and try to refute them but should not underestimate the potency of the acceptance barrier. Many have tried to change beliefs and attitudes only to experience economic frustration, as did Sears, which created a major marketing blunder by ignoring its changing customer market and letting Wal-Mart and K mart encroach on its market share. As of this writing, consumer indifference indicates that Sears' "everyday low prices" ad theme is falling mostly on deaf ears.[39] Sears faces a monumental uphill battle to survive in the 1990s.

Affective Responses *Affective responses* refer to emotions and feelings induced by the stimulus.[40] These feelings can be quite varied, encompassing fear, surprise, sadness, disgust, anger, anticipation, joy, and acceptance.[41] They also play an important role in mediating the process of acceptance. More will be said on this later.

Retention

As we have seen, a message often is so transformed as information processing progresses that it is quite different from what the sender intended. Now we reach the last step, *retention*, in which information is transferred into long-term memory. Marketers are increasingly turning to cognitive psychology to learn more about what happens during retention.

The human brain is divided into left and right hemispheres, each of which plays different roles. Evidence consistently indicates that the left hemisphere processes information sequentially, verbally, and logically, whereas the right functions spatially, intuitively, and wholistically.[42] This would suggest that message copy is processed more in the left hemisphere than in the right and visual and other executional elements more in the right.

Theories on memory structure abound. One currently popular theory holds that three different memory storage systems work in this way[43]:

1. A stimulus is first processed in *sensory memory,* at which time information is extracted about physical characteristics. Meaning is not attributed at this stage.

2. The input then goes to *short-term memory,* where it is temporarily held and analyzed for meaning. It is held there for no more than 3 to 10 seconds and then is transferred into long-term memory. The content that is *rehearsed* (i.e., the subject of silent, inner speech that analyzes and elaborates it) is transferred and vice versa. We referred to rehearsal earlier but used the term *cognitive responses.*

3. If the input survives the filtering in short-term memory, it enters *long-term memory* either intact or in modified form.

Much more could be said about various memory control processes such as retrieval and coding. Although additional information might be useful for general understanding, we now have a sufficient background in all stages of information processing to help us think more strategically.

ATTITUDE CHANGE AND PERSUASION

Following the definition of Petty and Cacioppo, persuasion refers to ". . . any instance in which an active attempt is made to change a person's mind."[44] The goal is always to influence thinking and behavior, and this is most frequently accomplished by changing a person's *attitude* or overall evaluation, pro or con, toward an object or person.

We will make clear in the next chapter that *attitude change is a valid marketing goal.* Our purpose here, first of all, is to describe in a general way how information is processed and used to bring about attitude change. In so doing, we will make an attempt to integrate much of the previous discussion in this chapter. The very word *persuasion,* however, also raises serious questions about manipulation, and these questions need to be addressed. We will do this in the concluding section.

Information Processing and Attitude Change

Marketing thinking has been influenced by the *Elaboration Likelihood Model* developed by Petty and Cacioppo.[45] In this model, a communication is persuasive to the extent that it affects brand attitudes by stimulating elaboration (defined earlier as issue-relevant thinking) during information processing.

When involvement is high, the *central route* to persuasion is the primary path. What this means is that the strength of *message arguments* becomes the primary determinant of attitude change. Put differently, arguments induce elaboration and lead to a reasoned opinion associating a brand object with desirable outcomes.[46]

The *peripheral route,* on the other hand, occurs when involvement is low or nonexistent. This means that there will be little or no elaboration; therefore, responses to secondary or peripheral factors, especially message execution, play a more important role than the arguments themselves. It has been common to refer to cognitive and affective responses to executional elements as *attitude toward the ad* (A_{ad}), as opposed to *attitude toward the brand* (A_B).[47]

Figure 4–9 is a simple diagram of how the central and peripheral routes to persuasion seem to work, based on available evidence. First, notice how each of the variables (involvement, attention, and so on) is separated by a dashed line. This line indicates a continuum between high and low. In other words, attitude change usually is brought about by a blend of central and peripheral route elements. Therefore, it is important to think of varying degrees between the extremes.[48]

What Figure 4–9 illustrates is that very high involvement leads to a voluntary search for information and subsequent attention, deep processing and elaboration, and dominance of strong message arguments in bringing about attitude change. In other words, all things being equal, *what you say is more important than how you say it.*

In very low involvement, quite the opposite is true. Attention is entirely involuntary and is directed mostly toward program elements and other factors. If attention is attracted and held at all, this is more an outcome of effective execution than content. The most that can be hoped for is that some message information (perhaps logo or main benefit) is processed at a low level and is held without elaboration or full awareness in memory.

This information has some significant implications for promotional strategy. When motivation and involvement are high, "reason why" copy becomes important. The goal is to get selling points across in such a convincing way that they will be deeply processed and *recalled* during the purchase decision process.

FIGURE 4–9

❖

How Information Is Processed and Used to Stimulate Attitude Change

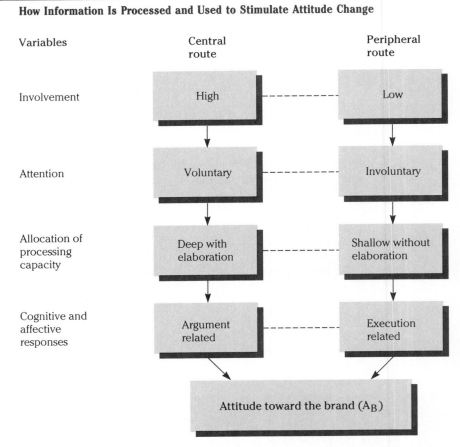

Variables	Central route	Peripheral route
Involvement	High	Low
Attention	Voluntary	Involuntary
Allocation of processing capacity	Deep with elaboration	Shallow without elaboration
Cognitive and affective responses	Argument related	Execution related

Attitude toward the brand (A_B)

Source: Adapted from Deborah J. MacInnes and Bernard J. Jaworski, "Information Processing from Advertisements: Toward an Integrative Framework," *Journal of Marketing* 53 (October 1989), pp. 1–23.

When these points are not processed and recalled, however, an interesting and captivating message can succeed in imparting some information that may come to mind at a later point. In this sense, it is especially important that the package and brand name be recognized at point of sale. You will learn in Chapter 6 that this is the primary objective when involvement is low.

We will have a great deal more to say about these considerations in later chapters. You will see many ways in which the growing marketing understanding of information processing can have real practical payout.

Manipulation

We have demonstrated how the consumer retains sovereignty through selective information processing and the formidable defense created against unwanted persuasion. Yet there always is the danger of manipulation defined by Em Griffin as the use of strategies that inhibit an individual's freedom of action and induce a response that otherwise would not be made.[49]

Deception

Outright deception, of course, is a blatant form of manipulation. A message is deceptive if it "creates, increases, or exploits false beliefs about expected product performance."[50] People are deceived if the *comprehension* of the message is something other than the literal truth, no matter what the message itself proclaimed. Over the years, authorities have been able to identify many ads that appeared to be truthful on the surface but left quite a different impression.

There are legal protections and remedies (discussed in Chapter 9) for such deception, but enforcement is spotty and inconsistent. Ideally, consumers must rely on the commonsense and goodwill of the marketer, but this is far from a perfect deterrent to deception. The best strategy always is *caveat emptor*—let the buyer beware.

Another type of deception is the use of various forms of message execution that dominate content and stimulate a response just because they were used. Examples include appeals to strong but relevant emotions, the use of distractions such as music or loud sounds, and so on. Consumers catch on to such gimmicks and rarely become repeat customers if they feel that "they have been had."

The following is an especially offensive sales tactic. "If you buy tonight, we have a special offer that is guaranteed to help your child do better in school." "Well, I don't know. . ." "You must buy tonight, because you don't want Tommy to look back and say you failed him. You never will get this low price again."

Notice how consumer logic is overwhelmed. Many people have immediately regretted making purchases in such a context. Fortunately, "cooling off" laws allow cancellation and rebate within the first few days after a sale, and these are an effective deterrent.

Subliminal Influence

In the 1950s, a great deal of interest was stimulated by a widely publicized report that consumers apparently can be induced to react to a certain type of advertising without knowing that they have been influenced. This has come to be known as *subliminal perception,* and it is an issue of concern to this day.

What Is Subliminal Perception?   A perception is said to be subliminal if sensation is induced below the *recognition threshold* defined earlier as that point at which a stimulus can be consciously classified. When identification or classification occurs at levels exceeding this threshold, they are said to be *supraliminal.*

There is no question that subliminal perception can occur,[51] and, as we will see later, it has been used by marketers.[52] But subliminal perception should not be assumed to occur unconsciously when a presentation is below the *absolute threshold* (that point at which conscious discrimination ceases).[53] The important question for us is whether or not subliminal presentation is a viable promotional strategy.

Subliminal Advertising   With this background, we can now evaluate the emotionally loaded issue of subliminal advertising. The controversy of the 1950s was triggered by reports of experiments by James Vicary.[54] Vicary claimed to have flashed the words DRINK COKE and EAT POPCORN on a movie screen at speeds well below the recognition thresholds of all audience members. This was supposedly done at a projection speed of 1/3000 of a second (far below even the lowest possible *absolute* threshold). Presumably theater sales of Coca-Cola increased by 57.7 percent and popcorn sales by 18.1 percent.

A virtual firestorm erupted when these results were made public. Cries from all quarters raised the specter of "Big Brother influence" and thought control. But matters subsided quickly once Vicary, previously a respected social researcher, admitted that his experiment was a hoax.

The issue was dormant until Wilson Bryan Key wrote a popular book arguing that erotic subliminal clues are planted in ads to stimulate subconscious sex drives for the purpose of increasing sales.[55] Key's book revived fears of thought control, which have been further enhanced by his latest book.[56]

Key has always focused his attention on liquor ads, many of which feature a closeup of a tantalizing drink poured over ice cubes. He claims that sexually oriented subliminal symbols are embedded in the ice cubes to increase the persuasive power of the ads. Although most people scoff at such an allegation, research has verified that this tactic can have the alleged effect. For example, when an ad for a well-known brand of scotch with sexual images imbedded in it was compared with a control ad, consumers rated the former ad higher in terms of credibility, attractiveness, sensuality, and likelihood of purchase.[57]

Figure 4–10 includes two different ads. Your assignment is to study them carefully, from the perspective of Key's comments. The liquor ad on the next page falls into the product category that Key most condemned. The issue is this: Do you see any sexual stimuli embedded in the ice cubes?

Frankly, we do not believe that anything of this sort appears in either ad. Let's be perfectly up front on this issue and restate once again that people

FIGURE 4–10

Sexy Ice Cubes?

Courtesy Thomas J. Lipton Co.; photographer: Ulf Skogsbergh

FIGURE 4-10

❖ **Sexy Ice Cubes?** (concluded)

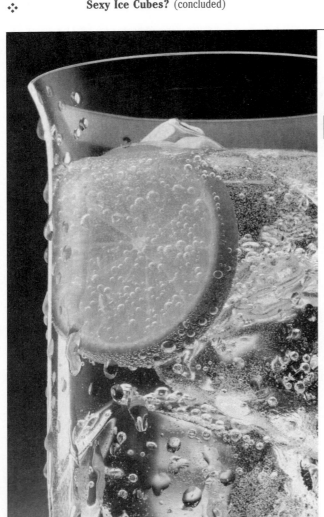

VODKA DRINKERS DEFECT TO RUM.

If we flat-out claimed that rum and tonic makes a better drink than vodka and tonic, you'd think we were biased.

Which is why we commissioned a "blind" taste test among vodka and tonic drinkers.

We asked them to choose between the best selling vodka and a selection of rums from Puerto Rico.

Each was mixed with tonic. But did that make things truly equal? Ours, after all, was a less familiar taste. Theirs was a tradition.

Yet, fully 47%—almost *half*—preferred rum and tonic to the tried-and-true vodka and tonic.

We assume that's because the rums of Puerto Rico, which are aged by law for one year, have a warmer, more alive character than vodka.

What else could explain such a defection?

RUMS OF PUERTO RICO

Courtesy Commonwealth of Puerto Rico

see and hear what they want to see and hear. Key may discern sexual symbols, but he is open to the charge that these are entirely a product of his own imagination. Here is an instance in which subjective semiology discussed in Chapter 3 can run amok.

Key has never produced evidence that such symbols, if they indeed exist, were consciously placed by the advertiser. We believe that the rebuttal by advertising executive John O'Toole (Promotion in Action 4–3) is well worthy of your careful reading.

Those Sexy Ice Cubes Are Back

❖
**PROMOTION
IN ACTION
4–3**

Wilson Bryan Key has written another book. More accurately, he has written the same book for the fourth time. Prof. Key once again cites examples of advertising people deliberately "embedding" the word *sex* and symbolic penises and vaginas into ad illustrations in order to reduce readers to quivering gobs of compliance.

He probes an ad for Kent cigarettes that I was involved with through every step of the creative production processes and asserts that we deliberately "embedded" the word "sex" in the male model's hair. He finds retouching that we never did and motivations in posing the model that I hope my daughters don't read.

Prof. Key even analyzes an ad in the American Association of Advertising Agencies' series to further public understanding of advertising. It is, needless to say, the one showing an on-the-rocks drink with the headline, "People have been trying to find the breasts in these ice cubes since 1957." An offended Prof. Key admits to finding no breasts in Tom McElligott's illustration, but he does perceive an erect penis.

All responses to Prof. Key's theories have been voiced to the point of tedium. I will not ask again what we would gain by relying on devices we could only define as "borrowed interest," or by questioning how a castrated penis could possibly result in favorable attitudes about a brand of scotch. Prof. Key's convoluted logic turns all of our denials and dismissals into admissions of guilt—to say nothing of increased book sales.

There is nothing so seductive as a conspiracy theory, be it the Russians turning our brains into lard by convincing us to fluoridate our drinking water, or Orson Welles's invading Martians.

Source: John O'Toole, "Those Sexy Ice Cubes Are Back," *Advertising Age,* October 2, 1989, p. 28. Mr. O'Toole is president of the American Association of Advertising Agencies. Reproduced by special permission.

Should subliminal stimulation be tried?   Undoubtedly, stimulus discrimination can be induced by presentation below the recognition threshold. In fact, subliminal presentation is being used commercially.[58] It has been found, for example, that subliminal suggestions on audio- and videotapes appear to help people lose weight or stop smoking. How well such subliminal suggestions work in general, however, is still open to question because reactions differ significantly from one person to the next.

Our assessment is that, to date, the effects of subliminal stimulation do not warrant its use in promotional strategy. We agree with Moore's conclusion:

> A century of psychological research substantiates the general principle that more intense stimuli have a greater effect on people's behavior than weak ones. . . . Subliminal stimuli are usually so weak that the recipient is not just unaware of the stimuli but is also oblivious to the fact that he/she is being stimulated. As a result, the potential effects of subliminal stimuli are easily nullified by other ongoing stimulation in the same sensory channel whereby attention is being focused on another modality.[59]

In short, it is enough to create understanding through persuasive communication without further adding to our difficulties by using an inferior, although exotic, strategy.

SUMMARY

This chapter picks up on an important principle from Chapter 3 which states that significant differences can exist between the meaning of a message intended by the sender and the meaning attributed by the receiver. The message is molded and shaped by the recipient through a sequence of stages in information processing.

Information processing has five basic stages: (1) exposure, (2) attention, (3) comprehension, (4) acceptance, and (5) retention. What takes place, however, is profoundly shaped by the degree of perceived *involvement* (perceived risk, social sanctions, or ego relatedness).

High involvement leads to actively processing relevant stimuli and avoiding the unwanted ones. Moreover, the *central route to persuasion* (primary emphasis on message arguments) is most appropriate to bring about attitude change when involvement is high, as opposed to the *peripheral route* (creative use of message execution) when involvement is low.

Exposure to stimuli occurs when one or more of the five senses are activated. The message is said to attract attention when information processing capabilities are focused and activated. As the stimulus is processed for its sensory and content characteristics, it then is given meaning through comprehension.

Persuasion does not occur, however, until the stimulus is accepted into existing cognitive structures (beliefs and attitudes). When this happens, existing beliefs and attitudes are modified or altogether new ones are formed. Processing terminates once this new information is transferred into long-term memory and is retained.

Information processing is highly selective in that people are free to see and hear what they want to see and hear. Unwanted exposure can be avoided. Selective attention can filter out nonrelevant information and facilitate entry of that which is viewed more positively. Needs, attitudes, and other cognitive factors strongly affect this process.

At other times, attention can be attracted and held without accurate comprehension. This is because our existing biases can cause us to distort the content and miss the point. Finally, inconsistent and unwanted information can be short-circuited by refusing to accept it into cognitive structures, whereas the opposite occurs when the input is seen as credible and relevant.

Even though consumer sovereignty is underscored, there always is concern about manipulation—interfering with a person's freedom of choice. This chapter showed that, short of outright deception, the consumer is quite capable of resisting manipulation and that the marketer has no magic power to bypass defenses.

REVIEW AND DISCUSSION QUESTIONS

1. Assume that a teenager cannot remember seeing ads for any brand of deodorant other than her preferred brand, even though she has finished paging through a consumer magazine replete with competitive ads, one of which was a two-page, four-color spread. How can you explain her response?

2. Try, if you can stand it, to pay close attention to a series of TV ads. Write down your own thoughts (cognitive responses), noting which ads are counterarguments, support arguments, and source derogation. When are source derogation and counterargumentation greatest? And when are you most likely to find support arguments?

3. Up to 20 percent of all TV viewers "zap" ads. You have been asked by Sears to design a series of TV ads stressing the everyday low appliance prices at Sears Brand Central. What strategies could you follow to minimize zapping?

4. Many critics today object to the amount of creative "gimmickry" and flashy attention-attracting devices used by advertisers. The point is, the critics contend, that good advertising should "sell," not "entertain." How would you respond to this point of view?

5. According to a leading critic, advertising has the power to influence people to buy unwisely—to induce them to act in a manner inconsistent with normal behavior. Do you agree? Why or why not?

6. Subliminal messages have been found to have persuasive power when they are embedded in either audio- or videotapes. You are the owner of a resort in a Caribbean country and have the opportunity to advertise your resort at subliminal levels in videotapes distributed by the government vacation bureau. Is this strategy likely to be effective? Are there ethical concerns that you should consider?

NOTES

1. John Antil, "Conceptualization and Operationalization of Involvement," in *Advances in Consumer Research*, ed. Thomas Kinnear, vol. 11 (Provo, Utah: Association for Consumer Research, 1984), p. 204.

2. See Giles Laurent and Jean-Noel Kapferer, "Measuring Consumer Involvement Profiles," *Journal of Marketing Research* 12 (February 1985), pp. 41–53.

3. Gary Putka, "People Invest Little Faith in Wall Street, *The Wall Street Journal*, September 25, 1989, p. B1.

4. A classic source is W. N. Dember, *The Psychology of Perception* (New York: Holt, Rinehart and Winston, 1961), ch. 2.

5. *American Demographics*, 11 (August 1989), p. 20.

6. Dennis Kneale," 'Zapping' of TV Ads Appears Pervasive," *The Wall Street Journal*, April 25, 1988, p. 21.

7. Phillip J. Kitchen, "Zipping, Zapping, and Nipping," *International Journal of Advertising* 5 (1986), pp. 343–53.

8. Jim Bounden, "Trouble Corralling the Grazers," *Advertising Age*, November 28, 1988, p. S–4.

9. Kitchen, "Zipping, Zapping, and Nipping," pp. 343–52.

10. "War Against Zapping," *Marketing News*, September 14, 1984, p. 1.

11. Patricia A. Stout and Benedicta L. Burda, "Zipped Commercials: Are They Effective?" *Journal of Advertising* 18 (1989), pp. 23–32.

12. R. D. Percy as quoted in Kneale, "Zapping of TV Ads," p. 21.

13. Scott Ward, David Reibstein, Terence A. Oliva, and Victoria Taylor, "Commercial Clutter: Effects of 15-Second Television Ads on Consumer Recall," in *Advances in Consumer Research*, ed. Thomas K. Srull, vol. 16 (Provo, Utah: Association for Consumer Research, 1989), pp. 473–78 and Wayne Walley, "Have:15s Hit Their Peak?" *Advertising Age*, November 13, 1989, p. 16.

14. For more detail see, James F. Engel, Roger D. Blackwell, and Paul W. Miniard, *Consumer Behavior*, 6th ed. (Hinsdale, Ill.: Dryden Press, 1989), pp. 268–376.

15. "How Important Is Color to an Ad? It's Not Just a Black and White Issue," *Tested Copy*, February 1989.

16. Larry Percy, *Ways in Which the People, Words, and Pictures in Advertising Influence Its Effectiveness* (Chicago: Financial Institutions Marketing Association, July 1984), p. 19.

17. Adam Finn, "Print Recognition Readership Scores: An Information Processing Perspective," *Journal of Marketing Research* 25 (May 1988), pp. 168–77.

18. For a good introduction to cognitive consistency theories, see Richard E. Petty and John T. Cacioppo, *Attitudes and Persuasion: Classic and Contemporary Approaches* (Dubuque, Iowa: Wm. C. Brown, 1981), ch. 5.

19. Cyndee Miller, "The Fur Flies as Fashion Foes Pelt It out over Animal Rights," *Marketing News*, December 4, 1989, pp. 2ff.

20. Homer E. Spence and James F. Engel, "The Impact of Brand Preferences on the Perception of Brand Names: A Laboratory Analysis," in *Marketing Involvement in Society and the Economy*, ed. P. R. McDonald (Chicago: American Marketing Association, 1970), pp. 267–71.

21. Scott Hume, "BK Sees Ad Awareness Slipping Away," *Advertising Age*, September 30, 1985, p. 12.

22. Bob Garfield, "N.E. Telephone Ads Are Real Bell Ringers," *Advertising Age*, June 5, 1989, p. 76.

23. "Warning: This Story Will be Miscomprehended," *Marketing News*, March 27, 1987, pp. 1ff.

24. Jacob Jacoby and Wayne D. Hoyer, "The Comprehension/Miscomprehension of Print Communication," *Journal of Consumer Research* 15 (March 1989), pp. 434–43.

25. For a helpful discussion of the categorization process, see Joseph W. Alba and J. Wesley Hutchinson, "Dimensions of Consumer Expertise," *Journal of Consumer Research* 13 (March 1987), pp. 411–54; and Joel B. Cohen and Kunal Basu, "Alternative Models of Categorization: Toward a Contingent Processing Framework," *Journal of Consumer Research* 13 (March 1987), pp. 455–72.

26. John R. Anderson, *The Architecture of Cognition* (Cambridge, Mass.: Harvard University Press, 1983).

27. See, for example, Mita Sujan and James F. Bettman, "The Effects of Brand Positioning Strategies on Consumers' Brand and Category Perceptions: Some Insights from Schema Research," *Journal of Marketing Research* 26 (November 1989), pp. 454–67; and Joseph W. Alba and Lynn Hasher, "Is Memory Schematic?" *Psychological Bulletin* 93 (March 1983), pp. 203–21.

28. See, for example, Ruthann Smith and Michael J. Houston, "A Psychometric Assessment of Measures of Scripts in Consumer Memory," *Journal of Consumer Research* 12 (September 1985), pp. 214–24.

29. See the evidence cited in Engel et al., *Consumer Behavior*, 6th ed., pp. 292–95.

30. For an excellent discussion, see Deborah J. MacInnis and Bernard J. Jaworski, "Information Processing from Advertisements: Toward an Integrative Framework," *Journal of Marketing* 53 (October 1989), pp. 1–23.

31. Robert A. Mamis, "Name Calling," *Inc*, July 1984, pp. 67–74.

32. Alex Taylor III, "Detroit vs. New Upscale Imports," *Fortune*, April 27, 1987, pp. 72ff.

33. See Richard L. Celsi and Jerry C. Olson, "The Role of Involvement in Attention and Comprehension Processes," *Journal of Consumer Research*, 15 (September 1988), pp. 210–24.

34. See Jack Honomichl, "Missing Ingredients in 'New' Coke's Research," *Advertising Age,* July 22, 1985, p. 1.

35. Sujan and Bettman, "The Effects of Brand Positioning Strategies."

36. The literature is extensive. For a description and review, see Engel et al., *Consumer Behavior,* pp. 387–89.

37. Manoj Hastak and Jerry C. Olson, "Assessing the Role of Brand-Related Cognitive Responses as Mediators of Communication Effects on Cognitive Structure," *Journal of Consumer Research* 15 (March 1989), pp. 444–56.

38. Scott B. MacKenzie, Richard J. Lutz, and George E. Belch, "The Role of Attitude toward the Ad as a Mediator of Advertising Effectiveness: A Test of Competing Explanations," *Journal of Marketing Research* 23 (May 1986), pp. 130–43.

39. "Missing the Market," *American Demographics* 12 (December 1989), p. 19.

40. Julie A. Edell and Marian C. Burke, "The Power of Feelings in Understanding Advertising Effectiveness," *Journal of Consumer Research* 14 (December 1987), pp. 421–33.

41. David M. Zeitlin and Richard A. Westwood, "Measuring Emotion Response to Advertising," *Journal of Advertising Research* 26 (October/November 1986), pp. 34–44.

42. Susan E. Heckler and Terry L. Childers, "Hemispheric Lateralization: The Relationship of Processing Orientation with Judgment and Recall Measures for Print Advertisements," in *Advances in Consumer Research,* ed. Melanie Wallendorf and Paul Anderson, vol. 15 (Provo, Utah: Association for Consumer Research, 1987), pp. 46–50.

43. See, for example, Lyle E. Bourne, Roger L. Dominowski, and Elizabeth F. Loftus, *Cognitive Processes* (Englewood Cliffs, N.J.: Prentice Hall, 1979).

44. Petty and Cacioppo, *Attitudes and Persuasion,* p. 4.

45. Ibid.; and Richard E. Petty and John T. Cacioppo, *Communication and Persuasion: Central Peripheral Routes to Attitude Change* (New York: Springer Verlag, 1986).

46. Charles S. Areni and Richard J. Lutz, "The Role of Argument Quality in the Elaboration Likelihood Model," in *Advances in Consumer Research,* ed. Michael J. Houston, vol. 15 (Provo, Utah: Association for Consumer Research, 1987), pp. 197–201.

47. Once again, the evidence is extensive. For current sources, see MacKenzie and Lutz, "An Empirical Examination of the Structural Antecedents of Attitude Toward the Ad"; Hastak and Olson, "Assessing the Role of Brand-Related Cognitive Responses"; and Engel et al., *Consumer Behavior,* footnotes on p. 445.

48. For a helpful argument on the continuum between extremes, see MacInnis and Jaworski, "Information Processing from Advertisements."

49. Em Griffin, *The Mind Changers* (Wheaton, Ill.: Tyndale, 1976).

50. Edward Russo, Barbara Metcalfe, and Debra Stephens, "Identifying Misleading Advertising," *Journal of Consumer Research* 7 (September 1981), p. 125.

51. For excellent reviews of the evidence, see Sharon E. Beatty and Del I. Hawkins, "Subliminal Stimulation: Some New Data and Interpretation," *Journal of Advertising*

18 (1989), pp. 4–8; and Nicolas E. Synodinos, "Subliminal Stimulation: What Does the Public Think about It?" *Current Issues & Research in Advertising,* ed. James R. Leigh and Claude R. Martin, vol. 11 (Ann Arbor, Mich.: University of Michigan Business School, Division of Research, 1988), pp. 157–88.

52. Jo Anna Natale, "Are You Open to Suggestion?" *Psychology Today* 22 (September 1988), p. 28.

53. Norman F. Dixon, *Subliminal Perception—The Nature of the Controversy* (Maidenhead-Berkshire, England: McGraw-Hill, 1971).

54. For a helpful review, see J. V. McConnell, R. L. Cutler, and E. B. McNeill, "Subliminal Stimulation: An Overview," *American Psychologist* 11 (1958), pp. 230ff.

55. Wilson B. Key, *Subliminal Seduction: Ad Media's Manipulation of a Not-So-Innocent America* (Englewood Cliffs, N.J.: Prentice Hall, 1972).

56. ————. *The Age of Manipulation* (New York: Henry Holt, 1987).

57. Natale, "Are You Open to Suggestion?"

58. Ibid.

59. Timothy Moore, "Subliminal Advertising: What You See is What You Get," *Journal of Marketing* 46 (Spring 1982), p. 45.

UNDERSTANDING THE CONSUMER

The following three chapters address the most important issue in promotional strategy—understanding the consumer. Errors or inaccuracies at this stage will doom all other efforts.

Consumer motivation and behavior are part of a complex field of study in its own right. We summarize the major insights and conclusions from this field with particular focus on the implications for promotional strategy. Of special interest is practical guidance in diagnosing behavior and thinking strategically.

Chapter 5 presents an overview of consumer decision process behavior and then concentrates specifically on extended problem solving (EPS). EPS is the reasoned action that takes place when a purchasing decision is of personal importance to the consumer, who is motivated to "make the right choice."

Most purchasing decisions, however, do not involve extensive reasoning. The majority are better described as limited problem solving (LPS). LPS occurs when personal relevance of choice is lower and the consumer has less incentive for evaluation and deliberation. Here the choice is often made at the point of sale from among many similar alternatives. LPS is discussed in Chapter 6, which also addresses habitual buying patterns.

Finally, the influence of the social environment is the subject of Chapter 7. In that chapter, you will discover the impact on decision processes of cultural and subcultural values, social class, reference groups, and family.

Understanding the Consumer: Extended Problem Solving

TWO SCENARIOS

The World of Fantasy and Pleasure

The following are two examples of consumer decision making, each of which offers different challenges for the promotional strategist.

High noon on Lido Deck, somewhere in the Caribbean: As the cotton clouds play hide and seek with the sun, the gleaming white 48,000-ton cruise ship, *Jubilee*, operated by Carnival Cruise Lines, slowly plies an ocean that is as flat as a tabletop. For the past hour, passengers hailing from Everywhere, U.S.A., have been staking out lounge chairs near the enormous pool, the center of shipboard activities during the day.

Joe Rotelli, 24, a light-brown-haired Eurodollar trader in snug swim trunks, strolls on the scene, flanked by his five buddies, who include a business manager for a car dealer, a foreign-exchange broker, and a New York City cop. "This is my second cruise in three months," says Rotelli, just one of the 400-plus singles among the *Jubilee's* 1,550 passengers. "When I showed my boys the video from the first cruise, they got excited. We booked this one two weeks after I returned."

Founder Ted Arison started Carnival at the height of the energy crisis with one aging transatlantic liner he christened the *Mardi Gras*. The marketing people dubbed the *Mardi Gras* the Fun Ship, and the strategy was born. The Fun Ship itself became the destination (a floating resort), a novel approach in an industry that still emphasizes the ports of call over the shipboard experience.

Courtesy Carnival Cruise Lines

To fill its ships, Carnival advertises heavily on TV. Last year, it spent $15 million on television advertising and promotion, more than virtually all the other players combined. It drives home the message that a Carnival holiday at sea is within reach of nearly every American.

Carnival is the most forceful marketer to travel agents in the industry, pushing the notion that a Carnival cruise is an alternative to a trip to Disneyland or Paris. Virtually all passengers who sailed on the *Jubilee* during the week of November 6 said that a travel agent had recommended Carnival.

Source: Faye Rice, "How Carnival Stacks the Decks," *Fortune,* January 26, 1989, pp. 108–15. Reproduced by special permission.

The World of the Mundane

Sarah Anderson is pushing her way down the supermarket aisles in her second shopping trip this week. Although she has several items on her shopping list, she, like many others, scans the shelves for a reminder of what she needs.

Courtesy Kimberly-Clark Corporation

An end aisle display for new and improved Kleenex facial tissue catches her eye. Although Kleenex is a household name for her as well as most other people in the store, Sarah usually buys Puffs Plus, a Procter & Gamble brand offering the benefit of softness.

Suddenly she is reminded of the commercials she has been seeing on prime time TV featuring the "Kleenex Kids" using the all-new, softer Kleenex as they play. She could even hum the jingle, "Baby, We're Going to Baby You." Her response? "Why not try it?" With little conscious deliberation, Sarah switched brands that day.

Kimberly-Clark Corporation introduced new Kleenex with a $7 million campaign using 30- and 15-second spots airing during daytime and prime time network TV and print ads in such popular magazines as *TV Guide, Reader's Digest, People,* and *Memories.* The expectation is that this product change will strengthen Kimberly-Clark's 49 percent share of this $1 billion market.

Source: Laurie Freemen, "Kids Tout a Softer Kleenex," *Advertising Age,* October 16, 1989, p. 12.

Joe Rotelli and most others do not decide to take a Caribbean cruise on impulse. First of all, taking a cruise requires a financial outlay of at least $500. In addition, many other options for fantasy, escape, and pleasure are available. Some careful thought usually goes into the decision to take a cruise and there is no question that friends, travel agents, and advertisements provide useful information.

Sarah Anderson, on the other hand, buys most items in the supermarket without much conscious deliberation. She picked up new Kleenex with little thought simply because it offered something new and different. Advertising did build some low-level awareness of this product and its benefits, and the point-of-sale display triggered a "Why not try it?" response.

These two vignettes contrast *extended problem solving* and *limited problem solving*. We will discover in this chapter and the next that the dynamics of consumer decision making are quite different in each case. Also, we will focus on the dynamics of repeat purchases and highlight the differences between actions based on *brand loyalty* as contrasted with *inertia*.

This chapter provides you an overview of the four types of decision processes—EPS, LPS, brand loyalty, and inertia—and discusses extended problem solving in more detail. Limited problem solving and habitual decisions are the subjects of Chapter 6.

The objective is not to make you an expert in consumer behavior in a few short chapters but to give you sufficient background in the dynamics of consumer behavior to make realistic strategic decisions.

AN OVERVIEW OF CONSUMER DECISION PROCESSES

Decades ago, John Dewey conceptualized decision-process behavior as *problem solving*[1]—thoughtful, reasoned action focused on need satisfaction. As Ajzen and Fishbein put it, "Human beings are usually quite rational and make systematic use of the information available to them. . . . People consider the implications of their actions before they decide to engage or not to engage in a given behavior."[2]

In general terms, consumer decision making follows the sequence shown in Table 5–1. The sequence can have major variations, however, from one situation to the next in terms of the extent to which each of these steps is followed. In the following pages, we will demonstrate that there are four options for consumer decision making: (1) initial purchase based on *extended problem solving (EPS)*; (2) initial purchase based on *limited problem solving (LPS)*; (3) habitual decision making based on *brand loyalty*; and (4) habitual decision making based on *inertia*.

The Initial Purchase

Visualize if you can a continuum representing an initial purchase decision anchored at one extreme by extended problem solving (EPS) and at the other by limited problem solving (LPS). Obviously, there can be a range of options between these poles.

Extended Problem Solving A decision process is referred to as EPS when careful reasoning, information search, and alternative evaluation are part of the process. As we have seen, EPS is likely when a decision is made to take a Caribbean cruise. EPS also is common in the purchase of stereos, expensive clothing, automobiles, and other situations when it is necessary to make *the* right choice.

In EPS, all of the stages in our decision-process sequence are followed. Multiple alternatives will be evaluated making use of information sources. Problem solving continues after purchase because the consumer has some clear expectations that the purchase must meet. If the purchase option is perceived as falling short of these expectations, substantial dissatisfaction can result in negative word-of-mouth communication to others.

Limited Problem Solving It is hard to imagine buyers of facial tissue engaging in much deliberation. It is more likely that most buyers will simplify the process by sharply reducing the number and variety of information sources and alternatives considered. Although each step in the decision-process sequence was followed in these two examples, the extent and rigor of their application vary greatly.

TABLE 5–1

The Five Stages in Consumer Decision Making

1. *Need recognition*—The consumer perceives a difference between the desired state of affairs and the current situation. This arouses and activates problem-solving action.
2. *Search for information*—The consumer acquires relevant information either from memory or from external sources.
3. *Alternative evaluation*—The consumer evaluates need-satisfying options from the perspective of expected benefits. The outcome narrows choice to the preferred alternative.
4. *Purchase*—The consumer acquires the preferred alternative (or substitute).
5. *Outcomes*–The consumer evaluates the chosen alternative after using it against the criteria of whether the product meets needs and expectations.

Sarah Anderson and others like her recognize that the differences between facial tissues are not large, regardless of what manufacturers say in their advertising. This is also the case with such products as gasoline, bread, and detergents. The actual decision often is made on such bases as "buy the brand with the lowest price"[3] or choose the brand that offers a new feature (color, for example). These purchases involve little or no information search, and alternative evaluation takes place mostly *after* purchase, not before.

Factors that Shape Problem-Solving Behavior   We encounter EPS most often when one or more of three conditions exist: (1) a high degree of involvement is experienced, (2) alternatives are differentiated in meaningful ways, and (3) the buyer has sufficient time for deliberation.

Involvement   There is usually little motivation to engage in EPS unless there is high involvement, defined in Chapter 4 as the degree of perceived personal importance and relevance accompanying product and brand choice within a specific situation or context.[4]

You will recall that involvement and personal relevance are personalized issues with some diverse roots:[5]

1. *Perceived risk of negative outcomes*. From time to time everyone has doubts or fears that their purchase expectations will not be met. Perceived risk is especially likely when the price is high.

This factor alone could have led Joe Rotelli to learn all he could about the options before his first cruise. Similarly, how would he and his buddies have felt had they been the only single baby boomers on the ship? This could have happened if they had chosen Sitmar, a cruise line with an average passenger age of 54 and a household income of at least $35,000.[6]

On the other hand, would you expect Sarah to have high perceived risk when trying new Kleenex? If it doesn't live up to expectations, so what?

2. *Social sanctions*. For many cruisers such as Joe Rotelli, the choice of Carnival versus other cruise lines could be influenced strongly by the line that is considered to be an "in" thing among their friends. It is pretty unlikely, however, that Sarah will pay much attention to what others think. To the extent that peer group influence becomes an important factor, involvement correspondingly increases.

3. *Ego relatedness*. Involvement increases to the extent that consumer actions are seen as enhancing or affecting self-image. Sarah's choice of facial tissue probably is of no importance to how she feels about herself; hence her choice requires little deliberation or problem solving. Joe, on the other hand, like most other cruisers, is probably motivated to make sure that the lifestyle onboard meets his most basic desires.

It is important to make clear that there is no such thing as a high involvement or low involvement product per se. Involvement is a highly personal issue, and it varies from one person to the next. It can be transient or enduring. Or it can be activated in certain situations and be totally absent in others.

The personal involvement inventory reproduced in Table 5–2 will help you to understand the dynamics of involvement. To understand its usefulness, think of the product or brand choices you have made in the past few days and rate them using these 10 factors. The higher the score, the greater the level of involvement.

Differences between alternatives   Joe Rotelli faced many options as he made his decision; each cruise line offered some major difference in ports visited and life on board ship. Also, he had many information sources to consult, including travel agents. Therefore, EPS is to be expected. Sarah, on the other hand, could choose from among many brands, some of which are essentially alike. There was far less need for conscious deliberation in her choice.

Time availability   EPS is inhibited when time pressures are involved. Joe and his friends, for example, could have been in a situation in which they made a spur-of-the-moment decision. In that case, there is far less opportunity for information search and alternative evaluation.

TABLE 5–2

The Personal Involvement Inventory ❖

Important to me	___ : ___ : ___ : ___ : ___ : ___ : ___	Unimportant to me*
Boring to me	___ : ___ : ___ : ___ : ___ : ___ : ___	Interesting to me
Relevant to me	___ : ___ : ___ : ___ : ___ : ___ : ___	Irrelevant to me*
Exciting to me	___ : ___ : ___ : ___ : ___ : ___ : ___	Unexciting to me*
Means nothing to me	___ : ___ : ___ : ___ : ___ : ___ : ___	Means a lot to me
Appealing to me	___ : ___ : ___ : ___ : ___ : ___ : ___	Unappealing to me*
Fascinating to me	___ : ___ : ___ : ___ : ___ : ___ : ___	Mundane to me*
Worthless to me	___ : ___ : ___ : ___ : ___ : ___ : ___	Valuable to me
Involving to me	___ : ___ : ___ : ___ : ___ : ___ : ___	Uninvolving to me*
Not needed by me	___ : ___ : ___ : ___ : ___ : ___ : ___	Needed by me

*Indicates that item is reversed scored. Items on the left are scored (1) low involvement to (7) high involvement on the right. Totaling the 10 items gives a score from a low of 10 to a high of 120.

Source: Judith Lynne Zaichkowsky, "The Personal Involvement Inventory: Reduction, Revision and Application to Advertising" (Discussion Paper 87–08–08, Faculty of Business Administration, Simon Fraser University, Burnaby, British Columbia, Canada). Reproduced by special permission.

Repeat Purchases

Our emphasis thus far has been on the initial purchase, but what happens when buying is repeated over time? Two general options are available: (1) repeat problem solving (EPS or LPS) or (2) habitual decision making.

Repeat Problem Solving   Assume for the moment that Joe and his friends had a bad experience aboard Carnival (you will recall that this was *not* the case). They are therefore likely to switch lines the next time they plan to take a cruise and to engage in EPS once again. Another reason they might switch is the desire to seek variety.[7] This reason is most likely when attractive unchosen options are available.

Habitual Decision Making   EPS demands an investment of time and energy and generally is the exception rather than the rule when choices are made. Habits are formed to simplify the process, but the nature of these habits differs depending on the extent of involvement. When involvement is high, we are more likely to use *brand loyalty,* as opposed to *inertia* when involvement is low.

Brand loyalty   Carnival could become the ongoing choice of many who are totally satisfied. Satisfaction in a product creates no incentive to make a switch. Obviously, strong brand loyalty is the objective of every marketer, but, as we will see in Chapter 6, few attain it on a lasting basis in today's competitive world.

Inertia   Sarah Anderson can buy new soft Kleenex on a regular basis simply out of inertia. She has no particular incentive to switch but may do so if a competitive brand offers a lower price or a new benefit. This type of buying habit is inherently unstable, and the result is a high level of brand switching.

DIAGNOSING CONSUMER BEHAVIOR

The manager at a major petroleum refinery who is responsible for marketing motor oil had a completely erroneous understanding of how consumers make their brand choices at the pump island. He based his strategy on the assumption that most decisions would be based on EPS, and his advertising gave strong "reason why" copy. Later he learned that nearly everyone assumed that all motor oil is alike and made their purchases through LPS. His misunderstanding resulted in a serious waste of marketing funds.

This mistake could have been avoided if the manager and his staff had been given better guidance as to how to diagnose consumer behavior. In Table 5–3 we have expanded the brief outline from Table 5–1 and have provided specific diagnostic questions to be used in strategic planning.

TABLE 5-3

A Research Outline to Diagnose the Nature of Consumer Decision-Process Behavior

Motivation and Need Recognition

1. What needs and motivations are satisfied by product purchase and usage (i.e., what *benefits* are consumers seeking)?
2. Are these needs dormant or are they presently perceived as felt needs by prospective buyers?
3. How involved with the product are most prospective buyers in the target market segment?

Search for Information

1. What product- and brand-related information is stored in memory?
2. Is the consumer motivated to turn to external sources to find information about available alternatives and their characteristics?
3. What specific information sources are used most frequently when search is undertaken?
4. What product features or attributes are the focus of search when it is undertaken?

Alternative Evaluation

1. To what extent do consumers engage in alternative evaluation and comparison?
2. Which product and/or brand alternatives are included in the evaluation process?
3. Which evaluative criteria (product attributes) are used to compare various alternatives?
   a. Which are most salient in the evaluation?
   b. How complex is the evaluation (i.e., using a single attribute as opposed to several in combination)?
4. What kind of decision rule is used to determine the best choice?
5. What are the outcomes of evaluation regarding each of the candidate purchase alternatives?
   a. What is believed to be true about the characteristics and features of each alternative?
   b. Are the alternatives perceived to be different in important ways or are they seen as essentially the same?
   c. What attitudes are held regarding the purchase and use of each alternative?
   d. What purchasing intentions are expressed, and when will these intentions most likely be consummated by purchase and use?

Now try your hand at diagnosis by returning to our example of Joe Rotelli and others who are about to consider their first cruise. You will seldom have sufficient information based on experience and marketing intuition to answer all questions. When this is the case, a clear need exists for pinpointed marketing research. Even though we have not yet discussed EPS in any detail, we believe that you will agree that most first-time cruisers have followed this type of decision-process behavior.

EXTENDED PROBLEM SOLVING (EPS)

In extended problem solving, *thinking leads to feeling, which leads to action*. The very nature of the decision often necessitates collection of information that is processed and stored. Various product attributes are weighed and evaluated. The consumer develops *beliefs* about different brands and

TABLE 5–3

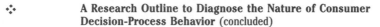

A Research Outline to Diagnose the Nature of Consumer Decision-Process Behavior (concluded)

Purchase

1. Will the consumer spend time and energy to shop until finding the preferred alternative?
2. Is additional decision-process behavior needed to discover the preferred outlet for purchase?
3. What are the preferred modes of purchase (i.e., retail store, in the home, or in other ways)?

Outcomes

1. What degree of satisfaction or dissatisfaction is expressed with respect to previously used alternatives in the product or service category?
2. What reasons are given for satisfaction or dissatisfaction?
3. Has perceived satisfaction or dissatisfaction been shared with other people to help them in their buying behavior?
4. Have consumers made attempts to achieve redress for dissatisfaction?
5. Is there an intention to repurchase any of the alternatives?

    a. If no, why not?

    b. If yes, does intention reflect brand loyalty or inertia?

Source: James F. Engel, Roger D. Blackwell, and Paul W. Miniard, *Consumer Behavior*, 6th ed. (Hinsdale, Ill.: Dryden Press, 1989), p. 473. Reproduced by special permission.

their ability to satisfy expectations, an evaluation pro or con (*attitude*) toward the action of purchasing each, and a *purchase intention*. This sequence is illustrated in Figure 5–1.

It will be helpful for you if we provide an overview of EPS using our diagnostic questions in Table 5–3. Table 5–4 summarizes everything discussed in the remainder of this section.

Need Recognition

All decision-process behavior begins with need recognition, which is defined as "perception of a difference between the desired state of affairs and the actual situation sufficient to arouse and activate the decision process."[8] For example, you may experience need recognition because you feel hungry (actual state) and desire to relieve those hunger pangs (ideal state).

FIGURE 5–1

The Stages in Extended Problem Solving

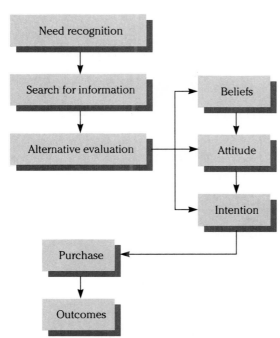

Source: Adapted from James F. Engel, Roger D. Blackwell, and Paul Miniard, *Consumer Behavior*, 6th ed. (Hinsdale, Ill.: Dryden Press, 1989).

Many factors can precipitate need recognition; one factor is *motive activation*. By *motive*, we mean a lasting disposition to strive to attain a specified goal or desired state. For example, you have been under a pile of work for a long period of time and desire some rest and relaxation. The

TABLE 5–4

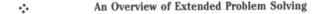

An Overview of Extended Problem Solving

Motivation and Need Recognition

1. High involvement and perceived risk.

Search for Information

1. Strong motivation to search.
2. Multiple sources used including mass media, friends, and point-of-sale communication.
3. Information processed actively and rigorously.

Alternative Evaluation

1. Rigorous evaluation process.
2. Multiple evaluative criteria used, with some more salient than others.
3. Alternatives perceived as significantly different.
4. Compensatory strategy in which weakness on given attributes can be offset by other attributes.
5. Beliefs, attitudes, and intentions strongly held.

Purchase

1. Will shop many outlets if needed.
2. Choice of outlet may require a decision process.
3. Point-of-sale negotiation and communication often needed.

Outcomes

1. Doubts can motivate need for postsale reassurance.
2. Satisfaction is crucial and loyalty is the outcome.
3. Motivated to seek redress if there is dissatisfaction.

Source: James F. Engel, Roger D. Blackwell, and Paul D. Miniard, *Consumer Behavior*, 6th ed. (Hinsdale, Ill.: Dryden Press, 1989), p. 474. Reproduced by special permission.

sense of deprivation that you feel triggers a state of discomfort known as *drive*, which, in turn, energizes goal-oriented behavior. A logical outcome here might be taking a few days off or even a cruise if you can afford it.

At other times, previous buying actions define an all-new sense of the "ideal," which makes the present situation seem inadequate. For example, new wallpaper can make existing carpeting look pretty shabby. Once it is replaced, in turn, something else may have to go.

Need recognition is also triggered by something that causes your present situation to be unsatisfactory. This can happen through changed circumstances such as suddenly realizing that you have no diet cola anywhere in your house or room. Or the washing machine fails to complete its full cycle and the repair will require some major financial outlays.

Targeting the Receptive This principle should come as no surprise: *promotional strategy has its greatest payout when need recognition already exists.* In other words, consumers are open and receptive to potential solutions.

Our initial goal, then, is always to isolate those receptive segments in which the probability of response is greatest and in which the advertiser has a competitive edge. Mothers of young babies, for example, have a pet peeve—leaky diapers. Kimberly-Clark Corp. product designers responded quickly to this need with a raised strip of padding for its Huggies brand of disposable diapers to effectively stop leaks around the leg openings. This redesign helped the company to maintain its 30 percent share in a very competitive market.

Strategies to Stimulate Need Recognition As you will recall, manufacturers of women's fashions found to their dismay during the late 1980s that their efforts to win acceptance for shorter skirts were a costly failure. Working women, in particular, let it be known loud and clear that they were not going to be manipulated into an unwanted wardrobe change. No amount of marketing firepower could reverse this resounding negative vote.

Nevertheless, skillful promotion can stimulate need recognition by *bringing the ideal state into sharper focus.* Do you find yourself feeling hungry as you contemplate Baker's "Deep, Dark Secret" in Figure 5–2? This need stimulation approach is commonly used and serves to change perceptions of the ideal state by highlighting a need that might be latent at a point in time.

Another strategy to stimulate need recognition is to take aim at a prospect's present choice or action and stress its inadequacies. What do you think of this appeal for the full-sized Chevy pickup?

Go forward with Chevy or backward with Ford. The key is Insta-Trac.℠ It lets you shift into four-wheel drive High and back to freewheeling two-wheel drive without slowing down, stopping or backing up. With Ford's Touch Drive you still have to shift the transfer case, come to a complete stop, shift into reverse and back up *at least* 10 feet to get from four-wheel drive into free-wheeling two-wheel drive.

The key to success lies in a product change that offers a unique product benefit that is perceived as significant and relevant. We believe that the benefit of instant shifting into or out of four-wheel drive has a chance of convincing at least some that it's time to replace their old truck.

FIGURE 5–2

❖ **Baker's Gooey Fudge Surprise**

Courtesy of General Foods, USA.

Don't lose sight of the fact stressed in Chapter 4 that absence of felt need carries with it little or no motivation to search for information. We referred to this absence as *involuntary attention*. The odds are always high that ads will be ignored altogether, regardless of the benefit offered, when felt need is absent.

Search for Information

Once a problem is recognized, the next stage in its decision process is to search for additional information. At times, a scan of information presently stored in memory (*internal search*) provides that additional information. When that is the case, the consumer switches out of EPS into LPS or habitual, routinized behavior.

Internal search will prove to be inadequate and lead to external search when:

1. The person has had little or no previous experience to draw on.
2. Previous choices have resulted in dissatisfaction.
3. A lengthy time period has passed since the last purchase.
4. The benefits offered by available alternatives clearly have changed.
5. The person has little confidence in his or her ability to make the right choice in a given situation.

Degree of Search   Consumers commonly engage in less external search than one might expect, even for such major purchases as furniture, appliances, and automobiles. For example, automobile buyers exhibit six levels of search behavior.[9] About 25 percent do not search at all, and only 5 percent use all the sources they can find. In another example, only about 50 percent of all men seek information when they are buying clothing.[10]

Research also indicates that search behavior varies from one demographic segment to the next.[11] Age is negatively correlated with search because older consumers are often brand loyal. Also, they can make use of experience gained over the years. Similarly, those with high incomes value their time greatly and are less prone to invest it in search activities.[12]

Sequence of Search   When consumers need and acquire more facts on the attributes offered by various brands, they process and use this information in two ways.[13] One way is *processing by brand* in which each brand is examined according to its various attributes before proceeding to the next brand. The other option is *processing by attribute* in which all brand information is collected and compared on an attribute-by-attribute basis.

The evidence thus far indicates that processing by brand is most common. This is especially probable in EPS, when the buyer has a high level of present knowledge or previous purchasing experience.

When research indicates that consumers follow this sequence, the best strategy is to place heavy emphasis on brand features and distinctions to be certain that the consumer doesn't miss any. Certainly this is the advertising tactic used by the Caloric Corporation (Figure 5–3). Advertising effectiveness in this kind of high involvement and extended problem solving is measured by *recall of brand name and product features and attributes.*

But it is entirely possible that processing by attribute will be used, especially in the early stages of decision making. Now the essential question is: "Which brands offer the features that are important to me?" For example, insurance companies generally offer discounts on homeowners insurance to retirees. A couple about to retire could be strongly influenced by an Allstate ad that ran several years ago claiming, "John Haight is 55 and retired and busy earning a discount on his homeowners insurance."

Use of Information Sources   Broadly speaking, information sources can be placed into two categories: (1) general and (2) marketer dominated. In each category, we find the use of both face-to-face communication and the mass media. An overview of the various options appears in Table 5–5.

The impact of any given source varies depending on the person and the nature of the decision. The following is a helpful typology to use when assessing media influence:

1. *Decisive effectiveness* — A major influence on choice.
2. *Contributory effectiveness* — Some role such as stimulating awareness or interest, but not a decisive one.
3. *Ineffective* — Exposure but no particular impact on outcome.

Media influence has been the subject of decades of research, and the sources are too numerous to detail here.[14] But we can give these major generalizations regarding media influence in the context of extended problem solving:

1. The various media are *complementary, not competitive.* People generally do not rely exclusively on one source.
2. The mass media, whether marketer dominated or not, most frequently have been found to perform a *contributory* role by providing such information as brand features and product availability. As we will see later, however, advertising properly conceived also can be *decisive* in many situations.
3. The general content media tend to be perceived as more credible than advertising and other marketer-dominated sources. As a result, they tend to have a greater contributory influence.

FIGURE 5-3

❖ You Can't Miss the Benefits Offered by the Caloric Range

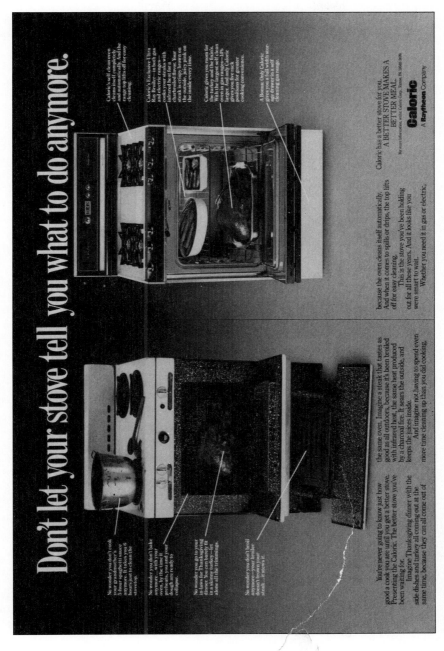

Courtesy Caloric Corporation

4. Personal selling often will have a *decisive* role when it is available.

5. Word-of-mouth communication from friends or relatives usually will have *decisive* impact and greatest total overall effectiveness in shaping consumer behavior. The primary reason is that information provided by a peer is regarded as more credible and trustworthy than anything the mass media can provide.

Personal Selling   Even in an age of mass merchandising, situations still exist in which point-of-sale negotiation or information exchange is needed. For example, the inclusion of energy-use ratings on appliances has proved to be of little value without additional explanation by a salesperson.[15]

It should come as no surprise to you that personal selling can be decisive in its impact. You will recall from Chapter 3 that interpersonal communication offers the significant benefits of instant feedback and opportunity to use various nonverbal signals.

What makes for effectiveness in personal selling? This is the subject of Chapter 18, but a study on the automobile sales person is worth noting here.[16] In the 1970s, flamboyant sales methods, not genuine concern for the buyer, were the norm. By the 1980s, just the reverse was found to be true. Now the pendulum has swung, forcing a real focus on the consumer's expectations. You will see clearly in Promotion in Action 5–1 how the growing presence of the woman car buyer has changed what happens in the automobile showroom.

In-Home Selling   More than half of all U.S. households now do some purchasing at home during a typical month. The strategies used to capitalize on this form of purchase (direct mail, telemarketing, etc.) are referred to as *direct marketing.* The consumers who respond to this type of selling prefer to avoid the costs, loss of time, and inconvenience of shopping in retail stores. Direct marketing is the subject of Chapter 22.

Advertising   Once a need is recognized, customers generally become more receptive to advertising that they might previously have ignored. Consumers

TABLE 5–5

❖   **The Information Sources Used by Consumers**

Source	One-on-One Communication	Mass Media
General Marketer-dominated	Word-of-mouth influence Personal selling Direct marketing	General media Advertising Promotion, Publicity Public Relations

often consult ads for information, although the informative role of advertising can vary. Here are some examples:

1. Print and TV ads were found to be the primary information sources used by purchasers of small electrical appliances and outdoor products.[17]
2. Nearly half of those interviewed in one study reported purchasing a product after exposure to a commercial or magazine ad. What were they looking for? Information on price reductions.[18]

The Woman Customer Takes Charge in the Automobile Showroom

❖
PROMOTION
IN ACTION
5–1

Women are taking over America's car lots. They bought 45 percent of the new cars sold in the United States in 1987, up from 23 percent in 1970. They influence 80 percent of all new-car purchases, according to studies by J.D. Powers and Associates of Westlake Village, California. Women could account for 60 percent of new-car purchasers by 2000, according to a 1986 study by *Cosmopolitan* magazine.

Car dealers need to be aware of the needs of women car buyers. "Women are less comfortable than men in dealing with the financial aspects of purchasing their car," according to a 1987 survey by J.D. Powers and Associates commissioned by *Family Circle* magazine. "Manufacturers and car dealerships who make women feel more comfortable with financial aspects could build a dominant market share among women purchasers."

Women are more brand loyal in car buying than men, according to Jayne Hamilton, the president and CEO of Market Development Associates and author of *How to Sell Cars and Trucks to Women.* Women pick up on showroom details that men usually ignore, according to Hamilton. They notice whether a showroom or service area is dirty or noisy. They are more aware of smells, decorative details, and the overall environment. And women will shop at three or four dealerships before making a final decision.

"The dealer is going to have to treat this new woman as her family doctor does in order to keep her business," explains Hamilton. "Women want to feel that the dealer is reliable, dependable, a good listener, and knowledgeable. Then they will gain confidence that this person will be able to diagnose the car or truck that will work best for their situation—and prescribe it." Once this relationship is established, "retailing becomes more customer-driven, and dealers will find that they have gained loyal customers."

Source: Frieda Curtindale, "Marketing Cars to Women," *American Demographics*. Used by special permission.

3. Those who rely most heavily on advertising are likely to be male, young, single, and employed.[19]

Does advertising play a contributory role or a decisive role in consumer decision processes? One can argue either way on this issue, but we believe the insights of Jack Trout and Al Ries are worthy of note:

> Apologists for advertising are fond of claiming that advertising doesn't sell anything. It only creates awareness. Other functions are responsible for sales. The facts suggest otherwise. For most products, awareness is not the issue, perception is. Brands like Coke, Pepsi, Chevy, Ford, Burger King and McDonald's already have awareness [ratings in the 90th percentile].
>
> To increase sales, a high-awareness brand must sharpen its perception in the mind. With the right name, the right positioning strategy and the right execution, advertising alone is the most powerful force in marketing. With other factors approximately equal, as they usually are in the real world, advertising alone can determine who will win the marketing war.[20]

In-Store Information   Many buying decisions are made at the point of purchase based on displays, labels, and other types of information. We will demonstrate that this source of information assumes even greater importance under limited problem solving, but it also plays a role in EPS.

The role of package labels is worthy of noting here. Information provided in this way can be decisive. A problem occurs when labels providing such crucial information as nutrition and safety are misperceived, used in part, or disregarded. Numerous studies over the years have shown that this can take place.[21] This means that manufacturers should stress in their advertising that a label must be read if the product is to be used as intended.

Public Relations and Publicity   Our reference here is to information that is marketer controlled but normally disseminated through the mass media. The objective is to influence sales by gaining public acceptance of company policies and products. Eastman Kodak, for example, flooded the general media with information on its new disk camera in the 1980s long before it began to advertise. This information dissemination proved to be an effective sales tactic, although the product was later withdrawn for other reasons.

General Content Media   The consumer can often gain valuable information regarding product features and comparisons through the general media. It is not uncommon for this source to be decisive in its impact. An example of the importance of the general media is the negative effect on the sales of some running shoe brands and the positive effects on others after publication of shoe comparisons in *Runner's World*.[22]

Word-of-Mouth Influence   Consumers frequently turn to others for advice about products and services. The transmitter of information is referred to as an *influential*. When are consumers most likely to respond to information from this source? Here is what we have learned from more than 30 years of research regarding word-of-mouth advertising:[23]

1. A product is difficult to evaluate using objective criteria. Therefore, the experience of others becomes a substitute for actual trial and use.
2. The person lacks the ability to evaluate the product or service.
3. Other sources, especially the marketer-dominated sources, are seen as having low credibility.
4. An influential person is more accessible than other sources.
5. Strong social ties exist between transmitter and receiver.
6. The receiver has a high need for social approval.

Anyone can serve as an influential if he or she possesses information that others do not have. In fact, most people play this role at some point in their lives simply because they have been a recent purchaser and are willing to share their experience.

The impact of word of mouth   Research consistently demonstrates that personal influence generally has a more decisive role than any other source, primarily because information from this source has greater credibility.[24] This is especially likely to be the case when the receiver initiates the conversion.[25] We also know that more than one-third of all word of mouth is negative and usually is given higher priority and assigned a greater weight in decision making.[26]

Some clues for promotional strategy   Positive word of mouth can be one of the greatest marketing assets. The opposite occurs, of course, when the content is negative. At the very least, monitoring whether or not word of mouth is occurring and what impact it has is essential for advertisers. Focus group research is often the best way of monitoring. Eight to 12 people are brought together and are guided by a monitor to discuss their experiences, motivations, values, and attitudes. If friends and relatives have shaped their decisions at all, this fact usually emerges clearly in discussion.

Sometimes positive word of mouth can be stimulated. One of the most used advertising themes is "Ask someone who owns one." It is even possible to trigger discussion of ads by using novel and interesting characters. Certainly the two bucolic spokesmen for Bartles & James wine coolers have become a part of American folklore, and there is little doubt that these spokesmen accelerated product trial.

At other times, the need is to curb word of mouth, especially when it has become negative. The Exxon Corporation triggered much public hostility by inept handling of the infamous oil spill incident in Alaska. After a long period of silence, company spokespersons were perceived to be denying all culpability for this incident. Not surprisingly, large numbers of consumers boycotted Exxon stations.

Much of the uproar could have been prevented by a clear and honest statement of responsibility backed by immediate remedial action. Failure to act in such a way has hurt many otherwise credible companies over the past decade. There seems to be an unwillingness to accept the fact that the general public is rapidly losing confidence and is less willing to forgive irresponsible action.

Alternative Evaluation

Four-wheel drive vehicles (known as 4×4s) designed for off-road perfor-mance represent a hot growth market in the automotive industry. Because many purchasers are first-time buyers, an EPS decision process is to be expected. What information is needed? How are available options evalu-ated?

Each buyer must arrive at a decision as to what attributes are really important. Is interior comfort important? Off-road handling? Low price? Abil-ity to switch instantly from two-wheel to four-wheel drive? In other words, *evaluative criteria* must be established to compare various alternatives.

Once these criteria are in place, information processing begins in ear-nest. You will recall from Chapter 4 that high involvement leads to what has come to be known as the *central route to persuasion* following the sequence of change shown below:

Beliefs ———> Attitudes ———> Intentions

This sequence is the heart of the *theory of reasoned action* first proposed by Ajzen and Fishbein.[27] Their theory has been affirmed by research since that time.[28]

First of all, *beliefs* are formed or changed reflecting the buyer's conclu-sions on how each alternative 4×4 brand measures up competitively. Then the total rating for each make forms an *attitude toward the act of purchasing that alternative.* Then, all things being equal, the potential buyer forms an *intention* to purchase the preferred make. We also must recognize that in-tentions can also be affected by social influences and conformity pressures. Chapter 7 presents more about the latter issues.

Evaluative Criteria   Alternative evaluation requires a set of evaluative crite-ria by which expected product attributes or benefits can be used to compare the alternatives under consideration. The alternative can be *objective* (price, durability) or *subjective* (relating to symbolic values such as youthfulness or status).

Evaluative criteria are often a product-specific representation of underlying motives. Considerable use has been made of psychographic research to explore consumer lifestyles through AIO questions (*A*ttitudes, *I*nterests, and *O*pinions).

What would be the most important expected benefits to a potential four-wheel drive truck purchaser who says, "I like to have the best in everything"? Such a customer most likely will make sure that he or she considers only those makes that rate highest mechanically. What would be most important to the person who agrees that "I'm not afraid to take risks when I do the things I enjoy the most"? Now the most important criterion might be "demonstrated ability to conquer the toughest terrain."

Shifting to a different purchase altogether, sun tanning was the "in" thing until the late 1980s when the evidence of the risk of skin cancer became unmistakable. Now sun lovers are increasingly motivated to avoid burning. To capitalize upon this shift in motivation, Plough, Inc., makers of Coppertone, changed its long-running advertising campaign picturing a small dog pulling at the bathing briefs of a young girl, revealing her tanning line. Coppertone now is positioned as the official suncare product of the Association of Tennis Professionals.[29]

The Alternative Evaluation Process   Now let's assume that marketing research has isolated a segment of prospective 4×4 buyers who use the following criteria (the numbers represent an averaged weighting of the importance of each):

Ease of shifting from two-wheel to four-wheel drive	(+3)
Engineered to handle rough off-road terrain	(+3)
Interior comfort of a passenger car	(+2)
Low frequency of repair	(+2)
Low price relative to competition	(+1)

Recalling our discussion in Chapter 4, information is processed via the *central route*, meaning that belief and attitude change takes place by active processing of message content itself. Message execution, although always important, is a secondary consideration in processing information. In central route processing, the individual forms cognitive responses reflecting the extent to which the appeals are accepted or rejected.

In addition, product information generally is processed by brand (PBB), with the individual making an decision on each evaluative criterion and forming a brand attitude. When involvement is high, most people will use a *compensatory strategy* in which a given alternative (a 4×4 make in our case) will not be rejected just because it fails to deliver on one or more criteria. Instead, weakness on a given attribute may be offset or compensated by strength on others.[30] Attitude toward purchase, then, is a summed total of ratings making use of all evaluative criteria.

Returning to our example, prospective buyers were asked to rate the five 4×4 manufacturers based on market share, making use of the five criteria they indicated were of importance to them. These ratings appear in Table 5–6. A score of +3 indicates the highest score for any given attribute, and −3 is the lowest mark.

You may be wondering how we arrived at the numbers at the bottom of the table labeled Attitude toward purchase. We used the formula given by Ajzen and Fishbein in the Theory of Reasoned Action[31] as follows:

$$A_B = \sum b_i e_i$$

where:

A_B = Attitude toward performing the behavior
b_I = Belief that performing Behavior B leads to consequence i
e_I = The person's evaluation of consequence i
n = The total number of beliefs

The formula states that the attitude toward the act of purchase is the sum total of belief ratings given for each of the attributes, taking into account their weights. For example, prospective buyers rate make A as tops (+3) in

TABLE 5–6

❖   **Summary of Consumer Attitudes toward Five Leading 4 × 4 Vehicle Manufacturers**

Attribute	Importance	Manufacturer Ratings				
		A	B	C	D	E
Two-wheel to four-wheel drive shifting	+3	+3	+3	−3	−2	+3
Off-road handling	+3	+3	+2	−2	−3	+1
Frequency of repair	+2	+2	+3	+1	−2	−1
Interior comfort	+2	+1	−2	−1	+3	−1
Low price	+1	+1	−1	+3	+1	+1
Attitude toward purchase		+25	+16	−12	−12	+9

terms of ease of shifting from two-wheel to four-wheel drive (an attribute rated +3, indicating that it is very important). These two figures were multiplied, giving a sum of +9. The formula was followed for the other four attributes, giving Make A a winning total score of +25, and so on.

Although these numbers may seem to be a bit abstract, look at the profile that is revealed:

Make A: Very strong on the attributes that count most: ease of shifting and off-road handling. A bit weaker on comfort and price, two factors that were not very important to those in this market segment.

Make B: Also well rated, but a bit weaker on off-road handling. Negative ratings on interior comfort and price do not affect overall evaluation very much.

Make C: Very weak on off-road handling and drive shifting. The high rating on low price does not offset the weaknesses.

Make D: Strong on interior comfort, but an also-ran in every other sense.

Make E: Strongest in drive shifting but otherwise very weak.

Some Clues for Marketing Strategy   Marketers have four strategic options for influencing the evaluative process: (1) feature the salient attributes; (2) minimize weakness by making the most of your strengths; (3) change the product; and (4) change awareness and perceptions.

Feature the salient attributes   Makes A and B are in the strongest position because of high ratings on the two attributes that count the most: drive shifting and off-road handling. The objective then is to reinforce this highly favorable market position by driving home product superiority. This is precisely the strategy followed by Mazda (see Figure 5–4).

Brand recall is the overriding objective of marketing strategy. This recall must go far beyond mere name awareness because the consumer will be influenced only if the brand name is associated with the most important expected product attributes. Accomplishing this association may require repetition because association rarely happens fully with only one or two exposures.

Management also faces the challenge of retaining a favorable image in a highly competitive market once it is achieved. Market share can erode virtually overnight. First, continual innovation must be used to maintain the competitive edge. Secondly, it is necessary to retain "share of mind" (i.e., present awareness and perception). The best strategy for this is consistency of message from one ad to the next.

Minimizing weakness   Make D faces a real dilemma because of its poor ratings on the three most salient attributes. If consumer perceptions indeed

FIGURE 5–4

❖ Engineered to Conquer the Great Divide

Engineered To Conquer The Great Divide.

Think of it as a brute with feelings. Like most 4x4 trucks, the Mazda B2600i is built to play rough. First off, it can handle nearly any off-road condition, from desert sands to rugged mountain trails. And since it's equipped with a 2.6 litre engine, the most powerful Four in its class, it doesn't just drive off-road—it conquers it. But what really sets the B2600i apart is how it feels to drive. Developed with Kansei engineering, it has been created to give you a driving experience you won't expect from a 4x4. A feeling of comfort, confidence, and control. In fact, it's so comfortable you may forget how tough it is.

But make no mistake, this truck is designed for toughness. And designed well, for it allows you to get into 4-wheel drive with the shift of a lever. And just as important, it allows you to return to civilization just as easily.

Test drive a B2600i. It'll feel out of this world. And odds are, it could take you there. For additional information, call this toll-free number: 800-424-0202.

mazda

It Just Feels Right.

Mazda 4x4.

© 1989 Mazda Motor of America, Inc.

Courtesy Mazda Motor of America, Inc.

144

reflect reality, all this company can do is to make the most of its strength (interior comfort) and hope to attract a few customers who consider this quality to be most important.

Another possible option, but a highly risky one, is to feature and promote an all-new benefit not presently offered by others. Perhaps it would be possible for this manufacturer to offer front and back wheel steering, an option limited to a few passenger cars. This might work if front and back steering is indeed perceived as a benefit. Marketing experience has shown, however, that this promoting of an all-new benefit can be an uphill battle. Read Promotion in Action 5–2 and discover why *Splendor* was not so splendid. The manufacturer was pushing against the consumer grain the whole way.

Product change   It is important to assess through further marketing research whether low ratings on salient criteria are, in fact, true. If Makes C and D are indeed weaker than their competitors in off-road handling, it is time for a product redesign. This then becomes a product policy problem, *not a promotional problem*.

Change awareness and perceptions   If Makes C and D in reality are competitive in drive shifting and off-road handling, the poor ratings indicate low consumer awareness. The challenge then is to revamp the promotional strategy. Both companies need to tell their stories on these features with much greater impact.

Purchase and Outcomes

Purchase and its outcomes are the last two stages in the decision process (Figure 5–2). Selection of the retailer or dealer often requires a purchase process in its own right, although in-home purchasing is rapidly growing in importance as we have stated previously.

Usually the alternative chosen at this stage will be consistent with purchase intentions established through alternative evaluation. But it is entirely possible that unanticipated circumstances such as lack of funds could lead to another opposite behavior. Also, purchase intentions can change when the product is not available, new information is encountered at point of sale, and so on.

The decision process does not terminate with the purchase, however. The buyer will compare the performance of the chosen product or service against expectations. If he or she concludes that the best action was taken, the response will be satisfaction. If the response is dissatisfaction, on the other hand, additional information is sometimes used to affirm that the initial choice was correct. Owner's manuals can be a real help in this respect.

If it appears that the product or service is defective, on the other hand, the buyer may complain and seek redress. Any failure by the manufacturer or service provider to act responsibly about a customer complaint can have decidedly negative word-of-mouth impact.[32] British Airways found this out

PROMOTION IN ACTION 5–2

Splendor Is Not So Splendid

The Colgate-Palmolive Company learned the hard way that no amount of marketing communication can move a product offering a benefit that customers do not perceive.

The Kao Soap Company, a Japanese firm, had achieved real success with a shampoo and conditioner that protect the cuticle in the hair shaft. Beauty salons in the United States had become aware of the need for protection of the hair cuticle, thus giving some clues that there may be a consumer market for this type of product.

Colgate and Kao jointly test marketed a version of the Kao product called *Hair Defense*. For various reasons, it fell far short of breakeven, which meant a return to the drawing boards. A revamped version was named *Splendor* and rolled out in western U.S. markets.

The result? Another failure. Part of the problem was the extreme competitiveness in the shampoo/conditioner market. It seems everyone was introducing new products. But this alone was not the explanation.

In a postmortem, Colgate speculated that cultural differences may have played a bigger role than previously thought. Japanese women have a long, daily regimen for hair care, using several different products. Oriental women are, perhaps, not as skeptical about claims and were more responsive to advertising. Certainly the Japanese advertising could not have been used in the United States. One Japanese TV spot showed someone holding a stick with nails in it slashing through the leaves of a fake palm tree. That was to illustrate what an average hairbrush does to the hair. The Kao product was suggested as an alternative.

Probably the major reason for the washout is that *Splendor* shampoo was doomed from the start. It was too complicated a concept to convey to consumers. The beauty salon market might have been something different.

One competitor felt the whole proposition was confusing from the beginning. Even if women had a hair cuticle problem, they probably were not aware of it, he observed. In his opinion, Colgate lost track of the end benefit women expect from a shampoo by its focus on the cuticle story.

Source: Adapted from Nancy Giges, "Splendor: Colgate's Hardy Haircare Washout." *Advertising Age*, May 30, 1985, p. 32. Used by special permission.

by experiencing heavy losses. The problem was so bad that the initials *BA* came to stand for "Bloody Awful."[33] Management turned the situation around, however, with a complete marketing overhaul. The company motto was changed to read, "To Fly, to Serve." The outcome represented a major switch to building maximum customer satisfaction, and both revenue and profits have increased dramatically.

North American businesses have faced growing consumer dissatisfaction, especially in the past decade. The crucial issue is that consumers perceive U.S. goods to be poorer in quality than imports. Many have now begun to feature quality as an advertising theme, making strong promises that changes have been made. The important question, however, is whether the products are actually better now.

Advertising and promotion must create *realistic expectations* that are backed by product performance. If what is promised is actually achieved, the company stands to gain market loyalty. If the product fails, the consumers' negative votes will soon be felt in market share. This point seems to be quite obvious. Why, then, do so many ignore it?

SUMMARY

This is the first of three chapters designed to help you understand the dynamics of consumer behavior. We viewed the consumer from a problem-solving perspective and pointed out that five basic steps are involved in the decision process: (1) need recognition, (2) search for information, (3) alternative evaluation, (4) purchase, and (5) outcomes of purchase, especially satisfaction or dissatisfaction.

The rigor with which these decision-process steps will be followed, especially on an initial purchase, will vary from one situation to the next depending upon (1) the degree of involvement (personal relevance), (2) the extent to which alternatives are differentiated, and (3) availability of time for deliberation. When involvement is high and the other two considerations are positive, decision process takes the form of *extended problem solving* (EPS). At the opposite pole on a continuum is *limited problem solving* (LPS) in which decisions are made with far less deliberation.

As purchases are repeated, however, decisions tend to become habitual. When involvement is high, habits are often based on *brand loyalty*. When brand loyalty is not a factor, buying habits mostly reflect *inertia* and are susceptible to change. The remainder of the chapter focused on EPS. The major characteristics of EPS as a decision-process strategy are:

1. It is motivated and activated by high involvement.

2. It involves strong motivation to search for information that is processed actively and thoroughly. It uses multiple sources.

3. Alternative evaluation is rigorous. Multiple evaluative criteria are used to compare various options. The resulting beliefs, attitudes, and intentions are strongly held.

4. Purchase often necessitates further decision process in choice of outlet.

5. Satisfaction is the crucial outcome of purchase. If the consumer is satisfied, consumer loyalty may be established. If this is not the case, consumers are often motivated to seek redress.

The chapter also discussed a number of implications for promotional strategy.

REVIEW AND DISCUSSION QUESTIONS

1. What are the essential distinctions between extended problem solving and limited problem solving? What type of decision process would you expect most people to follow in the initial purchase of a new product or brand in these categories: electric shaver, gold jewelry, soft drink, stereo equipment, men's underwear, women's lingerie, and flashlight batteries?

2. A product that used a synthetic substance as a substitute for leather failed in test market. Consumers said that it could not possibly have the same properties as leather, especially flexibility and ability to breathe. Could these perceptions be changed through advertising?

3. Sales of the Audi 5000 slumped drastically after an unfavorable exposé on the CBS "60 Minutes" program. It was alleged, erroneously as it turned out, that the manufacturer was responsible for unpredictable surges in acceleration that resulted in death-causing accidents. Consumer word of mouth became decidedly negative, and consumers blamed management for irresponsibility. What would you do in this situation if you were the North American marketing manager for this German company?

4. For a period of time, Isuzu cars and trucks were advertised in North America featuring a spokesperson, Joe Isuzu. Joe, as you may remember, made outrageous claims for Isuzu vehicles; his claims were always corrected by words shown on the TV screen as he spoke. Although many people loved these ads, their influence on sales appeared to be negative. Why do you think this took place? What implications can you draw for advertising strategy?

5. Carnival Cruise Lines has Project Tiffany in the works, calling for the company to build three luxury liners, all equipped with suites. Passenger capacity will be only 700, and everything will be done to compete at the absolute top of the line. Obviously, this is an entirely new concept for Carnival. How could marketing research among older, more affluent segments help Carnival to arrive at its product/service mix? What information would you want and why?

6. All evidence indicates that companies totally dedicated to product quality and customer service come out on top. Problems occur, however, in motivating designers and engineers to view the product from the consumer's perspective. As the CEO, you are becoming increasingly aware that consumers are rejecting your room air conditioning line because the designers and engineers did not consider the consumer. What can you do to bring about a changed orientation at the engineering and factory levels?

NOTES

1. John Dewey, *How We Think* (New York: Heath, 1910).

2. Icek Ajzen and Martin Fishbein, *Understanding Attitudes and Predicting Social Behavior* (Englewood Cliffs, N.J.: Prentice Hall, 1980), p. 5.

3. Wayne D. Hoyer, "Variations and Choice Strategies across Decision Contexts: An Examination of Contingent Factors," in *Advances in Consumer Research*, ed. Richard J. Lutz, vol. 13 (Provo, Utah: Association for Consumer Research, 1986), pp. 23–26.

4. John Antil, "Conceptualization and Operationalization of Involvement," in *Advances in Consumer Research*, ed. Thomas Kinnear, vol. 11 (Provo, Utah: Association for Consumer Research, 1984), p. 204.

5. See Giles Laurent and Jean-Noel Kapferer, "Measuring Consumer Involvement Profiles," *Journal of Marketing Research* 12 (February 1985), pp. 41–53.

6. "Let's Cruise," *American Demographics* 10 (February 1988), p. 21.

7. See Leigh McAlister and Edgar Pessemier, "Variety Seeking Behavior: An Interdisciplinary Review," *Journal of Consumer Research* 9 (December 1982), pp. 311–22.

8. James F. Engel, Roger D. Blackwell, and Paul W. Miniard, *Consumer Behavior*, 6th ed. (Hinsdale, Ill.: Dryden Press, 1989), p. 489.

9. See, for example, David H. Furse, Girish N. Punj, and David W. Stewart, "A Typology of Individual Search Strategies among Purchasers of New Automobiles," *Journal of Consumer Research* 10 (March 1984), pp. 417–31.

10. David K. Midgley, "Patterns of Interpersonal Information Seeking for the Purchase of a Symbolic Product," *Journal of Marketing Research* 20 (Winter 1983), pp. 174–83.

11. Sharon E. Beatty and Scott M. Smith, "External Search Effort: An Investigation across Several Product Categories," *Journal of Consumer Research* 14 (June 1987), pp. 83–95.

12. Joel E. Urbany, "An Experimental Examination of the Economics of Information," *Journal of Consumer Research* 13 (September 1986), pp. 257–71.

13. Itamar Simonson, Joel Huber, and John Payne, "The Relationship between Prior Brand Knowledge and Information Acquisition Order," *Journal of Consumer Research* 14 (March 1988), pp. 566–78; and James R. Bettman and C. Whan Park, "Effects of Prior Knowledge and Experience and Phase of the Choice Process on Consumer Decision Processes: A Protocol Analysis," *Journal of Consumer Research* 7 (December 1980), pp. 243–48.

14. For more detail, see Engel et al., *Consumer Behavior,* ch. 17.

15. John D. Claxton and C. Dennis Anderson, "Energy Information at the Point of Sale: A Field Experiment," in *Advances in Consumer Research*, ed. Jerry C. Olson, vol. 7 (Ann Arbor, Mich.: Association for Consumer Research, 1980), pp. 277–82.

16. "Unctious Auto Salespeople May Be a Thing of the Past, Study Suggests," *Marketing News,* November 23, 1984, pp. 1 +

17. "Study Tracks Housewares Buying, Information Sources," *Marketing News*, October 14, 1983, p. 16.

18. *A Study of Media Involvement* (New York: Magazine Publishers' Association, 1979).

19. "Whirlpool Corporation," in Roger D. Blackwell, James F. Engel, and W. Wayne Talarzyk, *Contemporary Cases in Consumer Behavior,* rev. ed. (Hinsdale, Ill.: Dryden Press, 1984), pp. 365–88.

20. Jack Trout and Al Ries, "The Decline and Fall of Advertising," *Advertising Age,* June 26, 1989, p. 20.

21. See Engel et al., *Consumer Behavior,* p. 501.

22. Sam Harper, "Athletic Shoe Surveys Run into Industry Dispute," *Advertising Age,* September 22, 1980, p. 22.

23. Engel et al., *Consumer Behavior,* p. 157.

24. For an extensive review, see Linda L. Price and Lawrence, F. Feick, "The Role of Interpersonal Sources and External Search: An Informational Perspective," in Kinnear, *Advances,* pp. 250–55.

25. Hubert Gatignon and Thomas S. Robertson, "A Propositional Inventory for New Diffusion Research," *Journal of Consumer Research* 11 (March 1985), pp. 849–67.

26. Marsha L. Richins, "Word of Mouth Communication as Negative Information," in Kinnear, *Advances,* pp. 697–702.

27. Ajzen and Fishbein, *Understanding Attitudes.*

28. See Blair H. Sheppard, Jon Hartwick, and Paul R. Warshaw, "The Theory of Reasoned Action: A Meta-Analysis of Past Research with Recommendations for Modifications in Future Research," *Journal of Consumer Research* 15 (December 1988), pp. 325–43.

29. "Coppertone 'Suncare' Strategy Targets Tennis Set," *Marketing News,* April 25, 1988, p. 2.

30. See Engel et al., *Consumer Behavior,* ch. 18.

31. Ajzen and Fishbein, *Understanding Attitudes.*

32. For a review of research findings, see Steven P. Brown and Richard F. Beltramini, "Consumer Complaining and Word of Mouth Activities: Field Evidence," *Advances in Consumer Research*, ed. Thomas K. Srull, vol. 16 (Provo, Utah: Association for Consumer Research, 1989), pp. 9–16.

33. For the story of BA's woes, see Kenneth Labich, "The Big Comeback at British Airways," *Fortune,* December 5, 1988, pp. 163–64.

Understanding the Consumer: Limited and Habitual Decision-Process Behavior

FREEDOM OF CHOICE ENSLAVES DAZED CONSUMERS

The woman is standing in the drugstore suffering from acute "consumeritis." This attack has been brought on by the excess of choices on the shelf before her. The chief symptom of the attack is mental paralysis, the total inability to make a decision.

She came here on a quest for a shampoo refill. But when she found that her usual brand was no longer available, she was tossed willy-nilly into the chaos of the modern-day world of shampoos.

What did she want after all? Which of the three-dozen options lined before her would make the dead follicles that grow out of her busy head come alive? A moisturizing formula? A body-building protein? A mysterious chemical soup of Elastin? Collagen? Keratin? Balsam?

She was compelled by the labels to ask herself some penetrating questions. Is she the type of person who needs her pH balanced? Or would she prefer her pH a bit off of kilter? Should she put essential fatty acids on her scalp? Does she want shampoo with a pectin extract? Or isn't that what she uses to make jelly?

This proliferation of personal products has turned shopping into a decision-making marathon. The competing claims of manufacturers have produced an information glut.

Informed consumers are propelled into examining their bodies in ever more minute detail. Does my skin need intensive care or not? Do I have plaque on my teeth or not? Ridges on my nails? Split ends on my hair? Am I normal or dry?

One thing is clear to the woman now at home and lathering the body-building protein into her scalp: What the advertisers call brand loyalty is a low-level consumer protest movement. It's our way of cutting through the bouts of decision making, avoiding the barrages of useless information. It's a defense against the need to waste energy differentiating things that barely differ.

Source: Ellen Goodman, "Freedom of Choice Enslaves Dazed Consumer," *The Columbus Dispatch*, October 9, 1987. Used by special permission.

Ellen Goodman's amusing comments underscore a basic consumer truth—most people usually cannot and will not devote the energy that extended problem solving (EPS) requires. Hal Kassarjian has humorously noted that consumers somehow "muddle through."[1] One way to cope with the information overload is to use limited problem solving (LPS), which greatly simplifies the decision-making process. Another way is to form buying habits based on either brand loyalty or inertia, both of which eliminate the need to deliberate.

We continue now where we ended in Chapter 5 and contrast LPS with EPS. Then we will shift the focus from the initial purchase to the purchasing routines under brand loyalty and inertia.

LIMITED PROBLEM SOLVING

Nearly everyone strives to simplify decision making by reducing the number and variety of information sources, alternatives, and evaluative criteria. All five decision-process stages outlined in Table 5–1 may still be followed, but there is a difference in the extent to which this takes place.

It is helpful to contrast EPS and LPS in summary form. Using the questions from Table 5–3, we have summarized EPS and LPS for you in Table 6–1.

In the arena of low involvement, making the "right" choice for reasons of high personal relevance and self-esteem is less essential than with high involvement. Available options are similar to one another in most essential characteristics, and there is little perceived risk in choice.

When she hears the cry, "Mom, we're out of detergent," Mom makes a mental note to buy laundry detergent when she visits the supermarket on her way home from work. Her decision rule is to buy the cheapest brand. She sees a display of new Tide with Bleach and recognizes it instantly from a two-page ad in *Good Housekeeping* (Figure 6–1). Also, she has a coupon

─────── 153 ───────
Chapter 6
Understanding the
Consumer: Limited and
Habitual Decision-Process
Behavior

giving her 25 cents off new Tide. Her choice? New Tide. Why not? What does she have to lose?

From your point of view, marketing of low-involvement products and services may not be very dramatic or exciting. But this example represents the everyday world of consumer buying. The majority of supermarket purchases are made in this manner, especially if the product has had some prior advertising exposure.

TABLE 6–1

An Overview of the Differences between Extended Problem Solving (EPS) and Limited Problem Solving (LPS) ❖

Extended Problem Solving (EPS)	Limited Problem Solving (LPS)
Motivation and Need Recognition	
1. High involvement and perceived risk.	1. Low involvement and perceived risk.
Search for Information	
1. Strong motivation to search.	1. Low motivation to search.
2. Multiple sources used including media, friends, and point-of-sale communication.	2. Passive exposure to advertising; information processing not deep.
3. Information processed actively and rigorously.	3. Point-of-sale comparison likely.
Alternative Evaluation	
1. Rigorous evaluation process.	1. Nonrigorous evaluation process.
2. Multiple evaluative criteria used, with some more salient than others.	2. Limited number of criteria, focus on most salient.
3. Alternatives perceived as significantly different.	3. Alternatives perceived as essentially similar.
4. Compensatory strategy where weakness on given attributes can be offset by others.	4. Noncompensatory strategy, eliminating alternatives perceived to fall short on salient attribute(s).
5. Beliefs, attitudes, and intentions strongly held.	5. Beliefs, attitudes, and intentions not strongly held.
	6. Purchase and trial primary means of evaluation.
Purchase	
1. Will shop many outlets if needed.	1. Not motivated to shop extensively.
2. Choice of outlet may require a decision process.	2. Often prefer self-service.
3. Point-of-sale negotiation and communication often needed.	3. Choice often prompted by display and point-of-sale incentives.
Outcomes	
1. Doubts can motivate need for postsale reassurance.	1. Satisfaction motivates repurchase because of inertia, not loyalty.
2. Satisfaction is crucial and loyalty is the outcome.	2. Main consequence of dissatisfaction is brand switching.
3. Motivated to seek redress if there is dissatisfaction.	

Source: James F. Engel, Roger D. Blackwell, and Paul W. Miniard, *Consumer Behavior,* 6th ed. (Hinsdale, Ill.: Dryden Press, 1989), p. 474. Used by special permission.

The least complex form of LPS is the *impulse purchase.* This form, an entirely spur-of-the-moment action triggered by in-store promotion and display, has become a worldwide phenomenon with similar underlying dynamics.[2] The decision process takes place on the spot with no prior deliberation, and it often represents *a search for variety.*[3] Also, many people make an impulse purchase if they are in a bad mood because they hope it will bring pleasure and excitement.[4] If alternative evaluation takes place at all, it occurs *after* the product is bought and used.

Need Recognition

The scenario in which need recognition occurs is usually quite straightforward: The stock of common household items is depleted, the car runs

FIGURE 6–1

❖   **New Tide with Bleach Is Launched**

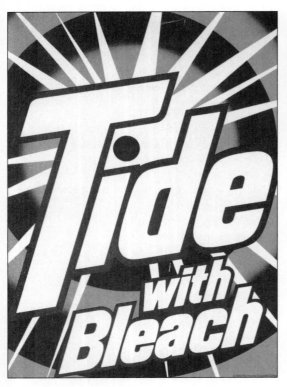

Courtesy Procter & Gamble

——— 155 ———
Chapter 6
Understanding the
Consumer: Limited and
Habitual Decision-Process
Behavior

low on gas, and so on. Advertising exposure can help generate some awareness of need.

Search for Information

When low involvement and little product differentiation exist, the need for active search diminishes and *internal search* (i.e., retrieving knowledge from memory) is generally sufficient.

Remember from the discussion in Chapter 4 that exposure to advertising and other forms of promotion is mostly *involuntary.* Perceptual barriers are not high, and information is accepted into memory without much effect on cognitive structure. Processing takes place via the *peripheral route,* meaning that the nature and form of the message tend to have more effect than its content per se.

It seems safe to say that the greatest impact of the two-page introductory ad for new Tide (Figure 6–1) comes from the full-page logo display rather than the "reason why" content. Exposure to the display triggers *advertising recognition* at point of sale. At that time, the ad and the display work together to cause the consumer to try the product. This recognition can happen even though most buyers do not remember having seen any ads.

Alternative Evaluation

Prechoice alternative evaluation consists, at most, of a quick comparison of competing brands in terms of one dominant evaluative criterion. "Gets out the worst dirt and stains." "Lowest price." "Contains mostly whole wheat flour rather than white flour." This evaluation generally takes place at point of sale and is done quickly using *noncompensatory* decision rules.[5] Information is processed by *attribute* rather than processed by *brand* as it is in the case of extended problem solving.

A noncompensatory decision rule states that a product's weakness in one attribute cannot be offset by a strength in another. This means that new Tide will be rejected if is perceived as being deficient in removing dirt and stains (assuming this is the dominant evaluative criterion), regardless of its strengths in any other dimension.

Noncompensatory decision rules take three forms:[6]

1. *Lexicographic*—All brands are compared in terms of one attribute (evaluative criterion) to determine a winner. If a tie occurs, the evaluation proceeds to the second most important attribute and so on.

2. *Elimination by aspects*—This strategy is very similar to the lexicographic form. The only difference is that cutoffs are imposed for the dominant attribute. If price is the dominant attribute, for example, a cut-off point

could be placed at $1.50 per package. Nothing over that amount is considered. Then the tie-breaking process continues as before.

3. *Conjunctive*—In this variation, cutoffs are established for each salient attribute and brands are compared one at a time. The failure of a product to meet the cutoff for any attribute leads to its disqualification. If, on the other hand, a brand meets all cutoffs, it is the winner.

These decision rules may seem unrealistic and overly mechanical to you. We recognize that few people *consciously* make these kinds of comparison, but evidence increasingly indicates that they are indeed used.[7]

Purchase

We have seen that point-of-sale influence plays an important role in making LPS decisions. In fact, research consistently supports the theory that supermarket shoppers use the shelves as their shopping list; they plan no more than one-third of their buying decisions.

Outcomes

The most rigorous alternative evaluation of a product takes place after it has been purchased and used. New Tide with Bleach makes this advertising claim: ". . . you'll have the cleaning power of the best Tide ever *plus* the whitening power of the best liquid bleach." If Tide fulfills these promises, the outcome will be the consumer's intention to repurchase, all things being equal.

Remember, however, that other acceptable alternatives exist and that the competitive scene is always changing. This means that intentions to repurchase can change as rapidly as they were made. If trial leads to dissatisfaction, the consumer will probably not complain or seek redress but will simply not repurchase. That will send a clear message to the manufacturer if enough consumers do the same thing.

Some Clues for Marketing Strategy

Attracting the LPS shopper truly is the central battle line of the competitive marketing world today. Marketers are finding to their dismay that older tried-and-true strategies are no longer effective. Promotion in Action 6–1 will give you insight into the challenges of competitive marketing.

Product Innovation and Change   The breakfast cereal industry is in turmoil. In 1983, Kellogg's market share hit its low of 36.7 percent, and a prominent Wall Street analyst evaluated Kellogg as "a fine company that's past its prime."[8] But the company regained at least four market share points, each worth about $42 million in sales revenues, although its market share slumped again a short time later.

157

Chapter 6
Understanding the
Consumer: Limited and
Habitual Decision-Process
Behavior

Like the other major players in the breakfast cereal field, Kellogg had largely ignored baby-boom-aged adults (middle 20s to early 40s) who had abandoned the breakfast table. Then Kellogg made a strategic decision to zero in on this market of 77 million adults. By using a strong pitch about the convenience and nutrition that cereal offers and by introducing a flood of new product entries, Kellogg helped stimulate a 26 percent increase by 1988 in cereal consumption in a supposedly "no-growth" market.[9]

Part of Kellogg's strategy was to search for market niches for technically innovative products. For example, it made a successful attack on Nabisco's

---

Stalking the New Consumer through "Micromarketing"

The good old days of mass marketing are gone forever. It used to be that large consumer products firms could advertise their products in standard and largely effective media (like soap operas on network television) and shoppers would go out and find the products on the shelves of largely cooperative retailers. No longer. Now the traditional shopper, the housewife, is out working, and family shopping may be done by any member of the family, from the mother on her way home from the office to the 16-year-old daughter. The burgeoning of options to network television has made the consumer harder to reach, even in the relatively predictable leisure hours. And retailers, also being forced to make more strategic stocking decisions, are demanding fees and hard data on consumer preference before allocating precious shelf space to new or marginal products.

Consumer goods companies struggled throughout the turbulent 1980s to meet these and other new challenges. One approach that is gaining favor is "micromarketing." The focus on micromarketing, rather than on the broad reach of national media, is on marketing through many avenues.

One aspect of this new approach is the appearance in national magazines of personalized ads that include the name of the subscriber. In another campaign, Kraft, General Foods, and Quaker Oats began in late 1990 unprecedented direct marketing campaigns to individual households. Based on the companies' own databases containing information on thousands of consumers, each began sending out coupon packages targeted to the buying habits of each consumer or household. The coupons are coded to allow the companies to track each household's redemptions, ultimately creating a dialogue with each consumer.

Sources: "Stalking the New Consumer," *Business Week*, August 28, 1989, pp. 54–55, and "KGF taps data base to target consumers," *Advertising Age*, October 8, 1990, p. 3.

Shredded Wheat market with such products as Raisin Squares and other fruit-filled shredded wheat cereals. Unfortunately, Kellogg later found itself unprepared for the sudden popularity of oat bran cereals and proved quite vulnerable to General Mills.

Admittedly, these examples may not seem like earth-shaking product innovations. But the strategy is to uncover market niches and experiment to see if a product can gain a foothold. As much as anything else, product change provides an opportunity to stress those magic words, *new and different*. This is how the battle is fought in "the world of the mundane."

The objective in marketing a product, then, is to differentiate its offerings sufficiently so that it can break out of the competitive noise and earn a new hearing. Management that neglects consumer research and product innovation will soon pay the price in lost market share. The following are two successful examples.

Amoco Corporation has tried to distance itself from the competition for premium motor fuel by offering a guarantee. It promises that regular users of Amoco Ultimate gasoline will have no problems with fuel systems or Amoco will pay for repairs. By making this promise, the company hopes to increase its 7.1 percent market share.[10]

Rubbermaid, Inc., maintains an annual sales growth of 15 percent by continually engaging in marketing research. The keys to product development are often identified by consumer focus groups.[11] In one focus group, participants complained that puddles of water form in the company's dish drainer, and the company responded by raising the back of the drainer to help water escape.

Advertising Strategy   As we discuss advertising strategy, bear in mind that information processing is largely involuntary. Also, information is processed via the peripheral route.

Stimulation of awareness   Advertising analyst Harry W. McMahan always contended that "the name of the game is the name. . . . Here is where all advertising starts and where so much of television advertising misses."[12] This statement merely confirms what marketers have always known: that there is a direct correlation between awareness and market share.[13]

Awareness of the brand name itself, however, is just a starting point. Marketers must also communicate the principal benefits of the product or service and establish them as valid need-satisfying options that may be worthy of the consumers' consideration at some point in time.

Brand recognition at point of sale becomes the marketer's central objective. If advertising has done its job, the consumer previously included the brand in his or her acceptable set of alternatives. This sets the stage for the consumer to try the product, especially if promotional incentives are provided.

————— 159 —————
Chapter 6
Understanding the
Consumer: Limited and
Habitual Decision-Process
Behavior

Notice the strong focus on brand and benefits in the ads included in Figures 6–1 and 6–2. You cannot miss the fact that new Tide (Figure 6–1) now has bleach and that Hellmann's (Figure 6–2) offers a cholesterol-free mayonnaise for the first time. Also, notice how clearly both the brand name and caffeine-free benefit are established for caffeine-free Diet Coke (Figure 6–3).

We cannot help wondering, however, whether the ad in Figure 6–4 conveyed an awareness of Vivid Thick Formula Bleach and its benefits. You have to be pretty motivated to move your eye from "the Brightest Kids in

FIGURE 6–2

Hellmann's Registers Its Name and Low-Cholesterol Benefit

Courtesy Best Foods, A Division of CPC International, Inc.

FIGURE 6–3

❖ Coke Delivers the One-Calorie Diet Coke Benefit

Courtesy Coca-Cola Company

FIGURE 6-4

What Makes These the Brightest Kids in America?

Courtesy Dowbrands

America" headline down to the much smaller image of the package and the brand name.

Memorability   In an overcommunicative society, many, if not most, ads simply get lost in the "noise." An ad may not communicate name and benefit unless it is memorable and stands out in some way.

What to say and how to say it? This question will plague us later in the book because there are no formulas to follow in designing effective ads. This problem becomes especially acute when involvement is low and brands are similar, because there really isn't much difference to emphasize.

Look at the ad for Maalox Plus in Figure 6–5. Let's face it; ads for self-medication products often head the list of consumers' most disliked advertising and fail to accomplish their intended purposes. Although the point of advertising is to be effective, not to be liked, there is no reason why brand name and benefit cannot be communicated in an enjoyable way as in some of the ads shown here. Most people can identify with the man in the picture in Figure 6–5. Also, the clever headline and bright photo liven information about the nutritional benefit of Fig Newtons cookies (Figure 6–6).

Memorability can be misused, however, if the execution gets in the way of the message. Do you remember the much-talked-about ads for Burger King featuring "Herb the Nerd?" "Where's Herb?" was the theme. Rather than think that poor old Herb had never been to Burger King, consumers associated his negative characteristics with the chain itself.[14]

We use the phrase "the Herb Factor" to label advertising that is carried away with irrelevant creativity. Trout and Ries put it well:

> Advertising can't differentiate your product without a position or "competitive mental angle." Beautiful singing and dancing by Burger King won't take a nickel's worth of business away from those golden arches. But a repositioning angle like hanging "kiddieland" on McDonald's will. There's always an angle and finding it isn't tough. Recognizing it is.[15]

Repetition   Repetition of brand name and benefit can be a fruitful strategy, and it is particularly helpful when involvement is minimal. Breaking through the competitive noise barrier always has low odds and may take many exposures. Therefore, repetition of brand name and benefit becomes important. More will be said about this in later chapters.

Changing media options   You read about the demands of micromarketing in Promotion in Action 6–1. The older strategy of relying on network TV and big circulation periodicals is far less effective today than in the past. Com

FIGURE 6–5

The Maalox Moment—A Good Registration of Brand Name and Benefit

Courtesy Rorer Consumer Pharmaceuticals

panies now target micromarkets by advertising on cable TV, in special-purpose, limited audience magazines, and on videocassettes.

H. J. Heinz Company's Ore-Ida Foods division has spent almost half of the advertising budget for its Steakumm sandwich meats on MTV in order to reach teenagers. This strategy alone helped reverse several years of market-share decline. As Anthony J. F. O'Reilly, Heinz CEO, put it, "We found this audience not through ABC, NBC, or CBS, but through MTV."[16]

FIGURE 6–6

❖   **Smart Cookies—Clear Communication of Product Benefits**

Courtesy Nabisco Brands © 1990

———— 165 ————
Chapter 6
Understanding the
Consumer: Limited and
Habitual Decision-Process
Behavior

O'Reilly's comment highlights the communicative effectiveness that draws advertisers to TV. Tentative, though not conclusive, evidence indicates that low involvement leads to increased information processing in the right hemisphere of the brain.[17] In turn, this processing takes the form of visual images as opposed to objective product information. What better visual medium to communicate a message is there than television?

Sales Promotion   Before a product can be evaluated, a consumer must have it to evaluate. The evaluation takes place during and after trial. Including coupons or other direct incentives as part of the advertising can increase the chance that the consumer will purchase and try the product. The Diet Coke ad in Figure 6–3 is an example of the use of incentives.

Advertising usually cannot do the selling alone, however. First, the package must stand out on shelves. New Tide with Bleach will be noticed simply because of its familiar orange package. Special displays are also a big help. Advertising uses incentives of all types: multiple packages at a lower unit price, coupons, free samples in home and at point of sale, and so on.

HABITUAL DECISION MAKING

We now turn from the initial purchase to the repeat purchase. As mentioned in the previous chapter, one possible decision-making strategy is *repeated problem solving,* either EPS or LPS. *Habitual decision making* is a more common strategy, however, because most of us cope with life by doing everything we can to establish routines.

If our choices prove to be satisfactory, we don't make other choices unless circumstances change. Figure 6–7 illustrates what happens when habit takes over. Once a person recognizes a need, the internal search into memory leads directly to the intention to repeat a previous choice without further deliberation.

Outcomes differ, however, depending on the extent to which the initial decision was made using EPS or LPS. For example, *brand loyalty* is an outcome of a satisfactory EPS decision, whereas *inertia* is the outcome of LPS (see Table 6–2).

Loyalty is a difficult habit to change. It can be a marketer's greatest asset because it erects barriers against the competition. One of the best indicators of loyalty is the response to this question: "What other brands would you consider if your favorite is not available?" The answer "None—I'll shop further" reflects strong commitment to a brand. At times several equally preferred brands may be available, and the consumer expresses loyalty by staying within this preferred set of options.

Inertia, on the other hand, is a nonstable habit reflecting little or no commitment to one brand over another. Often a purchase is made from among a group of satisfactory brands unless an incentive (reduced price or other promotional device) influences the choice. Repurchase is mostly a matter of convenience, and brand shifting is to be expected.

Brand Loyalty

Turn to Promotion in Action 6–2 and note especially the diagram on loyalty to various products. What do the first 8 or 10 products listed there have in common? You will find at least two of the three preconditions met for high involvement.

The first precondition is that the brands are different. Next, the perceived risk of failed outcomes is a factor in the purchase of film and over-

FIGURE 6–7

❖ **The Habitual Decision Process**

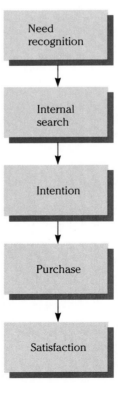

———— 167 ————
Chapter 6
Understanding the
Consumer: Limited and
Habitual Decision-Process
Behavior

the-counter medications. Finally, some of the items such as coffee reflect on self-image. You may wonder why we include coffee in this category. The reason is that a segment of consumers fear that a bad cup of coffee reflects on them personally.

The important point is that, for one reason or another, a large segment of buyers need to purchase the "right" thing. These considerations change as we progress down the list. Who will be loyal to a flashlight battery or a trash bag? If repurchase of such products occurs, inertia undoubtedly motivated the purchase.

Maintaining Brand Loyalty   As you would expect, brand loyalty can be lost quickly if it is taken for granted. The key to maintaining market share is an all-out commitment to continued innovation and customer satisfaction.[18] Economic history is littered with the wreckage of formerly popular brands.

Innovation, on the other hand, needs to be tempered with wisdom. As you will remember, the Coca-Cola Company nearly jeopardized its market standing by changing the tried-and-true Coke formula. Management seriously underestimated consumers' loyalty to the traditional formula and faced a market uproar. Management should have heeded a philosophy from folk wisdom: "If it ain't broke, don't fix it!"

In Coca-Cola's defense, however, market research documented changes in tastes in some segments. A much wiser strategy for Coke would have been to introduce alternate formulas for various segments with an altogether different label and promotion. Ultimately, Coca-Cola did this when it reintroduced traditional Coke as Coca-Cola Classic. The net effect on Coke's market share was positive after all the uproar died down.

Finally, maintaining advertising levels in relation to competition is strongly advisable. This concept is referred to as *maintenance of share of mind.* Its objective is to keep the brand and its principal benefit before the public eye. Without such an ongoing reinforcement of brand preference, many firms have experienced gradual erosion of market share in the face of competitive fire power.

TABLE 6-2

Brand Loyalty versus Inertia   ❖

Type of Purchase	Extent of Involvement	
	High	Low
Initial	EPS	LPS
Repurchase	Brand loyalty	Inertia

Consider the words of Clayt Wilhite, president of D'Arcy Masius Advertising Agency: "Every time 24 hours pass without any advertising reinforcement, brand loyalty will diminish ever so slightly—even for a powerful brand like Budweiser."[19] In recognition of this fact, Kraft General Foods stepped up advertising for its Maxwell House brand after stopping for a year in 1987. Dick Mayer, president of the General Foods USA

❖
**PROMOTION
IN ACTION
6–2**

The Consumer—Faithful or Fickle?

Betty Lombardi is a mild-mannered homemaker and grandmother in rural Hunterdon County, N.J. But put her behind a shopping cart and she becomes ruthless.

If Colgate toothpaste offers a tempting money-saving coupon, she'll cross Crest off her shopping list without a second thought. Never mind that her husband prefers Crest. When her supermarket runs a double-coupon promotion, she can boast that she shaved $22 off her bill by using coupons—never mind for what brand.

Although brand loyalty is far from dead, marketing experts say it eroded during the 1980s. Marketers themselves are partly to blame: They've increased spending for coupons and other short-term promotions at the expense of image-building advertising. What's more, a flood of new products has given consumers a dizzying choice of brands, many of which are virtually carbon copies of one another.

The Wall Street Journal's [1989] "American Way of Buying" survey found that most consumers switch brands for many of the products they use. More than half the users of 17 of the 25 products included in the survey said they're brand switchers (see the accompanying graph).

Nearly one-fourth of the participants aged 60 and older claimed brand loyalty for more than 10 of the 25 products in the survey; only 9 percent of those aged 18 to 29 had such strong allegiance.

People with high incomes also tend to be more brand loyal these days. Marketers speculate that more affluent people tend to lead more pressured lives and don't have time to research the products they buy for the highest quality and most reasonable price. An established brand name is insurance that the product will at least be of acceptable quality. It's sort of loyalty by default. The biggest wild card in the brand loyalty game is how will those hotly pursued but highly unpredictable baby boomers behave as they move into middle age. They grew up with more brand choices than any generation and have shown less allegiance so far.

169

Chapter 6
Understanding the
Consumer: Limited and
Habitual Decision-Process
Behavior

division, noted, "Even though brand loyalty is rather strong for coffee, we need advertising to maintain and strengthen it."[20]

Combating an Entrenched Competitor   As we have pointed out, brand loyalty can erode over time. Nevertheless, gaining an inroad into the market share of a strong competitor can be an uphill battle. As a result, many companies concentrate on increasing the loyalty of their own customers.

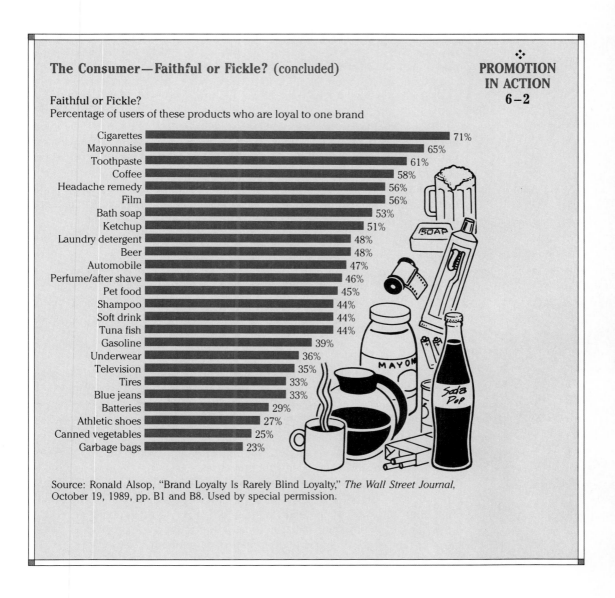

The Consumer—Faithful or Fickle? (concluded)

❖
**PROMOTION
IN ACTION
6–2**

Faithful or Fickle?
Percentage of users of these products who are loyal to one brand

Product	Percentage
Cigarettes	71%
Mayonnaise	65%
Toothpaste	61%
Coffee	58%
Headache remedy	56%
Film	56%
Bath soap	53%
Ketchup	51%
Laundry detergent	48%
Beer	48%
Automobile	47%
Perfume/after shave	46%
Pet food	45%
Shampoo	44%
Soft drink	44%
Tuna fish	44%
Gasoline	39%
Underwear	36%
Television	35%
Tires	33%
Blue jeans	33%
Batteries	29%
Athletic shoes	27%
Canned vegetables	25%
Garbage bags	23%

Source: Ronald Alsop, "Brand Loyalty Is Rarely Blind Loyalty," *The Wall Street Journal*, October 19, 1989, pp. B1 and B8. Used by special permission.

Tony Adams, vice president of Marketing Research at Campbell Soup Co., explains his company's strategy in this way:

> The probability of converting a nonuser to your brand is about 3 in 1,000. The best odds are with your core franchise. Our heavy users consume two or three cans of soup a week, and we'd like to increase that.[21]

To make inroads into the loyalty of a competitor, the best weapon is to feature a new and *demonstrably different* benefit. It will do no good to banner the words *new and improved* unless they are truly applicable.

As a case in point, Pillsbury Corp.'s Burger King division is the number two entry in the fast-food business, with a 17 percent market share compared with 36 percent for archcompetitor, McDonald's. Furthermore, Burger King's sales have been level for four years in a market characterized by an annual growth rate of 7 percent.[22] Nothing it has done as of this writing has made a lasting impact to increase its share.

Does this mean that McDonald's is invulnerable? In a sense, it is invulnerable to a competitor that offers the same product and service mix. But one newcomer, Burgers Direct, founded in 1988, has found a foothold. It offers a unique benefit—free home delivery of hamburgers in 30 minutes or less.[23] This benefit may give it only a small niche in the market now, but it is the same strategy that Domino's Pizza used to achieve strong inroads in its competitive arena.

Inertia

Purchasing habits based on inertia are highly unstable because consumers have no reason to remain loyal if competitors make it worth their while to switch. As we have stressed before, few manufacturers of low-involvement products would dare to advertise without bannering the word *new*. A product change, no matter how small, provides a reason to advertise heavily and induce trial through point-of-purchase promotion.

Procter & Gamble introduced Liquid Tide, aimed directly at Wisk, Lever Brothers' market-leading brand. By spending $50 million on advertising, the company stimulated a remarkable 10 percent increase in advertising recall for the brand name Tide.[24] By the end of the first year, Liquid Tide had gained a 6.8 percent market share. By then, Lever Brothers had matched Procter & Gamble in a competitive counterattack that actually increased Lever's share to 8.8 percent from its previous 8.0 level.[25]

If Lever Brothers had not fought back, its share would have undoubtedly eroded. The Liquid Tide advertising claims of "superior cleaning, water softening, and soil suspension agents," may be of little objective consequence to the consumer. What counts is that these words provided awareness of the new brand and encouraged consumers to try it.

171

Chapter 6
Understanding the
Consumer: Limited and
Habitual Decision-Process
Behavior

SUMMARY

Extended problem solving (EPS) discussed in the previous chapter occurs in only a minority of buying situations. This is due to the fact that involvement is low, alternatives are essentially similar, and time for deliberation is limited. The consumer is much more likely to base buying decisions on limited problem solving (LPS).

LPS involves minimal prepurchase information search and alternative evaluation. Even when the consumer recognizes a need, nearly any option will prove satisfactory. Nevertheless, it is possible to build some awareness of brand name and benefit by advertising, which activates a "why-not-try-it?" response at point of sale. Display, package design, and other forms of sales promotion trigger product trial. Competitors therefore have a strong incentive to introduce new products, suggest new uses for existing brands, and differentiate offerings through ongoing product change.

Once the consumer tries a product as the result of LPS and is satisfied with it, repeat purchases are most often made on the basis of inertia. Inertia reflects the common tendency to establish a buying habit simply to avoid further effort. This type of habit may endure unless competitors are successful in triggering trial. Brand loyalty does not exist with inertia, which is open to a high degree of competitive volatility.

On fewer occasions, buying habits are based on brand loyalty—especially when involvement is high and alternatives are differentiated. Competitors can find changing the habit of brand-loyal consumers to be difficult, with the result that some companies concentrate major efforts on maintaining the loyalty of their own customers. This requires continual vigilance in the form of ongoing innovation, quality, and advertising. A relaxed marketing posture can signal competitive vulnerability.

REVIEW AND DISCUSSION QUESTIONS

1. You are called in to serve as a marketing consultant for a soft drink company that is introducing a new line of fruit drinks featuring 25 percent real fruit juice. The brand name is well-known. What type of consumer decision process would you expect in this situation? How would that affect promotional strategy?

2. Would you expect purchasers to develop high brand loyalty once they have tried and liked this new fruit-based soft drink? Why? What difference would this make in ongoing promotional strategy?

3. Refer back to the battle between Liquid Tide and Wisk for market share (p. 170). If you were the brand manager for Liquid Tide, what would your

strategy be, given the apparent competitive standoff between these two brands?

4. Liquid Tide sales have grown in part from cannibalizing (taking sales from) traditional powdered Tide. Can this be prevented? What strategy would you suggest?

5. The "American Way of Buying" survey in *The Wall Street Journal* found that 53 percent of today's car buyers switch brands.[26] This has happened because of the explosive growth in the number of competing models and in the number of automobile showrooms. Also, American manufacturers have suffered from serious competitive inroads made by Japanese and European imports.

    You are the manager of a large Ford dealership in a major U.S. city and have been mandated by the owner to do all you can to retain a larger percentage of customers who have bought their cars from you. What will your strategy be?

6. Consumers over the age of 50 use a disproportionately large amount of aspirin but have been largely ignored by advertisers. Therefore, the Bristol-Myers Squibb Bufferin brand is being targeted for the over-50 crowd.[27] Advertising emphasizes that people over 50 can lead full lives despite occasional aches and pains that come with age. Print ads ran in women's service magazines and other targeted periodicals such as *Modern Maturity.*

    Design a point-of-sale strategy that will stimulate brand switching and trial to complement this advertising campaign.

NOTES

1. Harold E. Kassarjian, "Consumer Research: Some Recollections and a Commentary," in *Advances in Consumer Research*, ed. Richard J. Lutz, vol. 13 (Provo, Utah: Association for Consumer Research, 1986), pp. 6–8.

2. Prem N. Shamdasani and Dennis W. Rook, "An Exploratory Study of Impulse Buying in an Oriental Culture: The Case of Singapore," *Singapore Marketing Review* 4 (1989), pp. 7–20.

3. For a discussion of this interesting motivation, see Wayne D. Hoyer and Nancy M. Ridgway, "Variety Seeking as an Explanation for Exploratory Purchase Behavior: A Theoretical Model," in *Advances in Consumer Research*, ed. Thomas C. Kinnear, vol. 11 (Provo, Utah: Association for Consumer Research, 1984), pp. 114–19.

4. Meryl Paula Gardner and Dennis W. Rook, "Effects of Impulse Purchases on Consumers' Affective States," in *Advances in Consumer Research*, ed. Michael J. Houston, vol. 15 (Provo, Utah: Association for Consumer Research, 1987), pp. 127–30.

5. For a discussion of noncompensatory decision rules, see James F. Engel, Roger D. Blackwell, and Paul W. Miniard, *Consumer Behavior*, 6th ed. (Hinsdale, Ill.: Dryden Press, 1989), pp. 527–29; and James R. Bettman, *An Information Processing Theory of Consumer Choice* (Reading, Mass.: Addison-Wesley, 1979), pp. 181–82.

─────── **173** ───────
Chapter 6
Understanding the
Consumer: Limited and
Habitual Decision-Process
Behavior

6. Engel et al., *Consumer Behavior,* pp. 527–29.

7. See, for example, David Grether and Louis Wilde, "An Analysis of Conjunctive Choice: Theory and Experiments, *Journal of Consumer Research* 10 (March 1984), pp. 373–85.

8. Patricia Sellers, "How King Kellogg Beat the Blahs," *Fortune,* August 29, 1988, p. 54.

9. Ibid.

10. Julie Liesse Erickson, "Amoco Puts Guarantee in Writing," *Advertising Age,* August 21, 1989, p. 4.

11. "Profits on Everything but the Kitchen Sink," *Business Week* (Innovation 1989 insert), p. 122.

12. Harry W. McMahan, "TV Loses the 'Name Game' but Wins Big in Personality," *Advertising Age,* December 1, 1980, p. 54.

13. *Project Payout; A Review and Appraisal of the Pilot Study in Milgram's Store #40* (New York: Advertising Research Foundation, 1980).

14. "Marketers Blunder Their Way through the 'Herb Decade,' " *Advertising Age,* February 13, 1989, p. 3.

15. Jack Trout and Al Ries, "The Decline and Fall of Advertising," *Advertising Age,* June 26, 1989, p. 20.

16. "Stalking the New Consumer," *Business Week,* August 28, 1989, p. 56.

17. Banwari Mittal, "A Framework for Relating Consumer Involvement to Lateral Brain Functioning," in *Advances in Consumer Research,* ed. Melanie Wallendorf and Paul Anderson, vol. 14 (Provo, Utah: Association for Consumer Research, 1987), pp. 41–45; and Scott S. Liu, "Picture-Image Memory of TV Advertising in Low-Involvement Situations: A Psychophysiological Analysis," in *Current Issues & Research in Advertising,* ed. Claude Martin, vol. 9 (Ann Arbor, Mich.: Division of Research, Graduate School of Business, University of Michigan, 1986), pp. 27–59.

18. "Rediscovering the Customer," The Forum Corporation, 1988.

19. Ronald Alsop, "Brand Loyalty Is Rarely Blind Loyalty," *The Wall Street Journal,* October 19, 1989, p. B8.

20. Ibid.

21. Ibid.

22. John Sterlicchi, "Beefing up Burger King," *Marketing News,* August 14, 1989, p. 5.

23. Lynn Waldsmith, "How to Succeed in a Saturated Market," *American Demographics* 10 (November 1988), pp. 42–43.

24. Scott Hume, "P&G Ad Awareness Scores Fit to Be Tide," *Advertising Age,* March 25, 1985, p. 6.

25. Laurie Freeman, "Tide Hasn't Turned Yet," *Advertising Age,* November 18, 1985, p. 43.

26. Paul Ingrassia, "Is Buying a Car a Choice or a Chore?" *The Wall Street Journal,* October 24, 1989, p. B1.

27. Pamela Winters, "Bufferin Aims at 50-Plus," *Advertising Age,* October 23, 1989, p. 4.

Influence of the Social Environment

SITTING PRETTY

Everyone talks about couch potatoes, but no one talks about the couches. This may be a mistake. After all, if "cocooning" is the serious trend many claim it to be—if the baby boomers have finally tired of the social fast lane and are busy learning to be homebodies—the furniture business is poised for some potentially heady years.

"More people are staying at home, watching their VCRs, and eating take-in food," says Pat Grable, a spokesperson for Conran's, the New York City-based retailer of so-called lifestyle furniture and accessories. Conran's has, in fact, noticed an increase in demand for couches. "People are buying our most expensive and largest," says Grable.

Baby boomers have shifted the focus of their activity from the outside world to the inside world, moving away from a world they cannot control to a world that they can: their own homes. Combine this with the generation's long-established predilection for self-expression, and the home becomes an important outgrowth of the self.

This bodes well for those in the furniture business, but only if it understands with whom it's dealing. The baby boomers have long been used to a variety and quality of goods and service that the furniture industry as a whole has not been accustomed to supplying. An industry in which the highest-quality goods have always been reserved for professional decorators and their wealthy clients, and in

which consumer orders routinely entail months of waiting, is bound
to break down in the face of a maturing generation hell-bent on
expressing itself and not interested in waiting even a little.

Source: Jeremy Schlosberg, "Sitting Pretty," *American Demographics* 10 (May
1988), pp. 24–28. Used by special permission.

Chapter 5 stressed the fact that consumer decision-process models must
take into account the social influence on choice if intentions and behaviors
are to be predicted with accuracy.[1] You have just read about the shared
values of the baby boomers, the generation of 77 million people born between 1946 and 1964. The furniture industry is just one industry forced to
adopt an all-new approach to marketing to attract this specific market.

The purpose of this chapter is to help you understand the ways in which
the social environment affects consumer motivation and behavior. We begin
by focusing on culture—the broadest component of this environment,
stressing core values of Western culture and the extent to which they vary
from one subculture to the next. From there we show how cultural patterns
are maintained and transmitted through social classes and reference
groups. We end by exploring the impact of the nuclear family on consumer
choice through varying role structures and the changes that take place over
time.

THE CULTURAL CONTEXT

The word *culture* as used in the study of human behavior refers to "the
values, ideas, artifacts, and other meaningful symbols that help individuals
communicate, interpret, and evaluate as members of society."[2] Culture thus
provides a set of norms and shared beliefs that mold and shape what we do,
both individually and corporately. These values are learned early in life
through the process of socialization and hence are resistant to change. This
means, of course, that the wise marketer makes every effort to understand
values and adapt to them accordingly.

Some of marketing's greatest blunders, often quite humorous, have
been made when a marketer moved from one culture or subculture to another. The following is just one of the blunders. Some marketers from the
West have assumed that "thin is beautiful" is a universal value only to
discover that many underweight women in East Africa are struggling to add
pounds, not to take them off. Small wonder that weight loss products are
slow to take hold, especially in nonurban areas.

Such blunders sometimes reflect *ethnocentrism*, the philosophy that the values of one's parent culture are superior to those of another. Only after picking up the pieces from marketing wreckage does it become apparent that such judgments will lead only to failure on the word market.

Even more dangerous is an uncritical acceptance of what has come to be known as *global marketing* where essentially the same strategy is used in all contexts on the assumption that cultures are pretty much alike.[3] In 1984, the management at the Parker Pen Company discovered to its dismay that standardized advertising in 154 countries would lead to bankruptcy and reorganization.[4] Observers commented that this uniform approach represented the "lowest common-denominator advertising that tried to say something to everybody, but didn't say anything to anybody."[5]

It is far wiser to engage in *contextualized marketing*,[6] which considers cultural differences and adapts accordingly. It is encouraging that well over half of U.S. companies tailor their ads to European Common Market countries, compared with only 10 percent that did so in 1973.[7] The Coca-Cola Company, for example, produced 21 different versions of its TV ads featuring children singing Coke's praises.[8]

American Values and Their Influence on Promotional Strategy

Since most readers of this text are North Americans, our discussion will focus on American values and the role they play in shaping marketing action. Those of you from other cultures should look at this section as a case history in contextualized marketing and apply the principles to your own culture.

Core Values   It is important to grasp the basic values of a society even though those values differ to some degree in various subcultures. These values determine which products and services are appropriate, the ways in which they will be used, and the connotations given to advertising and brand names. The following are some of the values that lie at the core of American society.[9]

Material well-being   Achievement and success are pervasive motivating values from one generation to the next. Indeed, having all of the comforts and luxuries of life that success can bring is almost viewed as a right. This is brought home in the Lincoln ad in Figure 7–1: You *should* have knick-nacks like Ming vases and a Lincoln as your car.

Effort, optimism, and entrepreneurship   "We have one and only one ambition. To be the best. What else is there?" So reads a series of Chrysler Corporation

FIGURE 7–1

❖❖   **The Reward of the Luxuries in Life**

Courtesy Ford Motor Company

ads featuring, of course, chief spokesperson Lee Iacocca. Americans believe in an activistic attack on problems. Individual initiative, competition, and achievement are expected and rewarded. What appeal can be more potent than "You've made it—enjoy it" (Figure 7–2).

Humanitarianism   Americans have the outlook that it is important to help the underdog, to come to the aid of the less fortunate. What better way to do this than by contributing time and effort to a worthy charity (Figure 7–3)? Not-for-profit organizations use marketing in sophisticated ways, and Americans responded by giving over $104 billion to charities in 1988.[10]

Egalitarianism   There is widespread belief that everyone should have more or less equal opportunities for achievement. No doubt Chrysler chairperson and spokesperson Lee Iacocca has captivated the American public by the way in which he exemplifies rising from an ethnic immigrant background, overcoming his firing at Ford, and emerging successfully at Chrysler. The company is wise to feature this folk hero in its ads.

The Dynamic Nature of Culture   Core values are not held uniformly through society, and they also are in flux. Culture is dynamic and changing, and it is important to understand some of the reasons why this is true.

Declining family influence   In many societies, the extended family—grandparents, uncles, aunts, and so on—is the basic social unit. When this is the case, values tend to be stable and resist change. Western societies and much of the urbanized part of the remaining world have moved or are in the process of moving from the extended family to the nuclear family. Hence, one source of value stability is removed.

Even within the nuclear family, however, social influence is becoming fragmentary. Both adults are employed outside the home in well over half of all U.S. families, resulting in the phenomenon of "weekend parenting." Further, rising divorce rates result in the majority of children living at least part of their lives in single-parent homes. All of these factors taken together mean that children are less influenced by parental values, thus further undermining the stability of core values.

Changing influence of organized religion   Judeo-Christian religious institutions have traditionally played a large role in shaping American life. This influence is declining, however, as indicated by reduced church membership, attendance, and commitment to religious faith.

At one point, religion provided the foundation of values by which justice, science, the arts, and other dimensions of society were assessed. A sense of right and wrong was rooted in an affirmation of the supernatural.

FIGURE 7-2

❖ **Nothing Succeeds like Success**

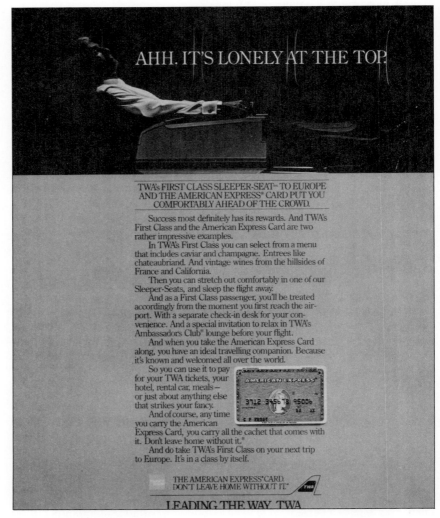

Courtesy TransWorld Airlines

Today right and wrong have become more relative and situational. The outcome of these changes is a marked diminishing of religious influence on the mainstream of life despite a continuation of religious forms and rituals in the majority of families.

In this same context, it should be noted that rejection of the religious institution does not necessarily imply diminished interest in the divine or supernatural. Quite the opposite is true in some quarters as is indicated by

FIGURE 7–3

Sharing Our Love

Courtesy Save the Children

the growing number of teenagers and young adults engaged in Bible study, satan worship, the occult, Eastern religions, and so on.

An enhanced role for education and media   Nature abhors a vacuum and something had to offset the diminishing role of family and religion. Education has stepped to the forefront, and one outcome is a highly educated populace in most quarters. Unfortunately, this outcome is partially offset by the failure of nearly half of inner city youth to finish high school.

Educational methods have undergone dramatic change. The teacher of today no longer is the product of the upper-middle class as was once the case. The result is communication of a wider spectrum of values and perspectives. Second, emphasis on memorization and description has decreased in favor of analytical approaches, questioning old solutions, and formulating new ones. Often education provides no correct answers, and rigid definitions of right and wrong are viewed as outmoded.

The outcome is an erosion of traditional values. Allan Bloom argued with conviction in *The Closing of the American Mind* that universities have abandoned teaching ethics and values that are part of the great traditions of philosophy and literature.[11]

Mass media, especially television, have also stepped into the vacuum and have become a primary teaching and value-shaping institution.[12] A child can be exposed to more in the way of world events, advertising, and other forms of persuasion in one day than his or her parents were in months. The media broaden perspectives and bring traditional values into conflict with the value montage of a rapidly changing world.

Changing Values between Generations   We have seen how traditional value stabilizers have been undermined with the result that change must be accepted as a way of life. This leads to some major differences from one generation to the next. Marketers are especially interested in how the baby boomers differ from those who preceded and follow them.

Preboomers   Only about 20 percent of all people alive today were born in or lived through the great depression of the 1930s. Those who remember those traumatic times were profoundly shaped by them. The relative deprivation of the depression and of World War II, which followed, was instrumental in forming such values as job security, individualism, patriotism, and material achievement. No wonder that the adult behavior of this generation has focused on material well-being and security.

Baby boomers   This generation[13] experienced childhood during the 1950s and 1960s. The critical lifetime experience of the elder boomer (born between 1946 and 1955), in particular, was shaped by such factors as the nuclear age, the civil rights movement, the paradox of continued poverty in an economy of affluence, ecological concern, the divisive effects of the Vietnam War, and a revolution in technology.

The influence of these events on the elder boomer has been accentuated by the declining influence of the nuclear family and deprivation centering around the absence of love and meaningful relationships. Thus, for many, current life motivations are highly focused on their own nuclear family and human relationships. Material achievement and a high standard of living are *assumed* because the economic climate encountered on entering the job market was highly favorable for upward mobility.

The younger boomer (born between 1956 and 1964) was affected by the same influences but faced quite a different economic challenge on graduation from college. The economy was in a state of recession, and employment and upward mobility were not guaranteed. Therefore, economic achievement is a more powerful motivator for the younger boomer. This group spawned the now largely discredited hedonistic lifestyle of the Yuppie.

The net result, of course, is that boomers differ from their parents. Boomers are more entrepreneurial and open to change. They have a high tolerance for diversity and desire for instant gratification. As you will read in Promotion in Action 7–1, these characteristics have some real implications for marketing.

One dominant motivation, the prime importance of the family, is common to both boomer segments. The home assumes a central role as a haven as boomers seek to turn inward in a rapidly changing world. In spite of high divorce rates, a successful marriage and a well-functioning family lie at the heart of the boomer's dream. Notice how effectively these important lifestyle themes are picked up by Hennessy Cognac (Figure 7–4).

It is interesting to note that boomers lead all age segments in their interest in philanthropies. They are willing to volunteer personally and to contribute financially.[14] This is a positive manifestation of greater interest in the welfare of others.

Postboomers   Not surprisingly, the generation of young adults born after 1964 has been labeled the *baby busters*. Whatever you wish to call them, those currently on campus and recently graduated show a different pattern of values as compared with the elder boomer but have much in common with the younger boomer.

The crucial lifetime experiences of postboomers have been affected by the energy crisis, massive inflation, growing tax burdens, and feminism. The moral philosophy now focuses on "help myself." Today, as General Foods Corporation proclaims in its ads for Crystal Light, it is "OK to believe in me" (see Figure 7–5). Now the individual is encouraged to take personal responsibility for success, hence the distinct turn to business and other career-oriented college majors.

Can Marketing Change Culture?   Some critics claim that the mass media and the marketing system are largely responsible for certain adverse effects of Western culture as we know it today.[15] Advertising, in particular, is identified as the villain that has brought about undue emphasis on materialism, eroticism, and so on.

We have argued thus far that *marketing must reflect the values of society.* This statement is based on our pervasive paradigm of consumer sovereignty in which the individual processes those stimuli seen to be relevant to values, motivations, and needs. Marketers have no choice but to adapt to them and certainly do not possess the ability to affect society in any major way.

❖
PROMOTION IN ACTION 7–1

Boomers: The Promised Land?

No social phenomenon has been more carefully chronicled, more thoroughly researched, or more shamelessly exploited than the baby boomers. As the advertising agency for BMW and Club Med, we have done our part.

If you care to memorize any single thing about baby boomers, memorize this! *Change* to a baby boomer represents opportunity—a positive force—something to be eagerly sought. *Change* to my father's generation was anathema, something to be avoided unless absolutely essential, a threat.

Age isn't the determining factor in appealing to baby boomers. Note their affection for old houses. What they crave is authenticity. They will go for fresh vegetables and natural-fiber clothes regardless of price. For years, we have trumpeted BMW's obsession for purity and functionality, as well as the company's abhorrence of gadgets and frivolity.

Baby boomers do not find the prospect of bloodless, plodding competence inspirational. On the contrary, it calls up visions of gray-faced serfs slowly grinding the wheels of a bureaucracy they loathe and consider a failure. An important concept to pin on the wall for both marketers and politicians is that baby boomers' mistrust of institutions runs very deep.

The implications for the future? We believe that no single group of Americans will ever generate as much fundamental change as the baby boomers will within the decade.

Our research indicates, for example, that the boomers are in the process of redefining the very idea of success itself. If success in the greedy '80s centered around the idea of how much money one made, success in the '90s will be about the ability to control one's life.

Source: Martin Ford Puris, "Lessons for Baby-Boom Futurists," *Advertising Age*, June 26, 1989, p. 24. Used by special permission.

FIGURE 7–4

My Favorite Name Is Dad ❖

Courtesy Schieffelin & Somerset Company

FIGURE 7–5

❖ **I Believe in Me!**

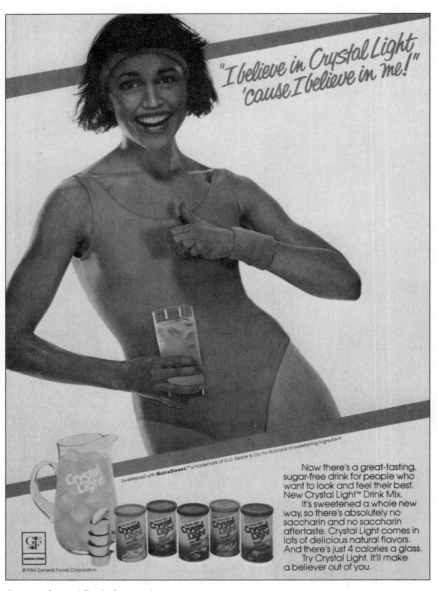

Courtesy General Foods Corporation

The marketing system as a whole, however, is another matter. We cannot deny that the cumulative impact of marketing efforts is another institutional determinant of value structures in much the same manner as family, religion, and education are. Although we find that marketing's critics often overstate their cases, they express a legitimate ethical concern that we will explore in more depth in Chapter 24.

Subcultures

Society as a whole has a great many ethnic subcultures with a distinct set of values and norms. Marketers are increasingly finding that they cannot treat Hispanics, Chinese, Koreans, and other groups as being an indistinct part of a cultural melting pot.

To illustrate what we mean, take the example of the Hispanic market now totaling nearly 20 million people in the United States. Those of Mexican origin are in the majority and are concentrated in the Southwest. The remainder are mostly Puerto Rican (about 15 percent) and Cuban (7 percent). Although most are bilingual, it is a great mistake to assume that they can be reached adequately in English. The majority speak Spanish in the home and think in Spanish.

The following is a brief sketch of some major distinguishing characteristics of Hispanics.[16] In general, they place a premium on quality and are brand loyal. Perhaps because many Hispanics are seeking status symbols to demonstrate that they have "arrived," couponing and discounting often fail in the Hispanic markets. The extended family accompanied by strong bonds of togetherness is of great importance. Appealing to individuals as a sales tactic usually fails.

Personal appearance is important to both sexes. The Hispanic male can be quite sensitive to image and will buy products such as cigarettes that connote "machismo." The Hispanic woman, on the other hand, is more emotional and will buy what she believes is best for her family.

Admittedly, this is an all-too-brief review of ethnic subculture, but it is important for you to recognize the sales potential that exists. Business firms are rapidly recognizing that Hispanic markets, in particular, can be quite profitable. The story of Hills Brothers' success in increasing coffee sales appears in Promotion in Action 7–2.

SOCIAL STRATIFICATION

Social class refers to the grouping of people who are similar in their behavior based on their economic position in the marketplace. Although this is often only a statistical way to describe people's status, social class can unquestionably be a powerful motivator.

Broadly speaking, an individual's social position is determined by several factors: (1) occupational prestige (often believed to be the most accurate predictor), (2) performance within an occupational class as evaluated by others, (3) social interaction and acceptance, (4) possessions, (5) value orientations, and (6) class consciousness. Income, by the way, is no longer

---

❖ PROMOTION IN ACTION 7–2

Hills Bros. Push Percolates from Bottom to Top

Of the nation's 19 million Hispanics, 32 percent reside in California, a state that accounts for roughly 20 percent of instant coffee consumption, says Laura Lynn Liptai, Hills Bros. coffee product manager. "You've got a big instant coffee market, coupled with a very big Hispanic community."

By conducting focus groups and performing quantitative analysis, the company discovered a market of "particularly significant users of instant, and we weren't even catering to it," stated Kenneth Hogue, Los Angeles division sales manager.

Hills Bros.' research revealed that many of the area's Mexican immigrants use instant coffee to make *cafe con leche,* a mixture of warm milk and instant coffee, and that many Hispanic parents serve the mix to their children. "A number of studies show that Hispanics drink 30 percent more coffee than the Anglo population," adds Ms. Liptai.

A decision was made to test Hills Bros. and MJB instant coffees in the Los Angeles area, where nearly 4 million Hispanics reside. The MJB spot, in which a mother takes an instant coffee break after sending her children off to school and husband off to work, uses the theme, "When it's time for coffee, savor the moment with a rich delicious cup of MJB." The ad played on the idea of mother and family, an effective pitch in the Hispanic market.

The Hills Bros. instant spot touched on a similar theme, focusing on Hispanic women as gracious hostesses. During a discussion of the just-finished dinner, the hostess says her recipe for coffee was simple: Hills Bros. instant. The guests agree that the coffee was perfect for *sobremesa,* the time spent talking at the table after the meal is complete.

Test results show a 15 to 20 percent increase in sales for both brands based on pre- and postevaluation studies.

Source: Adapted from Alice Z. Cuneo, "Hills Bros. Push Percolates from Bottom to Top," *Advertising Age,* February 13, 1989, p. S–1. Used by special permission.

an accurate measure for the simple reason that pay and social status are not necessarily correlated.

Value orientations and class consciousness all provide interesting data for the marketer. The data summarized in Table 7–1 will give you some idea of how these differ from one class to another. As you might expect, class consciousness is greater in the higher classes. When this is the case, advertisers can have a potent appeal using appropriate words and symbols. (See the two ads in Figure 7–6.)

Although social class often assumes greater importance elsewhere in the world, do not assume that it is dead in the United States. Gronhaug and Trapp found that consumers often associate brands with particular social classes and will buy those that most closely correspond with the social class image they have of themselves.[17]

Beer is a product with interesting social class perceptions.[18] In the past, it was largely considered to be a lower-class beverage. But beer has increased in social prestige over the years, largely, we believe, as a result of marketing efforts. Not surprisingly, brands vary in image. Heineken is primarily considered to be an upper/upper-middle class brand, whereas Old Style is perceived to be the product of the lower classes.

This stratification also occurs in retailing. Marshall Field has, at least in the past, been considered to be a store for the upper/upper-middle classes, and K mart is mainly seen as being a store for the working class.[19]

Space limits further description, but extensive evidence reveals important differences between classes in motivation, search, alternative evaluation, and purchasing behavior, which are worthy of your study.[20]

REFERENCE GROUPS

Before you read further, turn to Promotion in Action 7–3 on p. 194, which gives you the interesting story of how the products of Mary Kay Cosmetics, Inc., are marketed largely through personal influence. This illustrates the fact that all of us at times emulate the values and actions of those whom we admire highly. When attitude and behavior are affected in this way, others serve as a *reference group.*

How Reference Groups Function

Reference groups influence choice by exerting influence in three primary ways: (1) utilitarian (normative), (2) value-expressive, and (3) informational.

TABLE 7-1

❖

Social Classes Are Alive and Well in America

Upper Upper

Upper uppers are the social elite of society. Inherited wealth from socially prominent families is the key to admission. Children attend private preparatory schools and graduate from the best colleges.

Consumers in the upper-upper class spend money as if it were unimportant, not tightly but not with display either, for that would imply that money is important. For some products a trickle-down influence may exist between social classes. The social position of these individuals is so secure that they can deviate from class norms if they choose to without losing status.

Lower Upper

Lower uppers include the very high-income professional people who have earned their position rather than inherited it. They are the *nouveaux riches,* active people with many material symbols of their status. They buy the largest homes in the best suburbs, the most expensive automobiles, swimming pools and other symbols of conspicuous consumption, making them innovators and good markets for luxury marketing offerings.

Upper Middle

The key word for upper middles is *career.* Careers are based on successful professional or graduate degrees for a specific profession or the skill of business administration. Members of this class are demanding of their children in educational attainment.

The *quality* market for many products is the upper-middle class and gracious living in a conspicuous but careful manner characterizes the family's lifestyle. The home is of high importance and an important symbol of the family's success and competence.

Lower Middle

Lower-middle class families are typical Americans, exemplifying the core of respectability, conscientious work habits, and adherence to culturally defined norms and standards. They believe in attending church and obeying the law and are upset when their children are arrested for law violations. They are not innovators.

The *home* is very important to the lower-middle family and they want it to be neat, well-painted, and in a respected neighborhood. They may have little confidence in their own tastes and adopt standardized home furnishings—perhaps from Levitz or similar furniture stores. This is in contrast to the upper-middle consumer who feels freer to experiment with new styles and new arrangements and with the upper-lower consumer who is not very concerned about the overall plan for furnishing the home: The lower-middle consumer reads and follows the advice of the medium-level shelter and service magazines in an attempt to make the house pretty.

The lower-middle class consumer works more at shopping than others and considers purchase decisions demanding and tedious. He/She may have a high degree of price sensitivity.

Utilitarian (Normative) Influence   Reference group influence is strongest when it includes pressures to comply with *group norms* (i.e., stable performance expectations based on consensus). Many studies over the years have demonstrated how conformity pressures impact buying decisions.[21] Normative influences are especially likely to come into play when the product is socially conspicuous in use and when social acceptance is a strong motivator.[22]

Value Expressive Influence   Reference groups also can perform a value-expressive role when a need for psychological association is met by conforming to the values and behavior of others, even when there is no direct contact. The benefit hopefully is enhanced social image through the adopted values and actions.

TABLE 7–1

Social Classes Are Alive and Well in America (concluded)

Upper Lower

Upper-lower social classes exhibit a routine life, characterized by a day-to-day existence of unchanging activities. They live in dull areas of the city, in small houses or apartments. The hard hats are included in this class, with many members working at uncreative jobs requiring manual activity or only moderate skills and education. Because of unions and security, many may earn incomes that give them considerable discretionary income.

The purchase decisions of the working class are often impulsive but at the same time may show high brand loyalty to national brands. Buying them is one way to prove knowledge as a buyer, a role in which he/she feels (probably correctly) that he/she has little skill. This consumer has little social contact outside the home and does not like to attend civic organizations or church activities. Social interaction is limited to close neighbors and relatives. If he/she takes a vacation, it will probably be a visit to relatives in another city. Upper lowers are concerned that they not be confused with the lower lowers.

Lower Lower

The lower-lower social class contains people who may try to rise above their class but usually fail to do so. An individual in the lower-lower class often rejects middle class morality and gets pleasure wherever possible—and this includes buying impulsively. This lack of planning causes purchases that cost too much and may result in inferior goods. This person pays too much for products, buys on credit at a high interest rate, and has difficulty obtaining quality or value. This group includes highly distressed families, some who have habitual legal problems, and the homeless.

Source: James F. Engel, Roger D. Blackwell, and Paul D. Miniard, *Consumer Behavior,* 6th ed. (Hinsdale, Ill.: Dryden Press, 1990), p. 117. Reproduced by special permission.

FIGURE 7–6

 Social Status Can Be a Potent Appeal

I was born the second son.

I graduated second in my law school class.

And finished second in the Cannes-Marrakesh Rally (twice).

Recently, however, I acquired a Waterman.

How delightful to feel first, at last.

Pens write. A Waterman pen expresses. For more than a century, this distinction has remained constant. In the precise, painstaking tooling, for example. In the meticulous balancing. In layer upon layer of brilliant lacquers. In accents gilded with precious metal. Those who desire such an instrument of expression will find Waterman pens in a breadth of styles, prices and finishes.

WATERMAN
PARIS

© 1988 Waterman Pen Company

Courtesy Waterman Pen Company

Informational Influence   When assessing product or brand characteristics by observation is difficult, the opinions of others are often accepted as credible. Salespeople or experts featured in ads can provide these opinions.

Determinants of Impact

Three factors determine whether reference group influence will be a factor in a given situation: (1) social visibility, (2) public display and use, and (3)

FIGURE 7–6

Social Status Can Be a Potent Appeal (concluded)

Courtesy Austin Reed of Regent Street

the extent to which the product is a public luxury.[23] These three factors are depicted in Figure 7–7, and you will gain interesting marketing insights as you read through the four quadrants. For example, reference groups do not influence the choice of a man's suit but can have a strong effect on the brand of the suit.

FAMILY INFLUENCE

The family, in contrast to most of the larger social systems we have studied in this chapter, is a *primary group* characterized by face-to-face interaction. As such, it is a special type of reference group that becomes uniquely important in decision making. The family and its status affects promotional strategy in two significant ways: (1) influence on buying decisions and (2) influence on family life-cycles. Once again, our discussion must be brief.[24]

❖
**PROMOTION
IN ACTION
7–3**

The Mary Kay Model of Personal Influence

Prior to the late 1980s, you never saw any product manufactured by Mary Kay Cosmetics, Inc., on the shelves of a retail store. The 150,000 Beauty Consultants working exclusively through Home Beauty Shows are at the heart of the Mary Kay marketing strategy.

Part of the reason for this strategy is that skin care products must be appropriate for each person's skin condition and applied correctly. Each consultant is carefully trained to diagnose skin care needs through use of the Mary Kay Beauty Profile. Then the consultant actually uses and demonstrates all phases of the Five Steps to Beauty so that each potential customer can see what they do for her.

The Home Beauty Show strategy offers some potent additional advantages, however. It creates a sense of obligation to buy at least something. A hostess invites friends and relatives to participate in a social event in her home. When the hostess is viewed as credible, her endorsement of Mary Kay products does much to influence the receptivity of those who attend. Furthermore, the positive reactions of satisfied customers can stimulate the buying interest of others. In short, direct personal social pressure is both activated and used to benefit the company.

Source: James F. Engel, Roger D. Blackwell, and Paul W. Miniard, *Consumer Behavior*, 6th ed. (Hinsdale, Ill.: Dryden Press, 1990), p. 145. Used by special permission.

Influence on Buying Decisions

A family is not a buyer or user in the strictest sense of the word because only individuals buy or use products. But the family does function as a buying center with multiple roles:

1. *Gatekeeper*—the initiator and information gatherer.
2. *Influencer*—an opinion leader who influences the decision process and the final choice.
3. *Decider*—the person with the power and/or the financial means to decide how funds will be allocated.
4. *Buyer*—the purchasing agent.
5. *User(s)*—the final user(s) of the product or service.

It is necessary to discover who plays what role within a target market segment. For example, how does this work out in the purchase of children's toys?

FIGURE 7–7

The Determinants of Reference Group Influence ❖

Publicly consumed

Brand \ Product	Weak reference group influence (−)	Strong reference group influence (+)
Strong reference group influence (+)	*Public necessities* Influence: Weak product and strong brand Examples: Wristwatch, automobile, man's suit	*Public luxuries* Influence: Strong product and brand Examples: Golf clubs, snow skies, sailboat
Weak reference group influence (−)	*Private necessities* Influence: Weak product and brand Examples: Mattress, floor lamp, refrigerator	*Private luxuries* Influence: Strong product and weak brand Examples: TV game, trash compactor, icemaker

Necessity ————————————————————————— Luxury

Privately consumed

Source: William O. Bearden and Michael J. Etzel, "Reference Group Influence on Product and Brand Purchase Decisions," *Journal of Consumer Research* 9 (September 1982), p. 185. Used by permission.

The child is the user but the buyer is probably an adult. One or both parents may be a decider, but the kids can offer some pretty potent influence. Small wonder we see Bill Cosby urging kids to tell their parents to buy Jello puddings and Pudding Pops. Is there any doubt that this helps to swing the decision?

Anyone can take influencer roles. Although the males probably are still the usual deciders on the family car, children or wives can play a major role as gatekeepers of information and expertise, and as influencers.

The roles taken by husband and wife have been of interest to marketers because of the need to identify the partner with the greatest clout. Here are the possible variations in role structures:

1. *Autonomic*—equal decisions are made by each spouse, but each person acts individually.
2. *Husband dominant.*
3. *Wife dominant.*
4. *Syncratic*—most decisions are made with both acting cooperatively.

Recent research has shed light on the way in which role structures work.[25] Some product/service categories are wife dominant: women's and children's clothing, kitchenware, toiletries, groceries, and nonprescription drugs. The two categories found to be most husband dominant are lawn mowers and hardware. Autonomic decisions are found in many categories including women's jewelry, men's suits, sporting equipment, and stereos.

Family structures have changed over time to the point where decisions are increasingly being made jointly, especially those for high involvement options. This growth in syncratic decisions has been influenced by the increase in both the egalitarian status of women and the resources they command as working wives. Time pressures also can lead to autonomic decisions and specialized roles.

You should be able to quickly grasp the strategic implications of syncratic decision making. Vacation decisions are usually made syncratically, for example, thus making it necessary to appeal to both parties, stressing common interests.

The type of information featured in ads is also affected by role structure. The wife may be interested in appearance, convenience features, and space when buying an automobile, whereas the husband may have a greater concern for performance. These differences would call for two sets of appeals, one appropriately aimed at each.

Family Life-Cycles

Families change over time and pass through a number of stages. This is referred to as *family life-cycle.* Table 7–2 provides a good summary of the essential research on this subject and is worthy of your study.

Let's take one stage from Table 7–2 —the first group of empty nesters—
and examine something of its significance. Not surprisingly, disposable income is high because children no longer live at home. Furthermore, fixed
expenses are less at the very time in which investments and savings are
beginning to bear fruit. This is a sizable market segment with wealth and a
proclivity to spend.

Decision styles differ. Younger empty nesters have the experience and
ability to shop and find good values. They are also more prone to use the
mass media for information than reference groups. They expect greater
satisfaction in life and are good prospects for luxury goods, travel, health
care, and a wide range of financial services.[26] They are more prone to
sacrifice economy for comfort and will give their loyalty to the manufacturer
or retailer who earns it.

TABLE 7–2

Family Life-Cycles and Buying Behavior

Single Stage

Although earnings are relatively low, they are subject to few rigid demands, so
consumers in this stage typically have substantial discretionary income. Part of this
income is used to purchase a car and basic equipment and furnishings for their first
residence away from home—usually an apartment. They tend to be more fashion and
recreation oriented, spending a substantial proportion of their income on clothing,
alcoholic beverages, food away from home, vacations, leisure time pursuits, and other
products and services involved in the mating game.

Newly Married Couples

Newly married couples without children are usually better off financially than they
have been in the past and will be in the near future because the wife is usually
employed. Families at this stage also spend a substantial amount of their income on
cars, clothing, vacations, and other leisure time activities. They also have the highest
purchase rate and highest average purchase of durable goods, particularly furniture
and appliances, and other expensive items, and appear to be more susceptible to
advertising in this stage.

Full Nest I

With the arrival of the first child, some wives stop working outside the home, and
consequently family income declines. Simultaneously, the young child creates new
problems that change the way the family spends its income. The couple is likely to
move into its first home, purchase furniture and furnishings for the child, buy a
washer, dryer, and home maintenance items, and purchase such products as baby
food, chest rubs, cough medicine, vitamins, toys, wagons, sleds, and skates. These
requirements reduce family savings and the husband and wife are often dissatisfied
with their financial position.

TABLE 7–2

❖ **Family Life-Cycles and Buying Behavior** (concluded)

Full Nest II

At this stage the youngest child is six or over, the husband's income has improved, and the wife often returns to work outside the home. Consequently, the family's financial position usually improves. Consumption patterns continue to be heavily influenced by the children as the family tends to buy food and cleaning supplies in larger sized packages, bicycles, pianos, and music lessons.

Full Nest III

As the family grows older, its financial position usually continues to improve because the husband's income rises, the wife returns to work or enjoys a higher salary, and the children earn money from occasional employment. The family typically replaces several pieces of furniture, purchases another automobile, buys several luxury appliances, and spends a considerable amount of money on dental services and education for the children.

Empty Nest I

At this stage the family is most satisfied with their financial position and the amount of money saved because income has continued to increase, and the children have left home and are no longer financially dependent on their parents. The couple often makes home improvements, buys luxury items, and spends a greater proportion of its income on vacations, travel, and recreation.

Empty Nest II

By this time the household head has retired and so the couple usually suffers a noticeable reduction in income. Expenditures become more health oriented, centering on such items as medical appliances, medical care products that aid health, sleep, and digestion, and perhaps a smaller home, apartment, or condominium in a more agreeable climate.

The Solitary Survivor

If still in the labor force, solitary survivors still enjoy good income. They may sell their home and usually spend more money on vacations, recreation, and the types of health-oriented products and services mentioned above.

The Retired Solitary Survivor

The retired solitary survivor follows the same general consumption pattern except on a lower scale because of the reduction in income. In addition, these individuals have special needs for attention, affection, and security.

Source: James F. Engel, Roger D. Blackwell, and Paul W. Miniard, *Consumer Behavior,* 6th ed. (Hinsdale, Ill.: Dryden Press, 1990), p. 180. Used by special permission.

Recent developments in health research are a frequent basis for food advertising. These ads appeal both to beauty/weight concerns addressed by new low-fat products (top) and to the less glamorous dietary considerations of fiber and cholesterol (bottom).

I LOVED HAAGEN-DAZS BUT HATED ALL THE FAT AND CALORIES!

Élan. The premium frozen yogurt bar.

Metamucil fiber gives you 8 times more

of what you're eating oat bran for. (Without the fat and calories.)

Metamucil is natural soluble fiber—the same kind of fiber that makes oat bran so good for you. In fact, if you're looking for soluble fiber, Metamucil is one of the richest sources you can find.

Ounce for ounce, Metamucil fiber has eight times more of this remarkable health fiber than oat bran. That's right. Eight times.

And that's important. Because if you want the benefits of oat bran, you have to eat lots of it—far more than a mere muffin a day can provide!

That's how Metamucil can help. Metamucil is so concentrated, a single spoonful has as much

soluble fiber as nearly three oat bran muffins or two bowls of oatmeal. With absolutely zero fat and only five calories per spoonful (sugar-free).

Doctors have been recommending Metamucil as a source of extra fiber for regularity for more than 50 years. Medical researchers are finding out even more good news about soluble fiber and its benefits.

For better health, doctors say you should eat a balanced, high-fiber diet that includes plenty of soluble fiber. Adding Metamucil to your diet can make it easy.

Natural Soluble Fiber Metamucil. It can make a daily difference in your health.

The sales of nonalcoholic beverages like Buckler are on the rise because of increased concern and publicity over health problems associated with drinking and the obviously worrying issue of drunk driving.

LOOKS LIKE A BEER.
SMELLS LIKE A BEER.
TASTES LIKE A BEER.

SURPRISE.

It's Buckler Non-Alcoholic Brew from Heineken.

Now you can get the rich, refreshing taste of an import in a non-alcoholic brew—Buckler. But this shouldn't come as a surprise; it's brewed by Heineken. So the next time you'd really like a beer but could do without the alcohol, try Buckler. All the imported taste you want, and none of the alcohol you don't.

Imported by Van Munching & Co., Inc., New York, NY
BUCKLER CONTAINS LESS THAN 0.5% ALCOHOL BY VOLUME

In an age of quickly changing communications technology, this AT&T ad (top) appeals to readers on the basis of the company's longevity and stability. By the same token, this Wausau ad (bottom) matches the country's increased tendency to value tradition. The nostalgic treatment in this ad lends a comforting air to the idea of insurance.

As computers and other complex technologies become an increasingly large part of our lives, the marketers of new technologies have to find ways to overcome fear and indifference. One method, which these ads use, is to relate the complex to the simple. Thus, these ads equate new computer devices to something simple for uninitiated consumers to relate to: food.

This is what you pay for our modems.

This is what you get.

A lot of companies offer low priced modems. There's only one problem. They're not Everex. Our modems are engineered, not cloned. So you get built-in support features to make installation, testing and verification a breeze. They also come with the most comprehensive manuals in the industry. And our line covers everything from internals to fax modems. To find out more, call 1-800-821-0806 for the name of your nearest Everex Reseller.

Chances are, you'll get more modem than you need. For less money than you'd expect.

EVEREX

Imagine what a Canon Color Laser Copier could do with a pie chart.

The Canon Color Laser Copier 200 could do a lot for your business. And Digital Image Processing is the reason.

Now copies from graphics, slides and photos look more lifelike while text stays pure black. Reproduction is comparable to professional printing with 256 gradations per color and 400 dots per inch resolution.

And with 50% to 400% zoom and advanced editing, as well as automatic feeding and sorting functions and a quick 20 black-and-white copies per minute, it's one color copier that's all business.

To find out more, call 1-800-OK-CANON, or write us at Canon USA Inc., P.O. Box 3900, Peoria, IL 61614.

Canon COLOR LASER COPIER 200
The Digital Difference.

SUMMARY

This chapter has analyzed the impact of social environment on promotional strategy, beginning with culture, the broadest level, and working progressively downward to subcultures, social stratification, reference groups, and the nuclear family.

The chapter showed that certain American core values are generally common to all of its society. Among these values are individual achievement, entrepreneurship, and so on. Values differ, however, from one generation or subculture to the next, and this is especially true with the baby boomers. The individual firm has no choice but to accept these values as given and build on them in marketing strategy.

Social stratification is expressed in the form of social classes. We sometimes mistakenly view the United States as a classless society, but this is not the case. At times, class consciousness is a factor in the choices that people make.

Social influence is also expressed through reference groups, those entities whose standards are accepted as evidence about reality. Buying action is strongly influenced when pressures to conform exist and the individual is motivated to comply with them. When this is the case, social acceptance can be a potent promotional appeal.

Finally, the family was discussed from the perspectives of family role structures, decision styles, and life-cycles. First, the family often functions as a buying unit with various members performing different roles. It is especially important to identify and appeal to those who most affect the choices made, even though they may not be the purchasing agent.

Our focus then shifted to life-cycles, the changes that take place in motivation and behavior as the family progresses from early marriage through various stages to retirement. Major changes from one stage to the next present real opportunities for the sensitive marketer who understands those changes.

REVIEW AND DISCUSSION QUESTIONS

1. The trade press stresses the baby-boomer generation's common outlook and behavior as well as the differences between elder boomers (born between 1946 and 1955) and younger boomers (born between 1956 and 1964). You are assigned the responsibility to convince a largely baby-boomer community to vote positively for a waste disposal plan that features paper, glass, and aluminum recycling. What would your strategy be? Would it differ for younger and elder boomers?

2. The manager of a new brand of soft drink containing 25 percent real fruit juices is pondering whether to attempt to penetrate the Hispanic market in

California and other western states. What are the major considerations? If you were called in as a marketing consultant, what would your counsel be?

3. A well-known appliance manufacturer is introducing a new electric range product featuring a standard convection oven, a microwave oven, and an automatic timing system allowing each to be used simultaneously to deliver a completely cooked meal at a chosen time. The price is about $400 more than for a convection oven and a microwave oven purchased separately. It is believed that promotion should be aimed toward upper-middle-class families. Do you agree that the market is segmented by social class? What strategy do you recommend?

4. A line of men's suits displays on its label, "Made in America with All-Union Labor." How would receptivity to this appeal vary from one social class to the next?

5. The Levi Strauss Company has introduced a new line of all-cotton casual wear for young adults. Management is convinced that reference group influence is significantly high. How would this be expressed, in your opinion? What promotional strategy would you suggest?

6. A new line of relatively inexpensive and easy-to-apply wallpapers has been introduced by a company well-known for its quality paint and decorating products. Ads will run in *Family Circle, People*, and *Good Housekeeping*. What type of family role structure would you expect to be operable in making decisions to purchase this wallpaper? Would this affect advertising targeting and message? Why or why not? What strategy would be best?

NOTES

1. Social influence is an important component of reasoned action and multiattribute models. See Icek Ajzen and Martin Fishbein, *Understanding Attitudes and Predicting Social Behavior* (Englewood Cliffs, N.J.: Prentice Hall, 1980).

2. James F. Engel, Roger D. Blackwell, and Paul W. Miniard, *Consumer Behavior,* 6th ed. (Hinsdale, Ill.: Dryden Press, 1990), p. 63.

3. This term was popularized by Theodore Levitt, "The Globalization of Markets," *Harvard Business Review* (May–June 1976), pp. 106–18.

4. Joseph M. Winski and Laurel Wentz, "Parker Pen: What Went Wrong? Why Company Global Marketing Plan Floundered," *Advertising Age,* June 2, 1986, pp. 1 ff.

5. Ibid.

6. James F. Engel, "Toward the Contextualization of Consumer Behavior," in *Historical Perspectives in Consumer Research: National and International Perspectives,* ed. Chin Tong Tan and Jagdish N. Sheth (Singapore: National University of Singapore, 1985), pp. 1–5.

7. Julie Skur Hill and Joseph M. Winski, "Goodbye Global Ads," *Advertising Age,* November 16, 1987, pp. 16ff.

8. Ibid.

9. The discussion here closely follows Engel et al., *Consumer Behavior,* pp. 68–77.

10. "Charitable Giving Reaches All-Time High," *Fund Raising Management,* July 1989, p. 7.

11. Allan Bloom, *The Closing of the American Mind* (New York: Simon & Schuster, 1987).

12. The literature on this subject is vast. A good source is Charles R. Wright, *Mass Communication, A Sociological Perspective* (New York: Random House, 1986).

13. Must reading for those interested in knowing more about baby boomers is Cheryl Russell, *100 Predictions for the Baby Boom—The Next 50 Years* (New York: Plenum Press, 1987).

14. Virginia Ann Hodgkinson and Murray S. Weitzman, *The Charitable Behavior of Americans* (Washington, D.C.: Independent Sector, 1987).

15. See especially Michael Schudson, *Advertising, The Uneasy Persuasion: Its Dubious Impacts on American Society* (New York: Basic Books, 1984).

16. See, for example, Art Insana, "Spanish Flies," *Advertising Age,* special insert, 1989, pp. 18 ff.; and Marty Westerman, "Death of Frito Bandito," *American Demographics* 11 (March 1989), pp. 28 ff.

17. Kjell Gronhaug and Paul S. Trapp, "Perceived Social Class Appeals of Branded Goods," *The Journal of Consumer Marketing* 5 (Fall 1988), pp. 25–30.

18. Ibid.

19. Ibid.

20. See Engel et al., *Consumer Behavior,* chap. 4.

21. See, for example, Paul W. Miniard and Joel E. Cohen, "Modeling Personal and Normative Influences on Behavior," *Journal of Consumer Research* 10 (September 1983), pp. 169–180 and William D. Bearden and Michael J. Etzel, "Reference Group Influence on Product and Brand Purchase Decisions," *Journal of Consumer Research* 9 (September 1982), pp. 177–89.

22. Bearden and Etzel, *Journal of Consumer Research.*

23. Ibid.

24. For a thorough review, see Engel, Blackwell, and Miniard, *Consumer Behavior,* ch 6.

25. Mandy Putman and William R. Davidson, *Family Purchasing Behavior: II Family Roles by Product Category* (Columbus, Ohio: Management Horizons, Inc.: A Division of Price Waterhouse, 1987).

26. Mandy Puttman, Sharyn Brooks, and William R. Davidson, *The Expanded Management Horizons Consumer Market Matrix* (Columbus, Ohio: Management Horizons, Inc.: A Division of Price Waterhouse, 1986).

BASIC CONSIDERATIONS IN PROMOTIONAL STRATEGY

Now that we have thoroughly explored persuasive communication, it is time to explore in more detail the basic components of promotional strategy formulation.

Of course, the foremost consideration in any strategy is potential: the market's potential and the company's competitive positioning in it. These factors are discussed in Chapter 8, where we address competitive considerations and wrestle with definitions of the consumer segments (or market targets) where the opportunity is greatest, plus the key issues in the positioning of products relative to consumer needs and competitive products. This chapter lays the foundation for much of what follows in the book.

Next we will turn our attention to determination of promotional objectives (Chapter 9). We will look at the role of each element of the promotional mix in attaining those objectives. As you will see, the roles change sharply, depending upon whether the consumer believes the product or service requires extended problem solving, limited problem solving, or routine behavior.

The next consideration (Chapter 10) is budgeting and allocation. Traditionally budgets have been determined on a percentage-of-sales basis, but this can result in a grossly inadequate allocation. No phase of promotional planning presents greater challenges.

Ultimately, promotional plans are toothless without a strong organization to implement them. Chapter 11 explores the human resource dimension. Here, we cover the issues connected with the use of advertising agencies and other outside services.

Chapter 12 addresses the remaining major consideration—the legal climate. In a sense, laws and regulations "define the playing field" for all that we do. Therefore, we have summarized the chief constraints that you must know to stay within this "field."

Market Segmentation and Competitive Positioning

PASTA SAUCE MAKERS USE SEGMENTATION AND POSITIONING

Although true Italians may still cringe at the very thought of using pasta sauce from a jar, the $767.3 million pasta sauce market indicates that many Americans are using it. In an age when health and convenience often rule, pasta and ready-made pasta sauces are increasingly popular. According to Arbitron/SAMI, although 1979 sauce production totaled 545 million pounds, 1988 sauce production topped 1.93 billion pounds and sales increased 9 percent over the previous year. Ragu, Prego, Classico, Hunt, and Aunt Millie are the market's top five brands. According to figures based on the 52 weeks ended March 29, 1989, sales totals were $489 million for Ragu, $252 million for Prego, $61 million for Classico, $36 million for Hunt, and $26 million for Aunt Millie.

The high volume in the sauce segment attracts a lot of promotional dollars. According to the Leading National Advertisers, the top five sauce brands spent more than $52 million on advertising last year. TV accounted for $43.3 million of this media expense. New products and line extensions are prime targets for consumer promotions, with battles for market share and shelf space expected to be heated. Timothy Dunn, senior investment officer with PNC Financial noted, "It's a volume business. Name recognition is important, but I don't think people really see much difference between Ragu versus Prego. In bulk spaghetti sauces, people are probably not going to buy generic, but as long as it's one of the main brands, they'll buy whatever they can get a deal on." Keeping this in mind, the top five marketers use positioning and segmentation to increase their market share and sales.

Market leader Ragu, which holds half of the sauce market, spent $20.6 million on advertising last year, with $15.3 million going to network TV. Pursuing a strategy of protecting its market share, Ragu has remained "King of the Shelf" through its ability to quickly adapt to a changing market. Ragu and Chef-Boy-Ar-Dee dominated the national market until Hunt came out with Prima Salsa in the mid-1970s. The new sauce was positioned as "heartier," so Chesebrough countered with Thick & Zesty Ragu. Prima Salsa was pulled off the market by the early 1980s. Campbell introduced Prego in 1982, stressing its homemade taste. Ragu countered with its Homestyle line. When "chunky" became the rage in spaghetti sauce, Ragu introduced its Chunky Garden Style sauce with chunks of tomatoes and vegetables. "Thick and rich" were in style in 1987, so Ragu premiered its Thick & Hearty line. Ragu's versatility enables the leading sauce maker to effectively execute its strategy of keeping up with the market and maintaining its share.

Since its 1982 entrance into the market, Prego has positioned itself as a high-quality sauce that is "better than Ragu." Executing an image campaign, Prego ads feature a visual comparison with Ragu. Prego and Ragu are simultaneously poured over pasta; Prego is the thicker sauce. Gary Fassak, director of marketing of Italian Food Products at Campbell Soup Co., maker of Prego sauces, remarked, "We're trying to build long-term added value and get the word out that our sauce, in testing, tastes better than Ragu Old World Style." Campbell uses geographic segmentation. The company's regional marketing system tailors promotional programs for each of its 21 marketing areas. "The idea is to get some attention on what the local marketing needs are, particularly in the area of promotion. We try to tie back to the advertising, with the basic notion of Prego being a high-quality sauce."

Positioned as a line of authentic regional Italian pasta sauces, Classico stands apart from the other market leaders. Priced 40 to 50 cents above the other major brands, Classico is out to prove that class sells. Classico's promotional campaign centers on its regional Italian recipes, which are part of the sauces' packaging. The jars are shaped differently than those of other sauces and the label is designed for "old-world appeal." Classico targets the slightly upscale, 25- to 54-year-old segment that is willing to pay more for a premium product. TV ads are shot in Italy to further stress the product's authenticity. Maxine Houghton, marketing director for Prince Foods-Canning Division of Borden, describes the brand's strategy as a "pretty simple program of television and couponing to get trial and create awareness." Upscale magazines such as *Bon Appetit, Southern Living,* and *Sunset* have also been used.

Positioning itself as a traditional name in tomato products, Hunt uses couponing and promotions to retain its number four position. Hunt considers print an important advertising medium since recipes using its sauces can be featured to stimulate consumers' interest. *Good Housekeeping, Redbook,* and *Ladies Home Journal* are perennial favorites. In an attempt to distinguish its market position, Hunt is targeting the "busy family" market with Minute Gourmet, its new line of specialized sauces for the microwave. Each package includes one of six sauces and a cooking bag—consumers just add their choice of meat. The target segment includes busy singles, couples, and working parents.

Aunt Millie, a 42-year-old regional brand, captured the number five spot due to its solid base of loyal regional users. Sold in only 12 markets, Aunt Millie's sauce generated $26 million in sales last year with only $48,000 in ad expenditures, all of which went into newspapers. Positioning itself as the leading brand with "no sugar or starch added," Aunt Millie's original sauce has long attracted the health-conscious segment of one- and two-person households. Targeting "the sweet tooth of American children," Aunt Millie has developed a family style sauce that is sweeter and chunkier. According to Prince's Houghton, "Kids love sweet things and sweet sauces, so we brought Aunt Millie's Family Style out to attract the larger families that eat a ton of spaghetti sauce." This new segment should increase faster family volume usage.

Source: "Mangia!Mangia!" *Marketing & Media Decisions,* June 1989, pp. 83–93.

THE CONCEPT OF SEGMENTATION

The pasta sauce marketers discussed in the Promotion in Action at the beginning of this chapter are following a deliberate policy of *market segmentation: "The process of dividing large heterogeneous markets into smaller, homogeneous subsets of people or businesses with similar needs and/or responsiveness to marketing mix offerings."*[1]

In a sense, each of us is a distinct market segment because no two people are exactly alike in their motivations, needs, decision processes, and buying behavior. Obviously, it is not feasible to tailor a specific marketing mix to every individual. Thus, the objective is to identify groups within the broader market that are sufficiently similar in characteristics and responses to warrant separate marketing treatment.

Effective market segmentation requires three steps:

1. The identification of *criteria or bases* that are useful in forming the subgroups or segments of the market that are likely to respond differently to promotional activity or other marketing mix elements. This process is designed to identify *usable* market segment. Usable segments are ones that have sufficient size, have measurable potential, are reachable, and have different market response functions to marketing activity. Each of these aspects of usability is discussed later in this chapter.

2. The selection of *target markets*. This is the selection of the segment or group of segments for which a specific promotional program or programs and other elements of the marketing mix will be developed. The selected target segment or segments are those that offer the greatest opportunity for profitability given market and competitive conditions.

3. The development of a *competitive positioning* for the product or service offering within the selected segment or segments. This addresses the issue of how targeted consumers perceive your offering as compared to those of competitors.

These steps require a careful analysis of buyer motivation and behavior as discussed in the previous chapters and, in a sense, the identification of market segments is one of the most practical payoffs in marketing research. We will discuss each of these three steps in order in this chapter, but first we will discuss the issue of usable segments.

Criteria of Usable Segments

Frequently segmentation analysis produces results that are not of much use in promotional planning. Four criteria should be met: (1) the segment should be of *sufficient size* and market potential to warrant expenditure of marketing funds, (2) it must be possible to measure market potential in the segments, (3) it must be possible to *reach* the segment through available media, and (4) the segment should show clear variations in market behavior in comparison with other segments—the response of the segment to promotional variables must be different.

Sufficient Size If a total market consisted of 1 million persons, it is probably true that it has 1 million segments. Obviously, such a conclusion is of no use, because a segment must offer sufficient size and market potential to be of any significance. A leading manufacturer of paper products was confronted by this problem when it introduced a new and demonstrably different crayon in 11 test markets. Although the product appealed to a certain segment of users more than to others, it appeared that only 2 percent of a $30 million market could be captured. The possible sales revenue did not warrant the necessary expenditures to produce and market the product.

Measurability A key to assessing the size of a segment is the degree to which its purchase potential can be measured. For example, the market potential for machine vision systems in factory automation of circuit boards in the electronics industry is unknown. The size of paint inspection systems in the auto industry for the same machine vision technology is accurately known. The latter target is a more useful one for promotional planning because some sense of the likely payback is possible.

Reachability It is also critical that the marketer design a promotional program that can be delivered to the identified segment. For example, the marketers of Sunkist lemons found little or no demographic correlation with the heavy consumption of lemons. This made targeting heavy lemon users with demographic-based media such as magazines very inefficient.

Market Response Differences For any segmentation scheme to be useful, the consumers in the segments must in general respond differently to variations in promotional activity directed at the segment. Thus, we have Coke using a country version, a rock version, a blues version, and so on of its basic musical theme. The country music-oriented radio audience responds well to a country theme but not as well to some general theme or to a rock version. Without this variation between segments, the market segmentation has no point at all.

BASES FOR SEGMENTATION

A great variety of factors can be used to segment a market; many of these are itemized in Table 8–1. Bases in this table are classified as being geographic, demographic, psychographic, or behavioristic in nature. The first two classes describe the consumer's "state of being," whereas the third is related to the consumer's "state of mind."

Not all of the bases listed have proven equally useful in developing promotional strategies. Bases of a demographic or geographic type, together with selected psychographic and behavioral bases such as product usage rate, attitude toward brand, and preferred values and benefits, are the most widely used in current practice. Thus the discussion of bases for market segmentation will be limited to these, with particular attention being paid to the problems associated with measurement and analysis. Market

TABLE 8-1

❖   **Major Segmentation Variables and Their Typical Breakdowns**

Variable	Typical Breakdowns
Geographic	
Region	Pacific, Mountain, West North Central, West South Central, East North Central, East South Central, South Atlantic, Middle Atlantic, New England
County size	A, B, C, D
City or SMA size	Under 5,000, 5,000–20,000; 20,000–50,000; 50,000–100,000; 100,000–250,000; 250,000–500,000; 500,000–1,000,000; 1,000,000–4,000,000; 4,000,000 or over
Density	Urban, suburban, rural
Climate	Northern, southern
Demographic	
Age	Under 6, 6–11, 12–19, 20–34, 35–49, 50–64, 65 +
Sex	Male, female
Family size	1–2, 3–4, 5 +
Family life-cycle	Young, single; young, married, no children; young, married, youngest child under 6; young, married, youngest child 6 or over; older, married, with children; older, married, no children under 18; older single; other
Income	Under $2,500; $2,500–$5,000; $5,000–$7,500; $7,500–$10,000; $10,000–$15,000; $15,000–$20,000; $20,000–$30,000; $30,000–$50,000; $50,000 and over
Occupation	Professional and technical; managers, officials, and proprietors; clerical, sales; crafters, supervisors; operatives; farmers; retired; students; home-makers; unemployed
Education	Grade school or less; some high school; high school graduate; some college; college graduate
Religion	Catholic, Protestant, Jewish, other
Race	White, black, oriental, Hispanic
Nationality	American, British, French, German, Scandinavian, Italian, Latin American, Middle Eastern, Japanese
Psychographic	
Social class	Lower lowers, upper lowers, lower middles, upper middles, lower uppers, upper uppers
Lifestyle	Belongers, achievers, integrateds
Personality	Compulsive, gregarious, authoritarian, ambitious
Behavioristic	
Purchase occasion	Regular occasion, special occasion
Benefits sought	Quality, service, economy
User status	Nonuser, ex-user, potential user, first-time user, regular user
Usage rate	Light user, medium user, heavy user
Loyalty status	None, medium, strong, absolute
Readiness stage	Unaware, aware, informed, interested, desirous, intending to buy
Attitude toward product	Enthusiastic, positive, indifferent, negative, hostile

Source: Philip Kotler, *Marketing Management* (Englewood Cliffs, N.J.: Prentice Hall, 1988), p. 287. Reprinted by permission of Prentice Hall, Inc.

segmentation is not difficult to understand conceptually, but real problems may arise when applying the concepts.

Geographic Variables

Very significant differences exist in the usage of many products based on geographic location, both across countries and with the United States. Thus the utilization of a geographic basis to form segments is common. Indeed, one of the significant trends in promotional activity over the last several years has been the development of regionalization of promotional programs. The Frito-Lay Promotion in Action 8–1 is an example of the application of this regional approach to segmentation.

It is necessary to calculate the *relative sales possibilities* in the various potential geographic segments. For example, if a product is sold nationwide, how much promotional effort should be expended in Chicago relative to Phoenix? This key question can be answered only when *market potentials* are computed, for, as a general rule, effort is allocated in proportion to potential, all other things being equal.

Several different potentials might be computed for a given product: (1) volume attainable under ideal conditions (i.e., if all efforts were perfectly adapted to the environment), (2) the relative capacity of a market to absorb the products of an entire industry such as the major appliance industry, (3) the relative size of market for a company's type of product (i.e., sales of color television sets versus stereo sets), and (4) the actual sales a company can expect. The last category, of course, is the equivalent of the sales forecast for a firm, or the sales volume that can be expected if the firm continues on its present course. Potential, on the other hand, refers to sales possibilities rather than expected sales and is of greater significance for purposes of demand analysis. Although forecasting is necessary in determining allocations and budgets, it is beyond the scope of this book.

This is not to say, however, that potential is the sole basis for allocating resources because potentials for industry sales do not reveal the competitive structure of a market or the firm's ability to make inroads. Ann Arbor, for example, might appear to offer high potential, whereas, in reality, competitors are so entrenched that inroads would be impossible. Ideally, then, potentials must be augmented with information about the competitive structure as well as the firm's previous experience in the market. The goal, of course, is to make an optimum allocation of resources to alternative markets. This can be done only with great precision with a reliable estimate of the impact of a given level of promotional expenditure on market share. An array of markets in terms of potential provides a workable estimate of probable response to sales efforts. The methods used to compute potentials will be discussed in Chapter 10.

Demographic Characteristics

The market potential for any product is equal to the number of people who want or need that alternative and have the resources to obtain it. Motivation to buy is to some extent both determined and revealed by the demographic life position of the person (age, education, income, sex, and so on), as is ability to pay. Many possible demographic bases for segmentation are itemized in Table 8–1, but the most widely used are age, income, and sex.

Age A buyer's wants and ability to buy obviously change as he or she ages and passes through various stages in life, and this provides useful clues for marketing strategy. Jergens' Aloe & Lanolin proved to be most appealing to women over 35. This is not surprising, given the preference of younger consumers for a medicated skin conditioner. There would have been little to

PROMOTION IN ACTION 8–1

Geographic Segmentation
Frito-Lay Advances with Regional Marketing

Regional marketing is an increasingly popular strategy in our distinctly diverse nation. "Different strokes for different folks" is an old adage worth remembering. A product that does poorly in one area of the country may have great market potential in another. Matching regional interests with the right marketing mix can significantly increase a product's sales volume.

Frito-Lay is a firm believer in the regional marketing approach. After testing the regional idea in 1987, the snack food unit of Pepsi Co., Inc., decided to proceed full speed at the national level in 1988. Frito-Lay allocated 30 percent of its total 1988 advertising and promotion budget to regional marketing. Previous allocations had never exceeded 10 percent. Frito-Lay divided the country into seven zones. The marketing managers in charge of each zone were given greater decision-making authority. The company's Dallas headquarters facilitated local marketing decisions by providing more analytical assistance to each manager.

At first glance, Frito-Lay's impressive 50 percent share of the $7 billion salty-snack industry may not seem to demand such a specialized marketing approach. But stiff competition from local and regional snack companies alters this picture. According to Leo Kiely, senior vice president, marketing and sales, Frito-Lay may have a 50 percent share of the potato chip segment on a national basis, but the company's share is 30 percent or less in half of its markets. This is where the regional approach can build sales.

Steve Bryan, vice president, marketing planning, explained Frito-Lay's strategy: "We're approaching regional marketing from an evolutionary rather gain if the younger market had been the target of efforts to change preferences so the logical strategy was to target the older segment and capitalize on that opportunity. We noted in Chapter 2 that Carnival Cruise Lines targets two distinct consumer segments based on age. The Promotion in Action 8–2 notes the increasing economic importance of a segment clearly defined by age.

Income Income segmentation has long been used by marketers with generally favorable results. For example, the Jaguar is targeted to those making about $100,000 per year, and the media used include mostly national magazines and Sunday newspaper supplements appealing to this affluent segment. This effort is confined largely to the two coasts, reflecting the geographic segmentation of the market.

One must be cautious in assuming that income is a reflection of the consumer's social class. This obviously is not the case, given the high wages

---

**Geographic Segmentation
Frito-Lay Advances with Regional Marketing** (concluded)

❖
**PROMOTION
IN ACTION
8–1**

than revolutionary perspective. Our objective is to do what we need to do to be competitive by geography and to tailor our programs to customer needs."

Although Frito-Lay's initial efforts focused on price and promotion rather than separate regional advertising and product development, the company is very aware of different regional taste preferences. To capitalize on these differences, Frito-Lay is testing new flavors and line extensions in key regional markets.

Dwight Riskey, vice president, marketing research and new business, gave Doritos Salsa Rio as an example. The spicy tomato-flavor chip is being test marketed in the Northwest, where tortilla chips sell well. New Orleans, which has long preferred kettle-cooked chips, is an ideal test market for Crunch Tators, Frito-Lay's entry into the "hard-bite" potato chip segment. The company's regional strategy also sent the promotion of its Delta Gold potato chips to the Southeast, where lighter, golden chips are preferred.

Emmanuel Goldman, analyst at Montgomery Securities, thinks Frito-Lay is on to something: "Frito is carving up the country into various segments and targeting programs much finer than ever before. This strategy gives different pricing by region and a different product push. It's great for spot advertising. This is for real, and there's going to be more of it."

Source: "Frito Makes Regional Advances," *Advertising Age*, July 4, 1988, p. 21.

PROMOTION IN ACTION 8-2

Demographic Segmentation by Age
The Up and Coming Children's Market

The increasing number of dual-career couples has indirectly resulted in the increased buying power of children. In addition to the estimated $15.7 billion in spending money that children receive annually from their parents, ($6.2 billion in allowance and $9.5 billion for necessities such as bus fare and school lunches), children also influence the products and brands their parents buy. Some companies believe that this influence affects up to $50 billion in purchases each year.

This significant block of purchasing power is leading more and more businesses to concentrate on the children's segment of the market. Targeting children has several major advantages for marketers: The marketer can appeal directly to the children themselves; they can appeal to the children as a way to indirectly influence family purchases; and they can appeal to the children as future consumers by building brand loyalty early. McDonald's is one company that has already capitalized on this lucrative target market.

Regarded as a pioneer in this segment, McDonald's has been marketing to children for years. According to James McNeal, a marketing professor at Texas A&M University and author of the book *Children as Consumers*, McDonald's uses several different approaches to appeal to this market's various potential subsegments. The *Golden Book* coloring book is a direct appeal targeted at four- and five-year-old children. The book invites them to color people and things they encounter every day, such as police officers and fire trucks. The restaurant in the book is obviously McDonald's. Taking advantage of children's influential position, McDonald's uses advertising that encourages family trips to the restaurant.

McNeal believes that the future market is the strongest reason for targeting the children's segment of the market. By associating positive messages and experiences with its restaurants, McDonald's hopes to continue winning these children as customers, first as independent consumers and eventually as heads of their own families. According to McNeal, "You can see McDonald's appealing to kids to buy hamburgers, to encourage their parents to buy hamburgers, and creating brand recognition and preference so they buy hamburgers for themselves and their children later on."

Sources: "Children Come of Age as Consumers," *Marketing News*, December 4, 1987, pp. 8–9; " 'Kid Power' Put at $15.7 Billion," *Advertising Age*, August 15, 1988, p. 33.

now earned by those in the trades and various blue-collar occupations. There-fore, income by itself usually is not an accurate basis for segmentation.

Sex   It is obvious that some products appeal more to men than they do women, and vice versa. With the emergence of the working woman and greater female initiative as a result of the equal rights movement, women have become a target for more products.

Almost half of all cars sold in the United States are purchased by women for their own use; this requires major changes in the promotional activities of car companies. In addition, changing sex roles have resulted in the necessity to promote many grocery products to men as Promotion in Action 8–3 notes.

Demographics as a Clue to Lifestyle   Demographic data can provide some interesting insight into lifestyle differences between segments. For example, the heavy buyers of Kentucky Fried Chicken have this demographic profile:

Both spouses work.

More children than average.

Significantly higher family income than average.

Average educational attainment.

Middle-class occupational status.

It is not difficult to conclude that time is at a premium for members of this household. Undoubtedly, they are willing to incur the extra cost of purchasing prepared food in return for the gains in leisure time. Given the relatively high-income status, it is also probable that they would be responsive to buying with a credit card, and so on.

Figure 8–1 presents a Jordache Kids ad that is demographically based in terms of its target audience and theme.

The usefulness of both geographic and demographic segmentation working together is best illustrated in the description of Claritas' geodemographic target marketing system called *PRIZM*.[2] Using census and other secondary data on lifestyles, the system develops population clusters based on demographic information and ties these data back to a specific geographic location. The geographic analysis is available at the block group, census tract, minor civil division, postal carrier route, and ZIP code levels. The levels used in any particular case are those consistent with statistical reliability.

Based on this analysis, Claritas has divided the United States into 12 social groups and 40 lifestyle clusters. For example, two of the social groups are (1) "educated, affluent executives and professionals in elite metro suburbs" and (2) "mid-scale, child-raising, blue-collar families in remote suburbs and towns." Within the first social group above, two of the lifestyle clusters are "blue blood estates," and "money and brains." Within the second social group above, two of the lifestyle clusters are "blue-collar nursery," and "middle America." The names of the clusters are short-form descriptors. A detailed description of the characteristics of those composing these groups and clusters is available. In addition, the geographic location of all those assigned to a specific group or cluster is known to the group block, tract, or ZIP level as noted above. A customer or potential target customer can be assigned to a cluster based on the street address and then marketing activity can be directed to the relevant cluster's geographic location. For example, in the 77-square block area of Manhattan's ZIP code 10019, PRIZM can target eight different lifestyle clusters by specific blocks.

❖
**PROMOTION
IN ACTION
8–3**

**Demographic Segmentation by Sex
"Macho Marketing"**

To complement the last two decades' marketing emphasis on the working woman, today's marketers are targeting the shopping man. As men's and women's roles in society change, more and more consumer product companies want to gear their packaging design, as well as the products themselves, toward men. Hence macho marketing is seen as the trend of the 1990s.

Today's males are making an increasingly high percentage of all purchasing decisions, especially in the grocery stores. As a result, many organizations are identifying male market segment behaviors and related opportunities. While studying the product and packaging characteristics that appeal to this new all-male, macho consumer segment, Design and Market Research Laboratory of Carol Stream, Illinois, discovered the following trends:

1. Approximately 40 percent of shoppers in the supermarket are men.
2. About one-third of men do major food shopping alone, and another 25 percent shop regularly with their wives.
3. Some 80 percent of men do fill-in shopping in a month's period.
4. Almost 50 percent of men prepare complete meals for their families.

Men now account for 40 percent of all food-shopping dollars. The significance of this fact is underscored when one realizes that not so long ago, women spent 80 percent or more of those dollars. New opportunities exist. New approaches are needed.

Many different marketing mix components trigger the male purchasing decision, but packaging and display are seen as keys to the perception of a product and its benefits. Research is often necessary to develop a competitive

The power of PRIZM to aid promotion activity is high. PRIZM can be applied to retail location analysis, direct mail promotions and catalogs, media planning, and prospect identification. For example, a publisher of a very upscale magazine could mail a subscription promotion to only the relevant block addresses in the 10019 ZIP code of Manhattan mentioned above. A mailing to the other blocks would be a waste of money. The promotion efficiencies of this approach are large.

Worldstyle, a new fashion magazine, is convinced that the approach of PRIZM is effective.[3] *Worldstyle* has decided to use demographic data to target "the classiest zip codes" in the top 25 retail markets. The magazine

**PROMOTION
IN ACTION
8–3**

**Demographic Segmentation by Sex
"Macho Marketing"** (concluded)

package/product design. Packaging must create imagery that appeals to its target market segments while efficiently communicating essential product information. Macho packaging needs shelf impact and "easy finding power" to help male shoppers save time. Although the average time an American spends in the grocery store is 27 minutes, men tend to enter grocery stores with a finite shopping list and the intention to get those specific items and get out!

Research indicates that male shoppers are attracted to bold, linear packaging. They are not usually interested in coupons, detailed nutritional information, or recipes. Clear, identifying symbols are needed to create brand awareness and for ease of future recognition so that brand loyalty might be developed. Some researchers believe that men tend to be more influenced by the images created through packaging than by specific product information.

Kraft Pourable Salad Dressings decided to target the macho market. The packaging was redesigned accordingly, maintaining the brands' equity while strengthening the line's appeal to male shoppers. Unlike earlier shelf-impact strategies that stressed "shouting the package off the shelf," Kraft's three-step strategy involved letting the man know (1) what the product is, (2) what it does, and (3) how to use it. Kraft Salad Dressings' new bottle shape and label graphics are perceived as being more masculine. The distinctive bottles attract male attention because they are easily seen and are congruent with male values. Other products are expected to adjust accordingly as this market continues to evolve.

Source: "Research a Potent Factor in Reaching the 'Macho Market,'" *Marketing News,* September 26, 1988.

FIGURE 8–1

❖❖❖   **An Example of a Demographically Based Advertisement**

will be distributed strictly as a Sunday newspaper insert and will be zoned exclusively to women with household incomes of $25,000 and higher.

If initial estimates prove true, this strategy will provide a circulation of 3.3 million households and total readership of about 7 million, making *Worldstyle* the world's largest circulation fashion magazine. According to data from Simmons Market Research Bureau and Audit Bureau of Circulation, *Worldstyle* will reach 550,000 homes with incomes of over $25,000 in the New York City market alone. *Cosmopolitan* and *Mademoiselle* have circulations of 163,000 and 83,000, respectively, in this category.

Subtitled "The International Fashion Forecast Magazine," *Worldstyle* will target a certain upscale taste level by emphasizing a lasting, classic look and balancing high style with reality. Based on the newspapers' audiences, this target segment will share the following characteristics:

Median age of 36.5 years.

Average income of $41,950.

75 percent employed outside the home.

60 percent with a college education.

Women in this group are likely to fit *Worldstyle's* image. Many are established career women who have a professional need for classic clothes but do not have time to shop for them. Most appreciate and want both high quality and style, and they have the financial status to afford *Worldstyle's* fashions.

Psychographic Characteristics

In psychographic segmentation, consumers are differentiated on the basis of differences in patterns by which people live and spend time and money. These patterns represent consumer lifestyle. Some analysts include social class as a part of lifestyle (see Table 8–1), whereas others classify it as a demographic variable. For the most part, psychographics or lifestyle refers here to consumer attitudes, interests, and opinions (often referred to as AIO measurements) and the way in which these affect buying activities. For example, consider the heavy users of eye makeup. Demographically, they are younger and better educated than average and are more likely to be employed outside the home. This tells us something, but notice how much is added when users are differentiated from nonusers in psychologically graphic terms:

Highly fashion conscious.

Desire to be attractive.

Oriented to the future.

Interested in art and culture.

Interested in world travel.

Not home centered.

Relative rejection of the traditional.

These data, of course, say nothing about awareness or attitudes toward specific brands or types of eye makeup. Their usefulness in promotional strategy is in providing clues about the type of person the prospects are and the way they should be depicted in the message.

One could use this psychographic profile in a mechanical way and depict an overdressed woman with a man worshipping at her feet as they sit in an art institute in Paris with a letter from mother crumpled on the floor. Needless to say, this example is absurd, but an appeal to the wrong type of person and in contradictory settings will trigger selective screening of the message by the prospect.

Two companies have recently discovered psychographic segments that the cosmetic industry had previously overlooked: women concerned with their sensitivity to cosmetics and women who are unimpressed by sexy models and big names.[4] Bausch & Lomb has introduced a line of fragrance-free cosmetics for women with sensitive eyes. Rubigo Cosmetics has targeted women who have no "covergirl aspirations" but want to look good in their own way.

Sheila Rose, director of marketing and sales for Bausch & Lomb, said that her company estimates that 78 percent of all women have some sensitivity to cosmetics and that this sensitivity influences at least 33 percent of all women when they choose eye cosmetics. With its prominent reputation as a maker of optical products, Bausch & Lomb believes that cosmetics are a natural extension for the company and a good way to leverage the Bausch & Lomb name.

The new line is not limited to women who wear contact lenses. Many firms, including Aziza, have recently launched cosmetic lines exclusively for women who wear contacts, but not all women who wear contacts have problems with their cosmetics. "Obviously women with contact lenses are attracted to us, but there are other women who are concerned with the cosmetics they're wearing." Rose continued by saying that Bausch & Lomb wants to attract "all women who use cosmetics five times a week." The majority of this audience is projected to be between the ages of 25 and 45.

Rose Mary Worthen, executive vice president of Rubigo Cosmetics, remarked that many women look at famous models and say, "Okay, I'm at this age and no matter how hard I try, I'm not going to look like that girl." Worthen was a mother long before she went into cosmetics and believes that she can "fully appreciate what a working woman is looking for."

Rubigo does not want to neglect teenagers or older women. Worthen says that the cosmetic industry reaches further than the 18 to 34-year-old range. Older women want to look good too, and even 11-year-olds have significant buying power.

Both companies sought an upscale and fashionable image. They altered their packaging, displays, and product selection accordingly. Stylish colors took their place next to standard shades. Ad campaigns were designed and distribution channels were selected.

Bausch & Lomb went for the "slick" look. Its novel TV commercial shows no women, only the admiring looks of dashing men at a party. Print ads in *Vogue, Cosmopolitan, Glamour, Self,* and *Mademoiselle* feature the new products under the headline, "Introducing Bausch & Lomb cosmetics. The perfect blend of art and science." This embellishes but does not mar the company's "clean" image.

Rubigo went for a more classic look. The company's 1980 entrance into the cosmetic market was a great success. Its original product is its now-signature powder blush in an urn. These urns were sold exclusively in department stores and netted $3 million in sales during their first year. The company reduced the size of the urn in 1983 and went to mass merchandising. Its strategy was to become more visual and create an aura around the product. Rubigo's print and TV ads revolve around the distinctive urn, capitalizing on its target segment's desire for a unique and classy product.

Figure 8–2 presents examples of lifestyle-based themes. The British Knights ad captures the casual spirit of its youthful target market, and the Chemical Bank Private Banking ad gives the flavor of the luxury-based lifestyle of its target segment.

The makeup example above is an illustration of product-*specific* AIO analysis. That is, the AIO scales were tailor-made for the product. Another type of AIO scale is based on *general patterns* of lifestyle.

Table 8–2 presents the description of eight generalized psychographic segments prepared by Valentine-Radford Advertising from a statistical analysis of survey responses concerning (1) how people take control of their circumstances, (2) how they approach action, and (3) how they make judgments about information. Each of these segments is then correlated with brand usage, demographics, desired benefits, and other data to aid the selection of the best target market for specific products and services.

Evidence to date indicates that lifestyle segmentation is most appropriate when the following circumstances are present:

The product primarily offers psychological gratification.

Product performance cannot be evaluated objectively.

High involvement is present with most buyers.

FIGURE 8–2

❖   Examples of Lifestyle Themes in Advertisements

FIGURE 8–2

Examples of Lifestyle Themes in Advertisements (concluded)   ❖

Most of our clients are referred by a source far
more compelling than any advertising.

When it comes to innovative, responsive financial services, people of influence are recommending Private Banking at Chemical Bank.

In fact, our clients themselves are our single most reliable source of new client relationships.

If you wish to discover how your financial needs can best be met, please contact Chemical Bank, Private Banking, 30 Rockefeller Plaza, New York, NY 10112.

C 1989 Chemical Bank
Member FDIC

CHEMICALBANK PRIVATE BANKING

Advertising is the major tool in the marketing mix.

Consumers are willing to switch brands when not completely satisfied.

The product category is not dominated by one or two brands.

The product is not purchased primarily on the basis of price.

Behavioristic Variables

In this method of segmentation, buyers are differentiated on the basis of their knowledge of and attitude toward a product or its attributes, and of

---

TABLE 8–2

Eight Generalized Psychographic Segments with Some Demographic Correlates

1. *Traditionals.* Yield control, act first, and make fact-based decisions. Down to earth, practical, and conventional. Older, lower education and income, married, often retired.

2. *New middle Americans.* Take control, act first, make fact-based decisions. Very sociable, achievement oriented, concerned with living standards, and take moderate risks. Somewhat younger, well educated, high family incomes, fewer children.

3. *Home and community centered.* Yield control, think first, make fact-based decisions. Very conventional, prim, and proper. Exercise self-control, tend to go by acceptable rules of society, and not gregarious. Somewhat older, better educated, higher incomes.

4. *Rising stars.* Take control, think first, make fact-based decisions, intellectually curious but not socially gregarious. Have highest income and education and highest percentages of professionals, entrepreneurs, and be males and singles. Oriented to cultural activities.

5. *Good ol' girls and boys.* Yield control, act first, and make feeling-based decisions. Practical, down-to-earth, no nonsense, sociable yet cynical. Lower education and income. Like soap operas, game shows, and country and western music.

6. *Young socials.* Take control, act first, and make decisions based on feelings. Outgoing, warm, and intuitive. Low self-control—if it feels good, do it. Tend to be younger, less educated, have higher family incomes, and be more females.

7. *Moralists.* Yield control, think first, and make feeling-based decisions. Proper, detached, yet concerned. Older, lower education and income, factory workers, and homemakers. Attend church and exposed to religious media.

8. *Aging hippies.* Take control, think first, and make feeling-based decisions. Sensitive, fanciful, unrealistic, and imaginative. Younger and better educated. Unconventional living arrangements.

Source: "Ad Agency Develops Eight New Market Segments," *Marketing News,* August 26, 1987, p. 12. Used by special permission.

their response to and use of the product. It is finding widespread use. Our discussion here is confined to segmentation by benefits sought and by product usage rates.

Benefit Segmentation

Considerable attention was focused in earlier chapters on the attributes used (or benefits desired) by consumers in the process of alternative evaluation. In benefit segmentation, the first step is to determine these desired benefits. The consumer then assesses, from his or her perspective, whether or not available products fill the bill. If not, there may be a market niche that can be filled by careful product design and marketing strategy. In effect, then, the consumer sets the agenda.

Benefit segmentation played a large part in the successful introduction of Bacardi Tropical Fruit Mixers.[5] Market research, which included numerous focus groups, found an unmet consumer need that Bacardi could fill. Over the past five years, people have been drinking more light alcohol (e.g., rum and vodka) and less dark alcohol (e.g., bourbon and scotch), and drinking less alcohol overall. The popularity of tropical drinks has exploded in bars and restaurants. Bacardi saw that an easily accessible, in-home alternative would have vast market potential.

Lacking the specific expertise to develop and distribute the product, Bacardi entered into a partnership with Coca-Cola Foods, Inc. Bacardi brought its well-established name and Caribbean heritage. Coca-Cola brought a highly developed technical department, a well-established salesforce, and direct access to the grocery distribution system.

The two companies combined resources to produce a revolutionary new product that tasted homemade and was identical to the drinks purchased at bars and restaurants. In comparison to the powdered-mix alternatives on the market, Bacardi mixers provided superior quality at a lower per-ounce price. Coke and Bacardi chose the slogan, "Perfectly simple. Simply perfect." Advertising emphasized taste, convenience, and Caribbean imagery. Packaging stressed that the product was made by Bacardi and was a *mixer,* not an alcoholic beverage. This positioning communicated the product's superiority and separated it from everything else in its category.

How did these efforts add up? Within one year, Bacardi mixer sales were equal to the entire bottled mixer category. As Caryn McQuilkin, marketing manager for Coca-Cola Foods, Inc., stated, "What we ended up with is perfectly simple and simply perfect—a great product and a great price, with communication in terms of good advertising and beautiful packaging." By determining and fulfilling an unmet consumer need, Bacardi and Coca-Cola revolutionized the bottled mixer industry.

Product Usage Rates

It often proves useful to segment the market in terms of consumer usage rates for a specific product category. Different strategies then are required for those in various usage categories.

Nonusers of Product Category It is important to determine whether or not nonusers offer a potential market. Frequently the problem is only lack of awareness. If this is the case, an opportunity may exist to build familiarity through promotion and thereby lay the groundwork for later sales.

In other instances, a basically favorable attitude may exist but may be constrained by opposing forces from the environment. For example, if the problem is concern over financing, advertising or personal selling could possibly stimulate sales by promoting the offer of easy credit.

Most likely the analysis of nonusers will document segments that will not respond, regardless of the strategy. There may be a basic conflict between the company offer and evaluative criteria, lifestyles, and so on. Every attempt should be made to avoid such segments if possible, because the probable return would not be worth the expense.

Users of the Product but Not the Company Brand The purpose of this inquiry is to assess the probability of making inroads into competitors' markets. If their offerings or images are weak in certain respects or fail to satisfy important evaluative criteria, it may be possible to increase market share. On the other hand, competitors may be invulnerable in certain segments, especially if there is brand loyalty based on psychological commitment or centrality. The best strategy always is to *appeal to the waverers* (those whose commitment is diminishing) rather than to attack an entrenched competitor head-on.

Regardless of competitive market shares, many believe that the best strategy is to appeal to heavy users of the product class, often referred to as the *heavy half*. For example, the so-called heavy half of the beer drinkers' market (in actuality, this is 17 percent of the total market) consumes 88 percent of all beer; the heavy half in the market for canned soup (16 percent of the total) consumes 86 percent of the product sold. The assumption is that the heavy half is the most productive segment, and there probably is some merit in this viewpoint. Certainly the propensity to respond will be higher. Concentration on this segment has been made more feasible through use of data from syndicated research services showing the product consumption by audiences of various advertising media.

Efforts should not be concentrated on the heavy half, however, unless there is evidence that it is not feasible to turn nonusers into users and light users into heavy users. There should be an inquiry into why they buy or do not buy, what the product means to them, and other related questions. The answers to these questions may make it possible to win over buyers.

Users of Product and Company Brand The greatest asset possessed by any organization is its core of satisfied users, and the present user cannot be overlooked in promotional strategy. It is particularly important to monitor brand image and to clarify that the company offerings are still satisfying salient evaluative criteria better than the perceived offerings of a competitor. Any deficiencies should, of course, be remedied.

In addition, it is useful to monitor awareness of the company brand and competitive brands. In a highly volatile market, eroding awareness can be followed by a sales decline. A frequent advertising objective is just to maintain "share of mind"—that is, relative awareness vis-à-vis competitors.

It also may be possible to assess the potential for increasing brand loyalty among light to moderate users, for stimulating new product uses, for encouraging switching from competitive brands, and for preventing inroads by competitors, to mention only a few of the many possibilities.

Undertaking Segmentation Analysis

Many bases for segmentation have been analyzed in this section; none of these are applicable in every situation. Thus it is impossible to generalize with respect to the ideal approach. What emerges is the wide variety that is possible and the ways in which research imagination and creative planning can identify groupings that are a part of the total market. Promotional strategy requires a probing analysis to determine if viable segments exist. If these are present and recognized, they offer an opportunity for profit.

There are, however, two general approaches to segmentation analysis: a priori and post hoc. In the *a priori* approach, the marketer has a good reason to define the segmentation criteria in advance. We might be certain, for example, that the most frequent purchasers of our product category are women, or are people with incomes over $50,000. The *Worldstyle* magazine example discussed earlier is an example of the *a priori* segmentation approach.

In the *post hoc* approach, the criteria for segmentation are not decided in advance but rather are an outcome of the analysis itself. The first step is to develop a set of AIO questions that define the domain of interest to the marketer. This could be either a generalized or product-specific list. Second, a large sample of potential consumers is selected and asked to indicate their degree of agreement with the battery of AIO statements. Third, the respondents are clustered into homogeneous groups or segments on the basis of the similarity of their responses across the whole battery of AIO statements. They are clustered using one of a number of multivariate data analysis procedures that are appropriate for this purpose. Levi Strauss used the post hoc approach to define five segments in the men's clothing market, including "the utilitarian jeans customer," "the clothes horse," and "the trendy casual" segments. The eight groups identified in Table 8–2 also used the post hoc approach.

THE TARGET MARKET DECISION

Once the market has been segmented along the relevant bases or criteria, the marketing manager must make the target market decision. The target market decision relates to the selection of the specific segment or segments toward which promotional activity will be directed. The firm has three basic options in this regard: (1) undifferentiated marketing, (2) differentiated marketing, and (3) concentrated marketing.

Undifferentiated Marketing

If this strategy is followed, segments are in effect ignored, and one marketing mix is offered for everyone. All efforts are poured into building a superior image that will overcome these demand variations. Certainly the cost advantages to the approach are undeniable, as Henry Ford found when the Model A Ford was introduced in any color you wanted "as long as it is black." Ford, of course, had a near-monopoly on the market, but few firms enjoy that advantage today. As a result, undifferentiated marketing is exceedingly rare.

One variation seen more commonly is to target only the largest segment of the market, perhaps using the heavy-half concept. The problem is that this strategy appeals to most competitors—they concentrate in similar fashion and ignore smaller segments. The outcome is often that using this approach makes the marketer a sitting duck for competitors who differentiate and provide the desired option ranges.

Differentiated Marketing

In differentiated marketing, a firm operates in two or more segments and offers a unique marketing mix for each. This strategy has become quite common in larger corporations as is reflected in a trend toward multiple product offerings. It certainly offers the advantage of recognizing the demand variations that exist and capitalizing on them, in contrast with undifferentiated marketing.

Differentiated marketing is not without its disadvantages. For example, national marketers are finding that the latest marketing trend—regionalization—can be a costly and complex way to market their products.[6] Regionalization replaces national mass-marketing strategies with custom-tailored approaches in the hope that such localized targeting can boost market share in a slow growth environment. By segmenting the market into tightly focused areas, companies can design special advertising and promotional campaigns, and even develop new products—or new versions of existing products—that cater to local tastes.

Although the idea seems simple enough, implementing the strategy can be a major undertaking. As Thomas W. Wilson, Jr., a director of the McKinsey & Co. consulting firm, puts it, "Breadth of choice equals complexity; complexity equals increasing cost."

Adjusting products to appeal to regional tastes can lead to production headaches. Campbell's Soup Co. found this out the hard way when it decided to make a spicier version of its Nacho Cheese Soup in order to appeal to consumers in the West and Southwest. The regionalized recipe called for more jalapeno peppers—a lot more.

"When we first put them in the soup in large quantities, they created almost a gas cloud—it was virtually impossible for the workers to work with," said Larry A. Carpenter, Campbell's senior marketing manager for soups. "At one point," he joked, "we were considering gas masks."

Campbell was able to solve its problem with pureed peppers, and it is still one of the companies leading the way toward regionalization. The company has decided, however, that two versions of its Nacho Cheese soup are enough. "Beyond two, it gets a little too complex," concedes Mr. Carpenter. "You run into production problems and the risk of something going wrong."

Other companies experimenting with regionalization have found that it can also carry an expensive price tag. General Foods Corp. promoted its Maxwell House coffee brand by sponsoring a series of regional events, such as rodeos in Dallas and a show at Radio City Music Hall in New York. The company later estimated that sponsoring such varied events had cost two to three times as much as a single national promotion.

Indeed, the cost of running regional advertising can be prohibitive for some companies. Domino's Pizza, Inc., already offers different toppings for its pizzas in different regions of the country but doesn't publicize the fact. According to Douglas J. Dawson, a Domino's vice president, taking a regional approach "would blow our whole advertising budget."

Thomas J. Lipton & Co. agrees. Although Lipton has acquired a great deal of information about the preferences of tea drinkers around the country, the company is resisting regionalization. Instead, Lipton continues using the same tea blends and advertising themes nationwide. Ted Labiner, Lipton's director of creative services, defends the strategy, saying that "the economies of scale you get make it much more efficient to market nationally than regionally."

Concentrated Marketing

In the undifferentiated strategy, marketers target the whole market, while in the differentiated strategy, they target two or more segments. However, it is often wise to concentrate on one segment. The objective is to establish a larger share and focus resources on excellence in a more limited market. Numerous examples could be cited. One of the most notable is the success the Tandy Corporation has had with its Model 80 Radio Shack home computers. Although it has a great many competitors, the Model 80 has held a top position through continued product innovation, intensive distribution, and availability of service and software help.

The danger of concentration, of course, is that a market can dry up with amazing rapidity. Therefore, some diversification may be a wise policy to follow, especially if there is a high rate of product change.

The Choice of Approach

The fundamental basis on which the marketer selects one of these approaches to the segments available is a cost/benefit analysis. The marketer expects to generate additional revenue from a segment by more completely satisfying the needs of that group and by providing promotional activities that better match the segment. In doing so, the marketer incurs additional costs for new ads, new promotions, new sales-force activities, and so forth. In general, a unique program would be developed for a segment if the incremental revenue expected exceeds the incremental costs of serving it. Of course, other constraints such as financial resources, personnel limitations, and relationships of one segment to others need also to be considered. We see in the Lipton, Campbell Soup, and Domino's examples above the recognition of the limitations caused by the incremental cost of serving additional segments.

COMPETITIVE POSITIONING

Once the potential segments have been identified and the choice of segments to be targeted for promotion has been made, a need still exists to select a *competitive positioning* for the product or service in the minds of the consumers in the selected segments. *Competitive positioning is the perception that targeted consumers have of a firm's offering relative to competitors.* Positioning is often the most critical element in a firm's marketing strategy because it defines the intended perception of consumers of the firm's product or service. In addition, positioning directs the entire marketing mix of the firm. A clear positioning statement is key to the direction of promotional activity.

There are six basic approaches to positioning strategy: (1) by attributes, (2) by price and quality, (3) by use or application, (4) by product user, (5) by product class, and (6) by competitor.[7]

Positioning by Attribute

The most commonly used positioning strategy is to associate a product as having an identified level of a defined set of attributes, such as power, sportiness, caffeine, or color. Thus American Airlines is "the on-time machine," an attribute of great salience to air travelers, and Volvo takes the high position on the attribute "safety." See Figure 8–3 for ads associated with these companies.

Positioning by Price and Quality

Although price and quality may be thought of as attributes, they are so important that they warrant separate treatment. In many product categories, some brands offer more features, better service or performance, and use a higher price as a cue to the consumer that they have higher quality. Alternatively, other brands emphasize lower price with limited features to drive a value positioning. For example, BMW holds a premium-quality positioning, and GEO holds a value-based positioning.

Positioning by Use or Application

In this approach, the marketer attempts to position his or her brand as being associated with a particular use or occasion. For example, Gatorade took the "use with strenuous exercise" positioning when it was first introduced, and Hallmark took the positioning of being the card to send when you "care enough to send the very best."

Positioning by Product User

In this approach, the brand is associated with a specific user or class of users. For example, Cover Girl makeup has built a consumer franchise on a succession of well-known models such as Cheryl Tiegs and Christie Brinkley, and Miller Lite uses a group of former athletes in its advertisements.

FIGURE 8–3

❖❖ **Advertisements Designed to Establish a Competitive Positioning**

The On-time Machine.

American Airlines has achieved the best on-time record of the nine largest domestic airlines in each of the last five reporting periods.

And that's not all. Since on-time records have been kept, starting in September 1987, American has the best overall record of getting you where you want to go on time.

At American, we know what it takes to be the on-time leader. It takes an investment in maintenance of $1 billion a year to help keep delays to a minimum. It means monitoring our schedules daily to make sure the schedules we publish are accurate. And it means constantly looking for new ways to provide even more dependable service, day in and day out.

It's the kind of commitment you expect from American. The kind of commitment it takes to be the On-time Machine.

AmericanAirlines
Something special in the air.℠

Based on Department of Transportation data and the cumulative percentage of nonstop domestic flights arriving within 15 minutes of schedule for all reported airports for the nine largest airlines in terms of domestic revenue passenger miles, September 1987 through November 1989.

FIGURE 8-3

WHERE WOULD YOU RATHER SIT. BEHIND THE FRONT END OR IN IT?

Of these two family vehicles only one is required to meet passenger car safety standards.

Which might explain why the front end of a Volvo wagon is equipped with an impact absorbing "crumple zone" that helps protect its passengers. And why the front end of some minivans include impact absorbing components of a slightly different nature.

Your legs.

The fact is, minivans are not required to have many of the safety features found on Volvos.

That's because the U.S. Department of Transportation does not classify minivans as passenger cars.

Which is frightening when you think how many people tote their families around in them.

Volvos, on the other hand, are built with your family's safety in mind. So every Volvo wagon comes equipped with three-point seat belts in the front and back, a driver's-side Supplemental Restraint System and reinforced side-door crash bars.

Just a few of the safety features minivans are not required to have.

All of which leads us to the only logical conclusion. If the U.S. Department of Transportation doesn't consider the minivan a passenger car, maybe you shouldn't either.

VOLVO
A car you can believe in.

CALL TOLL FREE FOR YOUR CATALOG OF 1990 VOLVOS: 1-800-221-9136. © 1989 VOLVO NORTH AMERICA CORPORATION.

Positioning by Product Class

It is possible to position one's brand with respect to the product class in which it competes or to some associated product class. For example, the margarine brand I Can't Believe It's Not Butter has been positioned with respect to the associated product class butter. Weight Watchers brand foods have been positioned with respect to normal but more caloric foods.

Positioning by Competitor

In all positioning approaches, an explicit or implicit frame of reference is the competition. This is because an established competitor's image can be used as a reference point for another brand's positioning. In addition, how consumers perceive your brand relative to competitive offerings is most important, not how it is absolutely perceived. The relevant question is whether your brand is better than a given competitor in service cost, or value, or for use at snack time. We note that in the Volvo ad in Figure 8–3, the superior safety positioning is relative to competitors' minivans. Also the famous Avis campaign, "We're number two, so we try harder," is an example of the competitor as reference point for a positioning. Figure 8–4 presents a brand positioning map for automobiles on the attributes of sportiness and economy relative to the competitors.

It is also helpful to place segment ideal points on these maps to represent the demand structure relative to the product positioning. For example,

FIGURE 8–4

❖ **Product Positioning of Automobiles by Two Attributes**

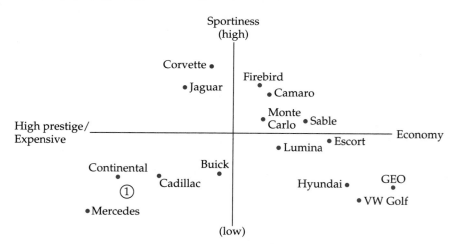

Source: Updated to 1991 brand and adapted from Yoram J. Wind, *Product Policy: Concepts, Methods, and Strategy* (Reading, Mass.: Addison-Wesley Publishing. 1982). p. 84.

the ① in Figure 8–4 represents the "luxury sedan" segment of the market. To the marketer, the positioning of the brands within the target segment is the key issue. Clearly, we want our brand to be closer to the ideal of the segment. The physical product, distribution location, package style, and promotion activity all help position a brand.

The importance of competitive positioning in overall marketing strategy and promotion is noted in Promotion in Action 8–4.

Competitive Positioning "Less Fare More Care": America West Airlines, Inc.

❖
PROMOTION
IN ACTION
8–4

Phoenix-based America West has positioned itself as an airline that provides "better-than-average service at a lower-than-average price, primarily to the frequent business traveler, through a hub-and-spoke system."

Airline industry consultant Edward Beauvais urged his clients to form a western hub in Phoenix. He believed that the West was being underserved by the major carriers and that the city's potential as a hub was great: Phoenix, the nation's ninth-largest city, was the only city of its size without a hub airline; combined with the region's good weather, the relatively uncongested air traffic at Phoenix Sky Harbor Airport would facilitate high schedule reliability; the city was growing, the Sunbelt was booming, and local traffic was heavy. When no one would listen, he took his own advice. In 1982, CEO Edward Beauvais and President Michael Conway of America West devised a business strategy for turning Phoenix into an east/west gateway linking California with a network of Midwestern cities.

Deregulation prompted a surge of new airlines. The increased number of competitors in the industry made the establishment of a market niche imperative for success. America West recognized and filled several unmet needs. Its philosophy was to serve overpriced, underserved markets. It was one of the few carriers that provided nonstop service to Phoenix. It provided "total California access" by serving all major and satellite airports in that state on a high-frequency, low-fare basis. It wanted passengers "to be able to go from our cities east of the hub to anywhere in California for about half of what they were paying before." Southwest Airlines was pursuing a similar strategy, so America West further distinguished itself: it targeted a small percentage of the population that accounts for a large percentage of all fliers—business travelers.

To attract business travelers and to show that low-fare airlines can still exude class, America West offered amenities such as convenient schedules,

Developing a Positioning Strategy

The development of a competitive positioning is a seven-step process:

1. Identify the relevant competitors; they may be brands within the product category or substitute products outside the category.

2. Determine how the competitors are perceived and evaluated; this requires marketing research to measure consumer perceptions. It may involve research to determine the relevant attributes for the positioning.

3. Determine the competitors' positions; all competitors, including our brand, are placed relative to each other; the use of a perceptual

**PROMOTION
IN ACTION
8-4**

**Competitive Positioning "Less Fare More Care":
America West Airlines, Inc.** (continued)

assigned seating, free alcoholic and nonalcoholic beverages, complimentary copies of *The Wall Street Journal* and *USA Today* at boarding gates, full interline baggage and ticket privileges, and frequent flyer benefits. Larger-than-standard beverage cups and premium brands of liquor add extra touches of class. Free luxury bus service is available between the Phoenix suburbs and an America West gate at the airport. Complete flight check-in service is offered at the bus terminals.

Beauvais and Conway further tailored America West for business clientele. The planes' burgundy, taupe, and blue color scheme was designed to create an "understated, businesslike" image. Although first-class seating is available on America West's long transcontinental flights, single-class service with a single, unrestricted fare is the rule for the rest of its routes.

Business travelers with unpredictable schedules seem to applaud the policy. Mark Coleman, senior vice president of market planning and advertising, noted that the policy "has a tremendous appeal for the business traveler—you know you're paying the same fare as everybody else on the airplane."

Coleman believes that America West's low fares are not the airline's main attraction. "Our schedule is 90 percent of our success. You have to give the customer convenience. Price is less of a factor." America West has established one of the best on-time records and lowest passenger complaint rates in the industry.

Excellent service contributes to satisfaction with single-class service and the low complaint rates. Believing that impeccable service should be a given, Beauvais structured America West so that its employees would be highly motivated. Cross-utilization, mandatory stock ownership, and profit sharing are among the company's built-in incentives. The airline distinguishes its positioning map such as that in Figure 8–4 is a common way to do this.

4. Analyze the consumers relative to their needs; the marketing research is designed to define an open and attainable position for our current product or new product.

5. Select the desired positioning; for example, we might desire to be the highest fiber cereal.

6. Implement a marketing and promotional program to establish the desired positioning.

Competitive Positioning "Less Fare More Care":
America West Airlines, Inc. (concluded)

**PROMOTION
IN ACTION
8–4**

cross-utilization program from People Express, saying that America West's purpose is to enable employees to experience first-hand how their work impacts each individual aspect of customer service, not to exploit their productivity. Employee ownership also helps to stave off corporate raiders and the industry's recent merger mania. (Employees own 18 percent of the company; executives control an additional 12 percent. An unwanted buyer must pay each employee up to 250 percent of annual wages.)

America West established a secondary hub in Las Vegas, creating a superhub in the Southwest. It also began a commuter service within Arizona. These moves enabled the company to feed traffic from small markets into its hubs. It can then integrate schedules to common cities, thus maximizing both direct and connecting service possibilities. When America West discovered that Chicago, New York, and Baltimore-Washington were not being heavily serviced from Phoenix by the major airlines, it defied the critics and expanded east. After a rocky start, these flights have developed into some of the carrier's most profitable routes. America West's recent bid to buy Eastern Airlines' northeast shuttle is further evidence of its strategic positioning for convenient, affordable business travel.

Sources: "America West Gambled and Won," *Air Transport World,* June 1984, pp. 60–64; "America West Continues Expansion with Transcontinental 757 Service," *Aviation Week & Space Technology,* March 2, 1987, pp. 42–43; "Dash 8 Fits Right in with America West's Boeings," *Air Transport World,* June 1987, pp. 214–15; "This Upstart Could be Flying a Bit Too High," *Business Week,* June 15, 1987, p. 76; "Surprise Attack," *Financial World,* November 17, 1987, pp. 136–39; "Air West is One of Deregulation's Big Winners," *Marketing News,* December 4, 1987, p. 26; "America West Is Flying High Again—But for How Long?" *Business Week,* February 6, 1989, p. 41; "America West Gains Time for Shuttle Bid," *The Wall Street Journal,* May 1989, p. A3.

7. Monitor the consumers' perception of our positioning. The marketer must continuously monitor the marketplace to see the impact of changing consumer tastes and competitors' new products or attempts to reposition themselves.

This is the general approach taken by America West in Promotion in Action 8–4.

KEY STRATEGIC CHOICES: SEGMENT TARGETING AND PRODUCT POSITIONING

The success of a promotional strategy depends on many details of media choice, creativity in ads, sales training, and so on. However, all of these depend on two key strategy choices. These are the choice of segment or segments to be targeted for promotional effort, and the designation of the position desired for the organization's product in consumers' minds. The choice of target segment determines where we will fight the promotional battles, and the designation of positioning determines what ammunition we've chosen to fight with. Indeed, in any given market, the segment target and the positioning choices will largely determine who our competitors are going to be.

SUMMARY

This chapter is the first of five chapters that lay the foundation for the development of specific aspects of advertising, sales promotion, trade promotion, and sales force programs. Segmentation and competitive positioning are the cornerstone elements of promotional strategy.

Segmentation is the process of dividing large heterogeneous markets into smaller, homogeneous subsets of people or businesses with similar needs and/or responsiveness to marketing mix offerings. Effective segmentation requires the identification of criteria or bases for the formation of the segments, the selection of target markets from the identified segments, and the development of a competitive positioning for the product or service within the selected segments. Usable segments have sufficient size to support a separate promotional program, must be measurable in terms of purchase potential, must be reachable by promotional vehicles, and must have different response functions to different promotional efforts and other marketing activities. Common bases for the identification of segments are geographic variables, demographic variables, psychographics variables, and behavioristic variables. Segments can be identified as either *a priori* or *post hoc.*

The choice of target markets falls into three general categories: undifferentiated marketing, in which promotional activity does not consider segment differences; differentiated marketing, in which different promotional programs are developed for the different targeted segments; and concentrated marketing, in which all promotional effort is directed at the one segment that is targeted. The choice of which and how many segments to target is based on a cost/benefit analysis of the increase in revenue in the segment against the increased cost of giving the segment a separate promotional program.

Competitive positioning is the perception targeted consumers hold of a firm's offering relative to competitors. It defines the intended perception of the product or service and gives direction to the development of promotional activity. Basic approaches to competitive positioning are by attributes, by price/quality, by use or application, by product user, by product class, and by competitor. Development of a competitive positioning requires the use of marketing research to identify relevant competitors, to determine consumer perception of these competitors and their positioning relative to the firm's offering, and to determine consumer needs and possible competitive positionings. The manager can then select a desired positioning and implement a promotional program to establish the desired competitive positioning.

It is critical that segmentation, targeting, and competitive positioning be done well for promotional methods to have their optimal impact.

REVIEW AND DISCUSSION QUESTIONS

1. For each of the companies featured in this chapter's Promotions in Action:
   a. Describe the bases for identification of market segments.
   b. Describe the target markets selected for a specific promotional program.
   c. Describe the competitive positioning of the product.

2. Describe how Avon could undertake a segmentation study of the makeup consumer using a *post hoc* approach based on AIO measures.

3. Survey data reveal that the market for a line of name-brand stereo units selling for a minimum of $200 is concentrated among males under 35, bachelors, located on the East and West coasts, college graduates, earning yearly $12,000 and over. How can these findings be used in promotional strategy?

4. Assume that researchers in a large New York advertising agency devise a valid measure of persuasion. Critically evaluate whether or not this measure can and will prove useful in planning the advertising campaign for a large household detergent account. Would the account director for a line of refrigerators and freezers use this measure differently than his or her counterpart on the detergent account?

5. Why are there no specific rules to follow in determining the best base for segmentation?

6. Select five ads from magazines for different product categories. Identify the product positioning taken by the product in these ads; name the relevant attributes and the rating on these attributes.

NOTES

1. Thomas C. Kinnear and Kenneth L. Bernhardt, *Principles of Marketing* (Glenview, Ill.: Scott Foresman/Little Brown, 1990), p. 103.

2. This section is based on Thomas C. Kinnear and James R. Taylor, *Marketing Research: An Applied Approach* (New York: McGraw-Hill, 1991).

3. "Fashion Magazine Targets Classiest Zip Codes," *Marketing News,* June 6, 1988, pp. 1–2.

4. "Two Companies Find New Faces in Cosmetic Market," *Marketing News,* April 10, 1989, p. 8.

5. Based on "Coke, Bacardi Use Segmentation to Develop a 'Tasteful' New Product," *Bank Marketing,* July 1988, p. 112.

6. Adapted from *The Wall Street Journal,* p. 21, col. 4, February 9, 1987.

7. This section is based on David A. Aaker and J. Gary Shansby, "Positioning Your Product," *Business Horizons* (May-June 1982), pp. 56–62.

Determination of Promotional Objectives

MILK FOR HEALTH

Milk's not for babies anymore—it's for sexy adults and brown-bagging kids. That's the message marketers and producers are sending in an attempt to build milk consumption by offering new products and using new advertising.

The main target is adults. Although per capita annual consumption totals 50 gallons for teenagers, that figure falls to 36 gallons a year for the 20- to 29-year-old group and 23 gallons a year for those ages 30 to 50.

The American Dairy Association will spend all its fluid-milk ad dollars to build consumption among adults. Two new TV spots poke fun at the lyrics, "Everybody knows milk's for babies," by zooming in on *adult* bodies—particularly teeth, bones, and skin—made beautiful by milk. "This time, we're not focusing on what we put into it—calcium, vitamins—but what you get out of it."

"Our research showed that everyone knows milk is good for them, but everyone—whether teen, young adult or senior citizen—also believes milk is for someone younger than me," said E. Hoy McConnel. "We wanted to shatter the myth that milk's for kids only by pointing out its relevance and benefits."

Source: Julie Liesse Erickson and Judann Dagnoli, "Dairy Industry out to Wake up Adults," *Advertising Age*, March 13, 1989, p. 30. Used by special permission.

The American Dairy Association has charted itself an uphill course—changing a stagnant trend in demand for fluid milk. Although the awareness of the benefits of milk consumption seems to be nearly universal, there is an overwhelming perception that milk is an appropriate beverage only for a younger person.

Advertising is being called on to achieve two objectives: (1) an increase in fluid milk sales and (2) communicating the benefits milk offers adult bodies, thereby changing the widespread perception that milk is for "someone else." Will these objectives be attained? One thing we can say for sure—the effectiveness or ineffectiveness of the campaign will be easily measured and clearly evident because of these unambiguous objectives.

The purpose of this chapter is to help you understand the steps involved in moving from the analysis of your situation to a realistic set of objectives for the promotion mix. Most of the focus here is on advertising and sales promotion; the specific considerations for personal selling and reseller support are covered in later chapters.

BACKGROUND CONSIDERATIONS

The objectives for promotional strategy always must be viewed in a broad marketing context. Prior decisions on market segmentation, decisions on other areas of marketing strategy, projected increases in sales and/or market share, and financial resources all shape and influence the role for promotion. These factors must be viewed as the *givens* within which promotion must function.

Market Segmentation

In Chapter 5, we discussed the results achieved by the Kellogg Corporation prior to 1989 once it made the decision to concentrate on the adult market between the ages of 25 and 49. The industry had previously written off this segment as being "health oriented joggers who never eat breakfast."[1] The decision to concentrate on this segment enabled Kellogg to raise its market share from 36.7 percent in 1983 to around 40 percent by 1989.

This market segmentation decision obviously paid off. Nevertheless, the age 25 to 49 segment is unduly broad in most situations. A broad focus obscures the fact that smaller market targets such as single adults, young families with children, and members of various ethnic groups exist.

What this means is that an initial market segmentation decision usually requires refinement if promotional strategy is to have a precise target.

Other Elements of Marketing Strategy

"This is Not Your Father's Oldsmobile." So rings the message in an advertising campaign by the Oldsmobile Division of General Motors. The campaign is even backed by a 30-day or 1,500-mile guarantee of satisfaction. The aim is to convert baby-boom buyers into repeat customers, thereby throwing off the stodgy image of GM's weakest division.[2]

Such positioning efforts may make for interesting advertising, but consider the fact that imports have made their greatest penetration in the baby-boomer segment.[3] Furthermore, at the onset of this campaign, Oldsmobile did not yet have a full line of models designed to be import fighters; as a result, much of what it offered at that time was largely what attracted "your father" to Oldsmobile.

This example illustrates that promotional strategy must build on prior decisions with respect to product design and features, pricing, and distribution. If these areas of the marketing mix have shortcomings, the promotional strategy is boxed in from the outset. There is no other choice but to work with what you have.

Sales and Market Share Goals

Sales and market share goals must also be part of the fundamental marketing consideration. Kellogg introduced Müeslix in November 1987 with a $33 million marketing budget. This European-style cereal carried a price of about $2.89 for a 14-ounce box in contrast to the $1.55 price for 12 ounces of corn flakes. Initial sales projections were $50 million.[4]

Where would the blame be assigned if sales fell short of this goal? (In actuality, sales were twice the expectation.) All eyes turn quickly to advertising. The advertising staff and agency could not walk away and point the finger elsewhere, even though it can be unfair to blame the promotional component of the marketing mix over others when marketing objectives are not met.

Many would counter that the role of advertising is to *communicate;*[5] hence, effectiveness can be measured only in communication terms, not by changes in sales. Undoubtedly, this is true up to a point. Without communication of brand name and benefits, little else can happen. It cannot be denied, however, that promotion is also assigned the legitimate role of stimulating trial and repeat usage, both of which translate into sales and market share.

Management is increasingly demanding evidence that *advertising and sales promotion impact buying behavior.* This means that a projected sales volume of $50 million must be translated ultimately into the behavioral outcomes of trial and/or repeat buying. Furthermore, methodology, especially electronic scanning, now exists to measure sales impact with greater precision.[6]

Obviously, at times it is unfair to blame advertising when sales fall short. As stated earlier, no amount of promotion can move a noncompetitive product. Furthermore, in some situations, the role of advertising is to create a change in product image over time, thus making it difficult to trace the immediate effect on sales.

To illustrate this point, look at the situation faced by the Lincoln-Mercury Division of Ford Motor Company in 1988:

> In 1988, Mercury placed dead last in "brand power"—a measure of such things as recognition and cachet—among domestic-car nameplates, according to Landor Associates, a San Francisco image consulting firm. In another Landor survey, some 76 percent of consumers didn't recognize the symbol Mercury adopted in 1984—a stylized "M" in a circle that many dealers deride as the "flying hockey stick."[7]

The challenge for Lincoln-Mercury is to change its image by using advertising communication. This could be a long-term effort given the extent to which this nameplate has dropped in consumer awareness. Although successful image building ultimately should translate into sales outcomes, it would be unrealistic to expect much at this initial stage.

What it comes down to is this: *Communication and sales both are legitimate promotional objectives.* We must ask management to recognize that sales are also affected by other elements in the marketing mix.

Financial Resources

How much can we spend? Obviously, the answers to this bottom-line question dictate both the nature and scope of promotional strategy. Nothing more need be said at this point since budgeting is the subject of the next chapter.

USING CONSUMER RESEARCH TO DEFINE THE ROLE FOR PROMOTION

All thinking about promotional strategy begins with segmentation analysis discussed in the previous chapter. You have seen how research can be used to delineate possible market targets using a number of segmentation bases. Now it is necessary to refine and sharpen this analysis so that we can answer two important questions: (1) What are the characteristics of our market target(s)? (2) What kind of decision process is undertaken in purchasing and using the product or service?

Description of the Market Target

Turn now to Promotion in Action 9–1, which describes the strategic thinking that led Bristol-Myers to target the over-50 market for its Bufferin brand. Notice that the overall target was narrowed, first of all, to heavy aspirin users. Second, it was narrowed even further to seekers of relief from occasional aches and pains. A possible secondary target aimed at those who use analgesics to reduce the risk of a second heart attack.

Now we need further descriptive information about each target segment. The following are the questions to ask of marketing research:

1. How is the decision-making unit defined?
2. What are the demographic characteristics?
3. What are the psychographic characteristics?

Getting the Most out of Life in the Golden Years

PROMOTION
IN ACTION
9–1

Bristol-Myers Squibb's Bufferin is abandoning heart-attack prevention claims in TV spots and is returning to its 1950s pain-relief message targeting older people. Angela Lansbury is its spokeswoman.

The theme emphasizes that people over 50 can lead full lives despite the occasional aches and pains that come with age. The major strategy shift reflects a trend to return aspirin advertising to its original pain-relief claims. The move comes in the wake of ads aimed at preventing second heart attacks, an effort that failed to boost aspirin unit sales or share of the $2 billion analgesic market.

Even more dramatic is that Bufferin is specifically targeting people over 50—a group that uses a disproportionately large amount of aspirin but for the most part has been ignored in advertising, said Bob Merold, analgesics marketing director at the Bristol-Myers Products unit. "No one is talking to these people; in advertising, everyone is 30 years old, except for the occasional arthritis spot where the person is 45."

Bristol-Myers hasn't abandoned heart health, however. Mr. Merold said the marketer will continue to advertise its heart message to the medical community and possibly in consumer print ads. The company will "strongly consider" advertising to prevent first heart attacks if the U.S. Food & Drug Administration approves that advertising claim.

Bufferin ranks fourth in the aspirin segment with about a 10 percent share.

Source: Patricia Winters, "Bufferin Aims at 50-Plus," *Advertising Age*, October 23, 1989, pp. 4, 116. Used by special permission.

Definition of the Decision-Making Unit   You will recall from Chapter 7 that members of the household can play different roles in the decision process:

1. *Gatekeeper*—the initiator of the buying process and information gatherer.
2. *Influencer*—expresses opinions that weigh heavily in the options that are evaluated and chosen.
3. *Decider*—exercises financial authority or power to dictate the final choice.
4. *Purchaser*—the shopper and buyer.
5. *Users*—the primary user(s) or consumer(s).

It is necessary now to determine whether such multiple roles are expressed within target households when the product or service is being considered. For example, it is possible that the most frequent ultimate user of Bufferin does not make the purchase. In that case, advertising should be targeted to either the decider or purchaser.

At times, those performing each of these roles could serve as a target segment. Here are a few examples of this:

1. *Gatekeepers*—The male decides when it is time to buy a new car; the wife has decided that the old couch has to go.
2. *Influencers*—The wife must use the car in her role as family driver; the husband loudly proclaims "any fabric color but baby blue"; the six-year-old who says, "Make sure it's Frosted Flakes, Mom."
3. *Deciders*—Mom visits many stores and comes home with the wallpaper pattern that she must "sell" to other family members; dad pays all the bills.
4. *Purchasers*—Dad always stops to pick up milk on the way home; anybody who's going to the drugstore.
5. *Users*—They could be anybody and everybody in the household unit, each of whom has different product expectations.

It is essential to sort these roles out because mistaken judgment can lead to unfortunate consequences. As an example, users of electric razors were surveyed to discover which colors they preferred. Much to the surprise of management, the color that most users chose turned out to be dead last in sales. The reason? Wives purchase the majority of electric razors as gifts for husbands, and their color preferences dominate, not those of the users.[8]

Demographic Characteristics   The term *demographics* refers to such objective descriptors as age, income, social status, education, and income. This information is the bread and butter of marketing research, and it plays an important role in the selection of advertising media. Once you have defined your target demographically, you can select media that have the same audience characteristics (see Chapter 15).

The target for Bufferin is quite broad and encompasses all people in the over-50 market who seek relief from occasional pain. Therefore, it is logical to use such media as *Modern Maturity* —the magazine reaching those over 50 who have joined the American Association of Retired People—the *Reader's Digest,* and so on.

Psychographic Characteristics   Those who are responsible for creating the message need more information than demographics. What kind of people are we trying to reach? What is their lifestyle? How should we depict them? Are they active, highly social, and outgoing? Or are they more interested in the family and home?

Research into consumer lifestyles has come to be known as *psychographics.*[9] Lifestyles are measured using a battery of *a*ctivity, *i*nterest, and *o*pinion (AIO) measures. The following are a few examples of the types of statements used to measure AIO (consumers responded using an agree/-disagree scale):

I consider myself someone who wants to get ahead in life.

Those who know me often think that I am shy and reserved.

To me, having a good time means an evening out with friends.

Weekly church attendance is important to me.

Statistical analysis is then undertaken to determine the extent to which these and other similar statements describe a particular market segment. The following are just a few characteristics of the over-50 segment that will be of interest to the marketers of Bufferin:[10]

They see themselves as being in the mainstream of life, not on the peripheries.

Convenience, not price, is a primary motivating factor.

Almost all say they prefer to buy a few high-quality items rather than more with less quality.

Nearly three-fourths are willing to pay more if merchandise is sold closer to home.

Writers and graphic artists now have a better picture of their customer. For example, he or she should be depicted as active, healthy, and involved. The Bufferin benefit is to free the customer from minor discomfort so that he or she can be on the go.

Moving to a different product category, Mazda Motors of America targeted the so-called neotraditionalists in its August 1989 introduction of the new and very sporty Miata.[11] Research indicated that this $15,000 car would attract a wide range of ages, especially older buyers yearning for a sports car and finally able to afford one. The company described the psychographics of its market in this way:

> "Neotraditionalist" is a term coined by Yankelovich, Clancy, Shulman to describe a lifestyle that embraces traditional values, such as family, but in a contemporary context of the social changes that have occurred over the past few decades. Neotraditionalists aren't faddish but seek solid products.[12]

Diagnosing Motivation and Behavior in a Target Segment

Now that we have defined the target segment (or segments), we must focus on motivation and decision processes. Will most prospective buyers make their decision on the basis of extended problem solving (EPS)? Or is limited problem solving (LPS) more likely? If buying is habitual, are buying routines grounded in loyalty? Or do they reflect inertia?

It is helpful to use a series of diagnostic questions to gain the needed insight. You will recognize the research outline in Table 9–1 from Chapter 5.

You make use of the outline in Table 9–1 as follows. The key decision makers review each question one at a time asking whether or not the needed information is available. If the answer is no, the focus of further market research is clearly defined. Once this process is completed, the role that promotion must play in both communication and stimulation of trial should be much more apparent.

Extended Problem Solving (EPS)   Five roles for promotion are possible when most people in the target market segment engage in extended problem solving.

Stimulation of need recognition   Need recognition exists, for example, when a consumer perceives that "the old car has had it and we must do something soon." If need recognition doesn't exist, promotion has no role. That means that promotion on occasion must be designed to bring about a perceived difference between "what might be" and "what is."

The Honda Motorcycle Division is attempting to change the image of motorcycling to make it more acceptable to a broader consumer public.[13] The 1989 campaign was positioned to change the "outlaw and burn-out" image that has plagued the industry. The campaign presented motorcycling as fun: "The wind in your face, the freedom of the open road, and the adventure of off-road riding."[14] If successful, this campaign could trigger need recognition that will ultimately lead to purchase.

Campaigns of this type often fail simply because promotion alone will usually not stem a downturn in primary demand. The American Dairy

TABLE 9–1

Diagnosis of Decision Process Behavior

Motivation and Need Recognition

1. What needs and motivations are satisfied by product purchase and usage (i.e., what *benefits* are consumers seeking)?

2. Are these needs dormant or are they presently perceived as felt needs by prospective buyers?

3. How involved with the product are most prospective buyers in the target market segment?

Search for Information

1. What product- and brand-related information is stored in memory?

2. Is the consumer motivated to turn to external sources to find information about available alternatives and their characteristics?

3. What specific information sources are used most frequently when search is undertaken?

4. What product features or attributes are the focus of search when it is undertaken?

Alternative Evaluation

1. To what extent do consumers engage in alternative evaluation and comparison?

2. Which product and/or brand alternatives are included in the evaluation process?

3. Which evaluative criteria (product attributes) are used to compare various alternatives?

   a. Which are most salient in the evaluation?

   b. How complex is the evaluation (i.e., using a single attribute as opposed to using several in combination)?

4. What kind of decision rule is used to determine the best choice?

5. What are the outcomes of evaluation regarding each of the candidate purchase alternatives?

   a. What is believed to be true about the characteristics and features of each?

   b. Are they perceived to be different in important ways, or are they seen as essentially the same?

   c. What attitudes are held regarding the purchase and use of each?

   d. What purchasing intentions are expressed, and when will these intentions most likely be consummated by purchase and use?

Purchase

1. Will the consumer spend time and energy to shop until the preferred alternative is found?

2. Is additional decision-process behavior needed to discover the preferred outlet for purchase?

3. What are the preferred modes of purchase (i.e., through retail stores, in the home, or in other ways)?

Association example at the beginning of this chapter is a case in point. Other beverages have replaced milk among adults, and this is not a recent trend. Changing consumer attitudes in this type of situation is a formidable challenge, and we will be surprised if the American Dairy Association's campaign succeeds.

Awareness of brand name   It is all too common for consumers to remember the advertising execution without recalling the brand name itself. When this happens, advertising investment will have little or no return. Promotion in Action 9–2 gives some interesting examples of serious failures in advertising communication.

The objective of advertising communication is to stimulate brand name awareness in the form of *recall*. This is because message content is processed in EPS using the *central route* in which information is weighed and evaluated in reasoned fashion. With little or no recall, advertising has missed the mark.

Attitude change   In earlier chapters, we stressed the importance of *attitude toward purchase* of a given brand. Attitude change now becomes an important communication objective.

Attitudes are formed on the basis of the extent to which the brand in question is perceived as measuring up favorably on those dimensions that are important in choice. When perceived deficiencies exist, they must be countered.

TABLE 9–1

Diagnosis of Decision Process Behavior (concluded)

Outcomes
1. What degree of satisfaction or dissatisfaction is expressed with respect to previously used alternatives in the product or service category?
2. What reasons are given for satisfaction or dissatisfaction?
3. Has perceived satisfaction or dissatisfaction been shared with other people to help them in their buying behavior?
4. Have consumers made attempts to achieve redress for dissatisfaction?
5. Is there an intention to repurchase any of the alternatives?

      a. If no, why not?
      b. If yes, does intention reflect brand loyalty or inertia?

Source: James F. Engel, Roger D. Blackwell, and Paul W. Miniard, *Consumer Behavior*, 6th ed. (Hinsdale, Ill.: Dryden Press, 1989), p. 473. Reproduced by special permission.

To illustrate what this means for promotional strategy, we return to the example in Chapter 5 of EPS decision making among first-time purchasers of a 4×4 pickup truck. Assume now that further market research has been undertaken; here is what it revealed:

1. Present 4×4 owners have substantial need recognition and desire to repurchase. The market share of the five leading brands is as follows: Brand A, 35 percent; Brand B, 30 percent; Brand C, 10 percent; Brand D, 8 percent; Brand E, 17 percent. Brand A owners showed the highest intention to repurchase with a rate of 78 percent; owners of Brand D showed the lowest intention with 30 percent.

2. *Motivation and Need Recognition.* Focus group research was undertaken among baby boomers who never have owned a 4×4. They indicated a real interest in the thrill and sense of power produced by off-road performance. Nearly all indicated that they would expect their vehicle to shift immediately between two-wheel and four-wheel drives. Also, many prospective buyers wanted to have the interior comfort and ambiance expected in a passenger car.

Use of the Zaichkowsky Personal Involvement Scale (Table 5–2) showed an average score of 8 of a possible 10, an indication of high involvement.

The Slogan's Familiar, but What's the Brand?

❖
**PROMOTION
IN ACTION**

Companies collectively spend billions of dollars a year trying to hammer home their advertising slogans. But it's the rare slogan that makes a lasting impression.

R. H. Bruskin Associates, a market-research firm in New Brunswick, N.J., finds that although people may recognize slogans, relatively few associate them with the right brand name. When the company tested a group of slogans recently with consumers, it found that 60 percent recognized "Never let them see you sweat," but only 4 percent correctly identified it with Dry Idea deodorant.

The recognition level for "Cars that make sense," was 32 percent; yet just 4 percent knew it was the slogan for Hyundai. Similarly, "American's business address" was familiar to 17 percent of consumers, but only 3 percent linked it with Hilton Hotels. One of the few slogans a majority of people matched correctly with the brand was Campbell's "Soup is good food."

Source: Ronald Alsop, "The Slogan's Familiar, but What's the Brand? *The Wall Street Journal,* January 8, 1988, p. 17. Reproduced by special permission.

3. *Search for Information.* Most baby-boomer prospects are motivated to search for information. Their primary sources are friends and relatives. Also, they remember reading ads in general interest magazines. Many have turned to such objective rating sources as *Consumer's Report.* Some have visited showrooms just to browse and collect information. Others are at the stage of discovering which features are important in differentiating alternatives.

4. *Alternative Evaluation.* Active alternative evaluation and comparison exist. The most important attributes of 4×4s are shown below in the attitude ratings. Attributes are evaluated in a *compensatory* way (weakness on one can be offset by strength on others).

Some people are uncertain how various alternatives differ. They are aware of the four or five leading brands and often mentioned Brand A as the market leader. Other people noted their concern that C and D do not shift easily between drives.

5. *Attitudes toward Five Leading Manufacturers.* The following table shows how the prospects evaluated the five leading makes:

Attribute	Importance	Manufacturer Ratings				
		A	B	C	D	E
Two-wheel to four-wheel drive shifting	+3	+3	+3	-3	-2	+3
Off-road handling	+3	+3	+2	-2	-3	+1
Frequency of repair	+2	+2	+3	+1	-2	-1
Interior comfort	+2	+1	-2	-1	+3	-1
Low price	+1	+1	-1	+3	+1	+1
Attitude toward purchase		+25	+16	-12	-12	+9

6. *Intention.* About 40 percent expressed an intention at least to test drive 4×4s in the next year. More than 60 percent expressed interest in Brand A, compared with only 20 percent interest in Brand D.

7. *Purchase.* Most people were willing to try many dealers until they find just what they want.

What does all this mean to the Brand D management? Several of the 1990 models have corrected previous deficiencies in drive shifting and off-road handling. Now the promotional objective becomes clear: *Change attitudes toward purchase of Brand D by changing the negative belief ratings on the dimensions of drive shifting and off-road handling.* Another objective is to *stress the uniqueness of Brand D in interior comfort.*

The following promotional objectives could emerge from analysis of marketing research data:

1. *Create an attitude.* This would be the challenge to reach new potential customers who have little or no information about alternatives.

2. *Modify an attitude.* Modification occurs when a brand is linked to a different motivation through a strategy of repositioning. This is what we have proposed for Brand D.

3. *Maintain an attitude.* Brand A is in the fortunate position of having the attributes that count. This favorable evaluation can be maintained by stressing superiority on drive shifting, off-road handling, and frequency of repair.

Intention change   All things being equal, a favorable attitude toward purchasing will be followed by an intention to buy. A positive change in intention is a common promotional objective, especially with frequently purchased products. Brand A is in the enviable position of attracting the majority who expressed an intention, whereas Brand B must offer special incentives (rebates, etc.) to stimulate a positive increase in the low level of interest expressed.

Behavioral change   Behavioral objectives are stated as increases in repeat purchases, switching to this brand, or first-time trial. The strategy for Brand A, for example, could call for maintaining its 25 percent market share by stimulating repurchase among 75 percent of present users. It also would make sense to aim at attracting some of Brand D customers by developing a point-by-point comparative campaign stressing Brand A's superiority on the most important attributes.

Finally, Brand A's promotional strategy could be designed to win at least 35 percent of those entering the market for the first time. Certainly Brand A has the awareness, image, and competitive strength necessary for such a level of penetration.

Limited Problem Solving (LPS)   If the market research analysis following Table 9–1 reveals limited problem solving, the following is a summary from Chapter 6 of the response characteristics you will notice:

1. Involvement is low and brands are perceived as being essentially the same.

2. There is little motivation to search for information. Exposure to advertising and other forms of marketing communication is described as *passive and involuntary.*

3. Alternatives are not evaluated rigorously, and a noncompensatory strategy is used. This leads to elimination of alternatives perceived as falling short on the most salient attribute(s).

4. Alternatives are evaluated more thoroughly *after* purchase rather than *before.*

5. Choice is often prompted by display and point-of-sale incentives.

Limited problem solving is precisely the situation that Liquid Tide faced when it was introduced in 1985. Its objective was to capture the number one place in the liquid detergent industry from Lever Brothers' Wisk, which had an 8 percent share.[15] Following are the types of promotional objectives that are appropriate with such an objective.

Recognition of brand name   Establishing the brand name as a widely perceived contender in the product category is essential. Remember that a first-time purchase generally is made on a "why-not-try-it" basis. For the purchase to be made, the brand name and logo must be *recognized* at point of sale.

Procter & Gamble achieved high levels of recognition for Liquid Tide, and advertising went one step further to establish high "top-of-mind recall." As a result of saturation advertising, 37 percent of potential customers mentioned Liquid Tide when they were asked which laundry advertising came to mind.[16]

It is important to be clear regarding the distinction between recognition and recall as communication objectives. With the reasoned action of extended problem solving, the consumer must *recall* salient information to be used in the deliberation process. Therefore, recall becomes the promotional objective.

The LPS purchaser, on the other hand, engages in little conscious deliberation. Although advertising can build some familiarity with brand and principal benefit, there may be little or no conscious recall of brand name or copy points. Yet a visual imagery has been stored in memory and can be activated by point-of-sale stimuli. This means that *recognition is the appropriate objective.* If some recall also occurs, as with Liquid Tide, this is a helpful added outcome.

Attitude change   Even though most alternative evaluation occurs after use, it is realistic to establish an objective that calls for awareness, expressed by recognition, of both brand name and principal benefit. In this case, our intent is to stimulate awareness that Tide now comes in liquid form. If the buyer has a preference for liquid over granular detergent, we have associated brand name with an important attribute, thereby influencing attitude.

You probably have grasped by now that attitude formation and change are less demanding tasks under LPS conditions. Message appeals will generate little counterargumentation and hence have a fair chance of entering into memory and changing beliefs if sufficient exposure has occurred.

Intention change   The only purchase intention in most LPS situations is the *intention to purchase product category, not brand.* Remember that brand preferences, if they exist at all, are generally not strongly held. About all that advertising can do is to feature a coupon or other incentive through direct action copy designed to bring about trial.

Behavioral change   The most crucial goal now is to *stimulate trial.* Everything possible must be done to get the product into as many hands as possible. Trying the brand once and evaluating it favorably can lead a customer to repurchase.

Procter & Gamble was successful in the introduction of Liquid Tide. With a $50 million investment in advertising and sales promotion, it achieved a 6.8 percent market share in the first year.

Trial stimulation is the objective for sales promotion. This means that the product must receive prominent display and point-of-sale promotional support. If these are not accomplished, the consumer's "why-not-try-it" response probably will shift to "why not try a different brand?"

Habitual Buying   All of us turn repetitive behavior into routine. Sometimes this behavior leads to brand preference based on high involvement. When this is the situation, the consumer has little incentive to change. Most often, however, repeat purchases reflect nothing more than inertia. Promotional strategy differs depending on these underlying dynamics.

Brand loyalty   Those firms fortunate enough to build substantial brand loyalty (there are relatively few in this position) face a continual competitive onslaught. The promotional objective calls for maintaining loyalty by stressing a consistent, readily identifiable theme and image. Competitors have found Budweiser to be almost invulnerable in part because of its image as "The King of Beers."

In other situations, constant innovation is the key to maintaining loyalty. This means that the primary function of advertising is to communicate the ever-changing benefits to the present market and to previously untapped segments. Awareness of changed product attributes becomes the objective.

Inertia   An LPS purchase is repeated mostly because of inertia and lack of sufficient reason to change. Brand preference is highly unstable and volatile. Consumers will switch quickly in response to coupon offers and other incentives.

Let's take the liquid detergent market as an example once again.[17] Even though Liquid Tide achieved a 6.8 percent market share, Lever Brothers' Wisk increased its share from 8.0 to 8.8 percent. Colgate Palmolive spent $25 million to introduce new Fab Liquid, further destabilizing the national scene.

Of the 21 remaining brands, 15 reported lower market shares. If matters weren't volatile enough, Procter & Gamble countered by introducing new Liquid Bold. It was positioned to offer the additional benefits of fabric softening and static control.

Market share is maintained in these situations by having sufficient reason to stress the word "new." Brand recognition is the most important advertising objective. Also, remember that competitors are not sitting still. Therefore, it becomes necessary to maintain competitive parity on the advertising scene. Often this parity is referred to as "share of mind." If awareness levels are allowed to drop, sales can quickly follow. Notice how quickly Lever Brothers matched P & G dollar for dollar.

THE STATEMENT OF OBJECTIVES

The statement of promotional objectives should include the following, each of which is stated within the time period covered by the campaign: (1) a definition and description of market target; (2) the expected outcomes in terms of trial and repurchase; (3) a clear message platform; (4) the expected communications results; and (5) the measurement methods and criteria.

Target Market

The statement of target market should include a definition of the decision-making role of the recipient, demographic characteristics, and a psychographic profile. A good example of target market is our earlier discussion of the over-50 target for Bufferin.

Message Platform

The message platform (sometimes referred to as the *creative platform* or *unique selling proposition*) is an answer to the question: *What exactly do you want to communicate to your audience?* It will usually be stated in broad terms, with specific details of execution left to artists and writers.

Eastman Kodak introduced its disc camera with this message platform: "The disc camera is decision-free, unique, and capable of letting you take pictures you couldn't take before."[18] It is specific enough to shape the message strategy without inhibiting creative execution.

You will also find a well-conceived message platform in the campaign undertaken by AT&T as it fought for survival in the long-distance telephone market. See Promotion in Action 9–3.

Expected Sales Results

The issue of sales versus communication outcomes was discussed thoroughly earlier in the chapter. Although advertising and sales promotion cannot achieve these outcomes alone, the expectations as to what can be accomplished in terms of trial and purchase should be specific. Here are examples of how these objectives are stated:

1. Generate a 29 percent trial rate in 20 metropolitan areas.
2. Achieve a 70 percent repurchase rate (10 packages per year) in the next 12 months.

Thank You for Calling AT&T

❖
**PROMOTION
IN ACTION
9–3**

The breakup of the telephone company in the United States is now legendary. AT&T Communications in Atlanta was left as the company's surviving long-distance supplier, but the door was opened wide for more than 300 competitors, ranging from IBM and RCA to smaller suppliers of every shape and variety. Through skillful promotion, AT&T was able to combat low brand awareness and price misperceptions while differentiating itself in this $45 billion market.

In 1983, only 5 percent of residential long-distance users recognized AT&T as a supplier. The company made a major attempt to build awareness with ads featuring Cliff Robertson; awareness reached 50 percent by the end of 1984.

But awareness was only the beginning. Next came the need to identify AT&T quality with the attributes people most want in a long-distance company. The objective shifted to communication of the distinctives of operator availability, the ability to call from anywhere in the country at any time, the ease of doing business, and a money-back guarantee. An important phrase here was *no surprises.*

At the same time, AT&T combated aggressive price competition by advertising its 40 to 60 percent off of peak discounts. In addition, it offered special new rates.

Once the campaign had built awareness and understanding, it shifted to asking customers to make a choice: "AT&T, the right choice."

Source: "Customer Contract Enables AT&T to Communicate Quality Message," *Marketing News,* November 22, 1985. Used by special permission.

Expected Communication Results

The objectives for an advertising campaign by a major oil company are the following:

1. Win new customers.
2. Increase station sales volume.
3. Increase the sales ratio of premium lead-free fuel compared with regular lead-free.

The Importance of Benchmarks   What is missing in the oil company's statement of objectives? First of all, it has no *benchmarks* (i.e., present market share, sales volume, and ratio of premium to regular).

Contrast this with the AT&T campaign in Promotion in Action 9–3. The benchmark was a 5 percent awareness of AT&T as a long-distance supplier in 1983. By the end of 1984, advertising had raised this awareness level to 50 percent, a clear indication of advertising success. Also, although the figures are not given, it is apparent that benchmarks were in place for awareness of such attributes as operator availability, ease of doing business, and money-back guarantee.

Extent of Expected Change   If you had been responsible for the AT&T long-distance advertising campaign, how much increase would you expect to achieve in the 5 percent awareness level? 20 percent? 50 percent? It is necessary to have some idea because the magnitude of expected change affects budget levels.

Turning once again to our earlier example of 4×4 vehicles, here are some feasible communication objectives:

1. Increase awareness of Brand A from 35 percent to 75 percent in the target market by the end of the introductory year.
2. Attain a 50 percent aided recall of the claim that Brand D now offers the benefit of instant drive shifting.
3. Create a change of attitude for Brand D from -2 to $+2$ on the attribute of easy drive shifting.
4. Change the percentage of prospective purchasers who state a preference for Brand B from 25 percent to 40 percent.

Benchmarks are in place in these examples and expected changes are specified. It is no great challenge to write such a specific statement, but how is a 20 or 30 percent awareness change translated into strategy? What does one do to achieve such levels?

We can give you no formula to follow in answering these questions. There is no substitute for past experience. In similar situations (if there are any), what results were achieved? What can we learn from these situations? Probably there is no way to avoid guesswork and some experimentation.

In our experience, we have not found many marketers who set objectives in concrete terms. Usually a benchmark or starting point will be clear, but no specific percentage of expected change is stated. This avoids setting numerical increases that can be quite arbitrary while at the same time allowing precise measurement of changes once the campaign has been carried out.

Measurement Methods and Criteria

We have tried to be explicit as to when recall is the best measure as opposed to recognition. This also needs to be made clear in the statement of objectives. Expecting high recall in a low-involvement situation in which recognition is the objective and vice versa could be totally misleading.

SUMMARY

The purpose of this chapter is to provide guidance as to how to move from marketing research and other background information to a statement of realistic advertising and sales promotion objectives.

An important initial issue is whether an increase in sales or market share is a legitimate goal for promotion. It is fair to state that promotion is the *communication* function of marketing. Yet communication must be related to stimulation of trial and repurchase, even though other elements of the marketing mix also affect sales. Therefore, both communication and sales objectives are important.

A statement of objectives has these components: (1) a definition and description of the target market, (2) a statement of the message (creative) platform, (3) the expected sales outcomes, (4) the expected communication outcomes, and (5) the measurement methods and criteria. The challenge is to state objectives so specifically that it is possible to measure outcomes unambiguously.

The majority of this chapter concentrated on the objectives appropriate for extended problem solving (EPS), limited problem solving (LPS), and habitual buying. When most consumers in the target segment use EPS, the objectives usually take the form of awareness of name and benefits expressed as *recall, attitude change,* and *trial.*

With LPS, on the other hand, advertising performs the primary function of stimulating sufficient name awareness and initial interest that the product will be *recognized* at point of sale. Trial is activated mostly by display and sales promotion.

Habitual decision-making behavior presents two different challenges. With brand loyalty based on high involvement, the objective is to reinforce preferences. When repurchase is motivated by inertia, however, competitive inroads are likely. Maintenance of awareness (share of mind) becomes an essential consideration.

REVIEW AND DISCUSSION QUESTIONS

1. "The reason we spend millions on advertising is to increase sales. What results have we seen in the last quarter?" This memo from the chairperson of the board of a California winery reaches you, the advertising director. How would you respond in a memo?

2. Now you are the advertising manager for a high-fashion women's wear chain and have received a memo identical to that in Question 1. Would your answers be different? Why?

3. The advertising campaign for a leading brand of camping items is based on this statement of objectives: "Our objective is to tell as many people as possible that camping is fun for the whole family and is inexpensive and easy." Is this sufficient? Are changes needed? If so, what would you suggest?

4. The advertising manager for a new brand of cat litter has $30 million to spend. Present levels of awareness for this brand are less than 10 percent in the 30 leading metropolitan markets. She is faced with the challenge of figuring out how much increase in awareness she can generate with this budget. This budget, by the way, is three times larger than in the previous year. What counsel can you give her?

5. One of the major competitors of AT&T in the long-distance market has mounted an aggressive campaign with an emphasis on better service at a lower price per call. The first market share results showed that top-of-mind recall of company name and advertised benefits increased from 35 percent to 48 percent. Management concluded that advertising was a resounding success, although a long-time senior executive expressed a dissenting view. He argued that awareness is not enough. What would your answer be?

6. A leading brand in the highly competitive headache remedy market has dropped in top-of-mind awareness from 31 percent to 20 percent because of competitive product introductions. What does this mean in practical terms? What implications do you see?

NOTES

1. Patricia Sellers, "How King Kellogg Beat the Blahs," *Fortune*, August 29, 1988, pp. 54–64.

2. Raymond Serafin, " 'Oldsmobile Edge': A Guarantee," *Advertising Age*, September 11, 1989, p. 116.

3. Paul Ingrassia and Gregory A. Patterson, "Is Buying a Car a Choice or a Chore?" *The Wall Street Journal*, October 24, 1989, pp. B7 and B8.

4. Sellers, "How King Kellogg Beats the Blahs," p. 60.

5. This is the basis of what has come to be known as DAGMAR (*d*efining *a*dvertising *g*oals, *m*easuring *a*dvertising *r*esults). See, for example, *Defining Advertising Goals*, ed. Russell H. Colley (New York: Association of National Advertisers, 1961).

6. Martha Farnsworth Riche, "Scanning for Dollars," *American Demographics* 11 (November 1989), p. 8.

7. Melinda Grenier Guiles, "Ford's Mercury Line Strives to Establish a Firm Identity," *The Wall Street Journal*, April 4, 1989, p. B6.

8. James F. Engel, Roger D. Blackwell, and Paul W. Miniard, *Consumer Behavior*, 6th ed. (Hinsdale, Ill.: Dryden Press, 1990), p. 39.

9. For a detailed review of psychographics, see Engel et al., chap. 12; and Martha Farnsworth Riche, "Psychographics for the 1990s," *American Demographics* 11 (July 1989), pp. 24–32.

10. "Tomorrow's Consumer," *American Demographics* 10 (July 1988), p. 22.

11. Raymond Serafin and Cleveland Horton, "New Mazda Ads Geared to Image," *Advertising Age*, June 12, 1989, p. 2.

12. Ibid.

13. "Honda Hopes to Win New Riders by Emphasizing 'Fun' of Cycles," *Marketing News*, August 28, 1989, p. 6.

14. Ibid.

15. Laurie Freeman, "Tide Hasn't Turned Yet," *Advertising Age*, November 18, 1985, p. 43.

16. Scott Hume, "P & G Ad Awareness Scores Fit to Be Tide," *Advertising Age*, March 25, 1985, p. 6.

17. Freeman, "Tide Hasn't Turned Yet."

18. "Credit Success of Kodak Disc Camera to Research," *Marketing News*, January 21, 1983, pp. 8–9.

The Promotional Appropriation

Chapter

10

DOES THIS PRODUCT (MANAGER) HAVE A FUTURE?

Mary Johnson was appointed product manager for Magic Care Skin Lotion (MCSL) in September 1989 and was given three weeks in which to recommend a promotional appropriation for the brand for the 1990 calendar year. To accomplish this task, she would have to project sales and profits for the coming year, but to do so, she would have to develop a marketing plan that specifies the appropriate level and nature of three types of promotional expenditures: consumer advertising, consumer promotion, and trade promotion. Johnson decided to begin by analyzing the history and results of MCSL's marketing strategy over the previous five years, with particular emphasis on the nature, effectiveness, and profitability of MCSL's various promotional efforts.

She found that the primary objective of MCSL advertising over the past five years was to increase sales by suggesting new uses for the product. An analysis of bimonthly advertising expenditures showed substantial period-to-period fluctuations. Johnson believed these data indicated the absence of a sustained commitment to consumer advertising as well as management's tendency to cut advertising expenditures during the fourth quarter to meet annual profit targets.

Media selection was more consistent with network television being the principal medium and receiving almost 40 percent of the promotional appropriation. Print media were used to announce special consumer promotions. Historically, MCSL brand management

263

had spent little on trade promotion. However, in 1988 and 1989, these expenditures increased rapidly as major retailers demanded more and larger slotting allowances to provide shelf space. In contrast, less money had been allocated to consumer promotions over the past three years. In 1988, for example, only two such promotions were run; one offered a cents off coupon and the other a self-liquidating premium.

Gross sales for 1987 were approximately $25 million with total promotional expenditures (excluding personal selling) of $5 million. During the past five years, sales had almost doubled while promotional expenditures had increased 50 percent. In 1988, the promotional appropriation was reduced to $4.5 million and sales remained about the same as the previous year. Expenditures to date in 1989 were about the same as for the preceding year, and sales were barely up to the levels for the same period in 1988. Profit contributions averaged about 30 percent of gross sales over the past three years but rose to 34 percent in 1988.

Johnson was faced with the problem of recommending not only a level of promotional expenditure but also a complete promotional strategy. Management had given her a free hand but had told her that the brand would be expected to show a profit increase of 10 percent in 1990.

Her first impression was that management might be "milking" the brand to increase short-run profitability by holding down promotional expenditures. To overcome milking she knew that she would have to show that the brand had enough growth potential to support investment spending. If she could not build a strong enough case to support this approach, she knew she would be the caretaker of a declining brand rather than the manager of a product with increasing sales.

Determining how much to spend for promotion is one of the most perplexing problems facing management today. Because of the large number of variables that come into play, as the Magic Care example illustrates, finding a solution is not easy. At best, the available methods to determine the promotional appropriation provide only rough approximations of the optimal expenditure level.

Before considering various approaches to the problem, it is important that we first understand something about the economists' notion of the optimal expenditure. With this background, it is possible to analyze existing appropriation procedures, to grasp the extent to which these methods approximate the ideal, and to analyze the potential of newer methods. This chapter focuses primarily on the problems inherent in determining the amount to be spent on advertising because of its often dominant role in the promotional mix. Of course, the modes of analysis applied to the problem of determining the amount to spend on advertising have application to determining expenditures for the other forms of promotion as well.

THEORETICAL FOUNDATIONS OF THE OUTLAY PROBLEM

Marginal analysis is a technique used in economics to measure the effect on output of an additional unit of input into a productive process. It is an ideal way to examine the outlay decision for advertising or any other demand stimulation activity. Figure 10–1 illustrates a situation in which units of an item are being produced. For the range of output under discussion, the cost of producing each additional unit is $2 (illustrated by the broken horizontal line). The price at which these units are sold over this range is $7 each (shown by the solid horizontal line). The vertical axes represent dollars per unit of production cost and advertising cost. Because this illustration deals with discrete numbers of units and dollars, we use the term *incremental* rather than *marginal* to describe additional units of product or dollars.

The price remains constant over the entire range based on the assumption that price seldom changes during any short-run planning period. Moreover, per unit production costs (incremental costs) are assumed to be constant at $2 over nearly the entire range of output. This cost rises sharply, however, at the point at which certain limits on plant capacity are reached. Costs of physical distribution of the product are included in the production costs.

Sales Response to Advertising Function   It may be difficult at first glance to determine which line in Figure 10–1 represents advertising costs per unit. The curve *AB* is the sales response to advertising function or a measure of the productivity of advertising. The incremental production costs and incremental advertising costs are determined by measuring the vertical distance between the horizontal lines and the sales response function. For example, the 100th unit produced has a production cost of $2 and an incremental advertising cost of approximately $3. Given a selling price of $7, the incremental profit earned by the sale of the 100th unit is $2 ($7–$2–$3).

Why curve *AB* first declines, then levels off, and finally rises over the range of output, may also be puzzling. The shape reflects the fact that a promotional campaign usually involves a substantial expenditure up front, and if only a small number of units are sold, the advertising costs per unit are high. In Figure 10–1, these costs are represented as exceeding the price per unit at low levels of output. The curve soon drops, however, as top prospects become customers and as the values of repeated messages and resulting consumer learning attract a broader group of consumers. However, as time passes, returns to advertising diminish because demand has, to a large extent, been satisfied and more advertising input is necessary to convert a prospect into a customer.

The Key Question How does one use marginal analysis to answer the key question, "How much should be spent on advertising or other forms of

FIGURE 10–1

❖   **Short-Run Determination of the Advertising Outlay by Marginal Analysis**

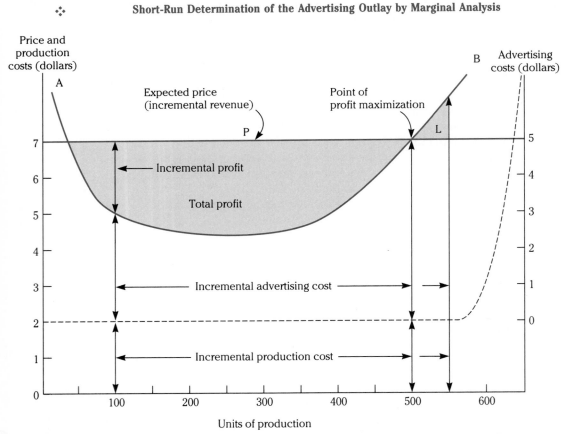

Source: Adapted from Joel Dean, *Managerial Economics* (Englewood Cliffs, N.J.: Prentice Hall, 1951), p. 356. Reprinted by permission of Prentice Hall.

promotion?" Notice that net profit is represented in Figure 10–1 as a shaded area marked "Total Profit." Incremental profit is produced when the sum of incremental production costs and incremental promotion costs is less than the incremental revenue gained by the sale of a unit of product. When the costs of producing and promoting an incremental unit exceed the incremental revenue, an incremental loss results. The answer to the question now becomes clear. *Keep adding incremental dollars for advertising or other promotion until the sum of the incremental costs of producing and promoting equals the incremental revenue.* This point is reached in Figure 10–1 where the advertising (or promotion) response curve intersects line *P* at 500 units of output. If additional funds were spent to sell 550 units, the incremental losses would be shown by the area *L* and would be subtracted from the profits previously earned. The point of maximum profit is reached at 500 units of output and thus the sum of all of the advertising and other promotional costs needed to reach this point would be the optimal promotional appropriation.

The Pros and Cons of Marginal (Incremental) Analysis   The value of the approach is that it directs the expenditures of dollars to that point at which incremental gains are offset by incremental losses. Figure 10–1 illustrates that because of the curvilinear shape of the advertising response function, not all dollars of input create the same sales response, and it emphasizes that net profit is the outcome to be maximized. Unfortunately, marginal analysis has limited applicability due to several problems. First, predicting the shape and position of the advertising response function is very difficult. That is because the function is a result not only of the inputs of the advertiser but also of consumer behavior and competitive activity. In addition, the aim of a great deal of promotion is not maximizing short-run profit but increasing consumer awareness, changing attitudes, or achieving other communication objectives.

Because marginal analysis is based on the short run, it overlooks the fact that promotion dollars continue to work in the future. Thus dollars spent in the past affect the response function in the present, and expenditures in the present will affect the response function in the future.

Simple Application   In spite of its shortcomings, the marginal approach can be used when the goal is short-run profit maximization and the relationship between sales and promotional input can be measured without too much interference from extraneous factors. Take for example the use of direct mail to sell a moderately priced product such as a textbook. Mailing lists of prospective customers in four categories—(A) librarians, (B) business executives, (C) professors, and (D) students—can be purchased, and the promotional material can be mailed to a sample of names chosen at random from each list. Based on the responses, the lists can be ordered in terms of their productivity. Let us say that the sample from list B proved most productive in that the ratio of its response to the number of names on the list was the highest, with samples C, D, and A being of diminishing effectiveness in that order.

The promotional material should therefore be mailed to list B in its entirety. When the responses have come in, say within 10 to 14 days, the total costs of the promotion (product costs, promotional material costs, list and mailing expense, and so forth) should be totaled. If the amount is less than the total revenue received, the next most productive list should be used. This process should be continued until the last list mailed does not bring in sufficient revenues to cover its associated costs. Unfortunately, in the real world one does not know when the optimal point has been reached until it has been passed.

Although marginal analysis is restricted in its application to those situations at which profit maximization in the short run is the goal, its theoretical underpinnings are most useful in appraising other methods of setting the appropriation. In the remainder of this chapter, we will look at some of these methods and indicate how a combination of them may approximate marginal analysis and thus give us a better answer to the question of how much to spend on promotion.

TRADITIONAL APPROPRIATION APPROACHES

Most methods for determining the promotional appropriation are what are called *top-down approaches* in which the total amount of dollars to be spent is determined and then this amount is budgeted to the various elements of the promotional mix by executive decision. Included as top-down approaches are such methods as (1) arbitrary allocation, (2) percentage of sales, (3) return on investment, (4) competitive parity, and (5) all you can afford.

In contrast to the top-down approaches, a sixth method, *objective and task,* is a build-up approach in which the costs necessary to achieve objectives are summed to obtain the advertising appropriation.

Before examining these methods in some detail, you should note the biggest national advertisers in the United States. Table 10–1 lists the top 100 national advertisers for 1988. The totals include expenditures for measured media including print, TV, radio, and outdoor. They also include an estimate of expenditures for unmeasured media.

Arbitrary Allocation

It goes without saying that allocation by arbitrary methods has always been common. The shortcomings of such an approach are numerous. For exam-

TABLE 10-1

The 100 Leading National Advertisers of 1988

Rank	Advertiser	Ad spending	Rank	Advertiser	Ad spending	Rank	Advertiser	Ad spending
1	Philip Morris Cos.	$2,058.2	35	Hershey Foods Corp.	$298.6	69	Kroger Co.	$144.1
2	Procter & Gamble Co.	1,506.9	36	U.S. Government	295.1	70	Seagram Co.	143.1
3	General Motors Corp.	1,294.0	37	General Electric Co.	276.6	71	Volkswagon AG	140.3
4	Sears, Roebuck & Co.	1,045.2	38	Toyota Motor Corp.	272.9	72	Paramount Comm.	139.2
5	RJR Nabisco	814.5	39	SmithKline Beecham	264.2	73	News Corp.	139.1
6	Grand Metropolitan PLC	773.9	40	Schering-Plough Corp.	262.2	74	CPC International	134.4
7	Eastman Kodak Co.	735.9	41	Campeau Corp.	260.5	75	Wm. Wrigley Jr. Co.	134.2
8	McDonald's Corp.	728.3	42	American Cyanamid Co.	256.2	76	Bayer AG	132.2
9	Pepsi Co Inc.	712.3	43	American Stores Co.	250.5	77	E.I. du Pont de Nemours & Co.	131.4
10	Kellogg Co.	683.1	44	American Express Co.	247.2	78	Texas Air Corp.	128.8
11	Anheuser-Busch Cos.	634.5	45	Honda Motor Co.	243.3	79	Noxell Corp.	126.7
12	K mart Corp.	632.0	46	Tandy Corp.	232.0	80	American Dairy Farmers	126.6
13	Warner-Lambert Co.	609.2	47	Dayton Hudson Corp.	230.2	81	Sony Corp.	125.9
14	Unilever NV	607.5	48	Pfizer Inc.	230.1	82	Goodyear Tire & Rubber Co.	124.6
15	Nestle SA	573.8	49	Nissan Motor Co.	224.9	83	Loews Corp.	123.8
16	Ford Motor Co.	569.8	50	IBM Corp.	214.4	84	Levi Strauss Associates	123.1
17	American Telephone & Telegraph	547.5	51	Hyundai Group	204.5	85	Columbia Pictures Entertainment	122.4
18	Chrysler Corp.	474.0	52	Campbell Soup Co.	202.5	86	Dr Pepper/Seven-Up Cos.	121.9
19	General Mills	470.1	53	Adolph Coors Co.	200.8	87	AMR Corp.	120.7
20	Johnson & Johnson	468.8	54	B.A.T. Industries PLC	184.1	88	Marriott Corp.	120.2
21	Bristol-Myers Squibb	430.7	55	BCI Holdings Corp.	180.2	89	UAL Corp.	120.2
22	J.C. Penney Co.	426.6	56	Revlon Group	177.3	90	Hallmark Cards	119.8
23	Quaker Oats Co.	423.4	57	American Brands	168.7	91	Citicorp	118.4
24	Ralston Purina Co.	421.0	58	Hasbro Inc.	164.5	92	ITT Corp.	115.9
25	Time Warner	409.7	59	Gillette Co.	160.5	93	Franklin Mint	114.8
26	May Department Stores Co.	399.7	60	Nynex Corp.	160.4	94	Wendy's International	114.2
27	American Home Products Corp.	393.2	61	Carter Hawley Hale Stores	159.8	95	Bell Atlantic Corp.	113.2
28	Coca-Cola Co.	385.1	62	Dow Chemical Co.	156.7	96	Delta Air Lines	112.6
29	H.J. Heinz Co.	340.1	63	Mobil Corp.	155.9	97	Whitman Corp.	111.7
30	Mars Inc.	339.7	64	Montgomery Ward & Co.	155.3	98	S.C. Johnson & Son	111.6
31	Sara Lee Corp.	326.9	65	MCA Inc.	153.7	99	Borden Inc.	110.5
32	Macy Acquiring Corp.	308.9	66	Clorox Co.	148.3	100	Subaru of America	108.0
33	Colgate-Palmolive Co.	306.6	67	Mazda Motor Corp.	146.7			
34	Walt Disney Co.	300.6	68	Philips NV	144.3		Note: Dollars are in millions	

Source: *Advertising Age,* September 27, 1989, p. 1. Used with permission.

ple, advertising frequently seems to serve as a vent for executive emotion and personality traits. One authority puts it this way:

> Noneconomic, or psychological, criteria by which management evaluates advertising also need to be understood . . . the function of advertising is highly cathartic, it is the focus of many strong emotional needs and drives relating to "self-expression" or aggressiveness . . . executive decisions on advertising philosophy and budget often may reflect as much the executive's psychological profile as they do the familiar economic criteria. The advertising philosophy and budget may be determined as much by personality as by profit maximization . . . each type of executive personality has a characteristic mode of feeling toward advertising in the light of this association of advertising with self-assertiveness or aggressive tendencies. Those who have either naturally or compensatorily induced strong self-expressive tendencies clearly tended to budget more for advertising. The latter tended to have wider swings in "intuition" or feelings of satisfaction or dissatisfaction.[1]

Moreover, the appropriation may in no way be relevant for promotion tasks. Proper management obviously focuses on profit maximization to the fullest extent possible.

Percentage of Sales

A commonly used method of determining an advertising budget is the percentage-of-sales approach. In its simplest application, this technique requires the calculation of the proportion of the sales dollar allocated to promotion in the past and then the application of this percentage to either past or forecasted sales to arrive at the amount to be spent. A fairly common variation is to allocate a fixed amount per unit for promotion, and then the appropriation is obtained by multiplying this amount by the forecasted unit sales.

The percentage of sales invested by advertisers can range widely. For example, data for 1989 published by Schonfeld & Associates indicated that manufacturers of special cleaning and polishing preparations (SIC 2842) spent 14.5 percent of sales on advertising while manufacturers of naval search and guidance systems (SIC 3812) spent 0.2 percent. It should not be inferred, however, that the firms noted determined their advertising appropriations through the use of the percentage-of-sales approach.

Two studies of company practices disclosed that many firms use the sales ratio as a fixed guideline for their expenditures.[2] The base figure is the sales volume projected or forecast for the period that the appropriation will cover. Many firms reported that the percentage used remains constant from year to year, and, in some cases, industry averages are taken as a point of reference. Variable ratios find favor with some companies, especially when new products are to be introduced.

The percentage-of-sales approach is widely used for several basic reasons. It is simple to calculate, and it is almost second nature for management to think of costs in percentage terms. Because the percentage-of-sales approach gives an illusion of definiteness, it is easy to defend to management, to stockholders, and to other interests. In addition, it is a financially safe method because expenditures are keyed to sales revenues, thereby minimizing the risk of nonavailability of funds. Finally, when it is widespread throughout the industry, advertising is proportional to market shares, and competitive warfare is made less probable. This competitive aspect is especially appealing to those who give strong credence to the human inclination to resist change.

It should be clear to the perceptive reader that the advantages of the percentage-of-sales approach are illusory. Most important is the inherent fallacy that appropriating for promotion as a percentage of past sales views advertising as the *result, not a cause, of sales.* This logical deficiency is widely recognized, and forecasted sales rather than past sales are more widely used. The use of forecasted sales, however, is fraught with circular reasoning because how can sales be forecasted without knowing how much is to be invested in sales-generating efforts? Basically, the fundamental and perhaps fatal weakness is that the focus is not on the promotional job to be done; deceptively simple and arbitrary means are substituted for the comprehensive analysis that must, of necessity, be undertaken to approximate the goals of marginal analysis.

The percentage-of-sales method, then, is seldom an adequate tool unless the environment is almost totally static and the role for promotion is unchanging from period to period—a highly unusual situation. This method should be used only as a starting point to calculate how many dollars would be allocated if conditions remain the same. Then the promotional objectives must be examined to fine tune the appropriation to the job to be done. More is said later about this use of percentage of sales.

Return on Investment

Advertising may be viewed as an investment in much the same manner as additions to plant or other uses of funds. Since dollar flows are not unlimited, advertising should compete for its share in the same fashion as alternative investments. This method seems to be especially logical for institutional advertising, which frequently is considered as an investment.

This type of analysis obviously is only an appealing exercise in logic because management can do little more than guess at the probable return from dollars invested. Nevertheless, it is true that payout analysis for other forms of investment is frequently as inexact, so its purpose no doubt is to admonish management to think of promotion in terms of larger organizational objectives. It is probable, however, that estimates of the return on dollars spent for promotion relative to other investments will be an impregnable barrier for some time to come.

Competitive Parity

Dollars are sometimes allocated by emulating competition and spending approximately the same amount, called *competitive parity*. Data for this approach can be found in advertising periodicals or can be obtained from the U.S. Internal Revenue Service and various trade associations.

Competitive parity offers the advantage that competition, a major component of the environment, is specifically recognized and adaptation to it is sought. In this sense, at least, competitive parity represents a small step past the percentage-of-sales method. It also offers the advantage that competitive relationships are stabilized and aggressive market warfare minimized.

Aside from coping with the variable of competition, however, this technique in no way recognizes other components of the promotion task, and the most gross oversight is the total lack of emphasis on the buyer. Competitive parity also assumes that all competitors have similar objectives and face the same tasks—a most dubious assumption. It further assumes that the competitor or competitors matched spent dollars with equal effectiveness; however, identical expenditures seldom imply identical effectiveness. Finally, the only data available to management, short of outright collusion or competitive espionage, are past expenditures. These data become useless, however, if the competitor changes its promotional mix. Future spending plans are seldom known, so the ability to match competitor expenditures will always be limited by available information.

In all fairness, it must be stated that few companies rely on competitive parity as the sole means of determining their appropriation. It should not be rejected totally as an appropriation approach because competitive efforts can be the dominant variable to be met in the promotional environment. The firm's objectives may by necessity be largely defensive in nature. Although it seldom is practical to match the competitor to the degree implied in competitive parity, this consideration will often weigh heavily in promotional strategy.

All You Can Afford

Occasionally it is reported that some firms determine their appropriation largely on the basis of available funds. It is not unusual that the need to show satisfactory profits in a given year limits advertising expenditures.

Also, upper limits are sometimes based on customary ratios between total advertising expenditure and forecasted sales revenue. When these are exceeded, the appropriation will be pared. In other words, management spends as much as it is believes the company can afford without unduly interfering with financial liquidity.

It cannot be denied that liquidity is an important consideration. Assume the situation shown in Table 10–2. With successive deduction of margins and other costs and a planned profit of 6 cents per unit, a residual of 13 cents remains for advertising, taxes, and other expenses. Assume further that it is determined that 10 cents will be allocated to advertising and that forecasted unit sales are 100,000. Then the advertising appropriation cannot exceed $10,000 unless funds are available from other sources. Management may be hard put to counteract financial necessity unless compelling reasons exist for expanding the appropriation by borrowing or other means, although management may, with considerable justification, propose "payout planning," a procedure to be discussed later in connection with new-product budgeting.

It is apparent that the $10,000 appropriation may in no way be related to objectives in that it may lead to either underspending or overspending. For this reason, it is seldom relied on exclusively except possibly in the case of new products or in situations in which it is grossly apparent that the firm has underspent in the past and that any amount of funds within reason will still generate a positive marginal return. Regardless of the situation, however, liquidity will always be an important factor, and management must be prepared with convincing arguments to justify requested increases.

TABLE 10–2

Computation of Promotion Cost per Unit

Selling price	$ 1.00
Retailer margin 30%	−0.30
Wholesalers' selling price	$ 0.70
Wholesalers' margin	−0.11
Manufacturer's price	$ 0.59
Manufacturer's production cost	−0.40
Revenue minus costs	$ 0.19
Specified 6% profit (on retail price)	−0.06
Residual for selling and other costs	$ 0.13

Objective and Task

No method discussed thus far stands up under close scrutiny, either because of failure to focus on the job to be done or because of the unavailability of needed data. This leads to the last major method of determining the amount to be spent on promotion—objective and task. In contrast to the methods discussed so far, objective and task refer to a build-up approach that aggregates the costs of performing those tasks needed to reach stated objectives to determine the total promotional appropriation. Of all the methods discussed, it has the most merits, and a recent study indicates that its use by leading consumer goods advertisers increased from 12 percent in 1975 to 90 percent in 1983.[3]

The objective-and-task approach is simple to describe. It requires only spelling out objectives realistically and in detail and then calculating the costs necessary to accomplish the objectives. Often financial liquidity will enter as a constraint on the upper limit of the appropriation. It is assumed that research will have been done to specify the tasks necessary to attain the objectives; all that remains is to put dollar estimates on these efforts.

On the face of it, one cannot argue with this approach. Truly it epitomizes the concept of marginal analysis in that it forces striving for the intersection of marginal cost and marginal return. It avoids the arbitrary decisions and the illusory certainty of other approaches and generates research-oriented analysis consistent with a modern philosophy of promotional strategy.

No matter how compelling the advantages, it must be stated that management frequently has no conclusive idea of how much it will cost to attain the objective or even whether or not the objective is *worth* attaining. What is the best way, for example, to increase awareness by 20 percent next year? Should a combination of network television, spot radio, and newspapers be used with hard-sell copy, or should these variables be changed? Obviously, all possible combinations of efforts cannot be evaluated, and it is perhaps impossible to isolate the *best* promotion mix. Nevertheless, what other alternative exists for profit-oriented management? There is no shortcut to experimentation and other forms of research if scientific management is to be implemented.

A realistic goal is to find an approach that seems to work well on the basis of research, estimate the costs, and then accumulate an appropriation by this means. It may not be the best mix of efforts, but it will no doubt exceed the estimate arrived at by percentage-of-sales or other arbitrary means. Measurement of results will then permit the accumulation of data that, over time, should provide an invaluable source of information for future appropriating with the objective-and-task method. The difficulty of the method cannot continue to be a barrier to its practice. More suggestions for implementation will be given later in the chapter.

CONCLUSIONS ON DETERMINING THE APPROPRIATION

Of the appropriation methods discussed, the objective-and-task approach most nearly approximates the ideal as provided by marginal analysis. Yet implementation of this approach is fraught with the difficulty of estimating the tasks necessary to accomplish objectives, to say nothing of costs. This approach requires a great commitment to researching the shape of the response to advertising for individual brands as an indication of interest (awareness, sales, etc.). In general, this response function has been found to exhibit decreasing returns as advertising expenditures are increased.[4] However, to make specific brand decisions on appropriations, specific research is necessary. The primary objective is to guarantee promotional accountability. Many companies have introduced semiannual, quarterly, or monthly reports for the purpose of reviewing decisions and introducing modifications where necessary. Procter & Gamble, Quaker Oats, Bristol-Myers, and North American Philips are all reported to have instituted this type of system.

IMPLEMENTING THE OBJECTIVE-AND-TASK APPROACH

The ideal approach to determining the optimal level of expenditures builds on the concepts inherent in marginal analysis. The logical procedure would be to establish objectives and then to experiment until determining the level of expenditure that most closely approximates the optimum. Larger firms commonly follow this procedure, although it can be time consuming and expensive.

In one three-year test experiment, a major petroleum company divided a large number of cities into three test groups and one control group. One test group received half as much advertising as normal; expenditures were twice the normal rate in another group, and three times the rate in the third. It was found that a 50 percent reduction had no great effect, whereas the greatest sales increases were in the double-expenditure markets. A tripling of the budget led to only minimal increases. Similarly, a six-year research program at the Anheuser-Busch Company comprising advertising variations in 200 geographical areas showed that it was possible to reduce advertising expenditures and still increase sales. Many believe, as a result, that experimentation is the only feasible approach, given management pressures for greater promotional efficiency and accountability.

Experimentation obviously is not feasible for most firms because of time and cost constraints. Therefore, some combination of the procedures mentioned above must usually be employed. A logical approach encompasses the following steps:

1. Isolation of objectives.
2. Determination of expenditures through a "build-up" analysis.
3. Comparison against industry percentage-of-sales guidelines.
4. Comparison against a projected cost figure based on percentage of future sales.
5. Reconciliation of divergences between built-up costs and percentage-of-sales figures.
6. Establishment of a payout plan where appropriate.
7. Modification of estimates in terms of company policies.
8. Specification of when expenditures will be made.
9. Establishment of built-in flexibility.

Isolation of Objectives

The first step in building a budgetary plan is to estimate the total market for the product category. These figures may be available from governmental sources, trade publications, or from market research firms such as A.C. Nielsen or the Market Research Corporation of America. Then it is necessary to estimate the share of the total market that the firm most likely can attain. Factors underlying this estimate are:

1. Product uniqueness—the advantages relative to competition and the ease with which they can be duplicated.
2. Number of competitors—it is difficult to obtain a large share in a highly fragmented market.
3. The spending pattern of competition—a large share is more feasible when competition has not been aggressive and is unwilling and (or) unable to become so in the future.

Estimated market share becomes significant in that it is possible to approximate necessary spending levels based on past industry performance, as is discussed later.

In addition, of course, communication objectives must be specified. These objectives should be combined into a comprehensive and specific statement on which a detailed plan of efforts producing measurable results can be built.

Expenditure Estimation through Build-Up Analysis

Once objectives have been specified, the next question concerns what is required to accomplish these tasks. This analysis, in turn, should encompass mass media expenditures (advertising and public relations), direct selling costs, and costs of stimulating reseller support.

Advertising and Public Relations   If the objective, for example, is to saturate the teenage market through repetitive advertising, it is clear that this objective will require a large budget for continued advertising in media that reach this market segment. In more technical terms, media strategy would be established to achieve *frequency.* On the other hand, the task may call for reaching as large a market as possible, in which case a wide variety of media would be utilized to attain *reach.* Reach and frequency requirements, therefore, are instrumental in determining the required appropriation. The basic approach is to "build up" or select the necessary media.

The analysis underlying media selection, which is complex, is the subject of Chapter 15. It is recognized that media analysis lies at the heart of the objective-and-task approach; in fact, Roger Barton, a widely quoted authority, does not even mention percentage-of-sales and other approaches in his discussion of budgeting.[5] He contends that the final budgetary figure is based on (1) definition of the types of media to be used, (2) the costs of individual media, (3) the frequency of insertions, (4) the media mix, and (5) other related considerations. This analysis is common to both advertising and public relations, although much publicity is achieved at no direct cost to the firm.

Direct Selling Costs   Next it is necessary to determine the required selling activities and resulting costs to reach wholesalers and retailers and to stimulate their promotional support. Computations are usually made by territory or other subunits of the firm when environmental situations are known to differ. Judgment armed with research data is the only tool available. Recourse must be made to historical records detailing efforts under similar sets of alternatives in the past and the costs that were incurred. In the absence of appropriate records, experimental research may be required.

The cost of efforts raises problems that require some discussion. A first step will always be to determine the total of fixed selling costs because, in all probability, they will change only slightly from period to period. A similar relationship may be found for semivariable costs that, for all intents and purposes, are fixed over large ranges of output. The problem comes in estimating variable costs, and detailed historical records are required for the estimates to have any meaning.

The problem of variable costs is clarified considerably if standard costs can be constructed for each activity. A cost standard is a predetermined norm for an operation intended to represent the costs under usual operating conditions. Standard costs frequently are based on time and duty analysis whereby time intervals required to perform an activity are translated into monetary terms. The availability of standard costs then permits the computation of a sales budget on the basis of estimates of the functions to be performed multiplied by the appropriate cost standard for each function. It might be discovered, for example, that the standard cost per sales call in territories 1, 7, and 9 is $10 and the best estimate of calls required during the coming year is 1,000, 1,200, and 870, respectively. The budgeted costs then would be $10,000 in territory 1 (1,000 × $10), $12,000 in territory 2, and $8,700 in territory 3.

Cost Standards   The two most widely used cost standards are cost per sales call and cost per dollar of net sales. Standards are also established frequently for the salaries and expenses of home office sales administration, the expenses of field supervision, the costs of home office and field office clerical efforts, and other related functions.

Even though standard costs are a significant aid, the applicability of standards depends greatly on the nature of the tasks performed. Clerical activities, of course, are routine, and it is not difficult to establish standards such as cost per invoice line posted. Creative selling, on the other hand, may be far from routine in that a sale may not be made until many preliminary customer contacts are completed. In such instances, it may be impossible to establish reasonable standards.

Stimulating Reseller Support   The point of departure is the history of trade efforts in the product category. What is the ratio of trade expenditures to the advertising of major competitors? What are the demands from the chains for "slotting allowances" to gain retail shelf space? In most situations, it is necessary to be competitive because more manufacturers seek support than can be accommodated by resellers. Additional costs to be considered include product samples, coupons, free goods, cooperative advertising, provision of point-of-sales and other displays, and so forth.

Comparison against Industry Percentage-of-Sales Guidelines

It is frequently found that *share of industry advertising,* sometimes referred to as *share of voice,* is a primary criterion of success, especially in marketing a new product. The share of industry advertising needed for a successful new product introduction in categories such as household goods, food products, and proprietary medicines is generally about 1.5 to 1.6 times the share of industry sales.

For example, if the sales objective for a new product is set at 10 percent of category sales, then the advertising appropriation for that product should be about 15 percent of the total category advertising expenditure.

The exact multiplier to use is a function of the strength of the brand; weaker offerings require higher multipliers such as 2 or 3. In addition, the effectiveness of the advertising campaign can also exert an influence. Exceptionally creative campaigns reduce the multiplier to less than 1.5. Most experienced promotion managers use results of previous product offerings as guidelines in determining the most effective multiplier and thus the advertising appropriation needed to reach the sales objective.

Comparison against Projected Percentage of Future Sales

It was suggested earlier that the percentage of sales devoted to promotion in the past is a useful starting point in setting an appropriation. These figures are readily available in conventional accounting statements, and breakdowns can be provided for sales territories and products.

The application of percentages to forecasted sales involves circular reasoning, to the extent that it is difficult to forecast sales without knowing the investment in promotion. As a result, this is not a sufficient basis for appropriating, but it does provide an estimate, all things being equal, of what would be spent if proportions were not altered to meet changed objectives. Thus it serves as a benchmark against which to compare the built-up budgetary sum.

Reconciliation of Divergence between Built-Up Costs and Percentage-of-Sales Figures

Once the projected percentage figures for the industry and the company, as well as those for built-up expenditures, are available, the focus can be on reconciling differences. If a 1.6 to 1 ratio is reasonable, given past industry experience in the product category, and projected spending is far in excess of the ratio, it may be necessary to revise premises, assumptions, and other factors to ascertain whether the projected figure is reasonable. The budgetary analysis is a continuing process of this type because only by accident will a sum be determined that is clearly the optimum appropriation.

Payout Planning

Frequently, extending the budgetary period is desirable, especially when new products are introduced, because one calendar year may not be sufficient to accomplish objectives. Strategy may encompass three to five years, and the appropriation must be viewed in that time perspective. Moreover, profitability may not be realized until the end of the period. In other words, the payout from the expenditures is expected to occur at a later point in time;

this extension of the planning period is frequently referred to as *payout planning*. Because it is most frequently used in introducing new products, further discussion of payout planning is reserved for a later section of the chapter.

Modification of Estimates in Terms of Company Policies

It is also pertinent to fine tune the appropriation figures to make the sums consistent with the overall framework of company policy and dollars invested in the other functions. Financial liquidity must always be considered, for there are bound to be financial constraints that cannot be exceeded, even in payout planning, regardless of logic or compelling necessity. Moreover, *too much can be spent* for promotion in view of the entire company situation. There is the possibility that advertising and selling can easily disturb orderly flows of manpower, inventory, and cash by borrowing sales from the future and introducing unwarranted fluctuation in other flows. The fact that the company is a system of related flows must never be overlooked, and dollars must be invested to maximize the response of the *system,* not the *function* itself. The danger to be avoided is suboptimization, which results when management loses sight of the system in which it operates.

Specification of When Expenditures Will Be Made

A well-developed appropriation plan requires the designation of when during the budgetary period dollars will be expended. This determination permits forecasting of cash flow requirements by the company comptroller to ensure that funds are available when needed. The choice of timing patterns for promotional input to the various media is a part of the overall promotional strategy. Whether these patterns will be continuous or pulsing or take some other form will be discussed in some detail in Chapter 15. We are concerned here with the impact of the selected strategy on a company's cash needs.

Building in Flexibility

The appropriation should never be viewed as a perfect map to be followed without variation. The dangers of inflexibility are analyzed at length in the management literature, and there is compelling logic for building in sufficient flexibility to allow for changing conditions. Markets are becoming more volatile, product planning deadlines are shortened, and many possibilities of tactical shifts by competition may occur. This flexibility may be provided by a 10 to 15 percent reserve sum that is not allocated until needed.

Adaptation to change, of course, requires maintenance of detailed records of results. More and more companies are now establishing a new management post—the advertising controller. He or she is appointed to be a watchdog over spending, with the result that performance may be more or less continually reviewed. Records are also useful as guides to future strategy decisions. Unfortunately, this type of record is seldom kept on any systematic basis, and this lack can serve as a real impediment to the application of the philosophy of marginal analysis.

Comments on the Suggested Approach

This section has not been presented with the objective of providing a formula that can be followed automatically. Rather, a step-by-step procedure has been suggested to approximate marginal analysis through the objective-and-task approach, and it must be adapted creatively and analytically to each situation. The final result should never be construed as being ideal because there may always be good reasons for major changes throughout the planning period. Also, the tendency to use the appropriation as a screen to hide inefficiencies must be guarded against. This danger can be avoided if top management insists on measuring results and evaluating the competence of personnel in performance terms.

A decision that faces management once the total appropriation has been determined is how to allocate it to various parts of the country. This so-called *geographic allocation* is an important issue if the best returns for the money expended are to be realized.

GEOGRAPHIC ALLOCATION

Geographic variables often provide a useful basis for allocating promotional expenditures. To use these variables it is necessary to determine the *relative sales possibilities* from one geographic area to the next. For example, if a product is sold nationwide, should twice as much effort be placed in the Chicago market as in Detroit, Michigan? Or should Detroit receive an equivalent allocation of promotional funds? Such questions can be answered only when *market potentials* are computed, for as a general rule, efforts are allocated in proportion to potential, all other things being equal.

Several different categories of potential might be computed for a given product:

1. Volume attainable under ideal conditions (i.e., if all efforts were perfectly adapted to the environment).
2. The relative capacity of a market to absorb the products of an entire industry, such as the major appliance industry.

3. The relative size of market for a company's type of product (i.e., sales of color television sets versus stereo sets).

4. The actual sales a company can expect.

The last category, of course, is the equivalent of the sales forecast for a firm, or the sales volume that can be expected if the firm continues on its present course. Potential, on the other hand, refers to sales possibilities rather than expected sales, and is of greater significance for purposes of demand analysis. Although forecasting is necessary in determining allocations and budgets, it is beyond the scope of this book.

Useful Measures The measure of potential that is generally found to be most useful is either category 2 or category 3 — market strength (capacity) for industry products or for types of products rather than the specific products of a firm. This is not to say, however, that potential is the sole basis for allocation of resources because potentials for industry sales do not reveal the competitive structure of a market or the firm's ability to make inroads. Detroit, for example, might appear to offer high potential, whereas in reality competitors are so entrenched that inroads would be impossible. Ideally, then, potentials must be augmented with information about the competitive structure as well as the firm's previous experience in the market. The goal, of course, is to make an optimum allocation of resources to alternative markets; this can never be done with great precision without a reliable estimate of the impact of a given level of promotional expenditure on market share. Nevertheless, an array of markets in terms of potential provides a workable estimate of the probability of response to sales efforts.

The methods used to compute potentials include (1) a corollary products index, (2) industry sales, (3) general buying power indexes, and (4) custom-made indexes.

Corollary Products Index

At times, it is possible to use the sales of another product as an indication of potential. Presumably the corollary product and the product in question are related in some way. If such a product can be found and its sales data are available, these data may be used as clues of expected variations in sales patterns of one's own product from one market to the next.

Residential building permits, for example, should be a realistic indication of the sales potential for bathroom fixtures. The danger, of course, is that association between one product and another does not mean that the two sell in direct proportion in different areas. As a result, this method should be used with caution, and in many instances it will be found to be inapplicable.

Industry Sales

This method uses sales of the industry or a major portion of it as the measure of potential. It is thus possible to clarify areas where the industry has made maximum penetration. The advantage is that it considers the experience of all competitors and avoids the error of considering only the circumstances peculiar to an individual firm. From the industry sales data, the share of market possessed by the firm can be computed easily, thereby arriving at a measure of sales possibilities.

Assume, for example, that industry sales are available and that a firm is discovered to derive 1.3 percent of its sales revenue from Connecticut, but that the total industry derives 3.4 percent from that state. It is clear that remedial steps are needed, and it is probable that a larger share of promotional dollars should be allocated to this state, all other things being equal. It is thus possible to capitalize on areas where industry products sell strongly and to avoid excessive promotion in the weak markets.

Unavailability of Data   One limitation of this method is the frequent lack of availability of industry sales data. In some circumstances (automobiles and motorboats are examples), license or tax records are a good source of this information. Trade associations such as the National Electrical Manufacturers Association also make such statistics available to their members.

Sales data, however, reflect only *what is,* not *what might be.* In other words, there is no certainty that available data measure untapped market opportunity for both the industry and the firm. Moreover, it is assumed that past experience is a good measure of the future. In some industries producing staple commodities, this may be true. It is doubtful, for example, that total sales of men's shirts vary drastically from year to year. In dynamic markets, however, the probable existence of untapped demand makes this an unsafe assumption. As a result, other types of indexes may be preferable.

General Buying Power Indexes

The index of relative buying power in various localities is a good indication of potential for many products. A number of data sources, including magazine circulation, are used for this purpose. This index is based on the assumption that those reading magazines have money to spend. No doubt this is often true, especially among subscribers to special-purpose periodicals. A manufacturer of fishing reels, for example, might find the circulation of *Sports Afield* to be a reliable criterion; similarly, manufacturers of photographic equipment selling to skilled amateurs could use *Popular Photography* for this purpose.

Total retail sales in various markets are also used for a buying power index. *Census of Business* data are issued periodically and are updated annually by *Sales & Marketing Management* and other publications for this purpose. Buying power should not be used, however, unless it is clear that there is high correlation between variations in total retail sales and variations in sales of the product under analysis.

Accurate Indexes   Usually the most accurate indexes are those that are constructed using several factors in combination. The best-known combination index is the *Sales & Marketing Management Survey of Buying Power* published annually. This index is derived by weighting population by two; effective buying income by five; and total retail sales by three. If the state of Illinois, for instance, were found to have 5 percent of effective buying power, a manufacturer using this index would allocate 5 percent of its promotional dollars to that state. Regardless of absolute sales volume, this state should generate about 5 percent of the total sales. Data are also provided by counties and cities so that a more precise allocation can be made. (See Table 10–3.)

A buying power index offers several advantages: (1) it is available in published form and can be used directly without additional computations, (2) the indexes are issued frequently and in considerable geographic detail, and (3) they may be used when other data that might be of greater use cannot be procured. A general index of this type, however, is not always appropriate. It is assumed that demand varies directly with this index, but this variance is likely to be correct only for those products whose demand rises or falls with purchasing power, regardless of other considerations. The demand for milk should not vary with buying power, and the use of snow tires is more associated with climatic conditions than anything else.

Custom-Made Indexes

It may be necessary to construct an index unique to a given product. In order to do so, it is necessary to isolate the important factors affecting demand, obtain data on these factors, and combine them into one index, with appropriate weights assigned to those with greatest influence. These factors may include any of the data mentioned previously. Buyer studies may be helpful, but the method usually depends more on informed guess than on scientific procedure.

For example, a large manufacturer of high-style belts, braces, garters, and jewelry found that the *Sales & Marketing Management* buying power index did not reflect the urban concentration of demand for its product. As a result, it used urban population (with a weight of three), retail sales (weight of three), and disposable income (weight of four). The result was a more precise indication of potential. Similarly, a brewery used the *Sales & Marketing Management* index to compute new-product potentials and found that sales in metropolitan areas did not meet expectations based on the

TABLE 10–3

Sales & Marketing Management Survey of Buying Power for Michigan
(1988 estimates)

METRO AREA County City	Total EBI * ($000)	Median Hsld. EBI	% of Hsls. by EBI Group: (A) $10,000-$19,999 (B) $20,000-$34,999 (C) $35,000-$49,999 (D) $50,000 &Over				Buying Power Index
			A	B	C	D	
ANN ARBOR	3,534,175	26,406	21.1	27.6	18.4	16.8	.1171
Washtenaw	3,534,175	26,406	21.1	27.6	18.4	16.8	.1171
*Ann Arbor	1,444,801	23,425	24.6	25.4	14.9	16.8	.0521
SUBURBAN TOTAL	2,089,374	28,471	18.7	29.0	20.9	16.9	.0650
BATTLE CREEK	1,747,790	25,912	21.0	27.8	17.8	15.5	.0554
Calhoun	1,747,790	25,912	21.0	27.8	17.8	15.5	.0554
*Battle Creek	627,946	20,619	23.5	25.6	13.3	12.2	.0201
SUBURBAN TOTAL.....................	1,119,844	29,739	19.2	29.3	21.1	17.9	.0353
BENTON HARBOR	1,785,076	21,651	24.7	28.4	15.5	9.6	.0594
Berrien	1,785,076	21,651	24.7	28.4	15.5	9.6	.0594
*Benton Harbor	88,327	12,886	29.8	19.6	7.2	3.9	.0066
SUBURBAN TOTAL	1,696,749	22,513	24.3	29.1	16.2	10.0	.0528
DETROIT	56,788,300	27,580	18.3	27.1	19.2	17.7	1.8451
Lapeer	803,402	27,881	18.6	31.3	21.4	13.9	.0237
Livingston	1,438,229	32,461	15.6	28.6	24.6	20.4	.0401
Macomb	8,023,766	26,440	19.8	34.9	19.9	10.8	.2926
Roseville	519,707	23,171	23.1	37.7	14.4	6.9	.0245
St. Clair Shores	1,322,998	30,164	15.6	38.5	25.7	11.2	.0506
Sterling Heights	884,644	26,740	19.8	34.2	18.8	12.2	.0279
Warren	1,712,766	26,081	20.3	33.6	20.1	11.2	.0646
Monroe	2,039,276	36,771	15.0	21.7	23.6	29.7	.0555
Oakland	17,936,947	35,394	14.3	24.6	21.4	29.2	.5661
Farmington Hills	1,329,800	42,744	10.8	20.8	21.6	39.5	.0373
*Pontiac	779,764	22,832	19.8	26.8	15.6	13.1	.0300
Royal Oak	1,121,079	32,408	17.4	26.9	22.4	22.7	.0348
Southfield	1,477,944	36,800	14.9	23.3	19.7	32.8	.0593
Troy	1,272,742	43,483	9.2	20.5	25.2	38.2	.0504
St. Clair	1,619,803	25,060	20.8	29.3	18.5	12.5	.0506
*Port Huron	374,725	20,107	23.5	26.5	14.2	9.5	.0152
Wayne	24,926,877	23,967	20.0	25.9	17.4	13.8	.8163
*Dearborn	1,247,749	28,125	19.9	24.7	19.7	19.4	.0514
Dearborn Heights	857,024	32,050	15.9	29.0	23.3	21.1	.0248
*Detroit	10,521,403	18,207	23.0	24.4	13.1	9.0	.3384
Lincoln Park	530,636	27,206	20.6	31.7	21.1	12.5	.0184
Livonia	1,453,245	38,021	10.8	26.0	28.3	27.7	.0535
Taylor	803,139	28,548	17.3	31.7	23.8	12.5	.0314
Westland	1,016,405	29,524	16.3	33.3	23.4	14.3	.0350
SUBURBAN TOTAL	43,864,659	30,991	16.5	28.2	21.6	21.0	1.4101
DETROIT-ANN ARBOR CONSOLIDATED AREA	*60,322,475*	*27,516*	*18.5*	*27.2*	*19.2*	*17.6*	*1.9622*

*Effective buying income
Source: *Sales & Marketing Management,* August 7, 1989, p. c. 91. Used with permission.

index. It was discovered that total retail sales have little relation to the sales of beer, and that the important determinants instead were the number of people over age 18, social class, and per capita consumption of malt beverages.

Such an index is often constructed in somewhat arbitrary fashion by selecting and trying those factors that seem to be relevant. A more sophisticated procedure is to experiment with a greater variety of factors and choose those that are found to have the greatest relationship to sales through use of multiple correlation analysis. Correlation analysis measures the extent to which two or more variables are related by assessing the variation in one variable (say industry sales) that is accounted for by the association between this variable and others (say disposable income and housing starts).

Computing Measures The task of computing measures of multiple correlation once was formidable, but electronic computers have greatly simplified the procedure. Once various combinations have been tried, measures may be readily compared. Assume that five series are tested and found to have coefficients of correlation with sales of 0.66, 0.81, 0.91, 0.84, and 0.87. The third (0.91) obviously is the best of the five, since a correlation of 1.0 is ideal. In reality, however, it is doubtful that a correlation of 0.91 will be found because this is an exceptionally high degree of relationship.

Probably this procedure is the most acceptable of all of those discussed in this section, but it also has its disadvantages. First, the correlation may be spurious—a coincidence rather than a cause-and-effect relationship. Moreover, it is assumed that past industry sales success will hold in the future, and it is obvious that this might not be so in a volatile industry in the early stages of its growth. Finally, the data needed may not be attainable or may be of questionable accuracy. Regardless of the problems, this procedure does focus on finding the combination of factors that offers the best relationship to sales, and as such it is likely to be superior to a more general index under most circumstances.

EXPENDITURES FOR NEW PRODUCTS

Some special considerations enter into the appropriation process for new products, in addition to those that have been mentioned. Payout planning assumes particular importance, and experimentation with quantitative methods is providing some interesting new insights.

Payout Planning[6]

A payout plan is a procedure that extends the planning period for longer than one year, and it has proved especially useful in evaluating the proper course of action in introducing new products. Most often it covers three years, but in the case of slow-maturing products such as proprietary medicines or when large initial expenditures are necessary, the payout plan may be extended to cover four or five years. The stages in payout planning are (1) estimation of market-share objectives, (2) assessment of needed trade inventories, (3) determination of needed expenditures, (4) determination of the payout period, and (5) evaluation.

Estimation of Share Objectives   It was previously mentioned that the first step in appropriating is to estimate the total market for the product category and then to assess the probable share to be captured by the firm. It should be noted that most new products reach their peak share and then decline to a lower level. Share builds slowly as distribution is achieved, promotion pressure is applied, and consumer trial is generated. Usually a brand will hit its peak share approximately 6 to 12 months after its introduction in a new area and will then level off or decline. It is then necessary to recycle the brand through product improvement.

This short life-cycle for low-involvement packaged goods makes it important to accelerate trial through heavy advertising expenditures in the first few months after introduction. Products are new only once, and this is the most important period in the life of a brand. The higher the peak share, the greater the probability that the brand will be a success. Of course, for high-involvement products, longer payout periods would be more realistic.

Assessment of Needed Trade Inventories   The company also makes money on what is sold to the trade, so the goods necessary to "fill the pipeline" must be added to consumer sales to get the total volume for this manufacturer. There are two general guidelines to follow:

1. The larger the projected volume, the shorter the number of weeks' supply necessary in trade inventories.
2. Most products lose pipeline sales in the second year through resellers' cutbacks unless share is climbing; this exerts a negative force on sales in that year.

Determination of Needed Expenditures   Several guidelines should be followed in arriving at the proper appropriation level based on experience:

1. The first-year budget should permit a heavy introductory schedule (13 to 26 weeks) followed by a sustaining schedule at least equal to the second-year advertising budget.
2. A good rule of thumb is that expenditures for the introductory schedule should be about twice the rate currently spent by competitors who have shares equal to the company's objective.

3. Carefully check expenditures on a per unit basis against competitors. The brand with the highest shares usually has a lower cost per unit, and vice versa.

Determination of the Payout Period In today's competitive marketplace, the trend is toward shorter payout periods. Most product development can be duplicated by the competition in a short time. There is also reason to believe that brand loyalty is not as great as it once was. Finally, there is a high rate of new-product failures. Long payouts are justified only when the projected life-cycle of the product is very long and the potential rewards are very big.

Two payout plans are shown in Tables 10–4 and 10–5. Notice that the new food product considered in Table 10–4 was projected to return a loss in the first year and pay out in the second year. The drug product considered in Table 10–5, on the other hand, was not expected to pay out until the fourth year. In the former example, the total promotional appropriation was highest in the first year so that maximum impact could be made, whereas the opposite is the case with the drug product, which matures more slowly.

Evaluation In evaluating the soundness of a payout plan, management usually directs attention to the first year (the year of heavy investment) and

TABLE 10–4

❖   **Payout Plan for a New Food Product (000s)**

	Theoretical Marketing Years		
	First	Second	Third
Total market (units)	50,000	52,000	54,000
Market share (%)	5.0	5.2	5.0
Volume (units)	2,500	2,704	2,700
Pipeline (units)	400	(50)	—
Total volume (units)	2,900	2,654	2,700
Total sales (@ $9)	26,100	23,886	24,300
Gross profit (@ $4)	11,600	10,616	10,800
Advertising ($)	6,500	4,000	4,000
Promotion to the trade ($)	8,000	2,000	2,000
Total advertising & promotion ($)	14,500	6,000	6,000
Gross trading profit ($)	(2,900)	4,616	4,800
Profit (% of sales)		19.3	19.8
Cumulative gross trading profit ($)	(2,900)	1,716	6,516

to the first year after payout is achieved. This latter year gives management an opportunity to assess the long-term rewards of the investments they have made in the other years. By comparison with other opportunities and with competitive products, it is possible to make an experienced judgment on the wisdom of the investment. Of particular importance are examination of profit margins and the financial implications of an investment of this size. Additionally, the net present value of cash flows may be calculated to determine the investment viability of the expenditures.

Adaptation   It must be emphasized that a payout plan is a theoretical financial plan calling for a national introduction at one specific point in time. Management has the option to make the plan fit overall company fiscal goals more closely by, first of all, picking the most propitious time to introduce a product. For example, introducing at the end of a fiscal year could fatten company profit for that year by accumulating the profits from heavy initial trade sales, while deferring the heavy introductory advertising expenses until the next fiscal year.

Companies frequently choose to introduce in waves. They might introduce in 20 percent of the market to start, and then 20 percent in the next two months, and so on. This has the effect of lowering the deficit position at any one point in time. There are other advantages, such as leveling production

TABLE 10–5

Payout Plan for a New Drug Product (000s)

| | Theoretical Marketing Years | | | | |
	First	Second	Third	Fourth	Fifth
Total market (units)	200,000	211,000	223,500	235,500	246,000
Market share (%)	2.0	3.3	4.4	5.6	6.7
Volume (units)	4,000	6,963	9,834	13,188	16,482
Pipeline (units)	700	750	780	800	800
Gross sales ($)	4,700	7,013	9,864	13,208	16,482
Gross margin (%)	7	7	7	7	7
Gross profit ($)	3,290	4,909	6,905	9,246	11,537
Advertising ($)	4,400	4,200	5,000	5,760	6,000
Promotion to the trade ($)	1,500	700	800	900	1,000
Total advertising and promotion ($)	5,900	4,900	5,800	6,660	7,000
Gross trading profit ($)	(2,610)	9	1,105	2,586	4,537
Profit (% of sales)	—	—	16.0	27.9	39.3
Cumulative gross trading profit ($)		(2,601)	(1,496)	1,090	5,627

schedules and correcting errors found in the first regions. The disadvantages are that it may result in shortening lead time over competition and that paying a premium to do regional advertising instead of national advertising might be necessary.

Evaluation of Payout Planning   Payout planning is being followed by an increasing number of firms. An assumption is made, of course, that environmental conditions existing during the first year will not change greatly during the planning period. Competition might enter and drastically change the competitive environment, to mention only one possibility. Also, it is assumed that the effect of promotional expenditures on sales can be estimated with some accuracy. Nevertheless, payout planning encompasses a managerial philosophy that has merit, for it makes a realistic attempt to implement the objective-and-task method without imposing arbitrary restrictions on funds in any given year. We must recognize, however, that given the increasing turbulence of the marketplace, payout periods may be decreasing. Instead of five-year plans, we may now have two-or three-year plans.

SUMMARY

This chapter has dealt with one of the most complex and important problems in the management of promotion. That is, how much should be spent to achieve planned promotional objectives? We started with a story about a product manager to illustrate the many variables that must be considered in arriving at an optimal solution to the problem. Next we looked at the marginal or incremental mode of analysis to discover the theoretical underpinnings of a solution aimed at profit maximization in the short run. We soon discovered that such an approach was applicable only under very restrictive conditions, although such conditions were present in certain classes of promotional situations.

In reviewing the traditional approaches to the problem, we found that most did not meet the twin criteria of *promotability* and *profitability*. In other words, the approaches suggested appropriations that were either not large enough to reach promotional goals or were so large that profitability was reduced. The objective-and-task approach seemed to meet the dual criteria best and thus received the support of the authors as the most appropriate approach. We spent considerable time discussing the means of developing such an approach and of checking it.

Next came the problem of geographic allocation of promotional effort. We illustrated the use of several indexes including the *S&MM Survey of Buying Power*.

Finally, we gave special attention to the determination of the promotional appropriation for new products. We discussed payout planning because it is required by many corporate controllers before funds can be provided for new-product introductions. We noted, however, that because of the increased un-certainty resulting from rapidly changing market conditions, the payout periods may be getting shorter than they were in the past.

We conclude with the belief that a systematic approach to the problem will provide better results than will using rules of thumb such as percentage of sales. We believe that even the best analysis cannot replace experience and good judgment when it comes to deciding how much to spend on promotion. Thor-ough analysis, however, can certainly sharpen one's judgment.

REVIEW AND DISCUSSION QUESTIONS

1. Imagine that your task is to determine the advertising appropriation for a new automobile to be introduced this coming fall. You have been impressed by the use of marginal analysis and would like to utilize it in your decision process. How should your thinking proceed with respect to the pros and cons of marginal analysis in the case at hand?

2. You have just received a copy of your advertising budget and have found that your boss has added several items that do not appear to be directly related to advertising and that seriously reduce the amount available to you for purchasing space in the print media and time in the broadcast media. How would you handle this situation?

3. Refer back to the Mary Johnson scenario at the opening of this chapter. Put yourself in her shoes. What could you do to make sure that your career was not damaged by management's insistence on a short-run milking strategy for the brand?

4. Given an annual sales objective of $40 million for a new health and beauty aid product, develop a hypothetical objective and task approach to deter-mine the promotional appropriation. Be sure to illustrate how you would use a build-up analysis as part of the process.

5. Assume that the advertising share of successful products in the soft drink industry exceeds sales share by about 2.1 to 1. You are the advertising man-ager of Twink, a new dietary soft drink. Would you abide by the customary ratio? What size appropriation would result if first-year sales were estimated at $8 million? What factors might lead you to depart from the customary ratio?

6. You are working for a large pharmaceutical manufacturer that requires pay-out planning before a new product can be launched. Assume that Table 10–5 is a payout plan that you developed given the company's five-year planning horizon. You are suddenly informed that because of increased market risk, the planning period has been reduced to three years with breakeven in year 2. Develop a new plan. *Hint*: Set up the old plan on a PC spreadsheet and see what works best for-a-three-year plan.

NOTES

1. Melvin E. Salveson, "Management's Criteria for Advertising Effectiveness," *Proceedings, 5th Annual Conference* (New York: Advertising Research Foundation), p. 25. Quoted with special permission of the Advertising Research Foundation.

2. Kent M. Lancaster and Judith A. Stern, "Computer-Based Advertising Practices of Leading U.S. Advertisers," *Journal of Advertising* 12, no. 4 (1983), p. 6.

3. Ibid., p. 6.

4. For a review of this literature, see Julian L. Simon and Johan Arndt, "The Shape of the Advertising Response Function," *Journal of Advertising Research* 20, no. 4 (August 1980), pp. 11–28.

5. Roger Barton, *Media in Advertising* (New York: McGraw-Hill, 1964), pp. 15–19.

6. This section was contributed by Robert Sowers, formerly senior vice president, Ogilvy & Mather, Inc.

Organization and Use of Human Resources

WHAT'S NEW? J. WALTER THOMPSON

An analyst recently asked Bruce Crawford, who returned to the advertising business as president of the Omnicon Group after four years of running the Metropolitan Opera, what had changed in advertising during his absence.

Mr. Crawford's reply was swift and short: "J. Walter Thompson."

Advertising people agree that Thompson, a proud old agency that was humbled in the mid-1980s by management turmoil and financial scandal, has returned to a position of eminence. Analysts and executives say the comeback has been achieved through cost cutting, management restructuring, and a wholesale change in the clubby, Ivy League culture of Thompson, 125 years old and one of the oldest agencies in the country.

An Instructive Transition The renaissance of Thompson is instructive, for it occurred during the nearly two years the agency has been owned by Britain's WPP Group P.L.C., the same company that upset the ad world this week with its audacious offer for the Ogilvy Group, another distinguished marketing name.

Among Thompson's best-known current campaigns are its soulful slices of Americana for Eastman Kodak film and comic ads featuring a degenerate dog pilfering Ken-L Ration's Tender Chops dog food.

At the time of Thompson's takeover in June 1987, operating margins at its parent company, the JWT Group, were hovering around 4 percent. The J. Walter Thompson Company finished 1988 with margins of 10 percent, the average for the ad industry. Financial analysts note that Thompson's margins improved when lower-margin companies such as Hill & Knowlton public relations were placed under WPP's banner.

The acquisition also hastened a flight of clients from the agency, including such prestigious names as Goodyear Tire and Rubber and Ford Motor, which dropped the agency in Europe, Brazil, and Venezuela, while keeping it in some countries. In all, Thompson suffered $450 million in account losses in the six months after the ownership change.

Last year the agency brought in $421 million in new business, by far the most in its history. Among the new business: Ford accounts in Taiwan, Australia, and New Zealand.

Source: Excerpted from Randall Rothenberg, "What's New? J. Walter Thompson," *New York Times,* May 3, 1989, pp. 25, 32. Used with permission.

Marketing organizations have been changing rapidly during the past decade. The increasing internationalization of business, the increased numbers of mergers and acquisitions, and the newer precepts of management have all served to change radically the way firms conduct their business. The above example about the venerable, conservative, Ivy League agency, J. Walter Thompson, is most enlightening. Indeed, since the article was written, the British WPP Group has succeeded in taking over the Ogilvy Group, so yet another story is to be written about changes in managerial style and corporate direction.

Our attention in this chapter is focused first on the organization but does not stop there, for only the very largest firms have all of the staff skills that they need. These firms also make considerable use of advertising agencies and other specialized resources, so we will describe the changing roles and operations of these service organizations so that you can gain insight into how they can be used effectively.

ORGANIZATIONAL REQUIREMENTS AND STRUCTURES

The conventional approach would be to give you a variety of organization structures, complete with boxes and arrows, and let it go at that. These are important, but more basic considerations should be reviewed first. These have to do with organizational dynamics—the *marketing spirit and vision.*

The Requirements of a Modern Marketing Organization

Jan Carlzon undertook a venture that most of us would never even consider. He took over as chief executive officer of the Scandinavian Air System (SAS) in the middle of the 1981–83 recession when SAS was losing $10 million a year and heading further downward. Under Carlzon's leadership, SAS quickly turned around and made $70 million on a sales volume of $2 billion. What was his secret? As Peters and Austin put it, the secret was "a return to old-fashioned service excellence, led by Carlzon's boundless spirit."[1]

Vision The central ingredient for organizational excellence is vision—"a whole new sense of where a company is going and how to get there."[2] Jan Carlzon inherited a dispirited airline exemplifying mediocrity, and he imposed on it a whole new standard of excellence. In his words, "We don't seek to be one thousand percent better at any one thing. We seek to be one percent better at one thousand things."[3]

Management authority Peter Drucker looms above his peers in terms of impact on the world business scene in the past half century. Yet his primary theme is amazingly simple—*the main role of a business is to create a customer.*[4] This is the philosophy that underlies Carlzon's success at SAS and the excellence exemplified by the firms described in Promotion in Action 11–1.

It may seem that we are stressing the obvious, but don't be deceived. One of the main factors that distinguish success is a consistent and all-embracing marketing orientation. A company can lose marketing responsiveness for two reasons: (1) a bloated bureaucracy that snuffs out innovation and (2) a play-it-safe mentality that tolerates inexcusable marketing foul-ups.

The principle is clear: To attain success, a marketing organization must be geared from top to bottom to respond and adapt to a rapidly changing environment.[5]

Customer Orientation Ukrop's 19-store chain of family-owned supermarkets, headquartered in Richmond, Virginia, doesn't sell beer, wine, or liquor, closes on Sundays, and stays clear of promotions such as double coupons. Yet the company has a 30 percent share of the metropolitan region's grocery sales and has beaten out national leaders such as Safeway. When asked about the success of Ukrop, one consultant says, "I think that far and away the most important thing that Ukrop does is to put their customer number one." Clerks are unflaggingly friendly, baggers insist on carrying shoppers' groceries, and a framed statement declares that the stores' mission is "to serve our customers and community more effectively than anyone else. . . ." The consultant went on to state, "A lot of people say that, but it's not done that frequently, and they do that."[6] We agree. Customer satisfaction must be the relentless goal of all organizations. Too many bad experiences result in lost customers and in squandering a company's most important asset.

The General Motors (G.M.) Corporation launched its much ballyhooed X-Car line in 1980 as a trump card in fighting the front-wheel-drive imports. Not long after the launch, reports began growing that brakes on some models were grabbing and resulting in potentially fatal swerves. G.M.'s response— "No problem." The company stonewalled growing consumer complaints and fought off government demands for a recall. In so doing, it may have won a battle but lost the war with many formerly loyal buyers. The X-Car line was phased out in 1986, by the way, because the market cast its negative vote.

PROMOTION IN ACTION 11–1

The First Ingredient in Reinventing the Corporation Is a Powerful Vision

As an economics student at Yale University, Fred Smith outlined a vision of an air parcel service free from the problems of piggybacking air freight services onto passenger flights. Although he got only a C on his paper, he went on to realize his vision in Federal Express, the leader of a $3 billion industry that was previously nonexistent.

SAS's president, Jan Carlzon, envisions a market in which, in the words of International Management, "the customer is always happy, costs are trimmed to the bone at the head office while more money is spent on service, businessmen are pampered without paying any extra on the standard fares, tourists fly for the price of second-class rail travel, and profits flow in like clear water from a mountain stream."

F. Kenneth Iverson's vision is to reinvent the steel industry into a high-tech business. Iverson, the chairman and CEO of Nucor Corp., was a pioneer in creating the minimill, the most productive dynamic element in the otherwise dying steel industry. Unlike other steel executives, Iverson is against import quotas and habitually undercuts foreign competition.

Control Data's simple, clear, and well-known vision was created by William Norris, the company's founder: "to address society's major unmet needs as profitable business opportunities." During the past 15 years, Control Data has moved six plants to inner cities, created 100 small-business centers, trained 5,000 disadvantaged people, and offered computer-based education in 20 prisons.

Source: John Naisbitt and Patricia Aburdene, *Re-inverting the Corporation* (New York: Warner Books, 1985), pp. 22–23. Used by special permission.

We are frank to say that without quality and excellence, promotional power is rendered impotent. As Jan Carlzon and the Ukrop brothers have demonstrated, this is first and foremost a top management responsibility. If this commitment is absent, competitive edge is lost, as American automobile manufacturers have learned to their sorrow. In all fairness, the quality of American automobiles has improved greatly since 1986. Recent survey data indicate that U.S. quality is almost equal to that of imports, but it will take time and effort to regain customers who were lost in earlier years when this was not the case.

Commitment to Innovation   In our discussion of consumer behavior in Chapters 5 and 6, we sounded the consistent warning that innovation is required if customer satisfaction and loyalty are to be maintained. Few firms have the assured luxury of strong loyalty based on involvement and commitment.

One of the greatest inhibitors of innovation is bureaucracy. In their study of organizational excellence, Peters and Austin found that innovation seldom is the output of formalized, rigid strategic planning complete with voluminous research, committees, and layers of approval. Rather, it is most often the output of a *skunkwork*. This interesting word has come to refer to a small team that is cut loose, backed with resources, and allowed to experiment. Strategic planning and careful evaluation are not ignored. The key is to cut the layers of bureaucracy so that something can be accomplished quickly enough to gain a competitive edge.

Furthermore, innovation never occurs without a managerial "champion." This refers to senior management committed to making the process happen. When it is absent, competitive mediocrity is inevitable.

Finally, the multilayered organizational structure is increasingly giving way to much more flexible systems so that impediments to creativity are removed. We will say more about this shortly.

Making People Productive   There is now general agreement that a top-down managerial style is giving way to an altogether different style designed to make people productive. This style is based on the commonsense principle that people work best when they chart their own destiny. Translated into practical terms, this means freeing people to set their goals and strategies within the organizational mission and objectives. In short, managers and workers throughout the organization are asked, "What will your goals and strategy be for this next period?" And they are held accountable for results.

The new style is referred to as *participative management.* Explicit account is taken of the fact that authority and responsibility must be pushed as close to the scene of action as possible. The experience of the Herman Miller Company noted in Promotion in Action 11–2 shows how powerful a management tool this approach can be. When employees can do what is needed to build quality products and to satisfy customer needs, increased market share and profits should follow. Of course, when an employee is allowed to exercise initiative, he or she must be willing to be measured on the basis of the results they have achieved.

PROMOTION IN ACTION 11–2

Hot Company, Warm Culture

Does this happen at most companies? A young woman, a line worker in an assembly plant, shows up at the chairman's office in a sour mood. Not only does she get in to see the boss, but he sits there and takes it when she snaps at him: "Don't you know that two production managers were just fired?"

At most American companies, even some that claim to use the participatory management principles currently in vogue, this young worker would not have made it past the security guards, let alone the chairman's receptionist. But at Herman Miller, Inc., the big office furniture manufacturer, Chairman Max DePree welcomed just such an employee. Not only did he look into her complaint, but he agreed that an injustice had been committed and rectified it. The two managers were offered their jobs back; the vice president who had fired them was asked to resign.

Such expectations require uncommon trust, and DePree and his forebears atop Herman Miller have built a thriving enterprise in large part because of the sturdy bridges that exist between management and employees. All hands are dedicated to fine design and insist on top quality.

At Herman Miller, all employees are organized into work teams. The team leader evaluates workers every six months, and then each worker in turn evaluates the team leader. On the plant floor, teams elect representatives to caucuses that meet periodically with line supervisors to discuss production shifts and grievances. If workers at these caucuses don't like what they hear, they can bypass the supervisor and go directly to the next level.

Everyone at Herman Miller knows the limits of this kind of management. Diane Bunse, a shift manager, describes the process as "participative, not permissive." Max DePree explains that Herman Miller is not a democracy: "Having a say does not mean having a vote." So managers have to be both firm in decision making and sympathetic in explaining why. Says Edward Simon, Jr., president and chief operating officer: "To be successful here, you have to know how to dance."

Source: Excerpted from Kenneth Labich, "Hot Company, Warm Culture," *Fortune*, February 27, 1989., pp. 74–78.

Without some form of participative management, innovation is unlikely to occur. If true participation is present, the form that the organization chart takes really doesn't matter.

MBWA   Have you heard this term? It has become a part of standard management parlance. It refers to *management by wandering around.*[7] This is a managerial style characterized by staying in touch with customers and with staff. The MBWA manager is quite the opposite of the stereotype of the "armchair general."

Managers at all levels (including the CEO) are expected to keep in constant touch, first of all, with customers. For example, they can pose queries such as "Why are you flying the Trump Shuttle?" "What do you like best?" "What can we do to make you happier?" These questions can be raised in person or through a guided interview with a focus group of a dozen or so customers. However it is done, management must know firsthand what is happening on the front line.

MBWA also means keeping in touch with people in the organization— their dreams, frustrations, and ideas. The concept is based on the premise that they too *will share the dream and vision.* It is expected that their work will be challenging and fulfilling if management is doing its job. Here again, this means that management must move from the office and be physically present where the work is being done. Questions must be asked. Suggestions must be taken seriously. Remedial changes must be made quickly when needed.

These comments may seem entirely too basic and obvious. Once again, we must point out that reality often paints a different picture. Customers are seen as a means to an end rather than the very focal point around which everything centers. Workers, too, are seen as means to an end rather than as full partners whose welfare and best interests are paramount.

Achieving Necessary Coordination   If a brand manager is unable to control and coordinate the elements of his or her marketing and promotional mix because of limitations on authority, confusion in the marketplace is likely to occur. If distribution is not coordinated with promotion, customers attracted by promotion may not find the product on supermarket shelves. If pricing changes are not communicated quickly and correctly to the salesforce, confusion will reign at all levels in the channels of distribution. Obviously, it makes sense to coordinate all of the activities needed to serve the consumer.

Fortunately, rigid organizational barriers are increasingly giving way to a networking style in which people draw from others at the same organizational level and receive support from many directions.[8] What this means is that old lines of authority and responsibility no longer are viewed as rigid, thus allowing cooperation and collaboration without fear of "end-running" the power structure. This reflects a growing commitment to flexibility and adaptability.

The Keys to Strategic Dominance   The company that will thrive in today's competitive environment will have these characteristics: (1) continual innovation and (2) topnotch customer service. These qualities, in turn, are fueled by the creative contribution of each person, made possible by an unwavering commitment to participative management. If any one component or combination is missing, promotional strategy is hampered from the outset.

Organizational Structures

The marketing function (and hence promotion) can be organized in two basic ways.

The Functional Structure   The most traditional form is the functional structure illustrated in Figure 11–1. This is seen most often in a single-product firm existing in a stable industry. Here the need is more for efficiency than innovation or adaptability, and this type of structure lends itself well to tight, centrally directed management.

The functional organization has the disadvantage that decisions are made by several functional managers who may or may not work together.

FIGURE 11–1

A Functional Organization

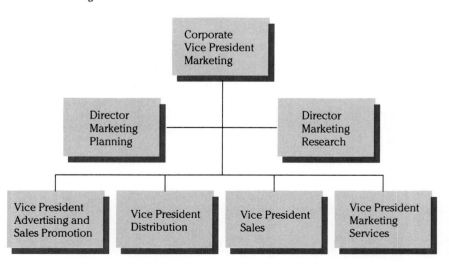

Equally important, innovation definitely is restricted. Usually levels of approval are required for each action. They tend inevitably to dampen initiative. The ability to adapt to competitive change is thus restricted. This factor, in itself, is leading to the decline of this type of structure.

The Product Organization   Over three quarters of the *Fortune* 500 companies are organized to place the product or brand manager in the central position of the organizational structure (Figure 11–2). This manager is given responsibility for profit performance and (we hope) sufficient authority to draw on the functional resources needed to achieve planned goals. The brand manager must accomplish six tasks. These include:

1. Developing a long-range and competitive strategy for the product.
2. Preparing an annual marketing plan and sales forecast.
3. Working with advertising and merchandising agencies to develop copy, programs, and campaigns.

FIGURE 11–2

A Product Organization

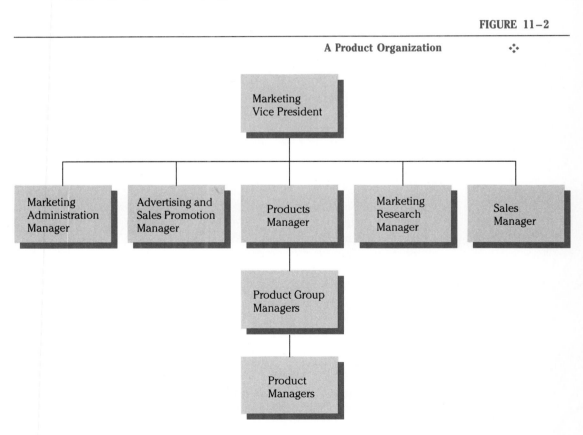

4. Stimulating interest in and support of the product among the sales force and distributors.

5. Gathering continuous intelligence on the product's performance, customer and dealer attitudes, and new problems and opportunities.

6. Initiating product improvements to meet changing market needs.[9]

You can see from this list how the product manager interacts with external promotional resources such as the advertising agency and sales promotion specialists.

Difficulties with the Product Management Form of Organization   Although the product management form of organization can undoubtedly facilitate participative management, given sufficient commitment from the top executives, it is not without its difficulties. First, product managers are often not given sufficient authority to carry out their responsibilities. If this is so, their task becomes one of persuasion and cajoling to gain support from others in the firm.

Second, the area of concern of product managers is so broad that they rarely develop expertise in any one area. They are thus at the mercy of experts within or without the firm who claim to know more about the subject at issue than they do.

Third, the product management mode tends to be more expensive than other types of organization. Each product is set up as a small business with a number of people on the management team. This team is duplicated for each product. To overcome this problem, Procter & Gamble decided to eliminate the position of advertising manager for most but not all of its 90 brands in late 1987. The company instituted the position of "category" manager to take the place of several advertising (product) managers. Two years later, it appeared that the brands that kept their managers did better than those that were under category managers. The category managers could not devote the needed attention to the individual brands, especially when interacting with the advertising agencies.

Procter & Gamble is reversing its policy and at least 15 associate advertising managers were recently promoted to advertising manager. It thus appears that managers at the product level are here to stay even if they are expensive.[10]

Finally, the turnover rate among product managers is high. The good ones get promoted and the poor ones leave. Thus it is hard to get continuity of management at the product manager level for periods of time exceeding two or three years.

Making It Work in Practice   Although the strictly functional organization is less desirable from the perspective of adaptability, participative management, and innovation than the product management organization, it, too can be made workable. The key is to have someone who is responsible for profit performance and who is backed with authority. Where this person is placed in a formal organization chart is relatively unimportant because the volatile competitive scene is forcing bureaucracies to give way to *adhocracies.* This means that regardless of the constraints of the organizational structure, improvisations are made to coordinate the resources necessary to accomplish the marketing task.

Peter Drucker puts his finger squarely on the issue:

> . . .the innovative organization builds a kind of nervous system next to the bony skeleton of the formal organization. Where the traditional organization is focused on the logic of the work, there is an additional relationship focused on the dynamics of ideas.[11]

Once again, we must stress that none of this will work, regardless of the structural shape, without the proper commitment of top management to innovation and excellence.

THE ADVERTISING AGENCY

Recognizing that they are unlikely to possess the range of services needed to mount a complex promotional campaign, firms of all sizes use advertising agencies. The agency originated as a broker of space for advertising media in the late 1800s, but it has changed dramatically since that beginning.

Organization of the Advertising Agency

Most full-service advertising agencies are organized around five basic functions as illustrated in Figure 11–3. The most important of these in terms of the allocated share of personnel and budget is the creative function. The people in this area develop the ideas and modes of presentation that make the advertisement.

A second important area is media, where strategies are planned and executed for placing advertising. The media department is responsible for the timing and geographic coverage of the advertising as well as for buying space in print media and time on broadcast media to ensure the most effective use of the promotional budget.

Closely allied with the media function is the operations area, which, in addition to handling the internal business of the agency, is responsible for billing clients and making payments to the various media. The traffic area (a subfunction under operations) physically handles and distributes the advertising copy, art, film, and other components of the advertising campaign within the agency and to the various media.

The research area is responsible for gathering and analyzing data to enable the agency to answer a variety of questions such as which is the most effective advertising theme, the best media mix, the most appropriate budget, and so forth.

Finally, the account management function is responsible for agency-client relations. In the daily task of producing advertising, the account executive on the agency side and the product manager on the client side are the parties who work together closely. The account executive works with the client (usually the product manager) to develop an effective marketing and promotion strategy. He or she then communicates the requirements of this strategy to the creative staff, the media planners, and others in the various support groups of the agency as are needed.

FIGURE 11–3

❖   **Organizational Chart of a Typical Advertising Agency**

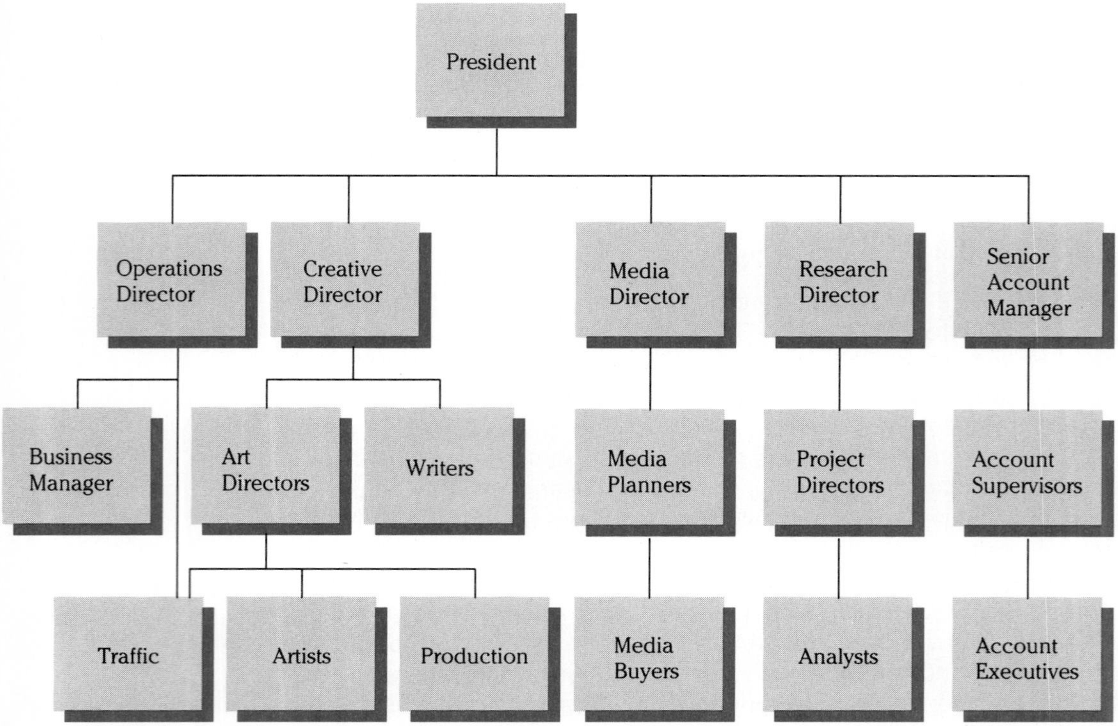

Large Advertising Agencies   Table 11–1 presents a list of the 30 largest advertising agencies ranked in terms of their worldwide billings. *Billings* refers to the costs of media time and space placed by the agency plus fees for extra services, which are capitalized (i.e., converted by formula) to give an estimate of their billings equivalent. The basic income of an agency is derived from a commission on billings; historically, this amount has been 15 percent but in recent years may have varied from that amount.

An ad placed by a large agency to promote its services is shown in Figure 11–4, but this is only a small part of its new business efforts. There is continual volatility and turnover in this industry because of aggressive solicitation packages. Often complete campaigns are prepared on a speculative basis to woo a potential client from its present agency.

Because the agency had its beginning as a media broker, the media themselves have long established a process of agency recognition before space or time orders will be honored. This recognition is presently based on proof that the agency has sufficient financial resources to pay space or time charges if its client defaults on payment. On occasion, proof might also be requested to demonstrate that the agency offers adequate personnel and facilities to provide proper client service. Generally, this approval is given pretty much automatically.

Until the 1950s, however, the approval process was much more controversial. This was due to a stringent requirement that the agency must accept compensation only through the 15 percent commission offered on space or time costs. In other words, agencies could not rebate any portion of this commission, thus preventing agencies from engaging in any kind of flexible pricing policies with their clients. A consent decree signed by five media associations and several associations of advertising agencies in the 1950s ended all prohibitions on commission rebates.

Principles of the Agency-Client Relationship

Through trial and error, four basic principles were established to serve as the foundation of the agency-client relationship. The first three are obvious and noncontroversial, but the fourth has become a major issue.

1. **Client Approval of Expenditures.** The agency is obligated to obtain prior approval for all expenditures made on the client's behalf. Without question, this is good business practice.

2. **Client Obligation for Payment.** The client is obliged to pay its space, time, and service bills promptly. The agency itself must pay all space and time billings even if client payment is not in hand. If the client is remiss in its obligations, it causes an unwarranted drain on the agency's cash flow.

TABLE 11–1

✥   The Top 30 Worldwide Agencies

Agency	Headquarters	Total Worldwide Billings (in thousands)		
		1988	1987	% Change
1. Saatchi & Saatchi Advertising	London	5,035,973	4,609,437	+ 9.3
2. McCann-Erickson	New York	4,381,000	3,418,495*	+ 28.2
3. Ogilvy & Mather Worldwide	New York	4,110,134	3,663,798	+ 12.2
4. Publicis-FCB	Chicago	4,052,000†	3,225,000†	+ 25.6
5. BBDO International	New York	4,051,222	3,664,493†	+ 10.6
6. Young & Rubicam	New York	4,023,000	3,360,000	+ 19.7
7. Backer Spielvogel Bates Worldwide	New York	3,804,784†	3,244,388*	+ 17.3
8. J. Walter Thompson	New York	3,686,616†	3,020,829*	+ 22.0
9. Lintas:Worldwide	New York	3,591,000†	2,900,000	+ 23.8
10. D'Arcy Masius Benton & Bowles	New York	3,218,694	2,598,141	+ 23.9
11. DDB Needham	New York	3,020,335	2,603,101	+ 16.0
12. Grey Advertising	New York	2,886,400	2,462,700	+ 17.2
13. Leo Burnett Co.	Chicago	2,865,087	2,461,794	+ 16.4
14. HDM	New York	1,938,000	1,507,000	+ 28.6
15. N W Ayer	New York	1,347,670	1,115,755*	+ 20.8
16. Bozell, Jacobs, Kenyon & Eckhardt	New York	1,283,000	1,325,000	− 3.2
17. Campbell-Mithun-Esty	Minneapolis	783,025	740,800*	+ 5.7
18. Ketchum Communications	Pittsburgh	776,000	660,000	+ 17.6
19. Wells, Rich, Greene	New York	729,900†	659,000	+ 10.8
20. TBWA	New York	691,900	549,516*	+ 25.9
21. Della Femina, McNamee WCRS	New York	660,456	590,079*	+ 11.9
22. Scali, McCabe, Sloves	New York	522,239	448,830*	+ 16.4
23. Chiat/Day	Los Angeles	500,000	350,000*	+ 42.9
24. Wunderman Worldwide	New York	444,700	414,807	+ 7.2
25. Tracy-Locke	Dallas	408,000	349,000*	+ 16.9
26. AC&R Advertising Inc.	New York	355,599	371,352	− 4.2
27. Ross Roy	Bloomfield Hills	346,000†	315,000†	+ 9.8
28. Hill, Holliday, Connors, Cosmopulos	Boston	334,958	289,638	+ 15.6
29. McCaffrey and McCall	New York	310,773	308,861	+ 0.6
30. Lowe Marschalk	New York	304,200†	304,200	0.0

Note: Agencies listed are those that control major operations in the United States.

* Restated 1987 billings
† Estimated figures

Source: *Advertising Age,* September 28, 1988.

3. **Forwarding of Cash Discounts.** Most media offer cash discounts for prompt payments. The agency is obligated to forward this discount to the client.

4. **Avoidance of a Relationship with Competitors.** Traditionally, the agency was forced to refrain from handling a directly competitive client. In return, the client was expected not to retain other agencies simultaneously. This may have worked in a simpler era when company mergers and multiple product lines were less common, but it is raising no end of problems at the present time. What should be done when one major firm is taken over by another and winds up having competitive brands? Or when a merger results in several agencies with the same corporate account? The dilemma is made crystal clear in Promotion in Action 11–3.

FIGURE 11–4

The Advertising Agencies Advertise

Crest is the #1 selling toothpaste in the United States.
NBC is the #1 television network.
Besides being #1, there's one other thing the two of them have in common.
Their advertising agency.

At DMB&B/USA, we do more than build brands. We build #1 brands.
Like Budweiser, Banquet, Cadillac, Crystal Light, Amoco and more. Dozens more. And there are many others we are working with to make #1.

So whether you're trying to become #1 in your category or trying to stay there, call Clayton Wilhite, President of DMB&B/USA, at 212-909-9036.
Because we can't work on your number until you call his.

DMB&B/USA
The One Behind The #1's.
Chicago, Detroit, Los Angeles, New York, St. Louis.
© 1989, D'Arcy Masius Benton & Bowles, Inc.

As one step in providing some clarity, the American Association of Advertising Agencies stated that the "ideal agency-client policy on account conflicts is one which is based on individual product categories rather than the total product line of any given client."[12] This would prohibit any single agency from handling directly competitive brands but would permit it to handle noncompetitive brands from clients who have product lines that are competitive with those that are in the agency.

In an interesting study, Herbert Zeltner found that 60 percent of 150 top managers in client and agency organizations believe that conflicts will increase sharply in the next few years, especially given the plethora of corporate mergers and takeovers.[13] About the only consensus was that brands competing head-to-head should not be in one agency. There was little agreement, however, on where to draw the line after that point. The need is to define exactly what is meant by *conflict.* The urgency of the problem makes it pretty certain that this must be done soon.

❖
**PROMOTION
IN ACTION
11–3**

Will Mergermania's Megamergers Produce Megaconflicts?

Ogilvy & Mather has invested years of time and talent in the General Foods brands it handles. But with Philip Morris' acquisition of GF, is it in trouble now on Brown & Williamson? And Benton & Bowles (yes, of premerger days)—is it now in trouble on its General Foods business because of the PM/GF deal, since PM also owns Miller Brewing, the competitor of Anheuser-Busch, which uses B&B since its merger with D'Arcy MacManus Masius? Could Leon Burnett USA possibly be in trouble on its longtime Kellogg account because it works on Philip Morris cigarets and PM now owns General Foods, which has Post cereals? Is Young & Rubicam in trouble on Kentucky Fried Chicken because that's owned by R. J. Reynolds Industries, which competes with PM, which owns GF, a large Y&R client?

And how about Y&R's Oil of Olay business? The fact is that Y&R's advertising alone built that once-small brand into a major national business. And when R-V extended the line with an Olay beauty soap, Y&R was forced to drop P&G as an agency client. And then Y&R replaced P&G on its roster with P&G archrival Colgate-Palmolive. And now P&G owns Olay. Will Y&R's investment in time and talent go for naught?

What many people would probably label as "trade press rumors" are in actual fact serious considerations at all too many client meetings. But should Y&R lose Oil of Olay or Kentucky Fried Chicken? Should O&M lose

Agency Compensation

Rapid changes are taking place in agency compensation methods. The plans used are (1) the commission system and (2) the fee system. It also is common to use these two in combination.

The Commission System Most media are commissionable in that the agency is paid 15 percent when it places an order for time or space. The 15 percent sum is entirely arbitrary when viewed from the agency perspective. It may or may not cover the costs of actual services provided. All costs of planning, designing, preparing, and placing ads are to be covered by the commission. Other services such as marketing research, direct marketing, sales promotion, and publicity are usually billed as an extra charge.

Direct marketing and sales promotion methods, however, do not qualify as commissionable because they are specially designed for the client.

Will Mergermania's Megamergers Produce Megaconflicts?
(concluded)

❖
**PROMOTION
IN ACTION
11–3**

lose Maxwell House because it handles B&W? Should D'Arcy Masius Benton & Bowles lose GF because it handles Budweiser? Getting ridiculous, isn't it?

That's why it's time for our major advertisers—the nation's largest, in fact—to realize that if they're to go on merging, they can't anchor themselves to inflexible or convoluted conflict policies. They must understand that corporate conflicts don't necessarily produce product conflicts. They should make public their views, and give agencies immediate votes of confidence. P&G should "credit" Y&R for that agency's role in the Olay success; PM should reassure O&M, and so on.

These big companies must reexamine their policies and make sure that as they acquire successful old brands, they don't let some musty old notions punish the agencies that helped bring those brands into prominence. The Association of National Advertisers will be holding its Diamond Jubilee annual meeting next month; wouldn't that be a proper place for some new policies to be enunciated? If they delay much longer, agency-business disruptions could become debilitating to the brands and the businesses they've built—or bought.

Source: "Needed: New Thinking on Conflicts," *Advertising Age*, October 14, 1985, p. 10. Reprinted with permission. Copyright Crain Communications, Inc. All rights reserved.

According to a 1986 study, fewer and fewer advertisers and their agencies are using the 15 percent media commission. Less than half (43 percent) of major media users responding to the survey said that they use the 15 percent commission. This percentage is down from 52 percent in 1983. Smaller advertisers are shifting to the fee system, and the larger ones tend to use a commission rate other than 15 percent.[14]

Because a sizable number of advertisers are still using the commission system, let us discuss it in some detail and then we will examine why the divergences and accommodations are taking place.

Pros and cons of the commission system   The commission system is defended by some advocates on the basis of its ease of understanding and administration. Moreover, they claim that the fixed amount of 15 percent avoids price competition among agencies. The argument is that an idea is difficult to evaluate in cost terms, and agency competition in terms of price is thus impossible. Finally, they hold that the agency is rewarded in proportion to the use made of its ideas—the more the space or time purchased, the greater the commission in total dollars.

Most of these arguments for the commission system dissolve on close analysis. The critical weakness is that a 15 percent commission may not be related to services performed by the agencies. It might result in overpayment or underpayment. Consider this example: The 15 percent system would seem to indicate that an ad running in a magazine charging $35,000 per page for advertising requires seven times the effort to produce as an ad running in a magazine charging just $5,000 per page for advertising. But this is just not so.

Another important weakness is that the commission system has provided an excuse for some agencies to avoid using accounting systems to justify their charges. To many advertisers, especially manufacturers, the absence of cost accounting is unthinkable.

Industry Adjustments

General Motors (GM) Corporation's divisions have gone to a sliding scale form of compensation to reflect more closely agency costs of producing advertising. The GM agency receives the traditional 15 percent only on the first $50 million of billings. A sliding scale takes effect over $50 million with the agency earning progressively lower commissions with additional expenditures.[15]

In addition to being a poor reflection of actual costs, the commission system has another bias. Unfortunately, it tempts agencies to place dollars in commissionable rather than noncommissionable media regardless of what mix will best achieve the client's promotional goals. In an attempt to overcome this bias and to see all of the promotional options available, Procter & Gamble, the nation's second largest national advertiser, changed its compensation structure starting with the 1990 fiscal year. Under its new policy, in addition to paying the 15 percent to traditional measured media, P&G will extend the commission to cover all of the other forms of sales promotion available ranging from mall events to ads on shopping carts.[16]

For further comment on the great commission debate, see Promotion in Action 11–4.

The Fee System   In this arrangement, the agency is compensated only by a fee based on costs plus an appropriate markup, with all commissions either rebated directly or deducted from the fee. There are benefits to both parties. From the client's perspective, the nature and extent of services to be utilized are negotiated, thus assuring that unnecessary expenditure is avoided. There always is the possibility that a commission represents overcharges. The agency also benefits in that cash flow is regularized. Moreover, there is greater incentive to recommend the noncommissionable media and to provide additional services. There now is assurance (that is not provided by the commission system) that compensation will be adequate.

This system requires precise cost accounting. Agency staff must keep accurate time records that become the basis for client charges. But such data should always be collected, no matter what the compensation system, to provide a picture of account profitability.

There has been a substantial shift toward the fee system during the past decade. The reasons for this shift include (1) inflation in media prices, which generated windfall earnings for many agencies, (2) increased cost consciousness among advertisers, and (3) increased performance in-house of work formerly done by agencies.[17]

The Current Situation   Given the increased acceptability of the fee system by advertising agencies and the continued use of the commission system, albeit with certain variations and adjustments, it seems that for the foreseeable future, the advertiser and the agency will use that combination of compensation methods that best suits the needs of the situation. The very large advertisers will press for some type of sliding scale commission or reduced commission plus bonus if certain goals are reached. Or, as in the Proctor & Gamble situation, they will pay commissions on some sales promotion activities that were formerly noncommissionable. For small advertisers, say those with billings under $3 million, agencies will probably negotiate a fee or a commission with a guaranteed minimum so that they will be certain of a profit after developing a campaign to meet the advertiser's goals.

The House Agency

Over the past several years, the trade press has reported that some large advertisers have removed their accounts from advertising agencies and have developed their own *house agency* to manage them. The motivation

---

❖

**PROMOTION
IN ACTION
11–4**

The "15 Percent" Debate: A New Look

Is the 15 percent commission system a relic of advertising's past?

Agencies tend to consider this question to be a roundabout way of saying, "You're making too much money." And, indeed, clients *are* looking for ways to save marketing dollars. The issue was recently addressed by a panel sponsored by a publication of the American Marketing Association in New York, and parts of the discussion were excerpted in AA's "Viewpoint: Forum" page May 1, 1989.

The subject brought forth some heated opinions, as can be expected whenever Al Achenbaum turns up among a group of agency executives. Mr. Achenbaum, the client consultant who is fast becoming to agencies what the Rev. Donald Wildmon is to TV programmers, chaired the panel discussion, which considered a related question: Can agencies convince their clients that advertising delivers the goods?

Several major advertisers now experimenting with new agency compensation systems have, in fact, built various types of incentives for agencies, but they aren't exactly sure what they should be rewarding. Should it be sales results? Ad test scores? Efficiencies?

Many marketers aren't totally convinced, said Mr. Achenbaum, "that marketing and advertising are really the revenue-producing part of the business." That job of convincing, he said, belongs to the agencies.

The standard line from agencies today, Mr. Achenbaum indicated, is "What is the value of a great idea?" That, he said, "doesn't cut any ice with clients. They want to know if they can get a rebate for a bad idea."

So the far-reaching reexamination of agency compensation goes on, cited as part of the problem, not the solution, or scored as a short-sighted, cost-cutting measure. But the debate is taking on a sharper focus.

This is clearly a cry for help from marketing executives: "Show me—show my management—that advertising works." It would seem that when the debate is argued on that basis, agencies should have an easier time of "selling" advertising's value and power—if one can assume that agencies *really* believe in it any more.

for this move has been the belief that the house agency could handle the account more effectively than a large independent organization serving many clients. Even more common has been the practice of the advertiser's taking over the media planning and buying function from the independent ad agency. These firms believed that they could economize on the cost of buying media.

Recent data indicate that although the numbers of accounts lost to house agencies has been increasing, the volume of billings involved favors independent agencies. Data for 1984 indicated that American Association of Advertising Agencies (AAAA) members lost 68 accounts with billings of $35.5 million. During the same year, they picked up 38 accounts with billings of $85.9 million.[18]

What appears to be affecting this shifting is the recognition that the economies of going in-house are not usually as great as expected. In addition, advertisers are discovering that independent agencies can offer a large staff with wide experience and objectivity. Even in those cases where there are some economies of media buying in-house, the advertiser discovers that these can be offset quickly by the loss of some of the other benefits offered by independent agencies. On the other hand, some advertisers appear to be pleased with their house agency operations and show no interest in shifting back to an independent agency.

Development of a Productive Working Relationship

Good working relationships between client and agency do not just happen—a real dedication to this end is required. Experience has established some important guidelines.[19]

Maintain a Top-Level Liaison   Top-level executives from both parties must communicate regularly to air issues arising as part of day-to-day operations. Most junior staff do not have sufficient background or status to modify operating policies or to put out fires. Minor misunderstandings can easily develop into major difficulties.

Evaluate Promotion in a Marketing Context   When sales drop, the blame all too quickly (and perhaps legitimately) is aimed directly at advertising. Then a quite common next step is to fire the agency—and repeat the entire process a year or two later. But advertising cannot maintain market share for long when the product lags competitively, prices are out of line, distribution is insufficient, and so on.

Part of the problem here is the inappropriate use of sales objectives. Although sales are a valid objective under certain conditions (see Chapter 9), advertising generally should be evaluated in terms of legitimate communications goals. These, in turn, must be agreed on by all parties in advance.

Now we are in a position to see if the agency has accomplished what it set out to do.

Do Not Abandon a Campaign Prematurely   One of the greatest pressures is to stop a productive campaign because executives (or their wives or husbands) are tired of seeing the ads. Every agency has its stories that seem funny when retold of how trivial preferences have led to the abandonment of a great campaign. It is necessary to recognize that everyone involved with a company quickly gets sick of the advertising because of sheer familiarity. But please note—*you are not typical of the average consumer.* Abandonment is appropriate only when there is a downturn in productivity.

Do Not Be Carried away by Creative Execution   Many years ago, David Ogilvy said, "Don't ask for great ads; insist instead on great campaigns."[20] Anyone can argue with details of execution and overlook the most important consideration in the process—*consumer benefit must be communicated clearly and memorably.* Nothing else really matters. Fortunately, this issue can be clarified by pretesting the advertising by using such methods as focus groups (see Chapter 16).

Emancipate the Agency from Fear   Some companies are known as "agency hoppers," making a change every year or two. What kind of output can they expect from an agency? They certainly will not get innovation. Why undertake the risk? Give them what they want! And that most likely will be mediocrity.

Also it is important to note that all agencies will fail at times. So evaluation should be based on the overall batting average. Any group will do its best when it realizes that a misstep will not necessarily be fatal.

We are not saying that an unproductive agency should be tolerated. That would make no sense. But it also must be recognized that an agency change is not necessarily a lasting solution. No one has a surefire formula; all mature marketing people are fully aware of this point and will take steps to make sure that the charge of poor agency performance has been verified before taking such drastic action.

Simplify Approval   The author of this chapter will never forget the travesty of a client "nitpicking to death" a campaign that pretested well and looked promising. First one client executive and then another added personal touches until the final output was nothing more than you would expect from a committee—bland advertising that had lost its cutting edge. The coup de grace was added by the chairman of the board when a member of his family was added as one of the actors in a commercial.

Remember our earlier insistence that authority and responsibility be placed as close to the firing line as possible. The client's marketing or brand manager should have the final say without further dilution. This also means, of course, that he or she will be held accountable for what happens.

Permit the Agency to Make a Profit   The operating margin is sufficiently small that most agencies will cut costs and avoid utilizing top talent if a client demands too much for what it pays. With no incentive to offer its best, the agency most likely will resign the account. It, too, has a right to make a reasonable return on investment.

USING SPECIALIZED SERVICES

Although full-service agencies still account for the bulk of the advertising business, over the years specialized firms have developed to offer limited services on a more in-depth and concentrated basis. These include (1) direct marketing agencies, (2) media-buying services, (3) creative boutiques, and (4) market research firms.

Direct Marketing Agencies

Direct marketing using such strategies as telemarketing, interactive video, and direct mail is not commissionable. Hence, it found its way into the full-service agencies only recently, largely by way of mergers. Nevertheless, numerous direct marketing shops have developed high skill and are worthy of consideration. Because direct marketing is growing dramatically, these agencies are getting increased use.

Media-Buying Services

The media-buying service initially appeared in the middle 1960s to provide help for smaller advertising agencies. A period of rapid growth has ensued, largely due to the growing complexity of media buying—brought about by the proliferation of specialized media to reach highly segmented markets. Today these organizations service both agencies and clients, who determine their own media strategies so that the sole role of the media-buying service is to execute the plan in optimum fashion. Historically, there has been a concentration in broadcast media, but this is rapidly changing. Compensation plans vary, but most consist of some type of fee averaging from 3 to 5 percent.

   The media-buying service has provoked controversy, much of it stemming from the traditional advertising agency, which has seen some departure of clients. Growth of media-buying service has continued unabated, however, and it would appear that continued media proliferation will make for a bright future for skilled media-buyers.

Creative Boutiques

The success of the media-buying service has encouraged the formation of specialized agencies whose sole function is to provide assistance in creative planning and execution. Media buying and other activities are left to the client. Compensation is a negotiated fee. The greatest use to this point has been for new-product development, print advertisements, and television commercials. Perhaps the most significant advantage is concentration of talent within one group, which can be focused as needed on specific projects. The number of such groups has increased over the past decade, but their growth seems to be leveling off, indicated by the fact that several leading full-service agencies are unbundling (charging separately for specific services) and are willing to provide creative services for a fee if that is all that the client desires.

Research Services

The significant role of marketing research has been stressed in this text, and expenditures for this purpose have increased dramatically during the past decade. The demands for technical expertise in this function have grown commensurately. Only a few advertisers have in-house capability for this purpose, and most make use of outside research agencies. These specialized organizations can provide services such as the following: interviewing and field supervision, sampling design, questionnaire construction, data analysis, specialized store audits, and so on.

Market Changes and the Advertising Industry

As we enter the last decade of this century, advertisers as well as advertising agencies face an uncertain future. The mass markets of the past have been fragmented into hundreds of smaller markets, and advertisers have been seeking new ways to communicate with them.

As new-product introductions increase and brands proliferate, the consumer is paying less attention to commercials on network television. Thus the advertiser seeking to persuade members of targeted market segments to buy his or her product is using an assortment of promotional tools ranging from in-store announcements, ads on shopping carts, couponing, direct mail, discounting, rebates, and so forth. The growth rates of billings and profits of many agencies have been cut in half because many of these promotional functions are noncommissionable or are handled outside the agency.

Another factor affecting the advertising industry is the increased economic power of retailers vis-à-vis manufacturers. This power shift, discussed in greater detail in Chapter 21, is largely the result of bar-code scanner technology, which provides the retailer with information on product movement that formerly was available only to the manufacturer. Armed with this information, retailers have been selling their shelf space to the highest bidder and requiring "slotting allowances" of up to $4,000 per store to get a new product on the shelves. These expenses come out of the manufacturer's total promotional appropriation and thus leave that much less for media advertising. A newspaper report on this subject stated:

> Last year, for example, Campbell Soup put 80 percent of the marketing budget for its dry-soup division into advertising inside stores. To give its agencies an incentive to use alternative media in their marketing plans, Campbell decided in August (1989) to pay them a commission for in-store ads. But the commission is less than 15 percent because Campbell is doing its own research and ad placement—work ad agencies used to do routinely.[21]

The Future of the Advertising Agency Given current market trends, it is likely that the advertising agency of the future will emphasize ancillary services to a greater extent. At the time of this writing, some major agencies stated that the provision of such services accounts for 30 percent of their corporate revenues. It is possible that in the not-too-distant future, over half of agency revenue will come not from media advertising but from providing other forms of sales promotion and from the sale of ancillary services such as market research.

On the other hand, some industry watchers who are more optimistic believe that the current stagnation in industry growth will be short-lived and will be replaced by a new surge of creativity. It is their prediction that smaller agencies will be the source of creative people of the stature of Leo Burnett and Bill Bernbach, who touched off the creative revolutions of the past, and that this new burst of creativity will get the advertising agency business back on a fast-growth track.

SUMMARY

This chapter has covered the important subjects of the organization of human resources and the use of specialized agencies. No matter how brilliant the strategy, everything can be sidetracked unless the organization, in its entirety, takes on a marketing orientation. Top management, in particular, must establish the climate and provide a vision.

Given that the goal of the firm is to create customers, it must have a pervasive commitment to innovation, quality, and excellence. A philosophy of participative management will allow these commitments to permeate the rank and file of the enterprise and increase employee productivity and accountability.

Two types of organizational structure—functional and product—were examined. Because product management organization has become so dominant, promotional management was discussed in that context. A product organization offers such great advantages of flexibility and innovation that it more than compensates for its disadvantages.

Few companies have the resources necessary to design and implement a full promotional program. For this reason, they make considerable use of advertising agencies and various other agencies specializing in direct marketing, media buying, creative design, and marketing research. The advertising agency was described fully in terms of its functions, compensation, and effective use.

Finally, the changes in the market that threaten the future of the advertising agency were discussed. The fragmentation of the market, the proliferation of new products, the seeking of new ways to communicate with consumers, and the shift in market power in favor of large retailers all mean that the era of the ever-increasing use of the mass media (especially network TV) is ending. Agencies that adapt to change most successfully will focus on improving their creative efforts and will seek to make up lost advertising revenues by the sale of ancillary services.

REVIEW AND DISCUSSION QUESTIONS

1. You have just taken control of a small service business employing 20 people. The business is not doing well, and you want to instill in the employees Drucker's theme that the purpose of a business is to "create a customer." How do you get this philosophy to permeate organizational ranks and become a reality?

2. The XYZ Corporation is currently organized on functional lines. The CEO has asked you to write a memo to him on the pros and cons of switching to a product form of organization. What key factors will you include in your communication?

3. Jane Hill, the product manager of Krispy Bits dog food, found herself at a disadvantage in that she did not have the necessary experience or expertise to appraise the research designs that she was getting from the company's marketing research people. What can she do, if anything, to minimize this disadvantage?

4. Imagine that you are seeking new business for your ad agency. The prospective client you are in contact with has the potential for $25 million a year in billings. Your agency has always used the 15 percent commission, but the prospective client states that she is interested only in a negotiated fee basis of compensation. How would you handle this situation?

5. Your full-service ad agency is being buffeted by clients who want to handle various parts of the advertising task in-house. This leaves you, in many cases, with the less profitable aspects of the business. What are the pressures for change? What can your agency do, if anything, to survive?

6. You are on the verge of signing a new client for your ad agency. In addition to the standard contract, the client wants a brief and simply worded statement of guidelines for developing and maintaining an effective working relationship between his company and your agency. What key guidelines would you include in the statement?

NOTES

1. Tom Peters and Nancy Austin, *A Passion for Excellence* (New York: Random House, 1985), p. xxi.

2. John Naisbitt and Patricia Aburdene, *Re-inventing the Corporation* (New York: Warner Books, 1985), p. 20.

3. Peters and Austin, *A Passion for Excellence,* p. 59.

4. For an excellent, concise statement of Drucker's thinking, see Peter F. Drucker, *An Introductory View of Management* (New York: Harper & Row, 1977).

5. See especially Tom Peters and Robert H. Waterman, Jr., *In Search of Excellence* (New York: Random House, 1982).

6. Associated Press, "Personal Touch, Traditional Values Help Family Grocery Beat 'Giants,' " *Marketing News,* June 5, 1989, p. 6.

7. See especially Peters and Austin, *A Passion for Excellence,* chap. 2.

8. Naisbitt and Aburdene, *Re-inventing the Corporation,* p. 62.

9. Philip Kotler, *Marketing Management: Analysis, Planning, Implementation and Control,* 6th ed. (Englewood Cliffs, N.J.: Prentice Hall, 1988), p. 709.

10. Laurie Freeman, "P&G Keen Again on Ad Managers," *Advertising Age,* September 25, 1989, p. 6.

11. Drucker, *An Introductory View of Management,* p. 536.

12. *The Ideal Agency-Client Policy on Account Conflicts* (New York: American Association of Advertising Agencies, 1973).

13. Herbert Zeltner, "Client Agency Conflicts," *Advertising Age,* March 5, 1984, pp. M64–68.

14. "Survey Shows Advertisers Quitting Traditional Commission System," *Marketing News,* June 20, 1986, p. 13.

15. Laurie Freeman, "Big Issue for 1988: Compensation," *Advertising Age,* November 23, 1987, pp. 1, 60–61.

16. Editorial, "P&G Levels the Playing Field," *Advertising Age,* February 27, 1989, p. 16.

17. Michael Cooper, "Agency Compensation: Fees vs. Commissions: A Conversation with Al Achenbaum," *Marketing & Media Decisions,* Fall 1984, pp. 109–116.

18. Stewart Alter, "Balance of Ad Trade Follows Full-line Shops," *Advertising Age,* December 2, 1985, p. 102.

19. We have benefited from many sources including David Ogilvy, *Ogilvy on Advertising* (New York: Crown Publishers, 1983), and *Confessions of an Advertising Man* (New York: Dell Publishing, 1963); and Kenneth Roman and Jane Maas, *How to Advertise* (New York: St. Martin's Press, 1976).

20. Ogilvy, *Confessions of an Advertising Man,* p. 92.

21. Randall Rothenberg, "Changes in Consumer Markets Hurting Advertising Industry," *The New York Times,* October 3, 1989, p. 1, 45.

Adaptation to the Legal Climate

CAMPBELL SOUP AGREES TO AD GUIDELINES IN NINE STATES TO SETTLE DISPUTE OVER CLAIMS

Campbell Soup Co. agreed to abide by advertising guidelines in nine states to settle a dispute over health claims made for soup in the company's "Soup Is Good Food" campaign. The challenge to the ads was brought in June 1988 by state attorneys general, who in recent years have increasingly asserted themselves as guardians of consumers' interests.

"The case against Campbell should put all food companies on notice that they won't get away with false claims about their products," said Hubert Humphrey III, the attorney general of Minnesota.

The attorneys general had alleged that Campbell misled consumers by highlighting the calcium content of its tomato and other soups when most of the calcium would come from the milk to be added to the soup. They also alleged that the fiber content of certain soups such as chicken noodle was misrepresented when they were pictured with the bean and pea soups that were the subjects of high-fiber claims.

Campbell, based in Camden, N.J., didn't admit to any wrongdoing. But the company agreed to pay $315,000 to cover the costs of state investigations and consumer education as well as to observe the guidelines.

The guidelines say that an ad focusing on one type of soup as a source of a nutrient can depict other soups only if they also contain that nutrient. They say further that if an ad features a nutrient in a recipe using a soup product, but the nutrient isn't in the product itself, the source of the nutrient must be disclosed.

The attorneys general never actually sued Campbell but used the threat of a suit to reach the settlement, called an *assurance of discontinuance.*

Campbell said it didn't pursue its case in the courts "because of the peripheral nature of the dispute" and because of the costs of litigating in different states. Besides Minnesota, the states involved in the settlement were California, Illinois, Iowa, Massachusetts, Missouri, New York, Texas, and Wisconsin.

Source: Excerpted from Richard Koenig, *The Wall Street Journal,* May 11, 1989, p. B4.

WARNING! Disregarding the contents of this chapter may be harmful to your well-being. The legal environment in which you will operate during the decade of the 90s is in a state of flux and unless you know what you are doing, you and your firm could be in big trouble. The reading may be tough going (even boring), but stick with it because you must know how the law will impinge on your freedom to act as a manager of promotion. As a brief example of what has been taking place at the close of the decade of the 80s, please consider the following news headlines:

Item: State attorneys general are filling the gaps left by deregulation at the federal level.

Item: The Federal Trade Commission has mounted a major attack against swindlers using telephones. Telemarketing fraud is estimated to cost consumers over $1 billion a year.

Item: A little noted Trademark Revision Act has become effective. It is now much easier for victims of "attack" advertising to sue.

Item: Federal Drug Administration aides are accused of taking bribes to hasten the approval of certain generic drugs.

Item: Manufacturers of oat bran products are charged with misleading consumers as to health benefits.

As you can see, lots of things are happening. Our goal in this chapter is to describe the legal environment as we see it today and to clarify the changes that are taking place with respect to new law and the interpretation of established law.

In addition, we want you to be aware of two major points: (1) The legal environment is in a state of constant change, and (2) ignorance of the law is no defense when you are charged with a violation.

Filling the Regulatory Vacuum   Federally imposed legal constraints on marketing in general and promotion in particular multiplied during the decade of the 70s. The high watermark of federal regulation was reached in the early 1980s. The Reagan administration had the general goal to deregulate business activity whenever possible, and Congress went along. Budgets of regulatory agencies were cut, and the regulators were told to concentrate on important cases and to stop harassing business about "minor" problems. Ironically, the regulatory vacuum that grew at the federal level has been filled to an increasing extent by regulatory activity at state and local levels of government as illustrated in the Campbell Soup case.

Because of the growing dispersion of regulation, the federal government is under increasing pressure to regain control. This pressure is being exerted in part by big business, which finds that it is easier to comply with one set of federal rules than with those of 50 states and hundreds of smaller governmental units. Whether or not the present administration and Congress will attempt to increase federal regulation of promotion and other business activities is not clear at the time of this writing.

In spite of the deregulatory trend, many laws and regulations that impinge on promotion are still in place. Although a review of the major ones in this text is necessary, the coverage cannot be exhaustive. Our goal is to provide enough detail to allow you to sense the current state of governmental and self-regulatory policies and to determine whether a proposed promotional campaign meets the requirements set by Congress and the various federal, state, and local regulatory agencies.[1]

PERTINENT LEGISLATION

Federal Legislation

Although laws and regulations to control promotional activities exist at federal, state, and local levels of government, the constitutional underpinnings of our judicial system give first precedence to federal statutes and federal administrative law. Thus in our discussion of pertinent legislation, activities at the federal level will dominate. However, when state or local regulatory efforts are of considerable importance, they will be noted.

A review of history indicates that prior to the 20th century, the doctrine of "let the buyer beware" prevailed with little or no buyer protection against false and deceptive methods of sale. Post office fraud laws were passed in 1872 to curb the use of the mails to defraud, but not until the passage of the Pure Food and Drug Act in 1906 and the Federal Trade Commission Act in 1914 did effective legal curbs exist. Unfortunately, the Food and Drug Act had limited applicability in that it required only that a correct description of contents be printed on the packages of patent drug items. This statute was superseded by the Federal Food, Drug, and Cosmetic Act of 1938, which will be noted later in this chapter.

The Federal Trade Commission Act   Unlike the first Pure Food and Drug Act, the Federal Trade Commission (FTC) Act of 1914 was the first truly effective legislation aimed at curbing promotional abuses and preventing unfair methods of competition. Thus, in one law, Congress provided for both consumer protection and antitrust surveillance.

The FTC Act set up a commission of five members and a staff of approximately 1,500 persons, divided among three bureaus: Competition, Consumer Protection, and Economics. An organizational chart is shown in Figure 12–1. The FTC's initial concern under Section 5 of the act was to prohibit unfair methods of competition in interstate commerce where the effect was to injure competition. The prevention of deceptive methods of promotion was only a secondary objective. However, over the years, as strengthened by several key Supreme Court decisions, the FTC increased its activities against false and misleading promotional activities.

The Robinson-Patman Act   In 1936, Congress passed this amendment to the Clayton Act designed to give the FTC broad powers to control discriminatory pricing practices. We will discuss the ramifications of this statute in some detail later in this text.

The Wheeler-Lea Amendment   This statute passed in 1938 significantly broadened the powers of the FTC.[2] Its contents are noted in Table 12–1.

Following the Wheeler-Lea Amendment, a series of congressional actions have required certain industries to provide special disclosures of information on their labels and in their advertisements to prevent consumer deception. Six laws are of special note because of the increased power they have given the FTC to control the promotional activities of firms in these industries. The names of these laws indicate the nature of the applicability:

Wool Products Act (1939)

Fur Products Labeling Act (1951)

Textile Fiber Products Act (1958)

Fair Packaging and Labeling Act (1966)

Truth in Lending Act (1969)

Fair Credit Reporting Act (1970)

FTC Monitoring   The FTC staff continually monitors all forms of interstate promotion. For example, television networks are required to submit typed scripts covering one broadcasting week each month. The FTC also processes a substantial number of complaints from individuals yearly.

The FTC holds a preliminary investigation if action appears to be required. Minor complaints may be turned over to the Division of Stipulation

FIGURE 12–1

The Federal Trade Commission

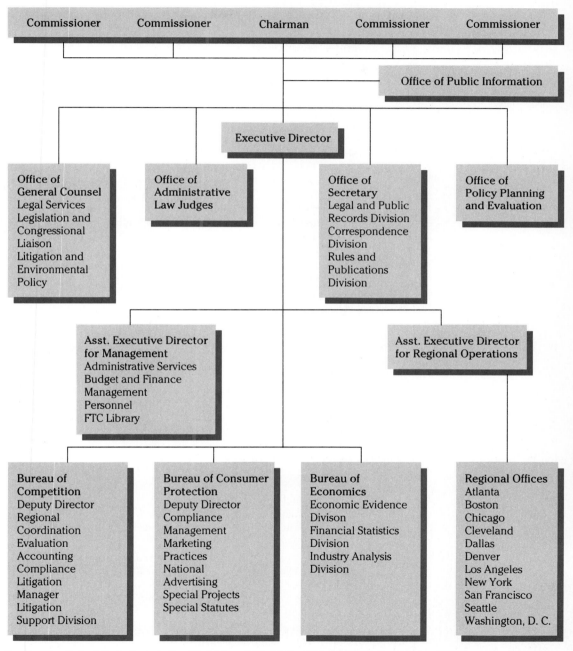

FEDERAL TRADE COMMISSION

| Commissioner | Commissioner | Chairman | Commissioner | Commissioner |

Office of Public Information

Executive Director

Office of General Counsel
Legal Services
Legislation and
Congressional
Liaison
Litigation and
Environmental
Policy

Office of Administrative Law Judges

Office of Secretary
Legal and Public
Records Division
Correspondence
Division
Rules and
Publications
Division

Office of Policy Planning and Evaluation

Asst. Executive Director for Management
Administrative Services
Budget and Finance
Management
Personnel
FTC Library

Asst. Executive Director for Regional Operations

Bureau of Competition
Deputy Director
Regional
Coordination
Evaluation
Accounting
Compliance
Litigation
Manager
Litigation
Support Division

Bureau of Consumer Protection
Deputy Director
Compliance
Management
Marketing
Practices
National
Advertising
Special Projects
Special Statutes

Bureau of Economics
Economic Evidence
Divison
Financial Statistics
Division
Industry Analysis
Division

Regional Offices
Atlanta
Boston
Chicago
Cleveland
Dallas
Denver
Los Angeles
New York
San Francisco
Seattle
Washington, D. C.

Source: "Your Federal Trade Commission, What It Is and What It Does," Federal Trade Commission (U.S. Government Printing Office, 1977).

TABLE 12–1

❖

Major Federal Legislation Affecting Promotion

1906 Pure Food and Drug Act

Requires the correct description of contents on the package of drug items.

1914 Federal Trade Commission Act

Prohibits unfair methods of competition to interstate commerce where the effect is to injure competition.

1936 Robinson-Patman Act

Empowers the FTC to control discriminatory pricing practices, including advertising.

1938 Wheeler-Lea Amendment

Provides that intent to defraud no longer needs to be proven.
"Unfair methods of competition" is expanded to encompass deceptive acts or practices.
The FTC receives jurisdiction over false advertising of food, drugs, and cosmetics.
The FTC is empowered to issue cease and desist orders.
The FTC is permitted to issue injunctions to halt improper food, drug, or cosmetic advertising when it appears that the public may be harmed.

1938 Federal Food, Drug, and Cosmetic Act

Empowers the FDA to investigate and litigate concerning advertising claims on the label or package of food, drug, and cosmetic items.

1946 The Lanham Act (The Trademark Act)

Gives the seller the exclusive right to use a trademark that it owns in a given line of trade. Sec 43(a) offers federal protection to businesses against many forms of unfair competition.

1962 Amendment to FDA Act

Authorizes the FDA to establish comprehensive procedures for premarketing approval of claims and labels for prescription drugs.
Provides for full disclosure of side effects and complications possibly associated with prescription drugs.

1966 Amendment to FDA Act

Gives the FDA power to seize shipment of goods on receiving evidence that its regulations have been violated.
Authorizes the FTC to institute its own court actions if the Justice Department does not act within 10 days of an FTC request.
Increases penalties for violations of cease and desist orders.
Permits the FTC to obtain preliminary injunctions against unfair or deceptive advertising.
Grants all federal regulatory agencies far-reaching information-gathering powers.

1975 Magnuson-Moss Warranty—FTC Improvement Act

Clarifies and strengthens product warranties.
Broadens the jurisdiction of the FTC and extends its rule-making authority.

1980 FTC Improvement Act

Requires FTC to submit proposed rules to Congress that would require a majority vote by both houses to become effective. (A recent Supreme Court decision has made this requirement questionable.)
Unfairness can no longer be used as a basis for rules restricting advertising.

1988 Trademark Law Revision Act

Prevents advertisers from misrepresenting the qualities or characteristics of "another person's goods, services, or commercial activities." Law effective as of November 1989.

for an informal, nonpublicized settlement. But more serious cases result in a formal complaint issued by the Bureau of Litigation upon the approval of the full commission.[3] A respondent has 30 days to answer a formal complaint, after which a hearing is held before an examiner. The examiner's decision may be appealed to the FTC by either side, and, in turn, commission decisions may be appealed through the federal courts. The FTC may issue a consent order whereby actions are enjoined but the respondent admits no guilt. A guilty judgment after formal proceedings, however, culminates in a cease and desist order. Consent orders and cease and desist orders are both binding.

The FTC on its own volition or at the request of an industry group occasionally calls a trade conference to establish a code of fair practice. The codes thus established may cover activities the commission deems to be illegal, such as the use of a fictitious list price or following unethical practices that are technically within the law.

The Alaska Pipeline Bill   In late 1973, the FTC was further strengthened by passage of legislation appended to the Alaska Pipeline Bill. The law authorized the FTC to institute its own court actions if the Justice Department does not act within 10 days on an FTC request, to increase penalties for violations of cease and desist orders from $5,000 to $10,000, and to obtain preliminary injunctions against unfair or deceptive advertising. In addition, the bill grants all federal regulatory agencies, including the FTC, far-reaching information-gathering powers.[4]

The Magnuson-Moss Warranty–Federal Trade Commission Improvement Act   This law passed in 1975 has two parts. The first deals with ways to clarify and strengthen product warranties to improve consumer protection. The second part is of special interest to managers of promotion because it broadens the jurisdiction of the FTC and expands its rule-making authority.

Certain changes such as the derivation of expanded powers for the FTC from statute rather than judicial review are clear. The impact of other changes is less clear. For example, Magnuson-Moss provided the FTC with rule-making authority permitting it to establish trade regulation rules that specify unfair or deceptive acts or practices that are prohibited. The term *unfair*, however, was neither defined nor clarified.[5]

FTC Improvement Act   In 1980, because of criticism of the FTC's rule-making activities, the second FTC Improvement Act was passed.[6] The first part of the act required the FTC to submit proposed rules to Congress, where a majority vote in both houses is required to become effective. Subsequently, the FTC issued a rule that would have required used-car dealers to disclose defects in the cars for sale. In 1982, both houses of Congress vetoed the rule, but the Supreme Court held that this method of restricting the authority of the FTC was unconstitutional. (The rule was never issued, however.) In 1983, a rule regulating funeral homes was submitted to Congress and became effective when Congress refused to act.

The Future of the Federal Trade Commission

At the time of this writing, the FTC is celebrating its 75th anniversary. Whether it will survive in its present form is doubtful. For example, over the 10-year period 1979–1988, the FTC workyear staffing levels have declined from 1,746 to approximately 900 as both the Reagan Administration and Congress reduced the FTC budget in an attempt to deregulate large portions of the economy. This reduction in personnel of almost 50 percent came in the face of ever-increasing workloads, especially in reviewing applications for mergers and acquisitions. According to a former FTC commissioner, Andrew J. Strenio, Jr., the quality of the FTC staff is high and productivity gains have been remarkable. But given the demands on its resources, the

**PROMOTION
IN ACTION
12–1**

Consumer Protection Frustrations

Telemarketing fraud costs consumers and businesses nearly $1 billion each year, according to a 1987 report by FTC Chairman Daniel Oliver. The commission has mounted a major attack against swindlers who have been using telephones to prey on consumers with some impressive results to show for these efforts. The bad news is that because of limits on FTC resources and legal authority, the efforts have not been nearly enough to turn the tide.

Since 1983, the commission has successfully brought more than 28 federal district court cases against nationwide telemarketing scams with aggregate sales of over $859 million. These actions have put some 165 individual and corporate telemarketers under federal order, and the FTC has obtained judgments for more than $91.8 million in redress for scam victims. To date, more than 6,500 of those victims have received redress checks ranging from $50 to $15,000 as a result of commission actions.

Unfortunately, telemarketing is not the only boom area for fraudulent operations. To name just one other, published estimates place health fraud in the range of $10–25 billion per year.

Source: Adapted from Andrew J. Strenio, Jr., "The FTC in 1988: Phoenix or Finis?," *Journal of Public Policy & Marketing* 7 (1988), p. 28. Strenio was a member of the Federal Trade Commission when he wrote the article.

agency can deal only with consumer protection in areas in which the violations are most flagrant.[7]

Decisions as to the agency's future must be made soon. If the FTC receives additional resources, it will reassume some control over regulatory actions that have become the domain of the various state attorneys general. If the FTC budget is constrained, it will play a lesser role than it does today and its responsibilities will increasingly be taken over by the Department of Justice and the various state and local agencies. Strenio believes that the latter situation would be unfortunate because the FTC is better qualified on the basis of its legislative charter to protect the consumer than the Department of Justice. In addition, as previously noted, federal regulations are easier to follow than a myriad of rules emanating from state and local governments.[8] Thus a good case can be made to strengthen the agency. On the other hand, in certain areas such as misleading advertising, litigators are moving to state courts, which are faster, less costly, and less technical than the federal courts. It may be difficult for the FTC to regain control.[9]

FTC Rule-Making   If the Bush administration and Congress increase the FTC budget, it will be interesting to see how far Congress will allow the agency to engage in rule-making, which is unpopular with powerful lobbies. For example, an FTC ruling as of September 1, 1989, swept away hundreds of state and local laws that regulated the sale of eyeglasses.[10] This ruling pits thousands of self-employed optometrists against the growing number of optical chains that dispense eyeglasses quickly and at generally reduced prices. Although Congress cannot exercise veto power over an FTC rule such as this one, too many rules that upset entrenched interests can cause Congress to put the brakes on the FTC by threatening to cut its budget.

Another constraint on the FTC's rule-making authority is that unfairness cannot be used as the basis for a rule restricting advertising. The vagueness of the definition of *unfair* and concern for the protection of commercial speech under the First Amendment caused Congress to limit the FTC's activities in this area.

The Lanham Act   The *Trademark Act,* passed in 1946, allows manufacturers to register their brand names and trademarks and thus gain a monopoly in their use. Section 43a of the Lanham Act has been the basis of several suits by brand owners who claimed that the value of their brand had been damaged by misleading comparative advertising by competitors.

The Federal Food, Drug, and Cosmetic Act   The earlier act of 1906 was supplanted in 1938 by the Federal Food, Drug, and Cosmetic Act. The Food and Drug Administration (FDA) is empowered to investigate and litigate advertising claims appearing on the label or package of food, drug, and cosmetic items. The FTC monitors all *other* forms of advertising for these products.

As a result of increasing pressures for more effective efforts to protect the consumer, the Hazardous Substance Labeling Act was passed in 1960. This law requires special disclosure on the label of household products that have toxic, corrosive, irritant, or similar characteristics. In 1962, still more regulatory power was granted the FDA with the amendment of the 1938 act to give the FDA authority to establish comprehensive procedures providing for premarketing approval of claims and labels for prescription drugs, as well as provisions that assure that advertising is consistent with permissible labeling claims. This legislation was especially aimed at gaining the full disclosure of side effects and complications that might be associated with prescription drugs.

The Fair Packaging and Labeling Act (1966) granted the FDA additional powers to require disclosure of information on labels of food, drug, and cosmetic products and to regulate packaging procedures that might tend to confuse consumers or make product comparisons difficult.

The FDA has the power to seize shipments of goods upon receipt of evidence that its regulations have been violated. Notable examples of seizure in recent years include shipments of frozen orange juice allegedly containing misrepresentation of contents and shipments of coffee containing false price information. Of course, in the situations where consumer health is endangered, the FDA has recalled entire batches of products, as it did when botulism appeared to exist in canned tuna, mushrooms, and soups.

For many years, the FDA and the FTC were antagonists because of the overlapping nature of their jurisdictions. In recent years, however, the two agencies have become close collaborators rather than rivals. The FDA with its vast scientific resources tests product efficacy. Although the FDA is limited to what goes on the label (with the exception of prescription drugs, where it also controls advertised claims), the results of its experimentation are used by the FTC as the basis of its charges of misrepresentation or fraud.

In 1962, with the advent of the new legislation, the FDA undertook a study of the effectiveness of all prescription drugs then on the market. Findings announced 10 years later resulted in removal from the market of several products that were deemed ineffective. At that time, the FDA began a similar study of over-the-counter products such as analgesics and antacids.

The FDA is a potent force in the regulation of product development and promotion by members of the food, drug, and cosmetics industries. One example of the FDA's ability to influence events is the end of the fish-oil supplement craze. Touted as helpful in combating high cholesterol and triglyceride levels, the fish-oil category reached sales of $45 to $48 million in

1987 with the major brands spending about $10 million in measured media. The FDA, however, questioned the use of fish-oil supplements by the general public. In the mid-1988, it sent a letter to some 100 fish-oil marketers stating that they were making advertising claims that they could not substantiate. The letter asked that claims cease under threat of legal action. Category advertising dropped to $2 million in 1988 with sales down to $35 million.[11]

During 1989, the FDA attempted to enact a set of guidelines that would allow food marketers to make direct health claims on product labels. Consumer groups as well as manufacturers have held up implementation of these guidelines for different reasons. A possible compromise approach may be to tell manufacturers what they can't say without forcing them to adhere to any specific wording. The list of approved subjects will be broadened but verification standards will be tightened. Marketers will probably be required to provide information on health claims to any consumer requesting such material.[12]

State and Local Regulations

Given the early inadequacies of federal regulation of promotion, *Printers' Ink* magazine in 1911 proposed a "model statute" for the regulation of promotion at the state level. At present, a substantial majority of the states have adopted this statute in whole or in modified form and thus spell out very clearly what practices constitute deceptive advertising. These statutes have changed over time to reflect changing values and practices.

The variety of local laws regulating promotion defy description. Some of these laws parallel the *Printers' Ink* model and others regulate house-to-house selling, advertising appeals, and the use of such media as billboards and signs.

The important aspect of state and local regulation is that given the reduction in resources allocated to the federal agencies, state and local regulators have taken up the slack in many situations. For example, in a California case, People v. Western Airlines, the court ruled that the state's deceptive advertising law applies to the airline's fare promotions. In Committee on Children's Television v. General Foods, parents were permitted to sue General Foods, Safeway Stores, and involved ad agencies for damages caused by encouraging the purchase of sugared cereals. As already noted, Campbell Soup Co. agreed to abide by advertising guidelines in nine states to settle a dispute over health claims made in the company's "Soup is Good Food" campaign.[13] Actions such as these noted above bear out the thoughts of one writer who states, "Thus, while the regulation of advertising continues, the venues for control have changed."[14] Table 12–2 illustrates the diversity of the challenges facing advertisers midway through the decade of the 1980s.

Self-Regulation

In 1971, the advertising industry in cooperation with the Council of Better Business Bureaus (CBBB) established an ambitious program of self-regulation. The goal of the program was to enable the members of the industry to respond more effectively to public complaints about national advertising. The coverage of the program was broad and in addition to matters of truth and accuracy, it also covered matters of taste and social responsibility.

The mechanics of the program, which are quite complicated, are illustrated in Figure 12–2. It can be seen that complaints about advertising are received by the National Advertising Division (NAD) of the Council, which evaluates them. The complaint is either dismissed at this point or the advertiser is requested to provide substantiation of its claims. Once again, the complaint may be dismissed, or if the substantiation is not acceptable, the

TABLE 12–2

⁚⁚ **Who's Challenging Advertising Claims**

Complainant	Forum	Product	Complaint	Status
American Home Products	Federal district court	Johnson & Johnson's Tylenol	Ads imply that ibuprofen causes stomach irritation	In discovery
Center for Science in the Public Interest	New York and Texas attorneys general	Kraft's Cheez Whiz	Ads say the pasteurized processed cheese is real cheese	Under investigation
	New York attorney general	McDonald's Chicken McNuggets	Ads say 100% chicken without saying product is fried in animal fat	Under investigation
General Foods' Oscar Mayer Subsidiary	Better Business Bureau*	Sara Lee's Bryan's bacon and bologna	Ads say products are No. 1 in the South	Advertising modified
New York Attorney General	Internal investigation	VLI's Today contraceptive sponge	Ads say the sponge has no side effects	Advertising modified

Although the FTC stance toward deceptive or fraudulent advertising was considerably narrowed under the Reagan administration to handle "only the most blatant cases," large national advertisers have not been let off the hook. Consumers and companies are seeking relief through the National Advertising Division (NAD) of the Council of Better Business Bureaus, Inc., as well as through the courts. Ironically, those large advertisers who welcomed the reining in of what appeared to them to be a too-active FTC are now having to face private challenges to their advertising claims that are even more difficult and costly to overcome than were those emanating from the public sector.

*National Advertising Division (NAD) of the Council of Better Business Bureaus, a self-regulatory group.

Source: Reprinted from *Business Week*, December 2, 1985, by special permission, 1985 by McGraw-Hill, Inc.

FIGURE 12–2

A Flow Diagram of the National Advertising Division (NAD) and National
Advertising Review Board (NARB) Self-Regulatory Process

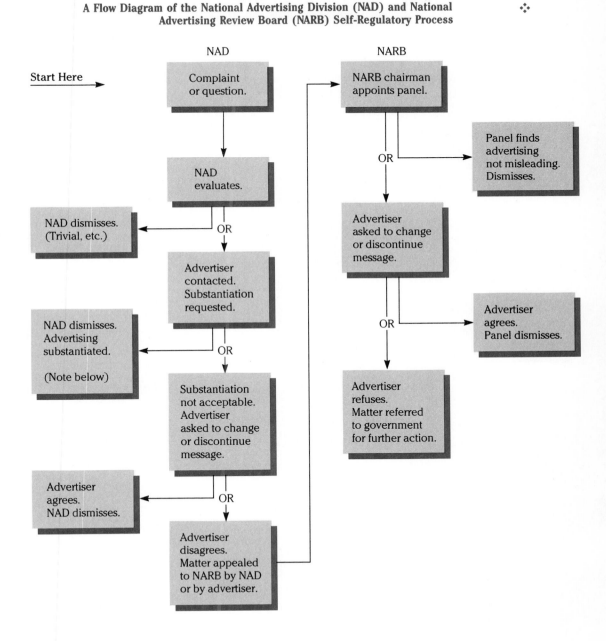

advertiser can be requested to discontinue its message. If the advertiser agrees to cease and desist, the case is terminated. If not, the matter can be appealed to the National Advertising Review Board (NARB) by either the advertiser or the NAD.

The NARB is composed of a chairman and 50 members representing various segments of the advertising industry and the public at large. In response to an appeal, the chairman may appoint a five-person panel to consider the case. If the panel finds in favor of the advertiser, the case is closed. If the panel finds that the ad in question is misleading, the advertiser is requested to modify or terminate use of the message. Refusal on the part of the advertiser to obey the findings of the panel results in referral of the complaint to the appropriate governmental agencies, and the findings of the NAD and NARB panel are made public. Figure 12–3 illustrates the responses of five companies to challenges from the NAD.

FIGURE 12–3

❖ **An Example of the Public Reporting of National Advertiser Participation in the NAD/NARB Self-Regulatory Process**

NAD Case Report

**National Advertising Division
Council of Better Business Bureaus, Inc.**

845 THIRD AVENUE, NEW YORK, NY 10022 · (212) 754-1358

⌐Copyright 1989· CBBB   Vol. 19 No. 4 — Pages 14-17   May 15, 1989

**PUBLIC REPORT OF NATIONAL ADVERTISER PARTICIPATION IN THE
NAD/NARB SELF-REGULATORY PROCESS ESTABLISHED BY BUSINESS**

APRIL CLOSINGS:

Appliances/Consumer Electronics: North American Philips Corp. (Improved Definition Television)

Children's Advertising Review Unit: Matchbox Toys, Ltd. (Pee-Wee's Playhouse and Accessories)
Worlds of Wonder, Inc. (Li'l Boppers Plush Animals)

Cosmetics/Toiletries: Bic Corp. (Bic Metal Shaver)
Pfizer Inc./Oral Research Laboratories, Inc. (Plax Pre-Brushing Dental Rinse)

Food/Beverages: Kellogg Company/Mrs. Smith's Frozen Foods Co. (Pumpkin Pie)

Travel/Accommodation: Hilton Hotels Corp. (HHonors Program)

ADVERTISING SUBSTANTIATED

NAD's findings are based on its own review and evaluation of advertiser's substantiation and, when necessary, on consultation with technical experts. The reports may not be used for promotional purposes. It is the policy of the Council of Better Business Bureaus not to endorse any company, product or service.

**BIC CORP.
Bic Metal Shaver**
Slater Hanft Martin, Inc.

Basis of Inquiry: Trade materials introducing the new Bic Metal Shaver were brought to NAD's attention by a competitor. The challenger maintained that the name "Bic Metal" was a misnomer since the product is made of plastic, except for the blade and metal guard bar and consumers might conclude it is non-disposable.

NAD referred the challenge to the advertiser and agreed to limit the inquiry, at this time, to the use of the term "metal."

Resolution: The advertiser indicated that the name Bic Metal was chosen to differentiate the product from other shavers in the Bic line of disposable shavers. The advertiser stressed that the advertising copy and the package label draw attention to the patented metal guard. Additionally, the fact that the product is sold only in five-packs should indicate to any consumer that these are plastic, disposable razors. The advertiser disputed the challenger's assertion that the term "metal" would indicate that the product is non-disposable.

Upon review of the package and advertising, NAD felt there

was no implication that the shavers were exclusively metal or non-disposable.

NAD agreed the claims were substantiated. (#2692)

**NORTH AMERICAN PHILIPS CORP.
Improved Definition Television (IDTV)**
Backer, Spielvogel, Bates, Inc.

Basis of Inquiry: Magazine advertising claimed: "No matter how good your conventional color television is, our IDTV is superior. By far. Because Philips IDTV (Improved Definition Television) will show you an image that has greater accuracy, better definition and less noise than any available today . . ." "Conventional TVs and monitors display 262 1/2 scanning lines every 1/60 of a second to 'paint' the image on the screen. With Philips non-interlace technology, the scanning rate is doubled to 525 lines. As a result, scanning lines become invisible and vertical resolution is improved by 40%."

Resolution: The advertiser provided a technical description of IDTV published for electrical engineers, a video catalogue containing details of the monitors and accessories, and an independent review of IDTV in a special interest magazine. The system uses two built-in tuners allowing display of a wide variety of picture-in-picture options, including picture recall. The advertiser explained there are 480 active vertical video lines in the frame compared to 330 lines in currently available interlaced pictures, resulting in a 40% improvement in vertical resolution.

NAD agreed the claims were substantiated. (#2693)

NAD Case Report 5/15/89 Page 15

ADVERTISING MODIFIED OR DISCONTINUED

The fact that advertising has been modified or discontinued, as reported below, is not to be taken as an admission of impropriety on any advertiser's part. In some cases, advertisers have voluntarily changed or discontinued advertising in cooperation with NAD's self-regulatory efforts. Other advertisers have discontinued challenged claims for their own reasons but have agreed not to run them again without furnishing appropriate substantiation. Reports may not be used for promotional purposes.

**HILTON HOTELS CORP.
HHonors Program**
Ogilvy & Mather

Basis of Inquiry: Advertisements promoting HHonors membership in February newspapers and March magazines claimed: "Get off to a QuickStart — act now and get a free weekend night. As an HHonors member, each time you use the American Express Card to stay at Hilton between now and April 30, 1989, you will receive a QuickStart Certificate for a future stay. It entitles you to a free Friday, Saturday or Sunday night when you stay the following night at the local corporate rate." A competitor brought the advertising to NAD's attention and maintained the potential savings were not as claimed since Hilton Hotels regularly offer weekend rates that average at least 50% less than the corporate rates. The challenger quoted an example where a guest would pay slightly less for two weekend nights, double occupancy, at the weekend rate than using QuickStart.

Resolution: The advertiser emphasized that the challenger's statement that Hilton weekend rates are greatly reduced as a regular rule was inaccurate. Only a small number of hotels in major metropolitan locations offer such weekend specials. The advertiser provided a copy of its current, revised advertisement and a sample QuickStart Certificate. All references to the "local corporate rate" had been changed to read "QuickStart rate." The advertiser stated the QuickStart rate for a two-night stay is lower than local corporate and weekend rates. The advertiser also noted that the QuickStart program allows for highest possible savings when members start their two-night stay on a Sunday and provided several specific examples to confirm the accuracy of the current claims. (#2694)

**KELLOGG COMPANY/MRS. SMITH'S
FROZEN FOODS CO.
Pumpkin Pie**
Leo Burnett Company, Inc./Chicago

Basis of Inquiry: Newspaper insert advertising claimed: "Mrs. Smith's Pumpkin Pie. The pick of the patch. Mrs. Smith's starts with fresh pumpkin, straight from the patch. Not canned pumpkin like other pies. That's why it's so fresh, so creamy, so tempting. Mrs. Smith's. It gives you a freshness cans can't." A television commercial contained similar claims.

Carnation, packer of Libby's canned pumpkin, brought the advertising to NAD's attention, and stated its belief that Mrs. Smith's pies are sometimes made with frozen pumpkin. The challenger also questioned the claim that the frozen product "gives you a freshness cans can't."

Resolution: The advertiser stated that it purchases fresh pumpkin direct from the growers. Some of the freshly processed pumpkin is used immediately and some is frozen until it can be made into pies. No canned pumpkin is used since, in the advertiser's experience, it could result in excessive thermal processing.

The advertiser also stated that advertising of this seasonal product is limited to the last quarter of the year and a decision has been made not to use the advertising at issue next season. If any of the claims at issue are made, substantiation will be furnished to NAD before the advertising is published. (#2695)

**MATCHBOX TOYS, LTD.
Pee-Wee's Playhouse and Accessories**
Berenter Greenhouse & Webster

Basis of Inquiry: A television commercial appearing on an independent station during children's programming hours opened with an "extraterrestrial" character reporting back to his leader about the assorted inhabitants of Pee-Wee's Playhouse. The alien says: "Your Greeness... the Earthlings are much more advanced than we imagined. They have chairs that talk... Windows that speak... Globes that teach... Birds that talk... Flowers that dance... And screens that walk." Throughout the commercial, the camera featured the various named objects, moving on their own, with a child interjecting as the voice of the different objects during the alien's report.

The Children's Advertising Review Unit (CARU) was concerned that, since the characters do move and talk in the television program on which these items are based, children might be led to believe that the toys in the commercial have such capabilities. Although some of the toy characters can move after being wound up, there were no hands-on scenes during the commercial which indicated this. The *Self Regulatory Guidelines for Children's Advertising* state: "Copy, sound and visual presentations should not mislead children about product or performance characteristics. Such characteristics may include, but are not limited to, size, speed, method of operation, color, sound...."

Resolution: In response, the advertiser stated that the commercial had been discontinued for business reasons unrelated to the inquiry, and that CARU's concerns would be taken into consideration when developing future advertising. (#2696)

Local Advertising Review Programs Because a great deal of advertising and sales promotion is local and cannot be effectively reviewed by a national organization, the American Advertising Federation (AAF) and the Council of Better Business Bureaus (CBBB) have approved an industry self-regulation program that operates at the local level. This local advertising review program (LARP) has as its goal improving truthfulness and accuracy of advertising and enhancing public confidence through voluntary means. At the heart of this program is a local advertising review committee (LARC) composed of equal numbers of groups affiliated with local advertisers, representatives of local advertising agencies, and the general public. The local advertising review process is shown in Figure 12–4.

FIGURE 12–4

The Local Advertising Review Process   ⋰

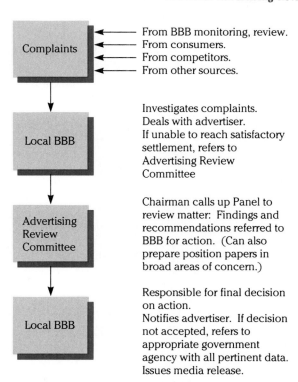

Complaints ← From BBB monitoring, review.
← From consumers.
← From competitors.
← From other sources.

Local BBB
Investigates complaints.
Deals with advertiser.
If unable to reach satisfactory settlement, refers to Advertising Review Committee

Advertising Review Committee
Chairman calls up Panel to review matter: Findings and recommendations referred to BBB for action. (Can also prepare position papers in broad areas of concern.)

Local BBB
Responsible for final decision on action.
Notifies advertiser. If decision not accepted, refers to appropriate government agency with all pertinent data.
Issues media release.

Source: *Local Advertising Review Program: Guidelines, Criteria & Implementation,* a publication of the American Advertising Federation and the Council of Better Business Bureaus, Inc., undated, p. 6.

IMPORTANT AREAS OF REGULATION

Although the vigor of regulatory activity by the federal government with respect to the promotional activities of business has diminished over the past decade, there is certainly more regulation today than there was 30 years ago. The special message sent to Congress by President John F. Kennedy in 1962 entitled "Strengthening of Programs for Protection of Consumer Interests"[15] can be said to have marked the beginning of an era. Certainly the years since the early 1960s have been marked with legislation and administrative actions aimed at promoting a fuller realization of the rights of consumers. In his special message, Kennedy enumerated the following four basic rights:

1. *The right to safety*—to be protected against the marketing of goods that are hazardous to health or life.

2. *The right to be informed*—to be protected against fraudulent, deceitful, or grossly misleading information, advertising, labeling, or other practices and to be given the facts needed to make an informed choice.

3. *The right to choose*—to be assured, wherever possible, of access to a variety of products and services at competitive prices, and in those industries in which competition is not workable and government

---

❖
**PROMOTION
IN ACTION
12–2**

NAD Slams Ward's Ad Claims

The National Advertising Review Board (NARB) has been asked to examine a dispute between the Council of Better Business Bureaus' National Advertising Division (NAD) and Montgomery Ward & Co. over Ward's "guaranteed lowest prices" ad claims. NAD contends that Ward's ads are potentially confusing to customers. NAD also wants to resolve the issue of price-matching policies with such claims as "We won't be undersold." Ward makes no effort to support the claim by systematically monitoring competitors' prices or by reducing the tag price of goods in stock. NAD said that Ward's proposal to add more disclosure statements to already complicated advertising materials and point of sale information did not resolve the complexities of the issues.

Source: Adapted from "NAD Slams Ward's Claims," *Advertising Age*, April 18, 1988, pp. 79, 82.

regulation is substituted, an assurance of satisfactory quality and service at fair prices.

4. *The right to be heard*—to be assured that consumer interests will receive full and sympathetic consideration in the formulation of government policy, and fair and expeditious treatment in its administrative tribunals.

As noted in the preceding sections, the Federal Trade Commission and the Food and Drug Administration are the major but by no means the only recipients of power to regulate promotional activity by business. We will discuss briefly some of the regulatory efforts of these two agencies and the philosophy underlying their actions.

Content of Advertisements

A large proportion of present and proposed regulation involves restricting or controlling the content of the advertisement. These questions of content include whether or not the advertisement is truthful, in good taste, respects the reader's right of privacy, and so forth. The FTC has been especially concerned with cases of deception, and the legislative branch of the federal government has passed laws that actually forbid the advertising of certain products in selected media.

Figure 12–5 illustrates the various steps taken by the FTC in handling misleading or deceptive advertising.

Misleading Representation   Many of the complaints issued by the FTC were aimed at stopping such overt deceptions as representing foreign merchandise to be of domestic origin, or claiming in the absence of proof that a wheat germ oil improves heart action. A more important issue from the viewpoint of the mass communicator, however, has arisen from a series of complaints issued by the FTC pertaining to how products are represented in television commercials.

The so-called sandpaper case stands as a landmark. The Ted Bates Advertising Agency claimed in a series of television commercials that Palmolive Rapid Shave would soften sandpaper sufficiently to permit shaving the sand grains from the paper. To illustrate this claim on television, a sheet of plexiglass covered with sand was substituted for sandpaper. The commission held that such a representation was false and misleading, but the respondents answered that the technical requirements of television present such difficulties that substitutes often must be made for materials used in commercials. They went on to point out that there was no intent to deceive and that such substitution in no way misrepresented product qualities. The FTC ruled as follows, however:

FIGURE 12-5

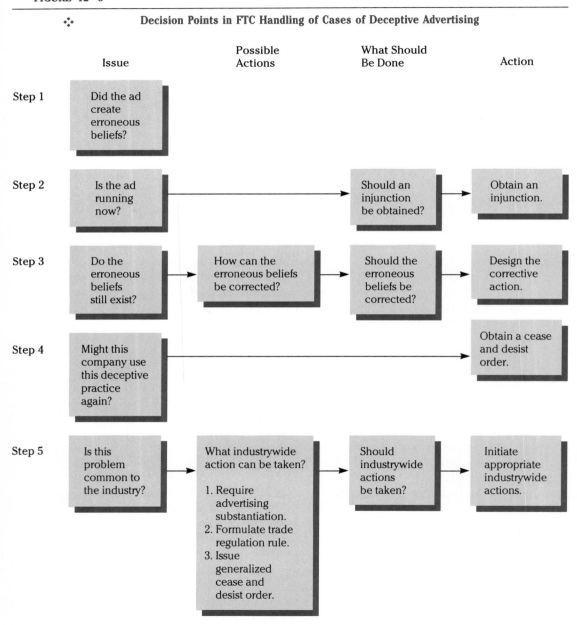

Decision Points in FTC Handling of Cases of Deceptive Advertising

The argument . . . would seem to be based on the wholly untenable assumption that the primary or dominant function of television is to sell goods, and that the commission should not make any ruling which would impair the ability of sponsors and agencies to use television with maximum effectiveness as a sales or advertising medium. . . . Stripped of polite verbiage, the argument boils down to this: "Where truth and television salesmanship collide, the former must give way to the latter." This is obviously an indefensible proposition. . . .

As a result of this decision, *both the client and the agency were prohibited from making any type of deceptive claim in the future.* Notice that the order issued was so broad as to prohibit future deception, although criteria defining deception were not in existence. The courts held that such a broad order was improper and remanded the case to the FTC to reconsider. A revised order was later issued. The commission was upheld by the federal courts with a final decision that the sandpaper mock-up used was deceptive. This finding does not mean that mock-ups and other artificial devices are prohibited; rather, it constrains the advertiser from using demonstrations that are likely to mislead.

Deception   The courts have traditionally held that advertising must be written so as not to deceive "the trusting as well as the suspicious, the casual as well as the vigilant, the naive as well as the sophisticated." In the sandpaper case, the product did not remove grains from sandpaper in the manner claimed in the television commercial. Doubts have been expressed, however, as to whether such a presentation really misrepresents product features in such a manner as to be harmful to the consumer. The problem is, of course, to define where puffing stops and misrepresentation begins.

Since the sandpaper case, the FTC has handled several similar situations. In one case, the FTC accepted an assurance of voluntary compliance from Lever Brothers Company, Inc., to discontinue certain TV commercials advertising its laundry detergent, All. The TV spots in question showed an actor wearing a stained shirt being immersed in water up to his chin. As the water rose the actor added the detergent and expounded on its efficacy. As the water receded the actor showed off his stain-free shirt. The FTC ascertained that the shirt had been washed in the interim by means of a standard washing machine and had not been cleaned by the immersion process.

The FTC accepted voluntary compliance, forestalling a more formal procedure, because it held that the commercial in question was of a "fanciful or spoofing" variety. The FTC held, however, that even these types of commercial can be misleading and suggested that any advertiser in doubt as to whether its commercial had the capacity to deceive should apply to the FTC for an advisory ruling prior to the disseminating the commercial for broadcast.

Puffing   Making exaggerated claims for a product or service is often the defense to a complaint of false or misleading advertising. For example, in cases involving misrepresentation and in those involving breach of warranty, the courts accept "puffing" as a valid defense. Legal writers have noted a move away from puffery as an acceptable defense. Recent court decisions indicate that it is not possible to know in advance whether statements will be held to be puffery and, therefore, advertisers must use exaggerated claims and statements only after careful consideration of the possible consequence.[16]

Comparative Advertising and the Lanham Act   With more and more companies engaging in comparative advertising, it is not surprising that some companies are striking back with legal claims against competitors who employ unsubstantiated claims or whose advertising deprecates the qualities of competitors' offerings. Although encouraging direct product comparisons, the FTC has generally not gotten involved with business-to-business advertising. In this area, a new law of comparative advertising was developed around sec. 43(a) of the Lanham Act (1946), which proscribes false description or representation. The plaintiff in several lawsuits proved that a competitor's false statements were likely to deceive a substantial portion of the intended audience.[17] (See Promotion in Action 12–3.)

   In November 1989, the little-noticed Trademark Revision Act of 1988 became effective. This statute makes it much easier for victims of what has been termed *attack advertising* to sue. Under the old Lanham Act, advertisers were prohibited from misrepresenting their own products. The new act prevents them from misrepresenting the qualities of another person's goods, services, or commercial activities.[18]

The Consent Order   Another important action against misleading advertising is the consent order. Several years ago, the FTC issued an order prohibiting the Colgate-Palmolive Company and its advertising agency from using "deceptive tests, experiments, or demonstrations to sell its products." The FTC specifically challenged the truthfulness of a water demonstration in a TV commercial for Baggies, the company's brand of plastic bag wrap.

   It should be noted that consent orders differ from orders in litigated cases only in that they do not constitute a finding nor do respondents admit to violating the law. The consent orders are fully as binding in forbidding respondents to engage in practices prohibited by the order. Consent orders cannot be appealed to the courts. Sixty days after their issuance, they become enforceable with fines up to $10,000 per violation.

The Fairness Doctrine   When the FTC was founded in 1914, Congress guaranteed it the power to proceed against "unfair methods of competition." In 1938, the Wheeler-Lea Amendment extended the powers of the FTC beyond unfair methods of competition to "unfair or deceptive acts or practices." This was the first legislative attempt to extend the jurisdiction of the FTC from manufacturers and competitors to include consumer protection.

The Magnuson-Morse Act (1975) supported what has been termed the *fairness doctrine* and its extension to rule development for consumer protection. The FTC wasted little time in exercising its new powers and proceeded to develop rules to regulate the advertising of ophthalmic goods (1978), vocational schools (1978), the funeral industry (1979), credit (1979), and used cars (1979). In addition, in February 1978, the FTC issued a staff report that recommended that advertising on television aimed at young children be restricted sharply.

U-Haul v. Jartran: Misleading Comparative Advertising and the Lanham Act, Sec. 43a

❖
PROMOTION IN ACTION 12-3

Marketers using comparative advertising have been given a stern legal warning that false and misleading statements can bring heavy damage awards. In U-Haul v. Jartran, Jartran had to pay $40 million in damages to U-Haul for deceptive statements in its advertising. The award was the largest under the Lanham Act, which prohibits unfair advertising practices. The Ninth Circuit Court of Appeals endorsed a novel damage formula that allows the plaintiff, U-Haul, to recover the amount that Jartran spent on corrective advertisements, rounded to the nearest million dollars and multiplied by *two*. One author believes that the award was out of proportion to the damages suffered by U-Haul and creates a dangerous incentive for monopoly-seeking, predatory litigation.

Sources: Ray O. Werner, "U-Haul v. Jartran Decision Gives Comparative Advertisers Warning," by *Marketing News*, April 26, 1985 p. 16; Garrett J. Waltzer, "Monetary Relief for False Advertising Claims Arising under Section 43(a) of the Lanham Act," by *UCLA Law Review*, 34 (February 1987), pp. 953–80.

The public outcry against limitations on commercial freedom of expression and the requirements to use "balancing" messages was so intense that in 1980 Congress passed the FTC Improvement Act, which put the use of the fairness doctrine on hold until 1984 when the limits on children's advertising were dropped. In 1987, Congress abolished the fairness doctrine completely. Since that time, it has attempted to reinstate the fairness doctrine. The first attempt was vetoed by President Reagan. At the time of this writing, Congress is making another attempt to pass a "fairness" law.

Advertising to Children   The current situation with respect to this topic is that the FTC still retains control over some of the technical details of commercial production. Given the lack of FTC control over other aspects of the problem, the three major TV networks have developed a set of guidelines to which advertisers must adhere (see Figure 12–6). Unfortunately, nonnetwork stations are considerably more lax than the networks, and advertisers are increasingly taking advantage of the situation.[19] In response, a Boston-based activist group, Action for Children's Television (ACT), has lobbied a bill through the House of Representatives that would limit the amount of commercial time in children's programs. The Senate will probably concur and President Bush is expected to sign the bill into law. He will most likely fulfill a campaign pledge and veto any attempt to revive the fairness doctrine.[20]

Obscenity and Bad Taste   It is difficult to define what is obscene or what is in bad taste. Generally, advertisers and the media have policed themselves to avoid advertising that might prove to be illegal or offensive, given present-day community standards. Because of many complaints about "sexually provocative" direct mail advertisements, Congress in 1967 passed a law entitled "Prohibition of Pandering Advertisements in the Mails." This act allows a householder to file a notice with the local postmaster requesting that certain advertisements not be delivered to his or her address. When notified by the postal authorities, the advertiser must remove the householder's name from the mailing list and make certain that no future mailings are sent to that address. A U.S. Supreme Court decision of May 1970 upheld the 1967 law and interpreted it so broadly that a citizen of the United States has the right to prevent a direct mail advertiser from sending anything at all one does not wish to receive.

Type of Product Advertised

Social conventions prevent certain types of products from being advertised. For example, hard liquor is not yet advertised on television, and only in recent years have women been seen in printed media advertisements for liquor. Social objection to advertising is diminishing, with the result that more freedom is being exercised not only with respect to what is being advertised but also with respect to how it is presented.

The most important restriction on the promotion of a product in the history of advertising occurred on January 1, 1971. After that date, the FTC was empowered to ban the advertising of cigarettes on radio and television.

FIGURE 12–6

Network Guidelines for Children's Advertising   ❖

A Sampling of Guidelines

Each of the major television networks has its own set of guidelines for childrens's advertising although the basics are very similar. A few rules such as the requirement of a static "island " shot at the end, are written in stone; others however, occasionally can be negotiated.

   Many of the rules below apply specifically to toys. The networks also have special guidelines for kid's food commercials and for kid's commercials that offer premiums.

	ABC	CBS	NBC
Must not overglamorize product	✓	✓	✓
No exhortative language, such as "Ask Mom to buy . . ."	✓	✓	
No realistic war settings	✓		✓
Generally no celebrity endorsments	✓	Case-by-case	✓
Can't use "only" or "just" in regard to price	✓	✓	✓
Show only two toys per child or maximum of six per commercial	✓		✓
Five-second "island" showing product against plain background at end of spot	✓	✓	✓ (4 to 5)
Animation restricted to one-third of a commercial	✓		✓
Generally no comparative or superiority claims	Case-by-case	Handle w/care	✓
No costumes or props not available with the toy	✓		✓
No child or toy can appear in animated segments	✓		✓
Three-second establishing shot of toy in relation to child	✓	✓ (2.5 to 3)	
No shots under one second in length		✓	
Must show distance a toy can travel before stopping on its own		✓	

Source: Joanne Lipman, "Double Standard for Kids' TV Ads," *The Wall Street Journal*, June 10, 1988, p. 25.

The amount of revenue lost by the broadcast industry has been enormous, and although some of the funds used for broadcast advertising have been shifted to other media, in total the cigarette industry has drastically cut back on advertising expenditures. In addition to the ban on broadcast advertising, the legislation also required that the cigarette label contain the statement, "Warning: The Surgeon General has determined that cigarette smoking is dangerous to your health."

The FTC also acquired the authority to monitor the cigarette industry's other advertising activities to see if a large buildup of promotion in non-broadcast media would occur. As noted above, no such buildup occurred, and this part of the law has remained inoperative.

Vertical Cooperative Advertising

Advertising in which the manufacturer shares the cost with resellers is called *vertical cooperative* or *co-op* advertising. This type of promotion is big business; an estimated $11 billion in co-op money was available in 1987 with about 40 percent of that amount going unspent. Manufacturers and retailers are both looking for ways to get more of it into circulation.[21]

Because payments for co-op advertising may be used as disguised price discrimination, an illegal practice under the Robinson-Patman Act, the FTC is quite vigilant in monitoring co-op programs to ensure their legality. The rules of the game were spelled out in a 1969 policy statement of promotional allowance and cooperative advertising that has been updated over the years. Word is out that after 20 years, the FTC is going to revise many of its old policies. For example, the FTC previously interpreted the 1980 FTC Act as outlawing refusal by a manufacturer to pay co-op allowances to resellers who sell at a discount. The proposed guidelines will make it less risky for a manufacturer to bypass a reseller who undercuts the manufacturer's suggested minimum resale prices.[22]

These proposed guidelines will be discussed further in Chapter 21, although at the time of this writing, the FTC has not announced the issuance date. At this point, it is sufficient to recognize that the proposed use of cooperative advertising requires careful study of the legal guidelines, which are, at present, in a state of flux.

Advertising and Competition

For over 20 years, the prevailing wisdom among economists and governmental regulators has been that a positive relationship exists between advertising levels and rising industrial concentration, primarily in consumer goods industries. Based, in part, on this thinking, the U. S. Supreme Court in 1967 upheld the FTC's order that Procter & Gamble divest itself of the Clorox Company, which it had acquired 10 years earlier. One of the principal

considerations involved in this decision was that the huge advertising outlays of Procter & Gamble and the promotional expertise it had at its disposal
substantially reduced competition in the liquid bleach industry.

Flushed with success, the FTC in 1971 accused four major cereal manufacturers of having a joint market monopoly. Kellogg, General Mills, General Foods, and Quaker Oats were alleged to have engaged in "actions or
inactions" over a period of 35 years that had resulted in a highly concentrated, noncompetitive market for ready-to-eat cereals. The FTC stated that
this had been accomplished by "proliferation of brands and trademark promotion, artificial differentiation of products, unfair methods of competition
in advertising and promotion, and acquisition of competitors."

After 10 years of extremely costly litigation, the FTC was not able to set
new legal precedents through the application of antitrust law to oligopolies,
and the case was dropped at the behest of the Reagan administration in
1982. In retrospect, it appears that competition in the cereal industry was
vigorous and effective and that the consumer has not suffered because of the
promotional resources and skills of the members of the industry. Indeed, the
whole notion that advertising can be harmful to competition has been questioned by recently published empirical studies that indicate no relationship
between levels of advertising expenditures and increased concentration or
decreased consumer welfare.[23] In spite of this evidence, however, heavy
advertisers with dominant market shares must be wary of the potential for
antitrust action. This issue will be discussed further in Chapter 24.

Remedial Alternatives

Various remedies for consumer protection may be classified into three categories: prevention, restitution, and punishment. Examples of preventive
remedies would be the FTC's Code of Conduct, or Trade Regulation Rules,
and the disclosure-of-information requirements in written consumer warranties as mandated by the Magnuson-Morse Act. An example of restitution
would be corrective advertising and of punishment would be fines or im-
prisonment.

Advertising Substantiation Another type of preventive remedy is *advertising substantiation,* a program developed by the FTC in 1971. The goal of this
program is to ensure that advertisers use only those claims for their product
or service offerings that can be supported by fact. Since the inception of the
program, companies in a variety of industries have been required to submit
proof of stated claims or terminate or modify the advertising message in
question.

Corrective Advertising For several years under the program for advertising
substantiation, complaints were settled either by furnishing acceptable

proof of claims or by signing a consent decree under which the advertiser agreed to modify or terminate the claim. In some cases as part of a consent decree, the FTC required that the advertiser devote a portion of its future advertising to what has been termed *corrective advertising.* In such advertising, the consumer had to be informed as to the true status of the product or service, and any misleading claims had to be corrected or modified.

In 1975, the FTC found that claims made for Listerine mouthwash by its manufacturer, Warner-Lambert Company, were false. The company had advertised for almost 50 years that Listerine could prevent common colds or lessen their severity. These claims could not be substantiated, and the FTC

TABLE 12–3

❖   **The FTC Attacks Fraudulent Medical Claims**

Washington—With two commissioners holding out for even sterner action, the Federal Trade Commission has added a therapeutic pain reliever to its list of medical treatments, the performances of which have failed to live up to advertising claims.

The FTC's proposed consent agreement with Biopractic Group Inc., Riegelsville, Penn., has resulted from a series of claims for Therapeutic Mineral Ice, a product that allegedly would reduce pain and inflammation from muscle sprains, arthritis, rheumatism, and other maladies.

Biopractic ads falsely claimed that various doctors, medical centers, and athletic teams—including the U.S. and Soviet Olympic track squads—had said Therapeutic Mineral ice was effective, the commission said, and that it stimulated the brain to produce beta-endorphin, which is a pain-relieving hormone.

Mineral Ice was sold through drug and health-food stores and chiropractors for $14.95 a 16-oz. container.

The commission's attempt to rein in more unsubstantiated ad claims represents another battle in its war on fraudulent medical aids and treatments that in recent months has included vitamins, hair restorers, diet aids, food supplements, and a toothpaste.

Under terms of the proposed agreement, Biopractic must have adequate substantiation for its ad claims and, to repeat its beta-endorphin claims, must meet standards of the Food and Drug Administration and present evidence from two well-controlled clinical tests.

Commissioners Patricia Bailey and Michael Pertschuk dissented from the majority opinion, arguing that the consent order should have been stronger.

They also felt that the commission's order, by suggesting that Biopractic in the future might be able to substantiate its claims, was overly lenient.

"There is no expectation whatsoever that what [Biopractic] said can be substantiated," a commission staff member said. "We don't believe they can be backed up, and we didn't think the commission was doing the public a service by leaving the door open to the future possibility . . . that they could come back and substantiate their claims."

Source: "FTC Ices Therapeutic Product Claim," *Advertising Age,* October 8, 1984. Reprinted with permission. Copyright Crain Communications, Inc. All rights reserved.

required that their use be terminated. In addition, Warner-Lambert was ordered to insert in the next $10 million of its advertising the statement, "Contrary to prior advertising, Listerine will not help prevent colds or sore throats or lessen their severity."

Warner-Lambert tested the findings of the FTC and its authority to order corrective advertising in the federal courts. In two cases brought before the Court of Appeals for the District of Columbia Circuit in 1977, the FTC was upheld both on its original finding that the advertising claims were false and on its authority to order corrective advertising. The corrective statement, however, was modified slightly in that Warner-Lambert was allowed to drop the phrase "Contrary to prior advertising" from the statement.[24]

Warner-Lambert took the case to the Supreme Court, which in 1978 refused to review the findings of the appeals court. Thus the powers of the FTC in both the areas of claim substantiation and corrective advertising have been upheld. Whether these powers have been effectively utilized in recent years is another question (see Table 12–3).

In a recent exhaustive study of the current state of corrective advertising, Wilkie et al. have come to the following conclusions:

1. Although the FTC's power to order corrective advertising as a remedy is not under question, it is significantly limited by certain legal criteria (see Table 12–4).

2. While it appears that corrective advertising has the potential to yield consumer benefits, past campaigns have been weak in consumer communications. Postcampaign research indicated that consumer impressions

TABLE 12–4

The Five Legal Criteria for Corrective Advertising ❖

Issue	Requirement for the Order
1. Orientation	The remedy must be prospective rather than retrospective in nature.
2. Goal	The remedy must be nonpunitive in nature.
3. Substance	The remedy must bear a reasonable relation to the violation in question.
4. Scope	The remedy must not infringe on the First Amendment rights of the firm.
5. Form	The remedy should be in the least burdensome form necessary to achieve an effective code.

Source: William L. Wilkie, Dennis L. McNeill, and Michael B. Mazis, " 'Marketing's Scarlet Letter': The Theory and Practice of Corrective Advertising," *Journal of Marketing* 48 (Spring 1984), p. 15, published by the American Marketing Association.

were not changed. This result is not surprising, given the fact that consumer effectiveness was not a prime concern of the FTC in the cases studied.

3. Such factors as the philosophical change in the FTC under a new administration, lack of a systematic FTC program, wide variations in terms of requirements, and the large role played by consent negotiations between the FTC and the respondent company, have all served to weaken the role of corrective advertising.[25]

It is obvious that, given the above findings, changes in the FTC philosophy and the approach to corrective advertising will be needed for a more effective remedy in the future for the problems that misleading advertising creates for consumers.

Other remedies (classified under the heading of restitution) include those that require advertisers to make affirmative disclosure about their products or services indicating the weak points of their offerings as well as the strong ones. Refunds to customers who have been misled and subsequently harmed, limitations of contracts, and cooling-off periods for consumers who buy from door-to-door salespeople are additional forms of restitution for consumer protection.

The final category of remedies includes punishments. The FTC has the authority to levy fines of up to $10,000 per violation of a cease and desist order. A defendant who refuses to obey an injunction may be found in contempt of court and sentenced to jail. Although the punishment remedy has been used sparingly in the past, it is an effective alternative that can be applied if attempts to protect the consumer through prevention and restitution remedies fail.

Regulation of Personal Selling

To this point, the discussion has dealt with the regulation of advertising. However, personal selling[26] activities also come under the surveillance of federal, state, and local laws. In the following sections, we will deal with a few of the major areas that should be of concern to promotion managers who are developing personal selling strategies.

Combinations and Conspiracies   The first of the major antitrust laws, the Sherman Act of 1890, prohibits combining or conspiring to restrain trade in interstate commerce. Because the courts have held that almost all commerce in the United States is interstate due to the inevitable movement of product and promotion over state lines, the applicability of the Sherman Act is extremely broad. The law prohibits, for example, agreements between two or more competing firms that provide for the division of a geographic market so that they are not rivals. Another example is the use of agreements by which competing companies set prices at specified levels. The most famous series of cases in this latter area occurred in the 1960s when several large electrical equipment manufacturers were found guilty of setting prices on electric power-generating equipment by means of a bidding formula.

Tie-in or Requirements Contracts   Certain contracts that require tie-in sales are deemed to be illegal under the Clayton Act of 1914 if the effect may be to restrict competition or to create a monopoly. For example, a manufacturer of laser printers cannot require that purchasers use only its brand of paper and toner if such a requirement might damage other sellers of similar supplies.

Sales policies that require buyers to deal exclusively with the supplier can also run afoul of the law. Please note that tie-in or requirements contracts are prohibited when their effect *may be* to restrict competition and create a monopoly. Thus even sellers with small market shares must be careful not to ignore these restrictions because the requirements for a successful prosecution under the Clayton Act are less stringent than under the Sherman Act.

Price Discrimination   The Robinson-Patman Act of 1936, discussed earlier in this chapter, prohibits the sale of goods of similar grade or quality to competing buyers at different prices when the effect may be to restrict competition or create a monopoly. When such effects have been determined to exist, the seller may utilize several defenses. These include (1) the fact that the price differentials reflect differences in cost of manufacture, selling, or delivery, (2) that the price differential was granted in "good faith" to meet the lower price of a competitor, and (3) a severe change had occurred in the market or marketability of the goods.

Brokerage Allowances   The Robinson-Patman Act also states that customers who buy directly from the seller without the use of brokers may not receive a payment or price reduction to reflect the nonuse of a broker. This is an idiosyncrasy of Robinson-Patman, which is really more an attempt to redress an imbalance of economic power between large and small firms than a pure antitrust law.

Promotional Allowances and Payments   Salespersons must be vigilant when offering promotional payments and/or allowances to customers who are competing with one another. The Robinson-Patman Act specifies that the value of such payments or allowances should be proportionally equal to the purchases made by each buyer. Thus, a customer buying $10,000 worth of goods in a year is entitled to twice the value in allowances and services as a customer purchasing $5,000 worth of product per year. In addition, all competing customers must be informed of the availability of the allowances or services.

Other Legislation In addition to its regulation of advertising, the FTC Act covers personal selling and sales promotion activities. It outlaws various means of "consumer deception," although it never exactly defines that term. Misrepresentation, "bait-and-switch" techniques, statements of salespersons that cannot be verified, or promises that cannot be kept can be in violations of the FTC Act. The Truth-in-Lending legislation means that all credit terms must be fully disclosed to the buyer. In addition, "cooling-off" legislation allows buyers of goods sold door-to-door to cancel purchases of $25 or more within three days after the sale.

Local laws that regulate personal selling and sales promotion are increasing in number. Of special concern are abuses by door-to-door salespersons, which have resulted in local "green river" laws that prevent salespersons from calling on homes without the permission of the occupants. Laws require persons in certain businesses to obtain licenses before they can sell within the area bounded by the local authority. These licenses can be required for door-to-door selling, panhandling, and sidewalk food service, and more professional businesses such as real estate and insurance agencies, which sell high-value products and services to the public.

SUMMARY

The purpose of this chapter was to provide a brief description of the current state of the legal environment in which marketers must operate. In addition, it reviewed some of the more pressing legal restrictions on promotion. The following are some of the key areas that have been considered.

Pertinent federal legislation and its development over the years was examined. Special attention was paid to the role of federal agencies in reaction to excesses that occurred during the deregulatory decade of the 80s. The move of the states into areas of regulation vacated by the federal government was also noted.

Of special concern is the future of the FTC and the FDA. Will these agencies receive the funding they need to fulfill their responsibilities? Can the Food and Drug Administration regain its control over the drug industry? Widespread cheating in the area of generic drugs with hints of payoffs to FDA personnel has clouded the reputation of this embattled agency.

We then turned to self-regulatory agencies and considered the roles of the National Advertising Division (NAD) of the Better Business Bureaus and the National Advertising Review Board (NARD) and its extension to the local level, the LARB. Questions were raised as to the effectiveness of these entities and whether or not their activities can moderate regulation of promotion by governmental agencies at all levels.

Additional topics covered included the fairness doctrine, advertising to children, co-op advertising, and the effects of promotion on competition. The chapter concluded with coverage of the various remedies available to a firm that has been found guilty of misleading the consumer.

In this chapter, we have covered some but not all of the issues you will face in the near term. Only a solid understanding of what has happened in the past will allow you to chart your course for the future. Be alert, have competent legal counsel, and, above all, be concerned with the well-being of the consumer. Experience has shown that this is the best orientation to guarantee success over the long run.

REVIEW AND DISCUSSION QUESTIONS

1. Imagine that you are the product manager of Healthbran, an oat bran-based breakfast cereal. You want to make some health claims for your cereal in the current advertising. Given the new role being played by the state attorneys general regarding health claims, what actions should you take to make sure that you will not run into trouble?

2. You are a young person in a marketing position at a large consumer goods company, and you are trying to decide among two candidates for the House of Representatives. One candidate supports the Fairness Doctrine; the other does not. What questions might you put to these candidates to help you to understand the issue more clearly?

3. Suppose that a competitor has been demeaning the quality of your brand in his or her advertising. What recourse do you have to stop the advertising and perhaps even to collect damages for the harm done to the image of your brand?

4. You have been called before the National Advertising Division (NAD) because it has received some complaints about your advertising. Specifically, you are charged with using a comparative price that was not realistic. What materials must you bring to the hearing? What are your rights if the NAD rules against you? Briefly outline the steps available to you in this self-regulatory process.

5. You are a toy manufacturer and want to advertise your product line to children on Saturday morning TV. What guidelines must you consider if you plan to buy time on the three major networks? Is there any difference in the requirements if you advertise on cable TV? Explain.

6. Imagine that you are an administrative law judge faced with the prospect of issuing a punitive ruling in the case of a manufacturer of a cough syrup who made false claims for the efficacy of the product. What remedies might you propose to assure that the consumer is protected and the manufacturer is properly penalized?

NOTES

1. For a more detailed background on legislation see, Ray O. Werner, *Legal and Economic Regulation in Marketing* (New York: Quorum Books, 1989); Dean Keith Fueroghne, *"But the People in Legal Said . . .": A Guide to Current Legal Issues in Advertising* (Homewood, Ill.: Dow Jones-Irwin, 1989); Louis W. Stern and Thomas L. Eovaldi, *Legal Aspects of Marketing Strategy: Antitrust and Consumer Protection Issues* (Englewood Cliffs, N.J.: Prentice Hall, 1984), chaps. 7 and 8; and Joe Welch, *Marketing Law* (Tulsa, Okla.: Petroleum Publishing Company, 1980).

2. Public Law 447, approved March 21, 1938, 75 Cong., 3d Sess., U.S. Stat. L., vol 52.

3. The issuance of a formal complaint may not be necessary in situations specified in the Magnuson-Moss Act of 1975 (discussed later in the chapter).

4. Public Law 93-153(1973).

5. Public Law 93-637(1975).

6. Federal Trade Commission 1980, *Improvement Act of 1980*, Public Law 96-2532.

7. Andrew J. Strenio, Jr., "The FTC in 1988: Phoenix or Finis?" *Journal of Public Policy & Marketing* 7 (1988), pp. 21–39.

8. Ibid.

9. Thomas J. McGrew, "The Shift in Advertising Oversight," *Ad Forum,* December 1984, p. 21.

10. Michael deCourcy Hinds, "Optical Industry Braces for Change under Deregulation," *New York Times,* April 22, 1989, p.16.

11. Patricia Winters, "Fish-Oil Sales Founder," *Advertising Age,* January 2, 1989, p. 9.

12. Dan Koeppel, "The FDA's Health Kick," *Adweek's Marketing Week,* April 10, 1989, p. 28.

13. Richard Koenig, "Campbell Soup Agrees to Ad Guidelines in Nine States to Settle Dispute Over Claims," *The Wall Street Journal,* May 11, 1989, p. B4.

14. McGrew, "The Shift in Advertising Oversight," p. 21.

15. *Congressional Record,* March 15, 1962, pp. 108,3813–3817.

16. Joshua Honigwachs, "Is It Safe to Call Something Safe? The Law of Puffery in Advertising," *Journal of Public Policy & Marketing* 6 (1987), pp. 157–70.

17. Steven A. Meyerowitz, "The Developing Law of Comparative Advertising," *Business Marketing* 70, no. 8 (August 1985), pp. 81–86.

18. Jeffrey A. Trachtenberg, "New Law Ads Risk to Comparative Ads," *The Wall Street Journal,* May 1, 1989, p. B6.

19. Joanne Lipman, "Double Standards for Kids' TV Ads," *The Wall Street Journal,* June 10, 1988, p. 25.

20. "Bush May OK Bill on Kids' TV Ads," *Marketing News,* March 27, 1989, p. 7.

21. Leslie Brennan, "How Retailers Are Putting It All Together," *Sales & Marketing Management* 140 (May 1988), p. 62.

22. Isadore Barmash, "FTC Plans Rule Changes on Co-op Ads," *New York Times,* February 21, 1989, p. D13.

23. E. Woodrow Eckard, Jr., "Advertising, Concentration Changes, and Consumer Welfare," *Review of Economics & Statistics* (Netherlands) 70 (May 1988), pp. 340–43.

24. *Warner-Lambert Co. v. Federal Trade Commission,* CCH P61,563 A-D.C., August 1977), and CCH P61,646 (CA-D.C., September 1977).

25. William L. Wilkie, Dennis L. McNeill, and Michael B. Mazis, " 'Marketing's Scarlet Letter': The Theory and Practice of Corrective Advertising," *Journal of Marketing* 48 (Spring 1984), p. 26.

26. This section borrows heavily from Robin Peterson, *Personal Selling: An Introduction* (New York: John Wiley, 1976), chap. 14.

ADVERTISING AND SALES PROMOTION

In Part 5, the first program element that we will discuss is the advertising message for sales promotion, in Chapter 13. We review what is referred to in the trade as the *creative strategy*. The focus is on a logical and pragmatic approach to what is the key element in the success of an advertising campaign—the message. Chapter 14 surveys the array of available advertising media, and Chapter 15 considers the basics of media selection.

The tools of marketing research find considerable use in advertising strategy. Chapter 16 analyzes research procedures used to pretest the message before it is placed in the media and the methods used to analyze the actual sales and communication effectiveness of the campaign.

Finally, Chapter 17 discusses the management of sales promotion activity.

The Advertising Message

GETTING DHL MOVING WITH GARY LARSON'S FAR SIDE

Securing a piece of the air-express business is increasingly difficult in today's crowded skies. Fierce competition in both domestic and international markets makes maintaining market share a feat and increasing market share quite a challenge. DHL Worldwide Express, the world's oldest and largest international air-express company, found itself with a paltry 5 percent share of the U.S. market and a major visibility problem. When competing giants FedEx and UPS began going after DHL's international market, finding an immediate solution was vital. DHL's answer: Humor a la Gary Larson.

Gary Larson, creator of "The Far Side," is possibly the hottest cartoonist in America. "The Far Side" is a wacky cartoon series based on "a warped world of funny and frequently grotesque people and other creatures doing and saying some pretty strange things." Wacky or not, "The Far Side's" popularity outgrew its original daily newspaper domain and Larson's distinctive cartoon characters can now be found in a series of books and on posters, calendars, and coffee mugs—and in DHL ads!

Dick Rossi, DHL's director of marketing services, acknowledged the inherent risks involved in using humor in advertising. "There's always a risk when you use humor. It tends to polarize your audience a little; there are those who get it and those who don't. But our research shows there's a relatively small number of people who don't like it." He equated the risk to doing anything unusual and said that DHL preferred taking the risk to doing what everyone else is doing and getting lost in the crowd.

Rossi explained the company's risky move: "We went to Larson primarily because we needed to get the DHL name out there. We needed a very quick boost in our visibility, to increase awareness and enhance our image. One thing you have to do in advertising, because there's so much out there, is to break through, and Larson does that very well. He has that impact."

DHL adopted a two-pronged approach. Its TV ads were designed for image building, and print ads were designed to deliver a specific message. Thirty-second TV commercials were produced for the nation's eight largest markets. These TV spots build an animated story around a "Far Side" cartoon. One spot features sagging birds laboriously flying across the screen to deliver packages for the other air-express companies. DHL's bird waves as it cruises by all of them in a jet plane.

DHL also placed full-page print ads in eight business and news magazines. Rossi explained that these ads were selected to fit two basic objectives: "One, explain that overseas shipping is different from shipping in the United States. Two, explain that DHL is the best at doing this, because of our experience, network, worldwide scope, and people." One popular ad features a strange-looking doctor searching his medical bag as he leaves a plane. The caption reads: *Suddenly, Dr. Frankenstein realized he had left his brain in San Francisco.* The major headline beneath the cartoon reads: *He should have shipped it DHL.* The ad copy goes on to humorously explain the relationship between the two statements.

Though revenue results are difficult to prove, the Larson campaign is succeeding. The ads have boosted DHL's image in America. The impact on TV markets is the easiest to measure. Rossi says, "Sales are better, growing faster in areas we're advertising in than in markets where we don't advertise." Since print ads are run in national magazines and the air-express industry is growing, it is harder to attribute increased sales specifically to the advertising. But general sales are up pretty sharply, indicating that DHL must be doing something right.

Source: "Larson's Humor Flies For DHL," *Industry Week*, April 3, 1989, pp. 33–34.

The DHL Promotion in Action at the beginning of this chapter illustrates the power of the advertising message to impact the market success of a firm. This development of advertising messages, called the *creative* aspect, is usually implemented by a copywriter and an art designer. They do their creative work based on the message strategy prepared by the advertising agency's account management team who work in conjunction with the client's marketing people. The copywriter and art director may also provide a support role in the meetings where the message strategy is formulated. This chapter is concerned with the development of advertising message strategy and with general approaches to the development of successful advertising messages. We begin now with a review of the elements of creative strategy. Then the subject of the actual advertising message is presented.

CREATIVE STRATEGY

The creative strategy, sometimes also called *copy strategy* or *copy platform,* is based on (1) the proper definition of the target market, (2) the objectives for the advertising, (3) the advertising strategy to reach the defined objective, (4) the support for the advertising strategy, (5) consideration of other elements belonging in the advertisement, and (6) the tone of the advertisement. The working definitions of these six elements is presented below. In addition, a potential application of them to the Simplicity Sewing Patterns Company is presented in Table 13–1.

	Creative Strategy or Copy Platform[1]
Target Audience:	This is an outline of who is the most likely candidate to be motivated to do something as a result of the advertising. Most often, it is stated in demographic and psychographic terms.
Objective:	What you want the advertising to do. Usually this starts with the words "to establish. . . ."
Strategy:	How you want the advertising specifically to accomplish the objective above. A good outline for this strategy statement is "to convince the target group to buy [use, prefer, or other verb] the Brand [substitute the name] instead of_____because_____."
Support:	This is the reason to believe the strategy. It can be either research that supports the strategy or an advertising "reason why."
Considerations:	This is where you would put other things that you would like to have built into the advertising if space or time allows. Usually this is not really pertinent to the discussion but would be nice to include. Quite often this is a client dictate.
Tone:	This is the philosophy of the advertising in tone form.

The creative strategy (copy platform) forms the basis on which the copywriter and the art director work to create the actual advertisement to be used in a campaign. Without having the six elements of the copy platform in place, the creative people lack the necessary guidance to develop advertisements that are effective in the marketplace. The Simplicity Patterns' copy platform presented in Table 13–1 points out a clear direction for the development of an advertisement. With the creative strategy in place, we can turn our attention to issues of the production of the actual advertisements, called the *creative execution*. A discussion of this topic follows.

CREATIVE EXECUTION

Although a correct strategy is essential to advertising success, this strategy in itself will never prove to be sufficient. There comes a point at which the strategy must be executed into the message. It is here that the creative ability of the writer or designer comes to the fore.

What is creativity? According to Webster, something is created when it is produced, formed, or brought into being. True creativity is *not* undisciplined imagination. Controls and discipline may be highly subjective, per-

TABLE 13–1

❖   **Application of the Six Elements Approach to Creative Strategy**

Simplicity Copy Platform	
Target Audience:	Women 18 to 34 with a college education
Objectives:	To establish Simplicity patterns as the quick and easy way for the target audience to obtain the clothes they want.
Strategy:	To convince the target group to buy Simplicity instead of shopping for clothing in boutiques and stores because Simplicity is the most efficient method of obtaining first-quality clothing with the right color and style.
Support:	Simplicity patterns eliminate the difficulty of searching for the right clothing because the target audience can select the fabric and color and because the patterns are current, durable, and active.
Considerations:	1. Easy-to-follow instructions 2. Can be made in a few hours 3. Sewing can avoid frustration
Tone:	Active, yet fashionable

Source: Professor Lawrence V. Johnson of the University of Kansas.

sonal, perhaps subconscious, almost secret, or covered up with a facade of "absolutely no control," but this does not mean that they do not operate powerfully in the creative personality. Creative work is largely conscious, deliberate, and *disciplined*. It is disciplined by the objective toward which it is directed and by the information and experience on which it is based. First the creator hunts for new information and details and arranges them into a pattern through discipline of thought processes. The creative process at each step is the same, whether the discovery is made as a contribution to science, music, technology, art, advertising, or some other area of interest. Rules or syntax can be developed, thereby keeping imagination within its most productive bounds.

Real communication does not occur until the message is attended to and correctly comprehended, retained, and acted on by members of the target market in the manner specified in the statement of advertising objectives. Results that fall short of this signify that true creativity was not achieved in the execution process.

This is not to deny the significant role played by the intuition and skill of the writer and designer. Comprehensive objectives provide the boundaries for creative work; they do not guarantee advertising success any more than staying within the sidelines of a football field guarantees a winning performance. Indeed, intuition and imagination are required, and it is this subjective element that differentiates ordinary advertising from great advertising.

The proper understanding of the likely persuasive power of advertising messages requires an understanding of potential impact of advertising on attitudes and behavior. This is our next topic.

Persuasion through Advertising: Influencing Attitudes and Behavior[2]

We know from Chapter 4 that the influence of any communication depends on what happens at each stage of information processing. An advertisement must capture attention, be accurately understood, be retained in memory, and be yielded to by the target audience in order to have persuasive impact. Yielding represents the persuasive impact of the advertisement. A key question, then, concerns what determines how much, if any, yielding occurs during information processing. Advertisers often focus on the *cognitive response* (i.e., thoughts) that occur during message processing. These thoughts are classified on three dimensions: valence, focus, and abstraction.

Valence represents the favorability of the thoughts. Positive thoughts in response to an advertisement are called *support arguments;* negative thoughts are called *counterarguments. Focus* refers to the content of the thoughts. Advertisers distinguish between thoughts focused on the brand versus those focused on the executional elements of the ad itself (e.g., picture, color, headline). *Abstraction* relates to the amount of elaboration reflected by the thoughts. The lowest level of abstraction would be thoughts that just play back a message. Greater abstraction would be demonstrated by thoughts reflecting the integration of various elements of the ad with each other or with one's own knowledge.

These classifications of thoughts are used as predictors of the attitudes formed following message exposure. The basic notion is that the persuasion impact of ads will be greater (more yielding) as cognitive responses become more favorable. Cognitive responses are certainly part of the persuasive impact of an advertisement but do not tell the whole story. We must also be concerned with affective responses as they relate to attitude and behavior change in advertising.

Affective responses represent the feelings that are elicited by the advertising. These types of "hot" responses, in contrast to the "cold" cognitive responses, are important in what is called *transformational* (as opposed to *informational*) *advertising*. Transformational ads attempt to "make the experience of using the product richer, warmer, more exciting, and/or more enjoyable, than that obtained solely from an objective description of the advertised brand."[3] Consider the California Raisin Advisory television ads as an example of such emotional appeals and resulting persuasion.

One of the most memorable campaigns to hit the airwaves was the California Raisin Advisory Board's television ads featuring raisins dancing to the sounds of Marvin Gaye's classic song "Heard It through the Grapevine."[4] The original idea behind the campaign was to enhance the product's appeal by emphasizing the nutritional value of raisins. This approach seemed quite sensible given the trend toward greater health consciousness that has swept the country during the past decade or so.

However, research revealed that consumers already appreciated raisins' nutritional properties. The problem was that consumers viewed raisins as plain and ordinary. As explained by Alan Canton, the board's advertising and promotions manager, "Nutritionally, they were appealing; emotionally, they were not appealing." It was hoped that the feelings evoked by the music and animated raisins would help overcome this limitation.

Did it work? Prior to the campaign, raisin sales had fluctuated between flat and declining. Sales jumped 5 percent after the campaign began.

Other examples of emotional appeals include AT&T's "reach out and touch someone," Pepsi's "get that Pepsi feeling," and Oldsmobile's "this is not your father's Oldsmobile" campaigns.

The importance of affective responses in persuasion are quite strongly supported by research findings.[5] They can be measured in advertising studies by asking respondents to write down the feelings that they experienced while processing the message, or by asking them how strongly they experienced various feelings on structured rating scales.

Many advertisers consider both cognitive and emotional responses to be important in persuasion to influence attitudes and behavior. Petty and Cacioppo's elaboration likelihood model of persuasion as outlined in Chapter 4 is useful in pulling all these elements together.

Advertising and the Elaboration Likelihood Model of Persuasion

A useful approach to understanding the persuasive impact of advertising is the Elaboration Likelihood Model (ELM), which was introduced in Chapter 4. The ELM states that the degree of elaboration in the form of issue-relevant thinking is the key determinant of the influence exerted by various communication elements. When elaboration is high, the central route to persuasion is followed where only those message elements (called *arguments*) relevant to forming a "reasoned" opinion are influential. So-called informational ads would apply in this case. Alternatively, the peripheral route to persuasion occurs under low levels of elaboration as elements (called *peripheral cues*) that are irrelevant to developing a reasoned opinion become influential. So-called transformational ads would apply here. Both arguments and peripheral cues are operative under moderate levels of elaboration.

Elaboration in turn depends on the person's motivation, ability, and opportunity during message processing (see Chapter 4). A person who is motivated and able and has the opportunity to elaborate will take the central route; the peripheral route applies when motivation, ability, or opportunity is lacking. Motivation was discussed in Chapter 4. Ability relates to such factors as intelligence, education, and product knowledge. Limits in these areas reduce the ability to elaborate. Opportunity concerns the situational environment at the time of exposure to the ad or to the elements of the advertisement itself that impact consumer information processing. For example, the advertisement may be shown during a distracting time in a television show, or music in the ad itself may distract the consumer.

Elaboration also relates to the level of involvement of the target consumer. High involvement consumers are impacted almost completely by the message arguments. In contrast, low involvement consumers are influenced by both arguments and peripheral cues. The ELM points out the importance of anticipating how much elaboration is likely to occur during message processing in developing persuasive advertisements. If elaboration is likely to be high, then more emphasis should be placed on compelling arguments to support the advocated position. In situations of expected low elaboration by consumers to the advertisement, other approaches that depend less on the degree of message processing are appropriate. These approaches include the use of a celebrity spokesperson or an emotional appeal.

Figure 13–1 provides a graphic overview of the ELM process. The antecedent conditions to advertising information processing are the need for a consumer benefit, the motivation, the ability to process information, the opportunity to process, and the advertising exposure itself. Information processing then occurs either through the central route or peripheral route to persuasion based on the degree of elaboration that is related to the attention to the advertisement and the capacity of the consumer to process information. Responses are then either cognitive or emotional with resulting attitude formation or change in the attitude toward the brand. The ELM provides a framework within which to evaluate specific approaches that may be used to present advertising messages. Related to these approaches are specific behavioral research findings that are useful in the development process of the advertisement message. We now turn our attention to some of these important findings.

Behavioral Research Findings for Advertising

Many relevant findings from behavioral research guide the development of advertising messages. These findings relate to (1) the characteristics of the

FIGURE 13–1

❖   Antecedents and Consequences of Brand Processing from Advertising

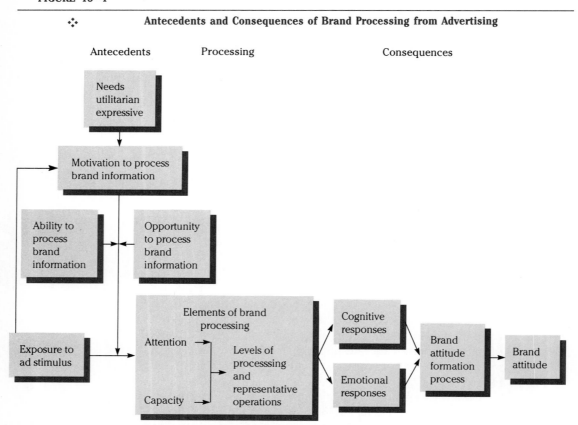

Source: Deborah L. MacInnis and Bernard J. Jaworski, "Information Processing from Advertisements: Toward an Integrative Framework," *Journal of Marketing* 53 (October 1989), p. 3.

message itself, (2) the attitudes toward the ad, and (3) characteristics of the consumer. Table 13–2 presents a summary of the most relevant conclusions to guide advertisers. These findings give more specific direction than the ELM for the actual development of advertising messages. They serve as a first floor to the foundation that the ELM gave us. We have not reported all relevant behavioral findings in Table 13–2 but only the ones we think are most relevant to message development.

However, even more detailed guidelines are needed by developers of advertising messages in terms of the specifics in forming the messages. These "upper floors" of the ELM foundation building are addressed in the last two sections of this chapter. We will now discuss a useful guide that presents a framework for types of creative executions and also examines when these different types of creative executions are appropriate. Finally, in this chapter, we present even more specifics about what works and what does not work in advertising messages. These latter guidelines are mostly based on the collective wisdom and research of advertising practitioners. We now present the framework on types of creative executions of advertisements.

A USEFUL GUIDE TO CREATIVE ASPECTS

Creative aspects of advertising hold a veto power over the effectiveness of a campaign. Good decisions in other areas can be wasted without meaningful copy, themes, presentation, and so forth. The marketing manager is likely not to be involved directly in the formulation of creative plans. This aspect is typically performed by the advertising agency. The manager is required, however, to approve and suggest changes in its creative efforts. To properly carry out this function, he or she needs a guide to what constitutes good advertising. The points to consider that are given here are based on the writings of Simon and have considerable practical usefulness.[6]

The analysis framework is based on developing links between product-market characteristics and advertising characteristics. To do this, one must first develop a classification scheme for both advertisements and products.

Alternative Advertising Approaches

The characteristics of ads that are important here relate to the way in which they attempt to activate buyers to action. Simon classified a number of activation methods. Some of them are:

1. *Information.* This type of ad presents straight facts. These facts are not presented in argumentative form, nor is the relevance of the facts explained. Classified and yellow pages ads are prime examples of this type of advertising, but many other examples exist, such as "round steak now 89

TABLE 13-2

Selected Behavioral Research Findings for Advertising

Characteristics of the Message

1. The more credible the source of the ad or the presenter in the ad, the more persuasive the ad. For example, certain celebrity presenters such as Bill Cosby have reputations as being credible.
2. Source credibility derives from expertise, celebrity status, gender fit with audience, physical attractiveness, likability, and similarity with the target audience.
3. The quality of claims in an ad impacts the persuasive level of the ad. The most effective claims focus on (a) dimensions relevant to target consumers, (b) factual information, (c) verifiable information based on search or experience, and (d) credible substantiation such as a test.
4. In low involvement situations, the more claims made, the greater the persuasive impact of the ad. That is, the quantity of claims serves as a persuasive cue under the peripheral route in the ELM.
5. Two-sided messages (those including pros and cons) increase perceptions of an advertiser's truthfulness and believability relative to one-sided messages (those presenting only the pros).
6. In new product introductions and in situations for a nonmarket leader brand, comparative ads (those that name another brand by name and make a direct comparison) outperform noncomparative ads, but this finding does not always hold.
7. Executional elements such as visuals, sounds, colors, and pace of the ad can impact its persuasive outcome, particularly ads designed to elicit emotional responses. Some of the detailed results related to these issues are discussed in the last section of the chapter.

Attitude toward the Ad

1. The ability of advertising to impact consumer attitudes toward a brand often depends on consumers' attitudes toward the ad itself.
2. In general, ads that are evaluated favorably (A_{ad}) can lead to more positive brand attitudes (A_b), although examples of disliked ads that sell a brand well do exist (e.g., the "Mr. Whipple" ad for the Charmin brand ran for 14 years).

Characteristics of Consumers

1. Differences in consumer motivation can influence the effectiveness of a particular persuasion strategy. Highly involved consumers are more likely to respond to informational ads. Little involved consumers are more likely to respond to emotional ads.
2. Ads will be more persuasive with a moderate level of arousal in consumers than with either little or greatly aroused consumers.
3. The higher the relevant knowledge level of consumers, the more receptive they will be to informationally rich claims.
4. Existing attitudes impact the receptivity to persuasion from ads. In general, persuasive communication is more successful in creating attitudes than in changing them. Current attitudes allow for more effective counterargumentation with the message. Product experience is an important element in the formation of the currently held attitude.

Source: Adapted from a review in James Engel, Rodger D. Blackwell, and Paul Miniard, *Consumer Behavior*, 6th ed. (Hinsdale, Ill.: Dryden Press, 1989), chap. 15.

cents per pound," or "City Center Motors announces the arrival of the new models." Figure 13–2 presents an example of an information ad.

2. *Argument or reason why.* This type of ad is structured in the form of a logical argument. The reasons utilized in the argument may be either facts or expected benefits to the consumer (social standing, and so forth). Figure 13–3 presents an example of an argument ad.

3. *Motivation with psychological appeals.* This type of ad uses emotional appeals. It tries to enhance the appeal of the product by attaching pleasant emotional connotation to it. The ad creates a mood. Selling points are then both explicit and implicit. Cosmetic, cigarette, and beer and liquor products are heavy users of mood commercials. Figure 13–4 presents an example of this type of ad.

4. *Repeat assertion.* This type of ad constitutes the hard-sell approach to activation. The statements made in these ads are usually unsupported by facts and so are the reasons why the statements hold. Two examples of this form are "Rolaids absorbs 20 times its weight in excess stomach acid," and "The little tablet is the more effective." The assumptions here are that people will believe a statement if they hear it enough and if they have no intrinsic interest in the product message. One is, then, just interested in getting across the line to remember. Nonprescription drugs are heavy users of this type of ad. Figure 13–5 presents an example of a repeat-assertion ad.

5. *Command.* This type of ad orders us to do something. For example: "When you drink don't drive," "Give the United Way," or "Drink Coca-Cola."

FIGURE 13–2

An Information Ad

FIGURE 13-3

❖   **An Argument Ad**

FIGURE 13–4

A Motivation-with-Psychological-Appeals Ad

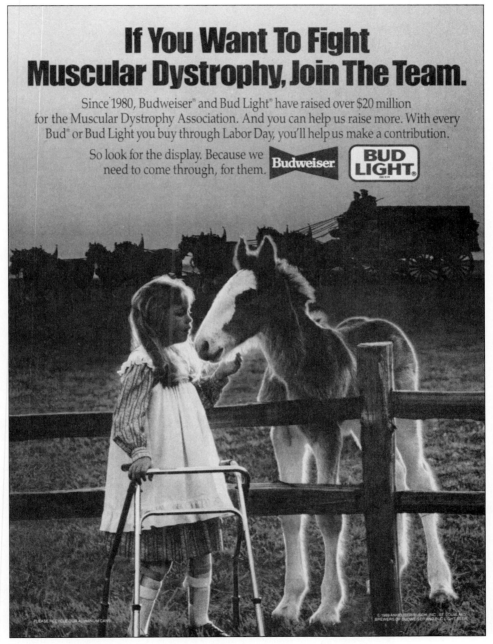

© 1989 Anheuser-Busch, Inc. Used with permission.

FIGURE 13–5

❖   **A Repeat-Assertion Ad**

The intent is to remind us to do something. The assumption is that the audience is suggestible. Command ads probably work best for products that are well-known and are generally well thought of by the audience. Figure 13–6 presents an example of a command ad.

6. *Symbolic association.* This type of ad is characterized as a more subtle form of the repeat-assertion ad. The intent is to get across one piece of information about the product. Here the product is linked to a person, music, or situation that has particularly pleasant connotations. The product and the symbol then become highly interrelated. Can anyone look at a picture of Gibraltar without thinking of what's-their-name? This type of appeal is obviously similar to emotional appeals. For example, beer is often associated with "good times with friends," a very emotional appeal. Both the emotion and the symbolic association are there. The first page of the color insert presents the classic Marlboro ad as an example of this approach. (See Promotion in Action 13–1.)

7. *Imitation.* This type of ad attempts to present people and situations for the audience to imitate (using our product, of course). The assumption is that people will imitate people whom they wish to be like or admire. Hence, we note the use of famous people in testimonials, status appeals, a group of young friends drinking beer, and so forth. Figure 13–7 shows this type of approach with Lynda Carter saying: "Your make-up can help hide a wrinkle. Mine can help prevent one."

We note that information, argument, and motivation are all directed at the conscious, "reasoning" parts of the mind. The others are directed at more emotional parts of the mind. Table 13–3 presents a summary description of the seven activation methods.

Choosing an Approach for the Product

Simon also notes a number of dimensions on which products and their markets may be classified. The choice of the market situation for a product by these considerations logically suggests how interest is to be activated. The positioning of a *product-market situation* on each dimension logically suggests an activation procedure.

1. *Industrial or consumer goods.* The information type and the argument type of ads are prevalent in industrial advertising. The complexity of the products, the dollar value of purchases, the risks of choosing a faulty product, and so forth, all dictate ads that provide facts and present logical arguments. The second page of the color insert presents an example of an industrial, argument ad.

For consumer goods, any one of the activation methods may still be appropriate. We must examine other dimensions before a more definitive answer can be reached. For consumer goods, then, we look at:

FIGURE 13–6

❖   **A Command Ad**

LUCY © 1952 United Feature Syndicate, Inc.

No Excuses Jeans Profits by Scandalous Association

The use of celebrity endorsers is among the most common forms of symbolic association advertising. Nike athletic shoes, for instance, are strongly identified with the excellence personified by their spokes athletes such as Michael Jordan and Bo Jackson. But, contrary to what you might think, some companies would prefer to be associated with scandalous, even unliked, celebrities.

No Excuses, a small jeans manufacturer, has achieved dubious but profitable notoriety for the infamous spokesmodels in their commercials. And they have done it with a budget that is miniscule by industry standards. The drawbacks to such a plan are obvious: the likelihood of alienating certain consumers groups, or being dragged through the media mud with celebrities of questionable character, for example. However, the advantages can be quick renown and inexpensive publicity.

With an annual budget of only $500,000, about enough to buy one and a half 30-second spots on "The Cosby Show" in 1990, No Excuses generated an invaluable amount of media attention.

No Excuses first received extensive media coverage for simply signing spokesmodels associated with high-coverage "scandals." Among the models were Donna Rice, infamous in 1988 for her Caribbean escapades with presidential candidate Gary Hart, and Marla Maples, companion to real-estate mogul Donald Trump. Even more publicity followed when most networks rejected the finished ads as too racy. Press conferences and articles in newspapers and magazines followed. The ads became overnight sensations without ever having been broadcast.

George Lois, whose Lois/GGK ad agency created the commercials was quite candid about the campaign strategy: "If we don't run one commercial, it still looks like we spent $50 million. How do you buy this kind of publicity we're talking about?" By making the campaign itself news, No Excuses gained free access to major media outlets and therefore spent even less on ad placement.

Many media officials were not happy about being the tool of No Excuses's manipulation, but, any mention, even this one, ensures the success of No Excuses's strategy. Some would argue that the No Excuses strategy does not measure up to the ethical and moral standards that should guide marketers in all strategic decisions. (See Chapters 12 and 24 for discussions of the legal, ethical, and social dimensions of promotional strategies.)

Source: Based on "Scandalous Ads Convert Rejection by Networks into Free Publicity," *The Wall Street Journal,* July 30, 1990, p. 85.

2. *What word best characterizes the product?* "Style," "mechanical," "sensory," "service," or "hidden benefit"? If "style," tend to use imitation, motivation, and symbolic association. For example, the advertising of fashion goods or beauty aids (see the third page of the color insert and Figure 13–7). If "mechanical," tend to use information and argument. Note the use

FIGURE 13–7

❖   **An Imitation Ad**

of statistical data in automobile and computer advertising (see Figure 13–8). If "sensory," tend to use symbolic-association motivation and imitation. These kinds of products appeal to all senses and need an appeal that goes beyond just words. Note the use of well-known people in cosmetic ads. For example, Chaz's use of Tom Selleck and Cover Girl's use of Christie Brinkley are classics. If "service," tend to use information and argument. People need to know that the service exists and rationally why they should partake of it (see Figure 13–9). If "hidden benefit," tend to use information, argument, and motivation. Lots of products have hidden benefits; examples are non-prescription drugs, all kinds of insurance, and foods, to name just a few. Buyers must be informed of these benefits and persuaded that they are important either with argument or by appealing to emotion (see Figure 13–10).

3. *Is it a necessity, a convenience, or a luxury good?* If a luxury product, we would likely use symbolic association or imitation. Luxury products are designed to give prestige and so we must create the aura of prestige in the ads. Also, the farther away a product is from being a necessity, the more likely we will have to create a demand for the product class. Motivational methods are, then, likely to be useful (see Figure 13–11 as an example of a luxury-good ad). The more necessary a product, the more likely activation methods other than motivation will be appropriate.

TABLE 13–3

Summary of Advertising Activation Methods ❖

	Activation Methods
Information	Presents straight facts without the relevance of the facts being explained.
Argument or Reason Why	Structured in the form of a logical argument, using either facts or expected benefits.
Motivation with Psychological Appeals	Uses emotional appeals to try to enhance the appeal of the product by attaching pleasant emotional connotations to it.
Repeat Assertion	Constitutes the hard-sell approach with the assumption that people will believe a statement if they hear it enough.
Command	Orders people to do something, assuming that the audience is suggestible.
Symbolic Association	A subtle form of the repeat-assertion ad that links the product to a person, music, or situation that has particularly pleasant connotations.
Imitation	Attempts to present people and situations for the audience to imitate, assuming that people will imitate people whom they wish to be like or admire.

FIGURE 13–8

❖   A "Mechanical" Product Ad Using an Argument Approach

4. *Stage of product class acceptance.* The newer the product class, the more people need information about it and reasons to buy it. We would then tend to use information, argument, and motivation (see Figure 13–12). As the product progresses through the life-cycle, people become less interested in hearing information about it. We then turn to use repeat assertion, imitation, symbolic association, or command.

5. *Stage of brand acceptance.* Even in an established product category, new brands must provide information, and therefore the early life-cycle methods are again appropriate (see Figure 13–13). The older brands utilize the later life-cycle methods.

FIGURE 13–9

A "Service" Product Ad Using an Argument Approach

Bob and I were having lunch the other day, and we started comparing brokerage accounts. As it turns out, I have a much better deal. I have Schwab One.

"Bob pays $80 for a brokerage account with checking. I pay zip."

Bob has a "cash management" account with a full commission broker. When he needs money, he can write a check.

So can I. But I don't *pay* for the privilege. I have a Schwab One brokerage account.

All the bells and whistles.

With Schwab One, I can invest in stocks, options, mutual funds, bonds—same as Bob.

I can write checks, use my free VISA® debit card, earn income on any between-investment cash, and borrow against my portfolio. Again, just like Bob. So what's the difference?

No annual fee. Low opening balance. Commission discounts.

There's *no* annual fee. While

Compare Schwab One to Similar Accounts	Annual Fee	Initial Deposit Required	24-Hour Service	Commission Discounts
Schwab*ONE*	Free	$5,000	Yes	Yes
Merrill Lynch Cash Mgmt Account	$80	$20,000	No	No
Dean Witter Active Assets Account	$80	$10,000	No	No
Shearson Lehman Financial Mgmt Account	$100	$10,000	No	No

Based on a survey conducted by Schwab in November, 1989.

Bob pays $80, I pay zip. And it only takes $5,000 to open Schwab One. That's cash, stocks, or any combination.

The bottom line?

Schwab One's a better deal. And

Bob agrees. When he switches to Schwab One, he'll save $80. And he'll save even *more* with Schwab's low commissions. Bob owes me one.

For free Schwab One information without sales pressure visit Schwab today or call:

1-800-537-5400

Charles Schwab

We give you more ways to succeed.

Member SIPC
©Charles Schwab & Co., Inc.

FIGURE 13–10

❖ A "Hidden Benefit" Highlighted by Using Argument and Motivational Approaches

FIGURE 13–11

A Luxury Product Ad Using a Motivational Approach

Courtesy of Doyle Dane Bernbach Advertising Agency and General Wine and Spirits Company

FIGURE 13-12

FIGURE 13–13

A New Brand Using an Argument Approach

Last year 358 Americans received their Ph.D.'s in electrical engineering. Presenting a VCR for the rest of us.

Let's face it: most VCR's are designed by engineers for engineers. But not the Goldstar compact GHV-5300. With its on-screen program-

The programming instructions for our VCR appear on your TV screen.

ming and random access remote control, this VCR is easier to program than tying your shoes.

As you can see, the instructions are clear, easy to understand and just as easy to execute.

And on-screen programming isn't our new VCR's only virtue.

It also comes with a

155 channel, cable-compatible tuner; an 8 event/365 day timer, stereo sound with Dolby,* and fully automatic controls that turn on, play, rewind and shut off all by themselves. So if you didn't spend your college days running around the inside of a dust-free laboratory, our VCR could be just your speed.

GoldStar

The brightest star in electronics.™

Company: Goldstar Electronics Int'l, Inc. 1990 Ad Agency: TBWA

6. *Price range.* If a high-priced item, tend to use information, argument, and motivation. People need reasons for spending so much(see Figure 13–14). The smaller the dollar amount, the more impulsive is the purchase, and so symbolic association, command, repeat assertion, and so forth become more viable (see Figure 13–15).

7. *Closeness to competing brands in objective characteristics.* A brand with great physical differences from its competitors allows the advertiser to say a lot about the physical product (see Figure 13–16). It can therefore make use of information, argument, and motivation. Items that vary little from brand to brand (beer, cigarettes, tuxedos must rely on other methods. For an example, see Figure 13–17).

8. *Repeatability of purchase.* Products with short repurchase cycles (for example, soap, coffee, and so forth) utilize symbolic association, command, repeat assertion, and imitation much more than those with long repurchase cycles (for example, diamonds). Information and argument become old hat for the former but are critical for the latter. Note the difference between Figures 13–14 and 13–15.

9. *Method of consummating sale.* The more direct action-oriented the ad (for example, mail order houses, Book-of-the-Month Club), the greater the need for argument and motivation methods. These types of ads must do the complete selling job and therefore can use many activation methods (see Figure 13–18).

10. *Market share held by brands.* If a brand holds a dominant position in a market, it has a lot to gain by expanding the whole market. One would, then, use information, argument, or motivation—the methods we associated earlier with early stages of the product life-cycle (see Figure 13–19).

Simon suggests that we identify the most important product-market dimension and then select an activation method with this in mind. Think of the ads you have seen lately for, say, beer and watches. Pick a brand and work through Simon's procedure. We think you'll be impressed with the usefulness of the framework. Table 13–4 provides a summary of the relationship of the product/market situation and the choice of activation method for the creative execution.

Within any of these advertising approaches there are millions of different ways to create the ad. The words, colors, and graphics of the ad can be used in infinite variety. Further, such things as humor, a well-known spokesperson (see Figure 13–7), or a "slice of life" presentation can be used. Thus Simons' scheme can aid our understanding but does not reduce the need for creativity.

FIGURE 13-14

A High-Priced Product Using an Argument Approach

Choose a diamond as valuable as the love you share.

An understanding of a diamond's qualities can add enormously to the value, beauty and pleasure of any diamond acquisition. And understanding quality in diamonds begins with the 4C's: Cut, color, clarity and carat-weight. It is the 4C characteristics that determine the value of a diamond.

If you're the kind of person who appreciates quality in every aspect of your life, from the wine you choose to the car you drive, you'll want to know more about quality in diamonds. Because diamonds of quality have more fire, more sparkle and scintillation. And they'll enhance your jewelry no matter what the design.

Your jeweler is the expert where diamonds are concerned. But your own understanding of diamond quality can help make your next diamond purchase even more special. So we've prepared a helpful brochure that takes only a few minutes to read. Not much, when you consider that a diamond is forever.

4C Your guide to diamond value. Consult your jeweler, or write for a copy of our informative brochure to Diamond Information Center, Dept. Q, 1345 Avenue of the Americas, N.Y. 10105.

A diamond is forever.

FIGURE 13–15

 A Low-Priced Product Using a Repeat-Assertion Approach

Courtesy of The National Federation of Coffee Growers of Colombia

FIGURE 13–16

A Physically Different Product Using an Argument Approach

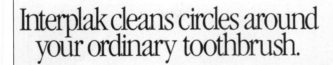

Interplak cleans circles around your ordinary toothbrush.

The Interplak™ Home Plaque Removal Instrument is one of the most important advances in home dental care since the invention of the toothbrush.

It doesn't look like an ordinary toothbrush. And it doesn't work like one.

After using the Interplak instrument just once, you'll be able to feel the difference immediately. Your mouth will seem fresher. Cleaner.

It cleans teeth nearly plaque-free.

Clinical studies show that manual brushing removes only some of the plaque that builds up daily on your teeth.

But those same studies show that the Interplak instrument cleans teeth nearly plaque-free and reduces gingivitis to improve the health of your gums. And the more plaque you remove, the more you reduce the risk of early gum disease and tooth decay.

Nothing fights plaque better.

Unlike manual and electric toothbrushes that only clean back and forth, or up and down, our ten tufts of bristles rotate 4200 times a minute.

Interplak tufts clean plaque from between teeth and under the gums.

And they reverse their direction 46 times a second to literally scour off plaque and stimulate your gums. When the tufts reverse direction, the bristles extend fully to clean deep between teeth and

under your gumline. And because the bristles are four times softer than the softest toothbrush, they're no more abrasive than manual brushing with toothpaste.

Ask your dentist about the benefits.

Dental professionals across the country have enthusiastically endorsed the Interplak instrument and they've recommended it to their patients. It's even accepted by the American Dental Association.

It's easy to use, cordless, and it recharges itself every time you place it in its stand. Plus you can buy color-coded, interchangeable brush heads for the whole family.

For more information, call toll-free 1-800-334-4031.

The Interplak Home Plaque Removal Instrument, from Bausch & Lomb.

A new way of brushing your teeth, with extraordinary results.

INTERPLAK HOME PLAQUE REMOVAL INSTRUMENT

FIGURE 13–17

A Product Not Very Different from Its Competitors Using a Motivation Approach

FIGURE 13–18

A Direct Action Ad Using Argument and Motivation Approaches   ❖

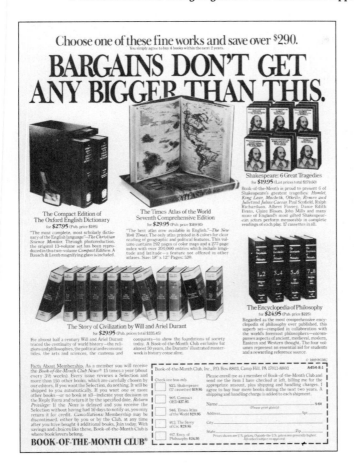

FIGURE 13–19

 A Dominant Brand Using an Argument Approach

Courtesy of Hewlett-Packard Company

TABLE 13-4

Choosing an Activation Method ∴

Product/Market Situation	Activation Methods
Classification of Product	
Industrial	Information, argument
Consumer	(Any activation method)
Characteristic Word	
Style	Imitation, motivation, symbolic association
Mechanical	Information, argument
Sensory	Symbolic association, motivation, imitation
Service	Information, argument
Hidden benefit	Information, argument, motivation
Type of Good	
Luxury	Symbolic association, imitation
Convenience	Motivation
Necessity	(Activation methods other than motivation)
Stage of Product Class Acceptance	
New product class	Information, argument, motivation
Old product class	Repeat assertion, imitation, command, symbolic association
Stage of Brand Acceptance	
New brands	Information, argument, motivation
Old brands	Repeat assertion, imitation, command, symbolic-association
Price Range	
High price	Information, argument, motivation
Low price	Symbolic association, command, repeat assertion
Closeness to Competing Brands in Objective Characteristics	
Large differences	Information, argument, motivation
Small differences	Repeat assertion, command, symbolic association, imitation
Repeatability of Purchase	
Short cycle	Symbolic association, command, imitation repeat assertion
Long cycle	Information, argument, motivation
Method of Consummating Sale	
Direct action oriented	Argument, motivation
Market Share Held by Brand	
Dominant position	Information, argument, motivation

DESIGNING AND PRODUCING ADVERTISING MESSAGES

In this chapter so far, we have progressed from (1) the development of a copy platform to (2) the application of the ELM of consumer response to advertising to (3) the stating of some useful behavioral findings for advertising and then to (4) the application of the Simon activation methods framework relative to the product/market situation to the development of advertising messages. A fifth level of knowledge in the development of advertising messages is the development of so-called creative "rules" of copywriting and art work as applied to advertising. These creative rules are based on the research of practitioners and on their collected wisdom. This is a level of implementation detail that transcends the main focus of this book. Thus we have placed these creative rules in the Appendix to this chapter.

Such creative rules have both value and danger. On the positive side, there is much known. David Ogilvy's books *Confessions of an Advertising Man* and *Ogilvy on Advertising* are typical of the research-based practitioners' creative rules. As Ogilvy noted:

> During a 10-hour train ride, I read the ads in three magazines. Most of them violated elementary principles which were discovered in years gone by— and set out in *Confessions*. The copywriters and art directors who created them are ignorant amateurs.
>
> What is this reason for the failure to study experience?
>
> Is it that advertising does not attract inquiring minds? Is this kind of scientific method beyond their grasp? Are they afraid that knowledge would impose some discipline on them—or expose their incompetences?[7]

On the other hand, the straight-forward application of these types of creative rules has danger also. Creativity cannot be put into a straight jacket. As Harry W. McMahan, another successful practitioner, stated:[8]

> Examples can help. Guidelines can help. But rules often lead the advertising novice astray. In our 20,000 commercials we can disprove almost any "rule." Why? Because . . . different product fields require different handling in communications and persuasion.

We judge the creative rules in the chapter appendix to be useful for those interested in that level of detail. We also expect the reader to approach their use with care, for sometimes real creativity comes from breaking the so-called rules.

ANALYSIS OF THE MESSAGE

With all the millions of possible creative executions for an ad, the reader may conclude that it is impossible to differentiate a good advertisement

Marlboro

Warning: The Surgeon General Has Determined That Cigarette Smoking Is Dangerous to Your Health.

Symbolic-association ads, like this classic, attempt to link the product to positive feelings. Here, feelings of courage, tradition, and strength might be generated in the viewer.

This product argument ad also manages to make an emotional appeal for the superiority of the product.

For Bill Demby, the difference means getting another shot.

When Bill Demby was in Vietnam, he used to dream of coming home and playing a little basketball with the guys.

A dream that all but died when he lost both his legs to a Viet Cong rocket.

But then, a group of researchers discovered that a remarkable DuPont plastic could help make artificial limbs that were more resilient, more flexible, more like life itself.

Thanks to these efforts, Bill Demby is back. And some say, he hasn't lost a step.

At DuPont, we make the things that make a difference.

Better things for better living.

REG. US PAT & TM OFF

Clothing is often promoted with style product ads, where the image conveys a sense of the product rather than specific information.

Advertising for men's clothing, traditionally more feature-oriented, is moving ever more toward the style product approach so common with women's clothing.

from a poor one. Yet there comes a time when such a decision must be made so that time or space can be bought. In part, this evaluation must be made on the basis of informed judgment, and some use also is usually made of copy tests (pretests).

Judgmental Analysis: Evaluation of Execution

An advertisement should be *memorable* in that it attracts and holds attention. It also must register its intended message and hence achieve its *persuasive* objective. The following questions are useful in assessing whether an ad is memorable and persuasive.

1. *Does the picture tell the story?* Given the large volume of competing advertising, no message has more than a fraction of a second to attract and hold the consumer's attention. Thus the visual portion of the message must register the message without sole reliance on words.

2. *Are the words appropriate?* Do they communicate product benefits in terms that are meaningful to the target audience?

3. *Is one clear theme registered by the total advertisement?* Rarely will attention be held for a sufficient period to register more than one or two ideas, so the emphasis must be on a single-minded presentation of the message theme.

4. *Is the brand name registered?* Many times the brand name is not stressed with the result that the reader or viewer fails to associate message and product.

5. *Is the tone appropriate?* In other words, is the style of message appropriate for the product? Demonstrations are best used with unique product attributes that can be illustrated. When this is not the case, the tone or impression left may interfere with the intended message. Humor is more appropriate when no unique product benefits are present; at other times, it may be entertaining but ineffective.

6. *Is the advertisement distinctive?* Does it stand out from the noise? The dangers of novelty have been stressed, but a message must have an element of distinctiveness to overcome mass media clutter.

Figure 13–20 presents a magazine ad recently produced by Carnival Cruise Lines. Take a chance at answering the six judgmental analysis questions above as they apply to the Carnival ad. What do you conclude? Perhaps you, like most advertisers, would be reluctant to rely completely on your judgment alone to make evaluations of advertising messages. For this reason, advertisers use pretests (or *copy tests,* as they are most frequently referred to in the trade). These and other advertising testing procedures are discussed in Chapter 16. Just to complete the thought, the

FIGURE 13-20

❖ **Carnival Cruise Lines Magazine and Television Advertisements**

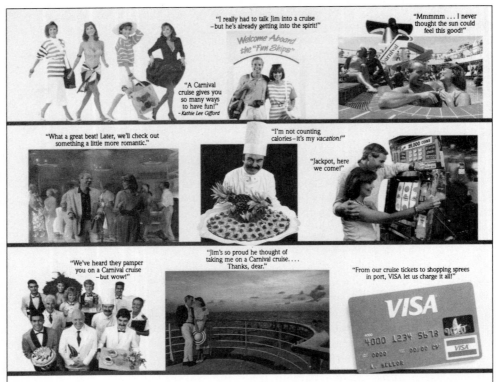

IF YOU'RE PASSING LIKE SHIPS IN THE NIGHT, IT'S TIME TO FIND EACH OTHER AT SEA.

When life's turning your loved one into a fondly remembered stranger, there's one way to get things back in perspective. Call your travel agent and reserve a Carnival® cruise. Just think of it. Experience playful days in the sun, charming tropical ports, exquisite food, dancing till dawn — sure to spark a new romance ... or re-kindle an old one.

Let us pamper you. Every "Fun Ship"® is a magnificent resort —

with so many things to do. How about roulette after dinner? Or an exciting Las Vegas revue? On Carnival, you know virtually all your costs up-front — your air fare, meals, activities and entertainment are all included in one low price! And you can charge your entire vacation on your VISA card. It's your best vacation value.

So when life's getting just a little too hurried, discover what happens when you glimpse the moon from a floating island of light. Carnival. When you're ready to find each other ... again.

See your travel agent for a 3, 4 or 7 day vacation from $395 per person, including air fare. Some restrictions apply. Prices higher in the West.

Experience the excitement of a Carnival vacation with our FREE 20 minute video. Send $3.50 for postage and handling to: Carnival Cruise Lines, Dept. 827, P.O. Box 9008, Opa Locka, FL 33054-9914.

THE MOST POPULAR CRUISE LINE IN THE WORLD.™

VISA It's Everywhere You Want To Be.®

Registered in Liberia and the Bahamas.

Carnival ad scored extremely well on copy testing procedures. Would you have judged this to be true a priori?

SUMMARY

This chapter has presented a five-step approach to the development of advertising messages. First, it is necessary to establish a creative strategy or copy platform that includes statements about target audience, objective, advertising strategy, support, other considerations, and tone. The second step involves the understanding of consumer response based in the level of involvement and elaboration, as conceptualized by the ELM. Third, we outlined some useful behavioral generalization for advertising. These guidelines provide some direction to advertising specifics but should be taken only as directions, not firm conclusions for any particular ad. Fourth, the Simon activation framework took us deeper into the actual production aspects of advertisement. Finally, the appendix to the chapter presents creative rules for copywriting and art production. These rules should be applied with care.

The end result of the development of advertising messages should be rigorously compared against the six judgmental criteria presented in the chapter. In addition, research-based copy testing of the specific ad is often needed.

REVIEW AND DISCUSSION QUESTIONS

1. For the beef ad in Figure 13–3, the Savin ad in Figure 13–8, and the Chanel No. 5 ad in the color insert, prepare what you believe the associated copy platform could be. This requires you to reason and speculate based on the actual advertising execution.

2. For the same three ads, are the principles of the ELM applied properly? What ELM–based outcomes would you expect from these ads? Why? What type of elaboration would you expect? Why?

3. From magazines that interest you, select three ads that you consider to be the best and three that you consider to be the worst. Apply the judgmental criteria to these ads. What do you conclude? Also apply the Simon activation appropriateness approach to these ads. What do you conclude?

4. If you have been assigned the Appendix to this chapter to read, apply the creative rules in the Appendix to the beef, Savin, and Chanel No. 5 ads in the chapter. Also apply these rules to the six ads you selected in question 3. What do you conclude about the usefulness of these creative rules?

5. "All these detailed copy platforms, behavioral guidelines, and creative rules of copy writing do is prevent the creative people from really being creative." Comment.

NOTES

1. This approach and material, with slight adaption, was provided by Professor Lawrence V. Johnson of the University of Kansas.

2. This section is based on an extensive presentation of this material in James Engel, Roger D. Blackwell, and Paul Miniard, *Consumer Behavior,* 6th ed. (Hinsdale, Ill.: Dryden Press, 1989), chap. 15.

3. Christopher Puto and William D. Wells, "Informational and Transformational Advertising: The Differential Effects of Time" in Thomas C. Kinnear, ed., *Advances in Consumer Research* 11 (Provo, Utah: Association for Consumer Research, 1984), pp. 638–43.

4. Diane Schneidman, "Perception-Altering Ads for Generic Foods Are Spread on the Grapevine," *Marketing News*, June 5, 1987, p. 15.

5. See, for example, David A. Aaker, Douglas M. Stayman, and Michael R. Hagerty, "Warmth in Advertising: Measurement, Impact, and Sequence Effects," *Journal of Consumer Research* 12 (March 1986), pp. 365–81; Julie A. Edell and Marian C. Burke, "The Power of Feelings in Understanding Advertising Effects," *Journal of Consumer Research* 14 (December 1987), pp. 421–33; Meryl Paula Gardener, "Mood States and Consumer Behavior: A Critical Review," *Journal of Consumer Research* 12 (December 1985), 281–300; Morris B. Holbrook, "Emotion in the Consumption Experience: Toward a New Model of the Human Consumer," in Robert A. Peterson, Wayne D. Hoyer, and William R. Wilson, eds., *The Role of Affect in Consumer Behavior* (Lexington, Mass.: D. C. Heath, 1986), pp. 17–52; Morris B. Holbrook and Rajeev Batra, "Assessing the Role of Emotions as Mediators of Consumer Responses to Advertising," *Journal of Consumer Research* 14 (December 1987), pp. 404–20; Patricia A. Stout and John D. Leckenby, "Measuring Emotional Response to Advertising," *Journal of Advertising* 15 (1986), pp. 35–42; David M. Zeitlin and Richard A. Westwood, "Measuring Emotional Response," *Journal of Advertising Research* 26 (October/November 1986), pp. 34–44.

6. This section is based on Julian L. Simon, *The Management of Advertising* (Englewood Cliffs, N.J.: Prentice Hall, 1971), pp. 169–206.

7. For the published insights of David Ogilvy, see David Ogilvy, *Confessions of an Advertising Man* (New York: Atheneum, 1963), and *Ogilvy on Advertising* (New York: Crown Publishers, 1983). The Ogilvy rules in the Appendix are from an internal publication entitled "Raising Your Sights! 97 Tips for Copywriters, Art Directors and TV Producers—Mostly Derived from Research," from Ogilvy, Benson, & Mather, New York. These rules are reproduced in the Appendix with special permission.

8. Harry W. McMahan, "Advertising: Some Things You Can't Teach—and Some You Can," *Advertising Age* (November 8, 1976), p. 56.

Designing and Producing the Mass Communication Message

The creative rules presented in this Appendix are based on the research and practical experience of practitioners, especially David Ogilvy. Not all advertisers agree with all these rules. Indeed, some successful advertisements have been known to break some of them. New research will also from time to time change some of these rules. We do not present in this Appendix all the points of disagreement about these rules. Thus the reader should learn from these practitioners' research and experience but should also use the learning with wisdom and care.

PRINT ADVERTISING

THE HEADLINE

The headline is often considered to be "what would be said if only one or two lines of space were available for the message." It must put forth the main theme or appeal in a few words. Considered in this context, there is no reason to make it less than a powerful selling message.

Without doubt, the headline shoulders a large part of the task of attracting the reader's attention. It should tell the whole story, including the *brand name* and the *promise* to the buyer. Otherwise, the advertiser is wasting money. Research shows that four out of five readers never get farther than the headline. The illustration also aids in attracting and holding attention, but readership studies repeatedly demonstrate that the headline is the major component in attracting attention. If it is not powerful, many good prospects will never get far enough into the ad to read the message.

Classifications of Headlines

Headline information serves various purposes. It may (1) provide news, (2) state product claims, (3) give advice, (4) select prospects, (5) arouse curiosity, or (6) identify product or company name.

News   This type of headline plays a role similar to its counterpart in the news story, for it often summarizes the point of highest interest in the copy. To command attention and arouse interest, such a headline must be pertinent and timely. It dispenses with cleverness and gimmicks and uses a direct, straight-selling approach. "Honda Number 1 in consumer satisfaction" is an example.

Product Claim   Featuring a product claim can be a good attention getter in that it appeals to the reader's self-interest. The claim should be significant and believable. A headline that says "This Tire Will Give You Good Mileage" would have less impact than one that says "This Tire Gives 30% More Mileage than Competitively Priced Tires." One might expect many brands of tires to give good mileage, but 30 percent more is something worth looking into.

   Although many successful headlines make claims, the use of this approach has been somewhat weakened by advertising that makes irresponsible statements. You should proceed on the assumption that the reader will be dubious. To ensure believability, take care to provide ample supporting evidence in the copy.

Advice   Advice given in a headline may be followed by a promise of results from product use. Such a headline is "You Owe It to Yourself to Try Slimmo Reducing Tablets," with a secondary headline featuring a claim: "Use Slimmo 10 Days and Lose 10 Pounds." A properly conceived advice headline appeals to the reader's self-interest in that it is aimed at helping him or her solve a problem or prevent its occurrence.

Prospect Selection   Because very few products are of interest to everyone, the advertisement should appeal only to potential customers. The headline is a principal device in the process of selecting prospects from among readers. Copy striving to reach everyone is usually so generalized that its effectiveness is lost. A headline that says "New Drug Aids Those Who Suffer from Asthma" would be a combination of *news* and *selectivity*. In other situations, the headline may be purely selective in purpose, as in the headline that says "Attention, June Graduates." The great majority of headlines are selective to some extent, regardless of emphasis.

Curiosity   Sometimes referred to as the provocative approach, the curiosity-oriented headline attempts to arouse interest by appealing to the unusual. It is hoped that the reader will be stimulated to read the copy text to find the answer to a "riddle" that is posed.

   The curiosity approach can be used when some aspect of the product is of such genuine and timely interest that the reader is predisposed to seek information. A headline that asks "Are You Protected from Atomic Pollutants?" would arouse interest on the part of many people and induce them to read the text for more information. Volkswagen has made effective use of this approach. In one of the most memorable advertisements in its campaigns, the headline read, "Lemon." Then the copy proceeded to explain the quality control procedures that prevent the customer from getting a "lemon."

The curiosity headline gives the copywriter great freedom to use his or her imagination, and its use can be tempting. However, some experts caution against the use of this approach in situations in which a direct-selling headline would be more appropriate. The curiosity type of headline too often is used for the sake of novelty alone, and, as was pointed out in Chapter 13, novelty without meaning is not creativity.

Product or Company Name   Occasionally the name of the product or company is used as the headline. This approach might be effective when the product is of such timely interest that the mere mention of the name is sufficient to arouse interest. In World War II a headline reading "Tires" would have attracted real attention from consumers in a market of scarcity. Substantial interest among many ethnic and racial groups can be obtained today by featuring members of that specific group.

Some Guides for a Persuasive Headline

A fair amount of published research is available that delineates the characteristics of effective headlines. Although there is general agreement on certain of these characteristics, they can be violated successfully in many situations. There is a real difference, however, between violating a known criterion intentionally and violating it through ignorance.

Researchers at Marplan have found that confining the headline area to a small portion of the advertisement and using only one or two lines of type will produce the highest readership.[1] In addition, David Ogilvy mentions the following criteria:[2]

1. On the average, five times as many people read the headline as read the body copy. If you haven't done some selling in your headline, you have wasted 80 percent of your client's money.

2. Headlines should appeal to the reader's *self-interest,* by promising a benefit. This benefit should be the basic promise of the product.

3. Inject the maximum news into your headlines.

4. Include the *brand name* in every headline.

5. Write headlines which force the reader to read your subhead and body copy.

6. Don't worry about the *length* of the headline—12-word headlines get almost as much readership as 3-word headlines. Headlines in the 6-to-12-word group get the most coupon replies. Better a long headline that sells than a short one which is blind and dumb.

7. Never change typeface in the middle of the headline; it reduces readership.

8. Never use a headline that requires readership of body copy to be comprehensible.

9. Never use tricky or irrelevant headlines.

10. Use words to select your prospects—like MOTHER and VARICOSE VEINS.

11. Use words which have been found to contain emotional impact.

KISS	DARLING	INSULT	HAPPY
LOVE	ANGRY	MONEY	WORRY
MARRY	FIGHT	FAMILY	BABY

It is also generally accepted that the headline must be simple and easily understood. Moreover, it must join with the other message elements in presenting a unified and coherent message.

COPY

During construction of the headline, ideas flow toward the next step—writing the body copy. An idea put aside as inadequate for the headline often becomes a subhead, a copy-block lead line, or the lead for successive paragraphs. The copy reinforces the headline and delivers the sales message.

Whatever writing form the copywriter chooses to express the selling points, he or she will find that there is an ever increasing demand for facts. It is a naive copywriter who does not include hard information on the product and its benefits throughout the message.

Classification of Copy Approaches

It is useful to classify copy approaches by manner of presentation. In *direct-selling news copy*, for example, the message is presented in a straightforward manner similar to the informative content of newspaper articles. New-product messages are typical examples. In contrast, *implied suggestion* gives the reader an opportunity to draw conclusions from the facts that are presented. Usually the facts are obvious enough to direct the reader to a favorable conclusion about the product or service.

In *narrative description,* the copywriter starts with an account of some human experience that presents a problem and the solution in terms of favorable orientation toward a product. In a related copy type, the *story form,* human experience is also used in a straightforward account of product use by a purchaser. It may also involve an analogy between a storybook use and the product itself.

One effective approach is to use *monologue* and *dialogue.* The monologue is a single subject, such as a person (animals are also used as ad characters) reporting on personal reactions to certain goods and services. The dialogue presents a conversation between two persons (or animals) who elaborate on the merits of the product. This can often be in the form of a *testimonial message.* The testimonial implies that the reader can emulate or imitate the person giving the testimonial. It is also a means of stating *authoritatively* that certain benefits can be found in using a product or service by following the exemplary behavior of those featured.

Humor can be very effective if the entertainment value of the presentation has real selling appeal to those who are exposed to the message. Messages that deal with food, drinks, and entertainment generally find this an appropriate form. More will be said shortly about the use of humor.

Finally, some use can be made of the *comic strip* or *continuity* forms. These have found growing use because of the popularity of children's television programming and fictional characters, but its effectiveness is limited by mechanical problems in production of the comic strip.

Some Copy Problems

The Use of Humor   As mentioned above, considerable use is made of humor, but this should not be regarded as an index of its effectiveness. Many agree with Ogilvy's statement: "Humorous copy does not sell. It is never used by the great copywriters—only by amateurs."[3]

Others would not take such a strong stand, but research findings seem to support the conclusion that humorous commercials generally are less effective than their nonhumorous counterparts. The Schwerin Research Corporation reports that commercials featuring *all* humor (less than 4 percent of all advertisements) seldom prove to be as effective as other approaches. However, some use of humor, in general, will help the commercial to perform better than a commercial with no humor whatsoever. The conclusion, then, is that humor at its best is used sparingly.

The purpose of advertising is *not* to entertain. Few advertisements can entertain and sell simultaneously; both elements are combined only through use of great skill.

Answering Competitors' Claims   Perhaps it is human nature for an advertiser to react defensively when attacked by a competitor. Although direct competitive derogation is seen infrequently, many advertisers indirectly attack competitors with their own strong claims of superiority.

There is real danger in a direct counterattack. If a competitor makes the claim, for example, that its make of automobile is the "quietest on the road," it has in effect appropriated that claim for itself. If it is answered by a counterclaim stating that "we also are quiet," the earlier statement is reinforced. If an appeal is answered, it gains credence.

Direct-Action Copy   Much advertising copy is designed to activate those in the final stages of their decision-making process as they move toward purchase. Similarly, the copy may serve to lead those now preferring a brand to purchase it more frequently and in greater quantities.

Among the many direct-action approaches are samples, contests, coupons and price offers, premiums, and combinations of related products. Some of the objectives to be attained are:

1. To obtain new triers and convert them into regular users.
2. To introduce new or improved products.
3. To increase brand awareness or awareness of a new package.
4. To increase readership of advertising by using coupons as attention-attracting devices.
5. To stimulate reseller support.

Success with the direct-action approach is most likely where brand loyalty is low. A buyer may actively seek a special incentive to buy, such as a price reduction. In addition, the direct-action method can be highly effective when the product or service being advertised possesses no distinct competitive advantage. For this reason, coupons and other incentives are a basic competitive tool among manufacturers of soaps, breakfast foods, cake mixes, and other items where no single firm can claim uniqueness and where brand loyalty is not especially strong.

The direct-action or "forcing" approach must be used with caution. When all competitors use this type of stimulus, the result cannot help but have a diminishing effect for any individual firm. Moreover, the person may buy only for the incentive and return to a preferred brand later, in which case a costly promotion has failed.

Experience indicates that the forcing approach should seldom be used when strong appeals can be made to product superiority. The Scott Paper Company abandoned couponing for this reason and was successful in its stress on the product line itself and its unique advantages for the buyer. Moreover, a strong stimulus to buy will have a lasting effect through increasing market share only if the product clearly demonstrates its differentiation in use. Many new products have been successfully introduced by direct-action means, but sales of an existing product with no apparent superiority are not likely to be affected greatly.

The direct-action stimulus clearly has a legitimate role when it has been indicated through research that a significant number of buyers require an additional stimulus for purchase action. It should not be used simply as a competitive fad but should be based on consumer research.

Slogans A slogan is a small group of words combined in unique fashion to embody the selling theme. In general, it will be short and to the point and feature the product name whenever possible. Through repetition, it may become associated with the product and its benefits, thereby provoking prompt recall of the advertising message.

Some slogans emphasize product performance, and the mention of the generic name is all that is needed to bring a powerful association to mind. Others are designed to emphasize product quality, such as the ageless slogan for Ivory Soap: "99 and 44/100 Percent Pure." A manufacturer may employ a slogan to minimize substitution of a competitor's product and stress confidence in quality. "You Can Be Sure if It's Westinghouse" became a well-known quality slogan.

Legal protection for slogans was granted in the Lanham Act of 1947. If the slogan is registered and certain additional requirements are met, legal protection is ensured. The detailed requirements of the act are explained in most basic marketing texts.

Some Guides for Persuasive Copy

Imagination, of course, must be disciplined to generate creative and persuasive copy. Although there is no universal set of steps to follow, there is substantial agreement with many of the following points mentioned by Ogilvy:

1. Don't expect people to read leisurely essays.
2. Go straight to the point; don't beat about the bush.
3. Avoid analogies—"just as, so to."
4. Avoid superlatives, generalizations, platitudes. Consumers discount them—and forget them.
5. Be specific and factual.
6. Be personal, enthusiastic, memorable—as if the reader were sitting next to you at a dinner party.
7. Don't be a dull bore.

8. Tell the truth—but make the truth fascinating.

9. Use testimonials. Celebrity testimonials are better than anonymous ones.

10. Don't be afraid to write *long* copy. Mail-order advertisers never use short copy—and they know exactly what results they get.

11. Make the captions under your photographs pregnant with brand names and sell.[4]

One could, of course disagree with some of these points. Some advertisers never use testimonials. Notice the several important basic criteria that are set forth. Persuasive copy should be (1) specific, (2) interesting, (3) believable, (4) simple, and (5) relevant.

If the copy surrounding an illustration or several illustrations does not make it apparent what the product's use or the benefit to the buyer may be, there must be a caption below the illustration. Research has generally found that the readership effect of a series of pictures with captions can be twice as great as body copy.

Nothing can lose a reader's attention more quickly than a general claim insufficiently supported by specific facts. "Chevrolet gets good gas mileage" is much less effective than "Chevrolet delivers 23.9 miles per gallon in the Mobile Gas Economy Run." Furthermore, the copy must contain relevant, meaningful information if it is to interest—not bore—the reader. Even interesting copy generally should not demand complex mental reasoning by the reader. It is much more effective if it focuses on a single theme.

The wording has much to do with the effect of the message on the recipient, for clumsy wording can violate the criterion of simplicity. Such words as *wonderful, powerful, time-saving,* and *finest* may lose their impact through overuse by advertisers, and the consumer is likely to reject them as being irrelevant. Good copy in most advertisements should amplify the headline, offer proof of what the headline claims, explain the product's advantages, and make clear what the reader is expected to do. It should in most cases end with an appeal to action, such as "visit your dealer now."

VISUAL ELEMENTS

The visualization of the basic theme is of such importance that one authority has suggested it be prepared before any other elements. According to this view, the most graphic, poignant, and appealing picture should be made of the theme; then the words are added. This is substantiated by a number of studies that demonstrate that the illustration is of critical importance in attracting and holding attention.

A number of methods can be used in creating the illustration—line drawings, cartoons, photographs, and artistic renderings of subjects. Photographs provide the most realism, but an artist's drawing may create a subtle mood or highlight an attribute of a product in use that may not be possible with photographs. In large part, the choice of the method will be made on a subjective basis by the creative team.

Classification of Visual Forms

Visual forms can be classified according to their features or techniques.

The Product Alone   Perhaps the simplest form of illustration is one in which the product is shown without background or setting. This method may prove powerful when the product has intrinsic characteristics that command attention. Precious jewels, high-priced automobiles, and similar distinctive items can attract attention without the use of background. At times, in fact, a background may distract from the product's impact.

The Product in a Setting   Not many products are of such distinction that they can be shown without background. The setting is chosen to show the product to advantage and, in many instances, the objective is to have the reader associate the quality of the setting with the product. In other situations, the setting may imply the pleasant and satisfying uses of the product.

The setting must be chosen carefully, for an incongruous background can lead to violation of the important criterion of believability. The low- or medium-priced car, for example, should not be shown in exclusive surroundings because the product would seldom be found in such an environment.

The Product in Use   This is perhaps the most widely used visualization. The power of suggestion is stimulated by this means because the reader immediately identifies with the product user and becomes the recipient of its benefits.

Benefits from Product Use   This method features the positive results derived from product use. It is hoped that readers will project themselves as ones who can benefit equally, especially if they have an acute need for the product.

Dramatizing Need   Frequently the need satisfied by a product is obvious, and visual treatment would be irrelevant. In other situations, the potential customer may realize that he or she has a need for the product when it has been illustrated. Moreover, effective visualization may dramatize the solution to an obvious and known need and thereby spur the reader to take action. Scouring pads, for example, are used mostly on pots and pans, but they also can be used to clean white-sidewall tires. The reader may have experienced difficulty in cleaning white sidewalls and may have never thought of scouring pads for this purpose. A dirty tire being made white can be a powerful illustration.

Explaining Product Uses   The illustration of a scouring pad in use dramatizes multiple product uses. Frequently there is limited market knowledge of product capabilities, and customers may refuse to buy because they don't know how to use a product. If they do buy, they may use the product incorrectly and get poor results. The visual treatment can be helpful in showing details of methods of use or the procedures to be followed.

Featuring Product Details   Often the advertising theme will center around an improvement in some detail of the product or its operation. The detail may be dramatized by changing the perspective to make one part proportionately larger than others or by presenting the product from an unusual angle to call attention to that part. Other methods are to show a cross section of the product or print parts of it in color.

Dramatization of Evidence   Evidence is often the lifeblood of effective advertising. Unfortunately, advertising too frequently has been handicapped by the use of unsupported claims. Many effective illustrations are created to support claims with factual evidence.

The Comparison Technique   This method may be used to point out certain product attributes that have competitive superiority. One variation is to show "before" and "after" pictures involving use of the product. The removal of carbon from engine valves after using a brand of gasoline for 6,000 miles is an example. Another method is to compare the results of using one product with the results obtained from another.

Dramatization of the Headline   The headline and illustration are usually closely related, and the illustration can effectively strengthen the headline by communicating in a picture what the headline states in words.

The Use of Symbolism   The winged feet of Mercury symbolize speed; Uncle Sam signifies patriotism. Advertising may make effective use of symbols to associate the product or service with the basic idea conveyed. Notice how often the cross is used in advertising products with Christian religious significance.

Some Guides for Persuasive Visualization

Studies on the use of visual elements to attract and hold attention have disclosed that greatest effectiveness results when:

1. The illustration is placed in the upper part of the page instead of being positioned below the headline.
2. The illustration is the dominant element in the layout.
3. Photography is used instead of art work.
4. People or things are pictured in proper proximity.
5. The colors used are vivid.[5]

In addition, Ogilvy offers the following suggestions that can generally increase the probability of attracting and holding attention.

1. The average person now reads only four ads in a magazine; it is becoming increasingly difficult to find readers. That is why it is worth taking great pains to find a GREAT illustration.
2. Put "story appeal" in your illustration.
3. Illustrations should portray reward.
4. To attract women, show babies and women.
5. To attract men, show men.
6. Avoid historical illustrations; they don't sell.
7. Use photographs in preference to drawings. They sell more.
8. Don't deface your illustration.
9. Use captions that are written the way people talk.
10. Don't use a lot of illustrations—they look cluttered and discourage a reader.
11. Don't crop important elements in your illustration.[6]

Some advertising artists would disagree with certain of these points; others would state different ones. Each would react according to personal experience and working knowledge.

The Use of Color   There is no question that using color adds to costs of space or time, printing, and production. Advertisers have found, however, that the extra cost is well rewarded for a number of reasons:

1. The attention-attracting and attention-holding power of the message may be increased sharply.
2. Contemporary social trends have encouraged experimentation in color in all phases of life, ranging from the factory to the home. Thus people have become responsive to innovative color stimuli.

3. Most products look better in color, especially food.

4. Color can be used to create moods ranging from the somber appeal to the freshness of greens and blues.

5. Color can add an image of prestige to the advertisement, especially if most competing advertisements are in black and white.

6. Visual impressions can be retained in memory, hence resulting in greater message recall.

Numerous studies have demonstrated the attention-attracting power of color. It is, for example, the one outstanding factor in stimulating high readership of newspaper advertisements.

Skillful use of color also can set the mood for the advertisement. Connotations of various colors include:

RED:	Anger, action, fire, heat, passion, excitement, danger
BLUE:	Sadness, cool, truth, purity, formality
YELLOW:	Cheerfulness, spring, dishonesty, light, optimism
ORANGE:	Fire, heat, action, harvest, fall
GREEN:	Calm, wet, spring, youth, nature, ignorance, immaturity
BLACK:	Mystery, mourning, death, heaviness, elegance
WHITE:	Cleanliness, purity, virginity

Color reproduction techniques have reached a high degree of refinement in magazines, and newspapers have made major improvements in its use. Increasing use has been made of preprinted inserts for newspapers, and real advances are seen daily in standard newspaper color procedures (run of press color). Inks have been standardized so that the advertiser can order certain colors and expect the same result anywhere the message is run. Moreover, production improvements have served to lower costs significantly, and the differential for the addition of color is now from 5 to 10 percent in newspapers. There is little doubt that it will be used in increasing amounts in a wide variety of newspaper ads.

RADIO AND TELEVISION

COPY

The discussion to this point has been concerned with printed advertisements. It is to be expected that broadcast advertising differs in certain details. Radio has become perhaps the most informal of all media, and this informality has permeated its advertising requirements. Frequently the commercial is not written word for word but an outline is given to the announcer, who then provides words and style. Heavy use may also be made of humor and whimsy.

Ogilvy makes these suggestions for the television commercial:

1. It is easier to double the selling power of a commercial than to double the audience of a program.

2. Make your *pictures* tell the story. What you *show* is more important than what you *say*. If you can't *show* it, don't say it.

3. Try running your commercial with the sound turned off. If it doesn't sell without sound, it's a feeble commercial. Words and pictures must march together, reinforcing each other. The words in your titles must be identical with the words spoken.

4. In the best commercials the key idea is forcefully demonstrated. But in the poorest commercials there is little or *no* demonstration.

5. The best commercials are built around one or two simple ideas— *big* ideas. They are not a hodgepodge of confusing little ideas; that is why they are never created in committee. The best commercials flow smoothly, with few changes of scene.

6. The purpose of most commercials is to deliver the selling promise in the most persuasive and memorable way. State your promise at least twice in every commercial.

7. The average consumer sees ten thousand commercials a year. Make sure that she knows the name of the product being advertised in your commercial. Show the package loud and clear. Repeat the brand name as often as you can. Show the name in at least one title.

8. Good commercials rely on simple promises, potently demonstrated. But promises and demonstrations can be made tedious and indigestible by logorrhea [excessive talkativeness]. Don't drown your prospect in words.

9. Make the product itself the hero of the commercial.

10. In *print* advertising you must start by attracting the prospect's attention. But in television the prospect is *already* attending. Your problem is not to attract her attention, but to *hang on to it*.

11. *Start selling in your first frame.* Never warn the prospect that she is about to hear a "friendly word from our sponsor." Never start your commercial with an irrelevant analogy. Never start with an interrupting device.

12. Dr. Gallup reports that commercials which set up a consumer problem, then solve it with the product, then prove it, sell four times as much merchandise as commercials which simply preach about the product.

13. Dr. Gallup also reports that commercials with a news content are more effective than the average.

14. All products are not susceptible to the same commercial techniques. Sometimes there isn't any news; you cannot always use the problem-solution gambit; you cannot always demonstrate. Sometimes you must rely on *emotion* and *mood*. Commercials with a high content of emotion and mood can be very potent indeed.

15. To involve a person emotionally you should be human and *friendly*. People don't buy from salespersons who are bad-mannered. Nor do they buy from phonies or liars. Do not strain their credulity. Be believable.

16. Movie screens are forty feet across, but most TV screens are less than two. Use close-up pictures instead of long shots. You have a small screen; get some *impact* on it.

17. You cannot bore people into buying your product. You can only *interest* them in buying it. Dr. Gallup reports that prospects are bored by "sermon" commercials, in which the announcer simply yaks about the product.

18. Television commercials are not for entertaining. They are for *selling*. Selling is a serious business. Good salespersons never sing. The *spoken* word is easier to understand than the *sung* word. Speech is less entertaining than song, but more persuasive. Persuasive commercials never sing.

19. The average consumer sees more than two hundred commercials a week, nine hundred a month, ten thousand a year. For this reason you should give your commercial a touch of singularity. It should have a *burr* that will cling to the viewer's mind. But the burr must not be an irrelevance. And it must not steal attention away from the PROMISE.

20. Whenever you write a commercial, bear in mind that it is likely to be seen by your children, your spouse—and your conscience.[7]

NOTES

1. "Basic Readership Factors," internal publication of Marplan Division of the Interpublic Group of Companies, Inc., New York.

2. David Ogilvy, "Raise Your Sights! 97 Tips for Copywriters, Art Directors and TV Producers—Mostly Derived from Research" internal publication of Ogilvy, Benson, & Mather, New York. Reproduced with special permission.

3. Ibid.

4. Ibid.

5. "Basic Readership Factors."

6. Ogilvy, "Raise Your Sights!"

7. Ibid.

Analysis of Mass Media Resources*

A.C. NIELSEN CHASES THE ILLUSIVE VCR VIEWER

Marketing research giant A. C. Nielsen Co. has revealed plans to begin testing a video cassette ratings system in the fourth quarter of 1988. The test will measure audience size and accumulate demographic data; it will also gather additional information, such as whether audiences fast forward through credits and plugs for coming attractions. Home-video companies currently have only a rough idea of how many people watch their releases and of who those people are.

Ten major home-video companies have already agreed to take part in the test and will pay a small fee to have their films included in the research. Nielsen will perform the test by piggybacking the videocassette ratings system onto its existing TV-ratings system, which consists of people meters placed in 4,000 homes across the country. The people meters record what programs are being watched and which family members are watching. Approximately half of these homes have VCRs, which will be specially wired with a small box for the test.

*The authors wish to thank Mr. Bernard Guggenheim, vice president of Lintas Campbell-Ewald, for his assistance in the preparation of this chapter. Also, we wish to thank the Media Department at Leo Burnett Advertising for providing data and other assistance.

Nielsen plans to brand all copies of 25 to 30 movie titles with an invisible code that can be read by the adjusted VCRs. The machines will be able to tell what parts of the tape are—or aren't—viewed while the people-meters record who is watching the film. The machines will also gather data on what TV programs are taped, how often taped programs are watched, and whether viewers fast forward through commercials.

Home-video companies hope that advertisers will be anxious to use the data and buy advertising time on the videotapes. According to Bill Perrault, national marketing manager for the Vestron video company, Vestron is hoping to put together more promotional tie-ins like the one it produced between Nestle and the movie *Dirty Dancing*. "But in order to do all of this, consumer goods companies and ad agencies want to know what the audience is and they want to measure its demographic composition," says Perrault. "The Nielsen ratings will give them the information they're used to getting from TV ratings."

Although other companies measure videocassette use, their systems have not been widely accepted, and advertisers have been reluctant to spend money on unreliable information. "Now, commercials on videocassette are very much an event," says Paul B. Lindstrom, vice president and product manager for Nielsen's home-video unit. But with the advent of reliable ratings, "the big money is likely to really start coming in," he says.

Source: Adapted from *The Wall Street Journal* August 17, 1988, p. 21.

The ever changing world of mass media is well illustrated by the Nielsen Promotion in Action on VCR audience measurement and audience behavior. It would have been considered to be ridiculous to ever consider measuring such audiences a decade ago.

The investment of dollars in the mass media to reach the desired audience with a minimum of waste and a maximum of efficiency requires careful quantitative and qualitative analysis and selection of media vehicles. Advertisers are constantly seeking new, more efficient media to reach consumers, as the chapter's opening insert shows. This chapter describes the range of media resources—types of available media and their characteristics—and the purchase of space and time. The next two chapters cover selection of mass media (media strategy) and evaluating advertising effectiveness.

EXPENDITURE TRENDS

In 1988, the total volume of advertising in the United States exceeded the $118 billion mark for the first time in history. As Table 14–1 indicates, newspapers are the leading media type with $31.2 billion in expenditures, followed by television with over $25.7 billion, direct mail with about $21.1 billion, radio with about $7.8 billion, the Yellow Pages with about $7.8 billion, and magazines with over $6.0 billion. All media have increased in advertising expenditures over the last decade.

It should be noted that the real increase in advertising volume is concealed by the increased cost of units of advertising. If inflation is taken out, there was about a 4 percent annual gain from 1968 to 1988. Additionally, we should note that the number of physical advertising units placed in various media has increased substantially.[1] Using 1968 as a base, the number of commercial placements on television has grown about 60 percent for spot television (local TV station buys), and about 45 percent for network television. The number of different brands advertised on television has grown about 50 percent during the same period, mostly in the spot market. In radio, spot commercial units are up about 60 percent, and network radio about 40 percent since 1968. Since 1973 magazine pages of advertising are up about 12 percent for national editions and 40 percent for special (regional or demographic) editions. Outdoor poster showings are up almost 40 percent since 1969, and newspaper advertising pages have increased by about 20 percent since 1960. This increase in units placed means that the fight to get consumers' attention is becoming more difficult. It is hard to get noticed.

The trend toward increased spending is expected to continue. Total yearly advertising expenditures are expected to reach over $150 billion by 2000. Advertising as a percentage of gross national product (GNP) declined from 2.20 percent in 1963 to a low of 1.97 percent in 1976. In 1988, this percentage had risen to about 2.37 percent.

NEWSPAPERS

Newspapers have long maintained first place among all media in terms of combined national and local advertising revenues. Newspapers are for the most part a local medium with daily circulation confined to the city of publication and immediately surrounding areas. The circulation of Sunday newspapers, however, frequently is much greater, often extending beyond state boundaries. There were 1,642 daily newspapers and 840 Sunday papers in the United States in 1988.[2]

The syndicated Sunday supplement is a distinct exception of the local flavor of newspaper editorial content. *Parade* and *Family Weekly* in effect are national sections inserted in more than 300 Sunday papers. Other supple-

TABLE 14–1

❖ **Advertising Volume in the United States in 1988**

Medium	Dollars (in millions)
Newspapers	
Total	$ 31,197
National	3,586
Local	27,611
Magazines	
Total	6,072
Weeklies	2,646
Women's	1,504
Monthlies	1,922
Farm Publications	196
Television	
Total	25,686
Network	9,172
Spot (national)	7,147
Syndicated Barter (national)	901
Cable (national)	942
Spot (local)	7,207
Cable (local)	254
Radio	
Total	7,798
Network	425
Spot (national)	1,418
Spot (local)	5,955
Direct Mail	21,115
Outdoor	
Total	1,064
National	628
Local	436
Business Publications	2,610
Yellow Pages	
Total	7,781
National	944
Local	6,837
Miscellaneous	
Total	14,531
National	10,461
Local	4,070
Total	
National	65,610
Local	52,440
Grand Total	$118,050

Source: *Advertising Age,* May 15, 1989, p. 24.

ments are local in editorial content and advertising. Some offer regional editions to permit insertion of advertising in a group of cities rather than purchase of the entire circulation.

Characteristics of Newspapers

Advantages   The use of newspapers as an advertising medium has the following advantages:

1. *Broad consumer acceptance and use.* Newspapers occupy a unique place in American life, according to studies. (See Table 14–2 for details.)
   a. Daily newspaper readership is high. Newspapers are read by 64 percent of all adults in the United States, and within the top 300 markets newspaper coverage includes 87 percent of households. Over one week's time, the daily newspaper has a cumulative reach of 90 percent of all U.S. adults. (See Table 14–2, part C.)
   b. Readership is 79 percent for college graduates and 42 percent for grammar school graduates.
   c. Newspaper reading increases with income. Of those making $40,000 plus, 75 percent read newspapers daily, compared to 47 percent of those earning less than $10,000.
   d. Of the readers, most claim thorough readership.
   e. Because so many readers go through newspapers on a section-by-section basis, the average page has a 49 percent chance of being opened by men, and 51 percent by women. (See Table 14–2, part E.)
   f. Weekend readership is also high.

2. *Short closing times. Closing times* refer to the deadline prior to publication by which advertising copy must be submitted. For daily newspapers, this period seldom exceeds 24 hours, thus giving the advertiser the opportunity to make last-minute changes. Closing dates for Sunday supplements, however, are generally much longer, usually ranging from four to six weeks.

3. *Improvements in color reproduction.* Standard newspaper color printing (ROP, or run of paper) has become widely available. Papers accounting for about 90 percent of total circulation offer black and white plus one ROP color; about 70 percent offer black and white and three ROP colors. Fine shadings and pastels are now possible but, because of the porosity of newspaper stock, truly fine color reproduction is difficult. The average costs for a full-page ad with black and three colors run about 31 percent above those for black and white.

Since high-quality color is so hard to achieve with ROP, use of pre-printed color advertisements on a heavier stock of paper is increasing. This procedure, called Hi-Fi color, is available in about 90 percent of the markets and usually runs about $29 per 1,000 circulation above the cost of black and white. The chief disadvantage is that Hi-Fi methods require preprinting on a

TABLE 14-2

❖   **Newspaper Statistics**

A. Cost and Coverage Cumulated by Top Market Groups*

Market	No. of Papers	No. of Homes (000)	Total Circ. (000)	Daily Inch Rate-B/W	Cost Per Page B/W
Top 10	133	28,290	19,075	$ 7,086	$ 780,949
Top 20	250	40,297	26,348	10,146	1,162,273
Top 30	348	48,563	31,764	12,434	1,435,709
Top 40	459	54,978	35,434	14,098	1,649,683
Top 50	544	60,305	39,911	15,691	1,849,153
Top 60	649	64,869	41,667	17,033	2,021,468
Top 70	725	68,762	44,152	18,216	2,169,690
Top 80	799	72,045	46,133	19,228	2,298,634
Top 90	860	74,901	47,778	20,030	2,394,160
Top 100	922	77,356	49,395	20,782	2,490,279

*Daily newspapers in each market are included on the basis of circulation rank until the combined circulations exceed 50 percent coverage of the market.

Source: Newspaper Advertising Bureau: ANM Circulation 1988–89; Standard Rate and Data Service, December 1988.

B. Newspaper Readership (Average Weekday)

Newspaper Readership (Avg. Weekday)	Adults	Men	Women
Total	64%	66%	62%
Age			
18–24	55	58	52
25–34	59	63	55
35–44	68	69	67
45–54	70	70	70
55–64	72	75	71
65 +	65	66	64
Education			
Graduated from college	79	83	75
Attended college	70	74	67
Graduated from high school	64	65	64
Attended high school	53	54	53
Did not attend high school	42	41	43
Household Income			
$50,000 +	77	79	75
$40,000 +	75	78	72
$30,000 +	73	75	70
$20,000–29,999	63	63	63
$10,000–19,999	56	56	57
Less than $10,000	47	46	48

Source: Simmons Market Research Bureau, 1988.

TABLE 14-2

Newspaper Statistics (concluded)

C. Newspaper Reach (Adults - Avg. Top 50 Markets)

	Net Reach of Leading Weekday Newspapers	
	Largest Circulation Newspaper	Top Two Newspapers in Circulation
Metro	45%	57%
ADI (areas of dominent influence)	35	46

Source: Scarborough, 1987.

D. Newspaper Readers per Copy

	Avg. Daily Paper		Sunday/ Avg. Weekend Paper	
Age	Men	Women	Men	Women
18-24	.12	.11	.13	.12
25-34	.21	.19	.22	.22
35-44	.18	.18	.19	.20
45-54	.13	.14	.12	.14
55-64	.12	.13	.12	.14
65+	.13	.17	.12	.16
Total	.89	.92	.90	.98

Source: Simmons Market Research Bureau, 1988; 1988 *Editor & Publisher Yearbook*.

E. Newspaper Readership by Section

	Percent of All Readers Generally Read	
	Men	Women
All Sections	50%	50%
Any Section	49	51
Business	21	17
Classified	17	19
Comics	17	21
Editorial	20	25
Entertainment	19	29
Food or cooking	12	28
General news	39	43
Home	12	23
Radio-Television	14	21
Sports	31	13
Other sections	15	23
Don't know	7	7

Source: Simmons Market Research Bureau, 1988.

continuous roll of paper, and it is impossible to have the cuts coincide with the end of the copy. Creatively, this usually requires a wallpaper type of design. This problem may be eliminated, however, by the use of still another process called Spectacolor, available in approximately 25 percent of the papers and costing little more than Hi-Fi. Preprinted inserts can be prepared either on ROP stock or rotogravure or other high-quality printing processes. These inserts are provided to papers, and the advertiser pays a special rate. Again the advantage is reproduction control.

4. *Increased geographic and market flexibility.* Newspapers are increasingly recognizing that one edition for a large market is not adequate to provide full local coverage. As a result, many papers now offer zone editions. The *Chicago Tribune,* for example, offers several zone variations and supplements corresponding to suburban areas. In addition, special-interest newspapers are becoming more established. Although many underground newspapers that started during the latter part of the 1970s have folded as U.S. society has changed, others have continued to flourish and have become more commercialized.

Perhaps the most significant trend, however, is the growth of community and suburban newspapers and the further segmentation of large central-city newspapers. Also, a selling company called U.S. Suburban Press, Inc. (USSPI) has organized about 1,300 suburban papers in over 40 markets into a one-order/one-bill package, thus simplifying the buying process.

5. *Communication advantages.* The printed page is often believed to offer greater prestige and believability, perhaps based on the adage that "seeing is believing." There is no convincing research to verify this claim, but it is known that print induces superior retention of complex factual material when compared with oral presentation. Also it is believed that print forces readers to become more involved in the subject matter by allowing them to grope to understand and to evaluate. Such involvement is less evident when material is presented in spoken form.

6. *Reseller support.* Newspapers are the most used of all media for the following kinds of reseller support:

   a. Cooperative plans whereby dealers share costs.
   b. Identification and promotion of the local dealer.
   c. Promotion of quick action through coupons.
   d. Other means to enlist dealer support.

Dealer enthusiasm for this use of advertising dollars often runs high.

Disadvantages   Newspapers also have disadvantages as an advertising medium, including the following:

1. *Rate differentials.* National advertising linage in newspapers has not realized as rapid gains as local advertising has. This lag is due in part to wide differentials between local and national (nonlocal) rates, in favor of

local advertisers. As might be expected, rate differentials have been under fire. Defenders of the differentials in rates claim several justifications:

    a. National volume is not as dependable as local retail volume and therefore costs more to handle.

    b. The national competitor will have a large edge over the local counterpart and hence should be penalized.

    c. National advertisers are requesting more merchandising assistance in the form of special promotion to dealers, assistance in advertising plans, and other services.

    d. It costs more to handle national advertising. Newspapers claim that these costs are from 20–25 percent higher because the 15 percent discount is granted to agencies (this is the standard method of agency compensation), a cash discount is given, and representatives must be paid to solicit nonlocal advertising. This latter charge is also incurred for local advertising.

The first three of the claimed justifications have little basis in fact. The widespread use of newspapers by many national advertisers on a continuing basis largely removes the charge of lack of dependability; the national and local firms seldom are competitors and in fact it is more common for the national advertiser to work in partnership with local dealers; and, finally, local advertisers seldom use an agency and therefore are prone to request more in the way of special services than the national firm. The payment of agency commissions, however, and the other costs are valid reasons for a nominal differential. The problem is that the usual differential is far in excess of this justifiable amount, and most newspapers at this point seem to be unwilling to change the status quo.

    2. *Costs of national coverage.* The costs of reaching a national market through newspapers can quickly become excessive. National coverage through this medium often requires an additional expenditure of 80 percent or more in comparison with network television and magazines. However, newspapers do provide better intensity of coverage of households.

    3. *Short life.* Newspapers usually are not retained in the home for extensive periods of time. As a result, little opportunity exists for repeat exposure to advertisements. This disadvantage is shared by all media, however, with the exception of magazines.

    4. *Reproduction problems.* Newspapers, of course, are printed on an absorbent paper stock, resulting in an inability to offer fine reproduction. In addition, the speed necessary to compose a daily newspaper prevents the detailed preparation and care in production that is possible when time pressures are not so great.

    5. *Small "pass-along" audience.* Generally speaking, newspapers do not generate larger audiences through sharing of issues by purchasers often referred to as *pass-along readership.* The pass-along audience of magazines may be substantial.

Buying Newspaper Space

Newspaper rates are usually quoted in detail in volumes published period-ically by the Standard Rate and Data Service (SRDS). The basic space unit for strictly local advertising is usually the column inch. The national rate, how-ever, is quoted in terms of agate lines (14 lines represent a column inch). The newspaper page consists of from six to nine columns, approximately 300 lines deep. The total number of lines is approximately 2,400. The tabloid page consists of about 1,000 lines with five or six columns.

Published rates vary if special treatment is specified. Color, of course, always carries a premium, as does location in a specific part of the paper. Unless otherwise specified, copy will be inserted on a run-of-paper basis.

For local advertising, gross space rates are usually converted to a com-mon basis for purposes of comparison. The milline rate, widely used for this purpose, is calculated as follows:

$$\frac{Line\ rate\ \times\ 1,000,000}{Circulation}$$

Rates are compared, then, in terms of costs of the circulation that is achieved. Otherwise an extremely low line rate might be deceptive if it fails to generate adequate circulation and advertising exposure. Also, milline rates are rarely used by national advertisers. They prefer to use a rating point measure, which is the reach of the paper times the frequency of insert, relative to cost.

Recently newspapers have developed "standard advertising units" (SAUs) as a way of simplifying national advertising buys. The American Newspaper Publishers Association has been the leader in this action. There are 56 different SAUs. Most major newspapers have indicated a willingness to use such a system. SAUs, implemented in 1984, represent different sizes of ads. Thus a national advertiser could prepare one ad for insertion in over 1,300 newspapers and have rates quoted on this basis.

Also the Newspaper Advertising Bureau has developed a "Newsplan" program whereby national advertisers obtain discounts in newspapers. Eight of 10 newspapers are cooperating in this plan. Both SAUs and Newsplan await effective implementation for easy use by national advertisers.

The Future of Newspapers

There can be little doubt that newspapers will continue to be vitally important as a local advertising medium. Two major trends will probably continue.

First, and most vital to the survival of the newspaper, is the development of increased technological sophistication. More than one half of the total newspaper copy in the United States is now printed on offset presses. The use of electronic technology is also increasing. Among the new systems is one that basically consists of a typesetting computer linked to a visual display monitor. It can be used for classified and display advertising as well as news copy. Previously entered copy can be recalled directly from memory files and can be paged.

The second major trend is the segmentation and diversification of the newspaper industry with the growth of suburban and community newspapers and the publication of different sections of large central-city newspapers.

Chain-controlled newspapers are also expected to grow in importance unless the federal government decides otherwise. Other newspapers are expected to expand into national distribution, such as the *Christian Science Monitor.* However, there are logistical problems. For example, *The Wall Street Journal* transmits copy to local plants via satellite, as does the national edition of the *New York Times. USA Today* was started by Gannett as a national newspaper and continues to increase circulation, but it has failed to attract enough advertisers to show a profit.

Of special concern are newsprint shortages and rapidly increasing costs. For example, the price of newsprint has increased from $175 to over $547 per ton in just 13 years. One solution to the problem that has been foreseen by many is broadcast of the local newspaper over two-way cable television. Hard copies could be made of items of particular interest through the use of a facsimile printer linked to the set. This appears to be a long time off.

Additional future concerns and prospects for newspapers include:

1. The acceptance of SAUs and associated growth in obtaining national advertising dollars.
2. Improvement in audience research. (See Chapter 15 for details.)
3. The potential display of newspaper pages on television screens in homes through cable hookups or direct transmission.

TELEVISION

Television, a marvel of the electronic age, grew into a dynamic marketing force in less than 20 years. The type of television under consideration makes a difference in any discussion; network program advertising differs substantially from advertising on local television stations. We will center first on the characteristics of television in general and then on the use of network program advertising versus spot (local) announcements.

In 1988 there were 1,388 operating television stations in the United States. The breakdown is as follows: 545 commercial VHF stations, 508 commercial UHF stations, 119 noncommercial VHF stations, and 216 noncommercial UHF stations. Most commercial stations are network affiliated, with only about 200 operating as independents.[3]

General Characteristics of Television

Advantages   The advantages of television as an advertising medium include:

1. *The combination of sight and sound.* Television, through its combination of sight and sound, provides audiences with a unique sense of participation and reality approximating face-to-face contact. As such, it commands full attention from viewers.

The combination of sight and sound is also advantageous because of the creative flexibility offered to the advertiser. Full opportunity exists for product demonstration and the amplification of selling points with audio presentation. In addition, color telecasting has the advantages of greater emotional impact and presentation of appetite appeal. Of the more than 90.4 million U.S. households now equipped with television, about 97 percent have color sets. About 8.7 million color sets are now in U.S. households, including some households with more than one color set. Of all television households, 63 percent have more than one set. Fifty-three percent of television households receive cable television programming.[4]

2. *Mass audience coverage.* Television is now in 97 percent of all 92 million plus U.S. households. Recent studies indicate that during an average day, 92 percent of these households will be exposed to television programming, and in the space of a week, this percentage reaches 98 percent. The average viewing time per day per television household is 7 hours and 2 minutes.[5] During an average week, the average television viewing time per television household is over 49 hours. Television is truly a *mass* medium. Table 14–3 presents a more detailed look at television viewing by providing data on some demographic characteristics of viewers by times of the day. Note that viewing is slightly less in higher income groups and among working women relative to other women.

3. *The psychology of attention.* The television viewer is in a sense a captive before his or her set. Most viewers give way to inertia and watch commercials rather than exert the effort to change the set to other program material. From this it can be inferred that they will be consciously exposed to a majority of advertising messages, with the result that at least one hurdle to promotional response is cleared. It must not be concluded, however, that exposure necessarily means favorable response. Response can be modified by the mechanisms of viewer's selective perception and retention discussed in earlier chapters. Low-involvement learning assigns television advertising even more power due to its ability to affect cognitive structure.

4. *Favorable consumer reaction.* Television is still a very popular medium with Americans. However, the percentage of households watching television over the last decade, especially network programming, has eroded. Using an index of 100 based on the percentage of households

TABLE 14–3

Television Viewing

Hours of TV Usage per Week

	Monday–Sunday			Monday–Friday	
	7-Day 24-Hr. Total	8:00– 11:00 P.M.	11:30 P.M. 1:00 A.M.	10:00 A.M. 4:30 P.M.	4:30– 7:30 P.M.
All Households	49.28	12.33	2.99	8.91	6.86
Households $30M+	47.29	12.49	3.01	7.76	6.34
Total Men	27.67	8.45	2.00	3.28	3.50
Men 18–49	24.83	7.51	2.05	3.33	2.77
Men $30M+ HH	23.26	7.81	1.82	2.02	2.73
Total Women	32.84	9.29	1.85	6.18	4.62
Women 18–49	29.18	8.23	1.99	5.23	3.63
Women $30M+ HH	26.92	8.38	1.71	4.43	3.60
Women employed	26.68	8.35	1.91	3.38	3.34
Women with children	30.58	8.39	2.01	5.98	3.78
Teens 12–17	23.42	6.66	1.35	3.54	3.74
Children 2–11	23.59	5.44	0.65	4.33	3.89

Source: A. C. Nielsen, *National Audience Demographics Report,* 1988 Average.

Households Using Television (Percent of U.S. TV Homes)

Monday–Friday	Oct.–Dec. 1987	Jan.–Mar. 1988	Apr.–June 1988	July–Sept. 1988	Oct.–Sept. Avg. Month
7:00–8:00 A.M. (ET)	19	20	19	16	19
8:00–10:00 A.M.	22	24	22	21	22
10:00–12:00 Noon	23	26	22	24	24
12:00 Noon–2:00 P.M.	28	31	26	29	29
2:00–4:00 P.M.	29	32	28	30	30
4:00–6:00 P.M.	38	41	35	35	37
6:00–7:00 P.M.	54	57	47	47	51
Monday–Sunday					
7:00–8:00 P.M.	58	61	41	48	52
8:00–9:00 P.M.	63	65	48	52	57
9:00–10:00 P.M.	63	65	53	56	59
10:00–11:00 P.M.	58	59	50	53	55
11:00–12:00 Midnight	41	42	41	41	41
12:00 Midnight–1:00 A.M.	24	25	29	26	26

Source: A. C. Nielsen, *Households Using Television Summary Report,* 1987/88.

watching television in 1977/78, the prime time percentage of households watching fell to 75, and the day network to 85 in 1987/88.[6]

Disadvantages Television also has certain disadvantages that affect its choice as an advertising medium:

1. *Negative evaluations.* There has been a growing tendency for programs to include more explicit sexual behavior and dialogue, more realistic violence, and free use of curses and vulgarity. Some groups have organized boycotts of sponsors they believe are supporting these shows.

2. *Nonselectivity.* Although there may be growing selectivity among television watchers, it is still difficult to reach precisely a small market segment using television as the medium. Variations in program content and broadcast time will obviously achieve some selectivity, especially through children's programs, sports programs with masculine appeal, or late-night talk shows, but more precise segmentation in terms of age, income, and interest is practically impossible on broadcast television. Cable television (CATV) may eventually allow for such segmentation if it continues to develop, as many expect it will. This is discussed further in the section on the future of television.

3. *Fleeting impression.* The television message crosses the viewer's consciousness only momentarily and then is lost. If for some reason the message did not register, the promotional opportunity has been lost. The opportunity does exist for reexposure, however, through multiple commercials over a period of time.

4. *Commercial clutter.* Once a problem chiefly in spot (local) television, the common use of 30-second and 15-second commercials, along with participatory buying by advertisers, has resulted in a greater number of different commercial messages in each program. The competition in each commercial break combined with the shorter time used in developing and communicating the message has many advertisers worried about the persuasive effectiveness of the commercial—the fear of being lost in the crowd.

5. *"Promo" clutter.* Another aspect of the general clutter problem relates to the networks' increased amount of hyping of their own shows. Again, getting one's message through to the consumer is made more difficult.

The Network Television Program

Networks are dominant in television for the reason that they originate most of the popular programs. The networks are confederations of stations in which each one is compensated at the rate of 30 percent of the gross commercial rate for programs carried in its area. Although it is assumed that each station will air most network shows, the station is free to originate local programming if a greater profit can be made.

Several smaller networks also offer shows on a regional or selective programming basis. The Hughes Sports Network makes available to subscribing stations coverage of sports events not covered by the major networks. The Christian Broadcasting Network, with headquarters in Portsmouth, Virginia, includes several stations nationwide that operate on a nonprofit basis to broadcast a wide variety of religious programming. Metromedia owns six television stations that compete with the major networks in New York and several other large metropolitan areas. The Fox Network represents a very real attempt to forge a fourth major network with its own first-run programming. Its success is still in doubt. In addition, the big three networks' share of the evening viewership fell from 90 percent in 1979 to 64 percent in 1989. The growing power of independent stations and cable programming is evident.

A recent development in the use of transmission by satellite was made by Turner Broadcasting's WTBS Atlanta, WGN Chicago, and WWOR New York. They are transmitting their own shows to cable systems in other regions of the country and have earned the name "superstations." Further, Home Box Office (a division of Time, Inc.) and others transmit "pay" movies and other events via satellite to cable operators for sale to connected households.

Advantages of Purchasing Network Time   The advantages of network television programming as a medium for advertising include:

1. *Excellent time availability.* The networks have virtual control over the prime-time programming (8–11 P.M. New York time). Federal Communication Commission (FCC) rulings regarding access to prime time put some limitations on network programming during that period, but the advertiser who wishes to reach a truly vast, nationwide audience at one time must necessarily buy time from the networks during prime-time hours.

2. *Simplicity of arrangements.* The time purchase is greatly simplified when network television is used. The mechanics of purchasing spot time can become exceedingly cumbersome and costly.

Disadvantages of Purchasing Network Time   The disadvantages of network time also must be considered:

1. *Costs.* Network television advertising is precluded for many because of the costs, although local spot announcements often can be purchased in network service times. In addition, commitments must be made well in advance, and modifications can be made only with great difficulty.

2. *Availabilities.* Even if smaller companies could come up with the money to buy prime time on network television, they might find it quite difficult to find time available, especially on highly rated programs. This situation may have eased to some extent with the virtual end of sole sponsorship

of any program by a single advertiser, but competition for the best programs still exists.

3. *Program mortality.* The rate of program mortality is traditionally high each season. There is no good way to determine in advance the probable success of a program, and too often time buys must be made on the basis of educated guesses. This is another reason why sponsorship of a single program has been largely replaced by time buying on a participating basis. The now-common network practice of program stunting, which uses specials and miniseries, has made the estimating process even more difficult.

4. *Variations in program popularity.* A program with a rating of 36 in one market (36 percent viewership) may produce a rating of only 10 in another market. The advertiser's market potential would match variations in program popularity only by accident, with the result that dollars can become allocated in such a way that potentials are not paralleled. A similar situation can result when program popularity does not parallel distribution. Occasionally, it is possible to purchase only part of the national coverage of a program, but this flexibility is the exception rather than the rule. To help deal with this problem, the Lintas Campbell-Ewald advertising agency developed a computer-based time-sharing system to facilitate the analysis and auditing of alternative network television schedules on a market-by-market basis.

Buying Network Time

Network time is quoted at varying rates, depending on the time of the day and season of the year. Prime-time rates are most expensive, of course. Approximately 65 percent of all stations are members of the National Association of Broadcasters (NAB), which permits its members to air commercials within the following guidelines:

1. *Commercials.* 9 1/2–12 minutes per hour in prime time and 16 minutes per hour in nonprime time. On children's weekend programs, 12 minutes per hour.

2. *Number of interruptions.*
   a. Prime time—two per 30-minute program; four per 60-minute program; and five per 60-minute variety show.
   b. Nonprime time—four per 30-minute period; one per 5-minute period; two per 10-minute program; and two per 15-minute program.
   c. Number of consecutive announcements—four for program interruptions and three per station break.

3. *Multiple-product announcements.* There is a 60-second minimum on multiple-product announcements unless they are so well integrated as to appear to the viewer as a single announcement. Local retailers are excluded from this rule. The NAB guidelines are usually followed, although NBC

added three minutes of commercial time to the "Tonight" show and 20 additional commercial seconds between 10 of its prime-time shows, to allow 62-second station breaks.[7]

The standing of the NAB code has been put in an uncertain state by a 1982 Federal district court ruling in the *United States* v. *National Association of Broadcasters* case. The government challenged four major NAB code provisions:

A limit on the amount of commercial material per hour.

A limit on the number of commercial interruptions per program.

A limit on the number of consecutive announcements per interruption.

A prohibition on the advertisement of two or more products in a single commercial if the spot is less than 60 seconds.

The court ruled that these provisions were a violation of the "conspiracy to restrain trade" provisions of the Sherman Anti-Trust Act. Rather than appeal this ruling, NAB agreed with the Justice Department in November 1982 to drop its guidelines. However, in the short run, major changes in commercial time and placement are not likely to occur because networks and local stations enforce their own codes that resemble the former NAB guidelines.

Because of the escalating costs of advertising, most television time is purchased on a participating plan by which program costs are shared by other advertisers. The 30-second commercial dominates, comprising 60 percent of all network advertising (up from 20 percent in 1970 and down from 74 percent in 1986). The average 30-second prime-time network television time slot in 1989 cost about $120,000, and daytime slots cost about $12,700. A 30-second slot on a top-rated prime-time series cost $225,000, whereas low-rated slots averaged $55,000. A 30-second slot on the 1989 Super Bowl cost $750,000. Obviously, these latter slots are not for the weak of budget. A widely used method of cost comparison is cost per 1,000 homes (CPM), which is based on the cost of the commercial time and the program ratings. Comparative numbers are presented in Table 14–6 at the end of the chapter.

Spot Announcements

Spot announcements are commercials shown on local stations, with the time purchased directly from the local stations involved. The network is not involved at all. Many of the disadvantages of network television can be overcome through use of spot announcements on local television stations purchased on a market-by-market (nonnetwork) basis. Time availabilities generally range from 10-second IDs (station identification breaks) to a full 60 seconds, although 30-second spots predominate.

Advantages of Spot Television   The use of spot announcements on television has some advantages for the advertiser:

1. *Geographic and time flexibility.* A key problem of purchasing network program time is the commitment to appear in nearly all markets where the program is aired even though market potentials may differ. Spot announcements are an effective alternative when the creative advantages of television are desired. Total costs are usually reduced through minimization of waste coverage.

2. *Reseller support.* Spot television also offers one of the advantages of newspapers in that it can be used effectively in cooperative advertising programs, for identification of local dealers, and in other ways to achieve dealer support.

Disadvantages of Spot Television   The disadvantages of spot announcements include:

1. *Chaotic buying procedures.* When local time is purchased, the buying situation can become chaotic. There is little uniformity in rates or in quantity discount plans. In addition, favored advertisers receive desirable time periods, and a personal relationship and difficult negotiations may be necessary to achieve the best time purchase. Firms representing many stations, such as the well-known Katz Agency, simplify these problems, but the difficulties remain so great that there is no shortcut to long experience in time buying.

2. *Commercial clutter.* An excess of commercials seems to be a problem for television in general, but the volume of nonprogram material appearing in station breaks is a real headache for the industry. Talent credits and announcements appear as trailers on network programs, several commercials are aired in the station break, and time must still be left for station identification and introduction of the next program. Not surprisingly, lower recall of brand advertising occurs when station-break commercials are used.

3. *Viewing at station-break periods.* It is well-known that the number of viewers declines during station breaks. Some leave the room, and the attention of those who remain is frequently attracted elsewhere. The total audience and viewer attention at station breaks may not be optimum.

Buying Spot Time

The purchase of network time involves only one contact; arrangements are considerably more difficult when local stations are used. The buyer either writes, teletypes, or telephones the station or its representative to request information on available time slots. These availabilities are then checked and communicated to the buyer, usually within 24 hours. The local stations guarantee protection in that advertisements for competing products normally will not be aired within 15 minutes of each other, but this practice is rapidly disappearing.

The listing of availabilities is always in writing, and a guarantee is given that the first buyer to make a request gets the time slot. Once the decision is made, the order is usually submitted by telephone and later verified in writing.

Costs are always quoted on a spot-by-spot basis, usually related to the time of day. Prime evening time usually carries the highest price and runs from 8 to 11 P.M. in all areas except the central time zone, where all classifications are one hour earlier. Stations affiliated with the network also quote fringe evening time from 6 to 7:30 P.M. and from 11 P.M. to 1 A.M. Daytime runs from sign-on to 5 P.M., Monday through Friday. In addition, it is common to quote a lower rate if the buyer is willing to run the risk that a competing buyer may later preempt the time spot. If one pays the full price, however, the buyer is guaranteed the time, and it is becoming increasingly common to reserve and hold desirable times over long periods by this means.

Most stations later verify, based on the program log, that the commercial actually was run. Following submission of this affidavit, the time bills become due. Third-party monitoring organizations such as Comtrac can be contracted to tape the broadcast to provide verification.

It is obvious that spot-time buying can be complex, and most agencies have specialists in this field. In addition, these complexities have been instrumental in the formation of specialized media-buying services. In order to manage the paperwork, many agencies are utilizing the computer, their own and that of service companies such as Donavan Data Systems.

The Future of Television

Several specific issues promise to bring about changes in television programming and advertising: (1) the growth of cable television (CATV), (2) videocassette recorder/players, (3) changes in network programming, and (4) overcommercialization. These issues are discussed below.

CATV The continued growth and sophistication of cable television may well have a dramatic effect on the television industry, dependent on the rulings and guidelines created by the FCC. The major function of CATV in its early days was to bring the regularly scheduled programs of commercial stations to areas beyond the range of their broadcast signals. Subscribers who formerly had poor reception and limited channel selection could, with cable hookups, receive clear pictures and a wide variety of channel selections. Now cable serves as an alternative to standard television by offering specialty channels such as movies, sports (ESPN—the sports network), Turner Broadcasting's 24-hour Cable Network News (CNN), music, and so on. (See Table 14–4, part C.) In 1988, there were about 8,500 operating systems reaching over 48 million subscribers, or 53.8 percent of television households.

Another attractive opportunity to CATV operators is pay television, which involves attaching to the subscriber's set a device that makes certain the pay TV broadcasts are impossible to view without the payment of a separate fee beyond the monthly subscription charge. This system would make possible truly specialized programming since only those subscribers who specifically decide to watch a particular program and are willing to pay a fee to do so will be in the viewing audience. If commercial time is made available, the segmentation potential could be at least equal to that of the magazine. Even without pay television, more precise segmentation should be possible once CATV begins to produce its own programs. Pay cable is on about 4,400 systems and reaches 28.1 million subscribers in 50 states.

Perhaps the most interesting recent development in TV technology is the Qube system, which is currently in test in Columbus, Ohio. Qube, which is owned by Warner Communications, offers the standard CATV services plus special stations with all-day children's programming, live nightclub shows, concerts, theater, and a 24-hour news station. In addition, Qube is set apart by offering viewers the ability to react to programs by pressing a button on an in-home control panel. At a designated moment, viewers push specific buttons to vote to rate shows, guess what play a football coach will call, and so forth. The results are put on the screen within 10 seconds. The potential to display ads and have viewers order products from their homes is also being developed.

The net result of the growth in CATV will be a fragmentation of the network and spot television audience, plus a decrease in audience size, with potential negative consequences on advertising revenues. However, for the cable networks to survive, they must also draw advertising revenues. To get these revenues, they must provide audience measurement numbers. Recently, ESPN and CNN both used A. C. Nielsen's Home Video Index to establish their audience sizes. The development of audience measurement techniques for CATV will be a major thrust of media researchers in the next few years.

Videocassette Recorders/Players   The use of videocassettes based on the same operating principles as cassette tape players is now common. Many companies are now marketing videocassette machines. In 1988, over 9 million videocassette recorder/players were sold, up from 1.6 million in 1981. The videorecorder releases viewers from the fixed time schedules for programs (time shifting). It is expected to greatly affect television viewing habits and to cause great problems for those attempting to measure the size of audiences of television programs. A show may be watched at any time using this system, since the viewer can automatically record any program for

TABLE 14-4

Cable Television Facts

A. NTI Sample: Cable Penetration by Market Divisions

	Cable	Pay Cable
Total U.S.	57%	31%
County Size		
A	51	33
B	64	33
C & D	59	26
Nonadults		
None	55	26
Any	60	39
Age of HOH		
Under 50	59	37
50+	55	23
HH Income		
LT $30M	53	24
$40M+	63	41
$50M+	63	42
No. of TVs		
1	52	24
2+	61	36

Source: NTI, *Cable TV: A Status Report,* November 1988.

B. Cable and Pay Cable Penetration

Year	Number* of Systems	Cable TV Homes†		Pay Cable Homes	
		Millions	% U.S.	Millions	% U.S.
1960	640	0.7	1.0	—	—
1970	2,490	4.5	7.5	—	—
1975	3,506	9.2	13.2	—	—
1980	4,225	17.7	22.6	7.6	9.8
1981‡	4,375	23.1	28.3	12.1	14.9
1982	4,825	29.2	35.0	17.1	20.5
1983	5,600	34.1	40.5	20.3	24.2
1984	6,200	37.3	43.7	21.7	25.6
1985	6,600	39.9	46.2	22.7	26.4
1986	7,500	42.2	48.1	23.1	26.4
1987	7,900	45.0	50.5	23.7	26.8
1988	8,500	48.6	53.8	28.1	31.1

* January of each year.

† November of each year.

‡ Change in Nielsen method for estimating cable homes.

Sources: A. C. Nielsen Cable Universe Estimates; NTI, *Cable TV: A Status Report;* and *Television & Cable Factbook.*

TABLE 14-4

❖

Cable Television Facts (continued)

C. Satellite-Fed Cable Services

Superstations	Subscriber HH (000)	Affiliates
WTBS	45,718	8,171
WGN	24,900	11,000
WWOR	12,302	2,499
WPIX	9,678	858
Pay Cable		
Home Box Office	15,900	7,400
Showtime	6,300	6,000
Cinemax	5,100	3,650
The Disney Channel	3,810	5,000
The Movie Channel	2,600	3,250
Basic Cable		
ESPN	47,800	9,500
CNN	46,238	11,860
USA Network	45,200	10,100
MTV	42,700	5,010
CBN Family Channel	41,642	8,215
Nickelodeon	41,200	6,195
The Nashville Network	41,051	7,335
Lifetime	40,800	3,600
C-SPAN	39,200	3,014
Nick at Night	36,400	3,285
The Weather Channel	36,100	3,240
Arts & Entertainment	36,000	2,600
The Discovery Channel	35,800	3,567
Headline News	32,693	3,228
Financial News Network	31,000	3,500
Video Hits One	27,900	2,140
Black Entertainment Television	20,000	1,200
Cable Value Network	20,000	1,850
FNN/Score	19,800	1,150
Turner Network Television	17,040	1,279
Home Shopping Network	16,059	1,396
C-SPAN II	15,400	539
The Learning Channel	12,800	930
QVC Network	12,600	931
FNN/Tel-Shop	11,000	950
The Travel Channel	11,000	300
The Inspirational Network	10,500	950
Silent Network	10,300	380
Eternal Word Television Network	10,100	461
The Fashion Channel	10,100	600
Country Music Television	8,000	862
Tempo Television	8,000	700
ACTS Satellite Network	8,000	365
Trinity Broadcasting Network	8,000	650

Source: *CableVision*, December 5, 1988.

TABLE 14-4

Cable Television Facts (continued)   ❖

D. Top 20 Designated Metropolition Area (DMA) Cable Markets

DMA	Cable Homes	Percent of TV Homes
New York	3,308,350	47.8
Los Angeles	2,231,670	46.5
Philadelphia	1,458,100	55.9
Boston	1,310,160	63.5
Chicago	1,264,410	40.7
San Francisco-Oakland	1,245,460	57.5
Detroit	816,980	48.2
Pittsburgh	783,190	66.5
Washington, D.C.	762,680	45.8
Seattle-Tacoma	753,620	60.1
Cleveland	737,780	51.3
Tampa-St. Petersburg	734,090	57.6
Miami-Ft. Lauderdale	699,370	56.0
Dallas-Ft. Worth	689,100	41.4
Hartford & New Haven	685,610	77.5
Houston	649,430	45.4
Atlanta	634,690	47.9
San Diego	590,890	70.5
Minneapolis/St. Paul	536,480	42.1
Orlando/Daytona	519,250	63.0

Source: A. C. Nielsen Cable Universe Estimates, November 1988.

E. Top 10 Cable Markets

Market	Cable Penetration (% of TV Homes)
Palm Springs	85.4
San Angelo	84.2
Santa Barbara-Santa Maria-San Luis Obispo	84.0
Victoria	82.5
Laredo	82.3
Biloxi-Gulfport	80.0
Honolulu	78.9
Hartford & New Haven	77.5
Eureka	77.5
Ft. Myers-Naples	76.9

Source: A. C. Nielsen Cable Universe Estimates, November 1988.

future viewing even if he or she is not at home. Prerecorded videotapes of movies and sports events are also available at prices between $10 and $80, or rental in the $1 to $5 range. Recorded television shows also give the viewer the ability to speed through the commercials in the program. They are able to "zap" the commercials while recording or playing back tapes. See the insert in this section. See the Promotion in Action at the beginning of this chapter for a description of Nielsen's attempt to measure VCR viewership.

Changes in Network Programming All of the developments discussed above would have a bearing on network programming. The major trend

TABLE 14–4

❖

Cable Television Facts (concluded)

F. Top 20 VCR Markets

Market	VCR Penetration (% of TV Homes)
Anchorage	84.3
Fairbanks	78.9
Las Vegas	74.3
Los Angeles	72.4
San Francisco-Oakland-San Jose	71.7
San Diego	71.4
Chicago	69.9
Reno	69.6
Sacramento-Stockton	69.3
New York	68.7
Atlanta	68.1
Boise	67.8
Honolulu	67.8
Washington, D.C.	67.7
Fresno-Visalia	67.6
Tyler	67.6
Dallas-Ft. Worth	67.2
Baltimore	66.7
Boston	66.3
Phoenix	66.2
Monterey-Salinas	66.2

Source: A. C. Nielsen VCR Penetration Estimates, November 1988.
Source: *Leo Burnett 1989 Media Costs and Coverage.*

created by the pressures of CATV and disk or tape systems would be toward more specialized programming, which would be necessary to fit into more selective viewing patterns. It has been predicted that the time spent watching television will continue to grow with increases in the number of television sets within each household. Since virtually each family member will have his or her own set, however, each will seek to watch a program conforming to his or her own interests. The decision will no longer have to be a compromise of family interests. Television ratings on individual programs will drop as the audience becomes segmented, and eventually television programming may well become similar to that of radio. Due to a more highly segmented audience, the cost per thousand individuals will probably increase, but the cost per thousand *prospects* should remain about the same or decline. There will be movement in this direction for the next few years, but broadcasting as it is today will probably persist for quite some time. Eventually, however, broadcasting may come to be referred to as *narrowcasting* to a highly segmented audience.

Overcommercialization   Many individuals believe that overcommercialization is already a very serious problem, especially during station breaks and local programming. With the growing use of 15-second commercials, split 30s, participating sponsorship, and multiple-product announcements, the situation on network television has also rapidly grown more cluttered. Clutter will probably be reduced through a growth of new stations and multiset ownership, which fosters expansion of local programming to segment target audiences, commercials customized to local market needs, and local service programming. For a while, though, the advertiser is going to have to compete with a clutter of other commercials to gain viewers' attention.

Overall, the future of television is one of great changes brought on by technology. The impact on advertising will be great in the long run.

RADIO

Radio, once considered to be a dying medium following the rise of television, has come back to exert a dynamic and vigorous competitive challenge. To underscore the extent of change, it has become almost totally a local medium, whereas it was dominated by networks prior to the onset of television. Moreover, there are more than four times more stations on the air today than in 1945. Radio networks came to exist primarily to feed newscasts to local stations and a limited variety of additional programs. Recently, however, network radio has come back to attain high listening levels. (See Table 14–5, part C.) The number of networks has grown from 4 in 1970 to 24 in 1988. In addition, FM radio, an unknown in 1945, has risen to over 90 percent penetration of U.S. homes and offers a new resource to the advertiser.

Characteristics of Radio

Advantages   Radio as an advertising medium has a number of advantages, including the following:

1. *The mass use of radio.* Of the over 528 million sets in use, 165 million are car radios, and 363 million are in homes. In 1988 there were 4,902 commercial AM stations, 4,041 commercial FM stations, and 1,301 noncommercial FM stations.

The availability of transistorized portable sets has enabled radio to become a medium that can be used anywhere. Within one week's time, radio will reach 95 percent of all people 12 and over in the United States. (See Table 14–5, part C, for details and other radio-listening facts.) In fact, during a single week, radio will reach well over 90 percent of all sex and age demographic segments of the United States. The exception is 6- to 11-year-olds, where reach is about 70 percent.

2. *Selectivity.* Radio has become a selective medium because local stations have differentiated the program formats to appeal to various consumer segments. As a result, it is possible to reach nearly any class of consumer in most markets. Of course, geographic flexibility has long been a strength of radio, as is true of all local media.

3. *Speed and flexibility.* Of all media, radio has the shortest closing period, in that copy can be submitted up to air time. This flexibility has been capitalized on by many advertisers. For example, quite a few travel-related companies found the radio to be helpful in keeping their potential customers aware of the effects of the weather and encouraging them to still use their services.

4. *Low costs.* For an expenditure of under $100 in most markets, any advertiser can purchase air time. Of all media, its cost per time unit ranks among the lowest.

5. *Favorable psychological effect.* Although the evidence is not unequivocal, there is some basis to the claim that there may be less resistance to persuasion over radio because many activities are directed by spoken word. Radio has also been found to produce greater retention of simple material than print, especially among the least educated. Finally, radio is easily attended to with little psychological resistance, but this casual attention can be a disadvantage when radio serves as musical background for other activities.

TABLE 14–5

Radio-Listening Facts

A. Percent Listening during Average Quarter Hour (Monday–Sunday)

	Men		Women		Teens
Daypart	18+	18–49	18+	18–49	12–17
6 A.M.–10 A.M.	20	20	20	20	12
10 A.M.–3 P.M.	19	21	19	20	9
3 P.M.–7 P.M.	16	18	15	16	14
7 P.M.–12 Midnight	8	9	7	8	13
Avg. 6 A.M.–12 Midnight	16	17	15	16	12

Source: RADAR, Fall 1988.

B. Percent Listening by Location (Monday–Sunday)

	In-home			Out-of-home Auto			Out-of-home Non-auto		
Daypart	Men	Women	Teens	Men	Women	Teens	Men	Women	Teens
6 A.M.–10 A.M.	41	67	75	31	15	15	27	18	10
10 A.M.–3 P.M.	25	44	54	27	18	21	48	38	26
3 P.M.–7 P.M.	28	44	61	41	31	22	31	25	18
7 P.M.–12 Midnight	54	67	74	27	20	14	19	12	12
Avg. 6 A.M.–12 Midnight	34	54	66	31	20	18	34	26	16

Source: RADAR, Fall 1988.

C. Potential Radio Audience

	Monday–Sunday, 6 A.M.–12 Midnight					
	Cumulative Audience			Avg. Qtr. Hour Audience		
	Men	Women	Adults	Men	Women	Adults
Total Radio						
Number (000)	81,899	88,061	169,960	13,311	13,825	27,136
Population percent	96	95	95	16	15	15
Network Radio						
Number (000)	68,378	71,609	139,987	7,860	7,934	15,794
Population percent	80	77	79	9	9	9

Source: RADAR, Fall, 1988.
Source: *Leo Burnett 1989 Media Costs and Coverage.*

6. *Reseller support.* Radio, along with newspapers and spot television, is also used on occasion with effective results to stimulate dealer cooperation and selling support.

Disadvantages Counteracting the advantages of radio as an advertising medium are these disadvantages:

1. *The nature of the message.* Of course, radio permits only audio presentation, a disadvantage for products requiring demonstration, the impact of color, or the other features of visual media. Furthermore, the impression made is momentary, and, as with television, it is impossible to reexpose the prospect except through multiple commercials over a period of time.

2. *Chaotic buying.* Spot radio and spot television share the disadvantage of chaotic and nonstandardized rate structures and the bookkeeping problems connected with the purchase of time. Once again, however, large-station representatives have simplified arrangements.

3. *Costs for national coverage.* As with all local media, the costs of national coverage can become substantial. Use can be made, of course, of network radio, and mass coverage is hereby achieved much more economically.

4. *Station fragmentation.* Unless substantial investments are made, it is difficult to achieve high levels of reach among mass audiences because of multiple-station fragmentation.

Spot and network radio rates are published by Standard Rate and Data Service. For stations subscribing to the code of the National Association of Broadcasters, 14 minutes of commercial time are permitted for each hour computed on a weekly basis, and the number of commercials is never to exceed 18 per hour or 5 per 15-minute segment. Many stations do not subscribe to the code, which is not binding, and offer a greater frequency of commercial time, much to the dismay of the advertising critics. This may be limited in the future by the Federal Communication Commission, which is now taking the position that licenses will not be renewed when stations broadcast commercials more than 18 minutes per hour for more than 10 percent of the broadcast day.

As with television, radio rates are differentiated into prime and secondary time. In radio, however, prime time covers the morning wake-up period and late afternoon drive-home time, when the most sets, especially car radios, are in use. The units of time available range from a few seconds to 60 seconds, thus affording great flexibility.

The cost per thousand homes reached is computed in a manner similar to that described for television. Although the accurate computation of network program ratings used to be difficult, RADAR (Radio All-Dimension Audience Research) was established in 1967 to help alleviate this problem, and the data on radio audiences available through RADAR are not too different from the Nielsen television ratings. Market-by-market audience information is available from the Arbitron Company. (See Chapter 15 for details.)

The Future of Radio

Radio may be characterized in the future by increasing network participation, more specialization, and further growth of AM and FM stereo. Network radio appears to be making somewhat of a comeback. CBS recently started the CBS Mystery Theater, and other old programs are growing increasingly popular when aired over local stations. Though this particular trend may be part of the overall mood of nostalgia, network radio is again exerting a greater influence through news and public affairs programming and giving advertisers more of a chance at national coverage.

Radio is one of the most segmented of the media. The ABC radio network is actually a combination of seven basic networks: contemporary, information, rock, talk, direction, entertainment, and FM. Almost every major market has an all-news station such as WBBM, Chicago, and some advertisers expect that eventually there will be nationally recognized frequencies where anyone in the major market areas of the country could turn for news, weather, or public affairs.

The growth and specialization of FM is expected to continue. AM-FM radios are already standard equipment on some automobiles, and the commercial production of radio sets that will handle only one band is expected to decrease rapidly. FM stereo is expected to achieve a much better market share over AM radio. This has caused a major thrust among some AM stations to broadcast in stereo. Regulations that prevented this have been dropped.

It is also expected that cable television may draw some audience away from radio in two ways: (1) new cable network will compete for some of radio's selective audience and (2) music-oriented cable presentations (MTV) will also compete.

MAGAZINES

Magazines have long been a significant medium and continue to show vitality, in spite of problems with paper shortages and postage rates increases. Magazines today reach nearly all market segments and cover a variety of special interests such as boating and photography. Some mass circulation periodicals continue to exhibit health despite the problems they face. There are about 2,422 consumer/farm magazines, and 5,000 business magazines.

Characteristics of Magazines

Advantages   The advantages of magazines as an advertising medium include:

1. *High geographic and demographic selectivity.* Once a nonselective mass medium, consumer magazines have attained a high degree of geographic selectivity. It is now possible to purchase one or more of 145 regional or demographic editions of *Better Homes and Gardens,* 301 editions of *Time,* 81 editions of *TV Guide,* and 70 editions of *Reader's Digest.* Twelve different consumer magazines with circulations ranging from 1.8 to 18.8 million offer 50 or more regional and demographic editions. Of 76 of the best-known consumer magazines in the United States, only 24 do not have any regional or demographic editions. Small premiums are usually charged for regional or demographic advertising, but the increased efficiency of the advertisement in reaching prospects usually is worthwhile. The magazine also becomes more an option for advertisers, such as banking institutions, that serve only a limited regional market.

Demographic flexibility has long been a major virtue of consumer magazines. Appeal can be made to distinct groups of buyers with special interests, and virtually any segment of the market in terms of age, income, or other demographic variables can be reached with a minimum of waste circulation. The editorial content of the publication is also tailored to the interests of the audience being reached so that the advertising is usually received by the consumer in a receptive mood. Figure 14–1 presents a description of demographic editions of *Time.* One may also buy so-called *magazine networks,* which are groups of magazines. One example is the City News Urban group composed of *Newsweek, Time,* and *Sports Illustrated.*

2. *The receptivity of magazine audiences.* Magazine readers appear more receptive to advertising than do television viewers. Younger segments of the audience also find magazine advertising more believable than the commercials they see on television. In the business press area, readers often read ads to stay on top of new developments in products.

3. *Long life of a magazine issue.* Syndicated research indicates that there are between three and four adult readers for the average magazine issue and that the reader takes more than three days to read the magazine and devotes 60 to 90 minutes to do so.[8]

Other advantages include (1) the selection of editorial content to match the nature of the advertising message and (2) the ability to reproduce ads in high-quality color.

The increased reading of magazines by those in upper income and educational levels is well established in survey findings and widely accepted as fact. The reach to prime prospects can be maximized by using the right publication for the purpose or, in some cases, a demographically selective edition of a popular magazine reaching many different groups of people.

Disadvantages   The disadvantages of magazines include (1) their inability to demonstrate the product in action, (2) their unintrusiveness relative to television and radio, (3) their limitation on geographic flexibility relative to television and radio, (4) their inability to display sound and motion, and (5) the lower levels of reach that go with repeated buys in a group of magazines compared to newspaper, television, and radio.

FIGURE 14–1

Example of a Special Edition of a General Magazine

Magazines can also be expensive. For example, the cost of a four-color page in the following magazines in 1989 was: *National Geographic,* $139,280; *People,* $75,485; *Scientific American,* $24,450; *TV Guide,* $104,600; *Business Week,* $49,760; *Time,* $120,130; *Good Housekeeping,* $95,105; *Self,* $30,550; *Vogue,* $34,010; *Road & Track,* $35,705; and *Sports Illustrated,* $101,760.

The Future of Magazines

The immediate future should see the continued growth of special-interest and special-audience magazines and continued difficulties on the part of magazines for general readership. The growth of the special-interest magazine is reflected in the number of new magazines in this area. In the 1980s, more than 400 new special-audience consumer magazines were introduced, including the science magazines *Discover* and *Technology Illustrated,* and women's magazines *Vital, Everywoman,* and *Lears.* Figure 14–2 demonstrates how magazines compete for special-interest markets.

The result of this trend for the advertiser will be a higher cost per thousand readers because of decreasing circulation. This will be offset by the ability to isolate a narrow marketing segment for whom the commercial message would have relevance.

The magazine industry is not without its problems, basically in the form of rising postage, production, and labor costs and paper shortages.

Partly as a result of shortages and partly due to inflation, production costs have risen steeply. Labor, paper, and ink costs have risen significantly. Magazines have continually passed these increases on to their readers and advertisers.

Finally, postal rates continue to climb, with the latest increase to take effect in 1990. A growing number of new magazines such as Time-Life's *People,* their new general-interest magazine, may be designed chiefly for distribution through newsstands and retail outlets. Not only are postal costs thus avoided, but the cost of maintaining a subscription department can also be avoided. The main problem is building and maintaining a consistent circulation. Most magazines, however, have no real alternative to the U.S. Postal Service at this time, and it appears that higher postal rates will just have to be survived. Attempts by a confederation of magazines to have their own mail service are just beginning to take shape. The success of this plan remains to be seen. Others such as *Better Homes & Gardens,* which uses private delivery services in 13 cities, seem committed to avoiding the Postal Service if possible. All of this has made the competition for shelf space at supermarket checkout areas more intense. One retailer noted that "the supermarket is the newsstand of today."[9]

FIGURE 14–2

Intermagazine Competition

the
®*seventeen*
years.

"This year, going back to school, I'll spend $864 on apparel, footwear and accessories." *

Furthermore, when a young woman in her Seventeen years is attracted to a brand, she stays with it. A Yankelovich study shows that 26% of women 20 to 34 still choose the same brand of bra they first chose as teenagers.

"If you want me to buy your merchandise, call Bob Bunge at (212) 407-9782."

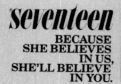

BECAUSE SHE BELIEVES IN US, SHE'LL BELIEVE IN YOU.

*Seventeen Back-to-School Study 1985

© Triangle Communications Inc. 1986

OUTDOOR ADVERTISING

Outdoor advertising is the oldest of all the media; outdoor signs were found in Pompeii and elsewhere in ancient times. It still is an important medium for certain specific purposes, and outdoor service is offered in most cities and towns. Approximately 210,000 standardized signs are available for use, and they had $1.4 billion in revenue in 1988.

Characteristics of Outdoor Advertising

Advantages Several unique advantages are enjoyed by outdoor advertising.

1. *Flexibility.* Outdoor advertising can be readily tailored to create a truly national saturation campaign or to high spot in selected markets or even in parts of markets. The frequency of exposure can also be varied from market to market to adapt precisely to variations in potentials.

2. *A mobile audience.* The buyer views outdoor advertising while on the move, and many of those exposed will be purchasers of the product within a short time after viewing. This last-minute promotion thus may serve as a link between previous advertising messages and a probable purchase as a reminder of a need, or as the required trigger for a pending sale.

3. *Relative absence of competing advertisements.* For the most part, outdoor signs stand alone and are not subject to the competition of other messages. Thus one source of distraction is removed, although it is apparent that outdoor surroundings substitute yet another and potentially more important source of distraction.

4. *Repeat exposure.* The opportunity for repeat exposure is great. It was found that a unit of sale reaches over 80 percent of all adults in the market in the first week. At the end of the month, 89.2 percent of the adults will have seen the message an average of 31 times.[10] These reach and frequency figures rise as income rises in that exposure to adults in high-income households is higher than average, and the average recall of message content is approximately 40 percent.[11] Thus the advantages of repetition are clearly achieved.

Disadvantages There are also certain disadvantages to the use of outdoor advertising:

1. *Creative limitations.* The fleeting impression permitted by exposure to a mobile audience limits copy to a few words or a single powerful graphic. Thus little more can be accomplished than a reminder or repetition of a brand name. When longer copy is required, outdoor ads cannot be used effectively.

2. *Mood of the viewer.* The consumer on the move is subject to many distractions, and prime attention is usually directed elsewhere. Furthermore,

he or she may be faced with the inescapable irritations of heavy traffic, heat, and dirt, and thus the opportunity for a successful advertising impact is diluted.

3. *Public attack.* Outdoor advertising is under attack from many sources. The terms of the Highway Beautification Act authorize the federal government to require states to provide control of outdoor advertising and junkyards on interstate and primary highway systems.[12] Title I of this act requires effective control of signs, displays, and devices within 660 feet of the right-of-way on interstate and primary systems. Other provisions restrict outdoor advertising in commercial areas and check proliferation of signs.

The major effect of this act on the outdoor advertising industry, which actually supported its passage, has been the elimination of posters in small towns and the forced merger of small advertising production plants into larger ones to assure financial survival. The clutter of business signs, which is a major concern of environmentalists, is not an aspect of outdoor advertising, since the owners of the respective business establishments have these signs constructed on their own property.

The industry is not guiltless in the unwise placement of signs, but it maintains that violations of good taste and of a strict professional code are the actions of an irresponsible minority, and the majority are in agreement with the need to prevent abuse.[13] To the credit of the industry, it has taken some positive action. A fairly extensive study was undertaken to assess the effects of the presence of billboards on peoples' reaction to the environment they see.[14] It was found that the majority of those who were vociferous about outlawing billboards were unaware when billboards were removed from a stretch of highway viewed in a laboratory. In addition, the presence or absence of billboards on the routes used did not prove to be critical in achieving "environmental quality"; the effect of removing utility poles had double the effect of removing billboards. However, it would be unwise to conclude on the basis of these limited results that consumers are indifferent to the presence or absence of billboards.

Purchasing Outdoor Space

Outdoor space is purchased directly from each outdoor sign company or from media-buying services specializing in outdoor, such as Out of Home Media Services, Inc. (OHMS). It gathers cost data and prepares estimates for any combination of markets, performs field inspections, and does the contracting.

Not all advertising agencies use OHMS because they may have complete departments equipped to handle outdoor contracts and billings. Space may also be purchased from any of the 700 individual outdoor companies, of course.

Space rates are published by OHMS. Quotations have always been made on the basis of the desired showing. A 100 showing, for example, is supposed to provide enough signs to reach 93 percent of the population an average of 21–22 times in a 30-day period; a 50 showing is supposed to provide sufficient signs to reach 85 percent an average of 10–11 times in this same period.[15] A 100 showing may require only one or two signs in smaller areas, but costs for some of these signs can run as high as $30,000 per month in larger localities. Unfortunately, in practice, a 100 showing is usually what the plant operator says it is. This is one of the reasons why the advertisers are searching for other rating devices.

Although the quotation based on showings is still used most often, the Outdoor Advertising Association of America (OAAA) has been promoting among its members a new rating system based on gross rating points. The OAAA maintains that this new system will give advertisers a more accurate basis for comparing outdoor advertising with the other media. Gross rating points are calculated by considering the number of "impression-opportunities" on the average week day, regardless of repeat exposures, as a percentage of the entire market. Therefore, if the locations of signs during a campaign allowed for 400,000 impression-opportunities (calculated by using government traffic reports) daily in a market of 500,000, the plan would deliver 80 gross rating points daily.

Standardized outdoor poster panels are approximately 12 feet high and 25 feet long with a copy area of roughly 10 × 23 feet. Copy is printed in 10 to 14 sections. Painted signs represent about 10 percent of all outdoor structures, although they account for more than 30 percent of total space billings. Recently much smaller poster panels (8-sheet so-called *junior panels*) have made an impact on streets in large urban areas.

The Traffic Audit Bureau (TAB) is the auditing arm of the industry and is responsible for traffic counts underlying the published rates. Effective circulation is computed as the average daily traffic having a reasonable physical opportunity to see the panels. Total gross traffic is therefore reduced as follows to arrive at effective circulation: 50 percent of all pedestrians, 50 percent of all automobile passengers, and 25 percent of passengers on buses or other forms of mass transit. Thus the 100 showing is based on *effective* circulation.

Several other organizations within the industry provide services to its members and to advertisers. The OAAA is the primary trade association; its members operate more than 90 percent of outdoor facilities in the country. One of the services of the OAAA is the Institute of Outdoor Advertising, a central source of information that also develops research, creative ideas, and methods for using the medium more effectively.

The Future of Outdoor Advertising

At least temporarily, outdoor advertising appears to have successfully withstood the attacks of the environmentalists. Its major problem is one it shares with most U.S. citizens—the probable extent of any future energy crisis. If auto traffic is significantly decreased in favor of public transportation, especially on trains and airplanes, outdoor advertising will be weakened. Continued growth is uncertain in the light of such developments. The attempt to develop small panels for urban use is one response to these potential problems. Also great strides have been made in the development of electronic display panels.

NEW MEDIA: VIDEOTEX

Technology based on cable television and computers is also opening up new media opportunities to advertisers. See the Promotion in Action 14–1.

TRANSIT ADVERTISING

Transit advertising has more than doubled its billings since 1969, and expectations were for an annual volume of about $100 million in 1988. Though it is still seen basically as a supplement to large advertising expenditures elsewhere, it is becoming an attractive option to many advertisers who have not used it previously.

Characteristics of Transit Advertising

Advantages   Among the advantages of transit advertising are the following:

1. *Opportune exposure.* Of those riding buses and subways, about half reported that their last use of transit was for shopping purposes. Moreover, 52 percent indicated some recall of inside-vehicle advertising, and more than 80 percent of those named specific products.[16] Thus this type of advertising can serve as an effective last-minute stimulus to a purchase.

2. *Geographic selectivity.* As a strictly local medium, transit offers the advantage of placing dollars in proportion to local market potentials. It also is used to provide extra advertising weight when required.

3. *High consumer exposure.* Exposure figures vary, of course, from transit system to transit system. It is believed that at least 40 million Americans ride transit vehicles every month. The New York Transit Authority alone claims over 152 million rides monthly.[17] A recent study of the Toronto transit system revealed that during one week, the unduplicated audience represents 52.4 percent of the total market and that, in the space of a month, the reach encompasses 67.5 percent of the market. The individuals making up this 67.5 percent coverage average 11 rides monthly.[18]

4. *Economy.* Transit advertising claims to be the least costly of all media. The cost per thousand inside-car exposures in the markets served averages between 15 and 20 cents, and for exterior exposure as little as 7 cents per thousand.

Disadvantages   Transit advertising also has some disadvantages:

1. *Weak coverage of portions of the population.* Although advertising is now available on the outside of vehicles, it is apparent that nonriders will not be exposed to the transit advertising on the inside of vehicles.

2. *Creative limitations.* The basic inside poster sizes are 11 × 28, 11 × 42, and 11 × 56 inches. Such small areas provide little opportunity for creative presentation other than short, reminder-type messages. Greater opportunities are presented by the use of outside displays, where it is possible to purchase the king-size poster, 2 1/2 × 12 feet in size. The standard exterior board is 30 × 144 inches. Creative opportunities are being expanded through the placement of exterior displays and such innovations as "Moods in Motion," in which an advertiser purchases all the space in the interior of the vehicle and hopes that the advertising in this setting will motivate the

**PROMOTION
IN ACTION
14–1**

Video Shopping Is Just around the Corner?

How has the advent of home shopping, banking, and mail service via computers affected advertisers? Utilizing their own television and telephone lines, consumers can subscribe to the videotex service and buy a keyboard so as to interactively make an airline reservation, send messages, or read a newspaper. But few consumers have subscribed to the services offered by such companies as Viewtron, Viewdata, and Gateway. Viewtron started in south Florida in 1983, and after seven years and a $30 million investment had only 3,000 homes subscribing to the service. Jim Holly, president of Times Mirror Videotex Information Services, Inc., who launched Gateway, said that "we create the medium for advertisers to gain exposure and revenue and they expand our content. The research shows people want to see advertisements." This medium allows advertisers to reach a very select audience and offer trials on new products. Companies such as Viewtron have charged $7,000 to $10,000 for small-market access, $30,000 to $60,000 for medium, and more for wider-ranging advertising. Yet advertising agencies haven't flocked to purchase ad packages. The agencies question the cost, given the limited viewer audience, and dollars already spent by their own research departments. Marshall Deckman, executive vice president of rider. Displays placed in transportation depots and terminals are also a part of transit advertising.

3. *Mood of the rider.* The usual bus or subway is frequently crowded, riders are uncomfortable, and attention often is directed toward reaching the destination as quickly as possible. It is doubtful that such an environment is ideal for advertising exposure, but little has been published to verify or refute this possibility.

4. *Availabilities.* Transit space is decidedly limited in quantity, and some satisfied advertisers use long-term contracts for space. The availability of space, then, may be unsatisfactory at times for the potential user.

Purchasing Transit Space

Published space rates are available in the appropriate SRDS listing. Costs are based on a system of showings similar to that used in outdoor advertising, although transit authorities are also monitoring closely the success of gross rating points as an alternative. The New York Subways Advertising Company will place an 11 × 28 card in all its 6,600 vehicles for a month for about

---

Video Shopping Is Just around the Corner? (concluded)

❖
PROMOTION IN ACTION 14–1

Wolf, Whitehill, Inc. Advertising, said that "until the audience is there, agencies can't justify the creative investment."

In order to increase the number of subscribers and therefore encourage advertisers, these videotex companies have offered rentals of equipment instead of purchase, as well as promotions on their catalog items. Martin Nisenholtz of Ogilvy & Mather Advertising has said that videotex "requires a new kind of creative presentation, which has to be involving, transactional, and entertaining."

The future of this new media resource? Communications Studies and Planning International said that by 1990 videotex could be in 30–40 percent of households and a $4 billion business. Booz Allen's research department projected videotex to be a $30 billion business with 30 percent household penetration. But the future of videotex appears to depend on the consumer. As International Resource and Development analyst Steve Weissman said, "Videotex isn't going belly-up, but its not setting the world on fire. The consumer notion has to become one of 'I have to have it.'" Perhaps the 1989 introduction of the Prodigy service provided to personal computer users as a service of a joint venture of Sears and IBM will give this medium a needed push.

$48,700, although discounts are available for contracts of longer periods. Exterior displays (30 × 144) are available on 400 New York City buses for about $51,000 monthly. Purchases may be made from either the individual companies or from centralized sources such as Metro Transit Advertising, a division of Metromedia.

The Future of Transit

The future of transit advertising is indeed bright. Any energy crisis that may prove hazardous to outdoor advertising can only add to the already healthy billings of transit advertising. The United States is growing increasingly conscious of its need for effective mass transit. Present systems are being enlarged, new ones such as the Bay Area Rapid Transit System (BART) of San Francisco have been completed, and the use of mass transit is growing rapidly. As mass transit grows, so will transit advertising.

THE NONCOMMISSIONABLE MEDIA

All of the media discussed thus far offer a 15 percent commission to advertising agencies, the standard means of agency compensation. Certain media do not provide this discount, however. These include direct mail, point-of-purchase advertisements, and advertising specialities.

Direct Mail

Direct mail is the third largest medium, ranking behind only newspapers and television and grossing over $20.9 billion in 1988, although this figure included both direct mail *selling* and *advertising.* The most widely used forms are personal letters, booklets, brochures, catalogs, circulars and fliers, and mail cards.

Direct mail offers several distinct advantages to the advertiser: (1) preconditioning prospects in advance of a personal sales call, (2) stimulation of selective local store patronage, (3) extreme flexibility in pinpointing prospects with desired timing, (4) no limitations on space or format, (5) little competition from other advertising messages, and (6) personal nature of the appeal, among others.

These disadvantages must also be considered, however: (1) high cost per thousand, (2) the difficulty of obtaining and maintaining a list of names, (3) the poor reputation of so-called *junk mail,* and (4) the creative skill required to create high readership. The high cost per thousand can be partially offset by the great selectivity offered, but in any event average production and mailing costs of 24 to 42 cents per unit (higher for first-class mail) cannot be avoided. The problems with mailing lists can be minimized by renting lists from brokers, publishers, and various advertising media.

Direct mail is used widely by small businesspeople, retailers, book and record clubs, catalog houses, magazine publishers, and the pharmaceutical industry. Insurance companies also use it to identify prospects and serve as sales leads, and it is a common medium for coupons, product samples, and other forms of "direct response" advertising. See Chapter 22 for a detailed discussion of direct marketing.

Point-of-Purchase Advertisements

Most advertising reaches consumers when they are not near a store and are in no mood to buy. Point-of-purchase (POP) stimuli reinstate earlier advertising suggestions and serve as final links in a purchase sequence. For this reason, point of purchase is an important medium. The largest users are manufacturers of soaps, packaged drugs, gasoline, beer, and liquors.

The roles of point-of-purchase advertising are:

1. It can trigger latent or postponed purchases.
2. It persuades shoppers to indulge in a treat.
3. It can trigger a desire to buy something special for family members.
4. It can break a pattern of shopping intent and release a flood of unplanned purchases.
5. It can evoke a feeling that items are on sale.

Some innovative point-of-purchase efforts have included recorded advertisements played over a store's public address system, special sales of 5 to 30 minutes announced over the public address system and identified by such devices as flashing lights (mounted on dollies so they can be moved from place to place), videocassettes to aid in making the sale of major purchases such as automobiles, and even motorized signs mounted on wires that travel around the store above the heads of the shoppers. These and other POP devices do increase sales; this is well documented.[19]

The importance of good point-of-purchase advertising can hardly be questioned. The difficulty, however, is stimulating retailers to use the many displays and banners they receive each month. Since this is a problem in working with resellers, it is discussed in depth in Chapter 21.

INTERMEDIA COMPARISON

The media types discussed in this chapter compete with each other vigorously for the advertisers' dollars. The basis on which they compete is

FIGURE 14–3

Drivetime. Walktime. Anytime is radio time.

It's the age of the headset phenomenon. People listening as they jog, walk, ride the train, play or shop. Hearing only the sounds of their radio. Hearing your message with no distraction. Catch someone like that on the way to shop, and you can get immediate buying action. Some trick in today's economy.

Add this growing audience to radio's big drivetime audience: 85 percent of all commuters who go to work by car.

Radio is big at home, too.

Surprise. Almost 60 percent of all radio listening is done at home. And the average household has 5.5 radios. It's no wonder radio reaches more adults in a day than television, magazines or newspapers. Even busy working women listen to radio an average of almost four hours a day—that's more time than they give any other medium.

Radio hits all lifestyles.

Radio goes with more people, more places, than ever before.

Young, old and in-between. In their cars, their homes, even on top of their heads.

Don't let your potential customers walk on by. Get your message into the streets. Get it on radio. For more information, call (212) 599-6666. Or write Radio Advertising Bureau, 485 Lexington Avenue, New York, NY 10017.

RADIO Red hot because it works.

FIGURE 14–4

An Advertisement by *The Sporting News* in Attempt to Compete with Spot Television

The way to a man's heart is through his sports.

For some men, sports is little more than a casual interest. But for others, it's a passionate love affair. And for 3.7 million of America's most avid sports enthusiasts, the magazine that fans the flames of their passion is *The Sporting News.*

The bible of sports for more than 100 years, *The Sporting News* is the only magazine that connects fans to every major sport every week of the year. Authoritative analysis. Insider reports. National perspective. When it comes to sports, no magazine delivers like *The Sporting News.*

The way to the hearts of 3.7 million avid sports fans is through *The Sporting News.*

The Sporting News' uncompromising weekly sports analysis attracts an audience of men who are active. Affluent. Well educated. And achievement oriented. In fact, *The Sporting News'* audience profile equals or exceeds *any* men's magazine—including *Sports Illustrated.*

	The Sporting News	Sports Illustrated
Male	91%	80%
Age 25-44 Index	131	119
IEI $40,000 + Index	181	160
College Graduate + Index	144	125
Professional/Mgrl. Index	126	108
Reading Days	2.2	1.9

But when it comes to the true measure of a magazine—the reading intensity that creates a dynamic ad environment—*The Sporting News* stands alone. As evidence, *The Sporting News'* 2.2 reading days is one of the highest in the men's category.

If you have a message you want men to take to heart, get serious. Serious about sports. Serious about men to whom sports is an integral part of their lives. Serious about the one magazine *real* sports fans love most. *The Sporting News.*

The Sporting News

Get Serious

1990 Simmons

TABLE 14-6

Media Cost Trends

A. Network Television — 1978 to 1988

	Avg. Cost/Commercial (:30)		CPM Homes	
	$000	Index	$	Index
Prime Time (Regular Programming)				
1978	64.8	100	4.41	100
1979	76.6	118	5.06	115
1980	74.3	115	4.94	112
1981	85.2	131	5.84	132
1982	88.7	137	6.44	146
1983	98.2	151	6.94	157
1984	110.9	171	8.08	183
1985	115.5	178	8.06	183
1986	124.7	192	8.94	203
1987	128.6	198	10.13	230
1988	121.0	187	9.46	215

	Avg. Cost/Commercial (:30)		CPM Homes	
	$000	Index	$	Index
Daytime				
1978	9.3	100	1.96	100
1979	10.8	116	2.15	110
1980	10.8	116	2.22	113
1981	12.3	132	2.47	126
1982	12.5	134	2.68	137
1983	14.0	151	2.70	138
1984	16.3	175	3.41	174
1985	16.4	176	3.48	178
1986	15.8	170	3.50	179
1987	14.8	159	3.11	159
1988	12.7	137	2.82	144

Source: A. C. Nielsen, NAC Cost Supplement, November of each year.

TABLE 14–6

Media Cost Trends (continued)

B. Spot Television— 1982 to 1988
Top 100 Markets

	Avg. Cost/Commercial (:30)		CPM Homes	
	$	Index	$	Index
Prime Time				
1982	69,832	100	8.87	100
1983	67,883	97	8.15	92
1984	73,989	106	9.40	106
1985	74,336	106	10.01	113
1986	71,458	102	9.57	108
1987	64,898	93	10.01	113
1988	76,838	110	11.58	131
Daytime				
1982	9,792	100	3.09	100
1983	8,523	87	2.64	85
1984	9,198	94	3.03	98
1985	9,955	102	3.32	107
1986	10,160	104	3.44	111
1987	9,663	99	3.77	122
1988	10,194	104	4.05	131

Sources: *Media Market Guide,* 1st Quarter each year; A. C. Nielsen, *DMA Planners Guide,* February each year.

C. Network Radio— 1975, 1980 TO 1988

	Cost per Adult Rating Point		CPM Adults	
	$	Index	$	Index
1975	1,585	100	1.10	100
1980	2,495	157	1.61	146
1981	2,668	168	1.69	154
1982	2,964	187	1.81	165
1983	3,245	205	1.93	175
1984	3,528	223	2.07	188
1985	3,832	242	2.22	202
1986	4,212	266	2.41	219
1987	4,501	284	2.55	232
1988	4,723	298	2.65	241

Source: *Marketing & Media Decisions,* August of each year.

TABLE 14–6

❖   **Media Cost Trends** (continued)

D. Spot Radio— 1978 TO 1988
Top 50 Markets

	Avg. Cost/Commercial (:60)		CPM Adults	
	$	Index	$	Index
Daytime				
1978	3,460	100	2.20	100
1979	3,984	115	2.57	117
1980	4,100	118	2.90	132
1981	4,305	124	3.04	138
1982	4,736	137	3.28	149
1983	5,091	147	3.50	159
1984	5,532	160	3.78	172
1985	5,901	171	4.00	182
1986	6,231	180	4.20	191
1987	6,505	188	4.37	199
1988	6,765	196	4.52	205
Drive Time—Morning				
1978	4,435	100	2.10	100
1979	5,071	114	2.43	116
1980	5,848	132	2.78	132
1981	6,140	138	2.91	139
1982	7,452	168	3.14	150
1983	8,011	181	3.35	160
1984	8,705	196	3.62	172
1985	9,286	209	3.83	182
1986	9,806	221	4.02	191
1987	10,237	231	4.18	199
1988	10,646	240	4.32	206

Sources: *Katz Spot Radio Planning Guide* for 1978 through 1981; Estimates based on *Marketing & Media Decisions* for 1982–1988.

TABLE 14-6

Media Cost Trends (continued)   ❖

E. Consumer Magazines— 1978 to 1988
Ten Selected Magazines

	Cost/Page 4 C		CPM-Circulation	
	$000	Index	$	Index
1978	537.7	100	5.88	100
1979	576.8	107	6.33	108
1980	653.2	121	7.34	125
1981	682.3	127	7.75	132
1982	740.7	138	8.49	144
1983	802.5	149	9.18	156
1984	834.8	155	9.68	165
1985	883.4	164	10.32	176
1986	906.5	169	10.92	186
1987	938.9	175	11.38	194
1988	973.9	181	11.79	201

Source: Standard Rate and Data Service, June 1978–1983 and September 1984–1988.

F. Daily Newspapers— 1977 TO 1987

	Inch Rate		Inch Cost/MM Circ.	
	$	Index	$	Index
1977	655.42	100	10.66	100
1978	714.29	109	11.61	109
1979	743.66	114	12.00	113
1980	899.71	137	14.46	136
1981	990.00	151	15.76	148
1982	1,091.24	167	17.46	164
1983	1,198.68	183	19.13	180
1984*	21,620.20	100	341.33	100
1985	24,050.21	111	383.17	112
1986	25,149.88	116	402.39	118
1987	25,079.46	116	399.19	117

*Newspapers converted from line to inch rates in 1984. Data are not comparable to previous years.

Source: *Editor and Publisher Yearbook.*

TABLE 14-6

❖ **Media Cost Trends** (concluded)

G. Syndicated Supplements† — 1978 to 1988

	Cost/Page 4 C		CPM-Circulation	
	$	Index	$	Index
1978	196,015	100	5.98	100
1979	215,070	110	6.44	108
1980	235,095	120	6.91	116
1981	266,480	136	7.81	131
1982	297,352	152	8.62	144
1983	367,655	188	10.00	167
1984	386,030	197	10.36	173
1985	426,235	217	11.58	194
1986	408,800	208	9.22	154
1987	439,900	224	9.65	161
1988	504,500	257	11.03	184

†*Parade* and *U.S.A. Weekend* only.
Source: Standard Rate and Data Service, June of each year.

H. Outdoor — 1979 TO 1989

	No. of Markets	No. of Panels	Monthly Cost* $000	CPM
1979	Top 300	15,000	2,412.7	$0.65
1980	Top 300	14,945	2,679.9	0.71
1981	Top 300	15,319	3,109.3	0.77
1982	Top 200	11,400	2,827.8	0.84
1983	Top 200	11,450	3,155.9	0.91
1984	Top 300	13,200	3,823.8	0.99
1985	Top 300	13,098	4,121.0	1.15
1986	Top 300	13,011	4,377.3	1.35
1987	Top 300	13,025	4,770.2	1.40
1988	Top 300	13,100	5,130.3	1.41
1989	Top 300	13,051	5,240.7	1.66

*100 GRPs in all markets.
Source: Institute of Outdoor Advertising.
Source: *Leo Burnett 1989 Media Costs and Coverage.*

Tracking Worldwide Media Trends

The construction of an effective communications network is a key marketing success factor in the increasingly global business world. Advertising agencies are major links in this network. In order to effectively serve international clients, ad agencies need an intimate knowledge of the current media trends in various foreign countries.

The international advertising market has great untapped potential. Projections indicate that the volume of advertising in the United States will soon fall behind the volume generated by the rest of the world. And this volume is fairly concentrated. Fifteen countries (the United States, Japan, the United Kingdom, West Germany, Canada, France, Brazil, Australia, Italy, the Netherlands, Spain, Switzerland, Sweden, Finland, and South Korea) accounted for more than 90 percent of all worldwide advertising expenditures as of 1985. These same countries also accounted for 61 percent of global gross national product. Anticipation of global trends among these countries, such as the dissolution of European trade barriers in 1992, will allow media professionals to more effectively serve their clients.

McCann-Erikson is one advertising agency that now tracks media data on a worldwide basis. One of the agency's major objectives is to determine which medium captures the largest share of ad expenditures. Its study examines television, radio, magazines, newspapers, and other media vehicles (cinema, outdoor, transit, direct, business-to-business, etc.). McCann-Erikson has found that newspapers hold the largest share in almost all of the countries studied, even the United States. Television accounts for a low share of ad expenditures in many of the European countries: 9 percent in West Germany, 5 percent in the Netherlands, 4 percent in Switzerland, 8 percent in Finland, and 17 percent in France. Several factors contribute to this trend: limited commercial TV availability, an extensive and well-established print industry, restricted TV commercialization policies, and stringent television time-buying guidelines. Government ownership of broadcast facilities is common in these countries and accounts for many of these restrictions. Privatization is a relatively new development.

The other end of this limited commercial television environment is a well-developed magazine and newspaper industry. This condition indicates a high literacy rate. There are over 1,220 consumer publications in both West Germany and the United Kingdom, and France and Italy each have over 900. At the other end of the spectrum, Brazil, with its low literacy rate, offers only 300 magazine titles while its struggling economy claims the lowest TV household penetration in the top 15 markets.   (continued)

❖
**PROMOTION
IN ACTION
14–2**

Tracking Worldwide Media Trends (concluded)

In amassing this and other media data, McCann-Erikson identified several key media trends:

1. The television medium will grow dramatically on both a household-coverage and usage basis. VCRs and the privatization of television channels will be major contributing factors.

2. Print media will also grow but at a slower pace. Improved economic conditions in Third World countries and subsequent improvements in education will increase literacy rates and increase the demand for print vehicles.

3. Advertising expenditures as a percentage of GNP will increase on a worldwide basis. Domestic markets will become saturated, and competitors will vie for limited supplies of advertising time and space.

4. The use of short-length (i.e., 15-second) TV commercials will increase globally. Although this practice is already common in other countries where air time has traditionally been scarce, U.S. advertisers, who are used to longer time slots, must find ways to communicate their message without sacrificing media and impact values.

5. Viewers' ability to bypass TV commercials is growing. The increasing use of remote controls and VCRs is reducing the number of commercials that television viewers actually watch, creating a new challenge for advertisers.

6. Major changes in political and economic structures will continue to encourage globalization. Eastern and Western Europe are prime arenas for these changes.

Pan-European media changes are expected to evolve more slowly than pan-European marketing changes. Differences in language and culture will inhibit media's reach potential. One proposed solution is to segment Europe by language and cultural similarities instead of by national boundaries. This would cluster countries on the basis of broadcast and print-circulation delivery. Possible clusters include Austria-Germany-Switzerland, France-Belgium-Luxembourg-Switzerland, Italy-Switzerland, Great Britain-Ireland-Northern Ireland, and the Scandanavian countries.

Source: "Mediology: Our Global Link," *Marketing and Media Decisions*, May 1988, pp. 108–15.

essentially to sell their own advantages while trying to highlight other media's disadvantages. Figure 14–3 presents an example of intermedia competition at a trade association level (the Radio Advertising Bureau). Individual media vehicles also present themselves against other media types as well as against other vehicles in their class. Figure 14–4 presents an example of this latter type of activity.

One of the most fundamental bases on which media compete is cost. Table 14–6 presents a comparison of media costs prepared by the media department at the Leo Burnett advertising agency for the period 1978–1988.

Care must be taken in interpreting these cost-per-thousand numbers because they are calculated on a *total* audience basis. Also, outdoor audiences are measured in terms of total people while others are stated in terms of adults, and television is stated in terms of households, whereas magazines are given by gross circulation, and so on. Of more interest to marketers is the CPM on *target* audience of the advertising program. Thus, for example for a particular target audience, the CPM for a specific television time could be higher than for a particular magazine. The use of the CPM target audience concept will be discussed in Chapter 15.

Keeping track of all this information about media is a complex and time-consuming task. With the increasing importance of global marketing over the last decade, this task has become even more complex. Promotion in Action 14–2 describes some of the efforts that advertisers are undertaking to track media worldwide. It is an exciting time to be involved with the advertising aspects of media

SUMMARY

The purpose of this chapter has been to condense a wealth of material on media characteristics, advantages, disadvantages, possible uses, and other factors that must be understood before discussing the media selection process itself. Of greatest importance is the way in which each of the media discussed is adapting to the current environment because the changes have been great. Understanding these changes enables a marketer to discuss meaningfully the methods by which media should be analyzed and selected.

REVIEW AND DISCUSSION QUESTIONS

1. The nationally distributed Sunday supplement seems to be losing ground in comparison with other media. What reasons can you see for this trend? Can it be reversed? Why?

2. The differential between local and national line rates is said by many to be triggering an exodus of national advertisers from local newspapers. Given

this fact, what reasons can be advanced for continuation of the differentials? Why, in your opinion, has there been so little change?

3. Contrast the milline rate and cost-per-thousand (CPM) formula. What advantage is gained by their use? What possible dangers can you see?

4. One of the distinct trends in the television medium is the rapid rise of CATV. What effects will this have on both local and national advertising in the future?

5. What are the implications for advertisers of the consumers' increasing acceptance of video recorder systems and video games?

6. Advertisers are showing a growing concern with commercial clutter in television and radio broadcasts. If clutter is allowed to continue, what might be the effects in terms of the consumer, as well as on the advertising copy and format?

7. The FCC is authorized to refuse to renew local station licenses if they fail to operate within broad guidelines of public interest. What are the advantages and dangers of this policy? What factors should the FCC consider in deciding license renewal?

8. Under what conditions might a 60-second television commercial be worth twice the cost of a 30-second version?

9. Radio continues its growth in advertising dollars. Do you think this steady upward trend will continue? Why?

10. What steps might be taken to save *Reader's Digest* from the same fate as *The Saturday Evening Post* and *Look?*

11. In what sense can it be said that magazines are a highly flexible medium?

12. With a *100 showing,* over 80 percent of all adults are reached with an average *frequency of 31.* What do these terms mean? Does this mean that outdoor advertising has unique advantages in terms of reach and frequency when compared with other media? What are the advantages of gross rating points (GRPs) as a substitute system of measurement?

13. There are frequent outcries that billboards should be removed entirely from the public roads. What arguments could you advance to refute this position?

14. For what types of products is transit advertising most suitable? Can it be used as a substitute medium for television and magazines?

15. Critics of direct mail advertising claim that the junk mail received in homes today is so excessive that government should step in to outlaw unwanted use of the mails. Would this be in the consumer's interest? Why?

16. It is sometimes said that point of purchase is the untouched "promised land" of advertising, the presumption being that it frequently is neglected. What roles can point of purchase play?

NOTES

1. Based on Bernard Guggenheim, "What the Research Shows about Actual Growth in Ad Volume," *Media Decisions,* March 1978, p. 90, and updates from various advertising agency media guides through 1989.

2. *1988 Editor and Publisher Yearbook.*

3. *Television Fact Book 1988.*

4. *Leo Burnett 1988 Media Costs and Coverage,* p. 5.

5. Ibid.

6. Ibid., p. 10.

7. The Code Authority of the National Association of Broadcasters.

8. Simmons Market Research Bureau at different years.

9. "The Magazines' Counter Attack," *Business Week,* March 29, 1982, p. 170.

10. "Reach and Frequency of Exposure of Outdoor Posters," study conducted by W. R. Simmons and Associates Research, Inc., for the Institute of Outdoor Advertising, Inc.

11. "This Is Outdoor Advertising" (New York: Institute of Outdoor Advertising).

12. Phillip Tucker, "State Implementation of Highway Beautification Act," Outdoor Advertising Association of America, 1968.

13. "This Is Outdoor Advertising."

14. "Measuring Human Response to the Urban Roadside," summary of a study conducted by Arthur D. Little, Inc., published by the Outdoor Advertising Association of America.

15. Estimates provided by Ogilvy Mather, Inc.

16. "The Transit Millions," New York Transit Advertising Association, and "Toronto Transit Rider Study," Daniel Starch Ltd.

17. "Transit Advertising Prospers."

18. "Toronto Transit Rider Study," p. 4.

19. For example, see Gary F. McKinnon, J. Patrick Kelley, and E. Doyle Robison, "Sales Effects of Point-of-Purchase In-Store Signing," *Journal of Retailing* 57, no. 2 (Summer 1981), pp. 49–63.

Media Strategy

MOTEL 6'S MEDIA MIX HELPS DRIVE THE CUSTOMERS IN

A fittingly laid-back marketing campaign transformed Motel 6 from a backwoods joke to a king of the road. Motel 6 now rules the economy segment of the $51 billion, 2.8 million-room lodging industry. This chain of self-proclaimed "cheap" motels (the 6 originally stood for $6-a-night) was founded in Santa Barbara in 1962. For years, marketing was a foreign concept to the entire lodging industry, and the economy segment was slower to catch on than the rest. Word of mouth was the major advertising medium. Random billboards were sprinkled along some highways, and economy motels were listed in lodging directories. Little else was done to attract customers.

For 24 years, Motel 6 was quite content with this minimal effort. Tiny regional chains were no match for the lodging giant. But competitors recognized a good thing when they saw it. Other super-cheap national chains began to appear, Motel 6's market share nose-dived, and occupancy rates bottomed out at 66.7 percent. Major changes were needed to rescue the fallen giant.

Kohlberg Kravis Roberts & Co. (KKR) bought Motel 6 in 1985. It hired Joseph McCarthy, a long-time lodging business executive, as president and CEO. McCarthy hired Hugh Thrasher as executive VP of marketing and development. The two set up the company's first marketing department and hired the Dallas-based Richards Group as their advertising agency. The agency waited 10 months to begin advertising. Customers had some major gripes with the chain and the Richards Group "didn't want to bring people in until the product was fixed." Phones were installed to attract the important business traveler segment; local calls were free and, unlike many chains in the industry, Motel 6 levied no service charge for long-distance calls. A reservation center was established in Albuquerque, New Mexico, and an itinerary-planning service was also made available. The national pricing structure was adjusted to each city's economy. Prices now range from $31.50 (e.g., Washington, D.C.) to $17.95 a night (Odessa, Texas). This allowed Motel 6 to offer services such as "free" local calls and TV hookups while remaining "the lowest-priced national chain on any corner." A family rate was added, allowing children under 18 to stay for free, and a credit card policy was implemented. When the ads started, they focused on each improvement as it came off the assembly line. A new image was being created.

People over 50 make up about half of Motel 6's customer base; two-thirds of these were retired. The company refers to them as "inveterate coupon clippers who could easily afford a Hilton or a Hyatt." As McCarthy points out, "It's just that these people take the "what do I really need" approach to travel. The segment of 18- to 35-year-olds on a tight budget is another large part of the company's customer base. The business traveler segment is also growing steadily. Half of this segment is self-employed; the other half is often on a per-diem expense account. Motel 6 is just what they need to fit necessary travel into their tight budgets.

Money was tight when Motel 6 began its media campaign in 1986. With a total promotional budget of only $1 million, radio seemed the only way to go. And it went far—so far, in fact, that when the budget was increased to $6 million in 1987 and $8 million in 1988, the company saw no reason to change its basic media plan. The fact that most people arrive at Motel 6 by car, truck, or motorcycle was a major factor in this decision. The company estimates that three-quarters of these customers make a "through-the-windshield" decision on where to stay each night and arrive without a reservation. Radio has a good chance of reaching them at this critical decision point.

The chain increased its number of billboards to 775, but it still believes that radio is the most effective way to reach these travelers. They first tested their media strategy with spot buys, and then expanded to network radio in 1988. In 1987, Motel 6 spent $7.63 million on spot radio, $1.73 million on network radio, and $321,900 on billboards, for a total of $9,677,600. In 1988 Motel 6 spent $1.9 million on spot radio, $9.1 million on network radio, and $400,000 on billboards, for a total of $11,347,600. More than 70 executions now air between 6:00 A.M. and 7:00 P.M. on most networks, including ABC, CBS, NBC, and TranStar. This covers the prime traveling hours.

Radio also created several unexpected advantages. Tom Bodett, the voice of Motel 6, has become something of a legend. Because people can't see Bodett, his ironic, real-folk voice becomes different things to different people. "Old people see him as a road-weary curmudgeon, younger people think he's one of them, and business-people frequently say in focus groups they hear a harried salesman." TV or print ads would destroy these advantageous illusions. Com-petitors bewail the fact that they didn't find Bodett first, and their attempts at imitation fall short. Another key to the ads' success is that they tell people it's okay to be cheap, pointing out the fact that money saved on a motel bill can be more enjoyably spent on gifts and entertainment. The occupancy rate of 73 percent for 1988 indi-cates that they agree.

Source: "King of the Road," *Marketing & Media Decisions,* March 1989, pp. 80–86.

The main problems faced in media strategy are selection of media vehicles and preparation of a media schedule. *Media selection* first involves a choice of media class or type: television versus radio versus magazines, and so on. Second, it involves the choice of specific vehicles within the media class: "The Cosby Show" versus "60 Minutes," *Newsweek* versus *Time,* and so forth. Other factors that are fundamental in media selection are (1) the requirements of creative strategy, (2) reaching the proper audience, (3) the requirements for reach versus frequency, (4) competitive factors, (5) cost efficiency, (6) qualitative factors, and (7) distribution requirements. *Media scheduling* is discussed with emphasis on geographical and seasonal scheduling.

THE REQUIREMENTS OF CREATIVE STRATEGY

The advertising requirements for the product often can easily favor or elim-inate certain media candidates. For example, it has been a long-standing agreement among broadcasters subscribing to the Code of the National Association of Broadcasters that liquor will not be advertised on radio or television. Moreover, the product may be so sensitive that good taste calls for its exclusion from certain media.

The product personality also will dictate media choice. The promotion of expensive French perfumes in *Mad* would clearly be inappropriate. The match between product prospects and media audiences would be poor, of course, but of even greater importance, association of the product with the magazine could affect its image adversely.

Finally, the requirements of the message may dominate the media decision. An automobile advertisement featuring acceleration and passing power requires a medium that dramatizes action for maximum creative impact; where movement is required, television or sales films are the only possible choices. Color might be specified to provide a more realistic representation of an automobile and to strengthen emotional impact. The finest color reproduction is available in magazines, although acceptable color can be purchased in both television and newspapers. Finally, a requirement for sound eliminates substantially all media except radio and television (although some direct mail promotions contain small recorded disks). There are many similar examples.

REACHING THE PROPER AUDIENCE

The pivotal consideration in media strategy is to select media vehicles that reach the target audience with a minimum of waste coverage. This is often referred to as *selectivity*. Computers make it possible to undertake selectivity analysis with considerable precision, conditional of course on the accuracy of available data. This means that the analyst must have a grasp of the nature, scope, and uses of available sources of audience data. Audience data are discussed in some detail here before focusing on their use in media planning.

Media Audience Data

All practical considerations aside, most analysts agree that it would be useful to have at least six categories of data for media planning and evaluation. The essential categories are (1) media distribution—the number of copies of a magazine in circulation or sets available to carry the advertising, (2) media audiences—people actually exposed to a medium, and (3) advertising exposure—people exposed to advertising units. In addition, data are also useful on (4) advertising perception—people aware of the message, (5) advertising communication—people affected by advertising, and (6) consumer response—people who make purchases.

The difficulty is that the roles of the medium and the message themselves intermix in categories 3 to 6. In these categories, it is difficult to determine whether people's awareness of the message is more attributable to layout, design, and wording than to the medium itself. Thus, only the first two stages focus on the *medium itself*, and media audience data are largely confined to these levels, as our discussion will be. A number of trade association and research supply companies are in the business of providing media audience data. The sections that follow discuss some of these organizations.

Media Distribution   Data in this category have long been available from such organizations as the Audit Bureau of Circulation (ABC). This organization is sponsored by national and local advertisers, advertising agencies, and publishers. It makes available sworn and audited statements of newspaper and magazine audiences. A publication must have at least 70 percent paid circulation (copies purchased at not less than one-half the established prices) to be eligible for membership and listing. Most publishers meeting this qualification are members of ABC.

Publications that distribute to special groups, perhaps on a free basis, are audited by the Business Publications Audit of Circulation (BPA). The functions performed by BPA closely parallel those of ABC.

The notion of total physical distribution of media vehicles quickly loses its significance when one moves out of the publications field. Although the Advertising Research Foundation has published a *National Survey of Television Sets in U.S. Households,* the most useful data on television and other media are confined largely to categories 2 and 3, with very little audience measurement data available on category 3.

These data are useful primarily in providing a verified audit of circulation claims. The figures are sometimes used as a guarantee for the rates established in magazine space contracts, but the data are of little additional use because there is usually a wide difference between physical distribution and audience exposure.

Media Audiences   Media audiences refer to the actual number of people exposed to a medium on both one-time and repeat bases. The methods of audience measurement are complex, as the discussion below indicates. In fact, the Advertising Research Foundation (ARF), a nonprofit industry organization, is almost always studying this subject.

Magazine audiences   The accepted definition of the audience of a given magazine is the number of people claiming to recall looking into an average issue. This definition is supported by evidence indicating that those who look into a magazine tend to be exposed to most of its contents. It should be apparent, however, that survey research often encounters response distortion. For example, it is not unusual for a respondent to deny reading a magazine that would appear to place him or her in a bad light in an interviewer's eyes, or to claim readership of a prestigious publication. To prove this point, we mention the report that the number of those claiming to be readers of a well-known prestige magazine can be more than 15 times the number of copies printed.

It is obvious that methods used to measure actual readership must be designed to minimize response distortion. The most commonly used approach, the editorial interest technique, encompasses an attempt to make respondents believe that they are helping editors to evaluate the appeal of various editorial features. No attempt is made at the outset to determine whether or not the respondent actually read the issue. The question is usually reserved until the end and is often worded as follows: "Just for the record, now that we have been through this issue, would you say you definitely happened to read it before, or didn't read it, or aren't you sure?" Questioning at the end of the interview and this careful wording are effective devices to guarantee a minimum of overclaimed or underclaimed readership.

Another approach used to assess magazine readership is to interview different samples of respondents every day for a period of time regarding "yesterday's reading." Confining the interview to yesterday's reading is intended to prevent memory loss. Extension of the interviewing period also permits useful estimation of the total readership of a given magazine over time. It is well-known, for example, that "issue life" (the time in which it continues to be read) may run into months.

Other advertisers believe that the best approach is the use of simple direct questions such as "Which magazines do you read?" The first step is to use benchmark studies using several techniques to determine the probability that claimed readership is accurate. From then on, it would be possible simply to ask respondents, "Do you read this magazine usually, regularly, quite often, seldom, or never?" and to modify the answers given by the probabilities of accuracy found from previous surveys. This approach offers an admirable degree of simplicity. Box A of Figure 15–1 contains five different versions of the questions often used in magazine research. The diversity of questions trying to measure the same thing is clear.

It is useful to distinguish four types of magazine readers (see Table 15–1). The classification relates to the source of the copy—whether purchased or picked up, and the location of reading—whether in-home or out-of-home. We define:

1. Primary readers: A and B.
2. Pass-along readers: C and D.
3. Out-of-home readers: B and D.
4. In-home readers: A and C.

FIGURE 15–1

Magazine Audience Research   ❖

Box A: Five Ways to Ask for Consumer Magazine Readership

1. Which of the magazines listed below have you read or looked into in the past month?

2. Which of these magazines do you read regularly; that is, at least three out of four issues?

Magazine	Read or looked into (past month)	Read regularly (3 out of 4 issues)
A	☐	☐
B	☐	☐
C	☐	☐
D	☐	☐
E	☐	☐
F	☐	☐
G	☐	☐
H	☐	☐
I	☐	☐
J	☐	☐

3. What magazines do you read regularly, that is, at least three out of four issues? (Please write in the names of the magazines.)

_____   _____   _____

_____   _____   _____

4. Next, the monthly publications. Next to each magazine, please check the box that describes how many different issues of the magazine, if any, you personally have *read or looked into* for the first time in the *last 4 months*.

Monthly magazine	Do not read it	Read now and then, but not in last 4 months	In the last 4 months, I have read			
			1 Issue	2 Issues	3 Issues	4 Issues
A	( )	( )	( )	( )	( )	( )
B	( )	( )	( )	( )	( )	( )
C	( )	( )	( )	( )	( )	( )
D	( )	( )	( )	( )	( )	( )
E	( )	( )	( )	( )	( )	( )
F	( )	( )	( )	( )	( )	( )

Readership can also be measured in terms of primary readers only (the person or household purchasing the magazine) or primary readers plus pass-along readers. In practice many agencies discount out-of-home and pass-along audiences.

Two major organizations are active in measuring total magazine readers, each using a different measure of reader. The first is the Simmons Market Research Bureau (SMRB). SMRB samples about 15,000 individuals annually. The readership measurement method is the "through-the-book

TABLE 15–1

❖ **Classification of Magazine Readership**

Source of Copy	Read in Home	Read Out of Home
Purchased	A	B
Picked up	C	D

FIGURE 15–1

❖ **Magazine Audience Research** (concluded)

5. For each of the magazines listed below, will you please check:
   (a) Whether or not *you personally* read the *most recent issue?*
   (b) Whether or not *you personally* read the *issue before that one?*

	Did you read the most recent issue? (Please check "Yes" or "No" for EACH)		Did you read the issue before that one? (Please check "Yes" or "No" for EACH)	
	Yes	No	Yes	No
A	☐	☐	☐	☐
B	☐	☐	☐	☐
C	☐	☐	☐	☐
D	☐	☐	☐	☐
E	☐	☐	☐	☐
F	☐	☐	☐	☐
G	☐	☐	☐	☐
H	☐	☐	☐	☐
I	☐	☐	☐	☐
J	☐	☐	☐	☐

editorial interest method." Respondents are shown logos of magazine titles and are asked to "pick out those you might have read or looked into during the last six months, either at home or at some place else." This is verified again later in the interview, after the respondent goes through a stripped-down version of each magazine.

SMRB also provides audience estimates for newspaper supplements, network television, and national newspapers. Also collected are usage patterns for products, brand loyalty, and some demographic and psychographic measures. A major competitor is Mediamark Research, Inc. (MRI). MRI draws a sample of about 30,000 individuals (15,000 in the spring and fall) and measures audience size with the "modified recent reading method." Here respondents are given a list of about 160 magazines and are asked to note the ones they have read during the most recent publication interval. This is done in two steps. First, a deck of cards containing magazines is sorted by the respondent to indicate those read in the last six months. The cards for the magazines read are then sorted to indicate those read in the last publication interval. With differences in the methods of audience measurement, and some differences in sampling procedures, it is little wonder that SMRB and MRI report different audience sizes. The result of this is a great controversy as to which is the correct estimate.

Newspaper audiences   The measurement of newspaper audiences involves essentially the same procedures as those reported for magazines. For example, a reader is defined as someone who has read a part of the medium being analyzed, and the time period covered generally does not exceed one day.

The Audit Bureau of Circulation's Newspaper Audience Research Data Bank (NRDB) offers such data. NRDB is based on data provided by cooperating newspapers in the top 100 markets. The data are collected by the newspapers themselves and made available to NRDB. To be part of NRDB, the study must meet both methodological and format standards. In general, advertisers must rely on newspaper-collected audience data. A significant supplier of newspaper audience research data is the Scarborough Company, which provides both syndicated data (much like MRI does for magazines) and custom studies.

Television audiences   Television audience data are frequently collected by means of a diary in which viewers record shows they have watched over a period of time. Several syndicated research services are widely used for this purpose, including A. C. Nielsen and American Research Bureau (ARB) for national audiences and Arbitron for local audiences. There is some use of coincidental telephone recall in which a sample of people is contacted by telephone during programs to establish listening or viewing patterns. Use is also made of the *audimeter,* which automatically records the number of television sets tuned to a particular channel.

The key problem with the *audimeter* is that it does not indicate the number of people watching a given television set, or the demographic characteristics of the audience. The response to these problems was the *people meter*. This is a device that is attached to the television set. It allows each member of a family to separately "log on" and "log off" television viewing time. The demographic characteristics of each family member are collected and viewing habits correlated with this demographic data. A. C. Nielsen is the leader in the development of people meters and maintains a people meter panel of 4,000 households.

People meters do not measure visitors to the household as part of an audience, nor are they attached to television sets smaller than 5 inches. In addition, they do not measure actual commercial viewership. Promotion in Action 15–1 illustrates one attempt to address some of these problems. If successful, passive people meters will provide the first measurement of actual exposure to the advertisement on television.

Radio audiences   A unique problem is presented by the fact that radios are used everywhere; hence, diaries and audimeters have not proved to be adequate radio audience measures. RADAR (Radio's All Dimension Audience Research) is now the accepted measurement procedure for network audiences.

In this measurement technique, two telephone panels are established, one in the spring and one in the fall. Each household is telephoned eight different times on consecutive days during the survey period and is questioned about radio listening habits for each quarter hour for the preceding 24 hours. Respondents also complete a standard questionnaire that gives such characteristics as age and sex. This permits a reporting of all radio listening and weekly cumulative audiences by subgroup within the population. At the local level, Arbitron dominates the ratings business, using a mail diary method. During the measurement period of a week, respondents are called twice to reinforce the proper completion of the diary.

Audiences of other media   Other media such as outdoor and transit advertising provide no information regarding audience evaluation since the total audience of the medium and potential for advertising exposure coincide. Research measures for these media are discussed in the next section.

Audience profiles   Up to this point, discussion has been confined to total audiences. Such data, however, are poor indications of the characteristics of the individuals reached. Today most media data are also classified in such terms as age, income, occupation, sex, geographical location, and product purchases. It is commonplace for the media planner to receive many such reports. In fact, the volume of information has grown to the point that computer storage facilities are a virtual necessity.

The Birth of TV Ratings for Advertisements— The Passive People Meter?

A. C. Nielsen Co., in conjunction with the David Sarnoff Research Center, is developing a "passive" people meter for measuring TV viewership. Although this device is designed primarily to measure programming viewership, its technology will enable Nielsen to measure commercial viewership much more effectively than Nielsen's current people meters. The system's projected time to implementation is three years. If the new meter is successful, national TV ratings for commercials could become a reality.

Nielsen's new system uses a device resembling a VCR. It combines a computer with a small camera and can identify individuals who are actually watching TV. It will be able to record both a person's presence in the room and his or her TV viewership at any given second, making it possible to record accurate TV ratings specifically for commercials.

The computer is initially "introduced" to members of the family. Using a form of artificial intelligence, it then matches characteristics to those it "sees" watching TV. One drawback is that the system is unable to record visitors watching TV.

Nielsen is committed to developing accurate commercial viewing measurements. Although the current people meters compile minute-by-minute viewing data, the new system will compile second-by-second viewing data. This precision is crucial in determining true ratings for TV spots. The company will tie this commercial viewing information to its "single-source" panel. By deriving TV viewing and purchasing information from single-source families, advertisers and agencies will be able to study the correlation between advertising and purchasing decisions.

According to Michael Drexler, executive vice president-media at Bozell, New York, "There's no doubt advertisers want this type of information. We've been trying to get audience measures for relevant exposure versus program ratings. We want it and we hope it is coming." Yet the ramifications of such a system are infinite. Both agencies and networks are already developing software capable of analyzing second-by-second data and tentatively pricing commercial inventory according to position within a commercial break. Networks will undoubtedly negotiate higher prices for certain key positions if the new data show a correlation between commercial viewing and the time a spot airs within a break. The current media pricing structure and buying process could be rendered obsolete.

Source: "Nielsen's New Meter May Give Ratings for Ads," *Advertising Age,* June 5, 1989, p. 1, as adapted from Thomas C. Kinnear and James R. Taylor, *Marketing Research: An Applied Approach,* 4th ed. (New York: McGraw-Hill, 1991).

It was formerly necessary to consult research reports published by individual media when profile data were needed. This is no longer necessary because of the widespread use of the syndicated research services that report audience profiles for television and magazines, the two leading national media.

Comments on Media Data   Ideally, it should be possible to estimate the third category of data on *advertising exposure* (not simply media audiences) for all possible media. Passive people meters are one attempt to do this in the television environment.

In addition, as was pointed out in Chapter 8, market targets can be defined in terms that go far beyond the usual demographic classifications. However, media profiles have not expanded to the same extent. There is an obvious need to enrich the data base through provision of data on the activities, interests, and opinions (AIO scores) of media audiences. Fortunately, there is every reason to anticipate that this will be done in the near future.

Using Media Audiences Data   The central task of media selection is to *achieve a media mix that reaches the target audience with a minimum of waste coverage and delivers exposure to the advertising unit in a proper frame of mind, apart from media content, so that the advertisement can perform its role.* The most demanding task is to match the target market with media audience, and this obviously requires a good data base.

With available data and computer technology, it is possible to utilize a number of characteristics of both the market target and media audiences in media selection. Thus, there is little excuse for failure to use audience research in building a media schedule, all other things being equal.

REACH AND FREQUENCY

Once determination is made of the extent to which a media schedule reaches the desired target market, it is important to determine both *reach* and *frequency*. *Reach* is the number of different target audience individuals or households exposed to the advertisement during a given period of time (often a four-week period is used). *Frequency* is the average number of exposures to the advertisement per individual or household target audience member during the same time period. A very useful summary measure referred to as *gross rating points* (GRP) combines both of these considerations; GRP is the product of *reach times frequency*. GRP is widely used as an indication of advertising weight or tonnage generated by the media schedule. Essentially, GRPs represent the achieved communication objective. Buyers use them as a ready reference point to determine what a buy is worth.

It is important to note that reach and frequency cannot both be optimized at the same time. When one goes up, the other must go down, *if the budget is held constant*.

An example will promote understanding of these concepts. Figure 15–2 represents the television viewing record over four weeks in 10 homes. Notice that all homes but home I were reached during the four weeks. This gives a reach figure of 9. There were 26 total exposures. If 26 is divided by the nine homes reached, this gives an average frequency of 2.9 exposures. GRP (reach times frequency) then is 261 (9 × 2.9).

The Problem of Audience Duplication

Reach was defined above as the number of different homes exposed. A given media schedule could fail to achieve reach by delivering multiple exposures to the same audience. If intensive coverage of the same group is

FIGURE 15–2

Reach and Frequency Patterns for Ten Television Homes over a Four-Week Period

Week	Message	A	B	C	D	E	F	G	H	I	J	Total Exposures
	1	x				x			x			3
1	2	x		x								2
	3		x		x		x	x				4
	4			x							x	2
2	5					x						1
	6					x						1
	7	x					x	x				3
3	8				x							1
	9		x		x							2
	10				x	x		x				3
4	11					x					x	2
	12		x								x	2
Total exposures		3	3	2	4	5	2	3	1	0	3	26

Source: Media Department, Ogilvy & Mather, Inc.

the objective, it is desirable to select media that reach essentially the same people; an opposite strategy is required to maximize reach. Therefore, *duplication* of audiences is an important factor.

In practice, the problem lies in estimating the extent of duplication present within a media schedule. Data for this purpose are far from ideal, although some estimates are provided by the various syndicated audience data services. The difficulty arises when a number of media are utilized because available data sources then are inadequate.

Using Reach, Frequency, and GRP Measures

The starting point is to establish a media objective, usually in terms of desired GRP levels. For example, 100 gross rating points a week is a relatively heavy advertising schedule. In a highly competitive market, it is not unusual to invest at this level or even higher levels. The media planner must specify the media GRP levels desired. Then the media buyer can fit together an appropriate schedule.

For example, the media plan for a food product called for at least 200 gross rating points and maximum reach using prime-time television commercials. The media plan depicted in Figure 15–3 delivered 205 GRP with a reach of 78.6 percent of all television homes. Hence it was entirely satisfactory, all other things being equal. Notice, by the way, that an equivalent GRP level could also be generated with much lower reach and higher frequency. Therefore it is necessary to specify both desired reach and GRP.

Guidance on which of several alternative plans would be most effective is also provided. Consider the data in Figure 15–4, which show the reach and frequency analysis for a luxury item. The best media plan includes monthly magazines; this is especially evident when plans 1 and 2 are compared. Also, plans 2 and 3 show that spot television is probably optional since the effects on reach and frequency are not great.

Finally, reach, frequency, and GRP measures can be an excellent guide to estimate budget levels through the built-up analysis discussed in Chapter 10. The data in Figure 15–5 part A, for example, give a general indication of the reach and frequency levels achieved by from 100 to 300 GRP in a four-week period with a television schedule. To take just one illustration, 100 GRP in daytime network television will reach, on the average, 56 percent of all television homes with a frequency of 1.8 times in a four-week period. The objective of a media plan for a convenience food item calls for 74 percent reach with a 2.7 frequency in the top 100 spot television markets using daytime placement. The 200 GRP level thus would be adequate. Figure 15–5 part B indicates that the gross cost for one GRP point in the top 100 markets on daytime television is $3,875. This would then yield a needed budget level of $775,000 (200 × $3,875).

Historically, reach and frequency were measures confined only to television and magazine audiences. Now data sources and computer technology permit estimates *across media* and between various market segments.

FIGURE 15–3

Reach, Frequency, and GRP Levels Produced by a Media Plan for a Food Item

	Total Announcements	Average Rating per Announcement
Schedule—four weeks		
1 announcement per week on "60 Minutes"	4	20.0%
1 announcement every other week on "Murphy Brown"	2	18.8
1 announcement every other week on "The Cosby Show"	2	25.0
1 announcement every other week on "Wide World of Sports"	2	18.7
	10	

Reach— 78.6 percent of all TV homes
Frequency— 2.6
GRP— 205.0

Frequency Distribution Number of Announcements	Percent of Homes	Cumulated Percent
0	21.4	—
1	21.6	21.6
2	22.4	44.0
3	15.4	59.4
4	10.0	69.4
5	4.8	74.2
6	2.9	77.1
7	1.2	78.3
8	0.2	78.5
9	0.1	78.6
10 +	0.0	78.6

Source: Media Department, Ogilvy & Mather, Inc.

FIGURE 15–4

❖

Reach and Frequency Analysis for a Luxury Product

Plan 1	Plan 2	Plan 3
Spot *People*	Spot *People*	No Spot *People*
newsweeklies	newsweeklies	newsweeklies
no monthlies	monthlies	monthlies
Schedule (2x)	(1x)	
1 Spot *People*	1 Spot *People*	2 *Time*
		1 *Newsweek*
2 *Time*	1 *Time*	1 *U.S. News*
2 *Newsweek*	1 *Newsweek*	1 *New Yorker*
2 *U.S. News*	1 *U.S. News*	1 *Sports Illustrated*
2 *New Yorker*	1 *New Yorker*	1 *Business Week*
2 *Sports Illustrated*	1 *Sports Illustrated*	1 *Sunset*
2 *Business Week*	1 *Business Week*	1 *Esquire*
		1 *Fortune*
	1 *Sunset*	1 *National Geographic*
	1 *Esquire*	1 *Holiday*
	1 *Fortune*	1 *Harper's*
	1 *National Geographic*	1 *Atlantic*
	1 *Holiday*	1 *Reporter*
	1 *Harper's*	1 *Town & Country*
	1 *Atlantic*	1 *Status/Diplomat*
	1 *Reporter*	1 *Commentary*
	1 *Town & Country*	1 *Venture*
	1 *Status/Diplomat*	1 *Réalités*
	1 *Commentary*	2 *The Wall Street Journal*
	1 *Venture*	
	1 *Réalités*	
	2 *The Wall Street Journal*	

User Groups	Reach	Frequency	GRP
Plan 1			
Total men	37	2.9	107
Own luxury, intend to buy	46	3.2	149
Income of $55,000+	65	3.5	229
Plan 2			
Total men	53	2.0	103
Own luxury, intend to buy	61	2.3	142
Income of $55,000+	77	2.9	225
Plan 3			
Total men	53	2.2	115
Own luxury, intend to buy	60	2.5	154
Income of $55,000+	77	3.3	249

Therefore, these measures are finding widespread use in media planning. Note in Table 14–6 that some media costs were reported on both a CPM and cost-per-rating-point basis.

FIGURE 15–5

Reach (R) and Frequency (F) Estimates and Costs at Various GRP Levels

A. Network TV Reach and Frequency (4-week period—households)

Averages for schedule in which the number of commercials is about twice the number of different programs. Evening estimates are for one or two network schedules; daytime estimates assume more than one network and show type.

GRP Levels	Prime		M-F Daytime	
	Reach	Frequency	Reach	Frequency
100	56	1.8	39	2.6
150	67	2.2	44	3.4
200	74	2.7	47	4.3
250	77	3.2	49	5.1
300	79	3.8	50	6.0

Source: Leo Burnett Television Reach & Frequency System, 1989. Reach based on averages for schedules for the average message-to-show ratio. Based on Nielsen People Meter Persons Cume Analysis, 1987.

B. Spot Television (costs cumulated by top market groups)

Markets	Percent U.S. TV Households	Prime Time Cost/Rtg. Point	Daytime Cost/Rtg. Point	Early Evening Cost/Rtg. Point	Late Evening Cost/Rtg. Point
Top 10	31	$ 4,364	$1,319	$1,480	$1,862
Top 20	44	6,253	1,985	2,262	2,887
Top 30	53	7,656	2,511	2,910	3,680
Top 40	61	8,489	2,816	3,289	4,185
Top 50	67	9,137	3,063	3,624	4,591
Top 60	72	9,678	3,283	3,884	4,928
Top 70	76	10,175	3,465	4,130	5,242
Top 80	80	10,614	3,621	4,331	5,484
Top 90	83	10,957	3,746	4,504	5,672
Top 100	86	11,272	3,875	4,656	5,859

Source: *Media Marketing Guide, Fall 1988*.
Source: *Leo Burnett 1988 Media Costs and Coverage*, p. 10. Used with permission.

COMPETITIVE CONSIDERATIONS

Competition can assume major significance in media decisions. At times, the advertising objective will call, for example, for maintenance of "share of voice." *Share of voice* is the dollar amount of advertising spent on a brand divided by the total dollar amount of advertising spent in this brand's product category. Thus, if we spent $5 million on our brand, and all the competitors in total spent $25 million (including our $5 million), our share of voice would be $5/$25 = 20 percent. This is especially likely in a situation in which the boundaries of a total market are more or less static and a number of competitors are offering essentially similar products.

The rationale underlying a share-of-voice objective is that market share will roughly parallel advertising share. In such situations, it is necessary, therefore, to analyze market share, share of total advertising expenditures, and share of advertising messages actually reaching prospects. Consider the data in Figure 15–6. The first column depicts share of market for competing brands, and the next column reveals the best estimate of share of advertising spending for television. Brands A and B are spending in proportion to market

FIGURE 15–6

Competitive Marketing and TV Advertising Shares of Nine Leading Brands

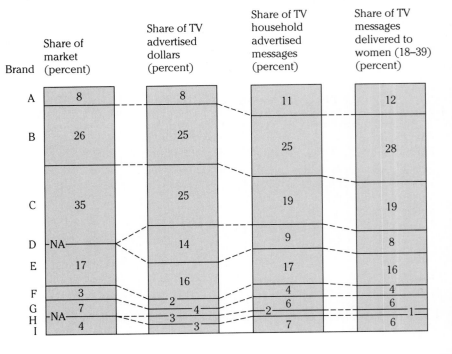

share, whereas the management of Brand C apparently believes that a dominant position can be maintained with a smaller proportional investment. Brand D apparently is a new product and is spending to attain an anticipated share.

Obviously, the quality of the advertising and other factors will affect the figures, but the data are quite revealing. It would appear, for example, that the Brand A schedule will lead to an increase in share of voice as well as a probable gain in market share. Brand B probably will remain stable, but Brand C may be in trouble. All other things being equal, it will be difficult to maintain market share with spending levels that lag competition to this extent. Finally, Brand D should be watched closely because it should achieve significant market inroads.

It should be stressed that this example represents a situation in which competition is a major factor, and this is not always the case. Nonetheless, competition is relevant in the majority of instances.

The third column in Figure 15–6 may be somewhat more puzzling. It provides an estimate of the *efficiency* of spending and is not necessarily equivalent to total dollar levels. With available data sources providing information on media audience, program ratings, and so on, it is possible to estimate the probable advertising exposure delivered by each firm's media schedule. Here Brand A is highly efficient in that an 8 percent share of spending delivers 11 percent of total messages. Brand C, on the other hand, apparently is choosing media that do not reach its prospects in that it has attained only a 19 percent share as compared with a 25 percent dollar share. These figures become especially significant when they are related to the key segment, messages delivered to women, appearing in the fourth column.

COST CONSIDERATIONS

Space and time costs are always important factors in media selection. These data usually appear in the volumes published by the Standard Rate & Data Service (SRDS). However, in practice, network TV and radio costs must be obtained from the network. Spot television and radio costs in SRDS are guides but are of little value for real planning or buying since buys are negotiated in terms of price. Because of this problem of actual prices being different from SRDS, two new services have developed. Conceptual Dynamics, Inc., publishes *Media Market Guide,* which among other things includes the cost for typical ad units by market. The second service is Spot Quotations And Data, Inc. (SQAD). This service provides real "street" prices for spot television in the top 51 markets. The measure provided by SQAD is the cost per household rating point (CPP) for a 30-second spot. SQAD averages the cost data from several unidentified agencies and combines them with the average of Nielsen and Arbitron audience measure for each market to give the CPP.

Recall from Chapter 14 that there are formulas (cost per thousand readers or homes, and the milline rate) that permit comparisons of the cost efficiency of various media. The logic of these formulas is that gross space costs must be refined by the audience reached per dollar spent before useful comparisons can be made across media.

The media planner then must obtain CPMs for target audience for every media vehicle under consideration. The computer can be used to combine audience measurement data, target audience designation, and the cost of an insertion to generate such figures. Figure 15–7 presents computer output from a run using Simmons's data for magazines. Note that the CPM target audience varies substantially depending on the target market specified. With computer technology, CPM's target audience can easily be calculated for many different target audience designations. Most of these programs allow *subjective* weighing of audience data to take into account the media planner's judgments about growth trends since the audience data were collected (see weight of 111.20 for *People*), and to allow the analysis of special editions (note three different special versions of *Time* in the output; each is subjectively assessed in terms of weight).

As useful as the CPM formula can be, it is often abused. First, it may be assumed that costs are the dominant consideration in media selection, whereas any of the other considerations mentioned thus far could be of great

FIGURE 15–7

❖ **Computer Output of CPM Target Audience Figures for Selected Magazines**

| **Target Market:**
$25M + Age 18–34
Population— 6665 (000)
Percent of Base— 4.47 | | | **Total Adults** | | | |
| | | | | **Reach** | | |
Rank	Cost	Weight	(000)	Percent Covg.	Percent Comp.	CPM
1. *People*	13,475	111.20	1243	18.6	9.7	10.84
2. *Time*	24,705	60.00	1317	19.8	10.6	18.76
3. *Time*	24,705	55.00	1207	18.1	10.6	20.47
4. *Time*	24,705	50.00	1098	16.5	10.6	22.50
5. *Newsweek*	38,160	100.00	1687	25.3	9.5	22.62
6. *Playboy*	40,745	100.00	1684	25.3	10.6	24.20
7. *Time*	53,195	100.00	2196	32.9	10.6	24.22
8. *Sports Illustrated*	34,010	100.00	1147	17.2	9.1	29.65
9. *Business Week*	18,760	100.00	547	8.2	14.3	34.30
10. *Esquire*	14,000	100.00	408	6.1	8.8	34.31
11. *U.S. News & World Report*	26,420	100.00	691	10.4	8.2	38.23

FIGURE 15–7

Computer Output of CPM Target Audience Figures for Selected Magazines
(concluded)

Target Market:
$25M + Age 35–49
Population— 6635 (000)
Percent of Base— 4.45

Rank	Cost	Weight	Reach (000)	Percent Covg.	Percent Comp.	CPM
1. *Time*	24,705	60.00	1162	17.5	9.4	21.26
2. *Time*	24,705	55.00	1065	16.1	9.4	23.20
3. *People*	13,475	111.20	571	8.6	4.4	23.60
4. *Business Week*	18,760	100.00	753	11.3	19.6	24.91
5. *Time*	24,705	50.00	968	14.6	9.4	25.52
6. *Newsweek*	38,160	100.00	1438	21.7	8.1	26.54
7. *Time*	53,195	100.00	1937	29.2	9.4	27.46
8. *Sports Illustrated*	34,010	100.00	1144	17.2	9.0	29.73
9. *U.S. News & World Report*	26,420	100.00	733	11.0	8.7	36.04
10. *Esquire*	14,000	100.00	287	4.3	6.2	48.78
11. *Playboy*	40,745	100.00	831	12.5	5.2	49.03

Explanation of Output

1. For each run, a "target market" is defined by the user based on some demographic variable: for example, the first run specifies 18- to 34-year-olds earning $25,000 and over as the target.

2. "Population" refers to the number of U.S. adults in this target; for example, 6,665,000 adults are in the target market.

3. "Percent of base" refers to the ratio of population as defined in item (2) above to the total U.S. adult population; for example, 6,665,000 is 4.47 percent of the total U.S. adult population (over 18).

4. Cost refers to the four-color, full-page cost of a magazine.

5. "Reach (000)" refers to the number of target market readers of an average issue of a magazine in thousands.

6. Percent coverage (*Percent Covg.*) refers to the ratio of reach to population; for example, for *People* magazine, it is 1,243,000/6,665,000 = 18.6 percent.

7. Percent composition (*Percent Comp.*) refers to the ratio of target audience readers of a magazine to total readers of a magazine; for example, 9.7 percent of *People* readers are in the 18 to 34 —$15,000-and-over target audience

8. "CPM" refers to cost per thousand target audience readers.

9. Weight allows the user to adjust the audience figures for a magazine. A weight of 100.0 means that the data on file are used as is in the calculations. *People* has been weighted up due to estimated expanded readership since the Simmons data were collected. Four different *Time* weights are presented. The 100.0 is the regular *Time* magazine. The other three weights for *Time* are for *Time Z*. This is so because Simmons surveys only measure readership on a national basis. Thus all special advertising editions of magazines (for example, *Time Z, Newsweek Executive, Business Week Industrial*) cannot be measured directly. What all publishers and users do in estimating readership is to simply take a percentage of the total readership when measuring demographic editions. *Time Z* is computed here by taking 50 percent, 55 percent, and 60 percent of regular *Time*. It was usual to use the 50 percent figure for $15,000 plus income and the 60 percent figure for $25,000 plus income.

importance, especially selectivity in reaching target markets. Furthermore, notice that the denominator of these formulas is circulation, readership, or viewership, none of which is modified to ascertain the number of prospects reached. A CPM of $2.83 could easily be a CPM for prospects of $20 because of inefficient coverage of the target market. Thus formulas of this type should be used only when the denominator is refined to generate *cost per thousand prospects reached* as it is in Figure 15–7.

Finally, it is difficult to interpret CPM figures under certain circumstances. CPM represents an average that treats all exposures the same, regardless of whether they are delivered to different people or represent increased frequency to the same people. As long as the repeated exposure is deemed to be of equal impact as the new exposure, CPM gives an advantage to a media vehicle that reaches a concentrated audience repeatedly. For example, it is possible to arrive at the same CPM with 10 percent of the people reached 10 times, 100 percent reached once, or 1 percent reached 100 times.

It can be concluded, therefore, that CPM must be used with caution. Cost efficiency is a useful criterion *only* when the other considerations mentioned in this chapter have also entered into the analysis. Even then it is only one criterion of an adequate media schedule, not the ultimate criterion, as many falsely assume.

QUALITATIVE MEDIA CHARACTERISTICS

The term *qualitative media characteristics* has come to assume several possible meanings. It is confined here to the role played by the medium or vehicle in the lives of the audience and with the positive or negative attitudes toward it and its advertising created by the medium or vehicle in its audience. This definition stresses the meaning of the medium to its readers, viewers, or listeners.

Qualitative values defy precise measurement and analysis, and existing data are sparse. Yet it should be clear that these characteristics form the mood in which advertising is received, and the resulting significance can exceed that of other factors that enter into media strategy. For instance, favorable attitudes toward a television personality can increase the effectiveness of advertising on that program.

As yet no continuing data sources can be used to assess the qualitative media characteristics across media classes. Rather, the analyst must rely on isolated research reports and his or her own judgment. Judgment, moreover, frequently will suffice. It is intuitively obvious, for instance, that the editorial environment and subjective values of the reader of the *Atlantic Monthly* are such as to be incompatible with the advertising of washday detergents. In other situations, however, the qualitative considerations are not obvious, and the need exists for more and better data. Fortunately, in this situation also, there is no serious methodological barrier to needed research.

A prime illustration of avoiding certain media environments is the recent action by some advertisers to remove their sponsorship from television shows or a specific episode featuring too much violence. Numbered among these companies are Procter & Gamble, General Motors, General Foods, and McDonald's.

DISTRIBUTION REQUIREMENTS

Distribution geography and stimulation of reseller support are considerations that can easily become dominant in certain situations.

Distribution geography refers to the density of distribution. Strictly national media would not be utilized if distribution were spotty across the country; local newspapers, radio, or television would represent a more economical media array. Promotional strategy also may call for heavy emphasis on dealer cooperative advertising whereby the dealer places local advertising, paid for in part by the manufacturer. Media choices in these cases are confined to local media by necessity, for the market reached by national media usually would substantially exceed that of the dealer. An identical situation is present when the manufacturer places advertising over the dealer's name without cooperative sharing of costs.

Promotional strategy at times dictates heavy reliance on personal selling to gain retail distribution, and advertising may be used as a door opener. It is often very effective for the company salesperson to point out to the retailer that the product has been nationally advertised in a prestigious medium; the pulling power of the advertisement thus becomes secondary to its role as a selling point to dealers. The sponsorship of network television programs and placement of advertisements in large-circulation magazines are popular strategies for this purpose.

Finally, it is frequently appropriate to advertise in consumer media for the sole purpose of stimulating dealer efforts. PepsiCo, Inc. for instance, sponsors such television spectaculars as the Miss America Pageant solely to serve as a rallying point for bottlers and a stimulus for greater efforts on their part.

The choice of media mix for Carnival Cruise Lines is presented in Promotion in Action 15–2.

SCHEDULING

Once the media to be used have been selected, it is necessary to determine the timing and allocation of advertising insertions. Of special importance are (1) scheduling by geographical region, (2) seasonal scheduling, (3) flighting (concentration of efforts in restricted time periods), and (4) scheduling within a chosen medium (size and location of insertions).

Geographical Scheduling

When the determination of geographical market potential was discussed in Chapter 10, the necessity to determine an *index of relative sales possibilities*

❖
**PROMOTION
IN ACTION
15–2**

Carnival Utilizes Its Media Choices to Enhance Impact

A typical media mix for Carnival Cruise Lines is as follows:

Magazines	$ 67,600
National Sunday magazines	29,600
Network TV	13,168,100
Spot TV	1,249,000
Network radio	—
Spot radio	—
Outdoor	1,900
Network cable	289,900
Newspapers	11,487,600
National syndication	—
Total	$26,293,700

The use of television provides the capability for Carnival to show the "fun" nature of the product and to build primary demand. Network shows selected are those with high target audience composition (see Chapter 2 for target description). These shows include afternoon soap operas and network news programs.

More detailed descriptive advertisements are presented in the newspaper ads that appear in over 200 markets, especially in the Sunday travel sections. This media allows Carnival to give information on schedules, itineraries, and prices. Tie-ins with specific travel agents are also possible with newspapers.

The magazines and the national magazines in Sunday papers selected include editorial-subject relevant and target-audience relevant ones such as *Cruise Travel, Travel-Holiday,* and *Modern Bride*. Magazines play a relatively minor reinforcing role in the Carnival media mix.

on a market-by-market basis was indicated. This index in turn serves as the foundation for geographical allocation of advertising dollars. The general principle is to allocate in proportion to market potential, all other things being equal. However, the "noise level" in major markets is higher than in smaller ones. Thus, more advertising weight relative to potential is usually placed in the larger markets.

Table 15–2 presents the geographical selectivity of the media plan for a convenience food item. Notice that allocations were made so that the schedule closely paralleled the index of brand use by county size.

The data in Table 15–2 provide only a very general indication of geographical selectivity. In addition, the agency utilized a computer program that permits media selection in proportion to market potential for each major metropolitan market. In this case, the projected percentage of sales in a given area became the target figure for total advertising impressions as well. Estimates were made of the necessary impressions for the entire fiscal year. These figures were then converted into gross rating points per week from which required dollar expenditure levels were estimated. In some cases, judgmental modifications were made when it was deemed advisable to ensure that certain markets should receive greater media weight than others. Finally, a computer printout compared original objectives for advertising impressions with actual media delivery. Some of the results were as follows:

Market	Target Impressions	Media Weight
Portland, Maine	1.7	1.5
Albany, New York	2.2	1.9
Milwaukee, Wisconsin	2.5	1.8
Los Angeles, California	11.2	11.9
Toledo, Ohio	0.9	1.1

Notice, first of all, that there was not an exact correspondence between target objectives and actual media weight, but the differences were so small as to be negligible. Also, the media schedule was evaluated in terms of GRP delivered, not the number of dollars spent. The dollar figure is not necessarily a good measure of *advertising message weight*, which can be estimated only from audience ratings.

Seasonal Scheduling

Because many products show seasonal variations in demand, the advertiser is compelled to introduce appropriate modifications in the timing of advertising throughout the year. In some instances, media weight is placed immediately prior to a seasonal upsurge so that maximum sales are generated at the beginning of the season. The promotion of air conditioning or heating equipment is a good illustration. In other instances, funds are allocated so that increases or reductions coincide closely with sales patterns.

The convenience food example indicated some slight seasonal variations in sales of the product. As the following data indicate, the media plan coincided closely with seasonal patterns:

Quarter	Percentage of Sales		Percentage of Media Weight	
June	26 }	55	34 }	57
September	29 }		23 }	
December	24 }	45	22 }	43
March	21 }		21 }	

Flighting

At times, media planners are forced to concentrate dollar allocations in certain time periods while cutting back at other times. This is referred to as *flighting,* and it is done to avoid spending at an inadequate level throughout the year. The objective is to achieve higher reach and frequency levels in a more limited period with the hope that the impact generated will carry over in the remaining periods.

Consider, for example, the data in Figure 15–8. Substantially higher reach and frequency levels are generated when the advertising is concentrated in 26 weeks rather than spread over 52 weeks.

Flighting offers the following advantages:

TABLE 15–2

❖

Geographical Selectivity of the Media Plan for a Convenience Food Item

County Size	Percentage in Sample Studied	Percentage of Users	Index of Brand Use (base 100)	Geographical Selectivity of Media Plan*
A	39.5	52.0	132	130
B	26.1	28.0	107	100
C	18.0	15.0	83	100
D	16.4	5.0	30	40

*Combination daytime television and three women's magazines.

1. Media rate and purchasing values such as better prices or discounts can be gained by concentrating ad dollars rather than spreading them.

2. There are communications values in concentrating advertising impact. A consumer awareness threshold that is impenetrable at light advertising levels can be crossed.

3. The availability of greater funds in shorter periods of time opens up new media strategy possibilities.

The first claimed advantage is rather apparent in that discounts increase in proportion to the concentration of dollars within a medium in a limited time period. Similarly, the third advantage can be a significant consideration in that a greater variety of media opportunities can often be presented. The second point, however, is more debatable. Obviously, a greater short-run impact can be made, but this may be at the sacrifice of continuing reinforcement during the interim periods. The net effect, therefore, can be the opposite of what is intended, especially if competitive efforts are strong.

FIGURE 15–8

Effect of Flighting on Reach and Frequency Levels

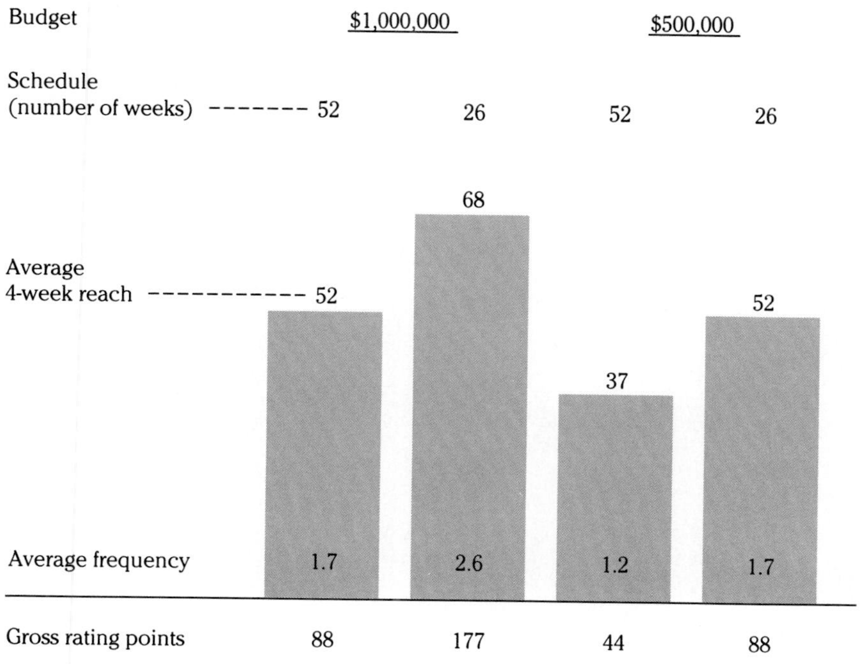

	$1,000,000		$500,000	
Budget				
Schedule (number of weeks) ------- 52		26	52	26
Average 4-week reach ---------- 52		68	37	52
Average frequency	1.7	2.6	1.2	1.7
Gross rating points	88	177	44	88

Flighting is probably most useful when available funds are inadequate to sustain a continued effort at adequate levels. Indeed, at times it might be the only feasible strategy when it is considered that spending at an unduly low level may result in little or no impact in view of competitors' efforts.

Many different flighting patterns (sometimes called *pulses*) are available. One scheme for classifying these patterns is presented in Figure 15-9. But which pattern is best?

The most effective pattern depends on the advertising communication objectives in relation to the nature of the product, target customers, distribution channels, and other marketing factors. Consider the following cases:

A *retailer* wants to announce a preseason sale of skiing equipment. He or she recognizes that only certain people will be interested in the message and that the target buyers need to hear the message only once or twice to know whether they are interested. The objective is to maximize the *reach* of the message, not the *repetition*. The retailer decides to concentrate the messages on the days of the sale at a level rate but to vary the time of day to avoid the same audiences. Pattern (1) is used.

A *muffler manufacturer-distributor* wants to keep his or her name before the public yet does not want the advertising to be too continuous because

FIGURE 15-9

❖

Classification of Advertising Timing Patterns

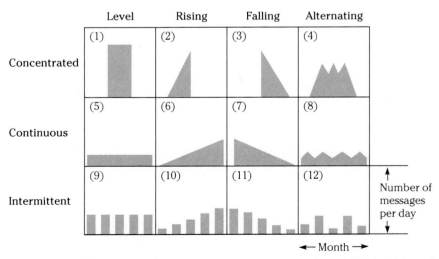

Source: Philip Kotler, *Marketing Management: Analysis, Planning and Control*, 6th ed. (Englewood Cliffs, N.J.: Prentice Hall 1988), p. 636.

only 3 to 5 percent of the cars on the road need a new muffler at any given time. The choice therefore is to use intermittent advertising. Furthermore, because Fridays are paydays for many potential buyers, it might be the best day to interest them in replacing a worn-out muffler. So the choice is made to sponsor a few messages on a midweek day and more messages on Friday. Pattern (12) is used.[1]

General rules should be used with care because promotion is a very situation-specific activity. A firm must be willing to experiment with its flighting pattern if it wants to determine the best one.

Putting the Media Plan Together

In the end, the marketer must combine quantitative and qualitative information about media, along with scheduling needs to make specific media choices. Promotion in Action 15–3 illustrates the outcome of this reasoning. Note the scheduling and the selection of different media depending on the target market for the advertising.

Scheduling within Media

Media scheduling necessitates specifying both the size of the space or time unit to be purchased and the location within the medium. These issues have been extensively researched, and it is now possible to advance a number of generalizations.

Size of the Advertisement The numerous studies of size of the advertisement on the printed page have made it clear that doubling size will not double results. In fact, readership increases roughly in proportion to the square root of space increase. This does not mean, of course, that a half page should necessarily be preferred over a full page. Size offers real advantages in greater power of attraction, more flexibility in layout arrangement, and greater opportunity for dramatic use of space elements. Moreover, the impact of larger space units on *attitude* may be greater, although existing evidence is not clear on this point.

The relative advantages of variations in the length of television or radio commercials defy generalization, although it is well-known that longer commercials are often preferred for the reason that creative presentation is simplified when time pressures are not acute. The shorter commercial is usually more demanding to produce, but the rising costs of television time in particular have forced many advertisers to abandon the longer advertisement. The shorter commercial can be equally effective if proper care is taken to prepare a direct and convincing appeal. In fact, 30 seconds can be *too much* time for some messages, and the shorter 10-second commercial can be more effective. For example, this trade-off between effectiveness and cost has resulted in a trend toward shorter television commercials over the last few decades. At one time, the 60-second commercial was the norm, but through the mid-1980s, the 30-second commercial became the dominant form. As Table 15–3 indicates, the trend of the last few years is toward the use of 15-second commercials.

Position of the Advertisement   From the numerous studies documenting the role of position on the page in printed media, the following generalizations have emerged:

1. It makes little difference whether the advertisement appears on the left- or right-hand page in either newspapers or magazines. The analysis of readership of the Million Market Newspapers, for example, presents this conclusion unmistakably. In fact, Starch has concluded

❖
**PROMOTION
IN ACTION
15–3**

Toy Marketers Select and Schedule Media

Given that toys and games are primarily seasonal in nature, most companies spend their ad budgets during the holiday season at the end of the year. As summer and spring arrive, though, there's usually another small push for outdoor products. Because the target audience is primarily the child, who will then convince the parent to make the purchase, advertising abounds on Saturday mornings and during afternoon specials. Magazines are often used to supplement the TV ads, whereas radio and outdoor advertising are rarely used.

James King, director of advertising services for Mattel, said that they "support 45 to 50 products in the fourth quarter. Each one has its own budget and media plan." Mattel, with a budget of over $40 million, spent the majority on TV with a 3 to 1 ratio of network over spot. The company has been increasing its expenditure of spot ads since King believed that "its flexibility allows us to adapt its use to shifting sales patterns regionally, and it gives us a better fix on local market opportunities." Network buys are on Saturday morning and afternoon children's specials; spots are in the after-school hours. Mattel's print buys are targeted toward mothers through women's magazines and children through a new magazine, *Muppets*.

The same pattern applied for Kenner, which spent $25 million ($16.1 million on network and $7.5 million on spot TV) with heavy expenditures on network Saturday morning and local afternoon children's shows. It ran one from 40 years of research that the primary factor in readership is the advertisement itself—what it says and how it says it.

2. In magazines, the greatest readership is usually attracted by covers and the first 10 percent of the pages, but beyond this the location of the advertisement is a minor issue.

3. Page traffic is high in nearly *all* parts of a newspaper, and position within the paper is of little significance.

4. Although position does not appear to be a crucial factor, some advantage accrues to the advertiser if the copy is located adjacent to compatible editorial features. Most newspapers and magazines attempt to ensure compatibility, and it can be specified by the advertiser for extra cost.

5. Thickness of the magazine has been found to exert only a slight effect on coupon returns and advertising recognition and recall.

6. A number of other generalizations result from a series of analyses of newspaper readership:

Toy Marketers Select and Schedule Media (concluded)

❖
**PROMOTION
IN ACTION
15–3**

unusual schedule in the month of October that included five consecutive evening ads at 7:30 P.M. to promote Strawberry Shortcake and Care Bear products.

Companies such as Fisher-Price have chosen a different strategy since it markets mainly infant and preschool products. Relying more heavily on print media than its competitors (spent $5.1 million), Fisher-Price reached its target audience of female parents. Ads ran in women's magazines, baby books, and *People*. Robert Moody, director of advertising, commented that "We've found print to be an efficient way to reach the adult audience."

But Fisher-Price still spends 60 percent of its budget on network, spot, and cable television. Moody said that "we use daytime network television (soap operas, game shows) and prime access in spot markets." The company's cable buy was on American Baby. Moody additionally said that "you must be aware of changes in the broadcast field and experiment with cable and syndication."

Hasbro also followed the industry's advertising basics with buying Saturday morning and afternoon TV spots, as well as ads in women's magazines. Dan Owen, vice president of marketing at Hasbro, said that "When the child gets to be five or older, the best results are achieved by advertising directly to the child. Toy purchases are 80 to 90 percent child initiated."

a. Position in the gutter (the inside fold) is no different from position on the outer half of the page.
b. Position on the page has little effect except when competing advertisements become especially numerous.
c. There are known differences in readership of different editorial features such as general news and sports by sex and age.

It thus appears that position on the newspaper or magazine page and location within the issue are minor considerations. There can, of course, be significant exceptions to these generalizations, but the advertisement itself appears to be the determining factor in high readership or coupon return.

Position in broadcast advertising has been researched to a lesser degree, at least insofar as published literature shows. It is known from the meager published evidence, however, that commercials frequently perform better when inserted as part of a regular program than at the station break, which often becomes cluttered. Location within a program seems to be especially advantageous for longer commercials. Many also believe that commercials at the beginning and end of a program are placed at a disadvantage because of the clutter of program announcements, production and talent credits, and other distracting nonprogram material. If this disadvantage appears to be important, the sponsor purchasing time on a participating basis would do well to specify insertion within the program. Others believe

TABLE 15-3

❖

Television Commercial Length

	% of Total Activity					
	Spot			Network		
	1986	1987	1988	1986	1987	1988
10 sec.	5.3	4.8	4.8	0.5	0.2	0.2
15 sec.	2.6	4.4	5.2	20.8	30.2	36.2
20 sec.	0.1	0.1	0.1	1.2	1.0	1.0
30 sec.	86.7	85.3	84.2	73.7	65.6	59.8
45 sec.	0.3	0.2	0.2	1.3	0.9	0.8
60 sec.	2.9	3.1	3.5	1.9	1.6	1.6
90+ sec.	2.1	2.1	2.0	0.6	0.5	0.4
Total	100.0	100.0	100.0	100.0	100.0	100.0

Source: Broadcast Advertisers Reports.
Source: *Leo Burnett 1988 Media Cost and Coverage*, p. 10. Used with permission.

that program commercial position is of no consequence, and not enough data exist to support either position.

SUMMARY

This chapter has investigated a number of factors that enter into media strategy, including requirements of creative strategy, audience selectivity, reach and frequency, competitive considerations, cost efficiency, qualitative factors, distribution requirements, and scheduling.

Clearly, it is impossible to present a conclusive set of steps leading to successful media selection in every problem. To do so would be to oversimplify relevant issues to an unrealistic degree. Media selection requires *research thinking* in that information must be sought at many points in the analytical procedure and utilized creatively and imaginatively. The considerations outlined above represent most of the major variables shaping the selection problem. A myriad of solutions is possible, depending entirely on these situational requirements.

REVIEW AND DISCUSSION QUESTIONS

1. The Tourism Bureau of France has hired you to prepare a media strategy for next year's advertising campaign to attract U.S. tourists to come to France. A media budget of $7.5 million has been allocated for this purpose. Prepare a media strategy for the bureau. Be sure to indicate (1) the dollar allocation across types of media (magazines, television, etc.), (2) the specific media vehicles you would recommend within the selected media types (*People, TV Guide,* ABC National News, etc.), and (3) the scheduling of the placement of the ads. Also be explicit in your assumptions about target markets, data, and so on.

2. Prepare a media strategy for the introduction of a new $55,000 sports car into the North American market by Ford-Jaguar, as per the preceding question.

3. The advertising agency for the Crummy Candy Company has submitted a media plan with the statement that "this plan is designed to achieve maximum frequency; reach is of little importance." The campaign is aimed at the market under 25 years of age, and the product being advertised is a popular chocolate bar that now has second place in market share in most local markets. Is frequency a desirable strategy for this type of product?

4. How can the media plan mentioned in question 3 be designed so as to achieve maximum frequency? What changes might be necessary if greater reach were desired?

5. Using the data in Figure 15–7, select the magazine mix for the media plan for a new male/female cosmetic line that is targeted at the first target market presented in the figure. Now select a magazine mix for the other target group. Assume that you have $1 million to spend against the specific target group.

NOTES

1. Philip Kotler, *Marketing Management: Analysis, Planning, Implementation, and Control*, 6th ed. (Englewood Cliffs, N.J.: Prentice Hall, 1988), p. 637.

Measurement of Advertising Effectiveness

CAMPBELL SOUP TRACKS V-8 TO NEW ADVERTISING SUCCESS

V-8 Cocktail Vegetable Juice is a well-established, tomato-based canned beverage marketed by the Campbell Soup Company. V-8 had shown substantial growth over the years and was a price leader in the red juices category. Management attributed this strong sales growth to the brand's advertising campaign that focused on V-8's superior taste relative to tomato juice.

When sales declined, advertising on the brand was discontinued in most markets. Management believed that diminishing sales trends were a sign of "advertising wearout." On two previous occasions, the institution of a new campaign had revived declining sales trends. Based on these past results, a new creative approach was developed.

To evaluate this new approach, the Campbell Soup Company conducted a series of studies for V-8 over a five-year period. The first of these studies was a controlled experiment to evaluate the effectiveness of the new "I coulda had a V-8" campaign and media mix.

The new campaign differed from V-8's previous campaign in two important factors. The new campaign was primarily based on television; the previous campaign had been primarily based on radio. Because of this, the new campaign required a significantly larger budget to achieve similar exposure goals. The controlled experiment was designed to evaluate the advantages, if any, of the new campaign.

The study was designed to evaluate both the new and old campaigns at the proposed higher budget using three different media mixes: a television/radio mix, prime time TV only, and fringe TV only. The old campaign was also tested using only radio. (The new campaign's design precluded a radio-only strategy.) A control component was also created using the old campaign, the old budget level, and the old media mix. The purpose of this control was to discern any "start-up" effects related to the mere act of advertising after a six- to nine-month hiatus. Based on the assumption that the start-up effect was independent of the actual campaign, the study allowed marketers to estimate campaign and budget effects by comparing a test cell with the control cell. The structure of the study is presented below.

Budget Level	Media Mix	New Creative	Old Creative
New Budget	TV/Radio	118.8* (2 markets)	111.2 (2 markets)
	TV Prime	121.8 (2 markets)	116.6 (2 markets)
	TV Fringe	113.6 (2 markets)	116.2 (2 markets)
	Radio	Not tested	107.2 (4 markets)
Old Budget	Primary Radio (Old Mix)	Not tested	110.0 15 markets (control)

*Entries are the ratios of cumulative actual sales to cumulative forecast sales in each market after three months, averaged over the markets in each cell and multiplied by 100. Under a null hypothesis of no treatment effect, the expected value of these entries is 100, assuming unbiased forecasts.

Selling Areas Marketing, Inc. (SAMI), defines experimental "markets" within geographical areas that receive their television signal from a central town or city. Because of this, a new media mix or advertising budget change can easily be implemented in a SAMI "market." SAMI also measures warehouse withdrawals on a monthly basis, by market, and for each size and brand in a particular product category. This allowed marketers to track V-8 sales for each market. Thirty-one SAMI markets were used in the experiment, 15 as control cells and 16 as various test cells.

Using the same media mix, response to the new campaign was 4 percent higher than response to the old campaign. The new campaign combined with the TV/radio and prime time TV media mixes corresponded to a 10 percent increase in sales relative to the control group. The study identified a definite relationship between strong consumer response and new creative presentation, media mix, and budget level. The power of causal designs in marketing research is evident.

Source: Joseph O. Eastlack and Ambar G. Rao, "Modeling Response to Advertising and Pricing Changes for 'V-8' Cocktail Vegetable Juice," *Marketing Science* (Summer 1986), pp. 245–59, as presented in Thomas C. Kinnear and James R. Taylor, *Marketing Research: An Applied Approach,* 4th ed. (New York: McGraw-Hill, 1991).

The V-8 Promotion in Action illustrates the use of a field experiment approach to measuring advertising effectiveness. This approach is but one of many available to the advertisier.

This chapter evaluates measures that are useful both in *pretesting* a message and in assessing its effectiveness following its placement in the media, as part of the whole advertising plan (*posttesting*). A persistent question is whether advertising effectiveness can be measured. The response in the past was mixed, but about 73 percent of advertisers use some type of effectiveness measurement.[1] Research orientation is becoming increasingly commonplace, largely because management is demanding proof that funds invested pay off. Measurement tools are being used with greater sophistication as new techniques are developed, although there is still room for substantial improvement.

Some believe that creativity and copy testing are incompatible. This position has little merit because creative imagination can produce *ineffective* copy. In reality, many artists and copywriters do not want to be held accountable for the productivity of their output. Part of the difficulty is that some managements use copy tests as a "report card." A better approach is to give artists and writers copy-testing results with the option to use them as they see fit and to reveal or not to reveal the results as they choose.

The authors believe, on balance, that the arguments for copy testing outweigh the arguments against it. The objective is not to find a definitive measure of communication success. The presently available methodology will not justify such a goal. Rather, all that can be provided is a good indication of whether or not copy will be comprehended and responded to as intended. Although this does not guarantee production of a good advertisement, *it substantially lowers the risk of failure*. At the very least, copy tests, if properly used, will differentiate a poor message from a good one. What they cannot do definitively at the present time is distinguish a *good* message from a *great* one. This type of fine discrimination awaits further methodological development.

AN IDEAL COPY-TESTING PROCEDURE: PACT

Of course, the reliability and validity of any copy-testing procedure need to be demonstrated. *Reliability* means that the procedure is free of random error. That is, the measure is consistent and accurate. *Validity* refers to the procedure being free of both random and systematic error. Validity addresses the question of bias and deals with the question: Are we measuring what we think we are measuring? Thus a reliable test would provide consistent results every time an ad is tested. A valid test would provide predictive power to the performance of the ad in the market.

Unfortunately, all too many suppliers of copy-testing services do not provide measures concerning these issues. Recently, 21 of the largest advertising agencies in the United States endorsed a set of principles aimed at improving copy testing. These principles are called *PACT* (*Positioning Advertising Copy Testing*). These nine principles state that a "good" copy testing system:[2]

1. Provides measurements that are relevant to the objectives of the advertising.

2. Requires agreement about how the results will be used in advance of each specific test.

3. Provides multiple measurements because single measurements are generally inadequate to assess the performance of an ad.

4. Is based on a model of human response to communication—the reception of a stimulus, the comprehension of the stimulus, and the response to the stimulus.

5. Allows for consideration of whether the advertising stimulus should be exposed more than once.

6. Recognizes that the more finished a piece of copy is, the more soundly it can be evaluated and requires, as a minimum, that alternative executions be tested in the same degree of finish.

7. Provides controls to avoid the biasing effects of the exposure context.

8. Takes into account basic considerations of sample definition.

9. Demonstrates reliability and validity empirically.

These are important recommendations that should be followed. In doing so, the reliability and validity of copy testing would improve greatly.

Table 16–1 is a classification of the most widely used measurement methods, classified first into those most useful in measuring response to the *advertisement* itself or its contents (awareness, comprehension, liking, and so on). The second classification differentiates actual impact of the message on *product* awareness, attitude, or usage. These data can be gathered under either *laboratory* conditions in which the respondents are aware they are being measured or *real-world* conditions, in which there is no awareness of the measurement process. In virtually all the testing procedures listed in Table 16–1, the results for the specific advertisement being tested are compared against (1) the *norms* for all ads in that testing procedure and (2) often against the norms for that particular product class and media environment.

CELL I: ADVERTISING-RELATED LABORATORY MEASURES FOR PRETESTING

In the category of advertising-related laboratory measures are those that yield data on attention, comprehension, retention, or response to the message itself in a laboratory-type research situation, as opposed to measures under real-world conditions. A variety of approaches that primarily measure the ability of a stimulus to attract and hold attention is discussed. The usefulness of what are fundamentally copy-testing procedures is greatest in pretesting advertisements, as was pointed out in Chapter 13.

1. The Consumer Jury

Consumers are frequently asked to analyze advertisements and rate their probable success on the assumption that "if laypeople are superior to the advertising expert in their conscious opinions as to the effectiveness of an advertisement, it is only because they are better judges of what influences them than is an outsider." Typically, 50 to 100 consumers from the target audience are interviewed, either individually or in small groups.

In one method referred to as the *order-of-merit rating,* a member of the jury (usually a sample of from 50 to 100 representative consumers) is asked to rank in order a group of layouts or copy blocks usually presented in rough, unfinished form and often mocked up on separate sheets. The juror might be asked these questions:

1. Which of these advertisements would you most likely read if you saw it in a magazine?
2. Which of these headlines would interest you the most in reading further?
3. Which of these advertisements convince you most of the quality of the product?

4. Which layout do you believe would be most effective in causing you to buy?

The questioning progresses from the second-best alternative to the worst. The verdict presumably indicates the relative effectiveness of each alternative presentation.

Order-of-merit rating is of questionable value for several significant reasons:

TABLE 16–1

❖   **Classification of Advertising Effectiveness Measures**

	Advertising-Related Test (reception or response to the message itself and its contents)	Product-Related Test (impact of message on product awareness, liking, intention to buy, or use)
Laboratory Measures (respondent aware of testing and measurement process)	**Cell I** Pretesting Procedures 1. Consumer jury 2. Portfolio tests 3. Readability tests 4. Physiological measures Eye Camera Tachistoscope GSR/PDR	**Cell II** Pretesting Procedures 1. Theater tests 2. Trailer tests 3. Laboratory stores
Real-World Measures (respondent unaware of testing and measurement process)	**Cell III** Pretesting Procedures 1. Dummy advertising vehicles 2. Inquiry tests 3. On-the-air tests Posttesting Procedures 1. Recognition tests 2. Recall tests 3. Association measures 4. Combination measures	**Cell IV** Pretesting and Posttesting Procedures 1. Pre- and posttests 2. Sales tests 3. Minimarket tests

Source: Adapted from the classification schema utilized by Professor Ivan Ross at the University of Minnesota.

1. It is probably asking too much of anyone to predict future behavior during and immediately after communication exposure.

2. Ranking of many alternatives can be exceedingly difficult, with the result that the ratings have little validity.

3. Some people have a tendency to rate one or two preferred alternatives high on all characteristics, just as they emphasize the good traits of a close friend while overlooking bad attributes. This distortion in judgment, called the *halo effect,* cannot be eliminated.

These problems are sufficiently serious that order-of-merit ratings usually are abandoned for more precise methods.

A better approach is to utilize some type of rating scale to elicit intensity of preference for each stimulus. No attempt is made to provide a ranking. In one example, advertisements were developed to influence public attitudes toward the Prudential Insurance Company and to cause people to think better of the company than of the insurance industry in general. Twenty-five attitude-scale statements were developed, focusing on aspects of the company and its operation. Respondents were asked to rate on a 10-point scale the degree to which the statements applied to most life insurance companies and then to the company whose advertisements they were viewing in disguised form, with company identity blocked out. The effectiveness of the advertisement was judged on the basis of the extent to which it induced a change in the rating of the company to make it more favorable than that for the industry. Meaningful differences were produced, and it was possible to isolate the most effective creative treatment.

The advantages of the scale are that it provides a basis to isolate dimensions of opinion; the technique is standardized and susceptible to comparison over time; it is reliable and replicable; full allowance is made for individual frames of reference; and problems of question-phrasing are eased. Also, norms giving average results by product class or even for previous ads for the same brand can be calculated. Almost all major copy-testing services give norm scores. Furthermore, determination of degrees of intensity of feeling provides a basis for ranking alternatives and assessing how well each performs against predetermined norms. Finally, the wording of questions reduces the danger that the individual will "play expert" and distort his or her reported opinion.

Consumer jury measures are widely used. Many experts believe that the artificiality of the questioning procedure introduces bias so that the ratings can have questionable validity. For this reason, more use is now made of the other measures discussed in this section as well as the real-world measures to be discussed later. A common variant of the consumer jury is obtaining consumer reactions to ads in a focus group interview.

2. Focus Groups

A focus group involves a moderator who conducts a loosely structured interview with 6 to 12 target consumers simultaneously. The moderator works from an interview plan but does not force structure on the discussion among the members of the focus group. The discussion usually starts with a broad discussion of the product category, and then the moderator gently directs the discussion to the brand of concern and then to the specifics of the advertising being tested. Example ads are typically shown to the focus group. The reactions of the members of the group in their discussion of the ad are then summarized.

The data so generated are qualitative in nature. No attempt is made to count the number in the group who prefer one ad over another. Thus, definitive conclusions are dangerous from focus groups. Some advertisers mistakenly believe that focus group results represent the whole market. Focus groups can be useful in giving creative directions to ads, giving insights into consumer motivations in the product category and their reaction to types of ads, and helping to identify ads that deserve further testing by more quantitative procedures.

3. Portfolio Tests

The portfolio test method requires the exposure of a group of respondents to a portfolio consisting of both test and control advertisements. The test ad is the one that the advertiser is interested in measuring the impact of; control ads are ones for which the testing company has response scores based on extensive testing over some period of time. These latter ads allow the advertiser to calibrate the effectiveness of an ad based on its score relative to the control ads' scores. In addition, the control ads allow the tester to identify a subject who is not attending to the advertisement assessment task. This identification is based on scores for the control ads that are far out of the norm for those ads. The principal criterion of effectiveness is playback of the content following exposure. The test advertisement that induces the highest recall of content presumably will be most effective in capturing and holding attention.

Portfolio tests are widely used, but vigorous attacks have been directed at the pretest use of this device. Critics contend that recall scores can vary from alternative to alternative for several reasons:

1. Variations can occur due to interviewing errors or memory defects, although this can be true of *any* research.
2. There may be legitimate differences between advertisements.
3. Differences may arise as a result of the consumer's interest in the products being promoted.

4. Recall scores may not be appropriate measures for low-involvement learning situations. Recognition is a better measure in these circumstances.

Variation for the second reason, of course, is the fundamental premise of the portfolio test, but some believe that interest in the product, the third cause, may be the most important problem. If so, the portfolio method clearly is not differentiating between advertisements on the basis of variations in creative treatment.

For the portfolio method to perform as claimed, scores on recall of the control advertisements should vary less from test to test than scores on the stimuli under analysis. Yet data have been reported to indicate that this relationship does not hold true, and it appears that product interest dominates all other factors. Apparently interest in the product seems to affect memory of the advertisements viewed and thereby obscures real differences between the stimuli.

These arguments against the portfolio test are plausible. Perhaps momentary reexposure to the alternatives viewed in the portfolio would sharpen memory and minimize distortions entering from product interest.

Regardless of the danger of memory distortion, this test serves its purpose well if recall data correlate with readership scores following investment of funds in the campaign. Each user must be satisfied that the predictive power of this device is sufficient to warrant the costs of research.

4. Readability Tests

Procedures are available to permit analysis of the readability of copy without consumer interviewing. The foremost method was developed by Rudolph Flesch, whose formula is in wide use.[3] The Flesch formula focuses on the human interest appeal in the material, the length of sentences, and the familiarity of words. These factors are found to correlate with the ability of persons with varying educational backgrounds to comprehend written material.

Readability of advertising copy is assessed by determining the average number of syllables per 100 words. These factors are then substituted into the Flesch formula, and the results are compared with predetermined norms for the target audience. It is usually found that copy is understood most easily when sentences are short, words are concrete and familiar, and frequent personal references are made.

Mechanical rules should not be observed to the extent that copy becomes stilted or unoriginal. The Flesch method is only a means to check communication efficiency, and gross errors in understanding can be detected and avoided. It should always be used, however, in connection with other pretest procedures.

5. Physiological Measures

Also within the advertising-related laboratory methods is a series of physiological measurement procedures.

The Eye Camera   For many years, it has been possible to track eye movements over advertising copy with the eye camera. The route that a person's eyes follow is then superimposed on the layout to determine which parts appear to capture and hold attention and whether or not various elements are perceived in the order intended by the creative person.

Eye camera results provide a guide in designing a layout so that the eye follows the intended path, but the findings contain a large degree of ambiguity. In the first place, exposure is undertaken in highly unnatural conditions, and it is questionable whether resulting eye movement patterns are what they would be when the consumer is not looking into a large apparatus. Furthermore, eye attraction does not necessarily reflect the person's thoughts or indicate success in capturing attention. Lingering at one point may also indicate difficulty in comprehension. For these reasons, the eye camera has never achieved wide usage. For it to be used widely, its validity must be proven.

The Tachistoscope   This laboratory device is basically a slide projector with attachments that allows the presentation of stimuli under varying conditions of speed and illumination. The tachistoscope has come to be a useful tool for many advertising researchers, especially in magazine and outdoor advertising. The Leo Burnett agency, for example, uses it to assess the rate at which an advertisement conveys information. The speed of response is recorded for various elements of an advertisement (illustration, product, and brand), and it has been found that high readership scores correlate with speed of recognition of the elements under analysis. Response to visualization seems to be especially important.

About 20,000 persons are tested with the tachistoscope each year at the Leo Burnett agency. The typical sample size is from 10 to 20, and no person is tested more than four times during any one year. As an indication of success, tachistoscopic measurement verified quick recognition of the Allstate Insurance Company name in an advertisement, a basic promotional objective, and the campaign built on this finding was believed to be highly successful. The only claim that Burnett researchers make, however, is that the tachistoscope measures physical perception; response from this point on is solely a function of the copy.

GSR/PDR   Galvanic skin response (GSR) and pupil dilation response (PDR) measure different aspects of attention attraction. GSR measures first the decline in electrical resistance of the skin to a passage of current and second changes in the potential difference between two areas of body surface. When GSR rises, it is believed to be an accurate indicator of *arousal* in response to a stimulus.

PDR, on the other hand, measures minute differences in pupil size and appears to be a sensitive measure of the amount of information or load processed within the central nervous system in response to an incoming stimulus. At one time, it was widely claimed that PDR measured emotional response, and several published studies purported to document that it could isolate attitudinal reaction to marketing stimuli. The weight of current evidence, however, makes this interpretation highly questionable.

A series of studies was undertaken using both GSR and PDR with a variety of audio and print stimuli.[4] It was found fairly consistently that good short-term and long-term retention occurs when both GSR and PDR are high in response to an advertisement. In addition, some tentative evidence indicates that GSR also correlates with attitude change, but this finding needs further investigation.

CELL II: PRODUCT-RELATED LABORATORY MEASURES FOR PRETESTING

Some techniques can be utilized under laboratory conditions to determine the effects of the message on consumer attitudes toward the product or service itself—such as awareness, attitude shift, and changes in buying intentions. Included in this category are the theater tests, trailer tests, and laboratory stores. These methods are fundamentally pretesting procedures.

1. Theater Tests

Theater tests are a means to assess changes in consumer product preference after exposure to advertisements. Typically, tickets are mailed to about 350 to 1,000 respondent households, to yield a sample of 250 to 600. Respondents are also recruited by telephone and mall intercept. ARS and ASI Market Research, Inc., offer these types of test. The research format is essentially the same for all testing sessions: people are invited to view new television shows with commercials inserted in the usual place. A drawing is held before the showing, and each consumer is offered a choice of various products as gifts. Product choices are noted, and then the show and commercials are viewed. Another drawing and offer of gifts is held after exposure, and changes in stated brand preference are noted. Written comments are also solicited on the programs and the commercials.

At first glance, it would appear that changes in stated preferences for gift products would in no way be meaningfully related to advertising exposure. Some rather dramatic conclusions, however, have been derived from the theater tests. Those campaigns rated as superior on the basis of changing product preferences tended to produce increases in sales as more dollars were invested in advertising. On the other hand, increased investment in inferior campaigns allegedly was found at times to *decrease* sales.

A definitive evaluation of the theater procedure must await disclosure of more details of validation research. Many advertisers and agency executives have voiced dissatisfaction regarding its predictive ability, although it has been successfully used by a number of firms.

Theater tests may tap a dimension of response that enables reasonably accurate prediction of advertising success, and for this reason it is in wide use. Respondents are presumably unaware that they are rating advertisements, and the tendency toward "buyer expertise" may thus be eliminated. Variations of this method are also in use.

2. Trailer Tests

Respondents may be brought to a central location, often a portable trailer or van set up in a shopping center, where they are shown several advertisements with or without surrounding editorial material or programming. Usually a comparative evaluation is made of two or more executions of the same theme. Respondents are told that the product can be made to different formulations and are shown copy describing each. Then they are asked to choose between the two formulations; questioning reveals what the commercial communicates. Although the technique is artificial, many believe that it is a useful way to measure comprehension of the copy. Furthermore, it is quite inexpensive.

3. Laboratory Stores

The laboratory store is a variation on the theater technique described above. Respondents are exposed to advertising under various types of conditions and are then permitted to shop in a small store. Usually coupons or chits that can be redeemed for actual merchandise are provided. In this way, actual product movement in response to advertising can be monitored.

CELL III: ADVERTISING-RELATED MEASUREMENT UNDER REAL-WORLD CONDITIONS FOR PRETESTING AND POSTTESTING

Procedures used in the second major category of technique depicted in Table 16–1, real-world measures, usually involve exposure under real-world conditions such as would normally be encountered in the consumer's home. Most researchers believe that the greater realism provided enhances the validity of the resulting data.

This section discusses the fairly extensive group of real-world measurements of response to or liking of the message itself. Some measurements are usually used to pretest the message prior to investment in time or space; others are usually used to posttest following airing or viewing. We begin our discussion by examining pretesting procedures.

Pretesting Procedures

1. Dummy Advertising Vehicles   Many testing organizations use a dummy magazine for pretesting purposes; such tests can result in accurate predictions of response. Editorial features of lasting interest are permanent items in this magazine; the only variations in the five yearly editions are test advertisements. Each printing is distributed to a random sample of homes in various geographical areas. Readers are told that the publisher is interested in evaluations of editorial content and are instructed to read the magazine in a normal fashion. A return interview focuses on both the editorial content and advertisements. Each advertisement is scored on recall, extent of copy readership, and whether or not the advertisement induces product interest.

The use of dummy vehicles is subject to the same criticisms as the portfolio test, but this procedure possesses the distinct advantage that advertisements are tested under completely natural surroundings—normal exposure in the home. Recall of content under such circumstances is likely to produce a more realistic indication of advertising success.

2. Inquiry Tests   Inquiry tests measure advertising effectiveness on the basis of return of coupons (from advertisements inviting readers to send for information) run under normal conditions in printed media. Different creative treatments may be compared in several ways: (1) by running coupons in successive issues of the same medium, (2) by running them simultaneously in issues of different media, and (3) by taking advantage of "split-run" privileges offered by some media whereby alternate copies carry different versions of the message. The split-run procedure is more widely used because all variables other than creative differences between stimuli are held constant.

The inquiry tests can focus on a number of creative variations: (1) one advertisement versus a completely different version, (2) variations in type or other elements of the same appeal, (3) summed inquiries compared over the total run of two or more campaigns, and (4) the effectiveness of different media when the same advertisement is run in each.

The advantages are apparent in that no interviews are required, and quantitative analysis of data usually presents no problems. As a result, the costs are not excessive. This approach, however, suffers from crucial limitations. First, the presence of a coupon attracts attention to the copy for this reason alone, and true differences in creative treatment can be obscured. Second, many people may read the copy and not return the coupon. Certain people are more prone to take this action than others, and "volunteer bias" can greatly overstate or understate the true effectiveness. One must constantly be aware that pretesting copy is very different from testing individual elements. For example, the advertising manager of International Correspondence Schools has searched extensively for pretesting techniques that can accurately predict at least the relative inquiry pull of various ads. Just as there seems to be no relationship between scores and coupon returns, none of these methods, when tested, has yielded data that would indicate any useful predictive ability. Finally, coupon return bears no special relationship to advertising effectiveness because changes in attitude and in awareness, the communication of copy points, and a host of additional responses are not tested.

It must be concluded that the disadvantages far outweigh the advantages of the coupon-return method for most purposes. The inquiry test should be used only when coupon return is the objective of the advertisement. When this is so, it is a completely valid measure of response.

3. On-the-Air Tests   Some research services measure response to advertisements that are inserted into actual television or radio programs in certain test markets. The "on-the-air" test is an example. The advantages and disadvantages are identical to those encountered in the use of dummy vehicles. In television, some of the best-known services used are Burke Marketing Services' Day-After Recall (DAR), Gallup and Robinson's Total Prime Time (TPT), and the Burke's AdTel cable system.[5]

DAR tests   DAR tests typically involve about 200 respondents who are contacted by telephone in any of 34 available cities and who claim to have watched a specific television show the night before. Measures are taken in both unaided and aided recall fashion. To begin with, respondents are asked if they remember seeing a commercial for a product in the product class of interest. If they do not, then they are asked if they remember a commercial for the specific test brand. Those who recall the ad in either fashion are asked what they recall about the specific copy points of the ad.

Total prime time   TPT is a service of Gallup and Robinson (G&R) that can test commercials that appear in prime time. They survey about 700 men and 700 women in the Philadelphia area. Qualified respondents are those who have watched at least 30 minutes of network prime time the previous night.

Another approach that is used is G&R's In-View. Here respondents are called in advance and are invited to watch the show in which the test ad will appear. About 150 men and 150 women are used in In-View, all from the Philadelphia area.

Measures taken for both TPT and In-View include:

1. Proved commercial registration (PCR) — the percentage of these who can recall (from company or brand cues) and accurately describe the ad.

2. Idea communication—the percentage of recallers who can recall specific sales points in the ad.

3. Favorable attitude—percentage of favorable comments about the brand offered by the respondent.

BehaviorScan Information Resources Inc. (IRI) developed BehaviorScan, which collects information that relates consumer purchases to television-viewing choices. By tracking family purchases at the grocery store through the electronic scanner system and placing meters on TV sets to monitor the selection of programs and TV commercials, IRI has developed a useful advertising research tool. BehaviorScan can also test various commercials by broadcasting them to selected homes and then monitoring grocery purchases to see if the ad induced the family to buy the product.

One of the most useful benefits of such a system is the collection of historical data. IRI puts such data into a software program and sells it to consumer product companies. For instance, brand managers at Colgate-Palmolive Co. used the software package to decide whether to market a new detergent using the developed advertising campaign. The company saved eight weeks and 35 percent of the cost of regular test marketing by avoiding test marketing research and using the information package sold by IRI instead. IRI hopes that in the future BehaviorScan will tell advertisers which shows give them the most for their advertising dollars in terms of reaching the right audience.

Both AdTel from SAMI/Burke and ERIN from A. C. Nielsen are testing services similar to the BehaviorScan approach. The main difference between BehaviorScan and AdTel is that AdTel uses cable television to place the different ads in different homes.

Posttesting Procedures

The following real-world tests of advertisements are usually performed on a posttest basis.

1. Recognition Tests The readership of printed advertisements has long been assessed using a standard technique called *recognition measurement,* which was developed by Daniel Starch. In 1989, Starch Irra Hooper, Inc., measured about 100,000 ads in more than 100 magazines and newspapers. The Starch method is described in detail because other related procedures are quite similar.

The nature of the Starch method   The Starch organization annually surveys approximately 30,000 advertisements in nearly 1,000 consumer and farm magazines, business publications, and newspapers. A national sample consisting of interviews in 20 to 30 geographical areas is chosen for each study. Although the sample is not a random selection, attempts are made to parallel the circulation makeup of each medium under analysis.

Interviewers are assigned a given number of readers over 18 years of age with certain demographic characteristics in terms of income and location. Studies usually include from 100 to 200 interviews per sex, and the quota for each interviewer is fairly small.

The interview is conducted in the respondent's home. The interviewer commences by asking whether or not the particular periodical has been read prior to the interview. If the answer is affirmative, the issue is opened at a page specified in advance to guarantee that the fatigue resulting from the interview will not unduly bias advertising appearing at the back of the issue. The respondent is then asked, for each advertisement, "Did you see or read any part of the advertisement?" If the answer is yes, he or she is asked to indicate exactly what parts of the layout and copy were seen or read.

Four principal readership scores for the sample are reported:

1. *Noted*—the percentage of readers who remember seeing the advertisement.
2. *Seen-associated*—the percentage of readers who recall seeing or reading any part of the advertisement identifying the product or brand.
3. *Read most*—the percentage of readers who reported reading at least one-half of the advertisement.
4. *Signature*—the percentage of readers who remember seeing the brand name or logo.

Several additional scores are also calculated and reported:

1. *Readers per dollar*—the number of readers attracted by the advertisement for each dollar invested in space.
2. *Cost ratios*—the relationship between readers per dollar and the median readers per dollar for all half-page or larger advertisements in the issue. A "noted cost ratio" of 121, for example, means that the copy exceeded the par for the issue by 21 percent.
3. *Ranks*—the numerical ordering of all advertisements from highest to lowest by readers per dollar.

Data are available on the readership of component parts of each layout, such as secondary illustrations, the company signature, or various copy blocks. Figure 16–1 presents an ad with readership scores placed on it. Note that this ad appeared in Chapter 13. Did you think then that it would score as highly as it did in effectiveness (recognition)?

The Starch method is a syndicated service, and other organizations offer similar services. In addition, individual advertisers and research consultants frequently conduct private specialized readership studies.

Analysis of the recognition method The recognition method, especially the Starch approach, is by far the most widely used means of measuring advertising readership. However, a growing number of criticisms of the technique have been published in recent years. These criticisms for the most part are based on significant methodological questions. The potential research pitfalls that have been reported involve (1) the problem of false claiming, (2) the reproducibility of recognition scores, and (3) sensitivity to interviewer variations.

The problem of false claiming The interview is conducted informally, with the respondent simply being asked to indicate whether or not he or she remembers seeing a given advertisement. It has been feared that the respondent could consciously or unconsciously give a completely false reply because no means exists to check its accuracy. Research has brought this problem into sharper perspective.

The Advertising Research Foundation undertook the Print Advertisement Research Methods (PARM) study. The Starch method, among others, was subjected to intensive impartial analysis. The syndicated services studied an issue of *Life* and reported readership as usual, and the PARM staff duplicated this research using a large randomly chosen sample. The readership results were then compared, and additional analyses were undertaken to shed light on the meaning of readership data.

The analysis of recognition by the PARM staff showed a surprising tendency for scores to remain stable over time. In other words, the scores showed little variation as the interval between the date of the claimed readership of the magazine and the date of the interview increased. If the recognition score truly measures memory, the scores should exhibit a reliable tendency to decline over time. For example, the recognition of meaningful data was 97 percent after 20 minutes, as compared with 75 percent after two days. The failure of Starch scores to show this pattern indicates the possibility that factors other than memory are dictating research findings and distorting results.

The PARM study indicated that interest in the product leads to substantial overclaiming of readership. In addition, the PARM study found that recognition of advertisements is significantly higher among owners of the

FIGURE 16–1

Starch Results for Metropolitan Ad

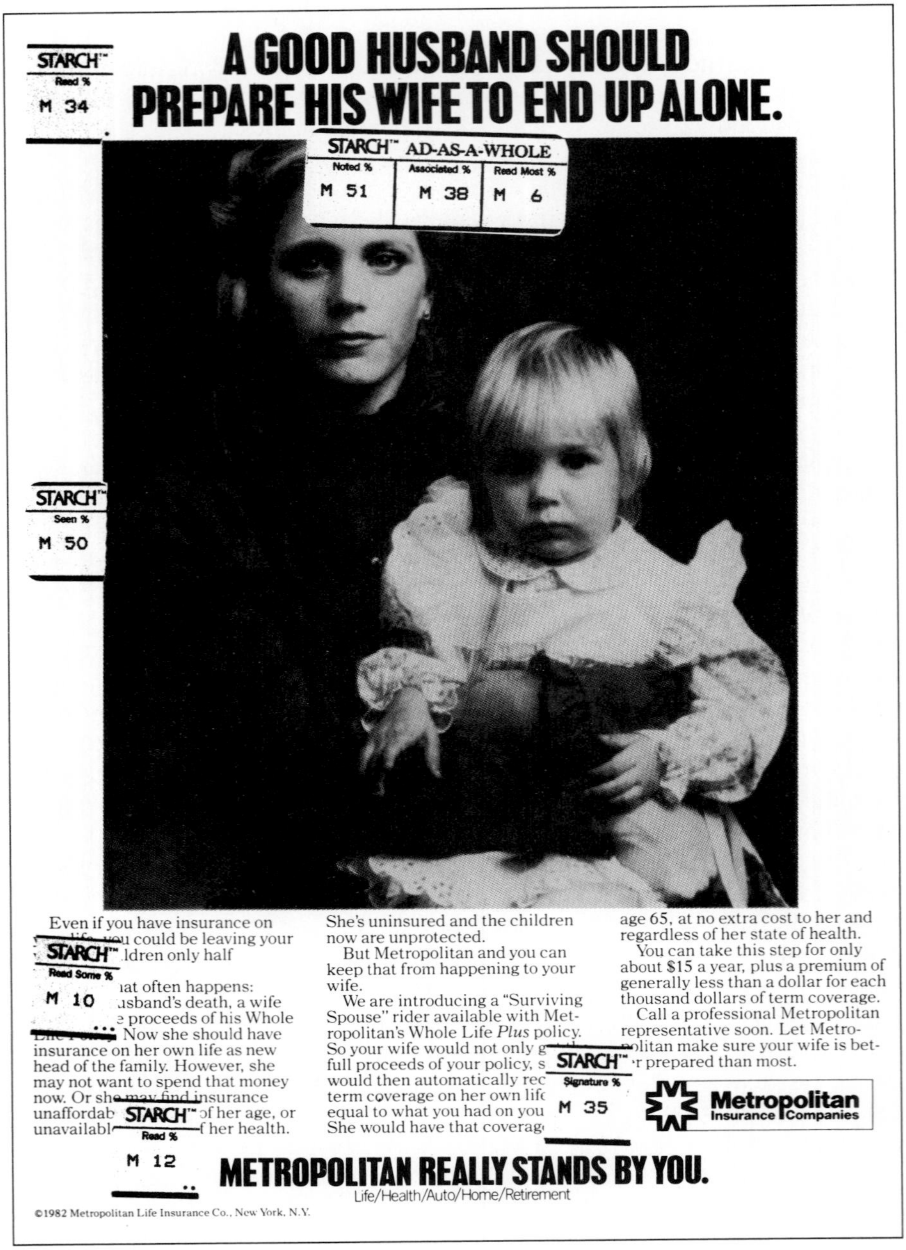

advertised product. These results taken together suggest the strong possibility that product interest markedly distorts memory and leads to false advertising readership claims.

It has also been discovered that some people seem to have a kind of generalized trait that leads them to overclaim readership. In fact, for those claiming recognition of advertisements they could not possibly have seen, the average noted score for all advertisements was 75 percent! This is referred to by psychologists as a *noting set*. It is related to multimagazine readership in that the greater the number of magazines read, the greater the incidence of false claiming. There are several reasons for this tendency:

1. Respondents may genuinely believe that they have seen the advertisement, whereas in reality they have seen a similar version elsewhere.

2. Respondents may be saying, in effect, that they would expect to have seen such an advertisement in the issue, so they inadvertently give an incorrect report.

3. Readership may be either underreported or overreported to impress the interviewer, especially if the report is seen as indicating social acceptability in some way.

4. Interview fatigue can easily lead to underclaiming.

The Starch organization has issued a vigorous rebuttal of the research discussed above. In the first place, it claims that there is no reason to expect a dropoff in recognition scores over time. On this point the logic is not clear, and the argument is not completely convincing. Starch does present data, however, that indicate that false claiming declines markedly if the respondent is told that he or she may not have seen all of the advertisements presented; he or she may exercise greater discrimination if this warning is given. Definitive research is obviously needed.

Perhaps all that can be done in the absence of further research is to utilize some type of controlled recognition procedure. In one of the most promising approaches, false advertisements are used to detect overclaiming, and respondents indicate the certainty with which they remember seeing and reading an advertisement. Overclaiming can be detected fairly reliably.

Reproducibility of recognition scores   The Starch organization, of course, uses a small national sample chosen by nonrandom means. Questions have arisen concerning the representativeness of this sample and the degree to which scores would differ if more rigorous sampling were used. The PARM study utilized a much larger randomly chosen sample so that these questions could be answered.

It was found that the average noted score in PARM interviews was 21.7 percent, as compared with the 26.4 percent average score reported by

Starch. Although there is a small absolute difference, the correlation was found to exceed 0.85 (1.00 is perfect). As a result of this close agreement, concern over the sampling procedure has abated.

Sensitivity to interviewer variations   Starch interviewers are trained not to point or to direct the respondent's replies in any way. Presumably such gestures could introduce bias. The PARM study analyzed the sensitivity of data to interviewer variations by using both experienced and inexperienced interviewers. Separate tabulation of results showed no significant differences in the noted scores produced by each group.

One might expect that the PARM results would be reassuring to the Starch organization because a potential source of bias in recognition scores apparently is not present. Starch also challenges this finding, however, by noting that interviewers develop tendencies that produce either overly high or overly low claiming by respondents. It is the opinion of the Starch organization that some of the studies criticizing the validity of Starch data have failed to control adequately for this factor.

Using recognition scores   Given the many unanswered issues about methods, what uses can be made of recognition data? Certainly the approach can be helpful in three ways:

1. Readership scores are at least a rough indication of success in attracting and holding attention because it goes without saying that an advertisement must be perceived before advertising objectives are realized.
2. The relative attention-gaining power of variations in creative treatment can be assessed from one campaign to the next or within the same campaign by controlled experiments.
3. The attention-gaining power of competitors' campaigns can be measured.

These data are most useful if an entire campaign is analyzed rather than each advertisement one at a time. It is possible, for example, that the individual score can be biased by an unrepresentative sample for a given issue or other random variations. These variations become neutralized when many stimuli are compared over time.

Perhaps the least effective use of recognition scores is to test the attention-gaining power of minor components within an advertisement. It is asking far too much of any reader to remember one's behavior in such minute detail.

Finally, these scores should not be projected to the entire market. The sample is not random, and for that reason no such projection can be made with measurable accuracy.

2. Recall Tests   Recall measures assess the impression of advertisements on the reader's memory according to the extent and accuracy of answers given, without exposure to the stimulus.

Unaided recall   The purest measure of memory relies on no aids whatsoever. The respondent might be asked, for example, "What advertisements have you seen lately?" Such a question is obviously difficult to answer because few respondents will retain such sharp recollections of advertising exposure that much detail will be recalled. Also, it is quite difficult to measure the impact of a specific campaign in this fashion because answers will vary over a wide range of products. For these reasons, unaided recall is seldom relied on as the only measure.

Aided recall   A practically limitless variety of means can be used to jog the respondent's memory and thereby sharpen recall. One might be asked, "What automobile advertisements do you remember seeing in yesterday's paper?" or "What brand of coffee do you remember hearing about recently?" The recall of a specific brand is a strong indication of the strength of the advertising impression.

The Gallup-Robinson impact test   The Gallup-Robinson test, perhaps the best known of the aided recall measures, is offered as a syndicated service. Basically, the technique involves five steps:

1. The person interviewed must recall and describe correctly at least one editorial feature in the publication under analysis.
2. The respondent is then handed a group of cards on which are printed the names of advertised brands that appear in the issue, as well as some that do not. The respondent is asked to indicate which of these products are advertised in the issue.
3. For each advertised brand the respondent recalls from the issue, she or he is interrogated in depth to assess the strength and accuracy of recall.
4. The issue is then opened to each advertisement the respondent recalls. The respondent is asked whether this is the advertisement he or she has in mind and if it is the first time he or she has seen it. If the respondent has not seen it before, the data are discarded in order to arrive at a "proven name registration" figure.
5. Information is gathered on the age, sex, education, and other details of the background of each person interviewed.

The interviewing usually commences on the day after the magazine appears. Responses are edited thoroughly to ascertain that the recall is genuine. The final score, *proven name registration (PNR)*, is adjusted by size of the appeal, color, placement on the page, and the number of competing advertisements in the issue.

The PARM study referred to earlier also analyzed the Gallup-Robinson approach. The correlation between scores produced by the PARM staff and Gallup-Robinson was 0.82 for women and 0.61 for men. Therefore, this technique was found not to be as fully reproducible as the Starch approach.

Gallup-Robinson scores were found to show the expected pattern of drop-off as time between reading the issue and the interview increased. For this reason if no other, it is quite likely that two different interviewing organizations would produce different results, for only by accident would all respondents be in exactly the same stages of memory decay.

The PARM study also detected that the Gallup-Robinson measure is highly sensitive to interviewer skill. The more inexperienced interviewer produced scores that differed significantly from those of the interviewer with greater experience, thus underscoring the need for rigorous training and tight field control.

It has been concluded that the PARM test in general verified that the Gallup-Robinson test truly measures memory, as its proponents claim, with a minimum of distortion from other factors (unlike the Starch measure). However, unnecessary secrecy surrounds the procedures used to edit and adjust the proven name registration scores. It would be possible to interpret the data with more accuracy if these facts were available.

Evaluation of recall tests   It is apparent that unaided and aided recall both offer minimum cues to stimulate memory, and it may be that memory is *understimulated*. The triple-associates tests (described below) and identification tests, of course, minimize this difficulty.

Understimulation of memory may not seem to be a problem. Consider the situation, however, when the advertised product is a convenience good and the objective is merely to register the name repetitively over a long period, or the situation involves low-involvement learning. In all probability, the respondent will not recall seeing the advertisement, but the objective still could have been attained. The point is that recall favors the distinctive appeals, especially those that are highly entertaining, and other high-involvement products. The danger arises when one assumes that a low score always implies failure to attract and hold attention.

Recall and position in the issue   It has frequently been believed that the position of the advertisement in the issue affects recall. For instance, it seems reasonable to expect that the advertisement close to the editorial section will be favored. It has been found, however, that the environment and location of the stimulus were not factors in recall scores. The content of copy and the visualization seem to be the dominant factors.

Finally, it cannot be assumed that the true "impact" of the advertisement has been isolated. This observation is pertinent because the Gallup-Robinson method is frequently referred to as "impact" measurement. If *impact* means the stimulation of buying behavior or successful attainment of other advertising objectives, aided recall in no definitive way is an indication of success. All that can be said is that high recall scores (perhaps 5 percent or more) reflect that a strong conscious impression was made and that attention was successfully attracted and held.

3. Association Measures   A time-honored measure of message recall is the triple-associates test. Respondents are asked the following type of question: "Which brand of gasoline is advertised as offering 'more miles per gallon'?" Two associates or factors are inherent in such a question: (1) the generic product (gasoline) and (2) the advertising theme ("more miles per gallon"). The third element, the brand name, is to be supplied by the respondent. The percentage of correct answers is thus a measure of the extent to which advertising has correctly registered a theme.

The triple-associates test can easily be modified to suit individual situations as long as it is confined to measurement of registration of a theme or a very abbreviated message. The communication of longer copy or advertising elements cannot be measured effectively with this technique. Also, registration of theme must not be taken as implying that advertising objectives have been achieved. All that can be said is that the advertisement communicated.

4. Combination Measures   It seems safe to observe that a recognition test *overstimulates* readers or viewers and that recall measurement *understimulates* them. It is possible, however, to combine these measures to capitalize on the strengths of each.

A controlled combination   One of the authors combined the recognition and recall procedures by removing test advertisements from their editorial surroundings, exposing consumers to the copy for a controlled interval, and asking for playback of copy and other features following exposures. Respondents were first qualified as being readers of the issue in which the advertisements appeared, and they were then exposed to five advertisements, one by one, for a short controlled interval. The advertisement was then removed from sight, and the respondent was asked to state whether or not he or she recalled seeing the advertisement. If the reply was affirmative, the respondent was asked to state in detail the major features, copy points, illustrations, and other components. Finally, one of the five stimuli was an advertisement scheduled for appearance one month following the date of the interview, and it was used to detect false recognition claims. The extent of false claiming was found to be minimal.

This procedure minimizes the overstimulation inherent in the Starch method. The interval of exposure appeared to be long enough to jog the memory but not long enough to permit further reading of the advertisement and false claiming. Furthermore, the recall phase verified the accuracy of recognition claims. Thus this type of measure seems to be a more accurate indication of readership than either recognition or recall measures used separately.

The Communiscope   The communiscope overcomes a disadvantage in the technique just described by mechanically controlling the interval of exposure. The communiscope is a portable tachistoscope that permits the presentation of stimuli at varying intervals of time. The advertisements are placed on slides and flashed at the correct interval. Playback of copy is then requested to verify the accuracy of readership claims.

The communiscope is sufficiently compact to permit its use in a home under normal conditions. Because of the opportunity for precise stimulus presentation, its use should increase in the future.

CELL IV: PRODUCT-RELATED MEASURES UNDER REAL-WORLD CONDITIONS FOR PRETESTING AND POSTTESTING

The most sophisticated and demanding of the various measurement approaches is field measurement of the effects of advertising. Sales test techniques, in particular, generally require considerable time and expense and hence are utilized mostly for purposes of posttesting the effects of an entire campaign. However, all of these procedures may be used on a pretest basis if one is willing to invest in a local tryout of a campaign (e.g., test market a number of creative executions). The pre- and posttests (to be described) are indeed widely used in the measurement of effectiveness.

Pretesting and Posttesting Procedures

1. Pre- and Posttests   When it is not possible to establish a clear-cut sales objective for advertising, the objectives usually are stated in terms of stimulation of awareness, attitude shift, or changes in preference. Whether or not the advertising has been effective requires measurement of changes in response of the initial attitude. Therefore, persons in a market segment will be tested before (pre) and after (post) exposure to the advertising.

Case studies of pre- and postmeasurement   We will first analyze several cases in which communication effectiveness was measured simply. Then the issues and problems related to the technique will be examined.

An association of tea importers and producers   The problem was an unfavorable attitude toward tea among many consumers, and the advertising goal was to generate a favorable attitude toward tea from a positive rating of 20 percent to 40 percent over five years. An attitude scale was developed, and studies were conducted annually to assess progress toward the goal. In each periodic assessment, the same attitudes scale was used, apparently with a different sample of buyers.

A small overseas airline   The advertising objective established was to communicate the attributes of a luxury airline to an additional 20 percent of the market segment in one year. Measurement consisted of mail questionnaires sent periodically to a representative sample of several hundred persons who were overseas-traveling customers of travel services in selected cities. The questions used were of the following type: "What airlines can you name that offer hourly service to _____?" Survey costs were small (several hundred dollars), and a high return was produced because a free booklet of interest to travelers was given as an inducement. At the end of one year, it was found that awareness of the company had increased 14 percent; the image of a luxury all-jet overseas airline was communicated to an additional 15 percent; and the proportion of those indicating they would seriously consider this airline for their next overseas trip increased 8 percent.

A pain reliever   The manufacturer of a leading brand of pain reliever had previously focused advertising on the theme of "fast relief." Because leading competitors were also doing this, it was decided that a new advertising objective should be to (1) hold the present level of awareness of the headache-relief theme (35 percent) and (2) increase awareness of the cold-relief message from 15 percent to 25 percent in six months. This strategy was undertaken in test markets. The results indicated that the headache message registration actually declined 2 percent at the outset but overall penetration of cold relief reached 28 percent at the conclusion, thereby exceeding expectation.

Analysis of the cases   The case examples discussed above have several aspects in common: (1) measurement of message penetration at the beginning of a period, (2) clear-cut communication goal, (3) another measurement either during or at the end of the campaign period, and (4) assessment of ensuing changes.

In general, the cases are representative illustrations of research-oriented advertising management. Some associated problems that may not be apparent to the reader are:

1. What is the nature of the sample studied at the beginning of the period? Is it representative? If it is intended to focus on prospects, where is such a list obtained? It may not be possible to draw a random sample

because of these problems, and, of course, the effect of nonrandomness is the inability to project the results to the universe being studied.

2. Were the people studied either in the interim or at the end of the campaign period the same as those chosen in the beginning? If so, the distinct possibility exists that the process of measurement may seriously bias later replies. The fact that respondents are asked for their opinions frequently causes them to think more deeply and change their opinions at a later time.

3. If the same people were not measured at a later point, were the samples studied clearly matched as to age, income, and other demographic variables? Even more to the point, is it known that the later samples studied possessed the same beginning attitudes as the sample used previously? Differences in any of these respects may vitiate the results.

4. Is it known what attitude changes would have occurred in the interim without advertising? Even when there is no intervening advertising, some percent of respondents will change their attitudes or brand preferences because of changes in the environment. In the same sense, it is essential to determine what nonviewers or nonreaders would have done before concluding that any changes are a result of advertising.

Until the above questions can be answered satisfactorily, conclusions cannot be drawn about the validity of the research. Basically, the only way in which these problems can be overcome is through utilization of an experimental design where attempts are made to control all the variables but one—in this case, the advertising used.

Experimental designs for ad tests   In a *controlled experiment,* the researcher intervenes to control for as many extraneous variables as possible. The independent variables (the ads) are exposed only to those the researcher wishes, and the results of exposure or nonexposure to the ads are measured (attitudes, preference, purchase, etc.). This allows for causal relationships between the ads and the results to be made. Usually it is necessary to use a test group and a control group. One group is exposed to the advertising and the other is not. The design is represented thus:

A Simplified Experimental Design	Experimental Group	Control Group
Premeasurement	Yes	Yes
Exposure to advertising	Yes	No
Postmeasurement	Yes	Yes

Changes that would have occurred in any event, without the exposure to advertising, presumably will be detected as differences between the pre- and postmeasurements in the control group. This change is subtracted from that noted in the experimental group, and the residual is the change attributable to advertising exposure.

However, the simple design above, sometimes called the *before-and-after with control group* design, may be grossly inadequate for this type of problem. As mentioned before, the simple fact of asking people for their opinions is known to change opinions later, and a very real source of bias is thus introduced by using the same experimental subjects for before-and-after measurement. One way to control for this factor is to use a four-group, six-study design, as illustrated in Table 16–2.

The use of four groups allows detection of the possible biasing effect of premeasurement. If, for instance, the effect introduced by advertising in the first experimental group is much greater than that in the second group receiving no premeasure, it is quite probable that the premeasurement biased later responses. In that case, the premeasurement of the first group under each heading would be compared with the postmeasurement of the groups receiving no premeasure.

No doubt the four-group, six-study design represents the ideal means to isolate the communication effectiveness of advertising. It would be a mistake, however, to fail to point out the difficulties arising when one attempts to use this "textbook ideal" research method:

1. Is it possible to establish *equivalent* test and control groups, especially when two or more of each kind are used to create the necessary four groups? Unless the answer here is yes, the research becomes questionable.

2. Is it possible to find equivalent groups, one of which is not exposed to the advertising? It may not be possible when a saturation campaign is being used. The individuals not exposed may be very different from those who are, and it may be exceedingly difficult to find typical groups of consumers who would qualify for this particular purpose.

TABLE 16–2

A Four-Group, Six-Study Design   ❖

	Experimental Groups		Control Groups	
	1	2	1	2
Premeasurement	Yes	No	Yes	No
Exposure to advertising	Yes	Yes	No	No
Postmeasurement	Yes	Yes	Yes	Yes

3. Is the information gained worth the cost? The more elaborate the design, the greater the research costs. The basic issue, then, is the return for the investment relative to less ideal designs, and this question is exceptionally difficult to answer.

The problem of finding equivalent groups becomes somewhat less crucial when the numbers in each are large. Difference in various dimensions may then be offset by the force of large numbers. The second problem also may be overcome when the campaign is confined to a select group of media. For instance, assume that dollars are invested in one television program. It may then be possible to find equivalent exposed and unexposed groups, but it must never be forgotten that those who watch the program may still differ from nonviewers in psychological outlook and other characteristics. Finally, the last question is the most difficult of all. Little more than advance hunches regarding the return for an investment in research is possible until more is known about the strengths and weaknesses of various research methods.

Comments on pre- and posttests It should now be apparent that the case studies above suffer from possible sources of bias, yet the application of experimental design also presents real problems. Probably it is safe to say that the kind of monitoring undertaken by the tea association and the airline is good practice if done on a routine basis. In other words, it is helpful to keep a running tally on the results of a campaign. This information, however, can never be a conclusive indication of success unless a control group of some kind is used.

The issue, then, once again revolves around the uses to which the research is put. Measurement without a control group provides a useful but rough indication of progress, and the strengths and weaknesses of the campaign can be pinpointed. If management uses these data with caution and fully recognizes that other factors in addition to advertising could be introducing change, the return of information for a minimum research expenditure can be worthwhile.

It is another matter, however, for management to take the results of uncontrolled research as a definitive indication of success or failure. The abandonment or continuation of a campaign theme involving millions of dollars should not rest on such a foundation. In this instance, experimental design procedures should be utilized. There are problems in methodology and possible sources of bias in experimental research too, but the chances for error resulting from the research methods used or uncontrolled factors are substantially reduced.

2. Sales Tests The question of whether the influence of advertising on sales can be measured has prompted much discussion in recent years, both pro and con. Consider, for example, the somewhat negative point of view in the following quotation:

> In essence, current sales figures are not the final yardstick of advertising performance unless one or more of these factors are present.
>
> 1. Advertising is the single variable.
> 2. Advertising is the dominant force in the marketing mix.
> 3. The proposition calls for immediate payout (such as in mail-order or retail advertising).
> 4. These conditions seldom prevail among so-called nationally advertised products.[6]

The point is that advertising is usually only one variable in the marketing mix, and it must pull together with the product, price, and distribution channel to produce sales. The contention is that the communication aspects of advertising are usually the only measurable results. As was noted in Chapter 9, this focus on communication has come to be referred to as DAGMAR (defining advertising goals, measuring advertising results).

DAGMAR, however, is referred to by some as a *philosophy of despair.* The argument is that communication goals are being substituted for the more relevant objectives of sales and profit and that communication comes from many sources other than advertising. Moreover, communication does not necessarily mean sales or profit, and examples are reported where one medium produced greater awareness or response but less sales or results than another. Therefore, some advocate testing the influence of advertising on sales and attaining profit objectives rather than on communication objectives.

It is useful to distinguish two distinct situations. The first is where one can directly attribute a sale to an ad. This is generally true in direct action ads, such as the Book-of-the-Month Club ad in Figure 16–2. A sales objective is relevant here and results are easily measured by the level of sales obtained. The more general situation is where direct tracing of sales results to ads is *not* possible. Here a legitimate controversy exists.

The controversy over whether the influence of advertising on attainment of sales objectives is measurable has been briefly described above. The authors do not take sides in the argument but believe it is pertinent to inquire into the possible ways in which the sales effectiveness of promotional dollars might be measured. These include the three discussed below: (1) direct questioning, (2) experimental designs, and (3) minimarket tests.

Direct questioning of buyers On occasion, it is fruitful to question buyers directly to define the factors that lead them to make a purchasing decision. For example, heavy television advertising for the *Living Bible* was undertaken in several test markets during the Christmas season. Direct question-

FIGURE 16-2

❖ **An Ad for Which Direct Tracing Is Possible**

The Story of Civilization for $20⁰⁰

The Story of Civilization by Will and Ariel Durant. 11 Volumes

Publisher's list price **$248⁵⁵**

You simply agree to buy four books during a year.

Book-of-the-Month Club® offers new members *The Story of Civilization* at extraordinary savings. It's your opportunity to obtain all 11 volumes for just $20—a set exactly like the one sold in bookstores for $248.55. To own it is to have at your fingertips a reference work of undisputed authority. To read it is to enjoy history made live with unfailing excitement and power. In fact, more than seven million Durant books have been distributed by the Club in American homes! It's hard to imagine a more valuable set of books for your home library, especially if there are students in the family.

Bookstore Quality at Book Club Savings

You conveniently shop at home at tremendous savings. Example: if you took *The Story of Civilization* for $20.00, bought six books and two Book-Dividends, you could save an average of $240—*including* postage and handling. And these are true savings, because every book is exactly like the one sold in the bookstores... the same size, paper, type and binding. Book-of-the-Month Club never sells small-size, cheap "book club editions."

Book-Dividends

Every book you buy earns credits which entitle you to select Book-Dividends at hard-to-believe savings. You enjoy savings of *at least 70%* on a wide selection of valuable books— from reference works to Rembrandt— when you remain a Club member after the trial period.

Additional Benefits

A distinguished collection of specially produced record albums—from Billie Holiday to Vladimir Horowitz...a wide variety of beautiful gifts and games... the best of children's books...a Club charge account with no service or interest charges...and much more...all made available *exclusively* to members.

"Our century has produced no more successful attempt to narrate the whole common story of mankind"–CLIFTON FADIMAN

I. Our Oriental Heritage. Ancient Egypt and the Near East. The Far East, early to modern times.

II. The Life of Greece. Explores all facets of Greek life from prehistoric times to the Roman conquest.

III. Caesar and Christ. The rise of Rome and Christianity and the collapse of classic civilization.

IV. The Age of Faith. Christian, Islamic and Judaic civilizations, 325 to 1300, including the Crusades.

V. The Renaissance. Italy's golden age, 1304 to 1576. A turbulent world of intrigue and great art.

VI. The Reformation. Europe's religious conflicts, from two centuries before Luther to Calvin.

VII. The Age of Reason Begins. Europe, 1558-1646. The age of Shakespeare, Rembrandt, Galileo.

VIII. The Age of Louis XIV. The brilliant era of the "Sun King," Milton, Cromwell, Peter the Great.

IX. The Age of Voltaire. Europe from 1715 to 1756. The world of Frederick the Great, Wesley, Bach.

X. Rousseau and Revolution. Europe from the Seven Years' War to the storming of the Bastille.

XI. The Age of Napoleon. France's domination of European history, from the fevers of the French Revolution to Napoleon's defeat at Waterloo. A history of European civilization from 1789 to 1815.

ing of buyers at point of purchase demonstrated high recall of television advertisements featuring Art Linkletter, although word of mouth was found to be the dominant influence on the decision.

The difficulties of direct questioning should be apparent. First, most people have great difficulty recalling the circumstances surrounding a decision. It is possible, of course, to minimize this difficulty by progressively taking the respondent back in time and asking him or her to restate the situation as completely as possible. For example, one may associate the purchase of a new automobile with a particular time of year, with particular family discussions, or with other events. Questioning can help one to recall the situation so that the influences on one's decision may come into sharper focus.

Even if the purchasing environment is clear in the respondent's memory, it still is doubtful that the role of advertising will be revealed. It seems to be natural for many to deny being influenced by advertising. This would presumably be admitting in some way to not being rational in buying. Moreover, advertising often works in virtually undetectable ways. Awareness might have been stimulated years before, and it is impossible for the buyer to restate this influence by introspection.

These problems are potent barriers indeed. For this reason, introspection by the buyer is seldom relied on to any great extent.

Experimental designs for sales tests   There is no satisfactory substitute for an experimental design to isolate the influence of advertising from the influence of other elements in the marketing mix. The application of experimental design to this problem, however, is complex, and the problems to be faced are many. They include (1) selecting the appropriate design, (2) selecting test and control markets, and (3) analyzing these results.

The appropriate design for sales testing   The before-and-after with control group experimental design is applicable for sales testing. This design uses several test cities and control cities. The procedure can be visualized from Table 16–3.

Sales usually are measured by auditing the inventories of a sample of stores, perhaps using the A. C. Nielsen store audit or a similar service. There is no need in this case for the more complex four-group, six-study design because no interviews are being made. As a result, there is little chance that premeasurement of sales will bias the results.

A sales test usually runs from six months to a year to permit time for advertising influence to be exerted. Several test and control markets should be used to minimize the danger that the markets chosen are later found to differ in some important aspect.

Selecting test and control markets[7] Every attempt must be made to assure that the markets chosen closely mirror the total market. In addition, the test and control areas must not differ in the following respects:

1. *Size*—Usually population areas from 100,000 to 300,000 are used. The areas must be large enough to encompass a variety of economic activities, yet not be so great that measurement and analysis of results are unduly costly.

2. *Population factors*—Areas with distinct and unique ethnic characteristics usually should be avoided. Milwaukee, Wisconsin, with its German stock, would be an unlikely area to test advertising for French wines. The more representative the area, the less likely it is to be rendered atypical by local disturbances such as strikes or layoffs. A one-industry town would be severely shocked by such an occurrence.

3. *Distribution*—The product must be readily available in retail outlets. If possible, retailers and wholesalers should not be informed of the test in order to prevent unusual sales activity on their part that would severely bias the results.

4. *Competitive considerations*—Competition in the test and control areas should not deviate from that usually faced in the entire market. The competitive climate during the test must be carefully monitored because any changes may render the test invalid.

5. *Media*—Full advertising media facilities must be available for use, or comparable media must be available in the test and control areas, and the media should not overlap with other markets (no "leaking").

Analysis of results   If the results of the experiment are those shown in Table 16–4, the results in the test city must be adjusted by the percentages for the control city to show the effect of advertising. Notice that the control city showed a definite decline in sales. If conditions were similar in both areas,

---

TABLE 16–3

A Before-and-After with Control Group Design for Testing the Sales Effectiveness of Advertising

	Test Markets	Control Markets
Before measure of sales	Yes	Yes
Introduction of advertising	Yes	No
Postmeasure of sales	Yes	Yes

it is necessary to calculate what would have happened in the test city without advertising. A 10 percent decline in the test city would give dollar sales of $360, whereas in reality the sales were $480. Therefore, $360 must be subtracted from $480 to give a net increase of $120. Thus the actual net increase is 30 percent in dollar sales and 31.7 percent in unit sales. The actual meaning of these changes must be assessed, using statistical tests such as the t test or chi square analysis.

These results are predicated on the assumption that all other things are equal. Again we must emphasize that variation in any factor, such as competition or retailers' efforts, that is present in the test cities and not in the control cities (or vice versa) will vitiate the experiment. If it appears that factors have not varied, however, the data should give a reasonably accurate measure of the influence of advertising on sales.

A multivariable experimental design In the above example, only one variable has been measured—the advertising campaign in the test areas. It is possible to study more than one variable at a time and in so doing to reduce the cost of repetitive individual experiments.

Assume that the research assignment is to analyze the relative attention-gaining power of four different media used individually and in combination. This problem would call for a factorial design. Although the mechanics of factorial design are clearly beyond the scope of this book, an indication of a possible structure for the experiment is given in Table 16–5. This design

TABLE 16–4

Comparison of Test City and Control City Sales Returns

City	Sales before Test Advertising (Feb. 1– Mar. 31)	Sales during Test Advertising (April 1– May 31)	Percentage Increase or Decrease	Adjusted Percentage Increase or Decrease
Control City A				
Dollars	$300	$270	− 10.0	
Units	300	250	− 16.7	—
Test City X				
Dollars	$400	$480	+ 20.0	30.0
Units	400	460	+ 15.0	31.7

Note: For purposes of simplification, only one test city and one control city have been used in this example. In actual practice, at least three test cities and three control cities are used.

has been used at Ford Motor Company, where it was reported that the data have revealed a definite relationship between advertising and sales but no significant advantage for any of the media tested.

Multivariable designs are elaborate, and the difficulties of controlling variables are compounded. The data must be analyzed by analysis of variance, a statistical technique that permits delineation of the significance of sales differences resulting from individual variables or from variables in combination. In addition, sales frequently are lost in areas where advertising is reduced; costs become high when test advertising proves to be ineffective; and it is costly to undertake the necessary rigorous analysis and interpretation of data. As a result, experimental designs, especially of such great complexity, are usually the province of the large advertiser. This is not to say, however, that such designs cannot be tailored to the means of the smaller advertiser.

Promotion in Action 16–1 describes a situation of the practical application of a multivariate experimental design when more than just advertising variables are operative.

Comments on experimental designs   Even though the difficulties to be faced are great, there is no doubt that proper experimental procedures will permit measurement of the sales power of advertising. Du Pont uses experiments regularly. In one experiment, for instance, industrial advertising was undertaken in all but two states, which then served as the control, and changes in effectiveness were assessed in both sections. Similar examples are reported by others. The use of new technology such as IRI's BehaviorScan and Nielsen's ERIN help in this process.

TABLE 16–5

⋄

Media Combinations in a 16-Cell Design

Combination	Area Number	Combination	Area Number
No media	1	Outdoor-TV	9
TV only	2	Outdoor-radio	10
Radio only	3	Outdoor-newspaper	11
Newspaper only	4	TV-radio-newspaper	12
Outdoor only	5	Outdoor-radio-TV	13
TV-radio	6	Outdoor-TV-newspaper	14
TV-newspaper	7	Outdoor-radio-newspaper	15
Newspaper-radio	8	Outdoor-TV-radio-newspaper	16

Obviously, more elaborate experiments will not be undertaken by the smaller advertiser with a local or regional market. The costs are simply too great at the present time. However, the experimental design need be only as elaborate as the problem being tested. In future years, advertisers of all sizes no doubt will begin to experiment, and the effectiveness of advertising should increase markedly.

Ahoy to Navy Advertising Research

❖
**PROMOTION
IN ACTION
16–1**

Market researchers conducted a study to evaluate the marketing effectiveness of the U.S. Navy recruiting program and to quantify the relationship between marketing efforts and enlistment achievements. This was done by estimating the impact of changes in the advertising budget and the size of the Navy recruiting force on Navy enlistment contracts for various categories of recruits. The study was based on a one-year, controlled experiment in which levels of Navy recruiters and advertising were systematically varied.

Researchers chose the area of dominant influence (ADI) as their analysis unit for the experiment. ADIs are geographical areas that receive their television signal from a central city or town. Electronic media-rating services assign individual counties to ADIs based on media-use patterns of sampled households. ADIs allow researchers to execute and measure changes in electronic advertising throughout the experiment. Twenty-six of the more than 200 ADIs in the United States were chosen as experimental markets because of their relative insulation. An additional 17 markets were chosen as control cells.

The Wharton Applied Research Center team assigned various treatment conditions to each of the 26 treatment markets. A number of characteristics differed across these markets: demographic, socioeconomic, levels of total military enlistments per capita, and the Navy's share of total military enlistment. Since the Navy Recruiting Command believed the last two variables were major factors in the effectiveness of marketing efforts, the market research team ensured that markets exposed to treatment conditions covered a wide variety of "total enlistment" and "the Navy's share of total enlistment" levels. Markets were classified in terms of these variables and were randomly assigned to treatment conditions. Treatment conditions included combinations of increasing or decreasing advertising by 50 percent or 100 percent, increasing or decreasing the number of recruiters by 20 percent, leaving advertising at prestudy levels, and leaving the number of

3. Minimarket Tests   There are ways to undertake full-scale experiments without the time and expense necessary for the market tests discussed above. One way is use of the so-called *minimarket*. Minimarkets or control markets are cities in which a marketing research firm has paid retailers to guarantee that they will carry a product that the research firm designates. These cities, which tend to be smaller and more isolated, include Akron, Duluth, Erie, Lubbock, Mobile, Boise, and Colorado

❖
**PROMOTION
IN ACTION
16–1**

Ahoy to Navy Advertising Research (continued)

recruiters at prestudy levels. Control conditions were created in the markets that maintained prestudy levels of both advertising and recruiters.

Detailed data were collected on the 42 chosen markets and divided into four broad categories—enlistment contracts, recruiters, advertising, and environmental variables. Monthly data were compiled for both Navy contracts and total Department of Defense contracts. This information was further sorted into the following categories: high school and nonhigh school, females, blacks, and two different mental groups. Navy recruiter data were collected on the basis of both applied person months and total recruiters present during each month. This information was divided into two groups: that for recruiters who were established in the recruiting function and that for recruiters who were in the first four months or last six months of their tour (when researchers hypothesize they are less effective). Advertising deliveries, measured by both gross impressions and dollars, were collected for each ADI and were categorized according to national print (further classified as magazines, newspapers, and direct mail), national electronic media (identified as TV and radio), local, and joint campaigns for all of the armed services. Four environmental variables were also taken into account: percent of unemployment, median family income, percent of black population, and urbanization (the percent of 17- to 21-year-old males who reside in counties with populations over 150,000). These variables served as blocking factors in the field experiment.

The experimental markets used, the structure of the assignment of treatment conditions, and the control markets used are noted in the diagram below.

Analysis of the data collected led to a number of conclusions. The number of recruiters did have a significant impact on enlistments. A recruiter's effectiveness was dependent on the recruiter's tenure. Only certain types of advertising expenditures were effective, with a wide variation in the degree of media impact. Socioeconomic factors also had major impacts on

Springs. The leading research services providing this type of procedure include IRI, Nielsen, and AdTel, a part of SAMI/Burke Marketing Services. AdTel utilizes a dual-cable CATV system and two balanced scanner panels of 1,000 households each. Because it is possible to control all variables except the one being tested over television, a precise measurement of effects is possible. (See earlier discussion of AdTel under on-the-air tests in Cell III Pretesting Procedures.)

❖
**PROMOTION
IN ACTION
16–1**

Ahoy to Navy Advertising Research (concluded)

enlistment. And in addition to increasing Navy enlistments, the Navy's marketing efforts expanded the total market for military enlistments.

	Recruiters −20%	Recruiters Same	Recruiters +20%
AD + 100%		Davenport-Rock Island	
AD + 50%	Tulsa	Washington	Boston
	Roanoke	Indianapolis	St. Louis
	Syracuse	Richmond	Charleston-Huntington
AD Same	Baltimore	Providence	Harrisburg
	Cheyenne, WY	Terre Haute	South Bend
	Laurel, MS	Springfield, IL*	Grand Junction, CO
AD − 50%	Wilkes Barre	Chicago	Dallas
	Phoenix	Pittsburgh	Louisville
	Odessa-Midland	Columbus, OH	Lansing
AD − 100%		Johnstown-Altoona	

* Additional control markets:

Nashville	Des Moines	Waco
Los Angeles	Youngstown	Sioux City
Charlotte	West Palm Beach	McAllen
Greenville	Chattanooga	Anniston
Knoxville	Huntsville	

Source: Vincent P. Carroll, Ambar G. Rao, Hau L. Lee, Arthur Shapiro, and Barry L. Bayus, "The Navy Enlistment Marketing Equipment," *Marketing Science* (Fall 1985), pp. 352–74, as presented in Thomas C. Kinnear and James R. Taylor, *Marketing Research: An Applied Approach,* 4th ed. (New York: McGraw-Hill, 1991).

SUMMARY

This chapter has examined the assumptions, strengths, and weaknesses of the various techniques for measuring advertising effectiveness. The use of some of these tools, however, does not shed light on the actual advertising response by the buyer. This may seem to be an obvious point, but it frequently is forgotten by users of research. A high Starch score, for instance, may be a favorable indication of success, but high readership does not necessarily imply a strong response, nor does it indicate a rising sales curve.

At the present time, no area of advertising research methodology is without important unknowns and doubts. As a result, no method can be used with complete certainty that it will always give desired results. The need for additional empirical research and improved methodology is apparent, yet this need is growing more rapidly than it is being met. It is strange that management is willing to devote funds to new product development but is loathe to improve the tools with which advertising is measured.

Given the state of the art, it is essential to advance a strong warning against the quest for certainty. Everyone has a tendency to assume that a quantitative finding is absolute—something on which to rely. The manager who relies on research data religiously without a skeptical, questioning attitude is falling prey to the false god of certainty. Such reliance may lead the manager to make wrong conclusions that can be costly. Moreover, an unquestioning attitude implies intellectual inflexibility, which has no place in advertising today.

REVIEW AND DISCUSSION QUESTIONS

1. Why are so many advertising testing firms unwilling to report the reliability and validity of their procedures as the PACT standards would require?
2. How does position in an issue affect recall of printed advertising messages?
3. What are combination measures? Are they an improvement over other approaches? In what ways?
4. Are measures of attracting and holding attention necessary to evaluate advertising success? Are they a sufficient measure for this purpose?
5. It is often overlooked that actual responses to advertising are more important in the final analysis than the attraction of attention. Why, then, is so much reliance placed on measures of attention attraction as opposed to more clear-cut indications of advertising effectiveness?
6. What are the major types of advertising response that can be measured?
7. Attempts to measure communications effectiveness are plagued with problems in research design. What are these problems?

8. Describe the experimental design approach to communications measurement.

9. What problems are encountered?

10. What is the basis of the argument that claims that advertising efffectiveness should be measured in terms of communication of a message rather than in terms of sales?

11. Can direct questioning of buyers isolate the effect of advertising on sales? Why or why not?

12. What is the essential distinction between laboratory and real-world measures?

13. Describe and discuss the usefulness of the various measures of opinion used in a consumer jury test.

14. Studies often show that recall is the most widely used measure of communication effectiveness. Many refuse to measure other stages of the communication process, such as attitude change or purchase. Why does this occur? What arguments could you present on behalf of attitude and/or behavior measurement?

15. Do you agree that laboratory measures, especially those focusing on the physiological aspect of attention, will see more use in the future? Why?

16. Describe the recognition method.

17. The Starch method for measurement of readership is widely used, as are other approaches. What precautions would you suggest in using findings of this type?

18. Unaided recall is rarely considered to be a powerful method to isolate advertising impact. Why?

19. The Gallup-Robinson impact test is one example of an aided recall measure. Describe and evaluate this procedure.

20. Recall tests often are hampered by "understimulation." What does this mean, and in what way is it a problem for researchers?

NOTES

1. Thomas C. Kinnear and Ann R. Root, *1988 Survey of Marketing Research* (Chicago: American Marketing Association, 1989), p. 44.

2. "21 Ad Agencies Endorse Copy Testing Principles," *Marketing News,* February 19, 1982, pp. 1 and 9; see also the complete PACT statement in the *Journal of Advertising* II, 4 (1982), pp. 4–29.

3. Rudolph Flesch, *The Art of Readable Writing* (New York: Harper & Row, 1974).

4. Unpublished studies under the supervision of James F. Engel.

5. This whole section is based on Thomas C. Kinnear and James R. Taylor, *Marketing Research: An Applied Approach,* 4th ed. (New York: McGraw-Hill, 1991), chap. 24.

6. Russell H. Colley, *Defining Advertising Goals* (New York: Association of National Advertisers, Inc., 1961), pp. 10, 12.

7. For a detailed discussion of experimentation, test marketing, and minimarkets see Thomas C. Kinnear and James R. Taylor, *Marketing Research: An Applied Approach,* 4th ed. (New York: McGraw-Hill, 1991), chaps. 9, 20, and 23.

Management of Consumer Sales Promotion

BASEBALL, OSCAR MAYER, AND . . .

Oscar Mayer Foods has blended traditional sales promotion with direct marketing techniques to put together a national promotional campaign with an all-American flavor. The company mailed a registration packet containing details for a special proof-of-purchase campaign called "Collect 'n Save" to 80,000 children's baseball teams and youth league leaders. The teams can sign up for the campaign and turn in proofs-of-purchase of Oscar Mayer products for a variety of baseball-related prizes—everything from Louisville Slugger bats for 100 proofs to actual electronic scoreboards for 7,930 proofs.

The company followed up the initial mailing by offering customers free baseballs, mitts, and bats via special free-standing inserts in newspapers. The inserts delivered details on the "Collect 'n Save" team program to an estimated 32 million homes and functioned as an additional lead generator. The ad material also contained cents-off coupons for hot dogs and cold cuts. "We wanted to do [the promotion] in a way that would appeal not only to kids, but also to moms," says Ray Klecker, associate product manager for the Madison, Wisconsin–based Oscar Mayer.

The integrated direct marketing-sales promotion approach evolved as the program progressed, says Klecker. The program's overall effect, he says, was to "establish a noncoupon emphasis for the brand image." Nearly 7,900 baseballs were given away as a result of the insert, and it generated 2,300 inquiries about the "Collect 'n Save" campaign.

"The role that direct marketing plays is that of having an identifiable, targetable group of leaders that can influence a group of kids and their parents to participate," says Barbara Weaver, an account supervisor in direct-response marketing for Chicago-based Frankel & Co., which developed the Oscar Mayer program. Responses from the initial mailing and insert were used to create a data base for future "Collect 'n Save" programs.

So far Oscar Mayer has given away 120,000 baseballs, and plans are already under way for additional free baseball offers. Frankel has designed extensive point-of-purchase materials containing information on the program, and retailers are being brought into the promotion by offering them free bats, gloves, and mitts if they create a major display. Oscar Mayer suggests that the equipment be donated to local teams.

In future years, the "Collect 'n Save" campaign may be extended to other sports such as soccer, hockey, and football. "But whether we'd get the same response, I don't know. We'd have to play it year by year," says Bob Weber, account director at Frankel. For now, the people involved in the program are pleased with the response and the benefits it offers to the young baseball players. "Even a few hundred dollars can mean [financial] success for a team," says Weber. By earning equipment in the "Collect 'n Save" program, teams free up funds for other essentials, such as paying umpires, he says.

Source: Adapted from *Advertising Age*, May 16, 1988, pp. S6–S7.

Sales promotion has been defined by the American Marketing Association as encompassing "those marketing activities, other than personal selling, advertising, and publicity that stimulate consumer purchasing and dealer effectiveness,"[1] and "as media and nonmedia marketing pressure applied for a predetermined, limited period of time at the consumer, retailer or wholesaler in order to stimulate trial, increased consumer demand or improved product availability."[2]

These activities occupy a gray area between advertising and personal selling, possessing characteristics of each promotional tool. For example, if a premium were to be offered to induce buyers to try a new product and the offer was made in an advertisement in a national magazine, how would you classify the activity? A well-accepted view is that the premium offer would be a sales promotion because of its nonrecurrent nature and because it was aimed at stimulating consumer *demand in the short run*. The communication of the offer itself in the national medium would be advertising.

SCOPE AND IMPORTANCE OF SALES PROMOTION

Sales promotion has been one of the most exciting areas in the promotional strategy field over the last decade. No text can truly capture the dynamic growth and excitement generated in sales promotion. Sales promotion includes consumer-directed "pull" activities such as product sampling, coupons, cents-off offers, refunds and rebates, contests and sweepstakes, premiums, and direct mail. It also includes wholesaler- and retailer-directed "push" activities such as cooperative advertising, promotional allowances, contests, incentive programs, point-of-purchase (POP) displays, management assistance, slotting allowances and fees, and trade shows. Figure 17–1 presents a conceptual framework to demonstrate the focus of these different

FIGURE 17–1

Consumer- and Channel-Directed Promotion

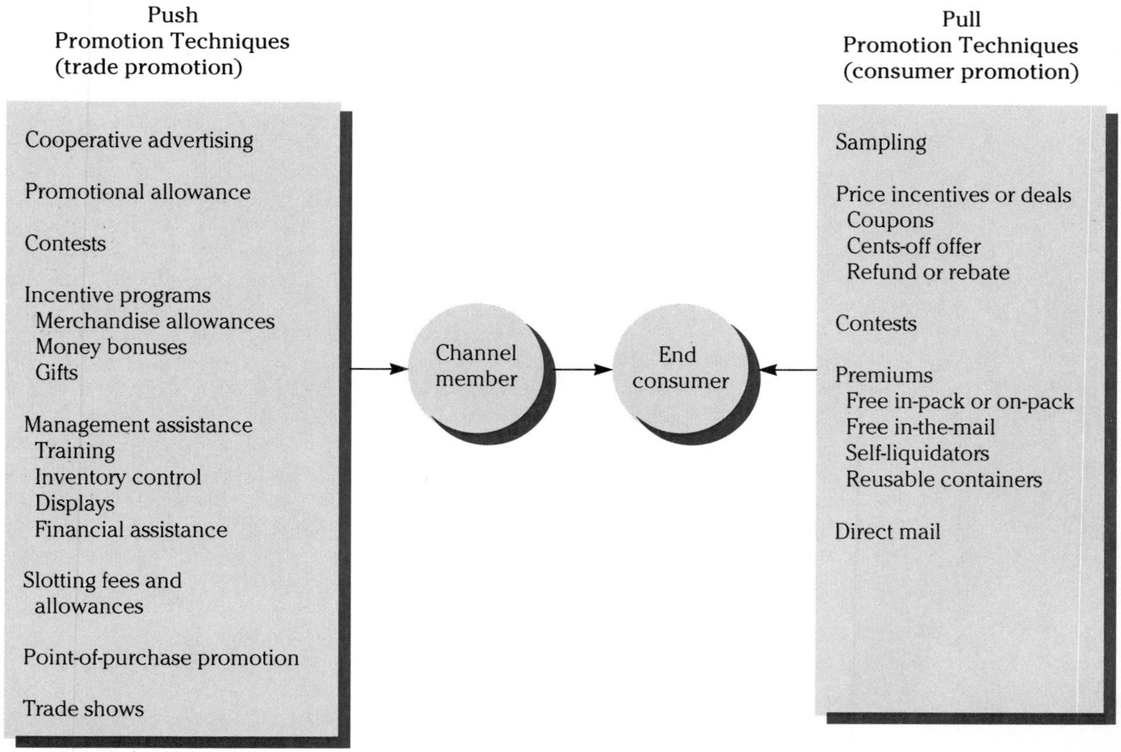

Push
Promotion Techniques
(trade promotion)

Pull
Promotion Techniques
(consumer promotion)

Cooperative advertising

Promotional allowance

Contests

Incentive programs
  Merchandise allowances
  Money bonuses
  Gifts

Management assistance
  Training
  Inventory control
  Displays
  Financial assistance

Slotting fees and
  allowances

Point-of-purchase promotion

Trade shows

Channel member → End consumer

Sampling

Price incentives or deals
  Coupons
  Cents-off offer
  Refund or rebate

Contests

Premiums
  Free in-pack or on-pack
  Free in-the-mail
  Self-liquidators
  Reusable containers

Direct mail

Source: Adapted from Thomas C. Kinnear and Kenneth L. Bernhardt, *Principles of Marketing,* 3rd ed. (Glenview, Ill.: Scott Foresman/Little Brown, 1990), p. 522.

sales promotion techniques. They are all designed to impact the end consumer, either directly (pull) or indirectly through the action of the channel members (push).

More money is spent in a year on these diverse activities that constitute sales promotion than is spent on advertising. The estimated expenditures on all types of sales promotion in 1988 totaled $124.5 billion.[3] Table 17–1 gives the breakdown of this total into its components. The growth rate in sales promotion dollars over the period 1980 to 1988 was 13 percent per year, and advertising expenditures grew at 10 percent per year. The percentage of firms' total advertising and sales promotion budgets spent on advertising was 31 percent in 1988, down from 43 percent in 1980. Retailer- and wholesaler-directed promotions constituted 44 percent of this budget in 1988, up from 35 percent in 1980. Consumer-directed sales promotions increased from 22 percent of this budget in 1980 to 25 percent in 1988.

Our discussion of sales promotion in this book is divided into three sections, presented in three different chapters. The channel-directed sales promotion activities, called *trade promotion,* are discussed in Chapter 21, "Working with Resellers: The Struggle for Channel Control." Direct mail activity is discussed in Chapter 22, "Direct Marketing." The remainder of this chapter discusses consumer-directed sales promotion activities, called *consumer sales promotion* or simply *consumer promotion;* as noted, discussion of direct mail is presented in Chapter 22.

TABLE 17–1

❖

Expenditure on Consumer and Channel-Directed Sales Promotion— 1988

Sales Promotion	Amount	Percentage
Direct mail	$ 21,115*	17
POP/Display	16,795	13
Premiums & incentives†	16,495	13
Meetings & conventions	33,526	27
Trade Shows & exhibits	8,040	6
Promotional advertising	10,833	9
Print/AV/Misc.	11,908	10
Coupon redemption	5,798	5
TOTAL	$ 124,510	100

*Dollars in millions.
†Includes Sweepstakes & Contests.
Source: Russ Bowman, "Dollars up but Cooling down," *Marketing and Media Decisions,* July 1989, pp. 123–26.

CONSUMER-ORIENTED SALES PROMOTION

Sales promotions are becoming such a popular marketing tool that some packaged goods giants are beginning to worry about the long-term effect they may have on brand loyalty.[4] The intense competition for retail shelf space and the desire on the part of brand managers to show quick gains in market share has had a snowball effect on promotional campaigns. Companies keep offering more coupons, bigger rebates, and more valuable sweepstakes prizes in an effort to draw customers from the competition.

This marketing approach neglects the brand images that some manufacturers have spent decades developing through advertising. "It's much easier to just give people a cents-off coupon so they'll buy your product instead of the next guy's," says David Hurwitt, marketing vice president at General Foods Corp. "Then he'll give even more cents off next month, you respond, and the war goes on."

Although a sweepstakes can be held for as little as $75,000 plus prizes, competition among companies is raising the ante. Procter & Gamble and General Motors Corp. worked together to offer a $9 million promotion that gave away 750 1988 Chevrolets. It was the most expensive promotion yet for either company. That amount is dwarfed, however, by the $40 million McDonald's gave away in its latest Monopoly game sweepstakes. Contestants in that contest tried to collect matching sets of game cards. Two top prizes of $1,000 a week for life with a guarantee of at least $1 million were given.

Advertisers are disturbed about this trend toward more expensive promotions. They are also worried that consumers are starting to take promotions for granted. When automakers offer rebates, their sales go up; when the rebate ends, sales drop while potential car buyers wait for the next round of rebates to start.

Companies also fear that heavy couponing, which represents a significant proportion of all sales promotion, is evaporating brand loyalty and turning retail brands into commodities. Some customers may not buy their usual brand if they don't have cents-off coupons for it. Marketers have also noticed an increasing tendency among shoppers who don't use coupons to simply buy the cheapest brand in the store.

Experts believe that to avoid these problems, companies will have to adjust the way promotions are being used. They say that promotions should be a part of an integrated marketing plan, supporting and enhancing product image and advertising. An example of such an integrated approach is the Pepsi Co-Paramount Pictures' joint campaign developed to promote Diet Pepsi and the videocassette of the movie *Top Gun.*

The Diet Pepsi *Top Gun* campaign combined numerous forms of sales promotion with intensive advertising. Coupons for Diet Pepsi were distributed, and the cost of videocassettes was discounted. Retailers received free cases of Diet Pepsi for every 10 videos sold. Television ads featured jet pilots drinking Diet Pepsi. A heavily advertised sweepstakes was held, with the grand prize being a ride in a P-51 with test pilot Chuck Yeager.

The campaign was a major success: more than 2.8 million copies of *Top Gun* were sold. This set a videocassette sales record that more than doubled the previous mark held by *Beverly Hills Cop*.

Despite such success, there is still a question as to whether consumers will become so spoiled by promotional giveaways that they will need additional inducements to buy some products. Companies are now realizing that their headlong rush into sales promotions may come back to haunt them.

One of the reasons that this potential excessive use of consumer promotions exists is that brand managers who are looking to have quick success are aware that promotions can produce quick jumps in market share.[5] According to Lou Houk, vice president of the Chicago sales promotion agency Frankel & Co., these marketers concentrate on getting immediate results instead of thinking about long-term strategy.

"A new brand manager comes in and says, 'What can I do to make a mark?' " explains Houk. "He can't fool around with the advertising too much because of bureaucracy and because the system is already in place. But he knows if he puts a consumer promotion together, all of a sudden market share will move."

Sales promotions are also usually cheaper than advertising, and their results are more easily identifiable. For example, a major national TV advertising campaign may target 50 percent of the households in the country at a minimum cost of $2 million. A promotional campaign using coupon inserts can reach as many households for only $1.25 million, and the effectiveness of the campaign can easily be determined by the number of coupons redeemed.

The level of use of consumer promotions by consumer goods companies is noted in Table 17–2. The growth in use since 1984 is evident. We also note that the firm not undertaking multiple consumer promotions in a given year is the exception.

An increasing number of companies are making efforts to curb the tremendous growth in sales promotions experienced in the last decade. Fed up with the spiraling costs and eroding brand loyalty associated with promotions, manufacturers are also worried that customers are being trained not to buy products unless they are on sale.

Other officials can also sense the marketing pendulum shifting back to advertising. Cutting back on promotions won't be easy, but these officials are determined to prevent sales promotions from spiraling further out of control. "We've been talking about it for years," said James Erceg, director of promotion and couponing services for Drackett Co., a unit of Bristol-Myers. "It's finally starting to happen."[6]

CONSUMER PROMOTIONAL ALTERNATIVES

The objective sought for the consumer promotion impacts the type of promotion that is appropriate. When new products are being introduced, three major types of sales promotion effort may be utilized: (1) sampling, (2) couponing, and (3) money refund offers. When the goal is to increase sales of an existing product, major alternatives include (1) price-off promotions, (2) premiums, and (3) consumer contests.

The remainder of this chapter discusses these alternatives in some detail and also considers the role of packaging as an important promotional tool.

Sampling

Consumer sampling is an effective but rather costly means of introducing a new product. As a technique, it is probably used more by large firms that produce broad lines of packaged consumer food or health and beauty items and engage in extensive advertising and personal selling on a national basis.

TABLE 17–2

Use of Consumer Promotions

Types of Promotion	% of Respondents Using in Each Year				
	1988	1987	1986	1985	1984
Couponing consumer direct	92	96	91	93	95
Money back offers/cash refunds	85	87	85	85	81
Cents-off promotions	74	69	70	78	64
Sweepstakes	72	66	72	77	73
Premium offers	68	74	58	79	82
Sampling new products	68	71	64	77	62
Sampling established products	63	65	57	76	36
Couponing in retailers' aid	63	57	45	56	40
Prepriced shippers	52	56	58	70	49
Contests	46	38	40	55	29

Source: *Donnelley Marketing Eleventh Annual Survey* as presented in Russ Bowman, "Dollars Up but Cooling Down," *Marketing and Media Decisions,* July 1989, pp. 123–26.

When used as part of a coordinated promotional campaign to introduce a new product, the catalytic effect of sampling on trial usage and subsequent repurchase can be sufficiently strong to more than defray the expense of sampling.

Distribution   The physical distribution of the sample either to resellers for redistribution to consumers or directly to consumers is a formidable task. Mail, house-to-house private delivery, distribution at point-of-purchase, and inclusion in the package of another product are some of the ways suggested to get the sample into the hands of the prospective customer.

There is little doubt that providing a free sample can break through the noise level and stimulate a higher rate of trial than can other promotional efforts. Such trial is not gained without the expenditure of a good deal of money, and unless the trials translate into repurchase, the sampling promotion cannot be deemed a success. Repurchase data may not be available for several weeks after initial distribution of samples and even if repurchase rates are high, it is difficult to determine how much influence the sampling promotion had on market results. What might be in order at this point would be a postintroduction market survey to determine how consumers were influenced to buy. Agree shampoo reached a leadership position in the market within six months of introduction and eventually obtained over a 20 percent share of the market by using mass sampling. Over 31 million samples were distributed.

Preliminary Research   Because sampling is so expensive, research is recommended prior to launching a full-scale effort. Information can be gathered as to the proper size of the sample, the most effective means of distribution, and so forth. During the test marketing of Gainesburgers by the Post Division of General Foods, for example, a one-patty sample of dog food was distributed to consumers at supermarket checkout counters. Repurchase rates after trial were disappointing, and market research indicated that dogs were still hungry after eating the patty and that the image of the product was that it was not a complete meal but rather a snack or treat-type product. The sampling strategy was changed so that two-patty packages of Gainesburgers were mailed to dog owners of record in the market area and the media advertising reinforced the idea that two patties were equivalent to one pound of canned dog food. Providing trial users with a sample adequate to supply a full meal to a dog and supplementing this trail with a copy platform of "Canned Dog Food without the Can" resulted in a very high rate of product repurchase after introduction and launched a new product category that over the years has shown remarkable growth and profitability.

Promotion in Action 17–1 illustrates some of the logistical dynamics and power of sampling.

Purpose of Sampling In other situations, sampling may not do the job. Customers will either disregard the sample or use it without switching their patronage. There can be many explanations for such a failure, but the first hypothesis that should be investigated is that the consumer could find no demonstrable difference in the new product that would motivate him or her to buy it. Sampling is most effective when the key attributes setting the new product apart from its competitors are difficult to describe adequately in print or visual media. Scent, taste, consistency, balance, and the like are selling points that can be effectively communicated by sampling.

On occasion, sampling will be used for other reasons. There have been some attempts to revive the sales of a slumping product, but the distribution of the sample rarely reverses the downturn. The cause most often lies in some marketing deficiency that should be remedied first. Also, some large firms use sampling as a defensive weapon to blunt the attempts of competitors to introduce new products through this means. Procter & Gamble, in particular, has utilized this strategy for decades, and its continuing domination in many product classes attests to the influence of its marketing muscle.

Generally, the advertiser will not undertake the sampling effort but will retain one of the variety of service firms in this field. One of the largest is the Reuben H. Donnelley Corporation, which distributes samples through mass mailings, handouts, or door drops. It also is possible to confine distribution to more selective audiences through Welcome Wagon and other specialized service firms.

Price Incentives

The use of a short-term reduction in price to encourage trial use of a new product or to stimulate demand for an established product is referred to as offering a *consumer deal.* Such deals are most frequently communicated to consumers by means of coupons and cents-off promotions. Figure 17–2 illustrates a deal in which the consumer can obtain a price reduction by presenting the coupons to the retailer at time of purchase. The coupon and cents-off promotions are used to stimulate further consumer response in the short run.

A somewhat different approach is shown in Figure 17–3. Here we see a price reduction of two thirds of the retail value of the item being offered to those customers who will send the coupon together with payment directly to the manufacturer.

The objective of all of these sales promotions is to increase product trial among prospective customers. The best results are obtained in those product categories in which the rate or repurchase due to brand loyalty is low. Where brand loyalty is high, small price differences are unlikely to overcome the perceived advantage of remaining with a preferred brand. In the first place, brand switching is often seen as having a high degree of perceived risk, with the result that the psychological cost of trying an unknown brand is too high. Furthermore, a price-induced trial may last for only one purchase, and basic brand preferences may remain unchanged. Usually when loyalty is high, relatively large price reductions will be required.

There is always the danger that offering consumer deals will become the standard competitive tool, in which case no competitor really benefits. All engage in it for mostly defensive reasons, and the consumer will wisely

❖
**PROMOTION
IN ACTION
17−1**

Sampling Corporation of America Gears up for Halloween

Sampling Corporation of America strives to "distribute samples and coupons in an environment that will maximize their usage and reinforce the brand name and existence." The Glenview, Illinois–based promotion company has conducted a special Halloween program for the past eight years. In honor of the holiday, millions of school children are given costumes, paper jack-o'-lanterns, and bright orange, black, and white plastic bags stuffed with coupons and product samples. Treats for their parents? Sampling and its customers think so.

The eye-catching orange, white, and black plastic bags feature a variety of Halloween figures intermingled with the logos of the participating brands. The real treats are inside: reflective safety stickers (for the kids to put on their costumes while trick-or-treating); a safety poster; a booklet for parents containing safety tips and ideas for simple costumes, makeup, and party games; and, of course, the coupons and product samples. Product samples usually include candy, snacks, an aseptically packaged juice box, and sometimes toothpaste.

Sampling Corporation distributes these Halloween bags free to local schools and school districts. Most schools hand out the sampling bags in conjunction with a safety speech given by a teacher or police officer. The National Safety Council lends its support as well. Bob O'Brien, director, public relations for the Chicago-based council, asserted that "our community safety department looked over the materials and made a number of recommendations on the safety advice. The idea of getting the message into the parents' hands is very valuable and we just don't have the horsepower to get into those households." This tie-in with holiday safety lends credibility to Sampling Corporation's program.

Do parents actually take the time to examine the bag's contents and read through the booklet? According to Cincinnati's Burke Market Research, the answer for most families is yes. For one participating brand, both brand adopt the strategy of purchasing the brand that offers the best deal at that point in time. No competitor really can gain differential advantage under these circumstances.

The consumer deal will most likely succeed under these conditions:

1. When the manufacturer has used the price incentive only infre- quently and at widely spaced intervals.

Sampling Corporation of America Gears up for Halloween concluded

❖
**PROMOTION
IN ACTION
17–1**

awareness and total advertising awareness increased by 40 percentage points—mainly due to unaided awareness. Brand usage increased 35 per- centage points and actual purchases of the brand increased by 20 percentage points. The packages' coupons were a great success as well, with 17 percent of consumers using them and 65 percent planning to do so in the future.

According to Stephen Kaplan, executive vice president, Sampling "can do something that major brands can't do for themselves. We can get prod- ucts and coupons home to parents through the schools." An increasing number of well-known companies are using Sampling to do just that. Eighty percent of each year's participants are repeat customers. This year's sam- ples include Kraft Handi-Snacks, Candilicious, and Del Monte Fruit Cup.

Best Foods, marketer of Karo corn syrup, found Sampling's program to be a great fit with its own marketing strategy. For several years, Karo had been trying to convince parents that Karo is a good medium for Halloween makeup; it's safer than masks, fun, and inexpensive. Jim Coyle, director- promotion planning for Best Foods, admitted, "It would have been difficult to communicate that usage [as makeup] directly to the user. We felt that if kids were sold [on the makeup idea], then they'd take it home to mom and dad." Sampling's Halloween promotion provided a great vehicle.

Sampling's growth is another mark of its success. The company now distributes its Halloween sample bags to 10 million 6- to 12-year-olds, cov- ering half the country's households with children in that age group. A similar program is being developed for summer safety. Sampling's revenues of $1.5 million for the 1987 fiscal year are up $450,000 from 1986. Revenues for 1988 are projected at $3 million.

Source: "Promo Dresses up for Halloween," *Advertising Age,* November 16, 1987, pp. S-12–14.

2. When the manufacturer avoids dealing as a strategy to force the retailer to stock in the hopes of offsetting acceptance of a price offer by a competing brand.

3. When the brand is relatively new.

4. When deals are not used as a substitute for advertising.

At all costs, deals should be avoided as a cure-all for declining sales. An ever-present tendency is to resort to the price incentive when the real prob-

FIGURE 17–2

❖

A Consumer-Oriented Price-Off Deal Implemented by Coupons Included in a Magazine Advertisement for Redemption by the Retailer

FIGURE 17–3

THIS PAGE IS WORTH $4.00

Take $4.00 from the regular $5.95* price of Hanes Alive® support pantyhose. And what do you get?

A darn good bargain for only $1.95. Why are we doing this? Because we believe that once you wear Alive, you'll find they look so good and make your legs feel so much better, that you'll never want to wear anything else. And that's what we're counting on.

How to get it.

We'll send you our most popular color, Barely There,™ (same as in photograph) in our most popular style. Just fill in the form below and send it with check or money order for $1.95 payable to HANES HOSIERY INC. P.O. Box 847, Rural Hall, N.C. 27045. Allow 4 to 8 weeks for delivery.

Orders cannot be filled for women under 4' 10" and 95 lbs. or over 5' 10" and 170 lbs.

NAME _____

ADDRESS _____

CITY _____ STATE _____

PHONE # _____ ZIP _____

HEIGHT Ft _____ In _____

WEIGHT _____
H46

Please do not send cash through mail. Offer valid with use of this form only and must include zip code. Limit one per family. Duplicates voided by computer. Offer expires June 30, 1978. Void where prohibited or otherwise restricted.
*Suggested retail price.

© 1974 Hanes Hosiery, Inc.

Hanes Alive Support.
Some women are more alive than others.

lem lies elsewhere in deficiencies in the marketing mix. Careful analysis must be undertaken before embarking on this strategy—to ascertain that there is a favorable probability of increasing brand loyalty. Often this requires an actual market test. Great care must also be taken to maintain normal advertising support, and the trade must be approached in such a way that its cooperation is both solicited and maintained. The result otherwise may be a financially abortive strategy or, even worse, the triggering of unnecessary and ruinous competitive warfare.

Couponing

The use of coupons as a means of sales promotion is very closely associated with price incentives. In fact, coupons are the major medium by which the manufacturer offers the consumer a price deal. If redeemed at a retail store, the coupon is used by the retailer and the wholesaler to gain reimbursement from the manufacturer.

The use of coupons as a sales promotion technique has increased dramatically in recent years. According to studies by the A. C. Nielsen Company, 5.3 billion coupons were distributed in 1962. In 1980, 90.6 billion coupons were distributed, 163.2 billion in 1984, and 221.7 billion in 1988.[7] In 1988, 7.05 billion coupons were redeemed for a redemption rate of about 3.2 percent.

The popularity of coupons is based on several advantages associated with their use. First, the use of coupons limits the price reduction to those customers who are sensitive to the price deal. All of the other customers continue to pay the regular price. Second, coupons enable the manufacturer to specify the time frame for the promotion. This enables coordination with other activities in the promotional mix. In addition, the time limit induces more immediate response from consumers. Third, since many products are losing their distinctiveness, the coupon offer may give the manufacturer something with which to develop a selective demand for a brand.

Distribution   Coupons are distributed in a variety of ways. Free-standing inserts that are leaflets of coupons inserted into a newspaper constitute 77.3 percent of coupon distribution in 1988, up from 59.9 percent in 1985. In 1988, newspapers got 7.8 percent of the distribution, direct mail 5 percent, in-/on-packages 5.2 percent, and magazines 2.4 percent. Redemption rates for various forms of distribution in 1988 were 3.2 percent for free-standing inserts, 4.9 percent for direct mail, 12.9 percent for in-package coupons, and 33.2 percent for on-package coupons.[8]

Cost   The cost of using a specific medium must, of course, be considered in relation to both the coverage offered and the redemptions expected. In addition, the financial liability associated with redemption of coupons seems to occur with differing time lags, depending on the medium used. Neilsen research indicates that "newspaper offers redeem faster than either pop-up or on-page magazine coupons; and pop-up magazine offers come in faster than on-page magazine coupons."[9]

In order to compare various coupon plans and distribution alternatives, many companies calculate the estimated cost-per-redeemed coupon. Since the redemption rates and distribution costs vary by method, each method will have a different cost per coupon. Table 17–3 presents a procedure for calculating these costs.

On average, cost per coupon redeemed is estimated to be newspapers run-of-paper solo, 55 cents; newspaper co-op, 37 cents; Sunday supplements, 75 cents; magazine on-page, 72 cents; magazine pop-up, 78 cents; and direct mail, 59 cents.

Although the couponing that we have been discussing in this chapter is consumer-oriented promotion, it is obvious that those strategies that require redemption at point-of-purchase cannot be executed without the cooperation of the retailers and wholesalers in the channel of distribution. The process of receipt of the coupons, their redemption, and subsequent submission to the manufacturer for repayment is costly. Although most retailers receive a payment of about eight cents per coupon handled, many complain that coupons cause more delay, expense, and general trouble than they ar

TABLE 17–3

Cost per Coupon Redeemed: An Illustration   ❖

1. Distribution cost	
10,000,000 circulation $\times$ \$8/M	\$ 80,000
2. Redemptions at 3.1%	310,000
3. Redemption cost	
310,000 redemptions $\times$ \$.25 face value	\$ 77,500
4. Handling cost	
310,000 redemptions $\times$ \$.08	\$ 24,800
5. Total program cost	
Items 1 + 3 + 4	\$182,300
6. Cost-per-coupon redeemed	
Cost divided by redemptions	58.8¢
7. Actual product sold on redemption	
(misredemption estimated at 20%) 310,000 $\times$ 80%	\$248,000
8. Cost-per-product moved	
Program cost divided by product sold	73.5¢

Source: Updated to 1990 by the authors from Louis J. Haugh, "How Coupons Measure Up," *Advertising Age,* June 8, 1981, p. 58. Reprinted with permission. Copyright Crain Communications, Inc. all rights reserved.

worth. The wise manufacturer makes certain that it doesn't overdo the use of coupons and that resellers are adequately compensated for their efforts when a coupon deal is used.

On the other hand, very often retailers are found to have engaged in misredemption practices in which customers are given some monetary benefit when they have not bought the product. This is a cost that must be considered—see Table 17–3. Until the computerized checkout using the universal product codes becomes standard practice, there is little the manufacturer can do but to press charges against those resellers who have been caught engaging in fraudulent practices such as misredemption.

Coupons have application beyond consumer package goods. A successful application of coupons into a nonconsumer package product category is illustrated by Promotion in Action 17–2.

❖
**PROMOTION
IN ACTION
17–2**

Mattel Puts Coupons into Play

After losing its first-place ranking in the $12.5 billion toy industry, Mattel, Inc., decided to enlist some strategies from the package-goods marketing manual. Aiming for the largest coupon promotion in toy industry history, Mattel hoped to boost its declining sales with more than half a billion dollars-off coupons during the industry's crucial holiday season.

Mattel USA President Robert Sansone, drawing on his 24 years of experience with General Foods Corp., came up with the idea. "Coupons are a tried and proven sales generator in other product categories but have never before been utilized as a key element in toy marketing." In an effort to regain lost ground, Mattel was willing to pioneer the idea and spent more money than ever on its promotional efforts. The company distributed about 582 million store-redeemable coupons worth between $1 and $5 for specific toys via direct mail, magazine ads, and consumer catalogs.

One of the campaign's key elements was a direct-mail coupon drop in both mid-October and mid-November. The drops covered 70 million U.S. households and delivered 315 million coupons. Each envelope delivered contained four or five coupons for popular Mattel products such as Barbie, Lady LovelyLocks, L'il Miss Makeup dolls, and Hot Wheels Speed Shift 500 race sets.

Another aspect of the holiday campaign focused on Mattel's new Disney-brand line of infant and preschool toys. To launch this new line, 150

Premiums

A *premium* is the offer of some type of merchandise or service either free or at a bargain price to induce purchase of another product or service offering. Although premium promotions vary greatly, their principal purpose is quite specific: to induce consumers to change the brands or amount purchased. The goal may be to switch consumers from their present brand to that of the promoter in order to gain trial use, with hopes of repeat purchase. Or the goal may be to induce present customers to increase their use of the brand or to purchase it in larger-sized packages. Premium promotions are effective in that they appeal to the very human desire to get a bargain. Their widespread use is shown in industry figures indicating that firms engaged in the supply and distribution of premiums grossed over $16 billion annually. The overuse of premiums is a concern in some industries.

**PROMOTION
IN ACTION
17–2**

Mattel Puts Coupons into Play (concluded)

million product-specific coupons were distributed. The coupons were part of an eight-page catalog that was distributed through both direct mail and insertion in October and December editions of parenting and women's magazines. A national brand tie-in promotion with 2-liter and 12-pack products from the Seven-Up Co. and Capri Sun fruit drinks delivered 117 million additional coupons. Mattel estimated that about 4 percent of the coupons will be redeemed.

Mattel supported its promotional blitz with a four-week flight of national spot TV commercials and heavy schedule of print ads. A Sunday comics ad featured in national newspapers launched a Hot Wheels "Instant Winner" game featuring a Ford Mustang convertible and matching child's minicar as a grand prize. Ad spending for 1988 was expected to remain at its 1987 level of $44 million. Although the company refused to divulge specific figures for unmeasured media spending—which includes couponing and various promotions—this category was expected to skyrocket past the 1986 figure of $14 million. After losses of $8.3 million in 1986 and $113.2 million in 1987, 1988's net income of $35.9 million is a major step forward and evidence that Mattel's strategy is at least contributing to its present goal of short-term profitability.

Sources: "Mattel Sets Big Coupon Effort," *Advertising Age,* September 26, 1988, p. 40; "Toyland Turnaround," *Forbes,* January 9, 1989, p. 168.

Effective promotion planners do not first choose a premium and then develop their creative strategy—they develop their creative strategy and then choose a premium that "fits" their overall program. Several recent cases exemplify this principle.

The first case is considered "an event/promotion that represents one of the largest premium orders of all time—diet Coke's 3-D glasses giveaway."[10] The 1988 Super Bowl's highly publicized halftime show was promoted as a 3-D extravaganza. Diet Coke capitalized on this event by producing a 3-D diet Coke commercial. The brand promoted both the halftime show and its unique ad by building off-shelf displays and distributing 20 million pairs of 3-D glasses as in-store premiums. Russ Bowman, a writer for *Marketing & Media Decisions,* provided a good example of this premium/promotion's effectiveness. The Friday before the Super Bowl, Bowman went to three different grocery stores in search of the coveted 3-D glasses. He checked the end-of-aisle displays and the Coke section in each store, and finally asked the manager at the third store if any 3-D glasses were to be found. Not only were all of the glasses gone, so were all of the 6-packs of Coke!

Several other premiums offered in early 1989 provided a good fit between the brand and the target consumer audience. Using a two-page spread in a Sunday newspaper supplement, Carnation's Friskies pet-food offered dog and cat owners 5 cents-off coupons and a "$36 value" pet-care grooming kit for only $9.95 with proofs-of-purchase. Kimberly Clark's Huggies diapers came up with yet another unique infant premium—the first national premium offer of a tape cassette of "personalized" lullabies produced by Playskool. A Valassis free-standing ad on January 29, 1989, offered a $1 Huggies coupon and a free personalized tape for 24 proofs-of-purchase. Another example was a character premium that has become a nationally recognized symbol: the California Raisins. The popular three-inch raisin figures were available for just 99¢ with a proof-of-purchase from any package of California raisins.

Premiums may be classified in terms of whether they are offered free or are to some extent self-liquidating (see Figure 17–4). In the latter case, the customer pays an extra amount that covers the manufacturer's out-of-pocket costs. Recent evidence indicates that with self-liquidating premium offers, consumers are less concerned with the amount they are required to pay than they are with whether or not they will be getting a bargain. One of the most successful self-liquidating premium offers was the Kool Cigarette promotion that offered a sailboat for $88 with the enclosure of 10 empty packages as proof of purchase. Over 20,000 customers ordered this premium.

Free premiums may range from toys offered for cereal box tops to towels packed in boxes of detergent. The item offered is carefully selected and often pretested to ensure that it will be sufficiently appealing to induce purchase. In most cases, the premium offered is not directly related to the main product as would be the case in a combination offer promotion. The ratio of free to self-liquidating premiums is about 55 percent to 45 percent, respectively.

Delivery and Redemption of Premiums   Premium promotions differ by mode of delivery or redemption. The most widely used mode is the "free-in-the-mail" approach. The offer is communicated to the consumer by coupons or by media advertising. Requests for the free premium are mailed to the manufacturer or to a premium redemption specialist where they are processed and deliveries are arranged. This process is quite expensive.

The alternative strategy of placing the premium in or on the package of the basic product simplifies premium delivery and stimulates interest at point-of-sale. The on-packaging premium has become increasingly popular as technology has enabled the use of blister or bubble packaging. With a

FIGURE 17–4

Example of a Self-Liquidating Premium Offer

blister pack, for example, the premium can be placed next to the main product without fear of detachment and loss. Yet the plastic packaging material allows the premium to be seen at point-of-purchase, thus stimulating consumer reaction. Of course, the use of the in- or on-pack modes of delivery require the support of the resellers. They must buy the promotional packs and display them so that they will be available when the national advertising communicates the promotion to the public. Closely associated with on-pack promotion is the use of the package itself as a premium. This topic will be discussed in the section on packaging.

The use of premiums is effective in gaining short-run trial use. However, unless the product offers a distinctive advantage to the consumer, trial use will not translate into repeat purchase. In that case, the premium promotion is simply providing a temporary boost to product sales. A better strategy would be to divert some of the promotional resources to product development activities.

Contests and Sweepstakes

Promotional activities that involve consumers in the advertising and merchandising activities of the manufacturer by gaining their participation in games of skill or chance are known respectively as *contests* (see Figure 17–5) and *sweepstakes* (see Figure 17–6). In comparison to other means of sales promotion, contests and sweepstakes are considered to be potentially as strong as the strongest premium offer (in-pack) and stronger than the weakest premium offer (self-liquidating).

A contest requires that the participant apply a skill in creating an idea, a concept, or an end product. Contests have been based on suggesting the best name for a new product, new uses for established products, or as in the case of the Pillsbury Bake-Off Contest, for creating and utilizing recipes to produce outstanding baked goods products. In contrast, sweepstakes are games of chance in which each participant has an equal chance of winning a prize from a rather extensive and expensive list of rewards. Care must be taken to prevent the sweepstakes from being considered a lottery, which is illegal in many states. Judicial review has indicated that the requirement that a sweepstakes entrant buy the manufacturer's product is not a "consideration" that would make the event a lottery. Even so, most firms that use sweepstakes allow contestants to use facsimiles of the box top or coupon as well as the real thing.

Contests and sweepstakes have many advantages, including their ability to gain a high degree of consumer involvement in the manufacturer's advertising and merchandising program. In addition, they can help gain support from resellers and often add excitement or interest to a lagging product or advertising theme.

FIGURE 17–5

Example of a Contest Promotion

Reproduced with permission © PepsiCo, Inc.

A well-conceived and well-run contest can have major benefit to the marketer. Consider the case of Eagle Food Centers.[11] Based in Milan, Illinois, Eagle Food Centers ran a highly successful campaign from April 15 to June 3, 1988. This campaign, "The Search for Eagle Kids," invited customers with children between the ages of 5 and 12 to describe why their child was the "perfect Eagle Kid" in 50 words or less. The prize for each of the 10 winning Eagle Kids was a $1,000 savings bond and an opportunity to appear in an Eagle print ad and TV commercial.

The Eagle Kid contest directly appealed to parents in Eagle stores' retail area, which included 105 stores in Illinois, Indiana, and Iowa. Colorful signs and point-of-purchase displays supported the contest in-store. Window dis-

---

FIGURE 17–6

❖ **Example of a Sweepstakes Promotion**

plays and "aisle danglers" featured cartoons depicting potential Eagle Kids. Each region designated special "Kid Days" when all children who visited Eagle stores received Eagle Kids balloons, buttons, bumper stickers, shoe-laces, license plates, and refreshments. "Kids Days" promoted the contest while generating awareness and support for local stores.

Customers were definitely aware. Phone calls poured in asking for ad-ditional information and inside advice on what type of photograph to send. Ray Myers, Eagle's ad vice president, stressed that the Eagle Kids campaign was not a beauty contest: "We tried to avoid 'professional' children, hoping to give recognition to kids who represented a true cross-mix of our custom-ers' families."

The contest was a great success. Eagle Foods received over 2,500 entries during the eight-week contest. The 10 winners were chosen throughout Eagle's marketing area. The end result was a diverse collection of children. The winning ad featured the Eagle Kids riding on a school bus while a voice-over described how children represent our future. Only subtle references were made to the Eagle promotion. According to Myers, Eagle Foods is "convinced this type of marketing effort helps us broaden our customer base and strengthens our positioning of the new Eagle Foods among this very important market segment." Jonathan Blum, general manager at Ogilvy & Mather Public Relations, Chicago, believes that the success of the Eagle Foods contest and other similar marketing campaigns by grocery retailers makes creative, family-oriented promotions a good bet for the future.

Sweepstakes are increasingly popular vehicles for increasing consumer loyalty and creating excitement in the marketplace.[12] A significant segment of the market believes that advertisements and cents-off coupons pale in comparison to free trips and automobiles. According to Charles Visich, a former marketing consultant and present senior vice president at Southland Corp., product promotion has turned into a giant lottery: "People are devel-oping a pot-of-gold-at-the-end-of-the-rainbow mentality." Jeff Conner, prod-uct manager for Heinz Ketchup, remarked, "The prizes are getting larger because people are desensitized to the small things. If you want to get their attention, you have to offer them something exciting."

The growing popularity and social acceptance of state lotteries gets credit for a lot of "contest fever." According to Visich, "Whenever somebody wins $23 million, it makes people who have never won anything think twice. The winners are glamorized on television. Society is telling us it's okay to participate." And thousands of consumers do participate in sweepstakes each year.

Sweepstakes have several advantages from a marketing point of view. As Visich points out, "The value of a 50-cent coupon is known in advance. But if I offer a trip to Hawaii, the incentive is much more exciting." Mailboxes full of junk mail and the seemingly endless parade of television commercials make it hard for manufacturers to make their products stand out. But Joe Namath offering tickets to a major football game is an attention-getter.

Companies often choose prizes for their promotional sweepstakes that tie in with their products. Pine-Sol disinfectant, which is marketed as a complete household cleaner, came up with the idea of giving away a free house. Pine-Sol's "Whole House" Sweepstakes awarded $250,000 in mortgage payments to its lucky winner. GE Lighting offered a free family vacation to Walt Disney World to see *IllumniNations,* GE's magnificent light display at Disney's Epcot Center. Prizes like these attract consumer attention.

A supermarket survey conducted by the Point-of-Purchase Advertising Institute found that two-thirds of all purchase decisions are made by customers in the store. This indicates that strong in-store display support is crucial for product success. As a result, separate sweepstakes are often set up for store employees to encourage more elaborate point-of-purchase displays. Although some companies require nothing more from employees than a mail-in card, others require photos of attractive displays. According to John Beh, national sales manager for GE Lighting, "Offering a contest where store managers can be rewarded for building special in-store displays drives additional volume." Prizes are sometimes given as reductions in merchandise costs so that the entire winning store gets credit.

Manufacturers win other benefits by going the sweepstakes route. An average of 3.2 percent of all supermarket coupons are redeemed today. Thousands enter sweepstakes, yet few are big winners. And sweepstakes are less expensive than giving stores straight cash merchandising allowances. Some prizes that have commercial tie-ins promoting a specific airline or hotel are special bargains. As one supermarket executive remarked, "That trip may be worth $5,000, but it may not cost the sponsor a dime. Think of the advertising impact to seeing the words 'Disney World' in 23,000 supermarkets nationwide. That has great commercial value." Even the manufacturers are lured by the offer of "something-for-nothing."

The use of contests and sweepstakes is not without its hazards. The folklore of marketing has many stories of contests and sweepstakes gone bad. Promotion in Action 17–3 speaks clearly to this issue. Great care in planning, testing, and implementing the details are needed for a successful promotion of these promotions.

PACKAGING

Although initially designed to provide protection for products as they move from producer to consumer, the product package has played an increasingly important promotional role in recent years. The recognition that the package is more than a protective container has boomed the packaging industry to an annual level of gross sales approaching $90 billion. No small part of that expenditure is to obtain the sales stimulation that well-designed packages can provide. In spite of the large role that packaging plays in promotional strategy, only a modest amount of literature is devoted to the subject. The remainder of this section highlights what is available. The promotional aspects of packaging can be both long term (like advertising) or short term (like most sales promotions).

Promotional Aspects

The prime promotional aspects of a package are its ability to identify a product from an array of competing goods and to convey information and meaning about the product. In those increasingly numerous situations in which consumer goods are sold with a minimum of clerk service or by self-service, the package is the salesperson. It plays the role of the attention getter or triggering cue that starts the sales process. It provides information about product attributes such as price, quality, quantity, instructions for use, warranty, and so forth. In addition, the package conveys meaning of an emotional or psychological nature. It can aid in the creation of product imagery. Package color and shape are very important for this purpose.

Package Color The use of color is one means by which a package conveys psychological meaning. White packages, for example, suggest purity and cleanliness, green packages suggest association with nature and thus natural ingredients, and blue packages indicate coolness, thus the use of blue on some menthol cigarette packs and on "Cold Water All" detergent. Red and yellow packages, in contrast, indicate a "hot" new product that demands consumer attention.

Package Shape The physical form of a package, in addition to providing protection and convenience, can also convey the psychological message deemed appropriate for the target market audience and the overall copy platform used in the advertising. For example, a successful promotion involved the packaging of a liquid cleaning compound in a container that was designed to be a miniature version of a 55-gallon industrial drum. The packaging and the TV advertising carried the message that the compound was strong enough to be used by a janitor engaged in commercial cleaning. The package design, needless to say, reinforced this message.

Another example of package shape is more Freudian in nature. It is the use of packages that are shaped as phallic symbols to create specific imagery for certain types of beauty aids. The general idea is to convey the emotional message that use of the product will increase one's appeal to the opposite sex. Look at the package shape for Pierre Cardin men's cologne, and Jōvan men's and women's colognes next time you are at the store.

**PROMOTION
IN ACTION
17–3**

Infamous Contest Blunders

John Steinbeck noted that *"the best laid plans of mice and men often go awry."* He could easily have been referring to recent promotional contests. Contest snafus are among the most noticeable and costly promotional errors, and despite careful preparation, recent years have brought us some "prize" blunders.

"The Scratch Gang" proved the undoing of Beatrice Co. in 1987. The company's *"Monday Night Football"* contest was designed as a game of chance. It ended up being a computer buff's playground. The object was to scratch silver-coated footballs off cards in the hope that they would match the number of touchdowns and field goals scored in eight actual Monday Night games. Computer whiz Frank Maggio cracked the contest code and discovered that 320 patterns were repeated in the cards. If he scratched off one line he knew what numbers were underneath. Maggio merely waited until after the games and then scratched off the correct numbers. Realizing that he could win up to $5,500 per card, Maggio recruited 20 friends for "The Scratch Gang." They collected and scratched 5,000 cards; 4,000 were winners. Beatrice cancelled the contest when it discovered this expensive loophole. The company claimed that the contest's defect nullified all prize claims, but millions of dollars worth of lawsuits were filed and immeasurable goodwill was lost.

Other companies have also fallen prey to unexpected contest quirks. PepsiCo, Inc. sponsored a spell-your-name contest with letters printed on bottle caps. The company thought a scarcity of vowels would guarantee few winners, but they forgot about Asian names such as *Ng.* General Mills, Inc., was forced to cancel an entire sweepstake when a printing error made every package a winner.

Kraft is the most recent victim of contest catastrophes. The company announced its "Ready to Roll" sweepstakes on June 11, 1989. Consumers in Chicago and Houston had the chance to match game pieces in free-standing inserts (FSIs) with pieces in Kraft Singles American cheese. The grand prize was a Dodge Caravan minivan. An incorrectly printed free-standing insert made at least 500,000 packages winners.

Seth A. Eisner, vice president-chief counsel for Kraft USA, explained the problem: "In matching-half games such as this, one half of each game piece

Infamous Contest Blunders (concluded)

is designated as the 'common' piece, and the other half is the 'rare' piece. The game pieces inserted into the packages were correctly printed, displaying the left half of the prizes as the 'common' half. The game pieces printed in the newspaper inserts were wrong because the right halves were mistakenly printed as the common piece."

Kraft declared the contest null and void when it learned that hundreds of consumers had game cards that matched the FSI game piece. They then devised an alternate compensation plan. All "winners" who sent their entries in by June 16 received cash prizes. Minivan winners were awarded $250; lesser amounts were awarded for other matching game cards. Kraft received nearly 21,000 valid entries, about 10,000 of which were minivan "winners." Each of the 21,000 valid entries was entered in the July 14 drawing for four minivans, plus bicycles, skateboards, and packages of Kraft Singles. Consumers who missed the deadline received a selection of coupons and recipe books. Kraft estimates the cost of pulling unpurchased packages off supermarket shelves, canceling the program, and paying consolation prizes to angry consumers will run about $3.8 million. Initially, the sweepstakes prizes were supposed to cost Kraft $36,000.

Although Kraft probably will not be able to recoup its $3 to $4 million goodwill gesture from any insurance policy, the monetary gesture has appeased many consumers. A Kraft spokeswoman noted, "Overall, we've gotten a really positive response from consumers thanking us and saying they thought the cash awards were very fair." Although the expected barrage of lawsuits has been filed, an attorney familiar with sales promotion cases asserted that Kraft would not be held legally responsible for paying the original claims from the game. "If a promotion is properly set up, the rules make clear that prizes need not be awarded in the case of typographical or mechanical errors, and awards will be made upon decision of judges, which are final."

Sources:"How Beatrice Lost at its Own Game," *Business Week,* March 2, 1987, p. 66; "Not Really 'Ready to Roll': Kraft Puzzles over Who Crashed Its Minivan Promotion," *Advertising Age,* June 19, 1989, pp. 1–74; "Kraft Snafu Could Cost $4 Million," *Advertising Age,* July 10, 1989, p. 53.

Package Size   By making different amounts of product available to different types of buyers, package size variation can increase the size of the market in many situations. Large-size "economy" packages can attract heavy users, and small-size "trial" packs can provide an option for light users or can induce trial use. The experience of the Morton Salt Company in placing its product in picnic packs barely an inch in diameter and in table-size packages the size of a salt shaker greatly increased market share and made it possible to differentiate a rather homogeneous product on the basis of packaging innovation.

Packaging to Meet Reseller Needs   Most of the discussion to this point has been concerned with the role of the package in filling consumer needs. What must not be overlooked, however, is that packaging plays an important role in gaining the support of resellers. Without such support, the product does not get the stocking and shelf position that is required if it is to succeed in the marketplace. In order to gain a fair chance of success in competition with thousands of other packaged items, three conditions must be met. First, the package must be durable and easy to handle by the reseller. Breakage, leakage, and the like must be minimized in order to save the reseller time and expense. Second, the package must be designed so that it can be stacked and displayed with a minimum use of shelf or floor space. Third, the package must aid in the sale of the product to such an extent that in combination with the rest of the manufacturer's promotion effort, the reseller's return per unit of space allocated will be in the acceptable range of profitability.

The case history of Sylvania's entry into the supermarket channel for sale of light bulbs illustrates how packaging design can gain support from resellers. Facing the problem of not having been in supermarkets previously and noting that, although light bulbs were a high margin item, they were not looked on with great favor by supermarket buyers because of the great difficulties involved in handling and displaying light bulbs, Sylvania created a packaging strategy that overcame reseller lack of enthusiasm for the product category. The company developed a shipping carton that not only protected the bulbs from breakage but also converted into a compartmentalized selling rack. In addition, bulbs of different wattages were color-coded by individual pack and placed in the appropriate compartment of the display. This use of packaging was most successful in gaining access to the supermarket channel for Sylvania.

The unique egg-shaped packaging and the specially designed display racks for L'Eggs pantyhose enabled Hanes to gain supermarket distribution for its product line. Again, attractive and attention-getting packaging that is also protective and a display strategy that maximizes return per square foot of allocated space are the secret of success when reseller support is vital.

Packages as Premiums As noted in a previous section, packages can be used as premiums. Instant coffee packed in containers that can be used as servers, cookies packed in jars that can be reused, and the like are all examples of how packages themselves can be used as a form of premium promotion. Figure 17–7 illustrates a promotion in which a specially de-signed canister was used to sell a product produced by Dunkin' Donuts. This type of package promotion is often used by instant coffee companies to promote short-term sales.

SUMMARY

This chapter has discussed some of those marketing activities encompassed by the term *sales promotion.* The growing importance of these activities was de-scribed and special attention was paid to such promotional alternatives as sampling, couponing, money refund offers, price-off promotions, premiums, and consumer contests. In conclusion, the role of packaging as a promotional tool was examined.

FIGURE 17–7

Illustration of a Premium Offer in Which the Package Is the Premium

REVIEW AND DISCUSSION QUESTIONS

1. For the Oscar Mayer, Sampling Corporation, Mattel, and Eagle Food Stores examples of consumer promotions in this chapter indicate:
   a. The likely objectives of the promotion.
   b. The rationale for selecting the specific consumer promotion type used.
   c. The role consumer sales promotion plays relative to other promotional tools.
   d. How the effectiveness of the promotion could be evaluated.
2. How could the contest blunders described in Promotion in Action 17–3 have been anticipated and thus avoided?
3. Do consumer promotions destroy brand equity that advertising creates? Comment.
4. From newspapers and magazines, select an example of each of the promotion types discussed in this chapter. Critically evaluate these promotions.
5. Suppose that Kraft is planning to introduce a new low-calorie version of its margarine. What consumer sales promotions would you use to support this entry? Be specific.

NOTES

1. American Marketing Association, *Marketing Definitions: A Glossary of Marketing Terms,* (Chicago: American Marketing Association, 1960), p. 20.

2. Peter D. Bennett, *Dictionary of Marketing Terms* (Chicago: American Marketing Association, 1988), p. 179.

3. Russ Bowman, "Dollars up but Cooling Down," *Marketing and Media Decisions,* July 1989, pp. 123–26.

4. This section is adapted from *Business Month,* July 1987, pp. 44–46.

5. Ibid.

6. *The Wall Street Journal,* February 3, 1987, p. 35, col. 3.

7. "A New Look at Coupons," *The Nielsen Researcher,* no. 1 (1976), p. 2, updated to 1988 from same source.

8. Ibid.

9. Ibid.

10. This section is based on "Premium Positioning," *Marketing & Media Decisions,* May 1989, p. 112.

11. This section is based on "Creative Campaigns Can Hit Baby Boomers Where They Live," *Marketing News,* October 10, 1988, p. 14.

12. This section is based on "Sweepstakes Fever," Forbes, October 3, 1988, pp. 164–66.

PERSONAL SELLING

In following the stages in promotional strategy outlined in Chapter 2, we have given considerable attention to the management of mass communication efforts. This part continues the discussion of management of program elements by considering problems inherent in managing the firm's personal selling resources. These resources provide for face-to-face contact with potential customers to inform them of new product or service offerings and persuade them to buy.

Although personal selling is used at every level in business, from the manufacturer to the retailer, this section is primarily concerned with manufacturers' use of a sales force to seek out new business by contacting end users or resellers. Many of the points discussed are applicable at all levels of the distribution channel.

The first chapter in this section deals with personal selling as a special form of interpersonal communication and with the nature of the selling task. The next chapter discusses the management aspects of building, training, deploying, and motivating a sales force. The third chapter considers evaluating results.

Personal Selling Strategy

OVERCOMING THE WILLY LOMAN SYNDROME

Has Willy Loman, the defeated and self-destructive protagonist of Arthur Miller's play *The Death of a Salesman*, become the symbol of the American salesman? Robert L. Montgomery, a former circus acrobat, college professor, author, self-made millionaire, and currently chairman of the Indianapolis ad agency of Montgomery, Zuckerman, Davis, thinks so and he's damned mad.

"Willy Loman has replaced Diamond Jim Brady, George Westinghouse, and Henry Ford as the image of American salesmanship," fumes Montgomery. "Why?" he asks rhetorically. "Because we've lost faith in the future and men like Brady, Westinghouse, and Ford sold the future while Loman was obsessed with the past. America was conceived out of molding a new and better tomorrow."

Montgomery attributes the decline of salesmanship to the growth of market research and points out that American business discovered research during World War II. "Companies thought that they could do away with salespeople and discover through market research what items customers were ready to buy."

As a result, says Montgomery, the effectiveness of salesmanship was reduced and companies began to offer what he calls *safe* products and services that market research told them that they could sell.

"Our success in the past was based on our ability to produce new and interesting products and then go out and sell them and we seem to have lost that ability. We've forgotten how to sell," continues Montgomery. "Salesmen today are selling the tried and true products of yesterday and they seem to have forgotten that the real salesman sells concepts, not products. We don't spend enough time creating an aura for our products and services, and we don't pay enough attention to building a perceived value in our customer's mind. It's not enough to explain logically why someone should buy your product: you have to appeal to the emotions. When someone builds my perceived value for his product, he's reaching me on an emotional level. Too much *product* knowledge and not enough *people* knowledge is what is really hurting salesmanship today."

Source: Excerpted from Doug Harper, "Strictly for Salesmen" *Industrial Distribution* (January 1987), p. 56. Used with permission.

Harper's ideas are interesting whether or not you agree that marketing research has had an adverse impact on personal selling. He may have had this opinion because of bad experience with unskilled salespersons. But he is also calling for a return to the real essence of personal selling—a true exchange of meaning between the salesperson and the customer.

Personal selling, properly done, can have high promotional impact because it targets only one person and offers immediate feedback of objections and reactions. Its value to the firm is underscored by the fact that more is spent on personal selling by all businesses in total than on other promotional efforts. In fact, it is estimated that many firms spend twice as much on personal selling as on advertising.

Although the use of personal selling is widespread in the aggregate, its importance in relation to other promotional tools varies widely with individual firms. In some situations, promotional goals are best met with advertising or sales promotion. In this chapter, we are most concerned with firms in which the overall marketing strategy requires heavy reliance on personal selling and the use of sales personnel to seek out buyers. Such firms are usually manufacturing companies, although many wholesalers use their salespeople to locate and cultivate new customers.

We must not forget, however, that most salespersons are employed at the retail level. Unfortunately, selling skills of retail salespersons range widely from top-notch to nonexistent. We hope that what we have to say in these chapters will be of use in improving retail selling effectiveness from the viewpoint of a promotional manager of a retail organization or of a manufacturer dependent on the selling skills of the company's retail resellers.

PERSONAL SELLING IN THE PROMOTION MIX

The sales strategy of a firm is essentially a communications process. The communication tasks to be accomplished by personal selling as part of the promotion mix determines the type and extent of personal selling activities required. Table 18–1 illustrates when the sales force is a major part of the promotion mix. It indicates that personal selling can do the job given the need to communicate about complex product or service offerings, when channel systems cannot do the job by themselves, when price is subject to negotiation, and when advertising cannot reach targets or provide sufficient information about the offerings.

TABLE 18–1

When the Sales Force Is a Major Part of the Promotional Mix

❖

Mix Area	Characteristics
Product or service	Complex products requiring customer application assistance (e.g., computers, pollution control systems, steam turbines) Major purchase decisions, such as food items purchased by supermarket chains Features and performance of the product requiring personal demonstration and trial by the customer (e.g., private aircraft)
Channels	Channel system relatively short and direct to end users Product and service training and assistance needed by channel intermediaries Personal selling is needed in "pushing" product through channel Channel intermediaries available to perform personal selling function for supplier with limited resources and experience (e.g., brokers or manufacturer's agents)
Price	Final price negotiated between buyer and seller (e.g., appliances, automobiles, real estate) Selling price and/or quantity purchased enable an adequate margin to support selling expenses (traditional department store compared to discount house)
Advertising	Advertising media do not provide effective link with market targets Information needed by buyer cannot be provided entirely through advertising and sales promotion (e.g., life insurance) Number and dispersion of customers will not enable acceptable advertising economies

Source: David W. Cravens, Gerald E. Hills, and Robert B. Woodruff, *Marketing Decision Making: Concepts and Strategy* (Homewood, Ill.: Richard D. Irwin, 1980), p. 384. Reprinted by permission of Richard D. Irwin, Inc.

THE INFLUENCE OF THE PRODUCT-MARKET SITUATION

To illustrate how the role of personal selling changes with various product-market situations, three short case histories are presented. They detail the experiences of a manufacturer of proprietary drugs, a manufacturer of personal computers, and a provider of specialized welding services.

Proprietary Drug Manufacturer

A manufacturer wants to launch a new cough remedy through retail drug-stores. Market research indicates that the market is geographically dispersed and that a large percentage of present users of similar remedies are potential buyers for the new product, which has several unique features. Cost analysis indicates that national advertising by means of newspapers, radio, and TV spots will provide the most economical coverage of the market. Accordingly, $2 million is appropriated for consumer advertising, $500,000 for trade promotion, and $200,000 for personal selling. Why the disparity in amounts, and what is the role assigned to personal selling?

The answer to the first question is that for the product type and the large and dispersed market, advertising and trade promotion can stimulate demand more economically than personal selling. Proprietary health aids that have hidden qualities may appeal to strong human emotions involved with health and well-being, thus making advertising especially effective. Moreover, the sales potential of the product promises sufficient revenues to sustain a costly advertising campaign. This situation is ideally suited to an emphasis on advertising in the promotional mix.

Personal selling effort is utilized, however, at three different levels in the channel: manufacturer, wholesaler, and retailer. The manufacturer has salespeople who call on large wholesalers and chain drug retailers. The advertising aimed at the household buyer meanwhile is creating a "pull" effect, and the primary task of the salesperson is to make certain that resellers have adequate stock. The selling task here is essentially order taking. But salespeople spend considerable time ensuring that wholesaler and retailer point-of-sales efforts are coordinated with the national advertising campaign.

The budget does not allow very much personal selling activity by the manufacturer, so the available effort is directed to customers who appear to offer the greatest potential. The great bulk of the orders is received by mail from interested wholesalers and retailers.

At the wholesale level, a different type of personal selling activity is taking place. The wholesaler sales force makes routine calls on members of the wholesaler's customer group. These salespeople carry catalogs and price lists describing thousands of items. Their essential function is order taking. If, however, the demand for the new patent medicine is being felt at retail and these salespeople are aware of the manufacturer's promotional plans, they may engage in some promotional selling aimed at getting the retailer to carry special stocks and to provide in-store promotional tie-ins.

Personal selling at the retail level is represented by the retail clerk or the pharmacist. They may suggest the brand to customers asking for that type of remedy. Since the product is being highly advertised, customers will probably ask for the remedy by name, thus reducing the personal selling task at retail to one of order filling. Retailer support, in this instance, is largely confined to providing ample display and counter space for the product.

Computer Manufacturer

After several years of research and development, a California manufacturer of personal computers developed a powerful portable computer. Due to limited production capacity and the desire to give consumers a great deal of personal attention at point of sale, the manufacturer decided to have only a few hundred dealers carry the line. A modest advertising campaign directed to the trade as well as to end users was planned. The bulk of promotional effort, however, was to be in the form of personal selling at both the manufacturer and retailer levels.

The manufacturer must develop a highly skilled group of salespeople whose principal task is to get several hundred of the best computer retailers in the country to stock, display, demonstrate, and sell the new computer. This will not be an easy task because the product type is totally different in a technical sense from anything previously made. The cost of the new product will be relatively high, and the demand is unknown. In this situation, the manufacturer salesperson must be an order getter. Creativity and aggressiveness are necessary if the salesperson is to succeed in gaining the best quality retailers in each market area.

Selling effort at retail is also very important. A potential customer for the new computer must be given a very thorough demonstration of how it operates. The retail salesperson must have knowledge of the product and persuasive ability to make the sale. The manufacturer's margin payment to the retailer must, therefore, include payment for the superior selling effort required.

Over time as the product moves along its life-cycle and enters a more mature stage, the personal selling task will change along with other elements of the marketing mix. The product itself will be better known by potential customers, distribution will be more intensive, price will be reduced, and the promotional mix will include a larger amount of consumer advertising and less personal selling effort.

From the manufacturer's standpoint, the need then will be to gain more sales from present retail outlets rather than to increase the coverage of the market. The selling task will become more routine, with greater emphasis on order taking and service. Similarly, at retail, the requirement for a creative selling job will have lessened. At all levels in the product channel, personal selling will give way to greater reliance on consumer advertising and price promotion.

Electron Beam Welding Service

A small company offers an electron beam welding service to industry. The electron beam technology, developed in the aircraft industry, had not gained widespread acceptance in the manufacture of industrial goods and consumer products, although it offered many advantages over conventional welding techniques.

The company hired a manufacturers' representative on an expenses-plus-commission basis to contact potential accounts within the market area. After two years, the owners found, much to their dismay, that the sales representative was not producing enough business to cover expenses. A reappraisal of promotional strategy was in order.

If the owners of this small company had analyzed their present customers in terms of information needs, they would have found that some required much more information than others. For example, buyers who had previously used the process or who had a relatively small job to be welded did not require much selling effort. On the other hand, those who were unfamiliar with the nature of electron beam welding or who had large and expensive jobs to complete required a great deal of information about the technical capability of the supplier, the price, and the delivery date for the finished work. In one case, it took six months of inquiry and negotiation to close a sale.

From this type of analysis, it would appear that although a manufacturers' representative might handle the routine buying situations, he or she would have neither the expertise nor the time to deal with more complex situations. Given such a set of circumstances, the owners of the welding service would either have to hire a salesperson of their own to engage in the complex selling task or, if such an addition were not economically feasible, they would have to assume the responsibility themselves.

Implications of the Cases

The three situations discussed above illustrate briefly how product and market influences affect the role played by personal selling in the promotional strategy mix. In the consumer market, as products mature, the role of personal selling is diminished, and advertising becomes more important. In the industrial market, as the product moves through its life-cycle, personal selling is generally a more important element in the promotional mix than is advertising. However, as the information requirements of industrial customers vary, so do the extent and nature of the personal selling task there.

WHAT DO SALESPEOPLE DO?

As the case histories indicate, there can be wide variations in environmental or strategic conditions that influence the role of personal selling in a given firm. Regardless of these variations, the work to be done by salespeople can be identified and described. For example, the salesperson must seek out or meet prospective buyers, discover customer needs and attitudes, and help customers to buy the product or service best suited to their needs. In helping the customer to buy, the salesperson must be prepared to supply generous quantities of information about product or service characteristics. The salesperson must also persuade the buyer that a particular offering is best suited to the buyer's needs and must act decisively to overcome buyer uncertainty by sensing how and when to close the sale. Follow-up after the sale is also important to ensure that buyers receive the fullest utility from the purchase and to prevent dissonance by assuring customers that they have made the correct choice.

Thus the essential tasks of personal selling consist of (1) locating and (or) meeting prospective customers, (2) discovering customer needs and attitudes, (3) recommending a product package to fill those needs, (4) developing a sales presentation aimed at informing the customer of product attributes and persuading the customer to buy the recommended package, (5) closing the sale, and (6) following up to ensure total satisfaction with the purchase.

Of course, all salespeople do not place equal emphasis on the various components of the selling task. This may be the result of inadequate performance or simply because the selling strategy requires a different presentation. It is essential that the selling task be clearly defined so the salesperson understands the nature of the job to be performed. Without this, evaluation of selling performance is impossible.

SALESMANSHIP

Salesmanship is a direct, face-to-face, seller-to-buyer influence that can communicate the facts necessary for making a buying decision; or it can utilize the psychology of persuasion to encourage a buying decision. Another way of looking at salesmanship is to consider it as a set of skills that can make personal selling efforts more effective. Because these skills are important in a noncommercial as well as a commercial setting, it is worthwhile to examine the subject in detail.

All of us are continuously selling our ideas and ourselves to others. In trying to land a job or gain the attention of a member of the opposite sex, we are engaged in selling.

Effective selling either in a commercial or noncommercial context requires a very clear understanding of the nature of interpersonal communication when one party is attempting to influence the response of another.

Buyer-Seller Interactions

There are a variety of influences on the way the buyer receives and interprets messages sent by the seller. The seller's appearance, personality, and level of knowledge about the product or service offered all have an effect. Buyer knowledge of the seller's company and familiarity with the seller on a personal basis also play a part in how the seller's message is received, and whether or not it is acted on. Even the buyer's immediate state of mind or of health can have a major influence on the buyer-seller communication process.

Given the large number of operative variables, research has been undertaken to provide insights into formulating an effective sales approach. In the life insurance industry, for example, it was found that prospects who bought insurance knew more about the salespeople and their companies, and felt more positively toward them, than prospects who did not buy. In addition, the greater the similarity between the salesperson and the prospect, in terms of physical, demographic, and personality characteristics, the greater the likelihood that a sale would occur.

Such findings may be useful when the number of potential customers is small, the sale involves a large outlay, and there is a possibility of matching salespeople and prospects. It is doubtful the strategy would be viable with large numbers of prospects, low-value unit sales, and limited ability to match sellers and buyers.

Different Selling Situations

Selling situations differ in degree of difficulty—a selling strategy developed for one situation may not be suitable for another. For example, we may classify selling goals as (1) order getting, (2) order taking, and (3) supporting.

The order getter engages in creative selling and aggressively undertakes a campaign to seek out potential buyers and make a sale. Order takers, on the other hand, operate on a more relaxed basis. They make routine calls on customers to maintain a continuing relationship. Their approach is a low-pressure one designed to enable them to live well with their customer group for a long time. It is a mistake to compare order takers unfavorably with order getters, for their goals are different. However, if a salesperson who is supposed to be an order getter performs as an order taker, management must step in to remind him or her of the need for creative and aggressive selling.

In the support category, selling activities are not aimed at getting or taking an order; missionary selling, technical support, and assistance in management or promotion fall into this group. These indirect selling activities build goodwill for the seller and help the order-oriented salespeople to close the sale.

It is obvious that the salesperson's task varies with the assigned role. But the position of the seller in the channel also has a profound effect on the nature of the selling job. Manufacturer salespeople selling to wholesalers or end users play a role different than that of wholesaler salespeople selling to retailers, or of retail salespeople selling to shoppers who come to their stores. And market characteristics as well as the product itself influence the basic selling task.

It is important, however, to recognize that the skill level required of the salesperson varies considerably over the range of selling situations. The quality of sales ability required in order getting is considerably higher than that required to take orders or provide service after the sale, although the latter activities also call for proper performance.

STEPS OF A SALE

Many authors who have written on the subject of salesmanship indicate discrete steps or stages. Although in reality the selling process is continu-

PROMOTION IN ACTION 18–1

The Golden Touch

Salesmanship is a people game, and great salesmanship is largely a matter of *feel*. Some people have it; some don't.

Nicholas Barsan has the touch. The top performer of 1986 among the 75,000 U.S. real estate brokers affiliated with Century 21, dashing, dark-browed Barsan, 47, was born in Rumania. He emigrated to the United States in 1968 and owned a wholesale food company and then a restaurant before he began selling property four years ago. In 1986, he moved $27 million of homes in Jackson Heights, Queens, netting $1.1 million in commissions. In this solidly middle-class New York City neighborhood, the average home sells for $225,000, so a fellow has to work to do that kind of volume.

Though a millionaire, Barsan still knocks urgently on strangers' doors, hungry for new business. He still hands out key chains and car window scrapers imprinted with his name, lest anyone forget it. But Barsan knows he can sell more homes with less effort by dealing again with customers he has already satisfied. So he calls on the people who bought their homes from him. "You ready to sell yet?" he asks. A third of Barsan's sales are to repeat customers.

Source: Excerpted from Monci Jo Williams, "America's Best Salesmen," *Fortune*, October 26, 1987, p. 124. Used by permission.

ous, with considerable overlapping of the steps, it is useful to consider the steps one at a time. In addition, we consider those steps described by Beach and others in writings that have endured the test of time.[1] The steps include (1) prospecting, (2) the preapproach, (3) the approach, (4) the presentation, (5) meeting objections, (6) the close, and (7) the follow-up.

Prospecting

In this, the first stage of the selling process, the salesperson attempts to locate prospective customers who are likely to have a need or desire for the products or services offered. In addition, the prospect must also be qualified to buy, that is, have the authority to enter into a purchase agreement and be financially able to pay for the purchase. The goal of prospecting, therefore, is to locate individuals who have needs that can be satisfied by the products and services offered by the salesperson and his or her company. The prospecting process is continuous because enough likely candidates must be provided to fully utilize the salesperson's time.

The systems that are used in prospecting are varied and numerous. One approach is termed the *snowball technique:* every prospect, regardless of whether she or he has made a purchase, is asked to recommend one or two additional prospects. Leads may also be elicited through advertisements containing coupons requesting further information about the product/service offering or from direct mail activities in which prepaid postcards are enclosed for the same purpose. These responses, then, provide leads for salespersons. When all else fails, the salesperson may adopt the *cold canvass* approach—he or she calls on a series of individuals, knowing little more about them than their name and address. The cold canvass approach is the least productive in terms of time and effort spent. If *planned* prospecting and selling are not taking up all of a salesperson's time, however, the marginal cost of cold canvassing is low, and the benefits will generally exceed the costs.

Preapproach

Once a prospect has been identified and qualified, the problem facing the salesperson is how to approach the prospect with the greatest effectiveness. Analysis of information gathered about the prospect's purchase behavior in the past, about the nature of current needs, and about alternatives offered by competitors can lead to the development of an approach strategy. These preliminaries constitute the preapproach step.

The Approach

This is the most easily identified step in the selling process: it occurs when the seller first meets the buyer. Unfortunately, too many selling processes start at this step without sufficient prospecting or preapproach effort. The approach must be carefully planned, especially if the salesperson is meeting the prospect for the first time. The goal of the approach is to secure the prospect's interest and attention. If this goal is not met, the selling process stops. The best the salesperson can do is exit politely so he or she can try again another day.

Approaches vary from the most widely used and least effective one of presenting a business card to the prospect or the prospect's secretary to the more imaginative approaches in which the salesperson uses product samples, premiums, or intriguing opening statements to capture the prospect's interest. Careful prospecting and preapproach planning should provide ideas for strategies most likely to succeed with a given prospect.

The salesperson will know very quickly whether an approach is succeeding. If the prospect invites the salesperson to have a seat or to continue with the presentation, the approach has worked. A polite suggestion that the salesperson leave because the prospect is very busy indicates that the salesperson will have to try again another time or with another prospect.

The Presentation

The objective of this step is to create in the prospect's mind a desire for the product or service offered. To achieve this, the salesperson must communicate as complete a story as possible about the product attributes and the benefits that the prospect will derive from it. The salesperson must gain the prospect's confidence as a prelude to effecting a change in the prospect's behavior. The seller must always be aware of the dyadic relationship in which he or she is involved. The seller must be the influencer; the prospect is the one who must act. To avoid making a decision, most prospects will raise objections as the presentation continues or will attempt to sidetrack the seller with extraneous remarks. The skilled salesperson will know how to anticipate and overcome objections and will be able to steer the discussion back to the topic at hand.

Some sellers use "canned" presentations—those that have been carefully developed and memorized. This approach has the advantage of completeness because the presentation has been pretested to make sure it covers the principal selling points. It lacks the spontaneity and flexibility of a noncanned approach, and thus its use is not recommended except in rather standardized selling situations in which relatively unskilled salespersons are being used.

Meeting Objections

Closely allied with the presentation step is that of meeting objections. Indeed, one could make a good case for combining this step with the preceding one. But because this skill is so important to the salesperson, we will look at it a little more closely. Objections can be handled most effectively if the salesperson knows what the true purpose of the objection is. For example, the prospect might object to some aspect of the product's physical design as a device to cover up the fact that he or she cannot afford to make the purchase at this time. In this case, even if the salesperson overcomes the stated objection, the sale will not materialize. Perhaps continued probing by the seller would uncover the true nature of the problem. Then a discussion about the possibility of extended terms or a leasing agreement might be fruitful.

In other cases, the best way to handle objections is to treat them as requests for clarification or for additional information. The prepared salesperson will anticipate objections and be prepared for them. Indeed, in such cases, overcoming an objection may impress the prospect and help to close the sale.

Closing the Sale

This is the step in which the goal of the salesperson is to obtain action, preferably a commitment on the part of the prospect to become a buyer. The skill of closing is perhaps the most important that a salesperson can possess but is also the most difficult to master. A seller who cannot close has been described as a "conversationalist." Part of the skill of closing is knowing when the prospect is ready to buy. When the prospect's questions pertain to delivery dates or credit terms, the time to close is at hand. The salesperson who is uncertain that the time is right might attempt a "trial" close that can be pushed to a complete close if the prospect appears willing to act or withdrawn if the prospect requires more information or more persuasion. Closing techniques differ widely, ranging from those that simply ask for the order to those that involve a promise to alter the offering to suit the specific needs of the buyer in order to gain the sale.

Closing is a skill, and preplanning the presentation and carefully monitoring the verbal and body language of the prospect can help the salesperson to develop that sixth sense that is so crucial to successful selling.

Follow-Up

Many salespeople end their selling efforts when the order is signed. This is a very serious shortcoming because the after-sale, or follow-up, stage is so valuable for removing any feeling of dissonance the buyer may have and for making sure that the buyer is receiving full utility from the purchase. Follow-up is the ideal time to suggest add-on sales of accessory equipment or maintenance items. The buyer is relaxed, committed, and thus fairly receptive to proposals to increase the investment and gain more advantages from the initial buy.

Even if no further business occurs during the follow-up, the salesperson's effort will be repaid many times over by uncovering problems that might have made future sales difficult and by cementing a relationship that will make future sales much more likely.

SUMMARY

This chapter has considered personal selling as a communication process and has examined salesmanship as a set of skills used by salespeople to improve their effectiveness. The steps of a sale as presented are based on a model that described by the acronym AIDA, standing for attention, interest, desire, and action.[2] Each step in the approach moves the prospect through the phases of buying readiness. Although many models could provide the basis for the analysis here, the AIDA approach to the stages of the buying process and the steps in the selling process as enumerated by Beach and others have withstood the test of time.

REVIEW AND DISCUSSION QUESTIONS

1. You are a promotion consultant trying to help a client develop a campaign for her product line. She does not have a clear idea of how personal selling differs from advertising as a communication process. How would you explain the differences to her?

2. You have just graduated from business school and are interested in a sales position. You have interviewed several companies and are impressed by the different emphasis that some companies place on personal selling as compared with others. How do you explain these differences?

3. In your search for a selling job, you are finding that different positions call for different types of selling activities or place different degrees of emphasis on various aspects of the selling task. How do you explain these differences? How do you find a job that places emphasis on what you like to do?

4. You have accepted a position and have been quite happy for a number of years. You especially enjoy the challenge of explaining how the products work and how they can save money for the user. Lately you are finding that everyone knows about your product, and you are facing stiffer and stiffer price competition. What is going on here? Is your firm in trouble? Should you seek another position?

5. John Jones is an excellent salesman who knows his product and his customers' needs. He does not do as well saleswise as does Jim Smith, who is

newer to the company and does not have Jones' breadth or depth of knowledge about the product or the market. In a discussion with his sales manager, Mary Worth, the suggestion is raised that Jones improve his closing technique. What is a closing technique? Is it hard to learn? Can one practice closing?

6. Fred Star is a fine auto salesman. He always stays in close touch with his customers after he sells them a car. He says that he must allay any hints of "cognitive dissonance" on the part of his customers. What is he talking about? What does one do to reduce the effects of this psychological state?

NOTES

1. Frederick A. Russell, Frank H. Beach, and Richard Buskirk, *Selling: Principles and Practices,* 11th ed. (New York: McGraw-Hill, 1982).

2. E. Jerome McCarthy and William D. Perreault, Jr., *Basic Marketing,* 8th ed. (Homewood, Ill.: Richard D. Irwin, 1984), p. 476ff.

Building the Sales Force

H-P BETS A BUNDLE ON OFFICE AUTOMATION

Considered the "sleeper" company to watch in the $10–$15 billion office automation (OA) market, Hewlett-Packard (H-P), Cupertino, Calif., is investing more than $650,000 in a special sales training program, Targeting the Office, that will eventually retool up to 2,000 sales representatives and their district managers. "We're committed to being a leader in the market," says Shirish Hardikar, office marketing programs manager, Information Systems Group, "and we recognize selling in the office environment requires different approaches than in the data processing world."

More than 400 H-P salespeople went through two-day courses last month; a bigger contingent will do the same in July. "Targeting the Office is designed to be an ongoing project," Hardikar says, "using the pace and style of the district managers."

A blend of videotapes, workshops, case studies, reports, and exercises on Hewlett-Packard's own touch-screen PC is used. Workshops and case studies focus on targeted accounts proposed by the salespeople and their managers.

H-P's internal office automation program and the productivity gains it has produced are cited as selling points representatives can make with their accounts. Example: The company's desk manager, electronic-mail software, that representatives use to exchange with each other notes on successful sales. Other office automation products from H-P include the HP 3000 minicomputer, a local area network (LAN) system, and several software packages.

Hardikar figures $500,000 was spent on developing the program and $150,000 will go for staging the courses. "On top of that," he adds, "is the substantial cost of having reps who won't be in the field selling for two days."

Source: *Sales and Marketing Management*, March 11, 1985, pp. 29–30. Used with permission.

This chapter and the one that follows deal with the management aspects of personal selling. Building and maintaining a sales force are complex tasks. The vignette above describes what Hewlett-Packard has done to bolster sales training to target the office automation market. Note the large expenditure of time and money invested to accomplish this task.

This chapter covers the recruitment, selection, training, and assignment of sales personnel, as well as their compensation and motivation. Chapter 20 deals with the evaluation and control of sales efforts.

BUILDING THE SALES FORCE

The creation of an effective selling organization must begin with a clear understanding of the nature of the selling task. The processes of recruitment, selection, and training will vary with the sales assignment. A job that involves calling on wholesalers to determine their stock needs and the promotion of a commodity-type product line is different from one in which the salesperson deals with diverse types of customers or products.

Those in the company responsible for recruiting, selecting, and training salespeople need a clear grasp of overall promotional strategy. The overall strategy determines the *kind* of selling required. The *kind* of selling, in turn, determines the personal qualifications needed by members of the sales force, as well as the methods of training, compensation, and motivation that are used.

Job Descriptions and Recruitment

Before recruiting activities can take place, the nature of the selling task must be clearly delineated. Management must prepare a carefully thought out and fully updated job description for every position on the sales force. An example of a job description for a farm machinery salesperson is given in Figure 19–1.

Once the specific kind of selling job to be filled has been determined, the search for a likely employee can begin. Currently employed salespeople,

FIGURE 19–1

Area Sales Manager's Job Description, Agricultural Systems and Machines

❖

Job Title: Area sales manager
Department: Marketing
Location: Western Region
Supervisor: Mr. Terrence Benet

Area consists of counties in northeastern Iowa and southeastern Minnesota. Travel away from home: estimated two nights per week.

General Description of Work:

Meet assigned management by objective (MBO) sales objectives in assigned sales territory by effective territory management including prospecting for, recruiting, training, motivating, and assisting Agrisystem Farm Machines Incorporated retailing dealers in the sales of Agrisystem structures and/or equipment manufactured by the company.

This is not a trainee position. Successful candidates will be expected to immediately assume full area sales management responsibility for meeting assigned sales objectives. While adequate product and sales training will be provided, the scope of this position requires a person who understands the sales and distribution of structures and farmstead equipment through a dealer organization as well as selling retail to farmers.

Major Responsibilities:

1. Make effective sales calls on existing dealers: train, motivate, and assist dealers in developing qualified sales prospects and selling plans that logically lead to the completed sale. Sell products on the farm as part of dealer training and assistance program.

2. With assistance from regional sales manager, analyze assigned territory for sales potential of assigned products; develop dealer prospects and/or effectively recruit new dealers for maximum product sales potential and service coverage within territory.

3. Train dealers in product features, benefits, effective selling techniques, installation, troubleshooting, and service, as required.

4. Collect accounts receivable from dealers and develop effective business relations between Agrisystem Farm Machine and dealerships as directed by regional sales manager.

5. Effectively implement Agrisystem Farm Machines' sales promotion programs, including local advertising, farm tours, field days, farmer meetings, and dealer meetings.

6. Prepare weekly written reports: territory sales progress, expense vouchers, promotion activity reports.

7. Develop annual management by objective plans for unit sales by product line, dealership area potential, county, etc., under direction of regional sales manager (revise plans quarterly).

Source: Gilbert A. Churchill, Jr., Neil M. Ford, and Orville C. Walker, Jr., *Sales Force Management,* 2nd Ed. (Homewood, Ill.: Richard D. Irwin, 1985), p. 492.

college students, and persons in business currently holding nonselling jobs are the prime prospects for sales jobs. The recruitment process, however, is a difficult one, for personal selling is not as attractive a career choice to many of the more talented or better-educated people as other alternatives. Many view a sales career in terms of long hours, frequent travel, and constant discouragement. The growing recognition of the value of the sales force as a resource of the firm has resulted in attempts by management to improve salespeople's working conditions and financial remuneration and to provide them with security for the future. Unfortunately, it takes time to change career images, and personal selling is still handicapped by the stigma of "hucksterism" and recollections of *Death of a Salesman.*

Sales Force Attrition   The problem of turnover also makes recruitment difficult. Undeniably, not all people who attempt a career in selling are successful. Those who are poor producers either become discouraged and drop out or are eventually terminated by their employers. Successful salespeople, on the other hand, may shift to other companies to improve their positions or rise to a position in sales management in the same company. Regardless of the cause of turnover, the net result is that openings in sales are frequent. Attrition because of failure or success means that the recruitment task must be continuous and closely attuned to the future needs of the selling organization. For example, if a company with a 200-member sales force loses 20 people a year, it must replace its entire sales force every 10 years!

Selecting Salespeople

Assuming that a continuing supply of applicants is available, the next step is selection. This phase is of great importance because success here can have a great impact on the effectiveness of the selling organization. Selection of qualified and motivated people results in more and higher-quality selling activity. It also reduces separation, either voluntary or involuntary. This in turn means less turnover and lower expense incurred by the firm.

Three tools are useful in the selection process: (1) the personal history statement, (2) psychological tests, and (3) the personal interview.

Personal History Statement   The personal history statement or application form is designed to elicit information about the prospect useful for initial screening. Conventional practice is to cover data such as:

1. *Personal data*—age, height, and weight.
2. *Education*—including a résumé of applicant's educational background, with data on performance, extent of self-support, and extracurricular activities.

3. *Experience*—prior employers, types of jobs held, and reasons for leaving.

4. *References from several sources*—former teachers, employers, and current acquaintances who can provide information about specific traits or abilities.

5. *Personality and motivation*—general questions about interests in hobbies, organizations, sports, and so on. The applicant may also be asked to explain why he or she is interested in selling as a career and why he or she chose the specific company as a possible employer.

A great deal of information about the job prospect can be gathered by means of a well-designed personal history form. Not only the specific information but its mode of presentation can give insight as to the type of candidate. If used as a preliminary screening device, the questionnaire must be designed to get the type of information *relevant* to the nature of the job. In addition, analysis and interpretation of the application form must be carried out by persons who are skilled in psychology, aware of the nature of the job, and involved in the design of the application form.

Psychological Tests   Perhaps the most controversial tools used in selecting salespeople are psychological tests. These devices are used to supplement the information gained from personal history forms and from the interview. It would, however, be unwise to view them as a substitute for the other selection options.

These tests are designed to provide insights about the applicant's intelligence, personality, and interests. Intelligence tests are perhaps the least criticized of all the tests in terms of reliability and validity. The problem is not with intelligence tests themselves but with the relation of a given level of intelligence to probable success in the sales position. It is clear that a minimum level of intelligence is required of salespeople and that perhaps higher levels are needed for successful performance in more technically oriented selling tasks. However, too high a level of intelligence for a given selling job may result in boredom and subsequent job dissatisfaction.

The successful use of intelligence tests is predicated on screening out extremely low and high performers for further investigation. If some relationship can be found between a range of intelligence and success in a particular type of selling job, then, of course, the tests assume predictive value.

Tests of personality, interests, and aptitudes appear to have greater relevance than intelligence tests. These tests deal with human traits that are important in a sales situation. Unfortunately, they are not easily validated—that is, shown to be successful in predicting success in a given situation. Tests are designed to predict, but often it is not clear just what they are predicting. What is required is that the user analyze the nature of the selling job in terms of the personality traits most likely to lead to success. Then the seller must construct a test to measure the existence of such traits or use a standardized test of some sort and engage in sufficient experimentation to validate the test or, more likely, the battery of tests. The goal is to be able to predict which persons from a group of applicants are most likely to succeed in a given selling situation. It is quite clear that this goal requires not only personnel skilled in psychological testing procedures but also time, money, and a sales force of sufficient size and turnover rate to provide opportunities for validation experiments. Smaller firms may utilize the services of testing consultants. It must be reemphasized, however, that without validation in terms of the particular selling task, testing should be considered only a small part of the selection procedure.

The Personal Interview   Another approach to selection is the personal interview. It is a flexible device and may be used for such diverse purposes as initial screening, as in college campus recruitment, or for final investigation prior to hiring.

The purposes of the interview include discovering traits not uncovered by the application or by testing, probing to find out more about interest and motivation, and evaluating such characteristics as personal appearance and oral expression. The interview may either be structured through a questionnaire or be unstructured, depending on the preference of management. Regardless of the type of interview used, management must provide well-defined criteria that can be used to evaluate the person being interviewed as well as to validate the interviewing process. This provision of criteria is especially important when selecting salespeople because interviewers often have many ill-founded preconceptions about the personality attributes of a good salesperson.

In order to prevent interviewer biases or preconceptions from lessening the effectiveness of the interview as a selection device, many firms have the applicants appraised personally by several interviewers. Regardless of the method, the personal interview can be a useful tool if it can be validated against later sales success. Such validation, in turn, requires a standardized approach. Traits that are important to the selling task at hand must be identified, and all the interviewers must agree on how the existence of these traits is to be discovered and measured.

Training Salespeople

The third component in building a successful sales force is training. After recruitment and selection of new additions to the sales staff, effort must be expended to prepare these people to assume their selling responsibilities. However, training must not be limited to new personnel—it is a continuing process encompassing all members of the sales force, old as well as new.

Training programs vary widely from firm to firm, and the type and extent of training required is a function of several factors, including:

1. The complexity of the product line and product applications.
2. The nature of the market in terms of buyer sophistication.
3. The pressure of competition and the resulting need for nonsales service.
4. The level of knowledge and the degree of the sales experience of the trainee.

Goals of Training   Regardless of the type of program required in a specific situation, the objectives of a training program for newly selected salespeople are quite clear: to make the salesperson more productive, to enable the salesperson to reach a sales norm more rapidly, and to reduce the rate of sales force turnover.

In terms of increasing selling productivity, training can:

1. Provide the product knowledge necessary for all beginning salespeople.
2. Introduce new products and new applications of old products to regular members of the sales force.
3. Point out opportunities in which the existing line can be used to satisfy customer needs.
4. Emphasize nonselling activities (e.g., information gathering) aimed at improving customer relations or cultivating selected accounts.
5. Increase salespeople's productivity by showing them how to utilize their time more effectively and how to engage in personal expense control.

Sales trainers are currently being asked to go well beyond developing and delivering basic skills programs for new hires to the sales staff. According to one expert, trainers must develop more sophisticated applications of product knowledge and market knowledge to respond to market changes, evolving technology, and strategic shifts such as a change in market targets. The goal of training should be to equip salespeople to function as an integral part of the customer's business. Experts say that the customer has supplanted the product or service as the driving force in sales.[1]

It takes considerable time for a new seller to become familiar with a territory. Not only is the learning process time-consuming, but also several months often must pass before the new person has the feel for the territory and can develop sales volume consistent with sales potential. The training program must be viewed as a means of supplementing the role of experience in the learning process. Its goal is to shorten the time span required between introduction of a new salesperson to a territory and his or her attainment of a satisfactory level of sales volume.

Because of the considerable expense involved in building a sales force, each salesperson represents a large investment of the firm's resources. When salespeople leave for one reason or another, the investment is lost. In addition, the replacement of an experienced salesperson by a new recruit results in a lag in sales volume until the new seller becomes experienced. Thus turnover, although inevitable, is expensive.

Training, both initial and continuing, may be viewed as an additional investment made to reduce the rate of turnover and thus the related costs and losses of revenue. Proper training may help the individual salesperson to be more successful by teaching him or her new sales techniques and approaches. Perhaps of even greater importance is the supportive role that training plays by indicating to the salesperson the concern of the company for his or her success. Thus it has a motivational role that may be as important to the building of a successful selling organization as its informational role.

Assignment of Sales Personnel

After recruitment, selection, and initial training at the home or district office, the new salesperson is assigned to a territory where he or she will come into

"Now this is called 'getting off your duff.'"

Sales and Marketing Management. October 7, 1985, p. 70. Copyright 1985. Used by permission.

contact with current or prospective buyers. In some situations, the salesperson will be assigned to a senior salesperson who will provide guidance and instruction. In other situations, the new seller may explore the territory alone, although under the general supervision and tutoring of the sales manager in the district.

The importance of proper assignment cannot be fully understood without considering the concept of *territory*. Although the term has a geographic meaning, it would be a mistake for a sales manager to think of a territory only in terms of its geographic boundaries. These boundaries are important in that they affect the distances that salespeople must cover and provide a basis for collecting data used in estimating sales potential or measuring sales performance. More importantly, the territory should be considered in terms of its customer content. The number and type of firms and their needs for various types of goods and services are the territorial attributes that are important in making assignments. Envisioning the sales territory as a set of actual or potential customers helps achieve the true goal of assignment, which is to match the selling resources available as effectively as possible with the buying needs of the target group of customers.

To achieve this goal, the assignment of new sales personnel must be well planned. Assigning a territory to an individual whose training and experience are insufficient to satisfy customer needs results in customer dissatisfaction and salesperson frustration. To avoid such problems, many companies design their sales territories around clusters of customers with similar needs for information and service. The actual location of the customer is of secondary importance as long as there are transportation services that can minimize travel times.

When the skill level required of salespeople varies greatly among the firms in the cluster or even within each individual firm, assignment of new salespeople may be facilitated by providing them with back-up support. Thus when new salespeople encounter selling situations that require more skill and experience than they can offer, more experienced senior salespeople can be called in from the district or home office.

Regardless of how the assignment task is handled by sales management, it is important that they recognize that it is not an easy task for a new person to begin selling effectively without continued support and ongoing training. Carefully matching the skill levels of new salespeople with customer needs and providing back-up support when necessary can avoid excessive rates of turnover among new employees and can maintain high levels of customer satisfaction while new salespeople are learning the skills of their trade.

Carnival Cruise Lines Example   Carnival Cruise Lines, which we have noted in previous chapters, provides an interesting example of how one company assigns new additions to its sales force. Because of the prospective acquisition of three new cruise ships in 1990, Carnival decided to increase the size of its sales force by 10 in 1989 and to assign these persons to the territories on the basis of the current travel agent base. Inasmuch as 99 percent of all cruise sales were made through travel agents, Carnival had concentrated on being "user friendly" to agents. In line with this policy, past experience indicated that an agent base of between 500 and 550 per representative was a "comfortable" number. Representatives were expected to make approximately 30 calls a week, varying call frequency with the potential of the agent to produce sales. Not being able to make 30 calls a week was taken as a signal that some reallocation of effort might be required.

A second consideration was the market share held by Carnival in each territory. These data were collected by Cruise Line International Association, which monitors sales of 40 cruise companies worldwide. Carnival's showing as average or lower than average in market share was considered another signal that corrective action might be needed. Third, the ratio of sales per 1,000 of population in a territory was examined to see how well that territory was performing compared to other territories. Management stated that the key to success was "to be sensitive to market expansion opportunities." For example, in 1985 20 percent of business was repeat; it was 30 percent in 1988. These data indicate a tendency to concentrate on reselling present customers. What will be needed to fill the growing capacity, however, is not such concentration but market expansion to attract new customers.[2]

SALES FORCE MANAGEMENT—COMPENSATION AND MOTIVATION

In the actual management of an ongoing sales organization, it is assumed that the sales force has an acceptable rate of turnover and that new people are being added to fill vacancies caused by terminations or territorial growth or a combination of both factors. It is also assumed that a training program is available for the newcomers as well as a continuing program of retraining for the more seasoned members of the sales force. Given this type of situation, the next aspect of sales force management to be considered is compensation.

Compensating Salespeople

Company policies that determine the level of payment received by salespeople have an important influence on the effectiveness of the sales force. Policies that are fair—that recognize variations in territorial sales potentials and reward individuals for a job well done—attract a better caliber of applicant and help keep more productive sellers satisfied. Thus well-designed and executed compensation plans can help to upgrade the quality of the selling force while reducing the turnover rate. This latter benefit means that the costs of recruitment and selection are lessened and the investment in training is utilized more effectively.

The goals of a good compensation plan have been stated in various terms, but most agree that the purpose is to gain the cooperation of the employees and further the interests of the employer. This is not an easy objective to achieve because individual self-interest on the part of a salesperson does not always coincide with the goals of the firm. Thus the most effective compensation plans are designed to provide an incentive for performing the activities the employer deems most profitable. These activities include making sales, of course, as well as providing service, cultivating new accounts, gathering market intelligence, and so on. The difficulty encountered in devising a good compensation plan is caused by the diverse nature of the typical selling job in terms of tasks to be performed as well as the breadth and heterogeneity of the product line or customer list. The complexity of the problem becomes especially evident when the dynamics of product-line development, customer turnover, and competition are added to this situation.

The starting point for appraising or redesigning a compensation plan is the all-important job analysis. A particular selling task must be analyzed in terms of the components of the task which, when performed well, lead to success. These are the components the compensation plan must spotlight to get more and better performance from the sales force. Second, an income analysis of the salespeople involved must be made. Will the compensation plan proposed provide competitive levels of income to members of the sales force? Will any members of the force receive a reduced income if the plan becomes operative?

A new compensation plan should not cause major short-term changes in the income of participants. Instead, it should change the rewards for performance of certain activities or for the sale of certain products over a period of time so that changes are evolutionary rather than sudden.

After a careful job analysis, including a definition of objectives for the compensation plan, a tentative approach can be developed and discussed with the salespeople. This step provides an opportunity for feedback—a chance to pick up new ideas from the sales force as well as to hear their criticisms. It also allows management to explain the way in which the plan will operate and to anticipate and assuage fears salespersons may have about the proposed plan's impact on their well-being. The plan proposed may be modified in view of the salespeople's suggestions and fears.

After preliminary analyses, the plan is ready to be tested. A test can be simulated by utilizing past sales records to see what earnings would have been if the new plan had been in force. Or the new plan can be put into effect in specific territories representing a range of competitive conditions and employee skill and experience. The second approach is preferred because it is impossible to tell how salespeople will react to a new plan until they actually work under it. Information from the actual test run can be used to improve the plan further and to indicate whether or not it should be fully implemented.

Components of Compensation   The methods of compensation are (1) base salary, (2) commission, and (3) bonus.

Base salary   The base salary is payment for certain routine activities performed by the sales force. It is a means of control by which management can require that a route be covered or that certain types of supporting activities be performed through guaranteed income. It also provides a cushion against large fluctuations in employees' income caused by conditions beyond their control. Hence, the greater the routinized selling activity or the larger the

---

❖
**PROMOTION
IN ACTION
19–1**

Marketer Makes a Million

America's highest paid salesman last year was a computer firm's vice president-marketing, who received more than $1.2 million, according to *Sales & Marketing Management* magazine's annual compensation survey.

Robert A. Bardagy of Comdisco, Rosemont, Ill., tops the magazine's compensation list, both in terms of salary, bonus commissions, and fees ($934,333) and overall compensation ($1,237,681).

But the biggest long-term gain realized last year was $636,599 by George H. Levine, vice president-marketing, Quotron Systems Inc., Los Angeles. Levine ranked No. 3 overall.

The average compensation for the top 115 sales and marketing executives with 104 publicly owned companies last year was $189,000, up 13 percent over 1983, the survey found. *S&MM* forecasts a 12 percent gain this year, compared to 6 percent average pay hikes for other corporate employees.

Pay raises, however, aren't automatic in sales and marketing, points out Matt S. Walton III, principal, Sibson & Co., Princeton, N.J. Only three-quarters of those surveyed typically receive compensation increases, and some suffer pay cuts, notes Walton, who helped prepare the survey.

The survey reflects the fundamental economic shift from the nondurable goods sector to the services sector, Walton said.

Source: Reprinted from *Marketing News*, September 27, 1985, p. 14, published by the American Marketing Association.

fluctuation in sales volume, the more the reliance is likely to be placed on base salary in the compensation mix.

Commission   A commission or percentage payment associated with the sale of certain items in the line is used by management to direct the sales effort to specific items (or customers). Rates of commission may be periodically adjusted to reflect changes in product or customer profitability or in the market environment. The role of the commission form of compensation is determined by the incentive requirements and the stability of sales volume. Customer needs for nonselling services place limits on the degree of sales incentive that management can blend into the compensation mix. With too much emphasis on incentive compensation, the salesperson becomes a "high-spotter," spending time with larger accounts and neglecting smaller ones.

Bonus   Bonus compensation is a more diffused type of incentive payment. Generally, bonuses are paid for exceeding a predetermined quota, although they may represent some allocation of profits based on performance and length of service. A bonus is a means of letting a salesperson share in the progress of the firm without making the payment as directly related to performance as is the case with a commission. The bonus may be very important in compensating technical representatives who back up salespeople by solving customer problems but who do not actually make sales.

   An actual compensation plan may call for any combination of the three components. The nature of the selling task and the requirements of the market that determine the role of personal selling suggest the emphasis to be placed on salary, commission, and bonus payments.

Objectives of a Good Compensation Plan   The following have been suggested as four general objectives of a compensation plan:

1. To attract and hold good salespeople.
2. To stimulate the sales organization to produce the maximum attainable volume of profitable sales.
3. To control selling expense, especially where there are major fluctuations in sales volume.
4. To ensure full attention to customer needs through complete performance of the sales job.

   Although the general objectives are common to all compensation programs, the relative importance of each one may change with respect to different firms or to individual firms in different stages of development. For example, the small firm just starting out may find that expense control is the most important objective of its compensation plan. On the other hand, a more established firm might find that competition requires a compensation plan that motivates the firm's salespeople to the complete fulfillment of customer needs.

In addition to the general objectives, individualized goals may be designed to achieve specific company marketing and sales objectives. The following goals have been suggested:

1. To encourage solicitation of new accounts and development of new sources of revenue.
2. To encourage full-line selling.
3. To stimulate the sale of more profitable products.
4. To hold a salesperson responsible for the profit contribution on sales where she or he can influence margins.

The specific objectives listed above are by no means exhaustive. Neither are they common to all plans for compensating salespeople. A truly effective program contains the means to reach goals common to all firms. In addition, it will be tailored to reach specific objectives that are an outgrowth of the resources, competition, and promotional strategy of the individual firm.

Carnival Cruise Lines Example   Carnival Cruise Lines uses a very effective approach to compensation. Its sales representatives have no caps on their earnings. They have realistic quotas and have direct input into the quota-setting process. Every effort is made to protect the present representative if an additional one is assigned to the territory. The company seeks to maintain its credibility with the representatives by keeping all promises it makes. A company executive stated that the key attributes of all successful Carnival representatives are intelligence, flexibility, the ability to listen, and hunger. The Carnival sales force has the least turnover in the industry; its members are loyal and have extraordinary esprit de corps.[3]

Motivating Salespeople

The very nature of the selling job requires that special attention be paid to the proper motivation of personnel. The seller who works alone and away from home faces considerable discouragement in daily routine. The depressing effects of loneliness and rejection usually require some type of supportive action from management. For some personalities, the selling task may be sufficiently intriguing to require little more in the way of motivation than a good incentive compensation plan and a new list of prospects. Such salespeople are rare, however, and the average member of the sales force requires some motivating efforts in addition to that provided by regular monetary compensation. The human traits of laziness and procrastination are as present among sellers as any other group in society, and managers have learned from experience that effort expended to overcome human inertia pays off in increased sales productivity.

The types of motivating action that might be taken by management are varied. Essentially, they may be classified as (1) additional incentive compensation, (2) career advancement, and (3) contests or other types of special sales stimulation promotions.

Additional Compensation This attempt at providing added motivation for the salesperson is predicated on the belief that monetary rewards are the most meaningful. The payment of special compensation in addition to the regular plan may be used to motivate salespeople to reach special short-run objectives in terms of sales volume, customer coverage, or product emphasis. Monetary rewards have the advantage of being direct, easily understood by employees, and readily administered. The question is simply this: Do they motivate salespeople to sell as well as other rewards such as those discussed below?

PROMOTION IN ACTION 19–2

How Much Is a Customer Worth?

The cost of replacing a customer can top $400 in the service industry, according to a survey by the Sandy Corporation, a Troy, Michigan, training and consulting firm.

Sandy Corp. mailed surveys to 5,400 service company executives to see how they handle customer service—and what it costs them when they don't do well. Among Sandy's findings were that banks lost about $80 in unrealized revenue every time they lost a customer, lodging and restaurants lost $21, and transportation companies lost $322.

In addition, the study found that it cost $100 in sales and marketing to replace customers in the banking and transportation industries, and $20 in lodging and restaurants. The loss plus replacement costs for banks was $180, lodging and restaurants $41, and transportation $422.

The survey also revealed that the major sources of customer dissatisfaction were, in order: a lack of responsiveness or the inability to resolve a problem, delays or interruptions in service, unfriendly employees, and errors in billing or delivery.

Source: Excerpted from "Short Takes," *Sales & Marketing Management,* May 1989, p. 23. Used by permission.

Career Advancement   In this approach, the better sales performers are offered transfers to more lucrative territories or are invited to join the ranks of sales management. Thus the income advantage of job betterment is combined with the prestige of a rise in the organizational hierarchy. The motivating appeal of job advancement is less immediate in its impact than a direct monetary payment. But the reward, if achieved, has longer-lasting benefits to the salesperson. The problem, of course, is the lack of immediacy of payoff.

Special Activities   Somewhere between the immediate and somewhat prosaic approach of direct monetary payoffs and the longer-run approach involving job advancement lies a range of special activities including contests and other types of special sales promotions aimed at increasing sales personnel motivation. Contests are especially popular among sales managers for this purpose. They view contests as a means to elicit extra effort to achieve short-run goals by means somewhat more dramatic than purely monetary payments. Contests may liven the competitive spirit of the salespeople, may involve wives and children, and may promise rewards such as travel or vacations with pay, which may have more general appeal than mere money.

Numerous dangers are inherent in the use of contests as motivators, however. Like any other form of stimulation aimed at getting extra effort in the short run, contests may lose their impact with continued use. The nature of some contests and other events may alienate the more serious and professionally oriented members of the sales force. Moreover, contests by their very nature engender rivalry among members of the sales organization and may thereby break down a close group relationship built over a long period of time. They must be used with care and never as a substitute for effective activity in the other aspects of sales force management discussed earlier.

Methods of Communication

Because salespeople work at a distance from the home office and are usually on their own a great deal, management has a special problem in establishing lines of communication to them. Written messages going out to the field and reports from the field flowing in are found in almost all sales situations, but there is a serious question as to the effect of this type of communication on employee morale or motivation. Certainly, a note from a superior congratulating a salesperson on a job well done will give the salesperson a feeling of being recognized and appreciated, but a routine written pep talk too often has little or no effect on motivation.

Recognition of the shortcomings of written communication has led many sales managers to use the telephone instead of the memo. Of course, personal contact is the best method of communication between salespeople and their managers. Traditionally, the sales manager has attempted to build a personal relationship with the individual salespeople. In fact, a psychiatrist, highly experienced in these matters, has indicated that sellers often view their sales manager as a parent figure and are quite disturbed emotionally when separated from this superior by transfer or promotion.

Organizational Variables and Their Impact on Sales

Policies and procedures that determine the patterns of organization of sales force management can have an important influence on sales force motivation.[4] For example, in the years preceding World War II, most sales organizations were highly formalized, highly centralized structures. Salespersons were considered as objects to be moved around the territories like chess pieces on a chess board, given their sales quotas, and discarded if they failed to produce. In reaction to this type of treatment, the concept of *human relations* developed in the postwar era. Scholars in this area stressed the importance of interpersonal relationships and the motivation of workers, including salespersons. "Management became less authoritarian and more participative. Sales executives began to realize that salespeople are individuals with emotions, personalities, expectations, and self-concepts."[5]

At present, organizational theorists recognize that neither of these extremes is effective in optimizing worker productivity and profitability. Effective management today requires a balance between the formalized hierarchical organizational structure and the human relations approach. The

TABLE 19–1

Two Models of Organization Theory ❖

Traditional	Current
1. More likely to be production oriented.	1. More likely to be marketing oriented.
2. Internally oriented.	2. Oriented toward external environment.
3. Highly formalized and inflexible.	3. Less formalized; more flexible.
4. Centralized authority.	4. Decentralized authority.
5. More levels of supervision and shorter span of control.	5. Fewer levels of supervision and broader span of control.
6. Major concern is toward the system; system becomes an end in itself.	6. Management relies on the workers rather than on the system; system is only a means to an end.
7. Orientation is toward how the job is done.	7. Results oriented: *did* you get the job done?

William J. Stanton and Richard H. Buskirk, *Management of the Sales Force*, 6th ed. (Homewood, Ill., Richard D. Irwin, 1983), pp. 46–47.

❖
**PROMOTION
IN ACTION
19–3**

What Makes a Top Performer?

What does it take to make it in selling today? A recently published survey by Learning International says that for salespeople, skills far beyond those involved in making a presentation are needed; for sales managers, it's the ability to plan and support their field people as never before. And, according to LI, most of us aren't making the grade.

For its survey, LI, a Stamford, Connecticut, training company, asked 3,200 managers, colleagues, and customers to judge 495 salespeople and sales managers they had worked with or with whom they had had recent business dealings. The respondents were asked to rate the subjects' effectiveness and for those they rated highly, to state what was special about their performance.

What makes a salesperson outstanding from the viewpoint of customers and others? Foremost is the ability to orchestrate events and bring together a selling team—the salesperson and whatever support people are needed to make the sale. Second is the ability to counsel clients based on a deep knowledge of the way they operate and what their product and service needs are.

To earn top status, the respondents said, a salesperson must also be skilled at problem solving and providing customer service, both being the secret for building long-term relationships. LI researchers add that learning these skills is in itself a long-term affair—most of the people who "won" the survey had been in sales at least five years.

Sales managers who were identified as most effective excel at the following:

1. Correctly analyzing customers' individual needs, developing sales goals that meet their company's own goals, and establishing territories for the people under them.

2. Mentoring their field people by skillful coaching and giving constructive criticism and full support.

3. Being strong communicators, not only with the field sales force but with upper management as well.

Source: Short Takes, *Sales and Marketing Management*, May 1989, p. 23. Used by permission.

organization is regarded as a total system, and decision-making theory is stressed. See Table 19–1 for a summary of contrasts between traditional and current models in organization theory.

Research by Churchill, Ford, and Walker and others has indicated that closeness of supervision, span of control, influence over standards, frequency of communication, opportunity rate (opportunity to be promoted to sales management), recognition rate, compensation rate, and earnings opportunity ratio (ratio of total financial rewards of the highest paid salesperson to the total rewards of the average salesperson) all influence sales force morale and motivation.[6]

It is beyond the scope of this text to explore this area in greater detail, but in reading the Promotion in Action 19–3, we hope that you will recognize that effective selling is an extremely complex activity. It is one that calls for bright, motivated salespeople and effective sales management. The high cost of personal selling and the inroads of competition mean that the days when a salesperson can be placed in a territory without any guidance or support are gone. To succeed takes a team effort with all eyes focused on the customer.

SUMMARY

This chapter has considered personal selling as a special form of interpersonal communication. Inasmuch as the salesperson is the key element in the communication process, the nature of his or her task was examined in some detail. In addition, the process by which a sales force is built into an effective promotional resource was examined. Furthermore, attention was paid to the compensation and motivation of the individuals who make up the selling organization.

In this chapter, the sales force was treated in the same manner as advertising was—as a "controllable." This implies that the type, amount, and direction of all promotional efforts are subject to variation in the short run by marketing management.

This view of personal selling as a promotional input subject to control in the short run is generally sustainable. However, a really effective selling organization cannot be built overnight. Thus, although short-run control is possible in terms of type of effort, extent of effort, or direction of effort, the truly qualitative aspect of the effort depends on a continuing process of recruitment, selection, training, supervision, and control. Good management is vital at each of these stages if the firm is to get the best payoff possible from its personal selling effort.

REVIEW AND DISCUSSION QUESTIONS

1. You want to hire three salespersons for your small software company. Outline a written job description and explain why a complete written job description is the foundation on which a sales force is built.

2. Seven persons have applied for the jobs described in your job description (question 1). You are now setting up a schedule for personal interviews. What dangers must you avoid when interviewing the applicants?

3. Of the seven persons interviewed (question 2), you are really interested in four of them but you want to be very careful in your selection. You are considering sending these applicants for psychological testing. What are the benefits and dangers of such a move?

4. You have hired three persons for the sales force and now must start to train them to perform in the field. What should be the goals of such a training program? Can sales training ever cease?

5. Imagine that two years have passed since you started your company and your sales force has grown to 20 persons. Your services are well-known in the market area and the nature of the selling task is changing. You are considering a change in the compensation plan to reflect these different conditions. What guidelines should you consider when proposing a new plan of compensation?

6. The compensation plan discussed above has been implemented and has resulted in a drop in sales force morale and in motivation. Is this normal? What can you do to alleviate the causes underlying these symptoms of salesperson dissatisfaction?

NOTES

1. Dick Schaaf and Tom Cothran, "Sales Training in the Era of the Customer," *Training: Sales Training Supplement,* February 1988, pp. 3–4.

2. Personal interviews (May 1989) and Faye Rice, "How Carnival Stacks the Decks," *Fortune,* January 16, 1989, pp. 108–16.

3. Ibid.

4. This section borrows heavily from William J. Stanton and Richard H. Buskirk, *Management of the Sales Force,* 6th ed. (Homewood, Ill.: Richard D. Irwin, 1983), pp. 46–47.

5. Ibid.

6. Gilbert A. Churchill, Jr., Neil M. Ford, and Orville C. Walker, Jr., *Sales Force Management,* 2nd ed. (Homewood, Ill.: Richard D. Irwin, 1985), pp. 447–49.

Evaluation and Control of Sales Force Efforts

CARNIVAL CRUISE LINES

Carnival Cruise Lines, the largest operator in the cruise industry, has had a revenue growth of 30 percent annually since 1980. In 1989, 60 sales representatives called on 35,000 travel agents to stimulate almost $600 million in sales. Two developments in 1989 were destined to impact the size of the sales force and the way it would operate in the future.

The first development was the purchase of Holland America Line's travel and tourism business that included four ships that operate in the Caribbean and Alaska, Westours, Westmark Hotels, and Windstar Sail Cruises. Holland America's 34 sales representatives called on 6,000 "core" agents who provided the bulk of the Holland America business.

Second, Carnival had three large cruise ships under construction with capacities of 2,050 berths each (based on two berths per cabin). The first ship was scheduled to begin cruising in March 1990 with the two other ships to follow approximately a year apart.

Carnival thus faced the problem of increasing the size of its sales force to maintain its revenue growth rate and to provide customers for the 75 percent increase in capacity coming on line over the next three years. In addition, Carnival management had to coordinate the operations of the Carnival sales force with that of the Holland America.

Role of the Representatives
Carnival representatives have the challenge of developing the leisure-vacation business and converting it into a Carnival cruise.

Competition is land-based resorts, sightseeing, and so forth. Carnival's strategy is to target middle-America and to sell the idea of the ship as the destination with ports of call being bonuses. The ships are designed to provide a range of activities such as dining and dancing, casino gambling, deck activities, health spas, and so on. The Carnival package includes round-trip airfare from anywhere in the country as well as meals and entertainment while at sea. The package is considered by those in the industry to be an outstanding value.

Working with Holland America Lines

Coordinating the efforts of the 34 Holland America sales representatives with the Carnival sales force was the second challenge facing management. At the time of the acquisition in early 1989, Holland America representatives called on many of the agents covered by the Carnival sales force. In fact, about 8,000 of the 35,000 agents gave Holland America some business. Carnival sales management developed a new incentive plan for Holland America representatives that made them responsible for bringing in 80 percent of the planned revenue goals for Holland America with the Carnival representatives being responsible for the other 20 percent. It was further stipulated that Carnival representatives would not cover the Holland America core agents as long as the Holland America sales force did its job. Sales efforts of both sales forces would be backed up by print and electronic media ad campaigns, sales promotion, the Carnival Agency Sales Service Department, and a newly developed Alaska Help Desk for travel agents representing Holland America.

In addition, the company holds about 100 sales receptions a year in various regions of the country. At these receptions, local travel agents are greeted by their sales representatives and, perhaps, a Carnival executive. They are wined, dined, and entertained while being given a pep talk about the advantages of selling customers on Carnival or Holland America cruises.

Source: Personal interviews (May 1989) and Faye Rice, "How Carnival Stacks the Decks," *Fortune*, January 16, 1989, pp. 108–16.

As the examples of Carnival Cruise Lines in Chapter 19 and in the chapter-opening vignette indicate, demand and competitive forces in the marketplace are constantly changing. Thus the evaluation of sales force efforts must be a continuous process. Like a servomechanism that can keep a machine operating within predetermined tolerances, the evaluative process can provide the information needed to control coverage patterns, call frequencies, and even sales objectives when necessary.

In the short run, evaluation can determine whether more specific objectives such as revenue goals and expense constraints are being met. Without such information, management cannot make the changes necessary to keep sales performance on budget in the short run.

In the longer run, evaluation is necessary in order to make better decisions about the number of persons to be employed at various levels in the sales organization, the hiring and training requirements, and the development of the sales budget.

Later in this chapter, a case history of Syntex Laboratories will be presented; it illustrates how the use of market research and modeling can aid in planning long-run sales force size and deployment over three to five years.

In addition to increasing sales force productivity, a continuing program of evaluation can improve the morale of individual salespersons by providing them with information as to what is expected of them and how they are performing relative to these expectations. Evaluation presents management with opportunities to praise good performance as well as to identify areas where help is needed to improve substandard performances. Evaluation is thus a very necessary requirement for the effective control of sales force efforts.

INFORMATION NEEDS

In developing a system of evaluation and control, the manager needs to decide what is to be measured. Of course, some information on individual performance is required in most situations. There are times, however, when information on group performance is also useful. This is especially true when the pattern of organization is based on the current model (described in Chapter 19). In still other cases, information about the performance of the entire sales organization is required.

It is the responsibility of the manager to evaluate the relative costs and values of different types of information and to adjust information-gathering procedures accordingly.

THE EVALUATION AND CONTROL PROCESS

Developing Performance Standards

Considerable information about the firm and its market is necessary for the development of standards for sales force performance. The firm must develop its sales forecast from data on market potential or aggregate demand for a specific good or service. This forecast is the best estimate of sales to be expected during a given period, assuming a given set of environmental conditions and a specific marketing plan or program. The sales forecast is thus the basis for the promotion appropriation. The forecast can, however, also be used as a starting point from which to develop sales goals or quotas for specific products, territories, or classes of customers. As such, it is vital to the development of criteria for performance evaluation.

Measurements of sales potential, however, should not be the sole basis for performance standards. Special territorial characteristics such as terrain or dispersion of customers must be considered, as well as special attributes of products, customers, and salespeople—if meaningful performance standards are to be developed.

With respect to characteristics of individual salespeople, some consideration must be given to the fact that not all salespeople perform in the same way. For example, the high-pressure type may do very well in the short run if results are measured in terms of sales volume in relation to potential. These methods may, however, lead to a decline in sales in the long run as customers tire of that approach. On the other hand, the low-pressure type may not score well on the basis of short-run performance but over the years may show a rising sales trend with regular, repeat customers.

**❖
PROMOTION
IN ACTION
20–1**

Why Sell Cases of Wine?

The senior management of a premium wine producer could not understand its sales force's insensitivity to the company's annual sales goal, which was measured in cases of wine. Although the sales staff worked hard to influence distributors' salespeople, the number of cases actually sold seemed to be of secondary interest. To the company, however, it was critical: The purchase of grapes, glass bottles, corks, and other costly product components were based on the annual case goals.

The winery had not set individual goals for its representatives. As a result, they were more oriented to customer relations than to the sale of a "hard number" of wine cases. Such omissions are not uncommon.

Assigning specific, quantifiable goals with associated cash rewards for achievement would provide clear direction to salespeople and their managers. Any number of specific goals could be applied.

Source: Excerpted from Stockton B. Colt, Jr., "Improving Sales Productivity: Four Case Studies," *Sales & Marketing Management,* May 1989, p. 10. Used by permission.

Because of the unique circumstances faced by each firm in terms of market potential, customer and product mix, competition, and qualitative characteristics of the sales force, the development of standards of sales performance must be closely related to the specific sales objectives previously planned.

Standards for Measurement of Performance

Quantitative Standards   The most commonly used standards are quantitative and are based on single ratios or combinations of ratios. Those expressed in quantitative form, however, are the easiest to calculate and to explain to salespeople. This latter factor is most important, especially when the performance standard is being used for incentive purposes as well as for control. Some ratios or measures commonly used include:

1. Sales volume as a percentage of sales potential.
2. Selling expense as a percentage of sales volume.
3. Number of customers sold as a percentage of total number of potential customers.
4. Call frequency ratio, or total calls made divided by total number of accounts and prospects covered.

There are other measures in addition to these, such as average cost per call and average order size, which can be part of the appraisal. The correct choice of measures to use in combination is best set by the sales manager to meet the needs of a specific situation.

Profit Contribution Standards   Most writers on the subject agree that the key measurement for setting standards is sales volume achieved in relation to sales potential. After all, the main objective of the sales force is to make sales, and without such sales, considerations of profitability cannot begin. However, more and more, the norms of sales performance are being combined with those of expense control so that profitability standards may be set. Perhaps the best way to control and appraise sellers' performance is by applying the techniques of distribution cost analysis. In this manner, not only can relative profit contributions of individual salespeople be measured but also standards can be set by which to judge such diverse factors as gross profits, product mix sold, customer mix, direct selling expenses, and the amount of sales promotion assistance going into the territory.

Distribution Cost Analysis   In very simple terms, a distribution cost analysis would be used to determine the gross margin contribution of each salesperson. This computation based on sales volume less cost of goods sold would give some idea of the *initial* profitability of the product mix being sold. From gross margin would be subtracted those expenses that can be allocated to the salesperson on a causal or benefit basis. This means that only those items that are *caused* by that person's activity or *benefit* him or her in terms of reaching goals (direct mail advertising, for example) should be charged against a personal gross margin contribution. The residual is the contribution to general overhead (not allocated to the territory) and to profit. This amount, often termed the *contribution margin,* is an excellent measure of the *relative* performance of individual salespeople. But, equally important, the technique allows the development of both revenue and cost standards based on actual as well as desired performance.

The contribution margin can also be used as part of a return-on-investment analysis. For example, if a certain territory produced a contribution margin of $80,000 on sales of $1 million and if $500,000 of company assets had been employed in support of the territory, the following return on investment (ROI) calculations could be made:

$$\frac{Contribution: \$80,000}{Sales: \$1,000,000} \times \frac{Sales: \$1,000,000}{Investment: \$500,000}] \; 16 \; percent \; ROI$$

The use of two fractions rather than one (contributions over investment) is to illustrate that the ROI is a function of both the profitability of the sales volume and the turnover rate. Thus ROI can be improved in a given territory by increasing sales with investment held constant, by increasing profitability of sales, or by reducing the investment needed to sustain the present level of sales.

By indicating the relative ROIs of various territories, the analysis can be used to appraise how well the various salespeople are doing, given the assets at their disposal.

Qualitative Criteria The setting of quantitative performance standards, whether based on revenue, cost, or other considerations, has as its major shortcoming the inability to measure activities and traits that may pay off for the salesperson in the long run. To make certain that these qualities are not overlooked in the appraisal process, many firms use a more subjective approach in order to develop norms of performance standards related to the qualitative aspect of the salesperson's job. In some cases, the sales manager or supervisor uses personal judgment in appraising how well the salesperson displays the desired traits. In other cases, a more formalized merit-rating checklist may be used.

Comparing Sellers' Performance to Standards

It is inevitable that some attempts will be made to appraise sellers' performance. Appraisals are needed to indicate where performance is substandard and to provide evidence to support salary adjustments or promotions. Appraisal also provides a good check on how well the sales force building process—selection and training—is being carried out. Last, but very important, is the beneficial effect that a well-administered appraisal program has on seller morale and motivation.

The difficulties encountered are numerous. The selling task itself is quite complex, and short-run effort by salespeople may not have immediate results. In addition, some of the results may not be measurable or may not be separable as a consequence of joint effort.

The appraisal process begins with a rather mechanical step. It is the comparison of the actual performances of salespeople or groups of salespeople with the performance standards previously developed. Data on actual performance may come from an analysis of company records or from special reports required of salespeople. Once the data are collected, the evaluation process can begin.

A brief example may be helpful here. Baker and Kent are two salespeople whose sales to date are $93,000 and $98,000, respectively. Their performances are to be measured primarily on the basis of sales in relation to sales potential, the latter being expressed as a quota figure, as follows:

	Sales to Date (in $000)		Percent Increase or Decrease	Quota in $000	Percentage of Quota to Date	
	This Year	Last Year			This Year	Last Year
Baker..........	$93	$ 80	+ 16	$170	55	47
Kent..........	98	104	− 6	200	49	52

If performance is measured on sales alone, it might appear that Kent is outperforming Baker. In terms of quota, however, Baker is performing better. Indeed, if the trends from last year are considered, Kent appears to be slipping while Baker's position is improving.

Although the relatively sparse data presented above can provide for some important analysis, it cannot answer all of the questions required for a complete performance evaluation. For example, the appraiser would need to know the relative profitability in the short run of the sales volume recorded. An analysis of gross margins less allocable expenses would provide the needed answers.

Current-period seller activities that may have payoffs in the future require the use of different standards of performance. Evaluation may take place on the basis of effort expended to gain new accounts or to cultivate old ones. Regardless of the approach, the objective is to gain some feel for the way in which the salesperson is performing the nonorder-seeking portion of the job.

In addition to the quantitative evaluation of the salesperson's performance, there is the appraisal of qualitative factors such as attitude, judgment, and appearance. Here the appraiser may use some sort of rating scale. It is good policy to have several people involved in subjective evaluation of salespeople to avoid bias on the part of those engaged in the rating process.

It cannot be stressed too strongly that the criteria, both quantitative and qualitative, used as the bases for appraisal must be consistent with the seller's task as *communicated by the written job description.* The selling job differs widely from firm to firm, and the appraisal process must be custom-made to fit the specific needs and goals of the individual selling organization.

Corrective Action

If the preliminary stages of the control process have been handled correctly, the sales manager should have a good idea of the relative performance of the salespeople under her or his supervision. The concept of relative performance is based on performance compared with predetermined standards. In those cases in which individual performances are well below the norms, the sales manager or supervisor can take corrective action. The philosophy underlying this action is that a better use of the resources (sellers) under one's control will increase the contribution of the sales organization to the goals of the firm. This objective might also provide the basis for remedial action where performances are substandard. Essentially, this involves helping the salesperson to utilize his or her most valuable resource—time—more effectively. After this type of remedial action has been undertaken, a second approach may be considered—the direction of activity to areas of greater opportunity.

Time-and-Duty Analysis   This approach to better use of a salesperson's time is an adaptation of the time-and-motion studies used by industrial engineers in the factory. With respect to time utilization by sales personnel, several generalizations can be made.

First, a measurable relationship exists between selling time and sales volume. In addition, the actual amount of selling time available to a salesperson in a typical day is very limited. Travel, waiting, small talk, customer service, and report writing all steal time from creative selling. A rule of thumb in some industries is that a sales representative spends about half of his or her time in contact with the customer and the other half in traveling.

Second, through careful training and scheduling, management can increase the time available for essential activities at the expense of nonessential ones. Indeed, the essential activities that management wants performed should be scrutinized carefully to see if they are, in fact, essential. For example, many companies ask their salespeople to aid in collecting past due accounts in their territories. If this is really an essential activity, no further question need be raised. In many cases, however, it would be better to use trained credit and collection personnel for collection activity, thus freeing the salesperson to concentrate on the selling task.

Third, in addition to increasing the selling time available, it is vital that that time be used effectively. For example, many sales managers find that when their sales representatives use genuine sales arguments or reasons to buy in their presentations to prospects, sales result with greater frequency than if the product is merely mentioned.

Of course, changing the selling approach is only one of the ways in which selling time can be made more productive. The point is that management will be in a better position to correct substandard performance if it knows how much selling time is available and how it is being used. Time-and-duty analysis is one way to get this information.

Routing If about half of the salesperson's time is spent in contact with the customer (perhaps with one-sixth of the time used for promotional selling and one-third of the time engaged in nonselling activity), the other half is spent in traveling. This travel time bears a very high hourly cost. If sales management make careful routing and travel plans in situations in which such control is feasible, the savings in time can be substantial. In any event, travel time can be made more productive by the salesperson using a car phone, by having sales training tapes available, or by simply using the travel time to plan ahead mentally for the next call.

REALLOCATION OF EFFORT

Changing the nature of the seller's task or of reducing travel time to allow more opportunity for creative selling is in a very real sense a reallocation of resources. When time is the scarce item, attempts are made to provide more of it for selling and to improve the utilization of that which is available. This attempt to optimize the performance of each individual salesperson in each territory may be only one approach by the sales manager to improve overall performance of the sales force. Certainly, corrective action should begin at the individual level, but time utilization is only a part of the story. The chances of success are also conditioned strongly by the sales targets chosen. If individuals are using their selling time effectively yet their performance is substandard, perhaps their effort should be reallocated to different products or to different customers. Further analysis of product types sold and customer classes covered may suggest whether the product mix or customer mix can be changed to improve the performance of the subpar salesperson.

However, the sales manager has one other alternative to consider. Briefly, that is whether to reallocate selling resources among the various territories that make up the market. Economic analysis provides the conceptual ideal for allocation of selling effort among territories. The rule for an *optimum* allocation is that the level of selling expenditures in each territory should be such that the incremental receipts per dollar of selling effort should be equal among all territories.

Although this standard cannot be applied precisely to the reallocation of selling effort, a simplified version may be usable. This is the rule that for an optimal allocation, the ratio of variable cost of personal selling to sales in each territory should be equal. For example, take two territories, A and B. An input of $2,000 in sales effort to each territory results in sales of $5,000 in A and $20,000 in B for a total of $25,000. Obviously, the response function of B is more favorable than that of A. Shifting inputs from A to B should result in a net increase in sales with no increase in selling costs.

The marketing or sales manager must know *how much* of a shift in selling expenditures among the territories is necessary to achieve the opti-

---

❖
PROMOTION IN ACTION 20–2

Time Management and Territory Management Differ

Most sales managers, sales trainers, and salespeople traditionally lump time and territory management together. But just putting them together without clear differentiation is a mistake. Although they interact, time management and territory management involve different skills and competencies. Time management requires "dancing" to avoid the crises, distractions, obstacles, and temptations that get in the sales representative's way. And while it's important to route yourself time-effectively—to handle emergencies by phone (rather than driving 100 miles out of the way) or to deal with customers who keep you waiting—time management skills are really only a minor part of the sales representative's job. The real issue and payoff come with territory management, allocating calls according to results, not just time. It means getting in front of the high-potential customers and prospects in the territory with optimum frequency, and maintaining or acquiring a targeted share of their business. And that requires intensive planning of more than just the number of hours in a day.

Source: Excepted from Warren Kurzrock, "A Cure for Sales Territory Trauma," *Training and Development Journal,* November 1985, p. 56.

mum allocation. A mathematical method for answering the question can be constructed based on two assumptions: (1) that relationships between total variable selling costs and sales in each territory are known from past experience and (2) that underlying factors that determined the relationship in the past have not changed significantly.

Sales Force Sizing and Deployment at Syntex Laboratories

In 1982, Syntex Laboratories, Inc. of Palo Alto, California,[1] embarked on a program to develop a series of models to aid in determining the optimum size of its sales force and how it should be deployed. Because the Syntex approach has been so successful in improving the company's sales and profit performance and because it illustrates how research and modeling can aid decision making with respect to sales force sizing and deployment in many industries, the Syntex case history is examined in some detail. The following material borrows very heavily from an article written by the persons who developed the model as well as from a Harvard case study.[2]

Syntex Corporation was founded in 1940 as a producer of topical steroid preparations prescribed by dermatologists and later of birth control products prescribed by gynecologists. By 1982, the company developed, manufactured, and marketed a wide range of health and personal care products.

"Where am I? Is this a Hyatt or a Ramada? Am I on I-91 or I-95? Sunbelt? Mid-Atlantic? Down East? Where the hell am I?"

Sales & Marketing Management, January 14, 1985, p. 67.
Copyright 1985. Used by permission.

Consolidated sales in fiscal 1981 were $710 million with $98 million in net income. Syntex Laboratories, the company's U.S. human pharmaceutical sales organization, was the largest Syntex subsidiary with sales in fiscal 1981 of $215 million and a strong profit performance.

In 1982, the Syntex product line was composed of seven major products grouped into four categories: nonsteroidal antiarthritic (NSAI) drugs, analgesics, oral contraceptives, and topical steroids. The NSAI product Naprosyn, introduced in 1977, was the third largest selling drug in its class in the United States. Other products included Anaprox, an analgesic; Synalar and Lydex, topical steroids for treating skin irritations; Norinal 1 + 35 and Norinal 1 + 50, oral contraceptives, which held a 10 percent market share; and Nasalide, a steroid nasal spray for treatment of hay fever and allergies that was not marketed until 1982.

Syntex Sales Force   The role of the Syntex sales force was to call on physicians and encourage them to prescribe Syntex products. During a sales call, the sales representative would provide a physician with samples and information about dosage levels and possible uses for various drugs. Typically, a sales representative would be able to describe or "detail" two or three products during one sales call; thus the generic term *detail salespersons* arose to describe sales representatives in the pharmaceutical industry who called on physicians.

In 1982, when the model building started, the Syntex sales force size was 433. Given the company's growth rate of 23 percent compounded since 1971, the question arose as to how much larger the sales force should be and how its efforts should be allocated over the various products and territories. The company situation was summed up by the then senior vice president for sales and marketing as follows:

> Our history had been one of increasing the sales force size in relatively small steps. I've never been really satisfied that there was any good reason why we were expanding by 30 or 40 representatives in any one year other than that was what we were able to get approved in the budget process. Over the years, I'd become impatient with the process of going to the well for more people every year with no long-term view of it. I felt that if I went to upper management with a more strategic, or longer-term viewpoint, it would be a lot easier to then sell the annual increases necessary to get up to a previously established objective in sales force size and utilization.[3]

In addition to the need of Syntex Laboratories for a long-term approach to optimizing the size of its sales force was corporate management's requirement for more analysis to support requests for major expenditures such as for sales force additions.

The Challenges of Model Building

Building a model to provide the analysis needed by management was, to say the least, challenging. No data were available to provide an empirical estimation of sales response to sales force size in the past. Thus an attempt had to be made to develop subjective estimates. Only a limited amount of time was available for such an attempt because the procedure was as yet unproven. In addition, because of the difficulties of reversing a decision on sales force size once taken, more than one set of estimating procedures was deemed necessary. Finally, if management were to estimate parameters, it was important that it be able to estimate response realistically. The model had to be complete and to utilize input from the managers who were to be involved in the implementation of the solution.

Initial Models With the help of outside consultants, company market research executives decided to develop two similar but separate versions of the model, each one to help estimate sales response to increased or decreased sales force size. The first model sought to determine the optimal number of sales presentations to be allotted to each Syntex product; the second sought to decide the number of sales representative visits to physician specialties. Thus the sales response to changes in emphasis on particular products as well as changes in efforts directed to specific market segments could be estimated. By estimating the effects of changes in sales force size independently of each other, the two models could provide convergent estimates and thus reduce risk.

Each model was based on an existing three-year strategic plan that assumed that sales force size would remain unchanged over that period. All other known environmental and competitive variables were included in the model, as well as hard data on cost per sales representative, expenses for sales management and general management, variable costs to produce and distribute the products, and data from company records as to the current allocation of sales force effort by products and market segments.

What was not known, however, was the sales response to changes in sales force effort over a future three-year period. The 1985 strategic plan was used because it gave enough time for new products to gain maturity and it provided a time period over which managers felt comfortable about estimating sales responses.

Estimating Sales Responses This part of the model-building process was carried out by means of a modified Delphi approach that used systematic, iterative surveys for forecasting based on independent inputs from selected respondents. At Syntex, the senior vice president of sales and marketing, the vice president of sales, two people from the market research department, two product managers, two regional sales managers, and two salespersons participated. At meetings worksheets were distributed so that each participant could estimate changes in sales for each of the seven Syntex products and nine physician specialties given varying levels of sales representative activity. The responses were tabulated and distributed to the group to serve as a basis for discussion of those areas for which the estimates diverged. After this discussion, a second set of worksheets was distributed. The summary of the second round showed that the group had reached a fine consensus.

Model Output During a three-day national sales meeting, the model was run and output presented. The results appeared to be reasonable and required only some fine tuning. Table 20–1 presents the input to the product allocation model, and Table 20–2 presents the "step report," which shows incrementally the products or segments that enter the solution as additional resources are added to the sales force. For example, step 35 indicates that given the addition of 9 sales representatives from step 34 for a total of 381, the additional resources should be directed to the product Naprosyn. Step 36 shows that 130 representatives should be added for a total of 511 representatives and the effort be directed to Anaprox. The reason for this big jump

TABLE 20–1

❖   **Model Input**

Maximum number of sales people: 1,000
Cost per rep by region: $55,498.70
Effort (details or calls) per salesperson per year: 3,677.4

	Naprosyn	Anaprox	Norinyl 1 + 35	Norinyl 1 + 50	Synalar	Lydex	Nasalide
Strategic adjustment factor (contribution) for each product:							
	0.811	0.633	0.837	0.837	0.616	0.616	0.616
Minimum effort (calls or details) for each product:							
	0	0	0	0	0	0	0
Response functions based on 100 for each product:							
Number of calls	47	15	31	45	56	59	15
One-half	68	48	63	70	80	76	61
Present number	100	100	100	100	100	100	100
50 percent more	126	120	115	105	111	107	146
Saturation	152	135	125	110	120	111	176
Normal planned effort (details) for each product:							
	357,853	527,581	195,443	88,817.7	101,123	110,351	210,225

TOTAL DETAILS: 1.59139M

TABLE 20-2

Step Report for Syntex Sales Force—Strategy for Fiscal Year 1985   ❖

Step	Number of Reps	Change in Reps	Sales (000)	Change in Sales (000)	Change in Marginal Contribution per Rep (000)	Allocated to
1	0	0	161,129	0	0	NA
2	115.0	115.0	297,965	136,836.0	909.5	Naprosyn
3	123.9	8.8	307,720	9,754.9	838.8	Naprosyn
4	132.7	8.8	316,326	8,605.8	733.4	Naprosyn
5	152.5	19.8	333,930	17,604.3	690.2	Norinyl 1 + 50
6	161.3	8.8	341,488	7,558.0	637.4	Naprosyn
7	163.5	2.2	343,136	1,648.1	572.8	Norinyl 1 + 50
8	172.3	8.8	349,757	6,621.4	551.5	Naprosyn
9	181.2	8.8	355,553	5,795.5	475.8	Naprosyn
10	190.0	8.8	360,626	5,073.6	409.6	Naprosyn
11	192.2	2.2	361,834	1,207.6	404.8	Norinyl 1 +50
12	201.1	8.8	366,280	4,446.1	352.1	Naprosyn
13	221.1	20.0	379,083	12,802.9	338.9	Synalar
14	223.6	2.5	380,596	1,512.6	317.2	Synalar
15	232.4	8.8	384,498	3,902.7	302.3	Naprosyn
16	234.9	2.5	385,797	1,298.5	264.5	Synalar
17	243.8	8.8	389,230	3,432.6	259.2	Naprosyn
18	252.6	8.8	392,256	3,026.3	221.9	Naprosyn
19	255.1	2.5	393,362	1,106.0	217.0	Synalar
20	257.6	2.5	394,386	1,024.2	196.9	Synalar
21	266.5	8.8	397,061	2,674.8	189.7	Naprosyn
22	310.0	43.5	409,278	12,216.9	179.7	Norinyl 1 + 35
23	314.8	4.8	410,602	1,324.7	174.0	Norinyl 1 + 35
24	323.6	8.8	412,973	2,370.5	161.8	Naprosyn
25	326.1	2.5	413,835	861.6	156.8	Synalar
26	335.0	8.8	415,941	2,106.4	137.6	Naprosyn
27	339.8	4.8	417,027	1,086.4	132.7	Norinyl 1 + 35
28	342.3	2.5	417,752	725.1	123.2	Synalar
29	344.5	2.2	418,217	464.8	121.7	Norinyl 1 + 50
30	353.3	8.8	420,094	1,877.0	116.6	Naprosyn
31	362.2	8.8	421,771	1,677.0	98.2	Naprosyn
32	364.7	2.5	422,383	611.6	95.2	Synalar
33	366.9	2.2	422,766	383.4	90.6	Norinyl 1 + 50

TABLE 20-2

Step Report for Syntex Sales Force—Strategy for Fiscal Year 1985 (concluded)

Step	Number of Reps	Change in Reps	Sales (000)	Change in Sales (000)	Change in Marginal Contribution per Rep (000)	Allocated to
34	371.7	4.8	423,586	819.5	86.5	Norinyl 1 + 35
35	380.6	8.8	425,088	1,502.5	82.2	Naprosyn
36	511.0	130.4	453,321	28,233.1	81.5	Anaprox
37	524.0	13.0	456,113	2,791.9	80.0	Anaprox
38	526.5	2.5	456,631	517.6	72.1	Synalar
39	553.8	27.3	462,174	5,543.1	69.7	Lydex
40	562.7	8.8	463,523	1,349.6	68.2	Naprosyn
41	564.9	2.2	463,843	319.5	66.3	Norinyl 1 + 50
42	569.7	4.8	464,514	670.7	60.7	Norinyl 1 + 35
43	572.2	2.5	464,953	439.9	52.9	Synalar
44	644.9	72.8	477,648	12,694.8	49.2	Nasalide
45	647.1	2.2	477,917	268.9	47.0	Norinyl 1 + 50
46	649.9	2.7	473,360	442.9	44.5	Synalar
47	654.7	4.8	478,910	550.1	39.3	Norinyl 1 + 35
48	657.2	2.5	478,286	375.6	37.1	Synalar
49	662.4	5.2	480,060	774.1	33.9	Nasalide
50	675.4	13.0	481,887	1,827.3	33.2	Anaprox
51	677.6	2.2	482,115	228.2	31.5	Norinyl 1 + 50
52	680.1	2.5	482,437	322.2	23.9	Synalar
53	685.0	4.8	482,890	452.9	23.0	Norinyl 1 + 35
54	690.2	5.2	483,544	653.5	19.9	Nasalide
55	692.4	2.2	483,739	195.3	19.0	Norinyl 1 + 50
56	705.4	13.0	485,259	1,519.6	18.3	Anaprox
57	707.9	2.5	485,536	277.7	12.9	Synalar
58	712.7	4.8	485,911	374.8	9.4	Norinyl 1 + 35
59	714.9	2.2	486,090	168.4	8.7	Norinyl 1 + 50
60	720.1	5.2	486,629	549.6	8.0	Nasalide
61	722.9	2.7	486,905	276.1	6.8	Lydex
62	735.9	13.0	488,170	1,265.0	5.9	Anaprox
63	738.4	2.5	488,411	240.5	3.8	Synalar
64	740.6	2.2	488,557	146.2	0.2	Norinyl 1 + 50
65	745.4	4.8	488,869	312.1	−1.4	Norinyl 1 + 35
66	750.6	5.2	489,331	461.8	−2.2	Nasalide

was that Anaprox was the marginal product to be allocated; its response function indicated that either 130 or no representatives be assigned to it. Tables 20–3 and 20–4 present the effects of 381 and 511 sales representatives on product presentations and sales dollars. Table 20–5 presents the effects of maintaining the present policy with 433 reps until fiscal year 1985. Note that the reallocation of 381 representatives produces better results than staying with the old allocations and with 433 representatives. The use of 511 representatives with reallocation of effort produces the best results of the three policies.

Conclusions

The following conclusions were developed after studying the various outputs of the models:

1. Until the size of the sales force approached 700, profitability would not be a constraint to adding representatives.

2. Syntex should grow from its current base of approximately 430 representatives by adding individuals who would focus on the primary-care audience (general practitioners, internists, and family practice physicians) rather than by redeploying the existing sales force.

3. Naprosyn was the largest product in the Syntex line, the most sales responsive, and the most profitable so that it should be the driving force behind almost all of the sales force sizing and deployment decisions.

4. Syntex should consider itself a major generalist company since optimal deployment would require that the greatest portion of a large sales force be directed toward the generalist physician audience.

Model Implementation and Results

During the three years following the presentation of the findings to the senior management and board of directors of Syntex Laboratories, 200 sales representatives were added. The number was constrained by the company's ability to train and deploy new representatives. By 1985, sales were $25 million higher than the strategic plan forecast and were directly related to changes in sales force size and deployment in the directions recommended by the model. The financial return on the sales force investment was 100 percent. The one-time out-of-pocket cost for developing and running the model was $30,000. It thus appears that a relatively small investment provided a highly profitable increase in the revenue stream for years to come.

The general technique used by Syntex is readily transferable to other situations and has been used by at least 10 other pharmaceutical firms and by other businesses that are highly dependent on effective sales force activity such as banks and chemical, steel, and rubber companies. One charitable organization is using the technique to allocate its limited fund-raising staff in such a way as to maximize its effectiveness.

TABLE 20–3

❖ **Output Report of the Sales Force Strategy Model Based on Policy of 381 Syntex Sales Reps by Fiscal Year 1985**

	Number of Reps Allocated	Presentations	Sales in Dollars
Product			
Naprosyn	257	943,432	308,029,056
Anaprox	0	0	5,475,000
Norinyl 1 + 35	58	213,211	22,019,448
Norinyl 1 + 50	29	104,966	38,048,152
Synalar	37	137,894	41,222,456
Lydex	0	0	8,614,000
Nasalide	0	0	1,680,000
Total	381	1,399,503	425,088,112

TABLE 20–4

❖ **Output Report of the Sales Force Strategy Model Based on Policy of 511 Syntex Sales Reps by Fiscal Year 1985**

	Number of Reps Allocated	Presentations	Sales in Dollars
Product			
Naprosyn	257	943,432	308,029,056
Anaprox	130	479,619	33,708,128
Norinyl 1 + 35	58	213,211	22,019,448
Norinyl 1 + 50	29	104,966	38,048,152
Synalar	37	137,894	41,222,456
Lydex	0	0	8,614,000
Nasalide	0	0	1,680,000
Total	511	1,879,122	453,321,240

SUMMARY

The evaluation and control of sales force efforts requires the development of performance goals and standards. Actual performance is then compared with these predetermined guidelines, and management appraisals are made on how well individual and group performance met the norms. The final step in the process is taking corrective action by changing the extent and (or) direction of sales effort and improving its quality.

The short-run goal of the evaluation and control process is to meet more effectively the firm's revenue and sales targets by improving the productivity and morale of the sales force. The long-run and more general objective of the evaluation and control process is to ensure that the sales force is the proper size and is trained and directed to make an optimum contribution to the overall long-term profitability of the enterprise. The Syntex Laboratories example illustrates how powerful (and profitable) the use of modern research techniques can be in aiding decision making in this area.

REVIEW AND DISCUSSION QUESTIONS

1. What are the key elements of Carnival Cruise Lines' personal selling strategy? How would you counter that strategy if you were a competitor such as Princess Cruise Lines?

TABLE 20–5

Output Report of the Sales Force Strategy Model Based on Policy of Continuing Present Policy of 433 Reps until Fiscal Year 1985

	Number of Reps Allocated	Presentations	Sales in Dollars
Product			
Naprosyn	97	357,853	202,001,792
Anaprox	143	527,581	36,500,000
Norinyl 1 + 35	53	195,443	20,113,592
Norinyl 1 + 50	24	88,818	35,992,408
Synalar	27	101,123	36,894,000
Lydex	30	110,351	14,600,000
Nasalide	57	210,225	10,471,728
Total	433	1,591,394	356,573,520

2. Imagine that you are the sales manager of a small sales force of 10 persons that sells computer services to law firms. Each salesperson has a geographic area to cover, but these areas differ in size and sales potential. Outline the basic steps that you would take to set up a system of evaluation and control of these efforts.

3. You are trying to develop a compensation system for the members of your company's sales force. You are especially concerned with rewarding those salespersons for activities that contribute greatly to the firm's profitability on a yearly basis. How would you go about measuring the relative profit contributions made by each salesperson?

4. One writer has noted that time is the most valuable commodity available to a salesperson. As a sales manager, what steps might you take to ensure that the time available to members of your sales force is used most effectively?

5. When you were a student in a leading business school, you studied many ways to solve resource allocation problems. Your boss has come to you for suggestions for realigning the current sales territories. What methodologies might be useful in tackling such a problem?

6. Compare and contrast the Carnival situation with the one at Syntex. What do these two situations have in common? On what points do they differ?

NOTES

1. Leonard M. Lodish, Ellen Curtis, Michael Ness, and M. Kerry Simpson, "Sales Force Sizing and Deployment Using a Decision Calculus Model of Syntex Laboratories," *Interfaces* 18 (January-February 1988), pp. 5–20.

2. D. Clarke, "SYNTEX Laboratories (A)," Harvard Business School Case number 98–584–033, 1983., p. 9.

OTHER FORMS OF PROMOTION

We proceed through the stages in promotional strategy outlined in Chapter 2 by giving further attention to the management of mass communication efforts. This part of the text continues the discussion of management program elements by considering problems inherent in gaining the support of independent resellers in the channels of distribution. By examining the task that resellers can be expected to perform, given their objectives and limitations as independent businesses, we can suggest how manufacturers might stimulate reseller promotional activity or improve, supplement, or control reseller promotional efforts.

The concluding chapters in this section deal with direct marketing (Chapter 22) and with supplemental forms of communication, such as public relations, publicity, and corporate advertising, that serve to bridge the gap between the firm and its many publics (Chapter 23).

Working with Resellers: The Struggle for Channel Control

WILL WAL-MART TAKE OVER THE WORLD?

In just a few years, Wal-Mart Stores will be the largest retailer in the United States. The only companies in its way are K mart and the floundering giant, Sears, and the gap is closing fast. Wal-Mart's 1,300 or so discount stores sell nearly $20 billion worth of goods a year— clothes, shoes, small appliances, cosmetics, and 50,000 other items. Even so, you may have never shopped in a Wal-Mart because the company is really just getting started. Early on, Sam Walton, the founder, focused on the small-town markets ignored by national discounters, and although the company now operates Wal-Marts in such cities as Dallas, Houston, St. Louis, and Kansas City, its trade area still includes only 25 states.

In 1989, as in 1988, Wal-Mart was scheduled to open 150 or so new stores. So sooner or later there's bound to be a Wal-Mart in your future. When you do step into your first one, don't get rattled when someone—probably an elderly retiree type—approaches you with a big smile and welcomes you to the store. This is the "people greeter," and every Wal-Mart has one because, well, it's the friendly thing to do. . . .

If all of this hospitality makes you think your company might like to sell something to Wal-Mart, a word of caution: Don't expect a greeter, and don't expect friendly. Plan on a tough trip over the river and through the woods and across a rock pile to a low-slung warehouse building in a town of 10,000 people. And even if you're a big deal at your company and have an appointment, don't be surprised if you're kept waiting an hour or two in a lobby filled with 150 molded-plastic chairs and mounted giant fish caught by brother Bud Walton. Unless you like cafeteria food, eat before you come, because Wal-Mart won't let you buy lunch or dinner or anything else for the buyer. And once you are ushered into one of the spartan little buyer's rooms, expect a steely eye across the table and be prepared to cut your price. "They are very focused people, and they use their buying power more forcefully than anybody else in America," says the marketing vice president of a major vendor. "All the normal mating rituals are verboten. Their highest priority is making sure everybody at all times in all cases knows who's in charge, and it's Wal-Mart. They talk softly, but they have piranha hearts, and if you aren't totally prepared when you go in there, you'll have your ass handed to you."

Source: Excerpted from John Huey, "Wal-Mart—Will It Take over the World?" *Fortune,* January 30, 1989, pp. 52–53. Used with permission.

The Struggle for Market Entry

As the Wal-Mart story indicates, manufacturers whose survival is based on their ability to get shelf space for their products from mass merchandisers face a considerable challenge. The shift of channel control to "power retailers" such as Wal-Mart, K mart, Safeway, Kroger, and A&P is accelerating bidding wars in which powerful supermarket and mass merchandising organizations auction their retail shelf space to the highest bidder. The manufacturer who offers the lowest prices or grants the most generous promotional allowances gets the slot on the retailer's shelf. The cost to "buy" the slot is so high for many firms that they have little left in their budgets for other forms of promotion. This situation has gotten so serious that some manufacturers are even asking for federal intervention. For an update on this topic, see Promotion in Action 21–1.

Technology and the Power Shift   Resellers are more dominant today because of technological advances. Bar-code scanners, computerized inventory control systems, and microwave relays can collect and feed store information such as sales and product movement to headquarters at the speed of light. The power shift in favor of large resellers is based on the fact that they now have the ability to acquire and utilize market information that previously was available only to large manufacturers. The new reality requires that manufacturers have a clear understanding of how the task of promotion through the channels must be shared, given the changes in channel power relationships. Without such an understanding, gaining meaningful promotional support from resellers will be very difficult.

In this chapter, we try to analyze the promotional role that resellers play and attempt to provide some guidance as to manufacturer policy in an era of changing power relationships in the distribution channels.

THE PROMOTIONAL ROLE OF RESELLERS

The promotional strategy of a manufacturer is a blend of the elements of advertising, personal selling, and sales promotion aimed at attaining specific marketing objectives. Under certain product-market situations, the optimal blend of the promotional elements may allow only a small promotional role for resellers. For example, the selling of candy bars or razor blades may require heavy expenditures for consumer advertising and for gaining widespread availability and display at point of sale. The manufacturer expects only that his or her myriad of resellers stock the goods and keep them on display.

In contrast, the marketer of a new model of a top of the line personal computer might require that an exclusive reseller in a given market call on

---

Grocery Retailers Get Tougher

❖
PROMOTION IN ACTION 21–1

Grocery retailers are gaining more ground in their power struggle with grocery product marketers.

At the Food Marketing Institute's annual Supermarket Industry Show in Chicago, it was apparent that retailers were no longer satisfied with merely controlling shelf space and promotional allowances. Instead, retailers are aiming at taking even more sales from national brands for their own house brands and demanding more control of in-store ad media.

Nabisco Foods Co. President-CEO William McKnight told food brokers in a speech before the FMI show that concentration of retail grocery trade power is intensifying so quickly that federal intervention may become necessary.

"The emergence of extra goodies like reclamation centers, co-op advertising fees far in excess of media costs, diverting, slotting allowances and other 'promotional expenses,'" he said, have given retailers the edge over marketers. Mr. McKnight called for "new rules for this promotion game."

Source: Excerpted from Judann Dagnoli and Julie Liesse Erickson, "Grocery Retailers Get Tougher," *Advertising Age*, May 15, 1989, p. 4. Used with permission.

potential business customers, provide leasing, training, and on-site repair services, and so forth. The promotional role of the reseller is considerably more complex under these circumstances.

In either case, the manufacturer concerned with gaining the needed support from the reseller organization must know what the role of these intermediaries is to be as a result of a given product-market strategy. Only with this information can the manufacturer evaluate the selling performance of wholesalers and retailers and consider ways to supplement or improve reseller performance.

The Impact of Manufacturer Promotional Strategy

Manufacturers often blame resellers for not being promotionally supportive. They do not realize that their own marketing strategies may discourage reseller effectiveness. For example, when manufacturers utilize multiple channels to reach various segments of the market, the manufacturers almost always increase the level of interchannel competition. One of the authors of this text, in a recent study, found that in the office furniture industry, many retailers resented manufacturer sales to end users on a direct basis or through architects and designers. Such resentments resulted in less enthusiastic support of these manufacturers' lines by retailers than of the lines of manufacturers who chose to sell only through the traditional dealer channel.[1]

In other situations, manufacturers who have created strong selective demand for their products may attempt to "pull" them through the channels with heavy investment in consumer advertising. Under this strategy, the reseller margins are slender and unless special promotional allowances are offered, the reseller will have little incentive to put much support behind the manufacturer's program other than to stock the item.

Manufacturers' pricing policies can also have an impact on the willingness and ability of resellers to engage in promotion of a specific brand or product. If the margin payment offered the reseller does not cover the costs of doing the promotional job that the manufacturer requires, then the average reseller will cut back on his or her efforts.

Effects of Product Evolution

In addition to the effects of manufacturers' promotional strategy, we must also consider the changes in the promotional role of resellers as the product moves through its life-cycle. Figure 21–1 illustrates some changes that occur as a hypothetical product moves through the key stages of its life-cycle.

In the *introductory* or *pioneering stage,* the demand for the product with respect to price is generally more inelastic than in the later stages of development. However, the manufacturer must make a considerable investment in promotion in order to educate consumers about the existence and uses of the product. In the *competitive* stage of the cycle, the product is challenged by substitutes produced by other manufacturers. The selling task changes from stimulating primary demand to stimulating selective demand. Price becomes more important as cross elasticity of demand (the sensitivity of demand for a product to changes in the prices of close substitutes) increases. The final phase of the cycle is the *mature* or *commodity stage.* When a product reaches the point at which market shares are relatively stabilized, where brand preference is low or nonexistent, and where price reductions will produce more profitable volume than will promotion, the product is said to have reached *maturity.* It has, indeed, become a commodity like salt, sugar, calcium chloride, or copper wire, and there is little need for promotion.

FIGURE 21–1

Promotional Strategy Changes over a Product Life-Cycle

Product life cycle	Introductory stage	Competitive stage	Mature stage
Demand	Stimulate primary	Stimulate selective	Stimulate selective
Price	High	Lower	Lowest
Distribution	Sparse	Selective	Intensive
Consumer promotion	Educate consumers	Differentiate brand	Remind consumers
Trade promotion	Get resellers to stock and display	Gain reseller promotional support	Tie-in with reseller services

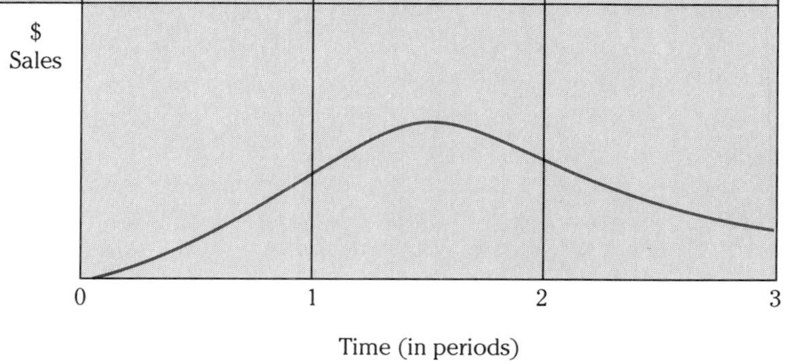

Time (in periods)

Introductory Stage   In the introductory stage of product marketing, a great deal of special selling effort is required to acquaint consumers with the new product type and to gain distribution at wholesale and retail levels. Some manufacturers sell directly to retailers in this stage, bypassing wholesalers until the need for special promotional effort has subsided. Other manufacturers use wholesalers but restrict distribution so that each wholesaler is willing to engage in the special selling required. Distribution at the retail level may also be on a highly selective basis to gain cooperation from individual retailers.

In those situations in which retail shelf space in supermarkets, mass merchandisers, and the like is needed, the role of the retailer is critical. Without "slotting" there is no availability to the market regardless of the attributes of the product. When introducing new products, manufacturers must direct most of their spending to trade promotion to gain reseller stocking and display.

Competitive Stage   As products pass from the introductory stage to the competitive stage, manufacturers' promotional tasks change from building primary consumer demand and gaining access to trade channels to stimulating selective demand for their specific brands. When the product reaches this stage in its life-cycle, manufacturers must recognize that wholesalers and retailers will require special incentives to continue promotional support. The reseller's task has changed from providing availability for a new product to routinely selling an established item. From the manufacturer's standpoint, unless selective demand for the product can be sustained through consumer advertising and sales promotion, resellers will not continue to support it. For example, the new scanning technology will alert the retailer to a slowdown in shelf movement for a given product and thus make it a candidate for replacement. In the competitive stage, therefore, promotional spending is aimed at sustaining consumer demand to maintain shelf space and position. Of course, to stimulate reseller support, trade promotion must be continued but with less intensity than was the case in the introductory stage.

Mature Stage   In the final stage of the life-cycle during which the product reaches maturity, brand preference weakens, physical variations among competing products narrow, and methods of production stabilize. In this stage, manufacturer strategy relies more on price than nonprice means of promotion. As the price spread among competing brands in the same category narrows, the opportunities increase for wholesalers and retailers to sell on the basis of their own patronage appeals. Service, delivery, credit extension, and so forth become the reseller's important selling points. The manufacturer should use promotion to tie the product to the services offered by the resellers.

Implications of Reseller's Promotional Role

As we have said, when the selling role of wholesalers and retailers is at a minimum, it is usually concerned with little more than order taking. As elements of "push" strategy enter the mix, however, the aggregate selling resources of the reseller family become of considerable importance to the manufacturer's promotional program. This situation is especially prevalent when the product being sold is a higher-priced, high-involvement good such as a major household appliance. In this case, the reputation of the retailer may be of greater importance to the customer than the brand itself. Clearly, the rules of the game change when one is dealing with expensive, complex, and infrequently purchased products as contrasted with those that are relatively simple, low priced, and purchased frequently, such as packaged grocery products and health and beauty aids.

It is also important to note that the nature of the reseller's task can change from the normal order of requirements. If resellers are assigned some of the extraordinary selling activities required in the earlier stages of the maturity cycle, the manufacturer must be sure to offer extraordinary profit opportunities. On the other hand, if the product has matured, the manufacturer should recognize that the role of resellers in stimulating selective demand is limited. The wise manufacturer analyzes a promotional program to identify the selling task that *resellers might reasonably be expected to perform.* Only then is the manufacturer in a position to formulate policies for improving or supplementing reseller efforts.

When the manufacturer has a clear idea of the role its resellers can be expected to perform, given the overall promotional program, and when it understands the ways in which its other pricing, product, and distribution policies can influence wholesaler and retailer willingness and ability to sell, it can consider ways to improve or supplement their activities. With respect to *improving* the selling performance of wholesalers and retailers, the manufacturer can consider (1) training programs for reseller salespeople, (2) quotas for resellers, and (3) assistance to resellers with respect to their advertising and sales promotion efforts.

In terms of *supplementing* reseller activity, the manufacturer might consider (1) using missionary (specialty) salespeople, (2) providing display and selling aids, and (3) scheduling special sales and consumer deals.

Two means are suggested for *controlling* reseller activity: (1) the selection of resellers and (2) the vertical integration of reseller outlets through ownership or by means of contractual agreements.

IMPROVING RESELLER PERFORMANCE

Training Reseller Salespeople

One of the most effective methods by which manufacturers can improve reseller performance is to assume part of the responsibility for training wholesaler and retailer salespeople. One writer states bluntly, "Generally speaking you [the manufacturer] will benefit from your distributor relationships more or less in proportion to the effort you put into training the distributor's sales [people]."[2] A study made by the National Industrial Conference Board further affirmed the contention that training of dealer salespeople was profitable for manufacturers. It was found that well-trained reseller salespeople built goodwill for the manufacturer as well as for the dealer—by recommending the right product to satisfy the customer's needs and by keeping customers informed about the advantages and uses of new products. Moreover, well-trained dealers maintained more adequate inventories and had better service facilities than did untrained distributors. Finally, well-trained dealers required less of the manufacturer salespeople's time so that those persons could make more calls per day.[3]

Training at the Wholesale Level   Although the generalizations stated about the value of training are valid for both wholesaler and retailer selling personnel, the objectives and scope of programs aimed at these two levels are different. The training programs at the wholesale level are intended to improve the salespeople's knowledge of the line and their selling techniques and often to train some to be management counselors for retailers. For example, one manufacturer of major household appliances has an extensive program to train the field representatives of its wholesale distributors. Courses held at the factory are given in such areas as product, business, and sales management; retail selling; handling used merchandise; service training; and general supervision of a sales territory. There is no charge for the courses, but the distributors must pay transportation and living expenses for their people in the program. Courses run for up to five and one-half days, and the trainees are worked hard. Heavy emphasis is placed on visual aids, and after factory training, each distributor salesperson is equipped with a sound-film strip projector and a wide variety of training films. These films are made under factory supervision and are sold to distributors at production cost for use in their own training programs for retailer salespeople.

Thus the objectives of a program to train wholesaler salespeople may be twofold—first, to provide them with knowledge about the product line and how it may be sold most effectively, and second, to prepare wholesaler salespeople to provide management assistance to retailers. This assistance may include training retailer sales personnel.

Regardless of the exact content of the manufacturer's training program, it is clear that a program for training wholesaler salespeople fills a gap that in many cases *cannot be filled by the wholesaler itself.* Because of either the pressures of day-to-day business or the lack of specialized sales management in smaller distributor organizations, many wholesalers will not or cannot do an adequate job of training, and the manufacturer can help perform this task. When the wholesaler does have training facilities and personnel, manufacturer assistance can make the program more effective and lighten the cost load.

Training at the Retail Level   Manufacturers' programs to train sales personnel at the retail level share many objectives with programs aimed at training wholesaler salespeople. Attempts are made to impart product knowledge to those who meet the public and to improve selling techniques. There are differences, however, because of the great dispersion at retail in terms of store size and location. A further complication is the stipulation of the Robinson-Patman Act requiring the manufacturer to offer promotional allowances or services (including those for training) to retailers on a "proportionally equal" basis. More is said about this requirement later in the chapter.

In spite of the difficulties in developing training programs for retailers, the manufacturer must take the initiative when high-quality retail selling is vital to success. For example, an association of mink breeders developed a promotional program encompassing both national advertising and point-of-sale activity. Unfortunately, the point-of-sale efforts were handicapped by a shortage of trained fur sales personnel. Moreover, even the larger retailers lacked the ability to develop a training program for their salespeople. To overcome this problem, the association developed such a program to accomplish the following:

1. Make a retail sales force as competent in selling mink garments as they are in selling ordinary cloth garments.

2. Dispel doubts in the minds of sales personnel regarding the meaning and significance of the association label.

3. Remove the fear that surrounds the selling of fur garments.

4. Emphasize the association image of quality.

Nine stores agreed to participate in the first training session, which lasted three days and was held on the store premises. The association specialists conducted a class for the first 30 minutes of each day and then spent the rest of their time on the selling floor. The program was followed by the visit to each store by a "mystery shopper" who monitored sales procedures and offered suggestions for improvement.

In another situation, a manufacturer of fine English bone china distributed its line through 1,500 selected jewelry and department stores. Although serving a national market, the company sales volume could support only a relatively small appropriation of $400,000 for advertising and sales promotion. Research studies had shown that the retail salesperson was highly influential in the sale of china but were sadly lacking in product knowledge or awareness of the type of information consumers wanted from them. Moreover, retail sales personnel did not give the line much selling "push."

To improve the caliber of retail selling and to gain greater support for the product line, the manufacturer developed a program for training retail sales personnel. It consisted of a 20-minute sound film presented by manufacturer salespeople at meetings held for about 1,000 of their retail accounts. The

PROMOTION IN ACTION 21–2

Hyster Gets Closer to Its Dealer People

Management at Hyster, the $422 million manufacturer of lift trucks and materials-handling equipment, is claiming to be the first to introduce a computer-based training system to a large dealer network. Moreover, managers say that the system, which uses Control Data's PLATO programming, costs just 20 percent of what was previously spent on training. Control Data claims computer-based training costs $2 to $3 per "contact hour" compared to the $15 to $20 per hour plus per diem expenses that traditional methods may cost, a strong inducement to Hyster, whose 43 dealers employ some 3,000 people. Dave Hoehn, Hyster's sales training manager, says Hyster looked at computer-based training "because we wanted to communicate with those 3,000 in a more efficient, timely, and consistent manner."

Because Hyster wanted self-contained microcomputers at each dealer location, the two companies agreed that Hyster would, in effect, become a marketing representative for Control Data. Hyster sold the hardware (a Control Data CDC 110 microcomputer terminal, keyboard, disk drive, and RCA videotape system) to its dealers, offering attractive financing. The company rented the software: programs on selling skills, products, and parts and service training created by Hyster and a generic Control Data course—combining video and PLATO—on sales techniques.

Training Fills Idle Time Compared to the expense and time out of the dealership required to fly personnel to week-long seminars (when and if film discussed fine china in general and was well received by sales personnel. To maintain continued contact with retail salespeople, the company developed a monthly sales bulletin providing product information, selling tips, and information about sales contests and informing retail salespeople of the national consumer advertising program.

These two examples of efforts to train retail sales personnel show that such a program is vital to the success of the manufacturer's promotional program when the product is such that the buyer must seek information and advice about it from the salesperson. In addition, it is clear that very few retailers have the means or the volition to initiate training programs for the sale of specific types of goods. Thus the manufacturer must assume the responsibility and the cost of training retail personnel if it desires an improvement in the quality and quantity of retail support. Moreover, this assumption of responsibility must be continuous because of the high rate of turnover of retail employees.

Hyster Gets Closer to Its Dealer People (concluded)

❖
**PROMOTION
IN ACTION
21–2**

their schedules permitted), computer-based training is on-site and ready whenever the dealer has a spare hour, Hyster says. If he or she gets interrupted, the computer holds the place until he or she can continue. Hyster's new training system makes use of the idle time certain dealer employees inevitably have while it allows others whose jobs preclude long absences from the dealership to receive extensive training for the first time. Seminar attendants often have varying degrees of experience, so the class's progress may sometimes be slowed to accommodate a few less skilled individuals. Hoehn says that with computer-based training, each dealer employee works at his or her own pace.

Hyster's sales staff found it easy to switch from traditional communication methods such as manuals, slides, and films, to computers. The new system eliminates the cost of printing and duplicating as well as the frequent headaches of immediately recalling material from dealers and updating and redistributing it.

Perhaps most important to Hyster is that the new system records each user's progress on program diskettes that can be reviewed by dealer management at any time. For the first time, Hoehn says, each individual's performance is being closely tracked, as is the effectiveness of Hyster's training.

Source: *Sales & Marketing Management*, August 13, 1984, pp. 30–31. Used with permission.

Quotas for Resellers

The establishment of quotas, if properly planned and administered, is a device that can improve reseller performance. Although the use of quotas to measure the performance of salespeople is quite common in a vertically integrated organization, the application of this technique to independent wholesalers and retailers is somewhat limited. One authority points out that:

> . . . not all sellers set quotas for their resellers. This results from one or more causes: failure to recognize that there is an underlying need to measure performance; difficulty in setting accurate quotas, especially where sales results may be far removed in time from sales effort, as for instance is often the case with the sale of costly industrial machinery; or lastly a realization of the inability to take any action if the quotas are not consistently met, as would be the case with the manufacturer whose product line would be of little importance to a reseller.[4]

An interview with officials of a home appliance manufacturer disclosed that quotas were used to measure the relative performance of independent wholesale distributors against sales branches. In addition, quotas were set for each sales division within the territory. Of course, in this situation, the manufacturer was granting exclusive agencies and could exert considerable influence in requiring distributors to meet quotas. Persistent failure to make the quota could well mean loss of franchise.

In cases in which the manufacturer's line is less important to resellers, the manufacturer's ability to encourage resellers to meet their quotas is weakened correspondingly. Even if the manufacturer cannot force distributors to meet quotas, however, the use of quotas to provide information on sales potentials can be a means to improve reseller performance. For example, the Atkins Saw Division of Borg-Warner Corporation offers its distributors a free market analysis of distributor territory. The purpose of this service is to aid distributors in accurate measurement of their sales performance, to help distributors establish quotas for retail dealers, and to get the resellers to work for a larger share of the available business.

Advertising and Sales Promotion Assistance

In addition to training reseller sales personnel and setting quotas for resellers, manufacturers can attempt to improve reseller efforts by assisting wholesalers and retailers in planning and executing their advertising and sales promotion programs. Such assistance may take the form of (1) cooperative advertising programs, (2) promotional allowances, (3) merchandising the advertising, (4) in-store promotions, and (5) contests and incentive payments for sales personnel.

Cooperative Advertising A program under which a manufacturer pays a portion of the reseller's local advertising costs is commonly called *cooperative advertising* (see Figure 21–2). Usually the manufacturer shares the cost of local reseller advertising on a 50–50 basis up to a certain limit, often a percentage of reseller purchases from the manufacturer. If, for example, the agreement specified a 50–50 share up to 4 percent of purchases, a retailer who had purchased $2,500 worth of goods from the manufacturer would be able to spend $200 on advertising them and would receive a $100 rebate from the manufacturer. Thus the net cost to the retailer would be $100.

An advantage of cooperative advertising to the reseller, in addition to the partial defrayal of the local advertising expense, is that under most programs, the manufacturer furnishes a good assortment of advertising layouts and stereotype mats for reproduction in the local press.

There are also disadvantages for the reseller. First, there is a tendency to promote a line more than it deserves simply because the cost is being shared by the manufacturer. Moreover, the nature of the advertisements may stimulate selective demand for the manufacturer's brand without increasing the patronage appeal of the store.

From the manufacturer's point of view, a well-planned cooperative advertising program can be useful. First, it involves the reseller financially. The wholesaler or retailer lays some money on the line to promote a given item. Even though the manufacturer matches the sum expended, the reseller has made an investment in promotion, and to protect its investment the wise reseller will make sure of three things: (1) that the stock of the item on hand is sufficient to back up the ad; (2) that the item (or items) receives adequate display at point of purchase and, perhaps, in the window; and (3) that the item (or items) advertised receives in-store selling support from the sales personnel. If a manufacturer's cooperative advertising program can get resellers to follow through in this manner, it is probably worth the trouble and cost of its administration.

For a more detailed view of a cooperative advertising program, we can look at one sponsored by the Palm Beach Company, a manufacturer of men's and women's summer-weight suits. In one year, for example, Palm Beach spent about $1 million for printed media advertising, with 60 percent of the budget for company advertising and 40 percent, or $400,000, for cooperative advertising with retailers. The bulk of the company advertising (80 percent) was placed in newspapers, with the remainder going to magazines and to trade advertising.

The cooperative advertising plan paid 50 percent of a retailer's cost for newspaper space, radio and TV commercial time, and billboard and car card space. Dealers could spend up to 4 percent of the net wholesale price of merchandise shipped to them, and they would be reimbursed up to a maximum of 2 percent.

FIGURE 21–2

1989 Motorcraft Advertising. Tuned in. Turned on. And turning up everywhere.

We're turning up the volume on Motorcraft TV advertising. Watch for it…and look for more Motorcraft customers in your store.

We produced new commercials that have impact so that 43 million presold Ford, Lincoln and Mercury vehicle owners get the message.

We scheduled the commercials on national sports programs during the time of year your customers are most likely to buy automotive parts.

We placed over 100 Motorcraft ads in major magazines—the ones we know they enjoy reading.

Better yet, we made it easy for you to turn up your own volume, simply by joining in. Just use our co-op TV and your Motorcraft Ad Planner ad slicks. Mention price—get 100% of your ad bucks back.

Now that our advertising has turned it on, Motorcraft Quality Parts are definitely part of your customers' program. Which is even more Peace of Mind℠.. for '89!

For details on how our advertising can help you, contact your Motorcraft representative. Or call 1-800-521-4114. In Michigan 1-800-482-4102.

Over 100 ads in hardworking publications rack up prospects, fast.

Hard-hitting national TV spots channel ready-to-buy customers your way.

Remember. Use co-op dollars and cash in on Motorcraft advertising, free.

Motorcraft *Ford*

QUALITY PARTS FOR QUALITY CARS℠

Palm Beach required that the ads include proper product labels and descriptions and be devoted exclusively to the promotion of Palm Beach products.

The really interesting aspect of this program is the intensity with which the company promoted its cooperative program to the retail dealers. Strategy included the following:

1. A magazine-size booklet informing dealers of the Palm Beach line and promotional program for the coming year was mailed in the spring.

2. In addition, the retailer received a 17×25-inch cooperative advertising service book containing descriptive material, ad layouts, reproductions of available mats, and suggested radio scripts. Plates for four-color ads were also available at cost ($20 to $35) to retailers who wished to advertise in color.

3. The 50-person Palm Beach sales force devoted a major portion of its time talking to retailers about tying in their local promotion with the Palm Beach national campaign. The sales force also planned balanced promotional campaigns for retailers, including display, direct mail advertising, and newspaper advertising.

As a result of the program, Palm Beach reported that 65 percent of available cooperative advertising funds were used by retailers. Careful records were kept, and salespeople—as well as top executives—of the Palm Beach Company called on stores whose advertising usage was far below the potential permitted by their sales volume. Every attempt was made to convince those retailers to make full use of the cooperative advertising allowance.

The Palm Beach program illustrates a situation in which a high level of reseller support is vital in reaching the manufacturer's sales objectives. The manufacturer has placed a major emphasis on cooperative advertising to gain the reseller support required. Moreover, the program was carefully planned and coordinated with the national advertising campaign. To make certain that retailer participation in the program was as extensive as possible, the manufacturer engaged in considerable personal selling effort to get retailers to increase their advertising. Although there are these advantages to such a program, there also are real problems, which are discussed later.

Promotional Allowances   In situations in which retail promotion is crucial to manufacturer success, payments may be made for types of reseller support other than media advertising. Such promotional allowances or payments are very often used to gain display at retail. Display is of great importance when the product sold is purchased on impulse or is unable to attract any "push" from retailers because of its limited contribution to overall retail profits.

The case history of Whitehall Laboratories, a well-known manufacturer of proprietary drugs, is a good illustration of the way one company attempted to improve reseller support effort for its products through the use of

❖
**PROMOTION
IN ACTION
21–3**

Simplot Wizardry Zaps Snack Market

J. R. Simplot made sales magic and spawned a host of competitors with its MicroMagic line of microwaveable snack foods.

Last year, after overcoming slotting allowances, one dismal product launch, and well-funded competitors, Simplot secured national distribution for the entire MicroMagic line. It now claims No. 1 or No. 2 shares in each product category it has entered, an industry rule of thumb for a successful product.

Today, the Idaho-based potato processor faces a new set of hurdles: eager competitors, media clutter, and what the company calls "power retailers."

Simplot has discovered what other product marketers already know: The real trick isn't in the product itself but in getting it on supermarket shelves and keeping it there. In the $331 billion grocery-marketing industry, however, even the best-conceived and best-funded products aren't guaranteed more than a trial shot at impressing supermarket buyers and consumers.

Tricks of the Trade   One of a food marketer's toughest challenges is balancing two audiences: the retailer who puts a new product on the shelf and the consumer who keeps it there.

"Through 1988, our emphasis had been on building distribution and that meant primarily trade marketing. But as competition develops, if you're going to protect the business, you've got to shift to the consumer," says Blaine Jacobson, Simplot's retail marketing manager.

"If the trade sees that you'll up the ante with them, they'll go around the table for the lowest bid. We chose to respond by developing a consumer base," he says.

But you can't neglect either consumers or the trade. In one case you end up with no brand loyalty; in the other, you get no shelf space," Mr. Jacobson says. "You can't have one without the other."

Although Simplot launched MicroMagic with a single product and little retail food experience, the company has learned to play the grocery-marketing game and negotiates with retailers to get what it wants. "In entering a market, we ask to get slotted, and with all our products shelved together, and a 90-day support plan from each retailer," Mr. Jacobson says.

Simplot will pay a slotting allowance of one free case of product per store. "We have paid cash in some cases, but only what the one case is worth to us, or about $10 per store," he says. "You've got to hold tight, develop a good slotting policy and stick to it."

Source: Excerpted Julie Liesse Erickson "Simplot Wizardry Zaps Snack Market," *Advertising Age*, May 8, 1989, p. S–6. Used with permission.

promotional allowances.[5] The company's line includes many well-known health and beauty aids among which was the best selling pain reliever, Anacin. Whitehall spent several millions of dollars annually on national advertising. To supplement this heavy "pull" promotion, 100 salespersons called on retailers who carried health and beauty aids.

A research study had indicated that point-of-sale displays using about 2½ square feet of counter space were especially effective in increasing sales. The company embarked on a program to get as many retailers as possible to utilize the special display. The key to the program was an allowance to the retailer of 5 percent of its purchases if certain promotional activities were performed.

Whitehall faced two problems. First, competitors offered equivalent allowances (or in some cases, even higher allowances), and it was difficult to gain retailer support because of the tremendous demand for limited counter space. Second, most druggists took the 5 percent allowance, but not all followed through with the placement of the display. It was evident that some type of action was required to get drug retailers to participate in the display program and to make sure that they kept the display on the counter for as long as they were collecting the promotional allowance.

This case illustrates both the need of a manufacturer to gain display at retail and the difficulties faced in sustaining such support. The promotional allowance is one approach to gaining special retailer support, but to ensure its success, special payments have to be backed up by the manufacturer's sales force. The competition for retailer display or advertising tie-in as well as the general inertia of most retailers required, in most cases, more than a mere payment. On the other hand, "push" or the use of personal selling effort by the manufacturer without special payment will not be as effective as "push" with a payment for special effort at retail.

Merchandising the Advertising   Have you ever gone into a store and asked to see a product that had been advertised recently on TV or in a magazine only to have been rebuffed by a salesperson who appeared not to know what you were talking about? Unfortunately, this experience is all too common. To prevent its recurrence, most manufacturers take considerable care to "merchandise the advertising." This is a process in which the manufacturer attempts to involve retailers in the national ad campaign by making sure that they are aware of the campaign schedule and contents, and by having the manufacturer's sales force make sure that retailers are stocking and displaying the products being advertised. The manufacturer also provides retailers with in-store and window displays that tie in to the national campaign and arranges for special cooperative advertising or promotional allowances. The manufacturer provides product selling-point information to salespersons, and so forth. The goal is to create synergy in that the effect of the coordinated efforts of both the manufacturer and the retailer will be greater than if each party worked alone. If when you enter a store to see an advertised item and find that it is on display and that the salesperson is knowledgeable about its features, the advertising has been effectively "merchandised."

An approach to gain reseller support that does not use cooperative advertising or promotional allowances is shown in Figure 21–3. It is essentially a strategy in which the manufacturer attempts to create strong selective demand for the brand by means of a pull strategy using consumer advertising. The trade advertising that you see in this figure exhorts the retailer to merchandise the advertising with heavy in-store support to take full advantage of the manufacturer's efforts.

In-Store Promotions   Other types of manufacturer programs to improve reseller demand-stimulation efforts may be aimed at achieving limited objectives over a short period of time. An in-store promotion developed by a manufacturer of nickel (widely used in the manufacture of stainless steel) is a good example.

The sponsor believed that if demand for stainless steel consumer products could be increased, the derived demand for nickel would be stimulated. A program was planned around department stores because research had indicated that they were the most powerful influence on consumer buying habits in the major market areas. The objectives of the program were (1) to spotlight stainless steel in the large stores, (2) to generate sales enthusiasm among retail sales personnel, and (3) to increase demand for stainless steel products and thus the derived demand for nickel.

The promotion was timed for February and was first run with 32 participating stores. Four-color, two-page ads were inserted in two leading shelter magazines in addition to local newspaper ads featuring the name of the cooperating department store in each of 32 market cities. The stores ran 103 newspaper ads featuring stainless steel, and many devoted key window space to the display of stainless steel items. Several steel manufacturers supported the nickel producer's national advertising effort.

Retailer cooperation was gained by offering the campaign to each store on an exclusive basis in its area. Nominal cooperative advertising allowances were granted, and each retailer was provided with a complete promotional kit. Sales training sessions developed for retail personnel featured a nine-minute training film produced for this purpose.

The results were so favorable that the in-store promotion was continued for three more years. Modifications in the program were minor, but retailer and industry participation increased greatly in each succeeding year.

FIGURE 21–3

A Reseller-Oriented Sales Promotion Aimed at Merchandising the
Advertising of the Manufacturer

A similar type of effort on behalf of Hilton Hotels was the Hilton "Follow the Sun" campaign.[6] Tie-ins were made with airlines and with the leading retailers in 15 target areas. The campaign sought to relate the Hilton Hotels' vacation and honeymoon facilities to the bridal promotions of the retailers. The promotion was built around a contest in which registrants might win a free honeymoon in the Caribbean or Hawaii. The participating stores were given a format around which to develop their bridal promotions and also benefited from the store traffic generated by the chance to win a free honeymoon.

Regardless of the method used by the manufacturer, in-store promotion must offer the retailer a quid pro quo or it will not succeed. Few retailers will put themselves out to support a specific manufacturer unless doing so promises a reasonable payoff. (See Figure 21–4.) Although an in-store promotion does offer a retailer a profit potential worthy of its effort, it must still be carefully planned by the manufacturer, and the execution of the program must be guided through to the end if best results are to be obtained. Once a manufacturer has concluded a successful in-store promotion on a modest scale, it is easier to expand the number of participants the next time it is run. Retailers have an effective grapevine that informs them on how their counterparts in other markets did with a specific promotion.

Contests and Incentives   To stimulate or improve the selling effort at retail, manufacturers may devise contests or provide special incentives for retail sales personnel. A contest or incentive plan is generally a part of a larger program and is aimed at motivating salespeople to participate in the selling campaign with enthusiasm. In the bone china case, for example, communication with the salesperson was established through the monthly sales bulletins. Shortly after the bulletin was first issued, it was used to announce a monthly contest based on the theme, "How I Made a Bone China Sale." Prizes were awarded to salespeople who sent in the best letters each month. The grand prize was a trip to England. Retail salesperson participation in the contest, which served to focus attention on the overall promotional campaign aimed at gaining retailer support, was unusually high.

Contests or incentive payments developed by the manufacturer can get out of hand. If used too frequently, contests can cause the salesperson to be more concerned with a payoff for good sales performance than with the merits of the product line itself. Salespeople begin to sell items because *they*, rather than the customers, will profit most from the transaction. This attitude, which may give the manufacturer a temporary increase in volume, does not necessarily provide a lasting benefit unless the product itself is superior. Too many manufacturers use incentive payments and contests to push products that are inferior to those offered by competitors.

FIGURE 21–4

A Reseller-Oriented Sales Promotion Aimed at Gaining Use of In-Store Display

Moreover, contests and incentive payments for retail sales personnel may conflict with the desires and objectives of retail management. Some retailers refuse to allow their employees to participate in manufacturer-sponsored contests or to accept incentive payments from manufacturers because they want to maintain control over their own selling activities. For a manufacturer's program of contests or incentives to succeed, it must have the approval of retail management. The program should basically serve as an attention getter to interest salespeople in the product line and the overall promotional campaign. Finally, it should be viewed as a short-run effort to support the overall program, not as a long-run substitute for product attractiveness or utility.

Legal Problems and Other Issues   The manufacturer's use of cooperative advertising programs, promotional allowances, and other forms of assistance is not without its problems. Especially serious are restrictions imposed by law. Sections 2d and 2e of the Robinson-Patman Act have perhaps the most relevance to promotional allowances and services as granted by sellers to resellers.[7]

These sections of the act define, in rather loose terms, the conditions under which nondiscriminatory payments or services can be made to members of a reseller group. Such payments or services are legal if they are granted on a "proportionally equal" basis. That is, their dollar value must be in proportion to the size of the reseller's purchases from the seller. For example, a reseller buying $10,000 worth of goods a year from a manufacturer is entitled to 10 times the value of payments or services (received from the manufacturer) as the reseller whose purchases totaled only $1,000.

Moreover, the seller's program must allow participation by all interested resellers. The nature of the seller's promotional strategy must not exclude competing resellers on the basis of size, geographical location, or other characteristics.

Revised guidelines issued in 1969 required among other things that (1) all competing customers, whether wholesalers or retailers, must be informed of the availability of a co-op plan; (2) the plan must be "functionally available" to all competing resellers on proportionally equal terms and must include more than one way for resellers to participate; and (3) the advertising media cannot quote higher rates than are actually charged to allow customers to claim greater payments than they are entitled to under the co-op plan.

New Guidelines Proposed   The Federal Trade Commission is expected to release new guidelines that revise the 20-year-old rules governing the use of promotional allowances including cooperative advertising. The new rules would make it less risky for a manufacturer to refuse to grant co-op ad allowances to a discount reseller who upsets the manufacturer's pattern of distribution. Another change expected by the FTC deals with the concept of *proportionately equal.* In the past, this meant that differences in allowances granted to competing resellers had to be proportionately equal to the dollar volume of purchases by the resellers. That is, if one reseller bought $1,000 worth of goods from the manufacturer and another bought $500 worth of goods, the first reseller could receive promotional support from the manufacturer that cost twice as much as that granted the second reseller. Under the new rules, a new concept, *value to seller,* would modify the proportional rule. This would mean that a reseller offering exceptional opportunity for promotion or for market entry would be allowed to receive value-based promotional allowances that exceeded those allowed under the former cost-based proportionally equal rule.

These changes [which, as of the date of this writing, have not yet been formalized], will cause a great deal of debate and could lead to new tests of the Robinson-Patman Act itself.[8]

SUPPLEMENTING RESELLER PERFORMANCE

In those situations in which *improving* the quality or quantity of reseller performance of selling activity does not succeed in reaching manufacturer promotional objectives, more direct action must be taken to *supplement* reseller effort. The manufacturer must assume some of the responsibility for selling and sales promotion at wholesale and retail levels. The utilization of missionary salespeople is one method of gaining greater activity at reseller levels in the channel of distribution. Provision of selling aids and price incentives are other methods.

Missionary (Specialty) Selling

The use of manufacturer salespeople to supplement the personal selling activities of resellers is known as *missionary* or *specialty selling.* In the sale of consumer goods, missionary salespeople are employed by manufacturers to contact both wholesalers and retailers. They check wholesalers periodically to determine if they have adequate stock. They call on retailers to inform them of new products, to arrange window and in-store displays, to provide advice on selling, to answer questions posed by the retailer and, in general, to build goodwill. If they take orders for merchandise, they usually turn such orders over to wholesalers for filling.

In the sale of industrial goods, missionary salespeople train distributor salespeople, demonstrate effective selling techniques by accompanying distributor salespeople on their calls, secure introductory orders from users, and assist distributor salespeople in closing those sales that demand greater technical knowledge or selling skill than the distributor salesperson has.

On the other hand, the use of missionary salespeople is probably not wise when other elements of the promotional program are weak. Missionary selling is an expensive undertaking for any manufacturer, and its use to cover up deficiencies in the product or in the distribution, pricing, or promotion strategies can be an unnecessary financial burden. In addition, excessive dependency on missionary selling can generate wholesaler resentment. When missionaries assume tasks such as routine order taking or delivery that could be performed by wholesaler salespersons, the wholesaler may believe that it is just a short step to his or her total circumvention. Even if circumvention is not the issue, wholesalers may resent the missionary salespeople infringing on the time of their sales force and preventing the most effective allocation of their salespeople's time.

There is little doubt that the correct use of missionary or specialty selling can improve or supplement reseller selling efforts. The problems that arise with their use, however, are often caused by using missionaries to *supplant reseller efforts where supplementation would suffice,* or by poor management of the missionary selling effort. The net result of improper use of missionary selling, regardless of its cause, can be less reseller promotional support rather than more.

Display and Selling Aids

Manufacturers' provision of display material for point-of-purchase use, mailing pieces for reseller distribution, dealer identification signs, and similar incentives are other ways to supplement reseller efforts. A manufacturer uses these promotional devices to stimulate demand for the product and to get an increased share of the dealer's promotional effort placed at the manufacturer's disposal.

The manufacturer usually has great difficulty, however, in getting resellers to utilize these display materials and selling aids. Based on the volume of material distributed to resellers, it appears that manufacturer response to nonuse of material is to double the quantity made available. Because resellers often do not know what to do with this great flood of material, it is not uncommon to find much of it in the refuse box in unopened cartons.

Several approaches are available to the manufacturer who requires some degree of product display or other cooperation from retailers. The payment of promotional allowances for display, the use of the sales force to obtain display and in-store promotion, and the practice of charging resellers a total payment for materials may help gain better point-of-sale display or selling effort.

Perhaps the most effective approach is that of pretesting dealer aids. An executive of General Foods reported the following:

> We made several field surveys . . . on the use to which our point-of-sale material was being put, and we reached some disappointing conclusions. We learned, for example, that on several campaigns last year, only half the material shipped out to the field was being used effectively. . . . It had not been checked with the field to predetermine its acceptance. We now have a continuous program . . . for periodic surveys of the grocery stores regularly contacted by our salesmen. . . . This system afforded us an accurate picture of the types and amounts of material which could best be used in these stores. . . . We are convinced that it is a waste of time, effort, and money to send point-of-purchase material to the field if we cannot demonstrate how it will work for the benefit of the store operator.[9]

Compaq Struggles to Fend off Big Blue

❖
**PROMOTION
IN ACTION
21–4**

In the past, IBM would bully its dealers into pushing sales of its machines. Compaq, with its reputation as the BMW of PCs, had to treat its outlets with greater respect. But now, Big Blue has dulled Compaq's marketing edge by cutting prices and becoming more generous.

Retailers who used to deal with IBM by phone now have field representatives nearby. IBM's direct sales force, with its knowledge of big companies' computer needs, now passes on customer leads. And IBM recently copied Compaq's lucrative incentive program, which last year gave dealers access to a pool of more than $65 million to buy advertising, hire technicians, and attend seminars.

IBM's moves sparked a clamorous divorce between Compaq and its second-ranking dealer, Businessland Inc., after the San Jose, California, retailer began paying some of its salespeople 5 to 10 times more commission for selling IBM machines rather than Compaqs. "A Businessland salesperson could not afford to eat by selling Compaq's products," grumbles Michael Swavely, Compaq's vice president for sales and marketing.

Compaq, which relies totally on dealers for sales, doggedly refused to extend a sweeter deal to one dealer than another. In February, Mr. Canion, CEO of Compaq, told Businessland that Compaq was yanking its machines off the retailer's shelves. It was a costly move for both: Businessland sold about $145 million of Compaq machines in 1988.

Source: Excerpted from Karen Blumenthal and Robert Tomsho, "An IBM Tagalong Sets Independent Course with Plenty of Risks," *The Wall Street Journal*, April 21, 1989, pp. 1, A7. Used by permission.

The Whitehall case noted earlier illustrates the difficulties of using promotional allowances to gain point-of-sale display. Because research had indicated that a new type of display increased sales as much as 150 percent in those stores where it was used for a 60-day period, Whitehall developed a bonus plan for its salespeople. This plan could result in a salary increase of as much as one-third for those salespeople who were able to get the stores in their territories to utilize the new point-of-sale displays. The extent of the payment to salespeople indicates the value of display to the company. This situation is of special interest because Whitehall was spending over $5 million annually, or 20 percent of sales, on national advertising. It appears, therefore, that even with extensive "pull," point-of-sale display is an important element of strategy.

Consumer Deals

When the manufacturer wishes to blend price promotion into its promotional mix to increase sales at retail, it may offer the buyer a temporary price reduction. Such reductions are known as *consumer deals* or, more explicitly, *price deals*. They differ from deals to the trade in that consumer deals attempt to create "pull," while trade incentives are aimed at getting reseller "push." Regardless of the target, a price deal is an attempt to exploit price sensitivity of demand. A study of the Chicago market provided the following information about price deals:

1. Off-season price reductions seem to be more profitable than in-season price reductions.

2. A high frequency of price promotions tends to make consumers overly price conscious.

3. Deals do not seem to be a good way to counter new brands offered by competitors, and they are not necessarily more effective if accompanied by product or package innovations.

4. Price dealing is more effective for new brands than for established ones, and it is almost always more effective if kept in proper balance with advertising.

5. No brand—even a well-established, nondealing, luxury brand—is invulnerable to price-deal competition if it has basic marketing problems, and price-deal promotion is never a cure for marketing problems.

6. When special promotional campaigns fall short of expectations, the manufacturer will do better to question its own planning and policy making than to blame the failure on "intractable" retailers.[10]

The last point above has special relevance to the stimulation of reseller performance because the use of price deals to buyers may hinder rather than help reseller cooperation. Poor scheduling, inadequate trade incentives, excessive frequency of deals, and the like may cause wholesalers and retailers to rebel. Interviews with several retailers indicated, for example, that the pressure on grocery retailers to shift inventories back to the manufacturers has been increased in part by the extra confusion and expense caused by a multiplication of deal merchandise.[11]

CONTROLLING RESELLER PERFORMANCE

The control of reseller promotional performance is considerably more difficult for the manufacturer than is control of its own sales force. First, the chain of command that exists in an integrated organization is replaced with a relatively unstructured network of communication connecting the manufacturer with independent intermediaries. Through this network flows a series of suggestions and persuasion rather than commands. (Of course, the greater the selective demand for the products of a given manufacturer, the greater the weight the suggestions will carry with resellers.) Second, resellers are both geographically dispersed and operationally diverse. No two wholesalers (or retailers) are really alike because each serves the market in a unique manner in terms of location, assortments carried, and demand-stimulation mix used. The manufacturer's loss of direct authority due to passing the title of goods sold to the resellers plus reseller dispersion and diversity makes manufacturer control of reseller activities a most difficult undertaking under ordinary circumstances.

The degree of control over reseller performance that manufacturers can exert reflects the importance of the manufacturer's line to the individual wholesaler or retailer. When the manufacturer engages in highly selective or exclusive agency distribution and has limited market coverage to make its line more important to its selected resellers, some degree of control over these resellers may be expected.

Adapting to the New Environment

When a manufacturer requires the broad market coverage and strong promotional efforts offered by mass merchandisers, selectivity of distribution is not a feasible way to gain influence in the channel. This leaves the other alternative: Make the line as important as possible by developing a strong consumer franchise.

Recent evidence supports the view that the most effective way for manufacturers to resist the demands of mass market resellers for "slotting allowances" and other "excessive" promotional payments is to build a strong selective demand for their brands through product quality and consumer promotion. Campbell Soup, for example, has a long-standing policy of not paying for slotting or shelf space.

Campbell Soup's director of promotion stated, "We use good marketing programs to show why customers should stock our products, regardless of the size of the category or our position in it," he says. "We try to show that we are not flooding the market with products arbitrarily, and we do consumer research and product testing to back that up."[12]

CPC International, whose product line includes such strong brands as Skippy peanut butter and Mazola oil, has also turned down requests for payment.[13]

In other cases in which the will to resist is lacking or the brand franchise is weaker, manufacturers are trying to work out a compromise with their retail distributors. At the Pillsbury Company, the vice president of marketing reported that company strategy is to work with retailers to gain access to stores' scanning data. By analyzing space allocations and pricing points, Pillsbury can help retailers merchandise categories and increase profit per linear foot in a category. By doing so, Pillsbury gains leverage over how retailers stock and allocate their shelf space.[14]

To aid manufacturers and retailers in this type of analysis, computer shelf-management programs are becoming available. Apollo Space Management Systems and Space Man are two examples of such programs. Although such systems are helpful in the short run, practices that will eventually increase manufacturer channel influence are improving product quality noticeably, reducing the frequency of price promotions, and communicating the selling points of the brands more effectively to the consumer.

Selected Resellers

A *control process* consists of formulating standards of performance, measuring performance, comparing actual results with the standards, and then taking action to correct substandard performances. If resellers are selected wholesalers or retailers for the line of a given manufacturer, the basis for control may be in the franchise agreement. In situations in which the manufacturer's franchise is extremely valuable (as in the sale of automobiles), the reseller may contract to supply data on sales volume, inventory levels, and general operating expenses. Such information may be used by the manufacturer to measure reseller performance against a variety of standards. Commonly used criteria include share of market, sales growth over time, and reaching goals or quotas. In addition, attention may be given to size of sales force, expenditures of advertising and sales promotion, and similar items.

Once arrangements have been made to monitor the reseller's performance in a quantitative sense (hopefully within the franchise agreement), attention can be paid to the qualitative nature of reseller performance. This aspect of reseller control does not usually require a contractual arrangement. A perceptive manufacturer's salesperson can report on how resellers are using promotional materials furnished by the manufacturer and whether resellers have effective training programs for their sales personnel. Moreover, the manufacturer or an independent agency, such as the Advertising Checking Bureau, can audit the reseller's media advertising for control of cooperative advertising payments or to measure the support being given to the manufacturer's line. Similar checking may measure reseller activity in setting up point-of-sale display or in sponsoring demonstrations or special selling events.

Nonselected Resellers

When broad distribution through many resellers is required, the manufacturer's problem of control is intensified. There is a limit to what the manufacturer may expect from any one reseller in terms of furnishing data or following a specific recommendation to improve performance. Measurement and control of reseller performance becomes less concerned with individual reseller performance and concentrates instead on the group performance of its resellers.

The manufacturer may attempt to classify the many resellers carrying its line by type of institution, location, size, ownership, and other criteria. Then a distribution cost analysis may be made to show the relative profitability to the manufacturer of different groups of resellers. One such study, made by a manufacturer of major electrical appliances, indicated the relative profitability of sales made through diverse channels of distribution and retail outlets. Thus, given a situation in which many resellers are used, measurement of reseller performance may help the manufacturer control *its utilization of specific groups of resellers* rather than the performance of individual resellers.

Some devices for the measurement and control of selected resellers can also be used with broad, intensive distribution. For example, manufacturer's salespeople may arrange for retailer use of point-of-sale displays and then check back to see if displays have been properly placed. Such a program was seen in the case of Whitehall.

Manufacturers may also take elaborate steps to check on cooperative advertising efforts of resellers. Members of a special department or outside agencies can be used to supplement internal efforts.

Knowledge of the levels of reseller inventories is vital to many manufacturers who engage in intensive distribution through many resellers. Unable to use their salespeople to take shelf and storeroom counts of goods, the manufacturer may avail itself of the services of an independent research agency to collect data on how rapidly products are moving off the retailer's shelves.[15] Without such information, the manufacturer might mistake an inventory accumulation by resellers for steady or rising consumer demand for the line.

Vertical Integration

Because of the limits on the control that manufacturers can exert over independent intermediaries, many producers have chosen to vertically integrate their channels of distribution through ownership of either all or part of the channel intermediaries. Through ownership, the manufacturer gains maximum control over the manner in which its goods are physically distributed and promoted in all of the channel stages.

Vertical integration by means of ownership can be a very expensive undertaking. Not only are the capital commitments enormous, but also unless the producer's product line is broad and sales volume is high, unit distribution costs will generally be greater in this arrangement than with traditional channels. For those firms engaging in vertical integration by means of ownership, the higher costs of physical distribution are accepted as a trade-off against the higher levels of promotional activity and customer service that can be provided by closely controlled resellers. Firms such as Sherwin-Williams (paints), Hart, Schaffner and Marx (men's clothing), Goodyear (tires), and Florsheim (shoes), among others, have found that vertical integration has been an effective channel strategy.

Distribution Programming

The vast majority of firms that do not have the economic capability to own their own resellers find themselves in an increasingly severe competitive struggle with their more integrated rivals. To counteract the advantages associated with vertical integration and to avoid having to make the needed financial commitments, many of these firms are adopting a strategy of "distribution programming" in which an integrated marketing system is developed by contractual agreements between a manufacturer and members of the reseller organization.[16]

The development of a planned, professionally managed distribution system utilizing independent resellers enables manufacturers to increase the effectiveness and efficiency of their distribution activities. *Distribution programming* has been defined as the development of a comprehensive set of policies for the promotion of a product through the channel. These policies are formulated by a joint effort between the manufacturer and the individual reseller in an attempt to negotiate a relationship giving both parties some of the advantages of vertical integration without the need for the manufacturer to purchase resellers.

Planned vertical marketing systems are rapidly displacing conventional marketing channels as the dominant mode of distribution in the U.S. economy. Planned systems are taking over because they avoid the loose relationships, autonomous behavior, and diseconomies associated with traditional channels of distribution. In addition, they do not require the capital investments associated with ownership systems. Yet these planned systems, being professionally managed and centrally programmed networks, preengineered to achieve operating economies and maximum market impact, can compete effectively with systems that are vertically integrated through partial or complete ownership of channel intermediaries.

TABLE 21–1

A Frame of Reference for Distribution Programming

Manufacturer's Marketing Goals	Retailer's Requirements

Based on a careful analysis of:
  Corporate capability
  Competition
  Demand
  Cost-volume relationships
  Legal considerations
  Reseller capability
  and stated in terms of:
    Sales (dollars and units)
    Market share
    Contribution to overhead
    Rate of return on investment
    Customer attitude, preference, and "readiness-to-buy" indices
	"Compensation" expected for required support (stated in terms of):
	  Managerial aspirations
	  Trade preferences
	  Financial goals
	    Rate of inventory turnover
	    Rate of return on investment
	    Gross margin (dollars and percent)
	    Contributions to overhead (dollars and percent)
	    Gross margin and contribution to overhead per dollar invested in inventory
	    Gross margin and contribution to overhead per unit of space
	    Nonfinancial goals

Manufacturer's Channel Requirements	**Distribution Policies**

Reseller support needed to achieve marketing goals (stated in terms of):
  Coverage ratio
  Amount and location of display space
  Level and composition of inventory investment
  Service capability and standards
  Advertising, sales promotion, and personal selling support
  Market development activities
	Price concessions
	  Financial assistance
	  Protective provisions

Source: From *Vertical Marketing Systems*, edited by Louis P. Bucklin. Copyright © 1970 by Scott, Foresman and Company. Reprinted by permission of the publisher.

Formulating a Strategy   The first step in formulating a strategy of distribution programming is careful analysis of marketing goals and requirements of the manufacturer and the needs of retail (and wholesale) resellers. These goals and requirements are outlined in Table 21–1. Note that they can be stated in quantitative terms, thus eliminating the danger of misunderstanding during subsequent negotiations between a manufacturer and individual resellers.

TABLE 21–2

❖   **Outline of a Programmed Merchandising Agreement**

1. Merchandising Goals
   a. Planned sales
   b. Planned initial markup percentage
   c. Planned reductions, including planned markdowns, shortages, and discounts
   d. Planned gross margin
   e. Planned expense ratio (optional)
   f. Planned profit margin (optional)

2. Inventory Plan
   a. Planned rate of inventory turnover
   b. Planned merchandise assortments, including basic or model stock plans
   c. Formalized "never out" lists
   d. Desired mix of promotional versus regular merchandise

3. Merchandise Presentation Plan
   a. Recommended store fixtures
   b. Space allocation plan
   c. Visual merchandising plan
   d. Needed promotional materials, including point-of-purchase displays, consumer literature, and price signs

4. Personal Selling Plan
   a. Recommended sales presentations
   b. Sales training plan
   c. Special incentive arrangements, including "spiffs," salesmen's contests, and related activities

5. Advertising and Sales Promotion Plan
   a. Advertising and sales promotion budget
   b. Media schedule
   c. Copy themes for major campaigns and promotions
   d. Special sales events

6. Responsibilities and Due Dates
   a. Supplier's responsibilities in connection with the plan
   b. Retailer's responsibilities in connection with the plan

Source: From *Vertical Marketing Systems,* edited by Louis P. Bucklin. Copyright © 1970 by Scott, Foresman and Company. Reprinted by permission of the publisher.

After the completion of the analysis, specific distribution policies can be formulated. Although quite numerous, the policy alternatives generally fall into three major categories: (1) those that offer "price" concessions to resellers, (2) those that provide financial assistance to them, and (3) those that provide some form of protection for resellers.

Using the mix of distribution policy alternatives available, and based on the prior analysis of goals and requirements, a programmed merchandise agreement must be developed for each type of outlet used in the pattern of distribution. This agreement, the result of joint deliberation between the manufacturer and a reseller, is essentially a comprehensive plan to distribute and promote the producer's product line for a period of six months or longer. An outline of such an agreement is to be found in Table 21–2. Its completeness is of special interest.

Subsidiary Plans After a clear delineation of quantitatively measurable goals, the agreement focuses on plans for inventory requirements, merchandise presentation, personal selling, and advertising and sales promotion. Finally, the responsibilities of both parties are enumerated, together with a schedule of dates on which certain performances are due.

Programmed merchandising agreements are fairly widespread in the following product categories: garden supplies, major appliances, traffic appliances, bedding, sportswear, cosmetics, and housewares. Manufacturers that use programmed merchandising include General Electric (on major and traffic appliances), Baumritter (on its line of Ethan Allen Furniture in nonfranchised outlets), Sealy (on its Posturepedic line of mattresses), Scott (on its lawn-care products), and Villager (on its dress and sportswear lines).

SUMMARY

Manufacturers' policies developed from diverse marketing strategies influence the role of resellers in the overall promotional program. Since personal selling activities make up the largest portion of promotional activity at wholesale and retail levels (with the exception of self-service stores), the maximum use of reseller potential can be made when the manufacturer emphasizes a push strategy. Regardless of the selling activity expected, if the *quality* of the selling performance by wholesalers and retailers is less than is desired by the manufacturer, the manufacturer may lend assistance to *improve* reseller performance.

Training programs for reseller salespersons seem to be one effective way in which manufacturers can upgrade the wholesaler personal selling effort. Such assistance is especially desirable when the product sold requires demonstration, installation, or a high degree of technical competence on the part of the reseller salesperson. Training is not recommended in cases in which the volume potential of the manufacturer's line is small in relation to the costs involved in setting up a suitable program.

Providing market information beyond what the reseller unit can gather for itself seems to help it allocate its selling efforts more effectively. Such information can point out where sales opportunities are not being exploited and how the reseller's performance measures up against that of other members of the reseller organization.

If the *quantity* of reseller effort is less than is deemed necessary to achieve manufacturer objectives, assistance may be provided in the form of missionary salespeople. These manufacturer efforts have as their objective the *supplementation* of reseller activity. When carefully supervised, such assistance can greatly increase the extent of sales effort aimed at wholesaler customers.

Under appropriate conditions, cooperative advertising programs are a very effective form of advertising assistance. They are especially helpful when, as with selected distribution, it is necessary to identify local retail sources of supply. Further, by getting distributors to invest their own funds in the local promotion of the manufacturer's brand, cooperative advertising programs may predispose resellers to carry better assortments of stock and to push the products advertised.

Manufacturer contributions that help resellers to do a better selling job themselves or encourage reseller promotion, such as display material or special deals, must be carefully integrated into the overall strategy, with special attention being paid to making these aids or deals fit the requirements of the *resellers.*

The manufacturer must be careful not to attempt to supplement wholesaler performance when efforts to improve it would suffice. Otherwise, the manufacturer will incur unnecessarily large promotional costs. Conversely, if additional selling effort is needed at the wholesale or retail level, manufacturer programs to improve the quality of current reseller performance will probably not fill the gap.

Manufacturer efforts to supplement or improve reseller performance may grow to take over functions typically considered to be reseller functions. Such shifting should not be permitted by the manufacturer unless analysis and experimentation indicate that efforts to supplement or improve reseller performance will not do the job. The manufacturer's assumption of tasks historically performed by wholesalers and retailers may suggest that it is considering their ultimate circumvention. The reseller who harbors such a suspicion is not likely to offer its selling support willingly.

The control of promotional activities by the manufacturer is much easier when control is under the manufacturer's direct supervision. The same is true with manufacturer control of the sales force. Control becomes more difficult when the effort is that of independent intermediaries who have purchased the manufacturer's product line for resale. Regardless of the degree of difficulty involved, the control process in either case is identical and consists of setting standards, measuring performance in light of these standards, and taking corrective action when actual performance is substandard.

The extent of control over resellers is a function of the importance of the manufacturer's line to them. Thus efforts to create selective demand through advertising or to reduce intrachannel rivalry by means of selective distribution should result in heightened manufacturer ability to control reseller efforts. If resellers are uncooperative for one reason or another, the manufacturer may use independent specialists to check on their performance. The manufacturer can always control its own channel strategy by careful selection of resellers, even if it cannot control their individual performance.

If a level of control is needed beyond that which can be expected from independent channel intermediaries, the manufacturer may engage in partial or complete ownership of its resellers. Because of the long-term financial commitments associated with vertical integration through ownership, an increasingly utilized alternative is vertical marketing integration by means of contractual relationships between manufacturers and individual resellers. The resulting distribution system provides many of the advantages of a system owned by the manufacturer without requiring a heavy investment in ownership. It also preserves the independence of the intermediary and allows the intermediary to provide the distributive economies that result from carrying the lines of several manufacturing sources.

REVIEW AND DISCUSSION QUESTIONS

1. As a manufacturer of high-speed cutting tools that are sold to the auto industry, you are very dissatisfied with the amount of promotional support that you are getting from your industrial distributors. Why might it be a mistake to place all of the blame on the distributors for the lack of support? What should your first step be in trying to rectify this lack of promotional effort on the part of your distributors?

2. The Johnson Company manufactures car telephones. When the product first came into being, Johnson set up a group of exclusive dealers in 30 key territories. These dealers received generous margins and were expected to engage in a great deal of "push" effort at the retail level. Recently, Johnson has noticed that similar products are showing up in a variety of outlets including discount houses and are being heavily advertised at a price much lower than that of its product. What is going on here? Is this normal? What should Johnson do?

3. ABC Food Products is trying to get distribution through the leading supermarket chains for its new frozen dessert, Koolcake. Formerly a new product

introduction required some free goods and special promotional allowances. Now ABC has been asked by one chain for an up-front payment of $2,500 per store for handling the new product. What is happening? Can ABC do anything to gain distribution without paying the "slotting allowance"?

4. Radio Ham, a manufacturer of amateur radio transmitting equipment, is complaining that the salespeople at the retail level do not know how to sell its products. It insists that the retailers train their personnel better. The retailers are telling Radio Ham that they have 200 other manufacturers to worry about and that Radio Ham will just have to do the best it can with what the retailers offer.

   Suggest a course of action for Radio Ham that might help ameliorate the problem. Why does the responsibility to take the initiative fall largely on Radio Ham in such a situation?

5. Imagine that you are a consultant to the Nadir Radio and TV Company, which manufactures radios and TV sets for sale to the public through a network of selected dealers. Nadir has been dissatisfied with the support it receives from its dealers. You are recommending increased use of cooperative advertising as a means to improve the extent and quality of reseller promotion. Explain how co-op advertising can be helpful to Nadir.

6. Your boss has asked for your opinion as to increasing control over retail distribution and promotion by means of distribution programming. How would you explain distribution programming and what would you tell the boss about the pros and cons of its implementation?

NOTES

1. Martin R. Warshaw, C. Merle Crawford, and Robert M. Tank, "Resolving Channel Conflicts in the Office Furniture Industry," *Business Marketing* 70 (March 1985), pp. 106–16.

2. Carl C. Gauk, "Training the Distributor's Salesmen," *Development of Dealer and Distributor Cooperation for Greater Sales*, Marketing Series no. 80 (New York: American Management Association), p. 4.

3. E. F. Higgins and J. F. Forgarty, Jr., *Training Dealers*, Studies in Business Policy no. 48 (New York: The Conference Board) p. 4.

4. Harry L. Hansen, *Marketing: Text and Cases*, 4th ed. (Homewood, Ill.: Richard D. Irwin, 1977), p. 475.

5. Ibid., pp. 615–17.

6. Described in personal correspondence with one of the authors.

7. Public Law no. 92, 74th Cong., H.R. 8442, June 19, 1936.

8. Isadore Barmash, "FTC Plans Rule Change on Co-op Ads," *New York Times*, February 21, 1989, p. D13.

9. W. P. Lillard, "Point-of-Purchase Promotion," *Proceedings, 6th Annual Advertising and Sales Promotion Conference,* Ohio State University Publications, College of Commerce Conference Series No. C–65, pp. 55–57.

10. Charles L. Hinkle, "The Strategy of Price Deals," *Harvard Business Review* 43 (July-August 1965), pp. 75–85.

11. Ibid., p. 82.

12. Rebecca Fannin, "Bring a Bag of Money," *Marketing & Media Decisions,* 22 (June 1987), pp. 38–45.

13. Ibid., p. 45.

14. Ibid.

15. The A. C. Nielsen Company's retail store audit is the best known of these approaches.

16. This section is based on an excellent article by Bert McCammon, Jr., "Perspectives for Distribution Programming," in *Vertical Marketing Systems,* ed. Louis P. Bucklin (Glenview, Ill.: Scott, Foresman, 1970), pp. 32–50.

Direct Marketing

UP TO THE CHIN IN CATALOGS

Lynn Rhatigan is the queen of catalog junkies. All her clothes, lingerie, shoes, furniture, books, videos, and cameras come from catalogs. So do her doorknobs, hair dryers, chandeliers, and videocassettes. Thanks to computer mailing lists, a shopper who buys just a few items from one or two catalogs is inundated with dozens more, from catalogs from reliable standbys to those that sell everything from evening wear for pets to musical lingerie.

It all started with couch-potato consumerism. The tremendous increase in the number of working women in the last 20 years expanded household incomes but cut shopping time. That led to a bonanza for such retailers as L. L. Bean, Lands' End, and homeware giant Wiliams-Sonoma. Their success, in turn, attracted a flood of imitators. Mail carriers say they sometimes have to make two trips a day to deliver mail to some people because they get so many catalogs.

Which catalogs will still be in mailboxes five years from now? "The companies who have product knowledge and treat the customers like kings," says Terry C. Gillette, founder of The Company Store catalog. Those that stay in the race should continue to see sales grow at twice the rate of store retailers.

Yet by then, home-shopping junkies won't be buying just from catalogs. Brownstone Studio is already experimenting with "video catalogs." And a number of on-line information services now offer a shop-by-computer feature. Mail carriers, your ordeal isn't over. Once the catalog crisis is under control, it will be time to start delivering those shop-at-home videos and software packages.

Source: Annetta Miller (with Lourdes Rosado), " 'Up to the Chin' in Catalogs," *Newsweek*, November 20, 1989, pp. 57–58. Reproduced by special permission.

What you have just read illustrates the growing importance of direct marketing—"an interactive system of marketing which uses one or more advertising media to effect a measurable response and/or transaction at any location."[1] Its most important tool is the *consumer database,* the all-important list of buyers and prospects who receive precisely targeted appeals.

For reasons to be made clear later, growing numbers of consumers prefer in-home shopping and buying. Therefore, direct marketing is increasingly used to bypass the retail shopping outlet. But it is also used as a valuable complement to more traditional channels because it enables the marketer to segment precisely and to reach consumers in multiple buying contexts. In this chapter, you will see how direct marketing, once considered to be a minor tactic, has emerged as one of the most valued promotional strategies.

A GROWTH INDUSTRY

The following are the bottom-line features that make direct marketing unique:[2]

1. *It goes directly to an identified person or household.* It does not go to a general audience as does most media advertising.

2. *The goal is some type of action.* That action can take the form of replying by return mail, sending a coupon, making a telephone call, and so on.

3. *Because the goal is specific action, results can be measured with precision.*

4. *It is interactive.* It involves a direct exchange of information and response between two parties.

5. *It makes use of a customer database.* A computerized record is kept of each customer's background, purchase patterns, interests, and so on. This provides an excellent source for targeting future marketing efforts with precision. As Tom Peters put it: "Database, database, database: it's where the marketing/customer-relations action is—and the money."[3]

Yearly in-home sales generated by direct marketing are estimated to be well in excess of $200 billion in the United States[4] and are growing rapidly elsewhere in the world.[5] The magnitude of direct marketing is further underscored by the fact that the estimated total expenditure on all direct response media in the United States equals two-thirds of all advertising, direct and nondirect.[6]

Furthermore, direct marketing is also used to raise funds for all sorts of nonprofit organizations. Almost $42 billion was raised in this way in 1988.[7]

Direct mail and telemarketing are the leading methods, each accounting for more than 40 percent of total expenditures, with the remainder being accounted for by interactive video and other methods.[8]

Many factors have contributed to the rapid growth of in-home buying:

1. Changing lifestyles resulting from the increased number of working wives, the greater attention to leisure, and the demand for more shopping convenience and service.

2. Growing distaste for shopping in overcrowded stores and malls — congested parking lots, uninformed salespeople, long lines, and so on. Promotion in Action 22–1 will give you a feeling for why so many shoppers are staying home.

3. The availability of credit cards.

4. Greater discretionary income resulting in higher service and product expectations.

Before proceeding further, we must state a fundamental principle: *Direct marketing usually achieves the greatest results when consumers are in the later stages of their decision process.* The primary intent is to elicit a buying (or giving) response, and effectiveness is measured in terms of return on investment (ROI). Every direct marketing effort is measured against this demanding criterion. This means that direct marketing ordinarily has not been used when the primary objective is to build awareness, change beliefs, and change attitudes. This premise is being rethought, however.[9] Consider these words by industry executive Malcolm Karlin:

> Getting results is important, but what you have to do is to be true to your product and brand. "Safe" techniques traditionally employed by direct marketers . . . diminish brand respect over the long haul.[10]

Some firms such as Xerox Corporation are gauging shifts in consumer attitudes toward products before and after direct mail to evaluate changes in consumer perceptions.[11] If this becomes a trend, the role for direct marketing will broaden.

THE DATABASE—THE KEY TO DIRECT MARKETING SUCCESS

Whatever the objective, most of the success of direct marketers depends on skill in locating and identifying likely prospects and building a responsive database. Assume that you are the marketing manager for a company offering a new weight-loss program on videotape. At this point, retail distribution does not seem to be the best strategy, and a decision has been made to try direct marketing. How do you build a database?

Two possibilities are available: (1) existing lists (an in-house list or names purchased from a list broker) and (2) geodemography.

Existing Lists   If you have sold teaching videos before and have retained customer names, this in-house list is your logical starting point. Generally such lists are computerized and can be segmented by recency of purchase

---

❖
**PROMOTION
IN ACTION
22–1**

Shoppers' Blues: The Thrill Is Gone

Marlene Dash would appear to be a marketer's dream come true. The corporate manager likes to dress smartly, both on and off the job. She owns a condominium in Chicago and takes pride in furnishing it well.

Yet Ms. Dash, in her mid-30s, loathes shopping. Lousy service and poor selections at many stores have turned a once-favorite pastime into what she calls a "frustrating" experience. These days she would rather exercise, visit friends, or read. "If you don't make it reasonably easy for me," she says, "I'm not going to waste my time."

Ms. Dash is far from alone. Shopping has become such a chore that more people hate browsing in stores than hate doing housework, according to the "American Way of Buying" survey conducted by *The Wall Street Journal.* Nearly a third of the 2,064 people interviewed by Peter D. Hart Research Associates said they "do not enjoy at all" window-shopping or browsing.

That feeling is amply confirmed by the spectacular growth of catalog companies that have stolen sales from retail stores for much of this decade. Yankelovich, Clancy, Shulman, a market research firm in Westport, Conn., warns clients that Americans' love affair with shopping is on the rocks: More than half the women it has surveyed in recent years, and an even larger percentage of men, say shopping for clothes is a hassle.

But underlying these complaints is a more far-reaching change: For many shoppers, the thrill is gone.

Source: Francine Schwadel, "Shoppers' Blues: The Thrill Is Gone," *The Wall Street Journal,* October 13, 1989, p. B1. Reproduced by special permission.

(purchase in the last few months or so), frequency, dollar amount, and type of products purchased.

Sometimes a house list also can be segmented psychographically. Spiegel, Inc., has developed accurate information that allows insight into the lifestyles of those on its house lists.[12] For example, one 35-year old single woman might be an impulse buyer who opts for trendy, high-fashion garments from Spiegel and also shops at Bloomingdale's or Neiman-Marcus. Another 35-year-old woman might be a "practical buyer" choosing value-oriented items at both Spiegel and J. C. Penney. Buying patterns such as these can reveal much about motivation and lifestyle.

Another possibility is to try existing lists available from a list broker. A starting point might be the purchase of names of people who have bought similar (or even identical) products through other sources. What do you think of this possibility?

> Weight-Loss Buyers of the "Nite-Diet" TV advertised program is offered for $45/M. The list of 95,070 is 90 percent women who are avid self-improvers, and they go after every opportunity to make themselves more attractive and healthy. They have responded to nationwide TV ads by sending for a month's supply of no-effect "Nite-Diet" pills. Dependable Lists, Inc.[13]

By "$45/M," this broker is saying that the list can be purchased for $45 per 1,000 names. There is good reason to think that these people might be prospects because of their demonstrated concern over diet and weight.

Another option is to approach a list broker for a *compiled list.* These lists are composed of names collected from a variety of sources such as census, home buying, car registration lists, and so on. It may be possible to infer interest from purchasers of collateral products or other related behaviors.

Before using any list, it is essential to test a sample of names prior to a full-scale rollout. The most common sample size for tests of this type includes 5,000 names. Testing the "Nite-Lite" TV list requires a total investment of $225 (5,000 at $45/M) plus printing and mailing. The entire list should be purchased only if sales response to the test sample gives a positive return on investment. Precise testing is a unique advantage of direct marketing.

Geodemography[14] The United States is geographically divided into more than 250,000 census tract block groups containing an average of 361 household units. These block groups are the heart of geodemographic segmentation systems such as PRIZM offered by Claritas, ACORN by CACI, and VISION by National Decision Systems.[15]

It is possible to classify each household within these block groups by demographic and psychographic characteristics and various activities such as buying behavior. Classification is made by using census data and other information collected for the block group and inferring that nearly all within that geographic segment are similar.

The objective, then, is to discover those geographic segments whose profile best matches that of your prospective customers. Once this is done, testing proceeds in the normal fashion.

DIRECT MARKETING STRATEGIES

Telemarketing Telemarketing has two phases: inbound (calls from the consumer) and outbound (sales calls direct to the consumer). There is no clear indication of the dollar magnitude of each, although it is estimated that they are about equal in dollar volume.[16]

Inbound telemarketing Seabreeze is part of the Clairol product group of Bristol Myers, which produces skin care, hair care, and hair coloring items marketed to salons and through retail stores. Only recently has Clairol joined the packaged goods manufacturers who are turning to direct marketing.[17]

Clairol ran four-color ads in the May 1989 issues of *Seventeen, Teen, Cosmopolitan, Mademoiselle,* and *Glamour* to reach an audience of 15- to 24-year-olds; TV commercials and in-store shelf talkers also were part of the media mix. Each ad gave information about a contest being conducted and listed the 3,000 sweepstakes prizes teenagers could win. The prospect was asked to look inside any Seabreeze carton especially imprinted with a telephone "bug" and to call an 800 number that was inside each box. Nearly 200,000 calls were received, and the name and address of each caller became a part of a database.

Bristol Myers' goal was to build a family of loyal buyers for the full line of company products. This database now is being used for ongoing direct marketing efforts.

The 800 number program uses an incoming WATS (wide area telecommunication service) system that is totally free to the customer. Successful case histories such as this one abound both in the United States and abroad.[18]

Many telemarketers also are making use of *audiotex*.[19] A computerized answering machine takes the incoming 800 number call that can be stimulated by ads in any medium. The machine asks questions and automatically records answers. In addition, full buyer information is collected. The answering machine dramatically lowers the cost per call when it is compared with the use of an operator.

One of the most effective uses of inbound telemarketing is for after-sale service. Nintendo of America, for example, receives about 50,000 inbound toll-free calls per week.[20] These calls are, of course, an ideal source of names for ongoing direct marketing of Nintendo products.

Outbound telemarketing   Telephone sales are becoming prevalent in both consumer goods and industrial marketing firms. A vast majority of *Fortune* 500 companies make at least some use of telephone sales.[21]

The Card Division of American Express offered by direct mail four $200 sculptures and followed each mailing with a phone call. Overall, the phone program produced more than $200,000 in extra sales, with an extremely favorable 8 percent expense/sales ratio.[22]

If you are going to use outbound telemarketing, here are some suggestions:

1. *Best results are achieved when the sales offer is a timely response to changing events.* "Mr. Smith, the stock market has jumped 50 points since the first of the month, and money market funds have slumped. We would like to show you how to increase your yield by switching to mutual funds now."

2. *You must know your prospect.* The author of this chapter lived in a brick home for years and received frequent calls from aluminum siding dealers. Nothing could scare them off—from sarcasm to threats.

The best outcomes often come from previous customers when your call is based on firsthand knowledge of their previous buying behavior. "Mr. Jones, your Mazda 626LX is now four years old, and I would like to invite you personally to see the new model." Sometimes it is possible to purchase lists of buyers of related items and use the same type of approach.

3. *Call at convenient times.* Does anyone appreciate being interrupted at dinner to hear about a new stock offering?

4. *State your offer and benefit at the outset.* You will have only a short interval to capture and hold the prospect's attention, and there is little room for delay.

Coping with growing backlash   More and more firms are making use of computerized, prerecorded presentations. Industry sources estimate that 7 million Americans each day receive an automated telephone sales pitch from around 190,000 solicitors.[23]

Apparently this tactic has had some success, but there is increasing evidence that a growing backlash may make it less attractive. According to Lorna Christie, director of ethics and consumer affairs at the Direct Marketing Association, "People are more annoyed about receiving unsolicited calls than [receiving unsolicited] mail."[24]

It hardly seems necessary to stress that telemarketing is successful over the long haul only when it is based in responsible professionalism. Everything we said about professional sales techniques in Chapter 19 also applies here. All too often, untrained people produce more alienation than sales.

Telephone solicitation is a legitimate activity that can provide real consumer benefit if it is done responsibly. Unfortunately, the frequency of discourtesy and abuse may be tainting the field for everyone.

Direct Mail   Mary Kay Cosmetics, Inc., has built a successful business via direct selling by nearly 170,000 beauty consultants who act as a sales force, but it also uses a direct-mail program to support consultants as they sell to segments of a 5 million-name database.[25] A consultant enrolls her customers in a program of quarterly direct-mail promotions.

Each direct-mail package promotes products and builds the image of the consultant (whose name is featured) as a skincare professional. The consultant is encouraged to make a follow-up telephone call after customers have received the direct-mail package. Those who take this step increase their profit from two to five times.

Similarly, an established shoe manufacturer and retail chain, Dunham's, has discovered the power of database marketing.[26] It has acquired more than 200,000 names from customers in the past few years, and it has seen a notable increase in store traffic since it began a regular mailing program.

As you no doubt are aware, direct mail is big business. The 10 leaders in worldwide sales are listed in Table 22–1. Why is this method so success-

TABLE 22–1

❖   **The Leading Mail-Order Companies Worldwide**

Rank	Company Name	Headquarters Country	Year Of Data	Mail Order Sales ($MMs)	Type of Merchandise
1	Otto Versand*	West Germany	1988	6,100	General
2	Sears, Roebuck & Co.	United States	1988	3,650	General
3	Quelle	West Germany	1988	2,900	General
4	Great Universal Stores	United Kingdom	1988	2,222	General
5	United Automobile Association Services	United States	1988	2,180	Insurance
6	Time, Inc.	United States	1988	1,997	Publishing
7	Bertelsmann	West Germany	1988	1,600	Publishing
8	Littlewoods	United Kingdom	1988	1,494	General
9	Tele-Communications	United States	1988	1,468	Cable
10	GEICO	United States	1988	1,430	Insurance

*Includes Spiegel

Source: "International Mail Order Guide," *Direct Marketing,* November 1989, p. 35. Reproduced by special permission.

ful? You may be surprised to discover that about two-thirds of the public enjoys opening their mail (including advertising). In fact, this has been found to be one of the most enjoyable activities of the day.[27]

The evidence overwhelmingly indicates that *direct-mail ads are read.* There have been numerous confirming studies published in such sources as *Direct Marketing.* Also, the author of this chapter has worked for years with nonprofit organizations using direct mail for fund raising. All of his research (which unfortunately is proprietary) indicates the same conclusion.

Then what about all the complaints about *junk mail?* We do not deny that much of the stuff received daily falls exactly into that category. As we will shortly discover, direct-mail success requires careful prospecting and the offer of relevant information. When this is not done, advertising goes nowhere, and the same is true no matter what medium is used.

The direct-mail letter   Read the letter in Figure 22–1 carefully. Is this a good letter? No one can say for sure just by looking at it because the ultimate proof lies in the return on investment that it generates. But there are some guidelines that will help you.

The first question always should be: *Is the recipient a likely prospect?* This takes us back to choosing a mailing list, which always must be a central consideration. The second question is this: *Does the offer provide a real benefit for the person who reads the letter?*

If your answers are positive, then, and only then, should you look into the details of the execution. Although no one has a precise formula, letters are tested in the same manner as lists. Does changing the headline, for example, stimulate greater buying response? Perhaps three different headlines will be compared in terms of ROI. Such comparison can be made with any part of the letter. The outcome is that any direct marketer can learn quickly what works and what does not.

Some of the most commonly used guidelines are given by Bob Stone in Table 22–2. Read them carefully and see what you think of the letter from GTE Sprint (see Figure 21–1).

1. The benefit is stated right at the outset—you will save money by using Sprint.
2. Specific details are given on what you will get, and these are backed up with comparative rates as proof.
3. You are told that you may have higher rates if you do not act.
4. The benefit is clearly restated in the P.S., as it should be.
5. Action is incited by the offer of a free hour of long-distance calling.

You will notice that "direct" is different from what you might have learned in creative writing class. Copy is clear and concise. Paragraphs are short. "Action" words are used. There is good reason for this. *Attention span is limited and you must get the benefit across quickly and succinctly.* We agree that long copy can be used *if there is consumer interest.* Still, this is different from writing a book or personal letter.

Curbing abuses   Consumers in many quarters are increasingly voicing concern over junk mail abuse. In particular, a 1988 study by American Express Company revealed that 90 percent of those surveyed believe that companies should disclose more about how they use their mailing lists. Also, 80 percent stated that information collected for one purpose should not be used for another.[28]

It should be pointed out that all direct marketers are required by law to protect the wishes of all persons who do not want their name sold for any purpose whatsoever. We doubt, however, that such provisions are well-known.

It seems clear that matters are reaching a point of diminishing returns. Our only conclusion is that too many direct marketers are disregarding return on investment and are basing their strategy on wishful thinking. If we

---

TABLE 22–2

❖   **Making Direct Mail Work for You**

Promise a benefit in your headline or first paragraph—your most important benefit. You simply cannot go wrong by leading off with the most important benefits to the reader.

Immediately enlarge on your most important benefit. Many writers come up with a great lead and then fail to follow through. Try hard to elaborate on your most important benefit right away, and you'll build interest faster.

Tell the reader specifically what the benefit is. It's amazing how many letters lack details on such basic product features as size, color, weight, and sales terms. Perhaps by being so close to the proposition, the writer assumes that the reader knows all about it—a dangerous assumption!

Back up your statements with proof and endorsements. If you can back up your own statements with third-party testimonials or a list of satisfied users, everything you say becomes more believable.

Tell the reader what might be lost unless action is taken. Here's a good spot in your letter to overcome human inertia—imply what might be lost if action is postponed.

Rephrase your prominent benefits in your closing offer. The stronger the recall of the benefits, the easier it will be for the reader to justify an affirmative decision.

Incite action, NOW. This is the spot where you can win or lose the battle to inertia. So wind up with a call for action and a logical reason for acting now.

Source: Bob Stone, *Successful Direct Marketing Methods*, 3rd ed. (Lincolnwood, Ill.: Crain Books, 1984), pp. 272–73. Reproduced by special permission.

One of the most familiar forms of direct marketing is the catalog. With the increased sophistication of direct marketing and telephone support, companies like Taylor Gifts (top) can, at relatively low cost, make sales to individuals, while others (bottom) aim for corporate buyers.

Magazine ads like this one that ask for direct action are an effective way of reaching a target audience.

HIM YOU KNOW.

THEM YOU SHOULD.

You know Washington, D.C. for memorials and monuments, but you'll want to know our other marvels as well. Here are a few:

Washington's well known stages and 14th Street theatre corridor offer premiere performances.

Step into shoppers' paradise where specialty shops and department stores offer marvelous merchandise.

And kids will love our parks, pandas and puppet shows.

Most museums are free and all D.C. hotels offer reduced weekend and holiday rates. Get to know D.C.'s other faces. Call 1-800-422-8644 or mail the coupon for a free brochure listing free annual festivals, theatres, parks, attractions, discounts for persons 60+ and reduced weekend rates for 91 D.C. hotels.

WASHINGTON
D.C.
MONUMENTS AND MUCH MORE
1-800-422-8644

FREE INFORMATION FOR READERS OF BusinessWeek

Want more information about advertisers in this issue?
If so...
1. Review the list of advertisers.
2. Circle the corresponding number on the postage-paid reader service card, complete the necessary information and drop in the mail.
3. Or, call toll-free Monday—Friday 8AM—5PM MST:
1-800-345-3550
When prompted, use keypad to enter this control number: **8299600** *

Offer expires September 17, 1990.

JAPAN

Special Advertising Section

ANNUAL REPORTS

1. Hitachi Ltd.
2. Mitsubishi Kasei Corporation
3. Sumitomo Metal Industries, Ltd.

PRODUCTS/SERVICES

4. Hotel Okura

5. Mazda Motor of America, Inc.
6. NEC Corporation
7. Nihon Keizai Shimbun, Inc.
8. Nikkei Business Publications, Inc.
9. Omron Corporation
10. Ricoh Co., Ltd.
11. The New Otani

No Postage Necessary If Mailed in the United States

BUSINESS REPLY MAIL
FIRST CLASS MAIL   PERMIT NO. 1217   BOULDER, CO

POSTAGE WILL BE PAID BY ADDRESSEE

BusinessWeek

P.O. Box 8829
Boulder, CO 80328-8829

BusinessWeek

July 16, 1990   BW-07/16-S
This card must be received by September 17, 1990.

PLEASE PRINT

Name

Business
☐ BUSINESS ☐ HOME   Address

City

State   Zip
☐ BUSINESS ☐ HOME   Telephone AREA CODE   NUMBER   EXTENSION

Please check one response for each following question.

1 Are you currently a Business Week subscriber?   A ☐ Yes   B ☐ No

2 What is your company's type of business?
1 ☐ Agriculture 2 ☐ Mining, Construction 3 ☐ Manufacturing, Processing
4 ☐ Wholesale, Retail Trade 5 ☐ Finance, Insurance, Real Estate
6 ☐ Government 7 ☐ Transportation, Public Utilities 8 ☐ Service Industries
9 ☐ Other—Please specify:

3 What is your title?
A ☐ Chairman of the Board   B ☐ President   C ☐ Vice President
D ☐ Treasurer, Secretary   E ☐ General Manager   F ☐ Division Manager
G ☐ Department Manager   H ☐ Other Manager   I ☐ Student
J ☐ Other—Please Specify:

4 How many employees in your company worldwide?
1 ☐ Under 100   2 ☐ 100-999   3 ☐ 1,000-2,499
4 ☐ 2,500 to 4,999   5 ☐ 5,000 to 9,999   6 ☐ 10,000 or more

Please circle number of item(s) for which you have specific interest:

1	2	3	4	5	6
7	8	9	10	11	

Magazines have recently begun to offer other services to advertisers, such as this reader response card (top), which allows interested readers to reach the advertising company. A more familiar form of direct marketing is the subscription forms (bottom) included in most magazines. Obviously, when you see one, the target market has been reached!

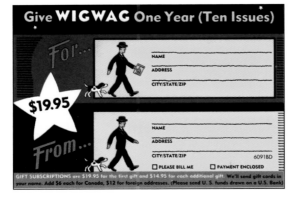

Give **WIGWAG** One Year (Ten Issues)

For...

$19.95

NAME
ADDRESS
CITY/STATE/ZIP

From...

NAME
ADDRESS
CITY/STATE/ZIP   6091BD

☐ PLEASE BILL ME   ☐ PAYMENT ENCLOSED

GIFT SUBSCRIPTIONS are $19.95 for the first gift and $14.95 for each additional gift. We'll send gift cards in your name. Add $6 each for Canada, $12 for foreign addresses. (Please send U.S. funds drawn on a U.S. Bank)

Other forms of direct marketing: special offerings in the Sunday paper that come in the form of FSIs (Free Standing Inserts) (top) and bulk coupon mailings that come to your home (bottom).

FIGURE 22–1

A Direct Mail Offer

GTE SPRINT

GTE Sprint Communications Corporation
500 Airport Boulevard, Suite 415
Burlingame, CA 94014

Choose new Sprint® Direct
Dial Service by

January 17, 1986

and you'll get a FREE
HOUR OF LONG DISTANCE
CALLING!

Mr. Anyone
Street Address
Illinois

Dear Mr. Anyone:

Illinois Bell will be sending you a letter and ballot soon asking you to choose your long distance telephone service.+

That's why I'm writing to you now...to offer some important reasons why we think GTE Sprint is your best choice.

First, you save as much as 30% over AT&T any time of the day, any day of the week on your calls to anywhere outside Illinois, and on calls to places like Peoria and Rockford within Illinois, too.

Here are examples of how much GTE Sprint could save you on calls made from the Chicago area:

Long Distance Calls from the Chicago Area to:	Time of Day	Minutes	Monthly Usage	AT&T	Sprint	% Savings
Los Angeles	Day	20	$75 - $149.99	$7.97	$6.83	14%
Peoria	Eve	3	$20 - $ 74.99	$ .81	$ .66	19%
Phoenix*	Night	15	$75 - $149.99	$3.45	$2.10	39%

See rate chart on Sprint Order Form for more information

Second, Sprint knows you want to hear and be heard clearly. That's why we spent $1.5 billion modernizing our network -- just to make sure you get the high quality you deserve.

Third, GTE Sprint's personal service representatives are available to receive your call, toll-free, 24 hours a day. That means you can always get

+ By order of the Federal Communications Commission, Illinois
  Bell must randomly assign a long distance company to any
  customer who does not make a choice.

have reached saturation, this will be clearly reflected in negative return on investment, and nothing is a better corrective.

Catalog Marketing   Most of the leading mail-order marketers listed in Table 22–1 use some type of catalog. The number of catalog companies is well in excess of 7,000, not including retailers. It is estimated that catalog sales alone increased 10 to 12 percent in 1989.[29] Catalog selling has also caught

FIGURE 22–1

A Direct Mail Offer (concluded)

your service questions answered any time of the day or night, any day of the week.

> Plus, with Sprint you'll continue to dial the same easy way you're used to dialing with AT&T, and you can use any type of phone -- pushbutton or rotary dial.

> So what does Sprint Direct Dial Service add up to? The best value you can get: savings + quality + service + convenience.

> Because we want you to <u>discover</u> <u>for</u> <u>yourself</u> all the good things we already know about Sprint, here's our special offer:

> <u>Sign</u> <u>up</u> for Sprint now and get the best value in long
> distance...plus <u>a</u> <u>free</u> <u>hour</u> <u>of</u> <u>long</u> <u>distance</u> <u>calling</u>!

<u>To</u> <u>choose</u> <u>Sprint</u>, <u>simply</u> <u>sign</u> <u>and</u> <u>send</u> <u>in</u> <u>the</u> <u>enclosed</u> <u>Sprint</u> <u>Order</u> <u>Form</u>. Or call 1-800-521-4949, ext. 870. We'll notify your local phone company that you've chosen Sprint as your long distance phone company.

> Then, when you receive your local phone company's letter and ballot, check "GTE Sprint" <u>to</u> <u>make</u> <u>doubly</u> <u>sure</u> they hear your choice of Sprint loud and clear!

> Whichever way you choose Sprint, <u>you'll</u> <u>get</u> <u>your</u> <u>free</u> <u>hour</u> <u>of</u> <u>long</u> <u>distance</u> <u>calling</u>!

> We know you'll be pleased with GTE Sprint. Now, more than ever, it's your best value in long distance service.

>   Sincerely,

>   *Barbara B. Press*

>   Barbara B. Press
>   Director, Residential Services

P.S.   Remember, if you do not select a long distance company, your local phone company has been <u>ordered</u> by the FCC to select one <u>for</u> you. <u>Act</u> <u>now</u>. Take a few minutes to read the enclosed brochure. Then <u>mail</u> <u>your</u> <u>Sprint</u> <u>Order</u> <u>Form</u> <u>or</u> <u>call</u> us at <u>1-800-521-4949</u>, <u>ext.</u> <u>870</u>.

> No-Risk Sprint Guarantee
>
> If, for any reason during your first 90 days of saving with Sprint, you decide to switch your long distance service back to AT&T, we'll cover any switching fee charged by your local phone company. (Confirmation of switch back to AT&T required. Offer subject to regulatory approval. Void where prohibited.)

on in Japan where sales totaled 300 million yen in 1985 (the latest year for which data are available), as compared with 90 million yen in 1975.[30]

According to data collected for Spiegel, Inc., Goldring & Company found that 90 percent of the public makes at least one catalog purchase a year.[31] The most frequent catalog users were found to be between 29 and 30 years of age, to earn above-average income, and to be highly educated. Interestingly, those buying seven or more times represented only 20 percent of the total, but they accounted for 60 percent of the sales. According to another study, the two main reasons for catalog use are "can't find the merchandise elsewhere" (63 percent) and convenience (56 percent).[32]

One of the most interesting catalog merchandisers is Sharper Image. Its focus is on the busy executive, and 90 percent of its sales come from its 1.5 million-name list.[33] This success story is described in Promotion in Action 22–2.

Sharper Image Targets the Executive

❖
PROMOTION
IN ACTION
22–2

When Richard Thalheimer got the idea to sell a digital stopwatch for joggers through an ad in *Runner's World* in 1977, he couldn't have predicted the success that a foray into mail order would bring. Today, Mr. Thalheimer's San Francisco-based Sharper Image is not only an innovative leader in the catalog business, but also it has spawned a chain of retail stores bearing that name.

Sharper Image is an idea for the 80s—proven by the number of imitators that have cropped up in the past couple of years. The items it offers couldn't be considered necessities, but they are the types of products people with a good bit of disposable income might want to own.

Representations of practical mindedness can be found in any of the monthly catalogs: Fitness systems, blood pressure monitors, aluminum luggage, leather bomber jackets, portable stereos, TV sets, and calculators.

"Our customers, at least the regular ones, tend to be professional men in upper-middle to high-income brackets," Sharper Image corporate communications representative Gavin Payne says. The house list of 1.5 million names was culled from repeat customers of lists compiled by brokers, a source the company occasionally still uses.

"Our customers are the kinds of people who typically don't have a lot of time to spend shopping around for things," he says. "They look to us to choose the types of things they're going to want to buy, and they trust us to get the best quality available."

Source: Betsy Gilbert, "Speciality Catalogs Cut through the Clutter," *Advertising Age*, October 17, 1985, p. 30. Reprinted with permission. Copyright Crain Communications, Inc. all rights reserved.

Other Direct Marketing Media   Direct marketers also use print and broadcast media, videotex, videocassettes, and house-to-house selling.

Direct action advertising   When advertising media are used to stimulate a direct buying response, the primary characteristic is an appeal to have the consumer call an 800 number or to return a coupon. Figure 22–2 shows a fund-raising appeal with a coupon keyed to show the magazine in which it appeared and the date of the issue.

Direct response television can be effective, especially through the use of cable TV on the local level.[34] For example, Black & Decker's household product group successfully experimented with two-minute commercials, as did Allstate Enterprises. The latter attempted to show in two minutes how a consumer could get travel and insurance benefits.

The usual form of response is a toll-free number, although handling arrangements can also be made with the carrying station for a fee as high as 30 percent of the selling price.

Most Americans, as well as increasing numbers of Europeans,[35] also have access to home shopping channels through cable TV. Home shopping channels were referred to as recently as 1987 as "one of the hottest revenue opportunities on the horizon." [36] By 1988, however, nearly two-thirds of the cable channel operators in the United States stated that home shopping networks are unimportant to the revenue growth of their channels.[37]

This gloomy outlook perhaps represents only a temporary slump; Schlossberg puts it this way:

> . . . shop-at-home TV has become more than a billion-dollar business with a loyal, repeat-buying, nearly cult-like following in its viewership, with the potential to reach nearly every home that has a TV set and a cable hookup.[38]

One of the ways to generate greater profitability is to feature higher-margin, specialty items similar to those offered in catalogs. J. C. Penney, for example, began an "electronic catalog" home shopping network in 1989 and has reached 6.5 million homes in a short time.[39] Therefore, there seems to be untapped market potential.

Videotex   Videotex is an electronic shopping medium that interactively links buyer and seller. Anything that can be typed on a computer keyboard can be transmitted to the home screen and copied if the TV set has facsimile capability. There are an estimated 1 million videotex users, but growth has been sluggish and slow.[40]

An alternative is interactive cable. The J. C. Penney Company has tested Telaction, which permits the buyer to communicate with a TV monitor by using a touch-tone telephone. This allows pictures and prices to appear on the screen, and the consumer can respond instantly. If this type of system catches on, interactive electronic media may grow in importance.

FIGURE 22–2

Fund-Raising through Direct Marketing   ❖

Sponsor a Child for Only $10 a Month.

At last! Here is a $10 sponsorship program for Americans who are unable to send $16, $18, or $22 a month to help a needy child.

And yet, this is a full sponsorship program because for $10 a month you will receive:
- a 3½" × 5" photograph of the child you are helping.
- two personal letters from your child each year.
- a complete Sponsorship Kit with your child's case history and a special report about the country where your child lives.
- quarterly issues of our newsletter "Sponsorship News".

ALL THIS FOR ONLY $10 A MONTH?

Yes—because we searched for ways to reduce the cost—without reducing the help that goes to the child you sponsor.

For example, your child does not write each month, but two letters a year from your child keeps you in contact and, of course, you can write to the child just as often as you wish.

Also, to keep down costs, we do not offer the so-called "trial child" that the other organizations mail to prospective sponsors before the sponsors send any money.

YOU CAN MAKE THE DIFFERENCE!

$10 a month may not seem like much to you—but to a poor family living on an income of $2.00 a day, your sponsorship really helps!

Will you sponsor a child? Your $10 a month will help provide so much:
- emergency food, clothing and medical care.
- a chance to attend school.
- counseling for the child's family to help them become self-sufficient.

HERE IS HOW YOU CAN SPONSOR A CHILD:

1. Fill out the coupon and tell us if you want to sponsor a boy or a girl, and check the country of your choice.
2. Or mark the "emergency list" box and we will assign a child to you that most urgently needs to have a sponsor.
3. Send your $10 in right now and this will eliminate the cost of a "trial child."

Then, in just a few days you will receive your child's name, photograph, and case history.

May we hear from you? Our sponsorship program protects the dignity of the child and provides Americans with a beautiful way to help a youngster.

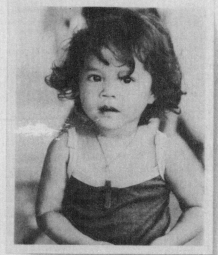

3-year-old Michelle was abandoned by her father. Soon after, her mother was forced to leave her in order to find work. She now lives with her grandmother in a hut with dirt floors and a grass roof.

Holy Land Christian **Mission International**   K6BA
Attn: Joseph Gripkey, President
2000 East Red Bridge Road
Box 55, Kansas City, Missouri 64141

☐ Yes. I wish to sponsor a child. Enclosed is my first payment of $10. Please assign me a ☐ Boy · ☐ Girl

Country preference: ☐ India ☐ The Philippines ☐ Thailand ☐ Costa Rica ☐ Chile ☐ Honduras ☐ Dominican Republic ☐ Colombia ☐ Guatemala ☐ Africa

☐ **OR, choose a child that needs my help from your EMERGENCY LIST.**

☐ Please send me more information about sponsoring a child.

☐ I can't sponsor a child now, but wish to make a contribution of _____ .

NAME_____

ADDRESS_____

CITY_____

STATE_____ ZIP_____

Member of American and International Councils of Voluntary Agencies. Our annual financial report is readily available upon request. Please make your check payable to Mission International. Your sponsorship gifts are tax deductible.

Holy Land Christian
Mission International

Video cassette recorders VCRs are finding creative use in combination with other media. You will recall our opening mention of the development of a video catalog by Brownstone Studio.

Also, Spiegel, Inc. has experienced good results by linking videos with printed catalogs.[41] Targeted to top customers, the video is sold for $12.95 and is accompanied by a $10 merchandise certificate plus a year's subscription to the company's *FOR YOU* catalog. Women are both entertained and taught how to chose garments that are most appropriate for their goals and lifestyle.

In-home personal selling House-to-house personal selling annually accounts for about 2 percent of all general merchandise sales but is declining. Two companies known for their large field selling force, Fuller Brush Company and Mary Kay Cosmetics, Inc., have been forced to change directions. Both are using other media such as telephone or direct mail to make primary contacts.[42] Skyrocketing costs and reduced availability of women at home during the daytime are the primary reasons.

MANAGING THE DIRECT-MARKETING PROCESS

Four remaining issues of direct marketing warrant some discussion: (1) agencies, (2) integrated strategies, (3) measurement of effectiveness, and (4) management of the database.

Agencies

Direct marketing finally has found its way into the traditional advertising agency. It was slow in coming, however, because this activity requires specialized skills. For this reason, specialized direct marketing agencies sprung up. The ad for Direct Marketing, Inc. that appears in Figure 22–3 offers a good primer in direct-mail writing.

Integrated Strategies

The ChemLawn Services Corporation saw the response to its direct marketing drop in the early 1980s as it faced increased competition. A new strategy called for TV spots guaranteeing the consumer a better lawn with a money-back guarantee. When that was combined with direct mail, the outcome was a 50 percent increase in response.[43]

This is a good illustration of the need to use general media to change beliefs or attitudes. When direct marketing is coupled with such efforts, it is reasonable to expect to reap attitudinal gains.

FIGURE 22–3

A Direct-Marketing Agency Markets Itself

29 direct marketing principles that work.

(Including an invitation to a free database marketing workshop.)

What works in direct marketing? At DMA, the direct marketing arm of Cunningham & Walsh, we've spent our careers finding out. Here are some of the things we've learned:

1. The letter is the most important part of a direct mail package. A good letter will invariably outpull the most impressive brochure.

2. ...and it must be written in the reader's self-interest. Resist putting irrelevant facts about you in your direct mail letter. Readers don't care that you're America's biggest or oldest or most respected.

3. Long copy usually works better than short copy. A mailing we did for Porsche + Audi contained a letter and a 1,500-word brochure. It sold more than $8 million worth of cars. The cost: $100,000.

4. The response device should summarize the sales story—sometimes it is the only part of the package that gets thorough reading.

5. A toll-free number raises response to a print or mail advertisement by anywhere from 10% to 150%.

6. Long headlines generally sell better than short ones. We introduced a cash management service for The Travelers with this headline: "Seven common mistakes in handling your money—mistakes you can correct with one simple step."

7. "If it ain't broke, don't fix it." If you've got a package that's working, keep using it until response goes down to the break-even point.

8. "More Information" is an offer, and it gets results—if your information is valuable or helpful.

9. You can fish the same waters again and again. In selling a service for Southern New England Tele-

phone, we went back to the same people over a two-year period. And none of the mailings drew less than a 4% response.

10. The offer can make the difference between success and failure. For Citibank we offered 1% more interest on 1-year CD's, and got $4,000,000 in deposits. Cost: $30,000.

11. Use your customer list for cross-selling. For Manufacturers Hanover, we offer their customers pre-approved loans. It has become a standard part of MH's marketing.

12. Keep refining your mailing lists. Your odds for success improve if you can use your own customer list supplemented by carefully chosen lists of prospects. (See principle #29.)

13. Track your customers. For Eastern Airlines, we've been tracking travelers for 15 years, and have built a database that identifies the 20% of their customers who account for 80% of their business.

14. Make your response device easy to fill out. The packages we do for Hoffmann-La Roche, Wyeth, J&J and Syntex ask doctors to check the medicines they prescribe most frequently. We regularly get responses over 40%.

15. Back up your mail with telemarketing. Surveys show that only

a third of the readers who intended to mail a coupon actually did. Telemarketing turns intention into action.

16. A "Take One" brochure must select prospects. A blind line will be taken by the curious, rather than by prospects. Also...

17. An envelope that hints at the offer is better than a "blind" envelope. When you tell at least part of your proposition on the envelope, the people who open it are prospects.

18. Always address your prospect by name. A simple 20-cent selfmailer was addressed to prospects by name. We got 1 1/2 responses for each dollar invested. The same package and offer addressed to "occupant" probably would have failed.

19. Fulfillment is important to repeat sales. Get the right product or information back to customers when promised. Delays cost customers.

20. Statement stuffers get a free ride on postage. But they get notoriously low reading because they will compete with bills or dividend checks. Use with care.

21. Time your print and TV ads to appear just before your direct mail goes out. This will lift response by 50% or more.

22. Place your direct response ad on the back page of the newspaper. It will get three times the response of the same ad placed inside the paper.

23. Involve your reader with a quiz. "How many of these money questions can you answer?" "How many of these services does your bank offer?" We have used the quiz successfully for clients as diverse as Volvo and The Travelers.

24. Use focus groups for fine tuning copy, not to supplant live market results.

25. Don't listen when someone tells you, "This always works" or, "This never works." Precedents make handy guide posts and experience is invaluable. But never ignore gut feelings, and your reactions as a consumer.

26. If you have something you don't want the reader to miss, put it in a picture caption, or a P.S. They are the best-read elements in an advertisement, a brochure, and a letter.

27. Keep it simple. Avoid fancy folds in the brochure that don't let the reader know where to go next. Avoid extra pieces that confuse the reader.

28. Don't be bound by the rules, these or any others. Go for breakthroughs. Don't be afraid of using your judgment. Trust instinct. Be willing to take a chance.

29. Build a database of customers and prospects. In 1984, Americans bought more than $200 billion worth of goods and services directly, and that figure is growing by 15% a year. Direct selling is the marketing arena of the future, and without a database you will be hopelessly outclassed. To learn more, complete and mail the coupon.

FREE DATABASE MARKETING WORKSHOP
An invitation to learn more (at your place or ours).
Call Norman Suslock at (203) 357-7895 or (212) 586-6348
to set up a time and place for your Database Marketing
Workshop, or complete and mail this coupon.

☐ I would like to have a workshop at   ☐ My place   ☐ Your place
☐ Please call me to confirm:

Name/title

Company

Telephone number   Best time to call

Address

City, State, zip code

Direct Marketing Agency, Inc.
The direct response arm of Cunningham & Walsh
One Dock Street, Stamford, CT 06902

Courtesy Direct Marketing Agency, Inc.

Measurement of Effectiveness

Return on investment, of course, is the single most important measurement[44] in direct marketing. It is computed as follows:

$$ROI = \frac{(SP \times RE) - TI}{TI} \times 100$$

where

$\quad SP$ = Selling price per unit

$\quad OM$ = Order margin per unit

$\quad RE$ = Replies per thousand

$\quad SC$ = Selling cost per thousand

$\quad TI$ = Total investment = $([SP - OM] \times RE) + SC$

$\quad ROI$ = Percent age return on investment

Assume the selling price per unit is $20 and the order margin (your return) is $10 per unit. We will further assume 20 replies per thousand letters (2 percent) and a selling cost of $185 per thousand. This would give an ROI of 3.9 percent. Given the fact that the cost of working capital (as of the time of this writing) is about 10 percent, this return is dangerously low. It tells us that our direct-mail letter has not produced as it should.

Immediate ROI, however, is not the ultimate measure. For example, an offer could generate a 10 percent or more initial return but fail to stimulate repurchase. In that case, the *attrition* rate is too high. This suggests that reduction of attrition rates is always a valid goal when repurchase is an option. This is measured simply as the percentage of repeat customers for any given period, usually a year.

No doubt you are asking just what is a good response rate for direct mail. Although a 2 percent rate probably is typical, we prefer to see a higher figure. It is usually disturbing to realize that 98 percent of your prospects can ignore you even though ROI is favorable. Rates of 5 percent or less, however, probably must be accepted as a good measure of reality unless you are working with a high-quality list composed of very interested people. In these instances response rates of 10 percent or more might be expected.

Managing the Database

The direct marketer's greatest asset is the database. The basic component, of course, is each customer's name and buying record. Here are some of the most essential facts to store in the customer file:

Name and address.

Source—how the name was acquired (from an ad, letter, etc.).

Personal information—how the person is to be addressed (first name, etc.).

Any demographic or psychographic data you might have.

Date and size of first purchase.

Motivation—the type of appeal to which they responded.

Every purchase recorded by dollar size.

Management is not especially interested in each customer record, per se, but makes considerable use of summary reports. Here are some of the reports that find greatest use:

1. *Monthly sales and ROI figures given by each specific appeal, medium, and creative package*—this is how to find out what is really working.
2. *List growth and attrition*—are we attracting new customers and holding those that we have?
3. *Purchase size*—upgrading size of purchase is always a realistic objective.

The database provides for no end of segmentation possibilities. For example, assume that telemarketing is showing high ROIs. Call up all who have bought by telephone in the past three months and appeal once again. Do the same if a particular type of direct mail or catalog works. Similarly, you can isolate customers who have responded to certain direct-mail appeals and press ahead with a related campaign.

Another good practice is to purge from the active mailing list those individuals who have not purchased at all during the past year. *Make sure, however, that the names are not lost.* It frequently is possible to reactivate lapsed customers at a later point in time.

It is safe to say that the successful direct marketer lives with these numbers. The reports reveal the dynamics of buying behavior and suggest no end of strategic possibilities. This seldom is possible without a database.

SUMMARY

This chapter has focused on marketing activities that are designed to produce some form of measurable direct buying response. Direct marketing is growing in importance as consumers find ways to circumvent the inconvenience of retail purchasing.

The list of names of prospects and buyers, referred to as the *database,* is the key to successful direct marketing. Several ways to build a database, including use of in-house lists, lists from other sources such as list brokers, and geodemography, were discussed.

REVIEW AND DISCUSSION QUESTIONS

1. "No way am I going to put my ad in a mailbox. It will get lost in that clutter and never be read. I'll stick with print ads as I always have." What is your comment?

2. Take an inventory of your mailbox during a given week. What have you received in the way of ads? Would you say that most who have written to you have a good idea of your background and interests? What, if anything, captures and holds your attention? What lessons can be learned from this?

3. Would you recommend telemarketing for an agency raising funds for drought relief? What types of people should be called? What are the odds of success?

4. Would TV ads or a 30- or 60-minute special be a better strategy for drought relief fund-raising? Why or why not?

5. You are the advertising manager for a high-fashion clothing designer that owns a highly exclusive store on the North Shore of Chicago. The store sells only its own creations. Would you consider any type of direct marketing? If so, what would you recommend?

6. In view of a growing backlash against some types of telemarketing, would you advise a stock broker to use this medium to find new customers? What would you suggest be done by this firm to avoid annoying those who are reached?

NOTES

1. "Direct Marketing—What Is It?" *Direct Marketing,* June 1985, p. 20.

2. A helpful and widely quoted booklet is: Vin Jenkins, *The Concept of Direct Marketing* (Melbourne, Australia: *Australia Post,* 1984).

3. Tom Peters, "The Era of Personalization Has Arrived," *Chicago Tribune,* October 16, 1989.

4. Jim Kobs, "Action Blends with Image-Building," *Advertising Age,* November 9, 1988, p. 78.

5. Arnold Fishman, "International Mail Order Guide," *Direct Marketing,* November 1989, p. 35.

6. *Direct Marketing,* September 1989, p. 4.

7. "Mail Order Top 250 +," *Direct Marketing,* July 1989, p. 36.

8. For a comprehensive overview of this field, see Bob Stone, *Successful Direct Marketing Methods,* 3rd ed. (Lincolnwood, Ill.: Crain Books, 1984), and William A. Cohen, *Direct Response Marketing—An Entrepreneurial Approach* (New York: John Wiley & Sons, 1984).

9. Kobs, "Action Blends with Image-Building."

10. Alison Fahey, "A Question of Image," *Advertising Age,* September 25, 1989, p. S–6.

11. Ibid.

12. Henry A. Johnson, "Computer Technology Is Key to Segmentation and Service," *Direct Marketing,* June 1985, pp. 66ff.

13. *Direct Marketing,* June 1985, p. 12.

14. See Dwight J. Shelton, "Birds of a Geodemographic Feather Flock Together," *Marketing News,* August 28, 1987, p. 13. For an excellent description of how geodemography is applied to fund raising strategy, see Daniel F. Hansler and Don L. Riggin, "Geo-Demographics: Targeting the Market," *Fund Raising Management,* December 1989, pp. 35–43.

15. Hansler and Riggin, "Geo-Demographics."

16. "Direct Marketing . . . An Aspect of Total Marketing," *Direct Marketing,* June 1985, p. 21.

17. "No Hand Ups Here," *Direct Marketing,* August 1988, pp. 16–18.

18. "Internationally Speaking," *Direct Marketing,* December 1988, pp 36–40.

19. For a brief description of how audiotex works, see *Direct Marketing,* April 1989, p. 96.

20. "The Power of Nintendo," *Direct Marketing,* September 1989, pp. 24–29.

21. Hubert D. Hennessey, "Matters to Consider before Plunging into Telemarketing," *Marketing News,* July 8, 1983, p. 2.

22. Stone, *Successful Direct Marketing Methods,* pp. 81–82.

23. John Osbon, "Abuses Draw Congress' Fire," *Advertising Age,* September 25, 1989, p. S–8.

24. Ibid.

25. Blair Stephenson and Jim Camey, "Glamorous Database," *Direct Marketing,* July 1989, pp. 54ff.

26. Gary W. Wojtas, "A Perfect Fit," *Direct Marketing,* November 1989, pp. 26–28.

27. The results were found in a nationwide Roper study quoted by Joseph Campana, "Chrysler Mail Campaign Gets Leads, Supports Dealers" (speech given at Direct Marketing Association of Detroit, October 6, 1983).

28. Osbon, "Abuses Draw Congress' Fire."

29. Amy Dunkin, "It's a Lot Tougher to Mind the Store," *Newsweek,* January 8, 1990, p. 85.

30. "The Japanese Yen for Non-Store Retailing," *Direct Marketing,* April 1989, pp. 24–28.

31. "Spiegel, Inc. (A)," in Roger D. Blackwell, James F. Engel, and W. Wayne Talarzyk, *Contemporary Cases in Consumer Behavior,* rev. ed. (Hinsdale, Ill.: Dryden Press, 1984), pp. 146–47.

32. "Mail-Order Frequency: Amount Rising Says Consumer Survey," *Direct Marketing,* March 1985, pp. 146–47.

33. Betsy Gilbert, "Specialty Catalogs Cut through the Clutter," *Advertising Age,* October 17, 1985, p. 30.

34. Linda Cecere, "TV Availabilities Put Squeeze on Marketers," *Advertising Age,* October 17, 1985, p. 19.

35. *The Wall Street Journal,* July 2, 1987, p. 1.

36. Judith Graham, "Home Shopping Loses Luster," *Advertising Age,* October 24, 1988, p. 52.

37. Ibid.

38. Howard Schlossberg, "Picture Still Looks Bright for TV Shopping Networks," *Marketing News,* October 23, 1989, p. 8.

39. Ibid.

40. James F. Engel, Roger D. Blackwell, and Paul W. Miniard, *Consumer Behavior,* 6th ed. (Hinsdale, Ill.: Dryden Press, 1990), p. 606.

41. Joyce K. Reynolds, "The VCR: Very Critical Resource," *Direct Marketing,* November 1989, pp. 51–53.

42. See, for example, Susan Garland, "Stores Brush Up Fuller's Image," *Advertising Age,* September 14, 1987, p. 107.

43. "Direct Mail Nurtured ChemLawn Rebound," *Advertising Age,* September 2, 1985, p. 61.

44. An excellent source for the mathematics of direct marketing is Stone, *Direct Marketing Methods,* ch. 15.

Public Relations, Corporate Advertising, and Publicity

EXXON'S PUBLIC–RELATIONS PROBLEM

The Exxon Corporation's reputation was bound to suffer after the *Exxon Valdez* ran aground off Alaska and dumped 250,000 barrels of oil into Prince William Sound. But experts in public relations say that Exxon seriously worsened the damage to its public standing by failing to seize control of developments after the spill and establish itself as a company concerned about the problems it had caused.

Exxon violated some cardinal rules of crisis management, practitioners of this new specialty say. They predict that the *Exxon Valdez* episode will become a textbook example of what not to do when an unexpected crisis thrusts a company into the limelight.

The crisis-management experts say Exxon failed to follow several well-established procedures:

1. The biggest mistake was that Exxon's chairman, Lawrence G. Rawl, sent a succession of lower-ranking executives to Alaska to deal with the spill instead of going there himself and taking control of the situation in a forceful, highly visible way. This gave the impression that the company considered the pollution problem not important enough to involve top management. In contrast, Ashland Oil's chairman, John R. Hall, went to the scene of the Ashland spill and took charge of the cleanup and publicity.

2. Exxon decided to concentrate its news briefings in Valdez, a remote Alaskan town with limited communications operations, complicating the problem of disseminating information. Even *Oil & Gas Journal*, hardly an industry critic, complained about this. "Exxon did not update its media relations people elsewhere in the

691

world," the journal said. Instead it "told reporters it was Valdez or nothing."

3. Top Exxon executives declined to comment for almost a week after the spill, increasing the impression of a company that was not responding vigorously to a major insult to the environment.

4. Public statements by the company sometimes contradicted information from other sources in the industry. At one point, an Exxon spokesman said that damage from the spill would be minimal, while others watching the spill were saying that the damage was likely to be substantial.

5. An advertisement that Exxon ran in newspapers around the country 10 days after the spill appeared too late, and although the company apologized for the spill, it did not accept responsibility. To some readers the ad seemed platitudinous and failed to address the many pointed questions about Exxon's conduct.

Exxon officials defend their handling of the incident, saying the first priority was getting the remaining million barrels of oil off the tanker. Asked why he did not go to Alaska, Mr. Rawl said at a news conference, "I'm technologically obsolete. Getting me up there would have diverted our own people's attention. I couldn't help with the spill; I couldn't do anything about getting the ship off the rocks."

But this emphasis on operations overlooked public reaction to the largest discharge of crude oil in the nation's history, crisis experts say.

Source: Excerpted from John Holusha, "Exxon's Public-Relations Problem," *New York Times*, April 21, 1989, pp. 21 and 28. Used by permission.

Public relations is a promotional management function that "uses two-way communication to mesh the needs and interests of an institution or person with the needs and interests of the various publics with which that institution must communicate."[1] Its purpose can be to inform various publics about certain aspects of corporate policy or to cushion the effects of a corporate crisis. The Exxon story that you just read is an example of opportunities lost because management was unable to formulate a crisis management plan on short notice and thus suffered what has been termed a public relations disaster.

In contrast, the manner in which Johnson & Johnson handled the 1982 crisis in Chicago in which seven persons died from poisoned Tylenol is a classic example of how management can respond to a crisis situation with the aid of a good public relations plan. The very active public relations program of Carnival Cruise Lines, which has kept its channels of communications open to several publics, played an important role in the recent acquisition of Holland America Lines. Both the Tylenol and Carnival campaigns will be discussed in greater detail later in this chapter.

The very term *public relations* means that a person or institution is engaged in persuasive communications with certain publics. These "publics" are analogous to what marketing strategists would call *target markets*. Table 23–1 illustrates the variety of target markets at which public relations messages might be directed and suggests representative objectives for public relations campaigns. As can be seen, some of the target publics, such as company employees, are internal to the firm while others, such as the stockholders, are external.

INTERNAL COMMUNICATIONS

Internal communication is designed to let employees know what management is thinking, as well as to facilitate communication in the reverse direction. At one time, organizations were small enough so that this could be

TABLE 23–1

Representative Objectives for the Public Relations Function to Target Markets

To Ultimate Consumers
Disseminate information on the production and distribution of new or existing products
Disseminate information on ways to use new or existing products

To Company Employees
Offer training programs to stimulate more effective contact with the public
Encourage pride in the company and its products

To Suppliers
Provide research information for use in new products
Report on company trends and practices for the purpose of building a continuing team relationship

To Stockholders
Disseminate information on: (1) company prospects, (2) past and present profitability, (3) future plans, (4) management changes and capabilities, and (5) company financial needs

To the Community at Large
Promote public causes such as community fund-raising drives
Disseminate information on all aspects of company operations with the purpose of building a sense of unity between company and community

done easily on a face-to-face basis, but this is no longer possible in most situations, and the need often exists for a formal communication program designed for purposes such as distributing information and building morale. Failure to provide such a program can have devastating effects on productivity, morale, and turnover.

Because the details of internal communication programs are beyond the scope of this book, only brief reference is made to the variety of media that can be utilized for this purpose. These are itemized in Table 23–2.

An example of the use of internal communications is the program by which the Atlanta Gas Light Company introduced its new corporate symbol to employees.[2] Following a series of mergers, the company was faced with difficult communications and public relations problems caused by the use of three different names in different parts of the state of Georgia. A need existed to design a company symbol that was so distinctive and identifiable that it would immediately identify the "gas company," no matter where or when it was seen. Once the new symbol was designed and adopted, it was necessary to inform employees of the program and to indicate how they could assist in building a more distinct public image. This took the form of stories in company magazines, letters to supervi-

TABLE 23–2

❖   **Media for Internal Public Relations**

Medium	Principal Advantages
Employee publications	Treats subjects in depth; visually attractive
Manuals and booklets	Flexible; complete in details
Newsletters	Easily prepared; low-cost coverage
Posters	Colorful; dramatic; attention-getting
Bulletin boards and information racks	Timely; strategically placed
Exhibits and displays	Highly flexible; attention-getting
Closed-circuit television and teleconferencing	Dramatic; attention-compelling; involves audience; good for training
Motion pictures and videotapes	Flexible; good for demonstration
Grapevines	Informal; timely
Speeches and meetings	Two-way communication; treats problems in depth
Advisory groups	Two-way communication; takes advantage of expertise

Source: S. Watson Dunn, *Public Relations: A Contemporary Approach* (Homewood, Ill.: Richard D. Irwin, 1986), p. 295.

sors, and personal visits by top executives of the company to key executives and operating staff.

EXTERNAL COMMUNICATIONS

As a part of the promotional plan, public relations is most concerned with external communications designed to enhance the image of the organization in the minds of its various publics—ultimate consumers, suppliers, stockholders, and the community at large. The image is the overall reputation or *personality* achieved by the organization in its public interface.

Image is of great importance for overall promotional strategy because it is the attitudinal background against which all organizational offerings are evaluated. If it is defective, a considerable competitive handicap results.

There is no denying that many, if not most, business firms are facing a growing public credibility crisis. This has been caused, in part, by the attacks from consumerists, government, and other critics. It is also true, however, that public antipathy has been aroused by numerous examples of product failure, outright deception, and various other forms of irresponsibility.

Some firms by and large ignore their public image. Many others, however, are quite sensitive to their public interface, and make wise use of corporate advertising, customer relations programs, and publicity. Table 23–3 illustrates the rich variety of media opportunities that is available for this purpose. Of special importance in the external campaign are (1) organizational symbols, (2) corporate advertising, (3) customer relations programs, and (4) publicity.

Organizational Symbols

Organizational symbols and names are significant in identifying the organization and differentiating it from competitors. Each symbol in Figure 23–1 is a type of shorthand stimulus that calls to mind a constellation of meanings every time it is seen.

Concern over corporate image has prompted a rash of symbol changes in recent years. In part, this has been brought about by mergers, as was the case with the Atlanta Gas Light Company. In other situations, management believed that established symbols projected an image that was no longer in keeping with the current environment or current organizational activity.

The symbol must identify the organization at a glance, or it has failed its intended purpose. Most of those illustrated in Figure 23–1 meet this criterion well. If there are one or two that you cannot identify, then the corporate symbol may be too abstract.

Although the identification value of the organizational symbol is obvious, many believe that changes have at times been instituted for the wrong reason. The sums spent for this purpose are often surprisingly high, and the minor changes introduced, quite frankly, usually do not justify the effort. In the final analysis, the primary reason for the symbol change often is simply to gratify the egos of top management. It is not by accident that a symbol change frequently accompanies a major turnover at the top.

Corporate Advertising

Corporate advertising differs from the types of advertising discussed previously in that it is aimed at benefiting the corporation rather than specific products or services. Although its purpose is to build awareness and favorable attitudes toward the whole firm, the problems of message design and media selection are quite similar to those faced in product or service advertising.

It has been suggested that corporate advertising may be divided into three major categories: issue or advocacy advertising, financial- or investor-relations programs, and general corporate image building.[3]

Issue or Advocacy Advertising   When a company is faced with legislative or social activity deemed to be threatening, issue advertising is one way to

TABLE 23–3

❖   **Media for External Public Relations**

Medium	Principal Advantages	Principal Limitations
Newspapers	Community prestige; intense coverage; control by audience; selectivity; staffing by professionals	Short life; hasty reading; poor reproduction of visuals
Magazines	Selectivity; long life; credibility of source; good reproduction	Lack of area flexibility; lack of immediacy; duplication of audiences
Television	Strong personal impact; mass coverage; believability; prestige; high memorability	Fleeting exposure; little audience segmentation; time limitation; emphasis on entertainment
Radio	Immediacy; selectivity; mobility	Fleeting nature of messages; audience fragmentation
Direct media	Selectivity; flexibility; personalizing	High cost per contact; difficulty in compiling mailing list; poor image
Special events and displays	Targeted to special audiences; attention-compelling	High cost per contact; requires specialized help in arranging

Source: S. Watson Dunn, *Public Relations: A Contemporary Approach* (Homewood, Ill.: Richard D. Irwin, 1986), p. 333.

present its side of the argument. The tobacco companies, for example, faced with increasing public pressure to limit smoking, have been engaged in heavy advertising to present the case for less government regulation. The Mobil Company has used, with great effect, the Op Ed page of the *New York*

FIGURE 23-1

Organizational Image Symbols

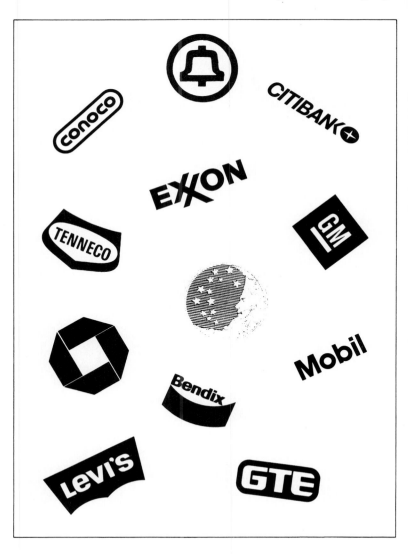

Times to defend itself against charges of excess profits and lack of interest in environmental protection. The U. S. Council for Energy Awareness is conducting a campaign to reduce the nation's dependence on foreign oil. An equally important goal of this organization is to promote increased use of nuclear power. Figure 23–2 is an example of an advocacy campaign supporting nuclear energy over oil.

Financial-Relations Advertising   This type of advertising strives to create awareness of and stimulate interest in a company or corporation among security analysts and potential investors. Many smaller companies find that

FIGURE 23–2

❖   **An Example of Advocacy Advertising**

JUST SAY NO.

America is hooked on foreign oil. Today, we import almost 40 percent of the oil we use—even more than in 1973, when the Arab embargo plunged us into gas lines, rationing, and recession.
    The more we can use nuclear energy, instead of imported oil, to generate electricity, the less we have to depend on foreign nations.

The 110 nuclear plants in the U.S. have cut our foreign oil dependence by over three billion barrels since 1973. And they have cut foreign oil payments by over one hundred billion dollars.
    But 110 nuclear plants will not be enough to meet our growing electricity demand. More plants are needed.
    To help kick the foreign oil habit, we need to rely more on

our own energy sources, like nuclear energy.
    For a free booklet on nuclear energy, write to the U.S. Council for Energy Awareness, P.O. Box 66103, Dept. SN09, Washington, D.C. 20035.

Nuclear electricity and energy independence

U.S. COUNCIL FOR ENERGY AWARENESS

Nuclear energy means more energy independence.

©1989 USCEA

Courtesy U.S. Council for Energy Awareness, Washington, D.C.

corporate advertising of this type is their only means to attract the attention of their various publics and to build a favorable image among members of the financial community. "One of the few pieces of concrete evidence of a link between corporate advertising and stock prices comes from the W. R. Grace 1980 television advertising campaign: their 'Look into Grace' series. The commercials highlighted the company's excellent business and financial attributes and then asked, 'Shouldn't you look into Grace?' After the commercials ran for 13 weeks in test markets, conventional studies of attitude and awareness indicated that familiarity and approval were at significantly higher levels than before the campaign."[4]

Image Building   Corporate advertising can be used to establish a company's identity or to change an image held by its various publics. The campaigns of GTE, TRW, and ITT are examples of efforts by companies that through acquisitions have gained many brand names. Consumer advertising of these brands does little to establish corporate identity or to create a desired image. One corporate campaign is described as follows: "GTE's ads present the company's technological achievements in telecommunications as surprising innovations. This leads to the response, 'Gee! No, GTE' and creates a link that (1) ensures association of the corporate name with the innovation and (2) works to eliminate the memory block inherent in perception of an acronym."[5]

On the other hand, when a company runs into problems such as those of the Manville Corporation (see Promotion in Action 23–1), a corporate TV blitz of $7 million may be needed to convey the right message. Another type of company image advertising is that in which the goal is to inform the public of the corporation's good citizenship. See Figure 23–3, in which Mobil Corporation describes its support of Maori art and literature.

Customer Relations Programs

Over the past decade, a growing interest in consumerism has motivated corporations to respond more effectively to customer needs and complaints. Many firms have established consumer relations programs. When Ford Motor Company recognized that consumers were favoring Japanese cars because of their perceived high quality, it introduced a company-wide quality assurance program. The fact that quality was now receiving top attention from all Ford employees was communicated to the public in ads like the one in Figure 23–4. The Chrysler Corporation's use of Chairman Lee Iacocca as its spokesperson offered customers a "Bill of Rights" including the right to a quality car, to long-term protection, and to friendly treatment, honest service, and competent repairs.

FIGURE 23-3

The prize of Maori culture

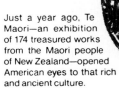

Just a year ago, Te Maori—an exhibition of 174 treasured works from the Maori people of New Zealand—opened American eyes to that rich and ancient culture.

The exhibition, sponsored largely by Mobil, originated at the Metropolitan Museum in New York and now is on display in San Francisco. It offers Americans what few of them had glimpsed before: what John Russell, in *The New York Times*, called "a race of master builders" and an art with "intimacy, a sure sense of scale and a regard for fine workmanship."

Now American readers have an opportunity to experience Maori culture anew with the publication of Keri Hulme's novel *The Bone People* (Louisiana State University Press, $17.95). The book was awarded Mobil's Pegasus Prize for Maori Literature in New Zealand after its selection by a committee of distinguished scholars. It also won the New Zealand Book Award and is a finalist in the competition for England's prestigious Booker Prize.

Publishers Weekly calls *The Bone People* "a first novel of distinct originality" that "tumbles out in an energized spill of narrative, poetry, dream and tribal lore."

The Bone People is the story of "three intimately realized, broken-winged people who are locked together in animosity and love," writes *Publishers Weekly*. Like Carson McCullers' characters, they are bound by their pain, their suspicion and—ultimately—their love. Unlike characters from cultures you may be more familiar with, these three also are bound by their Maori ties and their venerated ancestors—the bone people.

This sense of discovery is implicit in the Pegasus Prize for Literature, which recognizes authors of merit from cultures about which the American public often knows too little. Earlier prizes have been awarded in Egypt, Denmark, the Ivory Coast and the Netherlands. Next year's winning book will be from Indonesia.

It's our way of prizing other cultures, for the sake of ours.

Mobil®

Source: Reprinted with permission of Mobil Corporation.

FIGURE 23–4

Two Customer Relations Corporate Advertisements

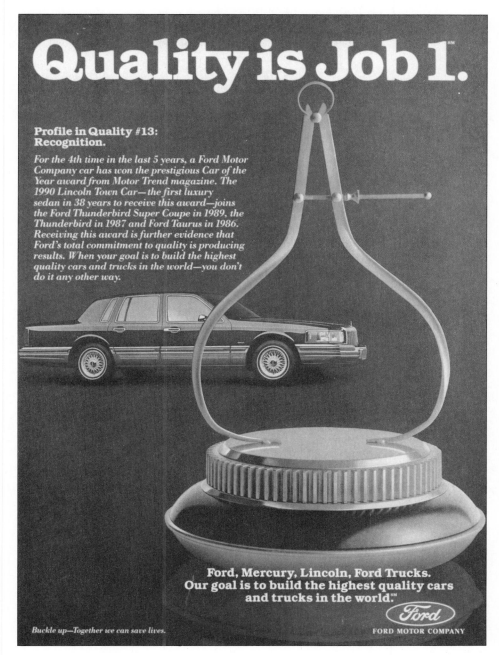

Courtesy Ford Motor Company

FIGURE 23–4

PUBLICITY[6]

Publicity is the provision of information designed to further the interests of an individual or organization in such a manner that the media uses the information without charge because they deem it of great interest to their audiences. The principal types of publicity are business feature articles, news releases, financial news, new-product information, background editorial material, and emergency publicity. Regardless of how well this material is prepared, without the cooperation of the press little information will reach the public. Given that there are over 100,000 editors in the United States and Canada, it is no small job for public relations people to keep the information going to the large number of persons who control the flow of publicity.

Manville Fights Image Woes with $7 Million of Ads

❖
**PROMOTION
IN ACTION
23–1**

Concerned that media coverage of its celebrated asbestos woes overshadow a bullish corporate story, Manville Corp. will have spent some $7 million on corporate advertising by the time its current campaign ends.

Manville expects it will have achieved 925 million gross household impressions and 70 percent cumulative net reach since the campaign began, says Robert H. Feeney, director of advertising and sales promotion.

Sports programming on the three major broadcast networks and cable's ESPN are designed to reach professional and managerial men, including specifiers of Manville's industrial and construction insulating materials. Major sports typically attract a 49 percent male audience compared to a 34 percent prime-time average, he notes.

Manville's three-spot pool features spokesman Jack Nicklaus. In two, he's at the St. Andrew's Golf Club in suburban New York City while he talks of Manville's building products or forest and filtration products. The third spot takes place in a simulated space mission control room. There he touts Manville's protective insulation for the space shuttle and the way the company uses the technology to improve earthbound automotive and appliance insulation. Mr. Nicklaus has been Manville's commercial spokesman for four years.

Mr. Feeney says that "the attitude tests we've taken show that our commercials convey the right message at the right time." Manville, previously Johns-Manville, hadn't run a corporate TV campaign since 1975.

Source: Cynthia R. Millsap, "Manville Fights Image Woes with $7 Million of Ads," *Business Marketing*, December 1984. Reprinted with permission; copyright Crain Communications, Inc.

Fortunately, the attitude of the press toward publicity is improving. To the surprise of several experts, a large proportion of editors queried stated that they found 50 percent of the publicity material received to be valuable for immediate or future use, and more than one-fourth of the editors said they would like to receive more.[7] On the other hand, the press is critical of the dissemination by business of irrelevant or poorly written news releases, or of releases that are little more than thinly disguised advertisements.

The wise public relations professional learns the press' editorial needs, policies, audiences, and operating problems. At the same time, the astute editor recognizes how publicity can be an important source of newsworthy information for his or her newspaper or magazine, or television or radio station.

The main avenue of communication with the media is through personal contact with editors, publishers, and feature writers of the print media— including wire services and syndicates, and news directors of radio and television stations. By making themselves available to the media, public relations people can increase the opportunities to have their material printed or broadcast. On rare occasions, the public relations people arrange a press conference. The purpose of such a conference should be the announcement of something very important, such as a new product introduction, a new pricing policy, a new acquisition, or a new chief executive. Press conferences called for inconsequential matters will result in lack of response when something of real importance occurs.

Other publicity methods include mailing press releases; giving press previews of new models or new facilities; and holding press-management luncheons where special reports can be given and the press can query the top corporate officers. At the luncheons, press kits containing mimeographed news releases, photographs, biographies, and background materials can also be distributed.

CASE HISTORIES OF SUCCESSFUL PUBLIC RELATIONS

The following two case histories illustrate the basics of strategy and execution in a public relations program. The first concerns the corporate response to the Tylenol tragedy;[8] the second, the announcement of the acquisition by Carnival Cruise Lines of the travel and tourism business of Holland America Lines.[9]

Public Relations Strategy for Rescuing Tylenol

In late September 1982, seven persons died in the Chicago area from taking extra-strength Tylenol capsules that had been laced with cyanide. Not until several days after the tragedy was it determined that the crime had been committed at the retail level by a person or persons (as yet unidentified) not affiliated in any way with the production process at Johnson & Johnson's McNeil Consumer Products Company, maker of Tylenol. At the time of the tragedy, Tylenol accounted for approximately 35 percent of all over-the-counter pain remedy sales. The product owed much of its success to the fact it contained no aspirin and was manufactured by a highly reputable pharmaceutical firm. It was heavily advertised and was recommended by many doctors for use by patients with a low tolerance for aspirin.

Immediately after the Chicago cyanide deaths, Johnson & Johnson withdrew all Tylenol capsules from distribution channels and urged retailers to remove them from their shelves. The company's share of the over-the-counter painkiller market fell to 6.5 percent the week following the tragedy because only tamper-proof Tylenol tablets remained on most retail shelves. The company's stock plummeted seven points on the New York Stock Exchange the day after the deaths were announced. Some prominent communication experts stated that the company would never recover from the adverse publicity. The chief executive of a large advertising agency, Jerry Della Femina said:

> I don't think they can ever sell another product under that name. There may be an advertising person who thinks he can solve this, and if they find him, I want to hire him, because then I want him to turn our water cooler into a wine cooler.

Competitors of Tylenol, fearing a possible backlash in public opinion, decided not to take advantage of the Tylenol crisis but to continue with their regularly planned promotion.

Johnson & Johnson decided to retain the Tylenol brand name and to launch a campaign to restore Tylenol's good reputation and its number one brand position. The following are the main elements of Johnson & Johnson's public relations campaign.

1. A policy of complete openness in response to news reports to warn the public not to take Tylenol capsules until the extent of the tampering was known and to make it clear that the company was not responsible for the poisonings.

2. A newspaper advertising campaign explaining that Tylenol capsules would be exchanged for Tylenol tablets.

3. Appearances by James E. Burke, chairman of Johnson & Johnson, on the Phil Donahue talk show and on the top-rated CBS news show "Sixty Minutes" to explain the company's concern and the measures that the company was taking to ensure the safety of the Tylenol tablets.

4. Low-key television commercials asking consumers to "trust" Johnson & Johnson.

5. A mailing of 2 million information pieces to physicians.

6. Personal calls on physicians, using an enlarged sales force.

7. Newspaper advertisements offering $2.50 off the purchase price of Tylenol.

8. New packaging with three safety seals for Tylenol capsules.

9. An offer of $100,000 for help in locating the person or persons responsible for the poisoning.

10. The introduction of a new television advertising campaign in early 1983 as a major part of a $70 million year-long campaign to promote Tylenol.

Tylenol had recaptured almost all of its market share by the beginning of 1983, even before the new safety-sealed Tylenol capsules had been introduced in all markets. Johnson & Johnson's total cost for its handling of the crisis was estimated at $100 million. By May 1983, Johnson & Johnson was running advertisements thanking the trade for helping Tylenol regain "a dollar level more than twice that of our closest competitor." A video press conference to announce the comeback was held simultaneously in 30 U.S. cities. Johnson & Johnson dropped its "continue to trust Tylenol" campaign to consumers in May 1983 and reinstated "You can't buy a more potent pain reliever" and "Trust Tylenol—Hospitals Do."

In 1983, the Public Relations Society of America gave its Silver Anvil Award to Johnson & Johnson and its agency, Burson-Marsteller, for their "extraordinary response to a recognized social responsibility."

Public Relations Strategy at Carnival Cruise Lines

As noted previously, Carnival Cruise Lines acquired the cruise, hotel, and land tour businesses of Holland America Lines in January 1989. To illustrate how a large corporation handles the communications to its various publics given an event of this magnitude, we present a brief case history illustrating how public relations served to fill needs that could not have been filled by the other elements of the promotional mix.

External Publics The day-to-day task of public relations at Carnival is to communicate with three external publics.

The first public is the trade press (*Travel Weekly, Travel Agent, Travel Trade,* and so forth). This audience is important because 99 percent of tour business originates with travel agents, and the trade press is an important communicator to the agents. In addition to the trade press, Carnival publishes in-house newsletters such as *Carnival Capers* (illustrated in Figure 23–5) and *Carnivalgrams,* which are mailed directly to agents together with releases for agents who publish their own in-house newsletters. In addition, the company publishes *Currents* magazine, which is distributed to past Carnival passengers and the travel agent community. This publication is aimed at creating top-of-mind awareness to Carnival passengers without bypassing the travel agents.

The second public is composed of travel editors and free-lance travel writers. These people develop materials that are printed in newspaper travel sections, general audience magazines, and travel guides.

The third public is the financial community. As a publicly held company with shares traded on the American Stock Exchange (ASE), Carnival must conform to SEC regulations by informing the financial community of any company happenings that have the potential to influence the price of the company's stock. Carnival uses, among others, the services of PR Newswire, which can alert the financial community on very short notice. Pertinent information is also sent by facsimile machine directly to the ASE.

Internal Publics This category includes all of the land-based employees (headquarters staff and sales representatives) as well as those operating the various ships at sea.

The Acquisition of Holland America Lines

On November 11, 1988, an agreement in principle was reached whereby Carnival would purchase the travel and tourism activities of Holland America Lines. A letter of intent had been signed and the proposed transaction was subject to the signing of a formal agreement, approval by directors and shareholders of each company, and the waiting period required under current antitrust legislation.

This information had to be communicated to all concerned publics. Special attention had to be paid to the financial community and the employees of both companies. Carnival did not want its employees or those of Holland America to be caught by surprise. A PR release was prepared (see Figure 23–6) and sent to the external publics. A letter explaining the impact of the acquisition was developed and was sent to all employees so that they would receive it at the same time the public announcement was made. Arrangements were made with Holland America management in Seattle to inform their employees in the same manner.

Access to the company president by the press was arranged. Network TV coverage (NBC "Today Show") and local Miami TV coverage were facilitated and a special video news release was developed. In addition, meetings were arranged between the chairman and president of Carnival and the top ex-

FIGURE 23–5

❖ **An Example of an In-House Newsletter**

Carnival Capers

Volume 15/No. 12   Carnival Cruise Lines   December, 1989

A Time For Thanks

The holiday period is the time of year when, traditionally, we take stock of things: where we've been, where we are, and where we're going.

We've come a long way from our inaugural voyage in 1972 when we ran aground. (The drink of the day was MARDI GRAS on the rocks!) 1989 has given us much to be thankful for:

- The acquisition of Holland America Line/Westours and Windstar Sail Cruises
- The terrific cooperation and "can do" spirit of their personnel — whether it's savvy senior management or a personable Alaskan tour guide
- The unique opportunity our sales force now has to provide you and your clients with a broad spectrum of non-competing vacation alternatives including our sparkling new Carnival Crystal Palace Resort & Casino on the Bahamian Riviera
- The outstanding support of tens of thousands of travel agents like yourself who bask in the glow of high

customer satisfaction from our array of vacation products
- Our new corporate offices — an entire 10-story building devoted to making Carnival as "user friendly" as possible for you to book us and work with us. Our state-of-the-art telephone and computer technology offers you what we believe to be the best service standard in the industry. (Our new address is shown at the bottom.)

We look to 1990 with keen anticipation. We eagerly await the inaugural of our newest SuperLiner ms FANTASY on March 2. (We even became an owner of the shipyard to insure that this splendid new vessel would be completed to our high standards.)

The FANTASY gives us a 25% increase in capacity ... the ability for you to have an additional 200,000 happy, satisfied customers.

All of us at Carnival Cruise Lines thank you for your past business and pledge to work hard to earn your continued support.

agent's corner

❝Recently a $9,000+ cruise we sold had to be canceled due to severe illness. The client got all his money back but we were left with nothing. We were not protected in the least. I bring this up now because of the foresight and forward thinking of Carnival Cruise Lines which sells the same kind of cancellation insurance as the other ship lines but also recognizes the fact that the travel agent who has performed all services required of him is left with nothing. Their trip cancellation insurance protects not only the client but the travel agent's commission. I have to applaud this thoughtful gesture on the part of our 'partners' and would hope that all cruise lines would institute such a program.❞

**Morton R. Mann CTC
Midwest Travel King, Inc.
Waukegan, Illinois**

Availability

Individual
- Mid-December on: Excellent for HOLIDAY, JUBILEE, CELEBRATION and FESTIVALE 7-day cruises, and CARNIVALE and MARDI GRAS 3- and 4-day cruises.
- Christmas on: excellent for TROPICALE 7-day cruises.

Group
- Excellent winter and spring group space available on all Carnival Cruise Lines' "Fun Ships."

**Note: Now is the time to begin booking individual and groups for the following exciting new products:
- 3- and 4-day cruises on the world's newest "Fun Ship" — the FANTASY.
- The January 7th TROPICALE and the March 25th JUBILEE special 13-day transcanal cruises.
- TROPICALE 7-day cruises from San Juan beginning January 20th.
- JUBILEE 7-day cruises from Los Angeles to the Mexican Riviera beginning April 8th.

Mystery Vacationers

$1,000 Winners
David Huff
AVENUES TO
TRAVEL, LTD.
Broken Arrow, OK

Jeanne Stephen
LIBERTY TRAVEL
Rockaway, NJ

Donna Munson
TEMPO TRAVEL
Parma, OH

$10 Winners
Kate Ricci
AMBASSADOR
TRAVEL
Altamonte
Springs, FL

Adele Kaehler
ROSENBLUTH
TRAVEL AGENCY,
INC.
Bala Cynwyd, PA

Winter Cruise-A-Thon

Space is still available at Travel Trade's 6th Annual Leisure Travel Conference and Winter Cruise-A-Thon in Fort Lauderdale on January 11-14, 1990. For information and reservations, call Travel Trade Publications at (212) 883-1110.

Back Of The Front

On the back of this month's Carnival Capers please find a quick reference guide for the products of Carnival Cruise Lines and Holland America Line/Westours, Inc.

Season's Greetings

Crystal Palace

Enclosed in this month's Carnival Capers please find the winter issue of Carnival's Crystal Palace Resort & Casino newsletter. The lead article features our newly created specialty suites including the Galactic Fantasy suite with a tariff of $25,000 a night. (Fully commissionable!)

Mardi Gras
Carnivale
Festivale
Tropicale
Holiday
Jubilee
Celebration
Fantasy

The "Fun Ships"

Registered in Panama & Liberia
**Important Carnival Cruise Lines
Telephone Numbers**
Carnival Place
3655 NW 87 Avenue/Miami, Florida 33178-2428

Individual Reservations		Group Reservations	
Nationwide	800-327-9501	Nationwide, Florida	
Florida	800-432-5424	and Canada	800-327-5782
Miami	305-599-2200	Fax	305-599-8664
Canada	800-327-9501		
Nationwide		**Executive**	
Hotline	800-327-2058	Nationwide	800-327-7373
Florida		Florida	800-325-1214
Hotline	305-325-1216	Miami	305-599-2900
Collect	305-599-2220	**Air/Sea**	
Reservations Hours		Nationwide	800-321-6666
Monday-Friday	8am-9pm	Florida	800-432-5424
Saturday	8am-8pm	**Sales/Service**	
Sunday	9am-7pm	Nationwide, Florida	
All Times are East Coast.		and Canada	800-327-7276

A MEMBER OF

CLIA
CRUISE LINES
INTERNATION
ASSOCIATIO

FIGURE 23–6

Carnival Cruise Lines Public Relations Releases

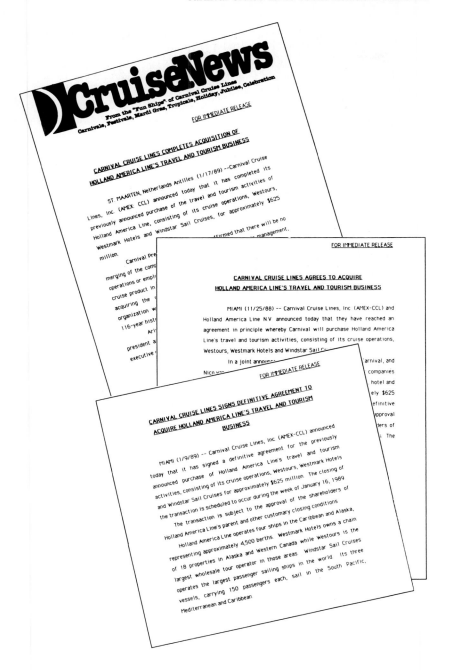

CruiseNews

From the "Fun Ships" of Carnival Cruise Lines
Carnivale, Festivale, Mardi Gras, Tropicale, Holiday, Jubilee, Celebration

FOR IMMEDIATE RELEASE

CARNIVAL CRUISE LINES COMPLETES ACQUISITION OF
HOLLAND AMERICA LINE'S TRAVEL AND TOURISM BUSINESS

ST. MAARTEN, Netherlands Antilles (1/17/89) --Carnival Cruise Lines, Inc. (AMEX: CCL) announced today that it has completed its previously announced purchase of the travel and tourism activities of Holland America Line, consisting of its cruise operations, Westours, Westmark Hotels and Windstar Sail Cruises, for approximately $625 million.

Carnival Pre... ...irmed that there will be no ...management.
merging of the comp...
operations or empl...
cruise product in...
acquiring the ...
organization w...
116-year histo...

Ar...
president a...
executive ...

FOR IMMEDIATE RELEASE

CARNIVAL CRUISE LINES AGREES TO ACQUIRE
HOLLAND AMERICA LINE'S TRAVEL AND TOURISM BUSINESS

MIAMI (11/25/88) -- Carnival Cruise Lines, Inc (AMEX-CCL) and Holland America Line N V announced today that they have reached an agreement in principle whereby Carnival will purchase Holland America Line's travel and tourism activities, consisting of its cruise operations, Westours, Westmark Hotels and Windstar Sail C...

In a joint announc... ...arnival, and
Nico v... ...companies
...hotel and
...ely $625
...efinitive
...pproval
...ers of
... The

FOR IMMEDIATE RELEASE

CARNIVAL CRUISE LINES SIGNS DEFINITIVE AGREEMENT TO
ACQUIRE HOLLAND AMERICA LINE'S TRAVEL AND TOURISM
BUSINESS

MIAMI (1/9/89) -- Carnival Cruise Lines, Inc. (AMEX-CCL) announced today that it has signed a definitive agreement for the previously announced purchase of Holland America Line's travel and tourism activities, consisting of its cruise operations, Westours, Westmark Hotels and Windstar Sail Cruises for approximately $625 million The closing of the transaction is scheduled to occur during the week of January 16, 1989 The transaction is subject to the approval of the shareholders of Holland America Line's parent and other customary closing conditions

Holland America Line operates four ships in the Caribbean and Alaska, representing approximately 4,500 berths Westmark Hotels owns a chain of 18 properties in Alaska and Western Canada while Westours is the largest wholesale tour operator in those areas Windstar Sail Cruises operates the largest passenger sailing ships in the world Its three vessels, carrying 150 passengers each, sail in the South Pacific, Mediterranean and Caribbean ecutives of Holland America Lines and several of the ship captains to explain the plans that Carnival had for improving the performance of the acquired businesses.

On January 9, 1989, a second release was prepared announcing the signing of a definitive agreement. On January 17, 1989, the third release was developed informing the various publics that the acquisition had been completed. (See Figure 23–6.)

The Commissioning of the *Fantasy*

In early 1990, the newest addition to the Carnival fleet, the *Fantasy,* was commissioned in Helsinki, Finland, where it was built. The first lady of Finland christened the ship and the ceremony was beamed by satellite to Cable News Network and to local Miami TV stations. The *Fantasy* began cruising in the spring of 1990, and Carnival wanted as much publicity as possible about the new ship coming on line.

Other Public Relations Activities

Carnival is a principal benefactor of the National Foundation for the Advancement in Arts, which provides support for newcomers in all areas of the arts. To raise funds for the Foundation, Carnival donated a three-day cruise to Nassau (Arts Fest at Sea) in January 1990 with all proceeds going to the Foundation.

The company also supports the New World Symphony Orchestra (Miami) led by Michael Tilson Thomas, which gives talented young musicians (ages 18 to 30) a chance to get a start in a symphony orchestra.

THE IMAGE OF PUBLIC RELATIONS

It is clear that much can be done to improve organization image through external public relations. Unfortunately, public relations is often undertaken as "window dressing" to gloss over and distort the true facts. The result is that the public relations industry itself has a bad image in many quarters, a reputation that is frequently quite deserved. Organizational accountability demands credibility in dealing with the public. To use the vernacular, anything less than this is rightly termed a *corporate ripoff.*

SUMMARY

This chapter has examined public relations, corporate advertising, and publicity as supplemental forms of communication. It noted the manner in which an organization can address its various publics, both internal and external, and communicate its policies and goals by means of an effective public relations program. Next we discussed corporate advertising and compared issue and advocacy advertising.

The chapter concluded with two case studies of successful campaigns showing how a total program utilizes all of the tools discussed previously and blends them into a communications mix that helps a company overcome adversity or handle a complex merger.

REVIEW AND DISCUSSION QUESTIONS

1. Your company has just experienced a disaster in that a leak in some piping at a large factory has spread poisonous gas over the countryside, injuring many people. You are in charge of public relations and must make immediate recommendations to the top management. Develop a short action plan based on lessons learned from the Exxon experience with the Alaskan oil spill.

2. Compare and contrast internal versus external public relations. Explain how management in the Tylenol situation utilized both of these activities to reach its goals.

3. The Todt Corporation, a large manufacturer of agricultural chemicals used for insecticides, has been besieged by activists who claim that the corporation's products are causing cancer in humans. The activists have no real evidence to support their claims, but they are raising a lot of public concern. The Todt Corporation has hired you to initiate a program of corporate advertising. What would you do in this situation?

4. How does public relations differ from publicity? How does one go about getting publicity?

5. What role does corporate imagery play in today's competitive environment? How does one go about developing a corporate image?

6. What role do you see for public relations activities in the decade ahead? Would you be interested in a career in public relation? Why or why not?

NOTES

1. S. Watson Dunn, *Public Relations: A Contemporary Approach* (Homewood, Ill.: Richard D. Irwin, 1986), p. 50.

2. Bertrand R. Canfield and H. Frazier Moore, *Public Relations: Principles, Cases, and Problems,* 7th ed. (Homewood, Ill.: Richard D. Irwin, 1977), pp. 70–75.

3. Thomas F. Garbett, "When to Advertise Your Company," *Harvard Business Review* 60 (March-April 1982), p. 100.

4. Ibid., p. 103.
5. Ibid.
6. This section borrows heavily from Canfield and Moore, *Public Relations*, ch. 7.
7. Ibid., p. 136.
8. Based on a case history in Dunn, *Public Relations,* pp. 20–21.
9. Based on personal interviews, May 1989.

EPILOGUE

The man [person] who knows right from wrong and has good judgment and common sense is happier than the man [person] who is immensely rich! For such wisdom is far more valuable than precious jewels. Nothing else compares with it. Have two goals: wisdom—that is, knowing and doing right—and common sense. Don't let them slip away, for they will fill you with living energy, and are a feather in your cap.

Proverbs 3:13–15, 21–22, *Living Bible*

From the perspective of the profit-making (or nonprofit) enterprise, promotional strategy is a valid and defensible activity. But can the same be said from the perspective of society as a whole?

At one time ethical, economic, and social considerations were a central concern in texts and courses. Unfortunately, a sampling of the current literature and of course content in business schools shows that this concern has died away. Have we fallen into the trap, "Anything goes as long as I can make a buck?" This seems to be the case in all too many quarters.

In this concluding section, we address serious issues that the responsible manager cannot evade. Ultimately, most of these issues can be resolved only by a personal sense of right and wrong.

Economic and Social Dimensions

POINT

There is a need in all market transactions to inform. With such information, markets are made more nearly perfect; the sovereignty of the consumer is served; and the latter learns where and by whom he is being served.

Source: John Kenneth Galbraith, "Economics and Advertising: Exercise in Denial," *Advertising Age,* November 9, 1988, p. 81.

COUNTERPOINT

Whatever advertising's direct effect in stimulating sales and making people buy more goods, it fully merits its reputation as an emblem of fraudulence. I do not mean fraudulence in the sense the Federal Trade Commission would recognize. . . . I take as emblematic the old McDonald's slogan, "We do it all for you." That, of course, is a lie. . . . [Advertising] does not seek to improve the lives of consumers except as a means to the end of sales.

Source: Michael Schudson, *Advertising, The Uneasy Persuasion* (New York: Basic Books, 1984), p. 10.

We have thrown you right into an argument that has raged for decades. Is promotion defensible from a moral, social, and economic perspective? Advertising, of course, draws the most fire because of its visibility. Therefore, it receives the most attention in this chapter as we address the effects of promotion on consumer behavior, new product introduction and prices, and competition and market structure.

As you will discover in this chapter, promotion is traditionally defended from the perspective that it performs these functions: (1) motivation of the consumer to increase standard of living, (2) provision of useful information to help consumers toward this end, (3) provision of a stimulus to produce new products at lower prices, and (4) prevention of monopoly and strengthening of competition. We will present both sides of the argument and will state our own opinion when it seems to be appropriate. Ultimately, however, it is up to you to evaluate whether a positive defense can be made.

These issues may seem remote to you at this stage, but they will not be for long. Today's business is increasingly being held accountable for all that it does. Let the words of Peter Drucker sink in:

> This new concept of social responsibility no longer asks what the limitations on business are, or what business should be doing for those under its immediate authority. It demands that business take responsibility for social problems, social issues, social and political goals, and that it become the keeper of society's conscience and the solver of society's problems.[1]

EFFECTS ON CONSUMER BEHAVIOR

Eminent economist John Kenneth Galbraith, once a highly outspoken critic of advertising, laments the fact that the gulf between established economic thought and the advertising industry is a wide one indeed.[2] He gets right to the heart of the matter:

> From the standpoint of strict economic orthodoxy, advertising verges dangerously on the subversive. . . . So long as wants are original with the consumer, their satisfaction serves the highest of human purposes. . . . But the foregoing holds only if wants cannot be created, cultivated, shaped, deepened or otherwise induced. Heaven forbid that wants should have their source in the producers of the product or service.[3]

Promotion is *persuasion;* it is *propaganda.* As Galbraith so clearly pointed out, these terms have taken on some bad connotations because both refer to communication that changes people. Change, of course, can have both good and bad outcomes.

Motivation to Increase Standard of Living   Conventional wisdom argues that motivational influences on the buyer are not sufficient to induce people to work, to produce, and to distribute the necessary goods. Some stimulus is required to influence them to attain higher incomes and to spend what they make on a rising inventory of goods and services.

Now the debate begins   Read the opposing arguments in Promotion in Action 24–1. Which do you favor?

The first perspective from Bogart maintains that promotion is necessary to fuel the process of increasing standards of living. The second from Schultze agrees that this does indeed take place, but he also contends in his writings (see Promotion in Action 24-2) that the process is self-defeating, that advertisers exploit the human condition and direct sentiments in ways that serve only the business firm, not the individual or society as a whole.

Belk has noted that in only the past 300 years has psychological well-being through discretionary consumption been within the reach of masses.[4] Despite some highly vocal charges by critics,[5] we agree with Richins that no conclusive evidence documents that advertising per se is a primary *causative factor.*[6]

Although advertising certainly is a major *contributing factor,* our opinion is that the causes can be found more readily by focusing on the nature of humans as acquisitive beings and on environmental conditions that favor economic development.

After a lifetime study of history, the Durants came to this conclusion:

> . . . the first biological lesson of history is that life is competition. Competition is not only the life of trade, it is the trade of life—peaceful when food abounds, violent when the mouths outrun the food . . . we are acquisitive, greedy, and pugnacious because our blood remembers milleniums through which our forebearers had to change and fight and kill in order to survive, and had to eat their gastric capacity for fear that they should not soon capture another feast.[7]

If this view is correct, we are constrained by human nature to live a self-centered life, according to the dictates of ego. Thus materialistic striving is a symptom of man's basic nature that, admittedly, is fueled and channeled by promotion. This, by the way, is the Judeo-Christian view, which proceeds from the premise that we are incomplete within ourselves, that we are sinners who cannot change apart from repentance, faith, and total commitment to a personal God.

The socioeconomic climate also is a major determinant. Taking North America as an example, we know the original settlers were forced to conquer a hostile environment. A work ethic was perpetuated and reinforced through the doctrine of individual effort inherent in the Protestant religion (i.e., the Puritan ethic).

In addition, a unique orientation toward the future resulted from a conscious revolt against the traditions of parent countries. Finally, individual initiative proved fruitful because of bountiful natural resources. Advertising is not required, therefore, as a primary incentive for work and achievement.

It is our contention that striving toward improvement of living standards is intrinsic. But there is no question that this motivation is reinforced by advertising and directed toward specific products and services. Therefore, promotional efforts do exert an effect on national income. It is entirely likely,

---

PROMOTION IN ACTION 24–1

Does Advertising Have Beneficial Effects on Standards of Living?

Point*

Apart from what a specific advertising campaign does for a specific product, there is a broader combined effect of the thousands of advertising exhortations that confront every consumer in America each day, a constant reminder of material goods and services not yet possessed. That effect at the level of individual motivation is felt as a constant impetus toward more consumption, toward acquisition, toward upward mobility. At the collective level, it is felt in the economic drive to produce and to innovate which fuels our economic systems.

Counterpoint†

Advertising exploits the human condition. Realizing that people are naturally covetous, that they form identities from the purchase and display of products and services, advertisers portray various styles of life and visions of reality, hoping to create and maintain meaningful images of people. They show us how to improve our social relationships, how to reduce our anxieties, and how to realise our most personal dreams. All of these things can be accomplished, they suggest, through buying and using particular products.

*Source: Leo Bogart, "Where Does Advertising Research Go from Here?" *Journal of Advertising Research* 9 (March 1969), p. 10.

†Source: Quentin J. Schultze, "Poets for Hire: The Ethics of Consumer Advertising," *Media Development,* 3 (1987), p. 3.

as Schudson[8] and others argue, that the *combined effect* of these efforts strengthens and intensifies materialistic strivings.

But what is the solution? Can we curb, or even eliminate, commercial efforts to persuade consumers? The late President John F. Kennedy proposed a four-part bill of consumer rights that had, at its heart, *the right to choose,* even as the late Clare Griffin argued, "Freedom for people to do foolish things."[9] If this right is removed or substantially altered, a step has been taken backward from a free enterprise system.

Provision of Buying Information   *The right to be informed* is another platform in Kennedy's bill of consumer rights. The traditional defense of advertising and selling is that they offer benefits to the consumer by providing information that is useful in buying decisions.[10] As consumer economist Hans Thorelli put it, "Informed customers are protected consumers—more than that, they are liberated consumers.[11]

Once again, attack and counterattack characterize the literature. Eminent semanticist Samuel Hayakawa leveled this charge:

> When my colleague, the teacher of home economics, says, "Buy wisely," she means thoughtful purchasing in the light of one's real needs and accurate information about the product; when advertisers say, "Buy wisely," they mean, "Buy our brand," regardless of your special situation or special needs.[12]

Empirical evidence seems to support Hayakawa by showing that less than half of all ads are truly informative in such terms as price, quality, performance, availability, and other objective criteria.[13]

The issue here centers, however, on what is meant by *buying wisely.* Critics seem to have some unspoken premises: (1) the only truly helpful information relates to price, performance, and other objective data; (2) the more information we have, the better; and (3) marketing efforts appeal to the "irrational." Here again, we will let the critics tangle (see Promotion in Action 24–2).

Our preference is to follow Snygg and Combs and base judgments on something other than personal opinion of what is irrational or inappropriate. We have shown in earlier chapters that consumer decision processes are enhanced by psychological associations and emotional appeals. Price, in fact, often is not a major purchase criterion.

Here is the determining principle: *The consumer must have access to information that is relevant in terms of the evaluative criteria used in purchase.* He or she alone makes the judgment as to what is relevant, and the economic system acts responsibly when that need is met. *None of us has the right to proclaim what is "rational" or "not rational" for another person.*

In our opinion, the system functions adequately in providing consumer information from a variety of sources, whether marketer dominated or not. The real challenge is to educate people on how to use the information they have.

The Issue of Deception   Nothing interferes more with the consumer's legitimate rights than deception. When it is practiced, consumers often make choices they would have avoided if the full truth had been known.

What is deception? Put simply, *deception* in advertising occurs if a message in any way creates a false belief or perception about product features or expected performance. The definition places explicit emphasis on *perceptions*. It is important to note this point because the Federal Trade Commission and other regulatory agencies have traditionally limited their inquiry to outright falsification. Many individuals, including one of the authors, have testified before the FTC that deception also can occur if the net impact is to mislead, regardless of what appears on the surface.[14]

❖
**PROMOTION
IN ACTION
24–2**

Wrestling with Rationality

Point*
Laying aside, for the moment, the objective facts about behavior that some of us have learned, let each of us look at his own behavior as we actually see it while we are behaving. We find lawfulness and determinism at once. From the point of view of the behaver himself, the behavior is caused. It is purposeful. It always has a reason. . . . When we look at other people from an external, objective point of view their behavior may seem irrational because we do not experience the [psychological] field as they do. . . . But at the instant of behaving the actions of each person seem to him to be the best and most effective acts he can perform under the circumstances. If, at that instant, he knew how to behave more effectively, he would do so.

Counterpoint†
Advertisers cajole, persuade, encourage, mystify, obfuscate, embellish, exaggerate, urge, wheedle, and admonish. They tell stories, create cosmic dramas, build clever arguments, and anthropomorphise products, and depict social relations. . . . Advertisers do these things principally to serve the client.

*Source: Donald Snygg and Arthur W. Combs, *Individual Behavior* (New York: Harper & Row, 1949), p. 12
†Source: Quentin J. Schultze, "Poets for Hire: The Ethics of Consumer Advertising," *Media Development* 3 (1987), p. 11.

There are three types of deception. The first and most obvious is an outright *lie,* a statement that can be falsified by objective information. The second is *claim-fact discrepancy* in which a claimed benefit must be qualified if it is to be understood (e.g., "50 percent off everything on our shelves [if you come in between midnight and 3 A.M.]).

The third and most insidious occurs when information processing leaves an erroneous impression about a product or service even though there has been no outright lie. A flagrant example is use of a credible spokesperson to motivate the consumer to trust an unworthy product.

The record of the free enterprise system on deception is spotty, and there always has been a need for regulation. During the 1960s and 1970s, there was considerable crackdown by government. Unfortunately, this regulation abated under the Reagan administration, apparently in the belief that the free enterprise system will provide correctives if it is left alone. This seems to reflect an unfounded optimism about human nature. We prefer a somewhat more rigorous regulatory atmosphere that supplies a consistent "well-lighted street." When the odds of getting caught are high, the deterrent is more real.

Consumerism   On balance, we believe that a better than passing grade can be given to the economic system from the perspective of consumer welfare and interest. Yet sufficient examples of excesses and abuses, including many not mentioned here, exist to give rise to the consumerism movement historically spearheaded by Ralph Nader.[15] Pressures have been strong indeed to correct such abuses as deception, defective products, and inadequate information.

The response of business to consumerism, on the whole, has been positive, but the record is mixed. For example, most manufacturers in the 1970s were hesitant to provide detailed documentation of advertising claims.[16] A common response was, "We do not propose to debate our advertising with you." Conditions have changed, however, to greater openness and sensitivity.

Our point is that promotion *can* and *does* perform a socially responsible and valid role when it is managed and conditioned by a genuine consumer orientation. Unfortunately, exceptions often speak so loudly that the public is understandably skeptical.

EFFECTS ON NEW PRODUCTS, PRICES, AND COMPETITION

The defenders of advertising have traditionally argued that economical access to a mass market has two important outcomes: (1) it provides the market access necessary to encourage innovation and (2) it lowers prices through mass production.

New Product Development   The primary contention here is that product development simply would not be feasible without access to a mass market. Certainly there is no argument against this premise, but it really is only the starting point to this issue.

You will recall the dynamics of consumer motivation and behavior under conditions of limited or routine problem solving. Because brand loyalty is pretty much nonexistent, marketers need to maintain "share of mind" through continual advertising. In order to have a message that attracts and holds attention, there always is pressure to produce something new. Innovation thus is a competitive necessity fueled by advertising.

There also is a strong incentive to produce better quality products. To see what happens when modern marketing is nonexistent, one need only turn to those economies that have recently moved away from their Marxist roots. Where previously there was little or no concern about consumers, matters changed dramatically. Branded and advertised products no longer can get away with shoddy quality that so characterized nonidentified, state-manufactured products. The consumer, of course, is the primary beneficiary.

The Effect on Prices   Marketers have traditionally contended that advertising lowers prices because of the advantages of economies of scale. The critic counters, however, that advertisers gain such a consumer edge that price competition no longer is necessary. Representatives of both sides speak for themselves in Promotion in Action 24–3.

Which side you take here depends on your theory of advertising effects.[17] If you subscribe to the view that *advertising gives market power*, a case can be made that market entrenchment leads to higher prices. If, on the other hand, you contend that *advertising provides new information*, it can be argued that the resultant competitive battle between entrenched brands can easily lead to lower prices. Probably there is some validity on both sides, but there is no definitive evidence one way or another.[18]

Lower prices   We must point out that total production and distribution costs can be reduced by advertising (providing the basis for lowered prices) only when a firm has excess capacity. If this is not the case, there will be no economies of scale.

Even if there are economies of scale, however, there is no convincing reason to expect that cost gains will be passed on to buyers. Until the mid-1960s, the differences in price between heavily advertised and nonadvertised goods were not large. In most cases, major industries were characterized by *oligopoly*—a few competitors producing similar products. Because price reductions are promptly met, nonprice competition usually prevailed.

But what a change in the 1990s! Few have freedom from voracious price competition. How common it is even in the ologopolistic airline industry for a smaller competitor such as Midway or Southwest Airlines to trigger a price war. And this is commonplace wherever one turns.

Higher prices It also can be argued plausibly that advertising can raise prices. It is entirely possible that competitive "share-of-mind" advertising, so

---

Does Advertising Lower Prices?

PROMOTION IN ACTION 24–3

Point*

The theory of the relationship between advertising and prices can be briefly summarized as follows:

1. There is not enough evidence available to judge whether for the economy as a whole advertising results in a net increase or decrease in manufacturers' selling prices.

2. If advertising is found to cause manufacturers' selling prices to increase, the magnitude of the price rise will be more than offset by the power of advertising to reduce distribution margins. Accordingly, on balance, advertising tends to reduce final consumer prices.

3. Advertising cuts distribution margins on advertised brands for two reasons: *first,* advertising causes goods to turn over rapidly so that they can be sold profitably with smaller markups, and, *second,* advertising creates product identity—which, in differentiated products, permits the public to compare prices between stores, thus setting a limit on the retailer's freedom to mark up.

Counterpoint†

Obviously, to the extent that partisan advertising alone creates brand loyalty, it creates a noncompetitive market situation. It is little wonder in recent years that we have seen a flight from price competition into promotional rivalry. . . . Not only the small company but the middle-sized company stands a decreasing chance to survive in a period when market survival depends upon the magnitude of promotional outlays rather than upon efficient production reflected in lower prices.

*Source: Robert L. Steiner, "Does Advertising Lower Prices?" in *Advertising's Role in Society,* ed. John S. Wright and John E. Mertes (New York: West Publishing Company, 1974), pp. 215–16.

†Source: Colston E. Warne, "Advertising—A Critic's View," *Journal of Marketing* 26 (October 1962), p. 12.

common when consumer involvement is low, adds to costs that must be covered by sales revenue. It is hoped that the great incentive for innovation will provide sufficient gains to offset this factor when it exists.

It is less convincing, however, to claim as did Colston Warne in Promotion in Action 24–3 that brand loyalty frees the marketer from price competition. We can only ask, "Where does such loyalty exist in today's market?" This point of view is further undermined by evidence demonstrating that brand-share stability generally is lowest among the most heavily advertised product categories.[19]

Effects on Competition and Market Structure   A main component in the defense of mass promotion is the premise that it facilitates and strengthens competition. It provides incentives for product improvements so that the firm has something to feature in its advertising. According to this point of view, it is difficult to gain monopoly position. If this incentive for innovation did not exist, market shares of existing firms would stabilize, and new competitors would have difficulty in gaining a foothold. For a sampling of opposing viewpoints on this issue, see Promotion in Action 24–4.

❖
**PROMOTION
IN ACTION
24–4**

Is Advertising a Barrier to Competitive Entry?

Point[*]
[speaking to the issue of advertising, entry barriers, and monopoly power] That competition is both vigorous and intensive among companies already in the market is clearly apparent from the marked increases in the number of products available and the significant changes that continue to take place in the market shares in most industries.

Counterpoint[†]
. . . The second most disturbing feature of advertising . . . lies in the area of monopoly power it has placed in the hands of the most substantial spenders (that is, investors in advertising). The national advertising outlay is not evenly divided among contenders for customers. It bulks with a very heavy weight at the top. It appears difficult, if not impossible, today to launch a new brand of food or drug without the outlay of as much as $10 million. If this is true, then what we face is a fantastic tax upon freedom of market entry.

[*]Source: Jules Backman, *Advertising and Competition* (New York: New York University Press, 1967), p. 8.
[†]Source: Colston E. Warne, "Advertising—A Critic's View," *Journal of Marketing* 26 (October 1962), p. 12.

If advertising reduces competition in this manner as contended, there should be high levels of advertising in those industries in which leading firms have a large market share, and vice versa. Although there are high levels of advertising in some situations (soaps, cigarettes, and others), it is not so in others, such as drugs and cosmetics.[20] Furthermore, there is no permanence of market share in those situations where it is true. Data have consistently shown that the top firms in one decade are in quite a different position in the next.[21]

In addition, an advertising-created barrier to entry should be revealed by a correlation between advertising levels and profitability. The evidence on this point reveals no consistent pattern.[22]

It cannot be denied that the heavy marketing investment necessary for survival is a deterrent to entry. But advertising should not bear this burden alone. It is more realistic to conclude that the requirements of large-scale operation are the fundamental deterrents to entry, and advertising is just one component.

To sum up, it is not possible to make a convincing case that mass promotion, *in and of itself,* creates entry barriers and promotes monopoly positions. Entry is always an uphill battle when such large investments are needed, but People Express, Hyundai Motors, Mitsubishi Electronics, and others have proven that it can be done. Who would have thought, for example, that a small designer in Seattle could dent the world of high fashion with, of all things, *sweat clothes*? This has been done successfully by Ellero, which makes use of specialty catalogs such as United Airlines' *Discovery* (see Figure 24-1).

Furthermore, you would have to look long and hard to find any firm with a guaranteed, monopolistic market position. Can you name any?

VALIDITY OF THE FUNDAMENTAL PREMISES

You will recall the two basic premises on which the defense of promotion in a free enterprise system rests: (1) a high and rising standard of living is a valid social goal and (2) profit is a valid measure of business performance. If either of these is found to be defective from a broad socioeconomic perspective, our case collapses.

Is a High and Rising Standard of Living Valid?　This premise is being challenged on two bases: (1) historical precedent and (2) environmentalism.

Historical precedent　Promotion in Action 24-5 presents two sharply divergent points of view. William Lazer, former president of the American Marketing Association, advocates the legitimacy of marketing's positive role in this respect, whereas Will and Ariel Durant see the materialism of today as symptomatic of a society in the last stages of decay.

FIGURE 24–1

❖   **Barriers to Entry Can Be Conquered**

Courtesy Ellero Ltd.

In the tension-filled era of the Vietnam War and its aftermath, the Durants' perspective was taken seriously. Public opinion polls reflected doubts about the materialistic course of free enterprise societies. There was widespread conviction, especially among young people, that the business system was accentuating the very forces bringing society to its knees. In that context, Lazer's assertions about the desirability of unrestrained materialism seemed naive at the very least, and perhaps even destructive if taken seriously.

The climate shifted dramatically in the 1980s. The very generation voicing such profound earlier concerns became baby boomers and, to the extreme, yuppies. The dominant values shifted to materialism and success. Quite a reversal!

What will be the climate of the 1990s? While there is a resurgence of social activism,[23] there does not seem to be an antibusiness climate. Certainly there is no diminishing of motivation to increase living standards. Once again, the perspective of the Durants and others[24] needs to be taken

---

❖
PROMOTION IN ACTION 24–5

Is a High and Rising Standard of Living a Valid Social Goal?

Point*

In our society, is it not desirable to urge consumers to acquire additional material objects? Cannot the extension of consumer wants and needs be a great force for improvement and for increasing societal awareness and social contributions? Is it not a part of marketing's social responsibility to help stimulate the desire to improve the quality of life—particularly the economic quality—and so serve the public interest?

Counterpoint†

Caught in the relaxing interval between one moral code and the next, an unmoored generation surrenders itself to luxury, corruption, and a restless disorder of family and morals, in all but a remnant clinging desperately to the old restraints and ways. Few souls feel any longer that "it is beautiful and honorable to die for one's country." A failure of leadership may allow a state to weaken itself with internal strife. At the end of the process a decisive defeat in war may bring a final blow, or barbarian invasion from without may combine with barbarism welling up from within to bring the civilization to a close.

*Source: William Lazer, "Marketing's Changing Social Relationships," *Journal of Marketing* 33 (January 1969), p. 6.

†Source: Will and Ariel Durant, *The Lessons of History* (New York: Simon & Schuster, 1968), p. 93.

seriously. Where do you stand on this? Will unrestrained commitment to materialism mean that developed societies will follow the paths to destruction of their ancestors?

Environmentalism   The world began to awaken in the early 1970s to the reality that its basic resources are not inexhaustible. In Western societies, ownership of such resources as air and water had come to be viewed as a common property right to be used by all, with the cost to be borne by society. The fallacies of such thinking were vividly brought to the forefront by Meadows and his associates known as the Club of Rome. They warned against the dire consequences of unchecked population growth, pollution, and exploitation of natural resources.[25]

These concerns became a rallying point of the environmentalism movement. Environmentalists broaden societal consensus beyond consumer satisfaction and focus it as well on *life quality.* They reject a marketing concept that centers only on meeting materialistic desires and strongly advocate the addition of societal and ecological considerations. Every indication is that these voices will grow in the 1990s.[26]

Here is the bottom-line question: *Is today's unchecked materialism mortgaging future generations who must live without necessary resources that are being selfishly squandered?* No one has a definitive crystal ball, but this is an ominous possibility.

Are There Any Solutions?   Some serious issues are raised here. But let's be honest: Is it probable that a social consensus will emerge calling for restrictions on the individual consumer and the free enterprise system? We think this is highly unlikely.

For this reason, some writers have rejected the viability of an economic system operating with unrestrained self-interest. At an earlier point in his life, economist John Kenneth Galbraith advocated an equalization of power between the social planning and marketing systems.[27] This, of course, would necessitate some form of socialism.

Certainly the world has had an object lesson documenting that Marxist socialism has failed to produce the economic utopia envisioned by its founders. The crumbling systems of Eastern Europe vividly underscore that only a limited ruling class prospered while the general public lived in deprivation and social needs were unmet. If this is what we mean by restriction of free enterprise, it is not likely that anyone will freely embrace it.

Those who advocate such radical change (and their numbers are declining) proceed on an all-important but unarticulated premise that mankind enters the world with no inherent predisposition to become self-centered and materialistic. The assumption is that self-centeredness is implanted and shaped by the environment.[28] If this is true, the logical solution lies in radical reform.

Others, including Will and Ariel Durant, take quite a different view of human nature, labeling us as "acquisitive, greedy, and pugnacious."[29] This, of course, is also the Judeo-Christian position that contends that people must change before the world will change. The Durants were not in the least bit optimistic that social surgery will solve the problem. Consider their words: "Nothing is clearer in history than the adoption by successful rebels of the methods they were accustomed to condemn in the forces they deposed."[30]

We agree with Galbraith's current position when he said that "perhaps this is not a socially perfect design for an economic system. It is, however, the one with and by which we live."[31] An economic system, after all, is only a reflection of the people who populate it. The ultimate solution to the real problems is responsible social action based on strong ethical and moral convictions.

Is Profit a Valid Measure of Business Responsibility?

The traditional position is that profits are an objective measure of the social value of ideas and that national consensus is found in market performance.[32] In other words, motivation to achieve long-run profit benefits society because of the necessity to meet the basic desires of both consumers and employees. If this is true, profit will be the reward for the enterprise that has been most successful in following the marketing concept and the principles of good management.

But does striving for profit allow for restraint that takes account of environmentalism and the other issues concerned with survival of a way of life? The eminent economist Kenneth Boulding has observed that there is a marked distinction between the profit system as an organizer of economic life and the profit motive in the "bad" sense of unadulterated lust for selfish gain.[33] Growing numbers today agree with Peter Drucker that the profit system functions successfully only when it is tempered by altruism or a sense of public responsibility.

Profit must, we believe, be defined to encompass more than mere financial attainment. Otherwise, business practices that operate counter to public interest may be justified when viewed from the perspective of history. The premise underlying the profit motive is that *business must be accountable for its performance*—accountable to owners and stockholders in the traditional financial sense but also to consumers and to society at large. It is time for this broader perspective to be taken more seriously.

STRENGTHENING THE FREE ENTERPRISE SYSTEM

We agree with Boulding that there is nothing inherent in a profit-motivated free enterprise system per se that demands a narrow selfishness and lack of identification with the broader concerns of mankind. The key is to adopt a proper attitude with respect to social and ethical responsibility.

Each person in business must take seriously the challenges our system faces. This requires an individual commitment to *ethical responsibility*— determination of *how* things should be and pursuit of morally justified courses of action. The question is no longer *whether* changes will occur in business practice but *how these changes will occur and what form they will take.*

Organizational Mission

Financial Accountability   A firm, especially if it is incorporated, outlives any individual set of managers. Present management must of necessity be oriented toward long-term financial survival. It cannot afford to extract a short-term monetary gain from shoddy merchandise or poor service because it must rely on repeat sales. In this sense, the firm profits when the consumers' interests are served.

Accountability to Consumers   Accountability to consumers, however, often requires going beyond the profit consideration. We referred earlier to President Kennedy's four-point bill of consumer rights: (1) the right to safety, (2) the right to be informed, (3) the right to choose, and (4) the right to be heard (redress). Consumerism as a movement has arisen because management has often been guilty of *one-way communication with the buyer; it is not listening to what is being said back.*

Manufacturers must be committed to developing safe, reliable products and to providing suitable means of redress when problems occur. An example of appropriate accountability is the Whirlpool Corporation, which initiated its "cool line" to provide immediate information on proper product usage and solution of minor difficulties. The company has also simplified and extended warranties and changed policies so that service can be given promptly when problems do occur.

Accountability to Society as a Whole   "It is increasingly recognized that business must divert some of its profits to help solve social problems." These were the sentiments of the president of Hunt-Wesson Foods in a speech made to an industry group.[34] Hunt-Wesson has acted on these convictions in many ways, such as financing improved medical care facilities in the inner city. It is only one of a number of firms that recognizes a broader social responsibility beyond that of financial returns. Indeed, survival—the basic goal of any enterprise—may demand expenditures and efforts of this type.

Phasing Accountability into Strategy Most organizations now assign reward to individual managers on the basis of sales performance, regardless of how much publicity they give to social responsibility. As H. M. Williams noted:

> Such an environment does not encourage any activity that does not maximize current profits. Nor does it recognize or penalize shoddy but temporarily profitable marketing and advertising practices. We do not make, nor in many cases do we know how to make or desire to make, estimates of the nonquantifiable or of the social and political implications of achieving plans.[35]

This is accentuated in the product form of organization, which decentralizes corporate and divisional responsibilities. Social concerns tend to be centralized at the headquarters level but do not find their way to those levels at which decisions really are made and implemented. The solution is for top management to initiate appropriate social and ethical considerations, to make compliance a part of the reward and punishment system, and to provide staff help in implementation at decentralized levels.

Cooperative Efforts

Because social and ethical responsibilities will never be met completely by individual organizations, a need exists for cooperative efforts. Certainly as a very minimum, an industry should provide a means for curbing false advertising as well as practices that are deceptive and unethical. Unfortunately, there are numerous codes of practice that represent nothing more than unenforced platitudes. Such superficial efforts, often undertaken to keep government at bay, do more harm than good in the final analysis, because they give a false sense of "having done something."

It is sometimes said that it goes against the grain of free enterprise to make cooperative codes of ethics compulsory, and to an extent we must agree. Nevertheless, it must not be overlooked that the mass media are intended for public use and are not the sole province of the advertiser. Government can present a convincing case for expanded activity to protect the public interest if self-regulation does not suffice. As never before, the advertising industry is faced with a challenge in this respect that cannot be ignored.

Cooperative efforts have taken the following forms: (1) Better Business Bureaus, (2) policing by advertising media, (3) cooperative improvement efforts, and (4) industry public service.

Better Business Bureaus Local Better Business organizations are sponsored by business firms to eliminate unfair methods of competition. They work with the national Better Business Bureau, which, among other things, publishes *Do's and Don'ts in Advertising Copy* to help advertisers steer clear of legal and ethical hurdles.

Individual customers or business firms initiate complaints to Better Business Bureau offices, and the action taken varies from publicity to legal action. The volume of advertisements and sales claims investigated each year is said to substantially exceed that processed by governmental enforcement agencies.

Policing by Advertising Media The media also have taken some positive steps in the form of industry self-regulation. Magazines and newspapers frequently turn down advertising that in their opinion violates good taste or is deceptive in its claims.

Most of the larger television and radio stations belong to the National Association of Broadcasters (NAB). The NAB issues a seal of approval to stations subscribing to its Code of Good Practice. This code is fairly rigorous in its provisions; it bans, for example, payoffs, rigged quiz shows, and deception regarding product characteristics. This is not to say that all areas of public responsibility are comprehended in this code. There have been numerous attempts to establish the NAB as a more definitive voice within the industry, and support for such an action may be growing.

Cooperative Improvement Efforts Industry associations of various types attempt to induce their members to adhere to ethical codes. The Proprietary Drug Association of America, for instance, enforces a code of ethics for its members, which handle more than 80 percent of all packaged medicines sold in the United States. Similarly, the Toilet Goods Association operates a board of standards to which members submit advertising copy. The board ensures that the copy is consistent with provisions of the Food, Drug, and Cosmetic Act and other legislation.

One encouraging cooperative effort is the National Advertising Review Board (NARB) sponsored by the Council of Better Business Bureaus and other organizations. Its organization and functioning were discussed in Chapter 12. As noted previously, the council's national advertising division receives and evaluates complaints against advertising. If an agreement cannot be reached, complaints are referred to the NARB for study by a panel.

Some have contended that NARB efforts have been too few and that its machinery grinds too slowly. There may be merit to this criticism, but hasty judgments also would be unwise. Further assessment of the NARB record must await longer service.

Industry Public Service   Some members of the business community have long been sensitive to their role in serving the public sector of the economy. The War Advertising Council was the first formal manifestation of this awareness; it was set up during World War II under the sponsorship of advertisers, agencies, media, and trade associations. The primary purpose was to stimulate the sale of War Bonds, and this objective plus others was given a real assist by the industry. This organization was later superseded by the Advertising Council.

The variety of public causes supported by the Advertising Council is impressive. Among the better known organizations and social issues given backing are (1) higher education, (2) the American Red Cross, (3) United Community, (4) the Radio Free Europe Fund, (5) the Youth Fitness program, and (6) the Smokey the Bear campaign to prevent forest fires. Costs are underwritten by advertisers, media, and agencies.

Further Cooperative Efforts   There are many additional unmet needs that require cooperative efforts, one of the most crucial being research directed toward a greater understanding of how information is received and used in a given culture. The restrictions of limited information, which hinder the effective management of advertising and promotion, have been noted throughout this book. Steps have been taken in recent years to dispel these constraints, but effort must go beyond this beginning. Basic research into all phases of promotional decisions is needed. Because the pressures of day-to-day management virtually preclude the necessary research efforts by individual firms, a cooperative industry research program is required.

In addition, industry can continue to meet its obligations through expansion of its activities on behalf of public causes. The tools of mass communication are ideally adapted to stimulating public awareness of unmet social needs, and the Advertising Council has done excellent work in this respect.

Finally, industry codes of ethics must become more than just platitudes stated for public consumption. Unless real enforcement provisions are established, such codes serve little purpose. If business is serious about cleaning its own house, it must do so through incisive action.

The Individual Manager   If the spirit of social and ethical responsibility discussed here is to be made operative, the commitment of individual managers to this end is required. This commitment, however, often requires a type of personal courage and sacrifice that many are not prepared to give because too many obstacles must be faced.

Evidence is mounting that today's competitive atmosphere is generating serious pressures to compromise personal ethics.[36] Corporate decision makers are facing a real dilemma.[37] It is not surprising that businesses are signing up for Ethics 101."[38]

Most managers encounter conflict when they discover that their youthful ideals and goals run counter to business operations that seem to be low on principle and high on expediency. This conflict is most severe for managers aged 34 to 42, and it often is manifested by an unwillingness to take on new problems and a desire to minimize the total demands of a job on one's life.

What is to be done when personal goals are found to be in conflict with organizational expectations? At one point in time, researchers at the California Institute of Technology gave this advice: "Take a tranquilizer, conform to the system, and realize that there are problems beyond your ability to solve."[39] Copping out is not a solution, however.

Obviously, ethical concerns can no longer be swept under the rug; they must be acted on if a way of life is to survive. This demands people who *dare to be different* — who are willing to seek solutions and act on their convictions regardless of personal cost. When such a spirit of innovation is absent, there is little basis for optimism about the survival of a way of life whose vitality stems from the exercise of individual initiative.

There are increasing examples of managers who indeed are daring to be different. Creative people in advertising agencies are demanding factual backup of advertising claims from their clients. Younger managers are not hesitating to voice their dissatisfaction with insulting advertising. Executives at all levels are refusing to give in when forced to behave illegally or unethically. The authors are personally familiar with a number of executives who have successfully taken their stands. Others, unfortunately, have taken their stands and paid the price of dismissal, but their personal integrity remains intact.

It must be assumed that each individual has arrived at a workable code of ethics. Some see no problem with subtle deception and other forms of legal but basically immoral business behavior. This speaks volumes about the content of their ethical codes. Far too many conclude that they will do what is necessary for themselves, regardless of the consequences, as long as they do not get caught. This is not the kind of ethical code that will make a real difference in today's world.

Ultimately everyone must come to grips with the eternal question of whether or not there are standards of truth that can govern behavior. Some say no — that truth is illusive and behavior should be based on the whims of the moment. Others place their roots deeply in religious conviction and guide their lives accordingly. Is religion out of place in the business firm? Some may say yes, but others are coming to a commitment that real ethics and morality pervade *all of life,* including life on the job.

Those who have found themselves — who have a workable philosophy of life — have a place to stand, from which they can dare to be different. Those who have not come to this point have little choice but to cave in when the pressures become great.

SUMMARY

This chapter has been devoted to a critical analysis of the economic and social role of promotion. The criticisms of this economic activity are far reaching, and the pros and cons were discussed in terms of their effects on prices, competition, consumer choice, and standards of living.

For the most part, the claimed social benefits of promotion are based on the premise that a high and rising standard of living is a valid goal. Once this premise is disavowed, the issues become more sharply focused because the materialistic society of today's Western world may be sowing the seeds of its own destruction. It was pointed out, however, that the economic system is merely a reflection of the basic motivations of its members, and the ultimate solution lies outside of business itself.

Nevertheless, there is much that can be done through a philosophy of business management that stresses not only financial accountability to owners and stockholders but stresses as well accountability to consumers and to society as a whole. Some suggestions were given that centered around the corporate mission, collective activities, and the role of the individual manager.

REVIEW AND DISCUSSION QUESTIONS

1. A well-known student of consumer affairs made the following statement to a group of home economists at a national meeting: "One of the greatest problems consumers face is lack of adequate information in making a purchase decision. They lack the know-how to be rational buyers, and business is not about to do anything to help them. The only hope is for government and other agencies to step in and give the consumer the information she needs." Comment.

2. Many proposals are advanced to reform the practice of advertising. Some have as their intent the elimination or reduction of the volume of advertising and hence a reduction of the socially detrimental effects of undue materialism. In your opinion, will this type of reform be a meaningful step in solving the basic underlying problems?

3. William Lazer has argued that marketing should work toward the end of helping the consumer to accept self-indulgence, luxurious surroundings, and nonutilitarian products. Do you agree?

4. The president of Hunt-Wesson Foods proposes that business must divert some of its profits to help solve social problems. However, this may serve to reduce the financial rewards to stockholders, thus giving rise to what might become a conflict of interest. Can this conflict be resolved?

5. In what sense are many criticisms of promotion really a criticism of poor management?

NOTES

1. Peter F. Drucker, *An Introductory View of Management* (New York: Harper & Row, 1977), p. 271.

2. John Kenneth Galbraith, "Economics and Advertising: Exercise in Denial," *Advertising Age*, November 9, 1988, p. 81.

3. Ibid.

4. Russell W. Belk, "Materialism: Trade Aspects of Living in the Material World," *Journal of Consumer Research* 12 (December 1985), pp. 265–80.

5. See Richard W. Pollay, "Quality of Life in the Padded Sell: Common Criticisms of Advertising's Cultural Character and International Public Policies," in *Current Issues and Research and Advertising* 9, ed. Claude Martin and James Leigh (Ann Arbor, Mich.: Division of Research, School of Business Administration, University of Michigan, 1986), pp. 173–250.

6. Marsha L. Richins, "Media, Materialism, and Human Happiness," in *Advances in Consumer Research* 14, ed. Melanie Wallendorf and Paul Anderson (Provo, Utah: Association for Consumer Research, 1987), pp. 352–56.

7. Will and Ariel Durant, *The Lessons of History* (New York: Simon & Schuster, 1968), p. 19.

8. Michael Schudson, *Advertising, The Uneasy Persuasion* (New York: Basic Books, 1984).

9. Clare E. Griffin, *The New Face of Capitalism* (Ann Arbor, Mich.: University of Michigan Graduate School of Business, 1961), p. 18.

10. See, for example, George J. Stigler, "The Economics of Information," *Journal of Political Economy* 60 (1961), pp. 213ff.

11. Hans Thorelli, "The Future for Consumer Information Systems," in *Advances in Consumer Research* 8, ed. Jerry C. Olson (Ann Arbor, Mich.: Association for Consumer Research, 1980), pp. 222–32.

12. Samuel Hayakawa, quoted in *Advertising Age*, December 25, 1961, p. 30.

13. Alan Resnik and Bruce L. Stern, "An Analysis of Information Content in Television Advertising," *Journal of Marketing* 41 (1977), pp. 150–53.

14. For a summary of this testimony, see John Howard and James Hulbert, *Advertising and the Public Interest* (Chicago: Crain Publications, 1973).

15. For a detailed review of contemporary consumerism, see James F. Engel, Roger D. Blackwell, and Paul W. Miniard, *Consumer Behavior*, 6th ed. (Hinsdale, Ill.: Dryden Press, 1990), ch. 25.

16. Arch G. Woodside, "The Documentation of Advertising Claims," *Scan* 21, no. 4, p. 18.

17. Robert Steiner, "Does Advertising Lower Consumer Prices?" *Journal of Marketing* 37 (1973), pp. 346–57.

18. Jules Backman, *Advertising and Competition* (New York: New York University Press, 1967), p. 144.

19. L. G. Telser, "Some Aspects of the Economics of Advertising," *Journal of Business* 41 (April 1968), p. 169.

20. Ibid.

21. Backman, *Advertising and Competition,* p. 113.

22. Ibid., p. 154.

23. For an interesting review, see Ronald Grover, "Fighting Back: The Resurgence of Social Activism," *Business Week,* May 22, 1989, pp. 34–35.

24. See especially Pollay, "Quality of Life in the Padded Sell."

25. D. H. Meadows and D. L. Meadows, *The Limit to Growth* (New York: Universal Books, 1972).

26. Grover, "Fighting Back."

27. See especially John K. Galbraith, *The Affluent Society* (New York: Houghton-Mifflin, 1958), and *Economics and the Public Purpose* (New York: Houghton-Mifflin, 1973).

28. This is the essential premise of B. F. Skinner, *Beyond Freedom and Dignity* (New York: Alfred A. Knopf, 1971).

29. Durant and Durant, *The Lessons of History,* p. 9.

30. Ibid., p. 34.

31. Galbraith, "Economics and Advertising," p. 81.

32. One of the leading advocates is Drucker, *An Introductory View of Management.*

33. Kenneth Boulding, "Ethics and Business: An Economist's View," in *Marketing and Social Issues,* ed. J. R. Wish and S. H. Gamble (New York: John Wiley and Sons, 1971), pp. 91–97.

34. Quoted in *Advertising Age,* February 23, 1970, p. 191.

35. H. M. Williams, "Why and How Are We Losing the Free Enterprise Battle?" *Advertising Age,* November 26, 1972, p. 34.

36. Geoffrey P. Lantos, "An Ethical Base for Decision Making," (unpublished manuscript, Fall 1986).

37. Daniel E. Maltby, "The One-Minute Ethicist," *Christianity Today,* February 19, 1988, pp. 26–29.

38. John A. Byrne, "Businesses Are Signing up for Ethics 101," *Business Week,* February 15, 1988, pp. 56–57.

39. *Sales Management,* May 1, 1969. p. 20.

Index

A

Absolute recognition threshold, 106
Abstraction, 362
Aburdene, Patricia, 296
Acceptance, 84, 99–102
Action for Children's Television (ACT), 342
Adams, Tony, 170
Admiral Cruises, Inc., 50
AdTel research service, 512, 513
Advertising; *see also* Promotion
   activation methods, 365-75
   advocacy or issue, 696–98
   analyzing messages, 390–93
   appropriations, 265–90
      geographic allocation, 281–86
      marginal analysis, 265–68
      new product payouts, 286–90
      objective and task approach, 274–81
      traditional approach, 268–74
   behavioral research findings, 364–66
   broadcast, 91
   to children, 342, 343
   choosing approach to product, 370
   communication, 243
   copy testing; *see* Copy testing
   corporate, 696–99
   creative execution, 359–60
   creative strategy, 359–60
   deceptive, 337–41
   definition, 13
   designing and producing message, 390,
     395–408

Advertising—*Cont.*
   impact on buying behavior, 243–44
   information source, 136–38
   low involvement, 94
   media; *see* Mass media *and* Media
   100 biggest national advertisers, 269
   persuasion, 361–63
   price effect, 724–26
   print advertising; *see* Print advertising
   regulation; *see* Regulation of marketing
     and promotion
   Simon activation methods, 365–75
   strategy, 158–63
   visual elements, 402–6
   volume in United States, 413–14
Advertising activation methods, 365–75
Advertising agency
   agency-client relationship, 305, 312
   compensation, 309
   direct marketing, 684–85
     future of, 317
   house agency, 312–13
   organization of, 303–5
   reseller assistance, 642–53
   specialized services, 315–17
   top worldwide agencies, 306
Advertising message weight, 489
Advertising recognition, 155
Advertising Research Foundation (ARF), 469,
   515
Advertising substantiation, 345
Advocacy advertising, 696–98

Affective responses, 102, 362

Aided recall, 519

AIO (attitudes, interests and opinions), 219
   lifestyle measurement, 247
   product-specific analysis, 221
   segmentation analysis, 227–28

Ajzen, Icek, 122, 140, 142

Alaska Pipeline Bill (1973), 327

Albers, John, 9

All you can afford method of determining
   advertising budget, 272–74

Alsop, Ronald, 67, 169, 251

Alternative evaluation, 128, 131, 140–45,
   155–56
   decision process behavior, 249

American Association of Advertising
   Agencies, 308, 311

American Hawaii, 48

American Honda Motor Company, 14–15
   advertisement, 16

American Marketing Association, 540

American Newspaper Publishers
   Association, 420

America West Airlines, 235–37

Amoco Corporation, 158

Arbitrary allocation method of determining
   advertising budget, 268–69

Argument ad, 367, 368, 375–78, 381, 383,
   385, 387, 388

Arison, Micky, 34

Arison, Ted, 32, 119

Association measures, 521

AT&T, 15, 17, 19, 257

Attention, 84, 90–96

Attitude change, 102–5
   information processing, 103–5

Attitude-scale statements, 505

Audimeter, 474

Audiotex, 674

Audit Bureau of Circulation, 469
   Newspaper Audience Research Data Bank,
   473

Austin, Nancy, 295

B

Bacardi, 225

Backman, Jules, 726

Bardagy, Robert A., 598

Barton, Roger, 277

Bausch & Lomb, 220, 221

Bayus, Barry L., 535

Bearden, William O., 195

BehaviorScan, 513

Belief, 97

Belk, Russell W., 719

Benchmark, 258

Bernhardt, Kenneth L., 541

Better Business Bureau, 734
   Council of, 332, 335

Blackwell, Roger D., 86, 129, 153, 191, 194,
   198, 250, 366

Bloom, Allan, 182

Blum, Jonathan, 561

Blumenthal, Karen 655

Bogart, Leo, 719

Bonus, 599

Boulding, Kenneth, 731, 732

Bowman, Russ, 542, 545, 556

Brand loyalty, 122, 126, 165–70
   habitual buyer, 255

Brand recognition, 143, 158–62, 250, 254

Brimley, Wilford, 30

Bristol-Myers, 245

R. H. Bruskin Associates, 251

Bucklin, Louis P., 662, 663

Bunse, Diane, 298

Burke, James E., 705

Business publications, 412

Buskirk, Richard H., 604

C

Cable television, 429–34

Cacioppo, John T., 102, 103, 362–63

Campbell Soup Company, 206, 229, 321,
   331, 499–501, 658

Canton, Alan, 362

Carlzon, Jan, 295, 296, 297

Carnival Cruises
   advertising, 391–93
   compensation, 600
   consumer decision making, 119–20,
   122
   media strategy, 488
   promotional strategy, 32–42
   public relations, 693, 706–10
   sales force assignment, 595–96

Carroll, Vincent P., 535

Catalog sales, 669, 680–81

Categorization, 96–98
   responses, 100–101

Category manager, 302

CBBB (Council of Better Business Bureaus),
   332, 335

Central route to persuasion, 363

Childrens' Television v. *General Foods,* 331
Christie, Lorna, 675
Churchill, Gilbert A., Jr., 589, 603
Claim-fact discrepancy, 723
Claritas, 217
Clayton Act (1914), 349
The Closing of the American Mind (Bloom), 182
Coca-Cola Company, 167
Coca-Cola Foods, Inc., 225
Cognitive consistency, 93–94
Cognitive responses, 101, 102
Cold canvass approach, 582
Color
  media advertising, 405–6, 413, 418
  packaging, 563
Colt, Stockton B., Jr., 610
Combs, Arthur W., 721, 722
Command ads, 370, 372, 375
Commission, 308–11, 599
Communication, 7, 59–78
  accuracy, 62
  advertising goal, 243
  definition, 61
  function of marketing, 13–14, 60
  kinds of, 68–74
  marketing, 74 – 78
  mass communication, 75
  personal selling, 74–75
  marketing mix, 20–25
  model of, 61–62
  price, 212
  product, 212
  promotional objective, 244
  sales force, 602–3
  semiotics, 64–68
Communiscope, 522
Community and suburban newspapers, 418
Comparative advertising, 340, 341
Compensation, 596–600
  base salary, 598–99
  bonus, 599
  commission, 569
Competitive parity method of determining advertising budget, 272
Competitive positioning, 230–38
  definition, 230–31
  key strategic promotional choices, 238
  strategy, 231–38
Comprehension, 84, 96–99

Concentrated marketing, 230
Connotative meaning, 65
Consumer deal, 547–50, 656–57
Consumer decision processes, 122
  alternative evaluation, 123, 140–45, 155–56
  diagnosing, 127–28
  habitual, 122, 126, 165–70
  information search, 123, 128, 131, 133–40
  initial purchases, 122–26
  need recognition, 123, 127–33, 154–55
  outcomes, 123, 129, 131, 145–47, 156, 250
  purchase, 129, 131, 145–47, 156
  repeat purchases, 126
  stages in, 123
Consumerism, 723, 732
Consumer jury, 503–5
Consumer sovereignty, 10, 84
Contests, 558–62, 564–65
  retail selling, 650, 652
  sales force motivation, 602
Contextual marketing, 177
Contiguity, 68, 70
Contribution margin, 612
Controlled experiment, 524
Cooperative advertising, 643–45
  legal problems, 652–53
Coordinated management of promotion mix, 30, 33, 41–42
Copy platform, 359, 360
Copy testing, 501
  experimental design, 524–25, 529–33
  laboratory measures, 503–10
  posttesting procedure, 513
  pretesting, 503–13, 522
  real-world measures, 504, 510–35
Corollary products index, 282
Corporate advertising, 696–99
Corrective advertising, 345–46, 348
Cost per household rating point (CPP), 483
Cost per thousand homes (CPM), 427, 452
  media strategy, 484–86
Cost standards, 278
Council of Better Business Bureaus (CBBB), 332, 335
Counterarguments, 361
Coupons as promotion, 168, 543–45
  inquiry tests, 511–12
Cravens, David W., 575
Creative boutiques, 316
Creative execution, 360–65

Creative platform, 256
Creative rules of copywriting, 390
Creative strategy, 359–60
Creativity, definition, 360
Cross elasticity of demand, 635
Culture, 176
    dynamic nature of, 179–82
    marketing as determinant of values, 184,
        187
Cunard, 47–48
Cuneo, Alice Z., 188
Curtindale, Frieda, 137
Customer database, 670, 672–74
Customer relations programs, 699, 701–2
Custom-made index of buying power, 284,
    286

D

DAGMAR (defining advertising goals,
    measuring advertising results), 527
Dagnoli, Judann, 241, 633
Database, 670, 672–74
    geodemography, 673–74
    in-house lists, 672–73
Davis, Donald, 6
Dawson, Douglas J., 229
Day-After Recall test, 512
Deception in advertising, 105–6, 722-23
Deciders, 246
Decision-making unit, 245–46
Decision process; see Consumer decision
    processes
Deckman, Marshall, 446
Decoding, 62
Della Femina, Jerry, 96, 705
Delphi technique, 619
Demographic segmentation
    by age, 212–14
    clue to lifestyle, 215, 217, 219
    definition, 246
    by income, 213–14
    by sex, 216–17
    target market selection, 246
Denotative meaning, 65
De Pree, Max, 298
Detail salespersons, 618
Dewey, John, 122
DHL Worldwide Express, 357–58
Dialogue copy, 399
Dickinson, Robert, 35
Differentiated marketing, 228–30

Direct action advertising, 682
    copy, 400–401
Directionality, 91
Direct mail advertising, 412, 450–51
Direct mail marketing, 676–80
Direct marketing, 669
    database, 670, 672–74
    direct mail, 676–81
    managing, 684–87
    return on investment, 686
    strategies, 674–84
    telemarketing; see Telemarketing
Direct marketing agencies, 315, 684–85
Displays, 654–56
Distribution cost analysis, 611–12
Distribution location, 25–26
Distribution programming, 660–61, 662
Dollar appropriation for promotion, 30, 33,
    36–37
Drexler, Michael, 475
Drive, 127
Drucker, Peter, 295, 303, 718, 731
Dummy advertising vehicles, 511
Dunn, S. Watson, 696
Dunn, Timothy, 205
Durant, Ariel, 719, 727, 729
Durant, Will, 719, 727, 729

E

Eagle Food Centers, 560–61
Eastlack, Joseph O., 501
Eastman Kodak, 138
Editorial interest technique, 470, 473
Effectiveness of promotional planning, 30,
    33, 42
Egalitarianism, 179
Ego relatedness, 87, 124
Eisner, Seth A., 564
Elaboration, 98
Elaboration Likelihood model, 103, 363
Empathy, 65
Encoding, 61–62
Engel, James F., 86, 129, 153, 191, 194, 198,
    250, 366
Erceg, James, 544
Erickson, Julie Liesse, 241, 633, 646
ERIN testing service, 512
Ethics, 732–36
    individual responsibility, 736
    industry associations, 734
    managers' responsibility, 735

Ethnocentrism, 177
Etzel, Michael J., 195
Evaluation of promotional strategy, 30, 33, 42
Exposure to communications, 84, 88–90, 155
Exxon Corporation, 691–92
Extended problem solving (EPS), 122, 123–47
    contrasted with limited problem solving, 152–53
    need recognition, 128–29
    promotional strategy, 248, 250–53
    target segment, 248, 251
Eye camera, 508

F

Fair Credit Reporting Act, 324
Fairness doctrine, 341–42
Fair Packaging and Labeling Act, 324
Family influence on values, 179, 194–96
Family life cycles, 196–98
Fassak, Gary, 206
Federal Food, Drug and Cosmetic Act of 1938, 323, 326, 329–30
Federal Trade Commission (FTC), 324–25
    Code of Conduct, 345
    cooperative advertising, 252–53
    deception in advertising, 722
    future of, 328–29
    Improvement Act, 327–28
    monitoring promotion, 324, 327, 344–48
Federal Trade Commission Act (1914), 323, 324, 326
Feedback
    analysis of, 78
    mass media, 77
Feeney, Robert H., 703
Fee system, 309–11
Financial-relations advertising, 698–99
Fishbein, Martin, 122, 140, 142
Fisher-Price, 495
Flesch, Rudolph, 507
Flighting, 490–93
Focus, 361
Focus groups, 506
Food, Drug and Cosmetic Act, 734
Food and Drug Administration (FDA), 329–30
Ford, Neil M., 589, 603
Ford Motor Company, 244

Free enterprise system, 732
    accountability of organizations, 732–33
    cooperative efforts by organizations, 733–36
    profit-motivated, 732
    public service by organizations, 735
Freeman, Laurie, 121
Frequency, medic schedule, 476–83
    effect of flight, 491
FTC Improvement Act (1980), 327–28, 342
Functional organization, 300–301
Fur Products Labeling Act, 324

G

Galbraith, John Kenneth, 717, 718, 730, 731
Gallup and Robinson (G&R) survey services, 512–13
    impact test, 519–21
Galvanic skin response (GSR), 508–9
Garrick, George, 89
Gatekeepers, 246
General buying power indexes, 283–84
General content media, 134, 138
General Electric, 21
General Foods corporation, 229
General Mills, 29
General Motors, 77, 296
Geodemography, 673–74
Geographic segmentation, 209–10, 213
Gidwitz, Ron, 6
Gifford, Kathie Lee, 35
Giges, Nancy, 146
Gilbert, Betsy, 681
Gillette, Terry C., 669
Goldman, Emmanuel, 9, 213
Goodman, Ellen, 152
Grable, Pat, 175
Griffin, Clare, 721
Griffin, Em, 105
Gross rating points (GRP), 476–81
Group norms, 191
Guggenheim, Bernard, 409

H

Habitual buying, 255–56
Habitual decision making, 165–70
    promotional strategy, 255–56
Hall, John R., 691
Halo effect, 505
Hannan, Michael, 46
Hardikar, Shirish, 587
Harper, Doug, 574

Hart Schaffner & Marx, 75
Hasbro, 495
Haugh, Louis J., 553
Hayakawa, Samuel, 721
Hazardous Substance Labeling Act, 330
Headline
    classification, 395–97
    guide for persuasive headlines, 397–98
H. J. Heinz Company, 164
Helene Curtis, 5–7
Hewlett-Packard (H-P), 587
Hidden benefit ad, 373–74
Hills, Gerald E., 575
Hoehn, Dave, 640
Hogue, Kenneth, 188
Holland America Line (HAL), 34, 35, 48–49,
    607–8, 706–7, 710
Holly, Jim, 448
Holusha, John, 692
Honda, 14–15
    advertisement, 16
Houck, Lon, 544
Houghton, Maxine, 206
House agency, 311–12
House-to-house personal selling, 684
Huey, John, 632
Humanitarianism, 179
Humor, 399
Humphrey, Hubert, III, 321
Hurwitt, David, 543
Hyster Company, 640–41

I

Iacocca, Lee, 697, 702
Icon, 64
Image, 695
    corporate advertising, 699–700
    public relations, 710
Imitation ad, 370, 374, 375
Impulse purchase, 154
Income segmentation, 213–14
Incremental (marginal) analysis, 265–68,
    274, 281
Index, 64
Industry sales method of computing sales
    potential, 283
Inertia, 122, 126, 166, 170, 255
Influencers, 246
Information
    in-store, 138
    search, 155

Information—Cont.
    source for advertising, 136–38
    processing, 155
Information ad, 365, 375
Informational influence, 193
Information processing, 84
    acceptance, 84, 99–102
    attention, 84, 90–96
    attitude change, 103–5
    comprehension, 84, 96–99
Information search, 128, 131, 133–40, 155
    decision process behavior, 249
    use of sources, 134–40
In-home selling, 136, 684
In-house list for direct marketing, 672–73
Innovation, 297
Inquiry tests, 511–12
In-store information, 138
In-store promotions, 648, 650, 651
Interactive electronic media, 682
In-view tests, 513
Involvement, 87
    attention, 103–4
    low, 94, 103
    problem-solving behavior, 124–25
Iverson, F. Kenneth, 296
Issue advertising, 696–98

J

Jaworski, Bernard, J., 104, 364
Johnson, Lawrence, V., 360
Johnson & Johnson, 692
    Tylenol crisis, 704–6
Job description, 588–89
Junk mail, 450, 677

K

Karlin, Malcolm, 671
Kassarjian, Hal, 152
Kellogg Corporation, 156–58, 242–43
Kennedy, John F., 336, 721, 732
Key, Wilson Bryan, 106–7, 109
Kimberly-Clark Corporation, 121, 129–30
King, James, 494
Kinnear, Thomas C., 475, 501, 541
Klecker, Ray, 539
Kneale, Dennis, 90
Koenig, Richard, 322
Kotler, Philip, 10, 210, 492
Kurzrock, Warren, 616

L

Labich, Kenneth, 298
Labiner, Ted, 230
Laboratory stores, 510
Language of artifacts, 68, 72
Language of kinetics, 73, 74
Language of space, 68, 71, 72
Language of time, 69, 73
Lanham Act (Trademark Act) (1946), 326, 329, 340, 341
Larson, Gary, 357
Lazer, William, 727, 729
Lee, Hau L., 535
Leo Burnett Agency, 508
Lever Brothers Company, 66, 170, 255–56
Levine, George H., 598
Levy, Sidney J., 66
Limited problem solving (LPS), 122, 123, 126, 152–65
    advertising strategy, 158–65
    compared to extended problem solving, 153
    impulse purchase, 154–55
    information search, 155
    marketing strategy, 156–58
    need recognition, 154–55
Lipman, Joanne, 96
Thomas J. Lipton & Co., 229–30
Living standards, advertising effect on, 719–20, 727, 729
Local Advertising Review Process (LARP), 335
Long-term memory, 102
Lower class, 191

M

McCarthy, Joseph, 465
McDonald's, 170
McElligott, Tom, 109
"Macho marketing," 214–15
MacInnes, Deborah J., 104, 364
McKnight, William, 633
McMahn, Harry W., 158, 390
McNeill, Dennis L., 348
McQuilkin, Caryn, 225
Magazine advertising, 414, 439–43
    advantages, 440–41
    audience research, 470–73, 476
    disadvantages, 441–42
    future, 442–43
    media selection, 469–73

Maggio, Frank, 564
Magnuson-Moss Warranty Act, 326, 327, 341, 345
Mahmarian, Robert R., 50–51
Mail order companies, worldwide, 676
Maintenance of share of mind, 167
Management by wandering around (MBWA), 299
Manipulation, 105–6
Manufacturers Hanover Trust Company, 10–12
Manville Corporation, 703
Marginal (incremental) analysis, 265–68, 274, 281
Market entry, 632
Marketing concept, 9–10
    promotional strategy, 10–13
Marketing manager, promotional issues, 43
Marketing mix, 20–25
    price, 21, 23
    product, 21
Marketing research, 43
    market segmentation, 208
    promotion role, 244–48
    services, 316
Market potentials, 211
Market segmentation, 207
    analysis, 227–28
    a priori approaches, 227
    behavioristic variables, 224–225
    benefit, 225
    competitive positioning, 208
    criteria, 208–9
    demographic bases; see Demographic segmentation
    geographic bases, 209, 211–12
    post hoc approach, 227–28
    product usage rates, 226–27
    promotional strategy, 242
    psychographic characteristics, 219–24
Mary Kay Cosmetics, Inc., 194
Mass communication, 75–78
    mass media, 76
Mass media; see also Media
    advertising volume in United States, 413–14
    cost trends, 455–61
    commissionable, 450
    direct mail, 450–51
    feedback, 77
    influence on decision making, 134
    intermedia comparison, 451–61

Mass media—*Cont.*
  magazines; *see* Magazine advertising
  newspapers; *see* Newspaper advertising
  noncommissionable, 450–51
  personal selling compared, 78
  point-of-purchase, 451
  promotional mix, 76–77
  radio; *see* Radio advertising
  selection, 467
  television; *see* Television advertising
  transit advertising, 447–50
  value shaping, 182
Mattel, 494, 554
Mayer, Dick, 168
Mazis, Michael B., 348
MCI, 15, 17, 18
Meadows, D. H., 730
Meadows, D. L., 730
Media; *see also* Mass media
  audience data, 468, 469
  audience research, 469–76
  competitive considerations, 483–86
  distribution, 469, 487
  general content, 134
  qualitative characteristics, 486–87
  reach and frequency, 476–83
  scheduling, 487–97
    flighting, 490–93
    geographical, 488, 490
    within media, 493
    seasonal, 489
    selection, 467
Media buying services, 315
Media Market Guide, 483
Mediamark Research, Inc (MRI), 473
Memory, 97
  theories, 102
Mertes, John E., 725
Metaphor, 68, 69
Micromarketing, 157
Middle class, 190
Miller, Annetta, 6
Miller, Herman, 298
Millsop, Cynthia R., 703
Miniard, Paul, 86, 129, 153, 191, 194, 198, 250, 366
Minimarket tests, 534–35
Missionary selling, 653–54
Moberly, Karen, 6
Monologue copy, 399
Montgomery, Robert L., 573
Moody, Robert, 495

Moog, Carol, 66
Moses, Elissa, 67
Motel 6, 465–67
Motivation, 127–28
  decision processing behavior, 248–49
Motivation with psychological appeals, 367, 368, 375, 378, 379, 386, 387
Myers, Ray, 561

N

Nader, Ralph, 723
Naisbitt, John, 296
Narrative description copy, 399
National Advertising Division (NAD) of CBBB, 332–36
National Advertising Review Board (NARB), 734
National Association of Broadcasters (NAB), 426–27
Need recognition, 123, 127, 129–33, 154–55, 249
Neotraditionalist lifestyle, 248
New product promotion expenditures, 286–90
Newspaper advertising, 413–21
  advantages, 415–18
  audience measurement, 473
  community and suburban newspapers, 418
  disadvantages, 418–19
  future of, 420–21
Nicklaus, Jack, 703
A.C. Nielsen company, 409–10
  Home Video Index, 430, 475
  research service, 535
Nisenholtz, Martin, 449
Noise, 62
Noncompensatory decision rules, 155–56
Normative influences, 191
Norris, William, 296
Norwegian Caribbean, 45–46
Noting set, 517

O

Objective and task method of advertising appropriation, 274–81
  implementing, 275–81
  media analysis, 277
Objectives of promotional planning, 30, 33, 36
Office automation (OA), 587

Ogilvy, David, 314, 390, 397, 399, 407
Ogilvy and Mather, 312–13
Oligopoly, 724
Oliver, Daniel, 328
On-the-air tests, 512
Order-of-merit rating, 503, 505
O'Reilly, Anthony J. F., 164, 165
Organization
  accountability, 732–33
  cooperative efforts, 733–36
  public service, 735
  requirements for success, 735
  structure
    functional, 300–301
    product, 301–3
Organizational symbols, 695–96
Oscar Mayer Foods, 539–40
O'Toole, John, 109
Outdoor Advertising Association of America
  (OAAA), 446
Owen, Dan, 495

P

Packaging, 562–63, 566–67
PACT (Positioning Advertising Copy Testing),
  502
PARM; *see* Print Advertising Research
  Methods study
Participative management, 297–99
Payne, Gavin, 681
Payout planning, 279–80, 286–90
Peirce, C. S., 64
People v. *Western Airline*, 331
Perceived risk of negative outcome, 87, 124
Percentage of sales method of determining
  advertising budget, 270–71
Perceptual defense, 93
Perceptual vigilance, 94
Peripheral cues, 363
Peripheral route of information processing,
  155
Peripheral route to persuasion, 363
Personal determinants, 99
Personal involvement inventory, 125, 251
Personal selling
  communication, 74–75
  compared to mass media use, 78
  definition, 13
  essential tasks, 579
  government regulation of, 348–50
  house-to-house, 684
  information search, 136

Personal selling—*Cont.*
  product-market situation, 576–78
  in promotion mix, 574–75
  steps to a sale, 581–84
Persuasion, 102, 361–63
  central route to, 103, 104, 363
  elaboration likelihood model, 363–64
  peripheral routes to, 103, 104
Peters, Thomas, 295, 670
Peterson, Ronald, 24
Petty, Richard E., 102, 103, 363
Point-of-purchase advertisements, 451
Point-of-Purchase Advertising Institute, 562
Portfolio tests, 506–7
Position in print media, 91
Premiums, 555–58
Price communication, 21
Price deals, 656–57
Price discrimination, 349
Price incentives, 547–50
Princess Cruises, 46, 52
Print Advertisement Research Methods
  (PARM) study, 515, 517–18, 520
Print advertising, 395, 413–21
  copy, 398–402
  headline, 395
  magazine; *see* Magazine advertising
  newspaper; *see* Newspaper advertising
Printers' Ink, 331
PRIZM, 215
Processing by attributes, 133–34
Processing by brand (PBB), 133–34, 141–42
Procter & Gamble, 170, 254, 256, 302, 344–45
Product communication, 21
Product life cycle, 634–37
Product organization, 301–3
Profit
  free enterprise system, 732
  as measure of social value, 731
Profit contribution standards, 611
Program elements, management of, 30, 33,
  37, 41
Programmed merchandising agreements,
  661–62
Promotion; *see also* Advertising *and* Sales
  promotion
  appropriation, 268
    geographic allocation, 281–86
    marginal analysis, 265–68
    new product payouts, 286–90
    objective and task approach, 274–81
    top down approaches, 268–74

Promotion—*Cont.*
 traditional approach, 268–74
 defined, 13
 effects on consumer behavior, 718–23
  buying information, 721–22
  consumerism, 723
  deception, 722–23
  motivation to increase living standards, 719–21, 727–30
 effects on new products, prices and competition, 723–27
 ethics, 733–36
 free enterprise systems; *see* Free enterprise system
 in-store, 648, 650
 market segmentation, 242
 objectives, 241
 profit as measure of social value, 731
 public service, 735
 role, 244–56
 sales and market share goals, 243–44
Promotional budget, 36–37
Promotional strategy
 dynamic nature of, 7
 examples of, 14–20
 habitual buying, 255–56
 marketing concept, 9–13
 market segmentation, 242, 244
 objectives, 256–59
  communication results, 258–59
  expected sales results, 257
  measurement methods and criteria, 259
  message platform, 256
  target market, 256
 stages in, 30–43
 values affecting, 177–87
Propaganda, 718
Proprietary Drug Association of America, 734
Prospecting, 582
Proven name registration (PNR), 519
Psychographics, 247
Psychographic segmentation
 AIO measurements, 219
 lifestyle, 219
Publicity, 138, 703–4
Public relations, 41, 138, 692
 case histories, 704–10
 external communication, 695–702
 image of, 710
 internal communication, 693–95, 710
 media, 696, 704

Public relations—*Cont.*
 publicity, 703–4
Public service by industry, 735
Puffing, 340
Pull activities, sales promotion, 541, 542
Pulses, 492
Pupil dilation response (PDR), 508–9
Purchase, 129, 131, 145–47, 156, 165
 decision process behavior, 249
 impulse, 154
Purchasers, 246
Pure Food and Drug Act (1906), 323
Puris, Martin Ford, 184
Push activities, 541, 542

Q–R

Quaker Oats Company, 29–30
RADAR (Radio's All Dimension Audience Research), 474
Radio advertising, 406–8, 412, 435–39
 advantages, 436–38
 audiences research, 474
 disadvantages, 438–39
 future of, 439
Rao, Ambar G., 501, 535
Rawl, Lawrence G., 691
Reach, medic schedule, 476–83
 effect of flight, 491, 492
Readability tests, 507
Reagan, Ronald, 342
Recall tests, 519–21
Recognition tests, 513–18
Recognition threshold, 106
Reference groups, 189, 191, 193–94
Regulation of marketing and promotion, 322
 areas of regulation, 336–50
 federal legislation, 324–31
 local advertising review programs, 335
 self-regulation, 332–35
 state and local regulations, 331
Religion, 179, 182
Repeat-assertion ad, 367–68, 371, 375, 384
Repeated problem solving, 165
Repeat purchase, 165
Research; *see* Marketing research
Reseller support, 13, 278, 632
 advertising and promotion assistance, 642–53
 consumer deals, 656–57
 controlling performance, 657–62
 display and selling aids, 654–56

Reseller support—*Cont.*
  legal problems, 652–53
  manufacturer strategy, 634
  missionary selling, 653–54
  nonselected, 659–60
  product life cycle, 634–37
  promotional role, 633–37
  selected, 658–59
  quotas, 642
  training salespeople, 638–41
Retention, 84, 102
Return on investment (ROI)
  contribution margin, 612
  direct marketing, 671, 686
  method of determining advertising budget,
    271–72
Rice, Faye, 120, 608
Richins, Marsha L., 719
Riskey, Dwight, 213
Robinson-Patman Act (1936), 324, 326, 349,
    639, 652
Rosado, Lourdes, 670
Rose, Sheila, 220
Ross, Ivan, 504
Rossi, Dick, 357, 358
Rothenberg, Randall, 294
Routing the sales force, 615
Royal Caribbean, 49, 54
Royal Viking, 49–50, 53
Rubbermaid, Inc., 158
Rubigo Cosmetics, 220–21

S

Sales and Marketing Management
  census of business data, 283–84
  survey of buying power, 284–85
Sales force
  application for job, 590–91
  assignment, 594
  communication, 602–3
  compensation, 596–600
  evaluation and control, 609
    corrective action, 614–15
    performance standards, 609–14
    routing, 615
    time and duty analysis, 614–15
  interview, 592
  job descriptions, 588–89
  management of, 616
  models used for sizing, 617–25
  motivation, 600–603
  reallocation of effort, 615–25

Sales force—*Cont.*
  reseller salespeople, 638–41
  selection, 590
  testing applicant, 591
  training, 592–94
Salesmanship, 579
Sales promotion, 13, 165; *see also*
    Promotion
  channel-directed, 542
  consumer-oriented, 543–45
  consumer promotional alternatives, 545–62
  definition, 540
  packaging, 562–67
  reseller, 642–53
  scope and importance, 541
  types of, 545
Sales territory, 595
  management of sales force, 616
Sales tests, 526–33
Sampling, 545–47, 548–49
Sansone, Robert, 554
Saporito, Bill, 75
Scandinavian Air System (SAS), 295
Schema, 97–98
Schlossberg, Howard, 682
Schudson, Michael, 717, 721
Schultze, Quentin J., 719, 720, 722
Schwadel, Francine, 672
Script, 98
Segmentation; *see* Market segmentation
Selective exposure, 89
Selective perception, 87
Selling Areas Marketing, Inc (SAMI), 500
Selling concept, 10
Semiology (semiotics), 64–68, 109
Sensation, 88
Sensory memory, 102
Service ad, 373–74
Seven-Up Company, 9–10
Shapiro, Arthur, 535
Share of industry advertising (share of
    voice), 278–79
Share of voice objective, 482–83
Sharper Image, 681
Sherman Act (1890), 348, 427
Shimmel, Howard, 89
Short-term memory, 102
Sigmund, Barbara, 83
Signs, 64
Silent language, 74
Simmons Market Research Bureau (SMRB),
    472–73

Simon, Edward Jr., 298
Simon advertising activation methods, 365–75
J. R. Simplot Company, 646
Sitmar, 46
Situation analysis, 30–36
Skunkworks, 297
Slogans, 401
Spot Quotations and Data, Inc. (SQAD), 483
Smith, Fred, 296
Smith, William, 46
Snowball technique, 582
Snygg, Donald, 721, 722
Social class, 187–89, 190–91
Social environment
    American values, 177–87
    culture, 176
    family influence, 194–98
    reference groups, 189–94
    social stratification, 187–89
Social norms, 65
Social sanctions, 87, 124
Spot announcement, 427–29
Standard Rate and Data Service (SDRS), 483
Stanton, William J., 604
Starch, Daniel, 514–18
Starch Irra Hopper, Inc., 514
Steinbeck, John, 564
Steiner, Robert L., 725
Stimuli, 91
    adaptation to, 94
    determinants, 98–99
    sensory memory, 102
Stone, Bob, 678
Strenio, Andrew J., Jr., 328
Subcultures, 187
Sublimal advertising, 106–10
Sublimal perception, 106
Support arguments, 361
Sweepstakes, 558, 560–62
Symbol, 64–66
    shared meanings, 65
Symbolic association ad, 370, 375
Syntex Laboratories, 617–25

T

Tachiscope, 508
Target market, 35, 208
    concentrated marketing, 230
    decision-making unit, 245–46
    demographic segmentation, 246
    differentiated markets, 228–30

Target market—*Cont.*
    key strategic promotional choices, 238
    marketing research, 244–48
    motivation and behavior diagnosis in target segment, 248–56
    psychographic characteristics, 247–48
    public relations, 693
    undifferentiated marketing, 228
Taylor, James R., 475, 501
Telaction, 682
Telemarketing
    backlash toward, 675–76
    direct marketing, 671, 674–76
    fraud, 328
    inbound, 674–75
    outbound, 675
Television advertising, 406–8, 412, 421–35
    advantages, 422–24
    audience research, 473–74, 475–76
    cable, 429–34, 682
    direct marketing, 682
    disadvantages, 424
    future of, 429
    networks, 424–27, 435
    spot announcements, 427–29
    videocassettes, 430
    videotex, 447, 448
Testimonial message as advertising copy, 399
Textile Fiber Products Act, 324
Thalheimer, Richard, 681
Theater tests, 509–10
Theory of Reasoned Action, 142
J. Walter Thompson Company, 293
Thorelli, Hans, 721
Time-and-duty analysis, 614–15
Times Mirror Videotex Information Services, Inc., 448
Toilet Goods Association, 734
Tomsho, Robert, 655
Top-down approaches to promotional appropriation, 268–74
Total Prime Time (TPT) tests, 512–13
Trademark Act (Lanham Act) (1946), 326
Trademark Law Revision Act, 326, 340
Trade press, 706–7
Trade promotion, 542
Trailer tests, 510
Transit advertising, 447–50
Traffic Audit Bureau (TAB), 446
Tragos, Bill, 96
Transformational advertising, 362, 363
Triple-associates test, 521

Truth in Lending Act, 324
Tupperware, 17, 20
Tylenol tragedy, 704–6

U

U-Haul v. *Jartran,* 341
Unaided recall, 519
Undifferentiated marketing, 228
Unique selling proposition, 256
United States v. *National Association of Broadcasters,* 427
Upper class, 190
Users, 246
U. S. Suburban Press, Inc., 418
Utilitarian influence of reference groups, 191

V

Valence, 361
Value expressive influence of reference groups, 191
Vertical cooperative advertising, 344
Vertical integration, 660
Vicary, James, 106
Videocassette recorders/players, 430–34
  direct marketing, 669, 684
Videotex, 447, 682
Visich, Charles, 561
Vision as requirement of organization, 295
Visual elements in advertising, 402–6
  color, 405–6

W

Walker, Orville C., Jr., 589, 603
Wal-Mart stores, 631–32

Walton, Matt S., III, 598
Waltzer, Garrett J., 341
Warne, Colston E., 725, 726
Warner-Lambert Company, 346
WATS (wide area telecommunication service), 674
Weaver, Barbara, 540
Weber, Bob, 540
Weber's Law, 88
Weiner, Joel D., 157
Werner, Ray O., 341
Wheeler-Lea Amendment, 324, 326
Whitehall Laboratories, 645, 647, 656
Wilhite, Clayt, 168
Wilkie, William L., 346, 348
Williams, Monci Jo, 581
Wilson, Thomas W., Jr., 229
Wind, Yoram, 234
Winters, Patricia, 245
Woodruff, Robert B., 575
Wool Products Act, 324
Word-of-mouth influence on decision making, 139–40
Worldstyle, 217–18, 227
Worthen, Rose Mary, 220
Wright, John S., 725

Y–Z

Yellow pages advertising, 412
Zaichkowsky, Judith Lynne, 125, 251
Zaichkowsky Personal Involvement Scale, 125, 251
Zapping, 89–90, 94
Zeltner, Herbert, 308